# Convergence of Litigation, Policy, and Standards: Building the Informed Practitioner in Education Abroad Risk Management

## About the Series

*Standards in Action* (2022– ) is a book series that seeks to bridge big ideas and foundational principles in education abroad to the creative approaches and practical tactics that can turn those concepts into reality. As our field seeks to face down hard challenges and reinvent instelf for the future, these books provide the inspiration and guidance needed to usher in the new era. The series is curated by Amelia J. Dietrich, Senior Director for Research and Publications, The Forum on Education Abroad.

Other titles in this series:
> *Voices from the South: Decolonial Perspectives in International Education*
> *Sustainable Eduation Abroad: Striving for Change*
> *A House Where All Belong: Redesigning Education Abroad for Inclusive Excellence*
> *The Half Yet To Be Told: Study Abroad and HBCUs*

ISSN: 2833-0595 (print)
ISSN: 2833-0579 (ebooks)
For more information, visit https://www.forumea.org/standards-in-action

*Standards in Action Series*

# Convergence of Litigation, Policy, and Standards: Building the Informed Practitioner in Education Abroad Risk Management

Editors
Julie Pollard and Kim S. Priebe

A publication of The Forum on Education Abroad

**THE FORUM**
ON EDUCATION ABROAD

The *Standards in Action* series is published by The Forum on Education Abroad, the standards development organization (SDO) for the field of education abroad as recognized by the U.S. Department of Justice and the Federal Trade Commission. For more information, visit www.forumea.org.

© 2024 The Forum on Education Abroad.

ISBN: 978-1-952376-41-2 (paperback)

ISBN: 978-1-952376-42-9 (ebook)

Library of Congress Control Number: 2024940771

Printed on demand to reduce waste.
First printing, 2024.

The Forum on Education Abroad
PO Box 425
Warren, Rhode Island 02885

The Forum on Education Abroad is hosted by Dickinson College.

www.forumea.org

# Contents

# Editors' Acknowledgments

## Julie Pollard

To the authors who have so generously shared your scholarship and time to create this book, you have my deepest gratitude. To the peer reviewers who contributed their subject matter expertise to bettering each chapter, please accept my sincerest appreciation. To The Forum on Education Abroad, thank you for believing in this project and making this knowledge accessible for the next generation. To my co-editor, Kim, words cannot express the value of your leadership in this project. You are a shining example of what it means to be an education abroad professional. I, and this field, are indebted to you.

I'd like to thank my mother for giving me both roots and wings to explore this world and my husband for sharing my passion for international education. Special thanks to Eduard Mandell who gave me so many opportunities and Duleep Deosthale who encouraged me to take them. To the many thought partners, colleagues, mentors, and friends who provided counsel over the years, your support is invaluable and deeply appreciated.

## Kim S. Priebe

I extend my sincere gratitude to all the contributing authors, futurists, and peer reviewers of this book. Your expertise, insights, and enthusiasm have been instrumental in realizing the vision of this book. Editing this book has been a labor of passion and deep collaboration, and I am indebted to everyone who played a part in creating this comprehensive resource that will benefit practitioners in the field for years to come.

To my husband, Jason, I am grateful for your unwavering support of my involvement in this project. To my sister and parents, whose interest and encouragement have fueled my determination and reminded me of the importance of pursuing projects we are passionate about. I extend my deepest gratitude to my friend and long-time colleague, Anna Hayes, who agreed to be my coauthor, and whose expertise, excellent editing skills, and collaborative spirit enriched our chapter beyond measure.

Special thanks to Amelia Dietrich at The Forum for her invaluable guidance and enthusiasm for this project. Your expertise and support were instrumental in navigating the complexities of bringing this project to fruition. Thank you, Melissa Torres and Marissa Lombardi, for believing in the importance of this book and backing this project!

Last but certainly not least, I want to thank Julie Pollard for extending the invitation to co-edit this book with her. Julie, your vision and leadership have been inspiring. It has been an honor and privilege to partner with you, a respected colleague and now friend, on this important project.

The Editors and The Forum on Education Abroad wish to convey their gratitude to peer reviewers who have generously given their time and subject matter expertise to strengthening this publication.

Marisa Atencio, Ed.D.

Sarah Schtakleff Ball, J.D.

Mark Beirn

Laura Boisvert Boyd, LCMHCS

Kenya Casey

Melissa Chambers

Ivonne Chirino-Klevans, Ph.D.

Gary Collins

Sean Cox, Ph.D.

Benjamin Cluff, Ph.D.

Kate de Blanc

Joseph M Debiec

Jeremy R. Doughty, Ph.D.

Andrea Drake

Laura Dupont-Jarrett, Ph.D., LP

Angie Edwards

William Ferreira, J.D.

Ariadne M. Ferro

Jennifer Fullick, Ph.D.

Seth Gilbertson, J.D.

Mariel Goble

Maureen Gordon

Staci Hagen

Dorothy Hassan, Ph.D.

Anna Hayes

Marcia Henisz

Sunanda Holmes, J.D.

Todd Holmes

Holly Hudson, Ed.D.

Morgan Inabinet

Elizabeth James, J.D.

Shaun Jamieson

Katie Johnson

Daniel Kampsen, J.D.

Julia Law

Barbara Lindeman

Miko McFarland

Breeda McGrath, Ph.D., NCSP

Meredith McQuaid, J.D.

Vinita Mehra, J.D.

Josh Meltzer, J.D.

Jessica Miller

Terence Miller, J.D.

Jaime Molyneux

Erin Nester

Krista Northup

Vivian-Lee Nyitray, Ph.D.

Allie Oberoi

Nancy Osborne
Michael Pfahl, J.D., Ph.D.
Debbie Pichla
Deb Reisinger, Ph.D.
John Simone, J.D.
Jamie Snow

Sarah E. Spencer
Christine Sprovieri
Vanessa Sterling
Laura Thompson, Ph.D., LPC
Catherine Winnie, Ph.D.
Olivia (Dan) Wu

The editors and publisher are also grateful to the following colleagues who reviewed the book upon completion and provided endorsements of its content: Avv. GianFranco Borio, Holly Hudson, Ed.D., Sabine Klahr, Ed.D., Carri Orrison, M. Colette Plum, Ph.D., and Adam Rubin.

# 1

## Introduction

### Julie Pollard and Kim S. Priebe

In recent decades, the field of international education has witnessed a significant evolution, driven by the increasing demand for quality experiences abroad and a growing awareness of the complexities involved in managing the health and safety of students participating in education abroad programs. The Forum on Education Abroad emerged in 2000 in response to these challenges, with a mission to promote high standards in the field and ensure the well-being of students. Founded by a group of passionate educators with expertise in the field, The Forum quickly became a leading voice in the realm of education abroad, offering resources, training, and a platform for dialogue and sharing of best practices among practitioners.

A pivotal moment in The Forum's history came with the development of the *Standards of Good Practice for Education Abroad*. Recognizing the need for a standardized approach to health and safety in international education, The Forum crafted a comprehensive set of guidelines designed to address the diverse needs of practitioners and the students we serve. These standards "are the only standards established by the Standards Development Organization (SDO) for the field of education abroad recognized by the U.S. Department of Justice and the Federal Trade Commission" (The Forum on Education Abroad, 2020), and serve as a benchmark for quality assurance, providing a roadmap for organizations to navigate the complex landscape of risk management in education abroad.

As showcased by recognized education abroad expert and Forum founder Kathy Sideli, in a podcast interview with William Hoffa (2015), the organization has consistently focused on fostering an informed and proactive approach to risk management in education abroad. Through initiatives like

1

specialized training, webinars, and publications, The Forum continues to empower practitioners to address emerging challenges and uphold the highest standards in health and safety. This book, *Convergence of Litigation, Policy, and Standards: Building the Informed Practitioner in Education Abroad Risk Management,* aims to further these efforts by connecting law and practice, using litigation in education abroad, as well as industry standards and policy, to inform and expand the education abroad scholar-practitioner's understanding of best practices in international risk management.

The education abroad field has supported students who have experienced physical harm (traffic accidents, drownings, robberies, sexual violence, etc.) and grappled with an array of natural disasters (tsunami and nuclear accident in Japan, volcano eruptions in Iceland, etc.); periods of social unrest (strikes, riots, demonstrations, etc.); political upheavals (coup d'états, civic violence, etc.); and the collective experience of responding to terrorism (Paris in 2015, the United Kingdom in 2017, etc.). We have long been expected to plan for and respond to incidents abroad in support of students' health and safety (The Forum on Education Abroad, 2020, clauses 4.2.2, 5.1.7, 5.1.8, 5.2.4, 6.1.11, 6.2.7, 6.2.8, 6.3.4). However, nothing prepared the field for the breadth and depth of COVID-19 and the upheaval it wrought for international mobility, reducing U.S. study abroad student numbers by 91% (Institute for International Education, 2022). The pandemic exposed the field to a new hypersensitivity around an enterprise's negligence liability due to the risk and crisis scenarios realized since March 2020.

In the wake of that upheaval, reflections from professionals in the field captured by the 2022 Forum State of the Field Survey identified the top 10 concerns facing the field in the year ahead:

1. Need for better funding for students
2. Supporting underrepresented students
3. Program costs and rising costs
4. Crisis and risk management
5. Student support services related to disability, wellness, or mental health
6. Adequate preparation of students
7. Current political climate
8. Helping students maximize their experience
9. Recovery and/or reinvention of the field after the COVID-19 pandemic
10. General health and safety (The Forum on Education Abroad, 2023)

The report also highlighted the gaps in training for our field. Respondents indicated that the top five skills required for their position but for which they did not receive training included finance/budget management, risk management, technology, crisis management, and outreach and marketing. It is important to note that among the top five were risk management (ranked second) and crisis management (ranked fourth) (The Forum on Education Abroad, 2023). Across all categories, the *State of the Field Survey* results included ample commentary related to high turnover and/or major restructuring in education abroad offices since March 2020. As editors, we started out our work on this volume in part in response to these challenges and gaps, as one of us (Kim S. Priebe) explored in *International Educator* in 2023:

> During and after the public health emergency, the field has experienced significant turbulence... In the education abroad space, the recent *State of the Field* comprehensive survey ... shows that turnover within the field is at an all-time high. Consequently, there is a loss of institutional knowledge and expertise in the field. A staggering 47 percent of respondents now find themselves tasked with risk management and crisis response responsibilities without having received sufficient training to effectively serve in the capacity of a primary risk manager. (Priebe, 2023)

Essentially, this means that even those offices that were able to retain their positions or have returned to full staffing are operating with many new and/or lesser experienced colleagues (The Forum on Education Abroad, 2023). As the field of education abroad advances and we train our newer professionals, it is important to develop awareness of the convergence of litigation, policy, and standards that inform best practices in operationalizing risk management in education abroad. We offer this carefully curated volume as a resource to help fill that gap. We believe that the intersections we explore throughout the chapters to follow will be helpful to new risk management professionals, their hiring managers and supervisors, and anyone working in education abroad who holds any level of professional responsibility for student safety and well-being in need of a primer or refresher to help them in their work.

*Convergence* includes 35 chapters featuring the expertise of 13 attorneys, three mental health practitioners, and scores of specialists in education abroad, international health and safety, DEI, international insurance, and global human resources. The book concludes with a chapter featuring the predictions of future risks in the education abroad space by 20 subject matter experts in their respective disciplines. As the fifth book in the Standards in Action book series, we are proud to offer a multifaceted approach to operationalizing the *Standards of Good Practice for Education Abroad.*

This book is not a comprehensive review of case law but is intended to identify themes through a sampling of cases and educate practitioners on mitigating risk through operationalizing these concepts. Further consultation should be sought from university legal counsel or outside counsel as needed.

The first section of the book is dedicated to U.S. litigation and laws affecting our duty of care for education abroad students. The chapters, authored by attorneys specializing in the chapter topic and education abroad and international health & safety professionals, break down U.S. cases and laws in an easily digestible manner, and explain the outcomes and how they apply broadly to our work. The chapters offer recommendations for best practices in the development and administration of education abroad programs. The second section of the book addresses international laws, case studies, and standards, and similarly offers an analysis of the lawsuit, law, or practice abroad and how we can apply those takeaways to our programming. The third section addresses the evolution of our understanding of risk and looks at various diverse topics impacting our work daily.

Before immersing oneself in how these elements intersect, it helps in first understanding them individually. The remainder of this chapter explains the structure and significance of litigation, policy, and standards separately. This foundation will facilitate exploring their convergence in relevant case law, laws, institutional policies, and standards as they apply to education abroad throughout this volume.

## Litigation

Litigation is the process of resolving disputes by filing or answering a complaint through the public court system. The Latin term *stare decisis*, meaning "to stand by decided matters," is a foundational principle of the rule of law (U.S. Congress, n.d.). Guided by this principle, judges are bound by the precedents in their own U.S. Federal District courts and may be persuaded by precedents in other circuits as a means of providing stability, predictability, and integrity to our legal system. For this reason, it is important to examine the relationship of past precedent in litigation outcomes to inform best practices in education abroad program operations. According to the American Bar Association (ABA) (2022):

> Stare decisis may be simple at its core, but there are nuances and limits in the way it is applied. For example, vertical stare decisis—the idea that the decisions of higher courts take precedence over the decisions of lower courts—is deeply entrenched in the American legal system. This idea is part of what makes the Supreme Court "supreme." By contrast, horizontal stare decisis holds that prior decisions made by courts at a particular appellate level (such as a federal court of appeals) should provide some precedent for cases heard by courts of the same appellate level. Horizontal stare decisis is generally seen to be less "control" when compared to vertical stare decisis. (para. 1)

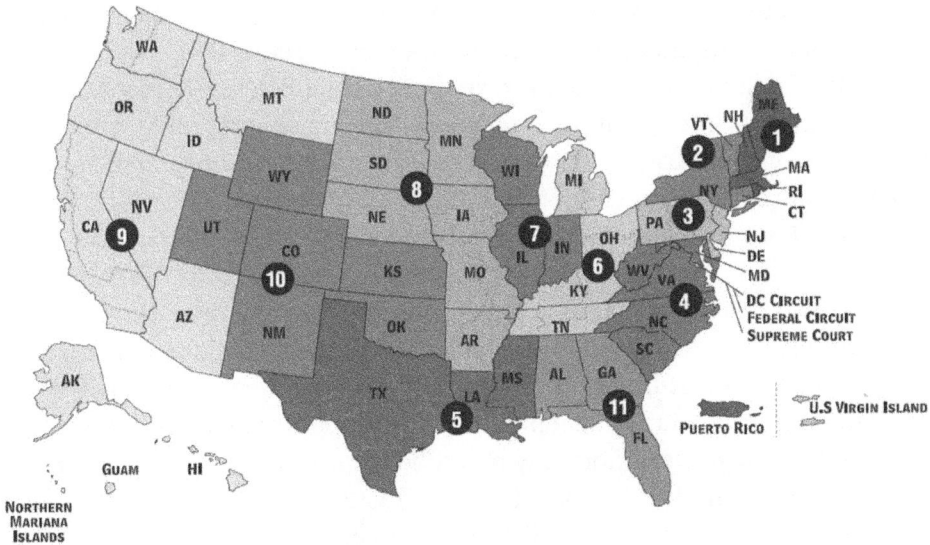

**Figure 1.1.** Map of the United States Showing Geographical Regions for the U.S. Court of Appeals and U.S. District Courts

The U.S. Federal Courts Circuit Map (Figure 1.1) visualizes the regions covered by each circuit court in the United States. Having a discussion with your legal counsel regarding the institution's response to any past litigation may provide background knowledge on court precedents and may yield greater understanding of your institution's risk appetite and risk tolerance.

## Policy

Organizations enact policies as a governing framework to set standards and expectations, hold responsible parties accountable, and respond to regulation and compliance requirements. Procedures are the operational processes required to implement the policy detailing who performs the procedure, what steps should be taken and when, and how steps should be performed (The University of Texas at Austin, n.d.).

Clause 5.1 of the *Standards of Good Practice for Education Abroad* (The Forum on Education Abroad, 2020) establishes this as best practice: "Each organization shall define policies, procedures, and guidelines ... to govern its programs and practices and prepare its personnel to apply them." The sub-clauses of this section go on to specify that policies shall be transparent and consistently implemented (5.1.1) and that organizations shall regularly review policies and their application to evaluate effectiveness (5.1.2).

An institution's international travel policy establishes a Duty of Care by defining the parameters of university-affiliated travel, including who is eligible for sponsored travel and what locations are permissible. Risk appetite and risk tolerance are crucial considerations for higher education institutions when developing policies for education abroad and international travel. Risk appetite refers to the level of risk an institution is willing to accept to achieve its objectives, such as expanding global learning opportunities in higher risk destinations. In contrast, risk tolerance defines the specific thresholds and limits of risk the institution is prepared to withstand without jeopardizing student safety or institutional reputation. Risk appetite and risk tolerance will differ across institutions and may be influenced by factors such as staffing, resources, funding, history of risk taking, institutional mission, and goals. See Chapter 30, "Who Can Go Where for What Purposes and Under What Conditions: Building an Institutional International Travel Policy," by Shaun Jamieson and Patrick Morgan (2024) for more details on travel policies.

## Standards

The Forum on Education Abroad was recognized as a Standards Development Organization for the study abroad field by the U.S. Department of Justice and the Federal Trade Commission in 2005 (Notice Pursuant to the National Cooperative Research and Production Act of 1993, 2004). In their current (sixth) edition, the *Standards* have been designed to be used for program design, professional development, establishing sustainable, accountable partnerships, and conducting program evaluations for continuous improvement and quality assurance. Throughout this volume, the authors connect best practice examples from their own work to The Forum on Education Abroad's *Standards of Good Practice for Education Abroad* (2020) utilizing their language:

- Shall indicates minimum requirements
- Should indicates recommendations
- Can indicates further possibilities for improvement

Responsible organizations shall utilize the *Standards* as "minimum requirements, quality indicators, and a framework for continuous improvement for education abroad" (The Forum on Education Abroad, 2020, p. 1). Moreover, collaboration and transparency are identified in the *Standards* (2020), stating "Collaborators shall discuss and clarify: managing health, safety, and security risks" (clause 4.2.2.), "Collaborators shall formalize all of the above in writing" (clause 4.2.3), and "Collaborators should evaluate for continuous improvement and clarification of responsibilities" (clause 4.2.4). Since the formation of the *Standards*, organizations and institutions have engaged in self-review or formal peer review of their programs (Redden, 2007), including policies and procedures that prioritize the health, well-being, and safety of students addressed by clause 5.1.7 (2020). These shall include "risk assessment and monitoring, tracking, responding to, and reporting critical incidents, written emergency plans and protocols, and insurance coverage" (The Forum on Education Abroad, 2020, clause 5.1.7). For more information on operationalizing standards, see Chapter 31, "Applying Standards to Travel Risk Management," by Henning Snyman, Hilary Douglas, and Gary Collins (2024), and Chapter 32, "Operationalizing Duty of Care in Education Abroad using The Forum *Standards*," by Kyle Rausch (2024).

We have compiled this volume because we believe knowledge should be shared and accessible. When we came together to work on this project, Kim recalled attending conference sessions as an early- to mid-career education abroad professional and occasionally heard lawsuits related to study abroad mentioned in passing, without much explanation or context. It struck her then, and we both agree today, that this was critical information that should inform our best practices. As education abroad professionals, the health, safety, and security of students are of paramount importance. We engage in this project with this in mind. Knowing that there are so many new professionals in the field, or people newly working in the risk management space, it is imperative that we learn from the past and embed these essential takeaways into our future practices to not repeat mistakes. In this book, *Convergence of Litigation, Policy, and Standards*, we aim to offer a comprehensive exploration of the critical intersection of litigation, policy, and standards, and recommendations for best practices in applying these to education abroad programming. We hope this book will serve as a tool to help train education abroad professionals, offering clear takeaways and direct application to best practices. This volume stands as a testament to our collective commitment to safeguarding the well-being of students and advancing the field of education abroad, ensuring that professionals are well-equipped to navigate the intricate landscape of litigation, policy, and standards.

# References

American Bar Association. (2022, December 16). *Understanding Stare Decisis.* https://www.americanbar.org/groups/public_education/publications/preview_home/understand-stare-decisis/#:~:text=Stare%20Decisis%E2%80%94a%20Latin%20term,and%20opinions%20from%20prior%20cases.

Hoffa, W. (Host). (2015, March 26). A Conversation with Kathleen Sideli. (No. 1) [Audio podcast episode]. The Forum on Education Abroad. https://archive.forumea.org/podcast/ep1-kathysideli/

Institute for International Education. (2022, November 13). U.S. Students Studying Abroad, 1989/90-2020-21. Open Doors Report on International Educational Exchange. https://opendoorsdata.org/infographic/u-s-students-studying-abroad-1989-90-2020-21/

The Forum on Education Abroad. (2020). *Standards of good practice for education abroad, Sixth edition.* doi.org/10.36366/S.978-1-952376-04-7

Priebe, K. S. (2023). Reflections on the NAFSA IE Competencies: Risk Assessment and Crisis Management. *International Educator.* NAFSA: Association of International Educators. https://www.nafsa.org/ie-magazine/2023/12/6/reflections-nafsa-ie-competencies-risk-assessment-and-crisis-management

The Forum on Education Abroad. (2023). *State of the Field Survey: Data from the Comprehensive 2022 Survey.* /https://www.forumea.org/uploads/1/4/4/6/144699749/forumea_-_2022_state_of_the_field_report_-_07.12.2023.pdf

The University of Texas at Austin. (n.d.). *Qualities of a policy in the Handbook of Operating Procedures ("HOP").* Policy vs Procedure. https://compliance.utexas.edu/policy-vs-procedure

United States Courts. *Geographic boundaries,* [U.S. Federal Courts Circuit map]. Retrieved April 8, 2024, from https://www.uscourts.gov/sites/default/files/u.s._federal_courts_circuit_map_1.pdf

U.S. Congress. (n.d.). *ArtIII.S1.7.2.1 Historical Background on Stare Decisis Doctrine.* Constitution Annotated. https://constitution.congress.gov/browse/essay/artIII-S1-7-2-1/ALDE_00001187/

# U.S. Cases and Laws Affecting Duty of Care for Education Abroad Students

# 2

# Understanding Legal Terms and Process in the Context of Litigation, Liability, and Risks in Education Abroad

Terence Miller, J.D. and Julie Pollard

## Introduction

In the 1960s and 1970s, general counsel positions in institutions of higher education (IHEs) were rare and often a board trustee was tasked with legal work, whether the occasional lawsuit or contact reviews (Jesse, 2024). In *All the Campus Lawyers*, Guard and Jacobson consider "lawyerization" an abbreviation for describing "the increased regulatory and litigation pressures facing institutions against the broader backdrop of the increasing operational complexity, public scrutiny, politicization and legislative interference with higher education" (2024, p. 4). The growing "lawyerization" of higher education can be attributed to federal, state, and local governments passing statutes, administrative agencies proposing regulations, as well as influence from accreditors, professional associations, and insurance companies (Guard & Jacobsen, 2024). "Today, the lawyer is not only in the meeting, but increasingly casts a deciding vote" (Jesse, 2024, p. 1). This speaks to the considerable power and influence university general counsel wields on campus, highlighting the importance of general counsel being a key partner for education abroad professionals.

Understanding legal concepts will provide adaptability in confronting risk and crisis management, build rapport with legal colleagues, and earn institutional confidence in operational risk management processes and decisions.

Risks in education abroad are complex, and when litigation does occur is often difficult to explore. The media involvement in incidents may misinterpret matters or are too vague to explore legal ramifications. Settlements, where both parties agree to terms and voluntary dismissal of litigation, are often not made publicly available, furthering the lack of clarity on outcomes and possible consequences for education abroad practitioners.

Erfle and Dietrich (2020) examined the mortality rate for U.S. students studying abroad, comparing the data to students studying on U.S. campuses, and found that college students studying abroad are less likely to die than college students studying on campuses in the United States. The complexity of risks that pose a significant danger to students' health, safety, security, and well-being while studying abroad is further examined in The Forum on Education Abroad's 2024 Student Risk Report (Dietrich, 2024). Data reported the most common incidents were property loss, physical health, and mental health distress, with "87.5% of incidents reported resulted in students returning to program, suggesting that incidents are responded to in such a way that generally allows a student to cope or recover and still pursue their educational programming after the incident" (Dietrich, 2024, p. 5).

United Educators, a membership-based organization of over 1500 institutions "committed to providing the coverage and tools needed to confidently operate your campus while managing education-specific risks," conducted a survey that identified institutions' most pressing risks (United Educators, 2023).

Top 10 Risks of 2023

1.  Data security
2.  Enrollment
3.  Recruitment and hiring
4.  Operational pressures
5.  Student mental health
6.  Funding
7.  *Facilities and deferred maintenance (*two risks tied for sixth)
8.  Regulatory and legal compliance (non-VAWA/Title IX)
9.  Title IX
10. External pressures (United Educators, 2023, p. 2)

*Student physical health and safety* ranked 14th while *Study abroad and other travel* tied for 16th in the survey results (United Educators, 2023). Education abroad risks mirror campus risks with the added complexity of occurring in a foreign environment with far less control than the home campus. Risk management measures will also differ significantly and require a subject matter expertise distinctly different from campus risk professionals.

Education abroad professionals are asked to assume various health and safety responsibilities, including understanding legal terms like the duty of care, reasonable care, foreseeability of harm, and proximate cause in the context of potential risks in education abroad programming. Employees are agents of their organizations, speaking and acting on behalf of the enterprise. From a strategic perspective, the relationship between employee actions and organization liability means education abroad employees are on the front lines of mitigating or enhancing risk for students studying abroad. This chapter will provide education abroad practitioners with an overview of legal terms and relevant case law, empowering them to suggest and implement standards mitigating risk and implementing leading practices according to their enterprise's risk tolerance level.

## Tort Law

A tort is an act or omission that gives rise to injury or harm to another and amounts to a civil wrong for which courts impose liability. In the context of torts, "injury" describes the invasion of any legal right, whereas "harm" describes a loss or detriment in fact that an individual suffers. (Legal Information Institute, n.d. c). Tort law, which varies by state, governs the rights of an individual who is harmed or suffered damages to pursue legal claims against tortfeasors, an individual or entity that commits the wrongful act (Kuersten & Lewis, 2023). Many states utilize the Restatement of Torts (second) as highly persuasive guidance and judges consider it an authority. Yet courts may not adopt Restatement principles into common law and they may not apply in all jurisdictions (Kritchevsky, 2010). The Restatement of Torts is a comprehensive legal treatise written by an independent organization of legal professionals dedicated to producing scholarly work to clarify, modernize, and improve the law. Restatements provide systematic and authoritative summaries of the general principles of law. Tort liability is a civil action and does not carry the same consequences as a criminal action. The civil court or jury will determine whether a tortfeasor committed a civil wrong against the injured party, shifting the burden of loss from the injured party to the party at fault. The legal remedy for tort liability is typically monetary compensation

(Legal Information Institute, n.d. b). Kuersten & Lewis (2023) expand further that tort law serves at least three distinct purposes:

1. It facilitates compensation for injuries resulting from wrongful conduct.
2. It can deter persons from acting in ways that may produce harm.
3. It can provide a way of punishing people who wrongfully injure others. (p. 1)

Over the past few decades, courts have exhibited an increased willingness to hold IHEs liable for campus-related injury, leading to tort liability ranking high among the issues confronting IHE administrators (Dall, 2003). Of the cases discussed in this chapter, the most common type of tort liability examined is negligence liability. Malveaux (2016), in researching study abroad student lawsuits against their educational institution and/or third-party agencies or vendors, coined the term "LARGEST 3 (Liabilities And Risks in Global Education and Study Travel)" to describe an observed pattern in those lawsuits. "Nearly all study abroad tragedies and lawsuits tend to be linked to three common risk types (1) medical risks, (2) sexual assault, and (3) supervisory neglect" (Malveaux, 2016, p. xvii). By its very nature, education abroad exposes students to various cross-cultural experiences that invite risk and expose participants to different risk environments creating tension between academic pursuits and risk tolerance. In the post-COVID world, this tension has caused the pendulum to swing to risk-averse education abroad programming, with IHEs seeking to reduce liability exposure in education abroad programming.

## Negligence Liability

A negligence tort refers to a legal claim against an entity for causing harm or injury due to negligent behavior (Legal Information Institute, n.d. c). "The liability issues relevant to study abroad programs are as broad as the expansive field of torts" (Johnson, 2006, p. 317). Claims in education abroad, such as "premise liability, intentional or negligent infliction of emotional distress, negligent misrepresentation, fraud, and negligent security," may share similarities to lawsuits involving the domestic campus (Johnson, 2006, p. 317). However, some are unique to study abroad, such as lawsuits concerning the duties owed to students when political violence and unrest occur, armed attackers take a bus hostage, or when dangers arise from the significantly different risk environment of a foreign country (Johnson, 2006).

In *Bloss v. Univ. of Minnesota Board of Regents*, a taxi driver raped a student on her way to a friend's homestay and the plaintiff "sued the University for negligence in its failure to secure housing closer to the [foreign program] campus, failure to provide transportation to and from campus, failure to adequately warn about risks, and failure to protect students from foreseeable harm" (*Bloss v. Univ of Minnesota Board of Regents*, 1999, p. 663 ). The appellate court held that the student's claims failed because the university had demonstrated that it was "entitled to statutory immunity in the exercise of its discretionary decision to create a cultural immersion program that placed students in host homes, relied on available public transportation, and provided a variety of student warnings and information" (*Bloss v. Univ of Minnesota Board of Regents*, 1999, p. 667). The *Bloss* decision clearly demonstrates that the Courts saw the value of cross-cultural education abroad experiences provided there were certain risk mitigation practices, including orientation and warnings to students regarding their environments. From an operational perspective, there is no one-size-fits-all approach to assessing the foreseeability of risks, rather, it is recommended to establish a risk identification and assessment process that accounts for the complexity of international environments. U.S. program providers should not strive to make a foreign educational experience the same as studying in the United States but shall take reasonable precautions to minimize the foreseeable risks of harm to program participants (Johnson, 2006). The Forum on Education Abroad's *Standards of Good Practice for Education Abroad* include the minimum requirement that an "organization shall have policies and procedures in place regarding security and risk management that prioritize the health, well-being, and safety of students" (2020, clause 5.1.7). It is then paramount to communicate identified risks and offer risk mitigation measures. The responsible party and the responsible organization "shall provide risk management, preparedness, and emergency response measures" (The Forum on Education Abroad, 2020, clause 5.2.4).

For a student or their heirs, beneficiaries or survivors to prevail on a negligence claim against the educational institution in court, the claimant (or plaintiff) must establish that the educational institution owed the student the duty of care, that the educational institution's breach of its duty of care was the proximate cause of the student's injury, and that the student has suffered injury or damages (Burch, 2010). Courts often use the Hand Formula created by Justice Learned Hand in *United States v. Carroll Towing Co.*, 1947, to determine negligence liability. If the probability of the loss (P) and the gravity of the loss (L) are greater than the burden of taking precautions (B), or B < PL, then the university will have a degree of liability (Gilles, 2001). Understanding the negligence standard that prevails across 50 different states can be examined by first reviewing judicial opinions. "What judges say about the negligence standard in appellant or trial court opinions may tell us precisely what the formal negligence standard is in that state and, possibly, the meaning of that standard as understood by the judges" (Kelley & Wendt, 2002, p. 592). You can also review the jury instructions on the negligence standards that judges in different states provide to obtain further insight.

## Duty of Care

Over the past 30 years, there has been an evolving sense of the duty of care a university has for its students (Lake, 1999). Duty of Care (DOC) is an enterprise's obligation to use reasonable care to promote employees' and students' well-being by protecting their safety and health from undue risks. DOC requires that a person acts toward others and the public with the watchfulness, attention, caution, and prudence that a reasonable person would use in the circumstances (Law.com, n.d.). A university can breach its DOC by failing to take reasonable care to keep its employees and students safe. If a person's actions do not meet this standard of care and there is a breach, the acts could be considered negligent, and damages may be awarded.

In *Wight v. Ohio State University* (OSU) (2001), a graduate student became ill during a university-led high-altitude expedition in Tibet. OSU took numerous mitigating steps to address the student's illness; however, the student died less than three months later due to complications from a lung infection. In the negligence suit, the court found that, based on the expert testimony and the evidence, Dr. Thompson performed his duties as a leader of the expedition in a reasonable manner. Accordingly, the court found that the plaintiffs had failed to prove that the defendant breached a duty owed to Wight (*Wight v. Ohio State University,* 2001). For a detailed discussion of this case, see Chapter 3, "Lessons from Legal Cases: Safeguarding Student Health & Well-Being in Education Abroad Programs," by Kim S. Priebe and Anna Hayes (2024).

In *McNeil v. Wagner College* (1998), the New York Court of Appeals found that because New York did not apply the doctrine of *in loco parentis* (that universities have supervisory and caretaking roles that parents otherwise would have) to universities, the university had no obligation to supervise the medical treatment received by the student. The student was participating in a Wagner College-sponsored Austria program when she slipped and fell on the ice. It was unknown whether, at the time of the injury, the student was actively participating in a curricular component of the study abroad program or whether she was pursuing her own interests. The student claimed that the study abroad program administrator "assumed a duty to act as interpreter for the student in the Austrian hospital and that she suffered nerve damage due to the administrator's failure to inform her of the treating physician's recommendation that she undergo immediate surgery" (Burch, 2010, p. 483). The student failed to show any duty assumed by the administrator in agreeing to serve as a translator (Burch, 2010). *McNeil v. Wagner College* (1998) represents an examination of an assumed duty of a college through an action of its employee in the absence of such obligation memorialized in a pre-trip waiver or consent forms, ultimately finding that the assumption of one task did not automatically mean the assumption of a special duty of care (Pfahl, 2021).

Duty of care is a question of law and therefore is a decision for the court (*Boisson v. Ariz. Bd. of Regents*, 2015). "DOC, being a question of law, is particularly amenable to resolution by summary judgment" (Parsons, 1997, p. 465), which is a decision made based on evidence and statements without going to trial. In *Regents University of California v. Katherine Rosen*, the defendants moved for a summary judgment, "arguing that postsecondary schools do not have a duty to protect their students from third-party misconduct" (2018, p. 894). Defendants challenged the order by petition through writ of mandate in the Second District Court of Appeals and it was granted. In *Regents University of California v. Superior Court of Los Angeles*, the Supreme Court reversed the Second District Court of Appeal determining that colleges and universities have a "duty to use reasonable care to protect their students from foreseeable acts of violence in the classroom or during curricular activities" (2018, p. 627). In *Boisson v. Ariz. Bd. of Regents* (2015), the plaintiff, the mother of a student studying abroad in China who traveled to Tibet on a noncurricular excursion and died of altitude sickness, tried to insert her expert's opinion as evidence in the determination of whether the University of Arizona had a DOC for her deceased son. The court held that the University of Arizona Board of Regents did not have a DOC because the Tibet excursion was not part of the education abroad curriculum. Determining whether a DOC exists is an issue of law for the court to decide, not experts per the court's decision.

## Breach of Duty of Care by Third Party

In Texas negligence law, liability "is premised on duty, a breach of which proximately causes injuries, and damages resulting from that breach" (*Thapar v. Zezulka*, 1999, p. 637). Therefore, whether a legal duty exists is a threshold question; if there is no duty, there can be no liability (*Thapar v. Zezulka*, 1999). As a general matter, there is no duty to control the conduct of third persons (*Greater House. Transp. Co. v. Phillips,* 1990). However, that general rule does not apply when a special relationship exists between the actor and the third person that imposes a duty on the actor to control the third person's conduct (*Greater House. Transp. Co. v. Phillips,* 1990).

Where students have sued their educational institutions for injuries caused by the act of a third party, courts have consistently applied Section 315 of the Restatement (Second) of Torts (1965), which provides:

> There is no duty to control the conduct of a third person so as to prevent him for causing physical harm to another unless:
>
> A special relationship exists between the actor and the third person which imposes a duty upon the actor to control the third person's conduct, or
>
> A special relationship exists between the actor and the other, which gives to the other a right to protection. (Bell, 1997, p. 235)

When determining whether a special relationship exists, courts have consistently held that the student–university relationship is insufficient to create a special relationship (Burke, 2010). In Kansas, it was decided that the student–university relationship does not in and of itself impose a duty upon universities to protect students from the actions of fellow students or third parties (*Nero v. Kan. State Univ.,* 1993). Those courts that have found that a special relationship exists have determined that, at the time of the student's injury, the educational institution's relationship with the student was the same as that of the business invitee, property owner, or landlord-tenant (Burch, 2010).

Since the special relationship in determining DOC is a state-by-state question of law, it has been interesting to watch the pendulum swing in higher education decisions from viewing students as autonomous adults to the more recent prevalent view that universities have a special relationship to provide a DOC to protect students from foreseeable harm even from third parties, especially in curricular activities (*Regents University of California v. Superior Court of Los Angeles,* 2018).

In *Fay v. Thiel College* (2001), a Pennsylvania Court found a special relationship existed for negligent liability of Thiel College due to a required signed emergency medical consent form even though a third party caused the breach. The court ruled that Thiel College did owe the plaintiff a special DOC as a result of the special relationship that arose between Thiel College and the plaintiff pursuant to the consent form. Thiel College's requirement for a student to sign an emergency medical consent form increased the institution's liability by evidencing a special relationship between the parties. This case is examined in detail in Chapter 3, "Lessons from Legal Cases: Safeguarding Student Health & Well-Being in Education Abroad Programs," by Kim S. Priebe and Anna Hayes (2024).

## Special Relationship

The landmark case defining an enterprise's special relationship incurring negligent responsibility for acts of a third party is *Regents University of California v. Superior Court of Los Angeles* (2018). In this previously referenced case Rosen, a UCLA student, had been attacked with a knife and sustained serious, life-threatening injuries by another student while working in a chemistry lab on campus. Concerns about the mental wellness of the attacker had been brought to the university's attention before the incident. The student made verbal and physical threats against other students and was ordered to seek therapy. It was alleged the defendants had breached their duty of care because they knew of the attacker's "dangerous and violent propensities," but failed to adopt reasonable measures to protect Rosen. In their decision, the California Supreme Court determined that public universities and colleges in California owe a duty of care to their students due to the special relationship between a university and its students to protect them from foreseeable acts of harm in the classroom or during curricular activities from known third parties such as fellow students (*Regents University of California v. Superior Court of Los Angeles,* 2018).

While *Boisson v. Ariz. Bd. of Regents* (2015) was decided before the Rosen case, it addresses the factors in Arizona and in other jurisdictions for determining whether an off-campus activity is deemed a curricular activity, including:

1. The purpose of the activity,
2. Whether the activity was part of the course curriculum,
3. Whether the school had supervisory authority and responsibility during the activity, and
4. Whether the risk students were exposed to during the activity was independent of the school involvement.

Additionally, the Boisson Court listed additional factors considered by courts in other jurisdictions, including:

5. Whether the activity was voluntary or was a required school activity,
6. Whether a school employee was present at or participated in the activity or was expected to do so, and
7. Whether the activity involved a dangerous project initiated at school but built off campus. (*Boisson v. Ariz. Bd. of Regents,* 2015, pp. 6-7)

For risk assessment purposes, these factors are instructive for determining whether an activity on an education abroad program would be considered part of curricular activities incurring DOC responsibilities and obligations and the designation of a special relationship if a third party causes harm during a curricular activity. Since determining a special relationship between university and student is more prevalent in court decisions within the last decade, education abroad professionals should assume that a negligence suit will proceed to the fact finding stage even when the harm is caused by a third party.

## Breach: Reasonable Care and Foreseeability of Harm

In determining whether an educational institution owed a duty of reasonable care to the student at the time of the injury foreseeing the harm giving rise to the injury, the *Patterson v. Sacramento City Unified Sch. Dist.* (2007) case shows the court balances the following factors:

> The foreseeability of the harm to the plaintiff, the degree of certainty that the plaintiff suffered injury, the closeness of the connection between the defendant's conduct and the injury suffered, the moral blame attached to the defendant's conduct, the policy of preventing future harm, the extent of the burden to the defendant and consequences to the community of imposing a duty to exercise care with resulting liability for breach, and the availability, cots, and prevalence of insurance for the risk involved. (Burch, 2010, p. 463)

Reasonable care requires that the educational institution maintain the premises in good order, including locks on doors and windows, warn students of criminal activity in the area, advise students on safety measures, and provide adequate security (Burch, 2010). In determining the measures reasonably necessary, most jurisdictions apply a totality of the circumstances test, while a minority of jurisdictions require that a similar prior criminal act occurred on the premises.

Is the harm foreseeable? For liability to arise, a particular risk must be so clear and probable that a reasonable person would be on notice of what is needed to be prevented and have some idea of what to do (Johnson, 2006). "Foreseeability of harm is the single most important concept in the law of negligence" (Johnson, 2006, p. 342). "Absent foreseeability of injury, there is no liability for failure to exercise care. As courts sometimes say, the question is not whether harm was "possible," but whether it was 'probable'—'probable' not in the sense of more likely than not to occur, but in the sense of being sufficiently likely than not to occur" (Johnson, 2006, p. 342).

An example where a university was not found liable for a lack of reasonable care was *Mattingly v. the University of Louisville* (2006). During a University of Louisville education abroad faculty-led program in Portugal, an unknown man raped a student. There was a delay in taking the student to a hospital and reporting the incident to the police. The court held that although the faculty advisor should have taken the student to the hospital and police quicker, the delay was insufficient to constitute a lack of reasonable care (*Mattingly v. the University of Louisville*, 2006). The students were warned during the orientation session to travel in groups, and the university housed the students in private dorms with locking doors. The university had no control over the alleged harasser or the context in which the harassment occurred.

"The breach of DOC and evaluating reasonable care for foreseeable harm are questions of fact for a jury" (Burch, 2010, p. 462). In *Jane Doe v. Rhode Island School of Design* (RISD) (2019), negligence resulted from the fact that the bedrooms in a rental facility for an education abroad program did not have locks on the bedroom doors in mixed-gender housing, resulting in the sexual assault of Doe, an RISD student. The court held that RISD undertook to provide accommodation for Doe in a foreign country, and Doe reasonably relied on RISD to act with due care. This undertaking and reliance altered the relationship between RISD and Doe to go beyond the university and adult student relationship, indicating a shift back to the doctrine of in loco parentis. This case is explored in greater detail in Chapter 4, "Housing Safety Considerations for Education Abroad," by Kyle Rausch (2024).

In *Munn v. Hotchkiss School* (2015), high school student Cara Munn traveled with a school group to China. During a hike, Munn contracted tick-borne encephalitis suffering long-term disabilities. The Connecticut Supreme Court found that the school had a duty to warn about or protect against the risk of a serious insect-borne disease in organizing a trip abroad, giving precedent to the notion that institutions have a duty to their travelers to warn about known risks and to take reasonable action to mitigate these risks. This case is discussed in detail in Chapter 3, "Lessons from Legal Cases: Safeguarding Student Health & Well-Being in Education Abroad Programs," by Kim S. Priebe and Anna Hayes (2024).

## Proximate Cause

A cause describes the reason something occurs, and the concept is used in many areas of law. There are two elements of causation in tort law; factual cause and proximate causation. Factual cause is often established using the "but for test," that evaluates if the tort would have occurred without an action or omission from tortfeasor (defendant) (Legal Information Institute, n.d. b). "Simply stated, 'but for' analysis requires the finder of fact to determine that the asserted harm would not have come to pass 'but for' the defendant's tortious act" (Rue, 2003, p. 2681). If the answer is yes, then the actions of the defendant are the factual cause of the tort. Proximate causation refers to a cause that is legally sufficient to find the defendant liable. Some courts have abandoned the "but-for" cause altogether and apply the doctrine of proximate cause (Legal Information Institute, n.d. b). Legal Information Institute defines proximate cause as

> an actual cause that is also legally sufficient to support liability. Although many actual causes can exist for an injury, the law does not attach liability to all the actors responsible for those causes. The likelihood of calling something a proximate cause increases as the cause becomes more direct and more necessary for the injury to occur. (n.d. b, paras. 1-2)

In *Wight v. Ohio State University* (2001), OSU graduate student Wight volunteered for a university-led high-altitude expedition in Tibet. The team lead, a faculty member from OSU, informed students of the rigors of high-altitude climbing and provided substantial information about the high-altitude illness before departure. Wight became ill due to altitude sickness and as the illness progressed and symptoms changed, the expedition leader followed normal procedures for monitoring and treating altitude-related illness. Wight died less than three months later due to complications from a lung infection. Wight's parents sued the university, alleging negligence. The court found that the death certificate did not support the plaintiffs' theory regarding the proximate cause of Wight's death and, in some respects, conflicted with that theory. Even if plaintiffs had established that the defendant breached a duty owed to Wight, there is no legal consequence for the breach of such a duty unless it is the proximate cause of an injury. The court concluded that the plaintiffs failed to prove that the defendant's alleged negligence proximately caused Wight's death. This case is discussed in more detail in Chapter 3.

## Assumption of Risk

"Assumption of risk is a common law doctrine that refers to a plaintiff's inability to recover for the tortious actions of a negligent party in scenarios where the plaintiff voluntarily accepted the risk of those actions" (Legal Information Institute, n.d. a, para. 1). Express assumption of risk is typically achieved through a signed waiver and may be treated by the courts as a contract issue. Waivers present a number of challenges from use of overgeneralized wording, being too long to be effective, and students not reading the content. Malveaux encourages a *healthy tension* between education abroad professionals and legal counsel, stating:

> When it comes to waiver construction, a natural opposition between coordinators and legal counsel has been widespread and long standing. In general, coordinators desire more program-specific language, non repetitive language, to produce a short, succinct, waiver. Legal counsel tends to want documents to be legally sound, without potentially leaving out official language; often that official language is repetitive and adds length to a waiver. Each side pushed for the most articulate document to protect participants and the institution. (2016, p. 157)

Relationships between education abroad professionals and legal counsel are explored in depth in Chapter 26, "Building the Partnership: Best practices in engaging counsel," by Ashley Krutz-Ordner and Miko McFarland (2024).

A case that illustrates the significance of a waiver in the event of a student death is *Thackurdeen v. Duke University* (2014). In 2012, Ravi Thackurdeen died in Costa Rica while enrolled in the Global Health and Tropical Medicine Program, a study abroad program administered by Duke University and Organization for Tropical Studies. At the end of the program, students were taken on a "celebratory trip" to a beach where Thackurdeen was pulled by a rip current and drowned.

Thackurdeen's parents argued that their claims of negligence and wrongful death are not barred by the doctrines of waiver and release because (1) claims for gross negligence cannot be released under North Carolina law, (2) the claims fall outside the scope of the releases, and (3) the releases violate a substantial public interest and are, therefore, unenforceable. The Thackurdeens asserted that the beach trip was unplanned, and was not a regular class, lecture, or field trip connected to the educational experience. Therefore, the beach trip did not fall within the scope of the program and the waiver does not release legal claims arising from it. The Duke waiver did not include beginning or end dates for the Global Health Program. Per North Carolina law, when a contract does not define term uses, nontechnical words are to be given their meaning in ordinary speech. The ordinary meaning of "program" in the context of the Duke waiver encompasses the entirety of the program and the beach trip was within the activity contemplated by the waiver. The court stated, "The surprise beach trip was a program sponsored event and was part of the Global Health Program. As such, it is not outside the scope of the waivers signed for either Duke or OTS" (*Thackurdeen v. Duke*, 2014, section 23). This case serves as a reminder to examine the reliance on waivers in the enterprise's overall assumption of risk strategy.

## Operationalizing Risk Management

In the *Standards of Good Practice for Education Abroad,* clause 6.1.11 states, "Responsible parties shall prepare students to manage their safety by providing resources related to concerns including, but not limited to:

- physical risks
- behavior
- property crime
- liability and legal issues
- sexual misconduct
- identity-based discrimination
- country-specific recommendations." (2020)

However, risk communication is only one step in operational risk management. The operational risk management process includes identifying risks, assessing those risks, determining the appropriate risk treatment, monitoring both the risk and the treatment method, and reporting incidents.

Responsible organizations should begin with assessing risks, meaning identifying any hazards or threats that may exist within a program or may exist because of the participants in the program and determining an appropriate treatment for the identified risk. In *Risk: A User's Guide,* McCrystal (2021) asks, "Does your structure make sense for what you're trying to do and for the environment in which you are operating" (p. 83), indicating that an internal organizational assessment of appropriateness of structure and resources should also be conducted. The U.S. Air Force first operationalized the risk assessment matrix, and it has become one of the most widely used qualitative risk assessment techniques adopted across industries for its simplicity, and effectiveness (Garvey & Lansdowne, 1998). A risk matrix identifies the probability/likelihood of the risk occurring is shown on the vertical axis, and the severity of consequences is displayed on the horizontal axis. The University of California Office of the President (n.d.) Enterprise Risk Management Office offers a risk assessment toolbox that helps support risk assessment. Excel-based worksheets help you identify and assess factors affecting the risks faced by your organization, including the likelihood of an incident, impact, severity, financial impact, and control effectiveness for a list of risks you create. The University of California Field Research Safety Center of Excellence (n.d.) produces a host of resources from the perspective of environmental health and safety, including a field operations safety manual that offers sections on planning, training, incident response and best practices for promoting safe teaching and research outdoors, at remote sites, and abroad. When identifying risks, it is important to examine the program holistically and consider subjective risks and objective risks that may occur in a location as a result of an activity or because of the participants themselves.

Risk treatment methods include various approaches from transferring the risk through waivers and insurance policies to relying on authoritarian bodies such as the U.S. Department of State or the Centers for Disease Control for guidance. A critical treatment method all education abroad professionals engage in is risk communication. The materials that promote, describe, and prepare students for programs are opportunities to communicate risk. The pre-departure preparations and onsite activities may include orientations, program guides, interactive modules, and/or training that serve as risk communication. Risk communication can provide timely, accurate, and relevant information to encourage awareness, improve knowledge, and increase understanding of the effects of risk. It contributes to transparency and accountability in the risk management process while promoting a shared understanding of responsibilities.

Continuous risk monitoring is a dynamic process that involves ongoing reviews of the risk treatment methods and encourages improvement. It builds awareness of what types of risks are being encountered, can serve to identify trends or patterns, and highlight opportunities for updates or further analysis. Benchmarking risk data with organizations such as the Overseas Security Advisory Council's (OSAC) Academia Sector Committee and The Forum on Education Abroad's Student Risk Report may provide further improvements in best practices throughout the field.

Institutional resources and support are essential for risk management in education abroad programming. Senior International Officers (SIOs) are key stakeholders in this work. In *Leading Internationalization* (2018), McQuaid and Klar identify three key areas where SIOs can provide leadership support of education abroad. (1) Appropriate Staffing; (2) Appropriate Orientation; (3) Appropriate Delineation of Responsibility. In order for responsible risk management practices to function effectively, these three areas are of critical importance. The Forum on Education Abroad and NAFSA: Association of International Educators convened a joint task force to "outline fundamental expectations for health, safety, and security in education abroad that could be easily understood by a variety of audiences, from participants to policymakers" (NAFSA and The Forum on Education Abroad, 2021, p. 2). This guidance provides robust considerations regarding the roles and responsibilities of all parties involved in education abroad; participants, support networks, responsible personnel, and responsible organizations.

Important components of a responsible organizational approach to risk management include

- Listening and responding to warnings and incidents
- Acting with integrity and investigating honestly
- Consistent enforcement and adherence to policy and continuous improvement of best practice
- Skillful, responsible communication and setting reasonable expectations

## Conclusion

The increasing complexity and scrutiny surrounding higher education institutions have led to a significant rise in legal and regulatory pressures, shaping the role of general counsel within these organizations. As education abroad programs become more prevalent, professionals in this field are confronted with unique legal considerations and responsibilities. From understanding negligence liability to assessing duty of care and breach of responsibilities, the legal landscape for education abroad professionals is multifaceted and demanding.

Negligence liability, a common legal concern, requires education abroad practitioners to navigate a broad spectrum of potential risks, including medical issues, sexual assault, and supervisory neglect. Recent court cases underscore the importance of implementing risk mitigation practices and establishing clear policies and procedures. Duty of care, which has evolved over the years, places a significant obligation on educational institutions to prioritize the safety and health of their students, whether on campus or abroad.

In operationalizing risk management, education abroad programs must go beyond mere risk communication and actively identify, assess, and monitor risks throughout the program lifecycle. By prioritizing proactive risk management practices and strong collaboration with legal counsel, education abroad programs can fulfill their mission of providing transformative experiences while safeguarding the well-being of students.

## References

Bell, T. W. (1997). *Restatement (Second) of Torts*. Internet Law. http://www.tomwbell.com/NetLaw/Ch05/R2ndTorts.html

Bloss v. Univ. of Minnesota Board of Regents, 590 N.W.2d 661, Minn Ct. App. (1999).

Boisson v. Ariz. Bd. of Regents, 343 P. 3d 931, 236 Ariz. 619 - Ariz: Court of Appeals, 1st Div. (2015).

Burch, K.M. (2010). Going global: Managing liability in international externship programs a case study. *Journal of College and University Law, 362*(2),455-510.

Dall, J.A. (2003) Determining duty in collegiate tort litigation: Shifting paradigms of the college-student relationship. *J.C. & U.L., 29,* 485-487.

Dietrich, A. (2024). *Student Risk Report: Data from Education Abroad Programs: January 1 - December 31, 2023.* The Forum on Education Abroad. DOI: 10.36366/R.2024SRR.1

Doe v. Rhode Island School of Design, 432 F.Supp.3d 35 (2019).

Erfle, S.E., & Dietrich, A.J. (2020) College student mortality on U.S. campuses compared with rates while abroad, *Journal of American College Health,* 68 (8), 900-905, DOI: 10.1080/07448481.2019.1634078

Fay v Thiel College, 55 Pa. D. & C.4th 353, (2001).

Garner, B. (2019) Black's Law Dictionary 11th edition Thompson West.

Garvey, P.R., & Lansdowne, Z.F. (1998) Risk Matrix: An approach for identifying, assessing, and ranking program risks, *Air Force Journal of Logistics, 22,* 18-21.

Gilles, S.G. (2001) On determining negligence: Hand formula balancing, the reasonable person standard, and the jury. *Vanderbilt Law Review, 54,* 813. Available at: https://scholarship.law.vanderbilt.edu/vlr/vol54/iss3/7

Guard, L.H., & Jacobsen, J.P. (2024) *All the campus lawyers: Litigation, regulation, and the new era of higher education.* Harvard University Press.

Greater House. Transp. Co. v. Phillips, 801 S.W.2d 523, 525, Tex. (1990).

Jamieson, S., & Morgan, P. (2024). Who can go where for what purposes and under what conditions: Building an institutional international travel policy. In J. Pollard & K. S. Priebe (Eds.), *Convergence of litigation, policy, and standards: Building the informed practitioner in education abroad risk management.* The Forum on Education Abroad.

Jesse, D. (2024 February 26). Repressive legalism. *Chronicle of Higher Education.*https://www.chronicle.com/article/your-colleges-top-lawyer-has-never-been-more-powerful?sra=true

Johnson, V.R. (2006). Americans abroad: international education programs and tort liability. *Journal of College and University Law,* 32(2), 309-360.

Kelley, P.J., & Wendt, L.A. (2002) What judges tell juries about negligence: A review of pattern jury instructions. *Chicago-Kent Law Review,* 77 (2), 587-682.

Kritchevsky, B. (2010) "Tort law is state law: Why courts should distinguish state and federal law in negligence-per-se law," *American University Law Review, 60*(1), Article 2. Available at: http://digitalcommons.wcl.american.edu/aulr/vol60/iss1/2

Kuersten, A., & Lewis, K.M. (2023). *Introduction to Tort Law.* Congressional Research Service https://crsreports.congress.gov/product/pdf/IF/IF11291

Lake, P. F. (1999). The rise of duty and the fall of in loco parentis and other protective tor doctrines in higher education law. *Missouri Law Review, 64*(1), 1-28.

Law.com (n.d.) Duty of care. In *The People's Law Dictionary.* https://dictionary.law.com/Default.aspx?selected=599

Legal Information Institute. (n.d. a) *Assumption of risk.* Cornell Law School. https://www.law.cornell.edu/wex/assumption_of_risk

Legal Information Institute. (n.d. b) *But-for test.* Cornell Law School. https://www.law.cornell.edu/wex/but-for_test

Legal Information Institute. (n.d. c) *Tort..* Cornell Law School. https://www.law.cornell.edu/wex/tort

Malveaux, G.F. (2016) *Look before leaping: Risks, liabilities and repair of study abroad in higher education.* Rowman & Littlefield.

Mattingly v. the University of Louisville, 3:05CV-H, 2006 WL 2178032, W.D. Ky. (2006).

McChrystal, S., & Butrico, A. (2021). *Risk: A user's guide.* Portfolio / Penguin.

McNeil vs. Wagner College, 246 A.D.2d 516;667 N.Y.S. 2d 397, NY App Div. (1998)

McQuaid, M., & Klahr, S. (2018). The senior international officer: Managing risk and liability. In D.K. Deardorff and H. Charles (Eds.), *Leading Internationalization.* Stylus Publishing.

Munn v. Hotchkiss School, 795 F. 3d 324, 2nd Cir. (2015)

NAFSA and The Forum on Education Abroad. (2021). *Responsible education abroad: Best practices for health, safety and security. (3rd ed.).* https://www.nafsa.org/professional-resources/browse-by-interest/responsible-study-abroad-good-practices-health-and-safety

Nero v. Kan. State Univ., 861 P.2d 768,778, Kan., (1993).

Notice Pursuant to the National Cooperative Research and Production Act of 1993-Forum on Education Abroad, Inc., 69 F.R. 69394 (proposed September 20, 2004) (filed November 29, 2004). https://www.federalregister.gov/documents/2004/11/29/04-26221/notice-pursuant-to-the-national-cooperative-research-and-production-act-of-1993-forum-on-education

Pfahl, M.R. (2021). Enhancing enforceability of exculpatory clause in education abroad programming through examination of three pillars. *Journal of College and University Law, 46*(1), 93-120.

Priebe, K. S., & Hayes, A. (2024). Lessons from legal cases: Safeguarding student health and well-being in education abroad programs. In J. Pollard & K. S. Priebe (Eds.), *Convergence of litigation, policy, and standards: Building the informed practitioner in education abroad risk management.* The Forum on Education Abroad.

Rausch, K. (2024). Housing safety considerations for education abroad. In J. Pollard & K. S. Priebe (Eds.), *Convergence of litigation, policy, and standards: Building the informed practitioner in education abroad risk management.* The Forum on Education Abroad.

Rausch, K. (2024). Operationalizing duty of care in education abroad using The Forum Standards. In J. Pollard & K. S. Priebe (Eds.), *Convergence of litigation, policy, and standards: Building the informed practitioner in education abroad risk management.* The Forum on Education Abroad.

Redden, E. (2007). The Next Frontier. Inside Higher Ed. https://www.insidehighered.com/news/2007/05/31/next-frontier

Regents University of California v. Superior Court of Los Angeles, 4 Cal. 5th 607, 413 P. 3d 656 (2018).

Rue, J.D. (2003). Returning to the roots of the bramble bush: The 'but for' test regains primacy in casual analysis in the American Law Institute's proposed restatement (Third) of Torts. *Fordham Law Review, 71*(6), 2679-2733.

Snyman, H., Douglas, H., & Collins, G. (2024). Applying standards to travel risk management. In J. Pollard & K. S. Priebe (Eds.), *Convergence of litigation, policy, and standards: Building the informed practitioner in education abroad risk management.* The Forum on Education Abroad.

Thackurdeenv Duke University & Organizational For Tropical Field Studies, Inc, 1:16CV1108 (M.D.N.C. Mar. 23, 2018)

Thapar v. Zezulka, 994 S.W.2d 635, 637, Tex. (1999)

The Forum on Education Abroad. (2020). *Standards of good practice for education abroad, Sixth edition.* doi.org/10.36366/S.978-1-952376-04-7

United Educators. (n.d.). *About United Educators.* Retrieved January 22, 2024 from https://www.ue.org/about-ue/

United Educators (2023) *Top risks report: Insights for higher education.*https://www.ue.org/4aef6e/globalassets/risk-management/reports/2023-top-risks-report-he.pdf

United States v. Carroll Towing Co., 159 F.2n 169,173, 2d Cir., (1947).

University of California Office of the President. (n.d.). Risk Assessment Toolbox. Enterprise Risk and Resilience. https://www.ucop.edu/enterprise-risk-and-resilience/erm/tools-templates/risk-assessment-toolbox.html

University of California Office of the President (n.d.). Field Research Safety Center of Excellence. https://www.ucop.edu/safety-and-loss-prevention/environmental/program-resources/field-research-safety/index.html

Wight v. Ohio State University, 750 N.E.2d 659, Ohio Misc. (2001).

# 3

# Lessons from Legal Cases: Safeguarding Student Health and Well-Being in Education Abroad Programs

**Kim S. Priebe and Anna Hayes**

Student health and safety are paramount concerns for education abroad professionals and program leaders. In order to ensure education abroad offices are developing and administering programs with student health and safety in mind, it is critical to understand the past for context. Three notable legal cases, *Wight v. Ohio State University* (2001), *Fay v. Thiel College* (2001), and *Munn v. Hotchkiss School* (2017), highlight the importance of implementing robust risk mitigation strategies to support the safety and well-being of students participating in education abroad programs, such as conducting site risk assessments and establishing clear emergency protocols, as well as protecting the institution through documentation and proper training of program leaders. The cases represent health and safety issues that can arise in a study abroad program, one of the three most common risks facing students while abroad (Malveaux, 2016). This chapter will examine the outcomes of these three cases and discuss how they should serve as a foundational basis for shaping risk mitigation best practices in education abroad.

## Wight v. Ohio State University

In 1997, Ohio State University graduate student Shawn Wight volunteered to participate in a university-affiliated research expedition at high altitudes in Tibet. Wight became ill at the higher altitudes and died less than three months later due to complications from a lung infection. His parents sued the university for negligence, claiming it failed to adequately monitor Wight's health during the expedition, leaving the student alone while being treated, failing to provide specific medical treatments, and failing to transport the student to a better evacuation site (*Wight v. Ohio State University*, 2001).

The court stated, "In order for plaintiffs to prevail upon these claims, they must prove by a preponderance of the evidence that defendant owed plaintiffs' decedent a duty, that it breached that duty, and that the breach proximately caused the death of plaintiffs' decedent" (*Wight v. Ohio State University*, 2001, p. 3). The court found in favor of the defendant, Ohio State University. The plaintiffs failed to prove a breach of duty given the thorough pre-departure information provided to Wight and others that specifically addressed the health risks in high altitude and the fact that the faculty leaders closely monitored Wight's health throughout the program, accompanying him down the mountain when they determined he needed to evacuate to a lower altitude, and offering advice on further evacuation (*Wight v. Ohio State University*, 2001).

Wight arrived in Kathmandu, Nepal, on August 5, 1997, and remained there for one week before he and the team began a three-day bus trip to the base camp at 17,500 feet of elevation. They remained there for six days to acclimatize, during which time "all of the American members of the expedition experienced symptoms of altitude sickness" (*Wight v. Ohio State University*, 2001, p. 2). Wight improved after three days, and on August 20, he began the ascent with the team to camp 3 at an elevation of 19,000 feet. After 13 days of acclimatizing and resuming normal camp activities, the research team continued their ascent to camp 4 at an elevation of 21,000 feet, where they spent an additional two nights (*Wight v. Ohio State University*, 2001).

On September 6, while at 23,000-feet elevation at camp 5, Wight complained of numb hands, became disoriented, and could not recall names. The team leads, Drs. Thompson and Yao, accompanied him back to camp 3, where he rested, regained his memory, and began feeling normal. Dr. Thompson determined that Wight needed to remain at the lower elevation for five additional days to recover before returning to camp 5. Drs. Thompson and Yao left Wight in the care of two field team leaders who monitored his health and regularly updated the team leaders at higher camps. Dr. Thompson was informed on September 15 that Wight had been experiencing pain under his ribs and intended to leave the expedition, at which time Dr. Yao provided funds for Wight to depart. On September 15, Dr. Yao suggested that Dr. Thompson descend to camp 3 because Wight's condition had become severe. Wight was unable to walk due to a swollen leg. The program leaders determined that Wight needed immediate evacuation to a medical facility. They accompanied Wight on the day-and-a-half journey to Lhasa, Tibet, where the local hospital admitted him. Wight's condition seemed to improve, at which time Dr. Thompson returned to the expedition site, leaving Dr. Yao in charge (*Wight v. Ohio State University*, 2001).

Wight's father arranged to have Wight medically evacuated to a hospital in Hong Kong, where he stayed for 10 days. The medical team advised Wight that he needed treatment for a lung abscess; however, he and his family chose to have him discharged and evacuated back to the United States. Following treatment at the University Hospital of Cleveland (UHC) in Ohio, Wight was discharged on October 31 "with the expectation that he would fully recover" (*Wight v. Ohio State University*, 2001, p. 3). According to court case testimony, on November 2, "Wight's condition suddenly worsened, and he was readmitted to UHC" (*Wight v. Ohio State University*, 2001, p. 3). He remained in the hospital until he died on November 28, 1997. His official cause of death was complications stemming from a lung infection.

In the ensuing case, the plaintiffs failed to prove a breach of duty of care regarding the university's oversight of Wight nor prove a proximate cause of death. The court records show that the university had informed the students of the rigors of high-altitude climbing and provided substantial information about high-altitude illness, including personal accounts from coworkers, a radio program featuring "medical experts discussing high-altitude illness and medicine" (p. 1), and a recording of an earlier expedition (*Wight v. Ohio State University*, 2001). The court determined that the university's expedition leader acted reasonably and decisively when Wight became ill, following appropriate procedures for monitoring and treating altitude-related illness, including moving to camps at lower altitudes, soliciting the opinions of multiple doctors, and evacuating Wight when his condition worsened. Given these actions, the court determined that "Dr. Thompson acted with the proper degree of care in responding to Wight's medical emergency and that [the] plaintiffs have failed to prove any negligence concerning the defendant concerning the choice of medical facilities" (*Wight v. Ohio State University*, 2001, p. 6).

## Fay v. Thiel College

Amy Fay was a student at Thiel College in Greenville, Pennsylvania, when she participated in a Thiel-sponsored faculty-led study abroad program in

Peru in May 1996. The group was in Cusco when Fay became ill, and she was taken to a medical clinic and admitted. The program's three faculty directors decided to proceed with a pre-arranged multiday excursion and leave Fay behind at the medical clinic (*Fay v. Thiel College*, 2001). They left Fay in the care of a friend of one of the program leaders, a Lutheran missionary not affiliated with Thiel College. Fay underwent a medically unnecessary appendectomy and, while under anesthesia, was sexually assaulted by the surgeon and the anesthesiologist (*Fay v. Thiel College*, 2001).

Fay, who did not speak Spanish, sought numerous alternatives to the surgery, requesting to call her parents, to be transferred to a hospital in Lima, and to fly home to the United States for her medical care (*Fay v. Thiel College*, 2001). All of her requests were denied, and the missionary authorized her surgery even though she was "not in any way related to Thiel College and was not in any way acting as an agent and/or representative of Thiel College" (*Fay v. Thiel College*, 2001, p. 2). Fay could recount being sexually assaulted because she had been given a local anesthetic and was fully conscious during and after her surgery (*Fay v. Thiel College*, 2001).

In the lawsuit, Fay alleged that Thiel College had a duty of care to her, and the program leaders "breached that duty by 'abandoning' her in the Peruvian medical clinic" (*Fay v. Thiel College*, 2001, p. 5). She maintained that the program leaders should have secured and overseen her medical treatment. Thiel College argued they were not liable because the student signed a liability waiver before the program. Thiel claimed they had no special relationship with the plaintiff beyond her being a student at Thiel College and acted reasonably by taking her to a medical clinic for care. Fay contended that the signed consent form created an expectation for a certain level of care, thus creating a special relationship between the parties.

Both sides testified that Thiel College required a signed waiver of liability and consent form to participate in the program. Citing a Pennsylvania Supreme Court 1996 ruling, the court decided the waiver was a "contract of adhesion" due to it being required in a "take it or leave it" manner, and therefore, invalid (*Fay v. Thiel College*, 2001). Furthermore, the court concluded that Thiel could not consider the consent form to be a waiver of liability form as the document did not expressly indicate its purpose as a waiver of liability (Pfahl, 2021). As per the findings in *Fay v. Thiel College* (2001), "a waiver of liability form must spell out the intention of the parties with the greatest of particularity" (p. 9).

More importantly, the court found that Thiel College owed Fay a duty of care due to the "special relationship" created by the consent form, which indicated that Thiel College would secure "whatever treatment is necessary, including the administration of an anesthetic and surgery" (p. 5), and that it was a requirement for participation in the program (*Fay v. Thiel College*, 2001). This consent form obligated Thiel to secure treatment and ensure a certain standard of care. Furthermore, the college did not continue communication with the student after leaving her. The court denied the defendant's motion for summary judgment, and the parties ultimately settled the case out of court.

## Munn v. Hotchkiss School

Cara Munn was a high school student at The Hotchkiss School in Connecticut and participated in a school-sponsored educational trip to China in 2007 at age 15. During the program, the students and faculty visited Mount Panshan. The excursion to Mount Panshan was listed in the program itinerary distributed to students before departure but included no description of the location as a forested area. In preparation for the trip, the faculty leaders provided students with a packing list, which included bug spray, but it was listed under "Miscellaneous Items" with other seemingly optional items (e.g., umbrellas and musical instruments). Additionally, students and their parents were inadvertently sent a link to the Centers for Disease Control and Prevention (CDC) information page for Central America rather than China, as intended (*Munn v. Hotchkiss School*, 2017).

While at Mount Panshan, most students and faculty leaders used a cable car to descend the mountain. Munn and several other students were permitted to walk down the mountain themselves. The students left the main paved path during the descent and became lost. While on the narrow dirt trails of trees and brush, Munn received numerous insect bites that later became itchy and swollen. Ten days after the hike, Munn began showing symptoms of tick-borne encephalitis. Court documents attested that as a result of these insect bites Munn was unable to communicate verbally due to her illness, experienced limited hand dexterity, which prevented typing, and had restricted control over her facial muscles, resulting in drooling, difficulties with eating, and socially inappropriate facial expressions. Despite retaining her intelligence, Munn also experienced impaired brain function that hindered the practical application of her cognitive abilities (*Munn v. Hotchkiss School*, 2017).

Due to their daughter's illness, Munn's family sued The Hotchkiss School, citing negligence on the part of the school for not warning the students and their families of the risk of insect-borne diseases. The United States District Court for the District of Connecticut initially ruled in favor of Munn and awarded Munn $10.25 million in economic damages and $31.5 million in noneconomic damages. The Hotchkiss School appealed the verdict to the Second Circuit Court of Appeals.

The Second Circuit Court of Appeals affirmed the lower court's decision, siding with Munn and citing that her illness was foreseeable. However, the Court could not determine "whether public policy supports imposing a legal duty on Hotchkiss" (*Munn v. Hotchkiss School*, 2017). Therefore, the Court certified two questions of law to be addressed by the Connecticut Supreme Court:

> (1) Does Connecticut public policy support imposing a duty on a school to warn or protect against the risk of a serious insect-borne disease when it organizes a trip abroad? (2) If so, does an award of approximately $41.5 million in favor of the plaintiffs, $31.5 million of which are noneconomic damages, warrant remittitur? (*Munn v. Hotchkiss School*, 2017, p.1)

In their responses to both questions, the Connecticut Supreme Court ruled in favor of Munn, stating that public policy does support imposing a duty on a school when it organizes a trip abroad, and the damages award is not excessive given the permanent and grave physical disability resulting from their negligence. The Connecticut Supreme Court stated that schools are "obligated to exercise reasonable care to protect students in their charge from foreseeable dangers" (*Munn v. Hotchkiss School*, 2017, p. 2), and that included insect-borne illnesses on study abroad programs.

The Connecticut Supreme Court applied a test to determine the existence of a legal duty. The test involves two aspects: first, whether a reasonable person in the defendant's position, knowing what that person should have known, would anticipate the likelihood of harm similar to the suffered harm of the plaintiff; and second, based on public policy, whether the defendant's liability for their negligent actions should encompass the specific result or the specific plaintiff (*Munn v. Hotchkiss School*, 2017). The Supreme Court also stated that many harms are foreseeable but do not necessarily result in damages. To demonstrate this, they outlined that the last step in determining duty involves deciding if the law's main principles say the person should be responsible for such outcomes. In considering whether the law suggests a duty, the courts examine four factors: (1) what participants typically expect in similar activities; (2) public policy of promoting involvement in the activity while considering the safety of those involved; (3) avoiding further litigation; and (4) what other jurisdictions have previously determined (*Munn v. Hotchkiss School*, 2017).

Similar to *Fay*, the Connecticut Supreme Court also addressed "special relationships," stating "the law of negligence typically does not impose a duty on one party to act affirmatively in furtherance of the protection of another" (*Munn v. Hotchkiss School*, 2017, p. 5), but an exception is when there is a "special relationship" between parties. In this case, a "special relationship" exists when one party assumes care of another party in a way that prevents the second party from protecting themselves as they normally would; there is a responsibility to ensure the person being taken care of is not hurt due to actions beyond their control. "At heart, the duty to protect derives from the simple fact that a school, in assuming physical custody and control over its students, effectively takes the place of parents and guardians" (*Munn v. Hotchkiss School*, 2017, p. 6). The Connecticut Supreme Court ruled that, in the context of a school-sponsored educational trip abroad with minor participants, program organizers are expected to provide adequate warnings to the participants and their parents about the risks of insect-borne diseases in the destination areas. The program organizers should also take necessary precautions to safeguard participants from these diseases. It is important to note that the outcome of this case may have been different had the plaintiff been a legal adult. Nevertheless, many lessons learned from this case apply to all education abroad programs, which will be discussed below.

## Direct Applicability to Education Abroad

The three cases, *Wight v. Ohio State University* (2001), *Fay v. Thiel College* (2001), and *Munn v. Hotchkiss School* (2017), each have clear takeaways that can be applied directly to education abroad operations and programming. In what follows, the lessons derived from the case law are organized to highlight the roles and responsibilities of two groups: (1) education abroad offices and (2) program leaders. Throughout the analysis and application of the cases to education abroad best practices, the terms "should," "shall," and "can" are used following The Forum on Education Abroad's (2020) *Standards of Good Practice for Education Abroad* and as established by the International Organization for Standardization (ISO).

### Education Abroad Office: Roles and Responsibilities

The education abroad office's responsibilities include having documented, accessible policies that clearly define the roles and expectations for program leaders, establishing emergency protocols, and developing program-specific safety assessments and risk mitigation plans for each location with their program leaders. Education abroad office personnel shall provide training to their leaders and pre-departure orientations to their students. They must also collaborate with their legal counsel to create and review any pre-program written agreements that need to be executed by the student before departure.

The Forum on Education Abroad's *Standards of Good Practice for Education Abroad* provide minimum requirements for education abroad programs, which include the expectation that an "organization shall have policies and procedures in place regarding security and risk management that prioritize the health, well-being, and safety of students" (The Forum on Education Abroad, 2020, clause 5.1.7). The *Fay v. Thiel College* case highlights the importance that an institution is obligated to do what it says it will. If the institution states it will "stand by the student," securing appropriate medical care and providing support, then the program leaders have a legal (and moral) obligation to do just that. A best practice would be to ensure that program personnel have clearly defined roles and responsibilities and know what is expected of them. Many institutions take this one step further and require their students, when under medical care, to be accompanied by program personnel affiliated with the home university or host program to ensure that adequate care is being provided.

Institutions administering programs abroad must ensure all programs have documented and regularly updated emergency plans and protocols (The Forum on Education Abroad, 2020, clause 5.2.4). Education abroad offices must ensure program leaders are familiar with these protocols and how to utilize them when an emergency arises onsite. In the case of *Fay*, before departure, the three program leaders from Thiel College, in consultation with their education abroad office, should have determined what to do if a student was unable to travel during the program as part of the emergency protocol planning, and in alignment with the *Standard's* clause 5.2.4 (2020).

Foreseeability of harm and the communication of all risks and mitigation strategies lie at the heart of *Munn* and *Wight*. In *Munn v. Hotchkiss*, the school's negligence in foreseeing the harm of insect-borne illnesses resulted in Cara Munn's irreversible health condition (2017). In *Wight v. Ohio State University*, the program leaders did foresee the risks of working in the high altitude of the Tibetan mountains. They were not found negligent because of the overwhelming clear evidence that showed they appropriately informed and assisted Wight during his illness (2001). The distinction between the two cases is that OSU took necessary steps to protect the students from foreseeable risks in *Wight*, whereas the Hotchkiss School did not provide the students with information to prevent harm.

A thorough risk assessment is essential to ensure program leaders are familiar with the risks associated with a proposed program or activity, as outlined by clause 5.1.7 (The Forum on Education Abroad, 2020). A thorough risk assessment analyzes the specific travel location(s) for concerns or risks related to, but not limited to, student accommodations, transportation, program activities and excursions, the local community, security of the area, modes of communication, and access to physical and mental health care and emergency services. The risk assessment should highlight the risks and identify mitigation strategies. The Overseas Security Advisory Council (OSAC) Academic Sector Committee and The Forum on Education Abroad offer examples of free risk assessment matrices that can serve as a resource (Overseas Security Advisory Council, 2021; The Forum on Education Abroad, n.d.). Program leaders can discuss their planned activities with education abroad or global health and safety office personnel and identify strategies to mitigate the known and foreseeable risks. In the pre-departure information, program leaders should ensure students are aware of any risks and advise on the specific precautions students should take to mitigate these risks during their education abroad program.

Many program leaders are not full-time education abroad professionals. Directing a program is often just one part of their academic work; thus, they may lack training and knowledge of industry standards. Nonetheless, they frequently remain the sole individuals present with students onsite, making crucial decisions about their well-being—a responsibility far exceeding their on-campus roles (Chieffo & Spaeth, 2017). *Fay* illustrates the importance of pre-departure training for program leaders, identified as a best practice in the field (NAFSA and The Forum on Education Abroad, 2021; The Forum on Education Abroad, 2020, clause 5.2.2).

Faculty and staff leading study abroad programs must be aware of their responsibilities in supporting student health and safety, and institutions must provide regular training for program leaders. Program leader preparation is "as much about defining the institutional role as it is about defining the additional responsibilities the director must assume" (Spencer & Tuma, 2002, p. 173). Education abroad offices (and global health and safety offices, if that resource is available at an institution) are responsible for training their program leaders, which should consist of informing program leaders of their responsibilities to the students and the institution and ensuring the leaders understand they have the support of the entire institution (Spencer & Tuma, 2002)—including the education abroad office, student affairs, legal counsel, Title IX office, and more—as well as their onsite staff, exchange partner, or partner provider for any assistance they need while on the program.

Program leader training sessions should include discussions of specific emergency response protocols, such as what to do when a student is injured or hospitalized and how to respond appropriately—in alignment with institutional policies—to common concerns, such as substance abuse or behavioral concerns. However, they should also emphasize that program leaders should never operate in a vacuum; a network of people and resources should be in place to support program leaders and the group of students in the crisis, and program leaders need to know how to engage that network. Education abroad offices must set the expectation that program leaders contact their home institution for support when incidents arise. Depending on the type of incident and established protocols, that contact may be via an incident report form, emailing their program coordinator, or calling an emergency phone number for immediate assistance.

*Wight* illustrates the need to sufficiently staff programs to ensure their ability to provide the expected duty of care. Depending upon the group size, type of activities, and support available on the ground, many institutions ensure there is always a minimum of two program leaders as a best practice. *The Guide to Successful Short-Term Programs Abroad* (Chieffo & Spaeth, 2017) published by NAFSA suggests having at least two program personnel once program enrollment reaches 20 students. As demonstrated by *Wight,* a second on-the-ground staff member can support a student during injury or illness, allowing faculty to continue leading the group.

*Wight* and *Munn* highlight the importance of comprehensive pre-departure orientations for students that address known and foreseeable risks associated with a location, share health and safety guidance from expert resources, such as the CDC, State Department, and OSAC, and explain how to use this advice to prepare to go abroad. In *Munn,* students should have been given correct CDC information and advised to use insect-repellant during the pre-departure orientation, but the school only included it as a "miscellaneous" item on their packing list. The home institution is responsible for providing pre-departure orientations for students, ensuring they inform students of the risks and how to navigate them while abroad, per NAFSA and The Forum on Education Abroad (2021) and highlighted in *Standard* 6.1.11 (The Forum on Education Abroad, 2020).

The *Fay* case is especially significant for education abroad professionals and higher education professionals broadly because it is illustrative of a "special relationship" that can be formed between institutions and students. In requiring students to sign a consent form that permitted the institution to authorize medical treatment, Thiel College created a "special relationship" between the institution and student, thereby owing the students a "special duty of care" regarding medical treatment (Hoye, 2006; Kaplin & Lee, 2014). *Fay v. Thiel* (2001) shows that institutions can be liable for breaching that duty (Pfahl, 2021). We also learned from *Fay* that informed consent forms and liability waivers must be specific and explicit in their intent to be enforceable (Friend, 2017).

Nearly two decades ago, expert advice was to collaborate with the institution's legal counsel to craft waivers that attempted to absolve the institution and its employees from any liability for injury or damage that students might experience during the program (Hoye, 2006). However, we have seen a shift away from waivers of liability toward using assumption-of-risk agreements to ensure that students are advised of the risks associated with their activities abroad and have an opportunity to make an informed decision to assume said risks (and sign the agreement) (Pfahl, 2021). Pfahl (2021) makes the case:

> Instead of being reduced to a perfunctory component inwardly protecting the institution, waivers and releases should be viewed as the culmination of a process through which the participant is aware of the risks, understands the risks, has voluntarily agreed to assume the risks, and has voluntarily agreed to release the institution from the consequences of the program in consideration for the opportunity to participate in the program itself. For its part, the institution should engage the student in an examination of the reasonably foreseeable risks throughout the course of the education abroad experience and provide the student with the resources through which the student can knowingly and voluntarily assume the risk, while also taking personal steps to mitigate the dangers inherent therein. (p. 112)

Agreement to the terms of any release should be made "knowingly, voluntarily, and with valuable consideration" between the parties (Pfahl, 2021, p. 96). Institutions should consider incorporating assumptions of risk into their process so that students can be informed and agree before completing their application, or at the very least, upon acceptance and before committing to a program.

## Program Leader Roles and Responsibilities

Program leaders are best equipped to do their job well if the education abroad office clearly defines their role and informs them of their expectations. Education abroad offices can offer workshops and training for new program leaders that provide an overview of roles and responsibilities, including but not limited to "communication protocols, participant health, well-being, safety, and security, [and] emergency management and response" as outlined in *Standard* 5.1.5 (The Forum on Education Abroad, 2020). Institutions may wish to consider requiring program leaders to sign a contract outlining their formal responsibilities to clarify expectations on both sides.

As discussed above, a comprehensive risk assessment is essential and can be created by either education abroad personnel or the faculty leader (Hoye, 2016). Program leaders should be familiar with the program location and shall develop a plan to address known and foreseeable health and safety issues with their education abroad office personnel. A risk associated with short-term programs is that program leaders may have never traveled to a location before leading a program. They may need more familiarity with the local language, culture, and customs. As discussed with *Wight*, the faculty were very familiar with the location, knew how to identify and mitigate altitude sickness, and had specific protocols and communication plans to follow if needed.

In the case of *Fay*, even if one of the faculty members had stayed behind, they still may have had limited ability to advocate for Fay as they may have lacked sufficient language skills. Education abroad administrators and program leaders should create a plan to address this type of scenario in advance and, if possible, avoid it entirely. A recommended best practice would be to require programs to contract with an education abroad program provider organization or trusted exchange partner institution to ensure local expertise is available for program support. Additionally, travel assistance providers such as International SOS and On Call International have medical professionals and translators available 24 hours a day. These experts are often contracted through the home institution (Hoye, 2006).

Suppose program leaders are unfamiliar with the destination where they will be leading an education abroad program. In that case, they should complete a site visit at least 6 months before the program's departure date to familiarize themselves with the area and any available onsite support services and to inform their risk assessment and mitigation strategies. The *Wight* case highlights why this familiarity is essential, particularly for field expeditions and other activities in remote areas.

Upon arrival, program leaders should provide students with an orientation reinforcing the pre-departure orientation information, reviewing the established emergency and communication protocols, and, as in the case of Ohio State University, highlighting location-specific concerns and providing guidance on minimizing their risks. As with *Wight*, *Munn* underscores the importance of providing exhaustive and accurate information to students before program departure and once again onsite. Clause 6.1.11 of the *Standards* states, "Responsible parties shall prepare students to manage their safety by providing resources related to concerns including, but not limited to, physical risks, behavior, property crime, liability and legal issues, sexual misconduct, identity-based discrimination, and country-specific resources" (2020). In this case, the program leaders at Hotchkiss failed to properly inform students how to prepare for the risks associated with the trip on multiple occasions—by not informing them that Mount Panshan included a forested area, not expressly requiring bug spray with DEET on the packing list, not reminding students to apply bug spray, and by providing a link to the incorrect CDC page.

## Summary

The outcomes of *Wight v. Ohio State University, Fay v. Thiel College, and Munn v. Hotchkiss School* offer valuable insights into best practices for risk mitigation in education abroad. As noted, institutions must engage in due diligence and risk assessment to identify and mitigate the risks associated with all aspects of their education abroad programs and take a comprehensive and proactive approach to risk management in education abroad. Additionally, pre-departure education, informed consent processes, and appropriate support and resources while abroad should be required to aid students in maintaining their health and safety. Hoye (2006) advises institutions to work proactively

> to attempt to reasonably reduce the risk of reasonably foreseeable injury and harm to students, faculty and staff in the first instance. For these reasons and others, colleges and universities should consider investing greater resources in preventative law, pro-active risk assessment, training, education and orientation for students, faculty and staff in the context of international study abroad programs. (p. 20)

Malveaux (2016) sums it up nicely, "The lesson is clear – all institutions [engaged in] study abroad should have risk-averting documents in place with language specifying clear and accurate risks specific to that individual region, accompanied by instructive orientation sessions" (p. 31).

The outcomes from the three cases explored in this chapter underscore that education abroad offices and program leaders must conduct comprehensive risk assessments, provide students with thorough and accurate pre-departure information, ensure that appropriate levels of supervision are in place, and administer appropriate training and instruction related to local laws and customs. The Forum on Education Abroad's *Standards* (2020) referenced in this chapter are tools with which all education abroad professionals should acquaint themselves. The lessons learned from *Wight, Fay,* and *Munn* can help education abroad offices safeguard the health and well-being of their students while participating in study abroad programs.

## References

*Bloss v. University of Minnesota*, 590 N.W.2d 661 (Minn. Ct. App. 1999).

Chieffo, L., & Spaeth, C. (Eds.). (2017). *The guide to successful short-term programs abroad* (3rd ed.). NAFSA: Association of International Educators.

*Fay v. Thiel College*, 55 Pa. D. & C.4th 353 (2001).

Friend, J. (2017). Mitigating organizational liability: A review of U.S. case law and regulations. In P. C. Martin (Ed.), *Crisis management for education abroad* (pp. 121–153). NAFSA: Association of International Educators.

Hoye, W. P. (2006, Feb.). *Legal issues influencing international study abroad programs.* [Conference session]. 27th Annual National Conference on Law and Higher Education, Clearwater Beach, FL, United States.

Kaplin, W. A., & Lee, B. A. (2014). *The law of higher education, 5th edition: Student version.* Wiley.

Malveaux, G. F. (2016). *Look before leaping. Risks, liabilities, and repair of study abroad in higher education.* Rowman & Littlefield.

*Munn v. Hotchkiss School,* 326 Conn. 540, 165 A.3d 1167 (2017).

NAFSA and The Forum on Education Abroad. (2021). *Responsible education abroad: Best practices for health, safety and security.* (3rd ed.). https://www.nafsa.org/professional-resources/browse-by-interest/responsible-study-abroad-good-practices-health-and-safety

Overseas Security Advisory Council. (2021, January 21). *OSAC Risk Matrix.* [Member access only]. https://www.osac.gov/Content/Report/0dc9b6d3-aeb2-4f76-932a-15f4ae952eb3

Pfahl, M. R. (2021). Enhancing enforceability of exculpatory clauses in education abroad programming through examination of three pillars. *Journal of College & University Law, 46*(1), 93. https://heinonline.org/HOL/P?h=hein.journals/jcolunly46&i=102

Spencer, S. E., & Tuma, K. (Eds.). (2002). *The guide to successful short-term programs abroad.* NAFSA: Association of International Educators.

The Forum on Education Abroad. (2020). *Standards of good practice for education abroad, Sixth edition.* doi.org/10.36366/S.978-1-952376-04-7

The Forum on Education Abroad. (n.d.). *Resources for the Standards.* [Member access only]. https://web.forumea.org/atlas/portal/web-content/1257

*Wight v. Ohio State University,* 112 Ohio Misc. 2d 13 (2001).

# 4

---

# Housing Safety Considerations for Education Abroad

**Kyle Rausch, Ed.D.**

Many aspects of planning education abroad programs require an intentional risk assessment to demonstrate that an institution or organization has fulfilled its duty of care obligations. Among the most critical elements of program development is the choice of accommodation for participants. Arranging specific accommodations creates a special duty of care, especially for programs that are organized by an institution or organization (e.g., faculty-directed programs, third-party provider programs, etc.). As participants are often unfamiliar with the location and local culture of where a program is based, appropriate accommodations promoting students' well-being must be vetted and sourced.

The 2021 legal ruling in *Doe v. R.I. Sch. of Design* underscores the duty of care that institutions and organizations have in vetting and securing safe housing accommodations. In this case, Jane Doe, a former student of the Rhode Island School of Design (RISD), participated in a RISD three-week art program in Ireland. On the program's first night, Doe was raped in her bedroom by a fellow program participant who entered her room through bedroom doors that did not lock. The court found that

> The relationship between RISD and [Doe] gave rise to a duty on the part of RISD to exercise reasonable care in providing secure housing to [Doe] for the Ireland Program. RISD undertook to arrange for housing for [Doe] in Ireland, and [Doe] reasonably expected that RISD would exercise due care in fulfilling this undertaking. (*Doe v. R.I. Sch. of Design*, 2021)

Several interesting elements of this case further speak to RISD's duty to exercise reasonable care in securing housing. First, RISD managed and controlled all aspects of the program. Their contract with the local housing provider did not require the housing provider to ensure the housing was safe (The Forum for Education Abroad, 2020, clause 5.1.8). Additionally, a RISD professor proposed the Ireland program and it was their responsibility to safeguard the welfare and care of the RISD students participating in it. These points highlight institutions' elevated levels of duty of care when coordinating faculty-directed programs and the importance of documenting health and safety responsibilities in contracts with vendors. It is also critical to ensure that program leaders are aware of their health and safety responsibilities and are trained to carry out these responsibilities (The Forum for Education Abroad, 2020, clause 5.1.5).

The oversight is made more problematic by the fact that keys to lock the doors were available. However, no one from RISD checked the students' rooms to see that a key was required to lock the doors. Furthermore, students were not informed that there were keys they could request to lock the doors.

Finally, there was precedent for RSID's negligence, given that a similar incident occurred in 2013. During the summer of 2013, a student reported that a sexual assault had happened in RISD housing while studying abroad in Rome. The student housing was in a single building with multiple floors. The school housed students of all genders together. Students were assigned bedrooms that did not have functioning locks on the doors. RISD officials were made aware of this sexual assault. The facts are very similar to those of Jane Doe's assault less than three years later. RISD officials acknowledged that students in mixed-gender housing could be at an increased risk for sexual assault and that lockable bedroom doors are critical for students' safety and security, thereby making this a foreseeable risk, an important point within the legal context (*Doe v. R.I. Sch. of Design*, 2021). RISD acknowledged its negligence when its Lieutenant of Public Safety for Support Services stated that students had a reasonable expectation that RISD would provide them with safe and secure housing with secure buildings that limited access by strangers.

Taken together, the findings of the RISD cases underscore the importance of vetting housing accommodations and training program leaders in their duty to oversee student well-being during an education abroad program. Rape and other forms of sexual assault are but some of the many incidents that can occur without proper health and safety oversight in accommodation sourcing. However, they are not the only issues related to housing safety. The RISD case has been preceded by other important legal cases regarding incidents in housing for education abroad programs.

In 2000, Rocky Paneno, a student at Pasadena Community College, studied abroad in Italy with Academic Programs Abroad Ltd. Paneno suffered serious injuries, including paralysis, after falling six stories from his apartment's balcony due to a portion of the balcony railing giving way (Ashmann-Gerst, 2004). Ensuring that the infrastructure of program housing is in good condition and that there are essential safety features are other critical parts of the vetting process.

Given the variety of countries, cultures, contexts, and objectives of education abroad programs, there are many considerations and stakeholders to balance. The following sections outline some of the more common housing options and their risk management considerations along with a reflection on the roles and expectations of key stakeholders in the selection of housing for education abroad programs.

## Types of Education Abroad Housing and Associated Risk Management Considerations

Institutions and organizations are often operating programs in a variety of locations with different variables like program size, student needs, and program objectives. Accordingly, there is no one-size-fits-all approach to selecting accommodations for education abroad programs. However, there are best practices to vet accommodation options while balancing the needs of an individual program and its participants.

Common vetting practices include:

- Touring facilities on a regular basis
- Verifying essential safety features: fire alarms, fire extinguishers, marked escape routes, carbon monoxide detectors, doors (internal and external) and windows that lock
- Reviewing neighborhood crime statistics
- Conducting background checks, where legally and culturally appropriate
- Identifying easily accessible, quality medical facilities
- Ensuring access to reliable and safe transit options

In addition to these general practices, specific types of accommodation options warrant additional risk mitigation measures. The following are some more frequently used housing options for education abroad programs. For each type of housing, common risk management considerations are offered to help guide education abroad professionals in their vetting procedures. It is important these considerations are taken in combination with professionals' own institutional and legal contexts.

## Homestays

From a cultural immersion perspective, homestays are often considered among the most favored housing type for education abroad programs. The ability for students to live with a local family and learn about the host culture and language provides rich opportunities for cultural competency development. However, homestays require a formal vetting process to promote the safety and well-being of students.

There have been cases in which students have been victims of rape committed by a member of the homestay household (Guernsey, 1997; Schecter, 2012). Accordingly, program staff should obtain background checks, where possible, for each household member in addition to in-person interviews conducted by a member of the program planning team familiar with the local culture. These interviews will also identify families who are a good fit to host students with diverse identities and who may have documented accommodation needs.

Onsite staff should tour homes where students will be staying to ensure the homes have the essential safety features and access previously mentioned. The distance of the homestay from staff members who can offer support in an emergency must also be considered. An evaluation should be given to students after each program to continually assess the homestay for future students.

## Apartments

Independent student apartments (or independent living arrangements in other rented or leased spaces, for that matter) can be an effective accommodation option for programs that need to house a group of students in locations where homestays might not be available or for which the program objectives are in line with giving students a more independent housing option. Students can build closer connections with their peers, and these relationships can promote their safety in other aspects of the program. However, with less direct supervision of students, there may also be additional opportunities for student behavioral issues to arise. Onsite staff should have a protocol for responding to such issues and consider mitigation strategies.

Since conducting background checks on neighbors is impossible, it is important for program staff to get a general understanding of who neighboring residents are by speaking with property managers or landlords and those who live in the neighborhood. In addition to supporting the vetting process, it helps ensure that the neighborhood will be a good fit for international university students. As with homestays, apartments and other independent living locations should be a reasonable distance from onsite program staff who can assist in an emergency.

In cases where apartments have individual owners and are not managed by a property agency, it may be prudent to conduct background checks of landlords and ask for references where legally allowed. Students should be informed who their landlord is and know the proper procedures for reporting any complaints or needs of urgent attention regarding the property.

### Student Residences

Student residences can be an economical option, especially for longer-term programs. Additionally, students may have an opportunity to build relationships with local students and participate in local student life activities. While there may be a general assumption that student residences are relatively safe, a formal vetting process should still occur since *standards* of what is reasonably safe may differ across cultures and local ordinances.

At some institutions, students in residence halls may have a curfew. While this maybe designed to promote student safety, how the curfew is imposed should be discussed. As an example, the author learned from a student participating in an English-teaching program at a South Korean university that the entrance doors of their residence hall were locked with chains each night for curfew. This meant that students would have to escape via an old escape ladder in the event of a fire or other building-wide emergency. This led to a discussion with the institutional partner about our institution's health and safety expectations and local practices to better inform our housing selection for students.

Upon arrival, building staff should provide an orientation reviewing the building's policies and safety plan. Additionally, as indicated in The Forum on Education Abroad's *Code of Ethics*, students must be informed of the local laws, cultural norms, and customs (2020, p.52). This includes the protocols for reporting sexual harassment and misconduct.

### Hotels and Hostels

For some short-term programs, hotels and hostels may be the most practical and sometimes economical option. In these cases, the location of the hotel or hostel is of paramount concern. Program organizers should ask the hotel staff about known incidents in the neighborhood and review crime statistics. This will prove helpful in Clery Act reporting responsibilities. See also Chapter 8 of this volume; "Clery Act and Title IX Extraterritorial Application (And Why the Federal Approach Is the Floor, Not the Ceiling)" (Storch and Stagg, 2024). It can also be insightful reading traveler reviews of the property on travel websites.

Hotels and hostels should feature marked emergency exits, have fire alarms and escapes as appropriate, and adhere to local codes and inspections.

Where possible, rooms should have safes where participants can store valuables. Upon arrival, students should have an orientation highlighting the emergency exit plans. Guidelines and rules about alcohol use should be shared if there is an onsite bar.

In the case of hostels, it is best practice to reserve rooms for the sole use of program participants instead of sharing rooms with nonprogram travelers. In every case, program leaders (including student assistants) should be roomed separately from student participants.

For both hotels and hostels, it is essential that doors have locks and that students are only placed in adjoining rooms unless there is a lock on both sides. It may be prudent to recommend that students travel with a door wedge for added protection against break-ins. Consider that reserving specific rooms could be seen as an institution having control of the location and thus having implications under the Clery Act.

### "Vacation Rental" Properties

With rental property websites such as Airbnb and Vrbo being popular platforms to organize short-term accommodations, their use in education abroad programs has increased. The ability for college and university faculty and staff to look for housing from abroad is useful and can often be an economical option. However, it can be challenging to vet accommodations from pictures. Although reviews from past travelers can be helpful, they are not a substitute for having toured a property and neighborhood. Additionally, it may be challenging to determine who bears liability for specific incidents that can occur. The legal counsels of institutions or organizations may have concerns or prohibitions about renting from websites such as these since their terms and conditions may need to meet institutional or organizational standards.

### Independent Housing

Program participants, whether student, faculty, or staff, may have reasons for requesting independent housing. In these instances, institutions are advised to consider their risk tolerance threshold in relation to who the traveler is and what resources are available to them onsite. Legal counsel may recommend a release form.

### Stakeholders in Education Abroad Housing Safety

There are many stakeholders to consider when coordinating housing for education abroad programs: students, faculty members, partners/providers, onsite staff, host families, and locals living in the neighborhoods where students are housed. Balancing the needs of these stakeholders and the realities and constraints within each context can be challenging. Weighing the roles and expectations of these stakeholders can help inform housing selection.

## Students

As the direct beneficiaries of the accommodation used by a program, students represent the primary stakeholders. Appropriate housing must be sourced to promote a positive learning environment that aligns with broader program learning and intercultural objectives. Additionally, students expect to be lodged in comfortable and safe accommodation that provides for their basic needs.

Accounting for students' identities is an important step in the housing selection process. For instance, nontraditional-aged students participating in a program that enrolls primarily traditional-aged college students may expect a single-room option. Nonbinary and transgender students may have preferences about which gender of students they are housed with, as could their cisgender peers. As highlighted earlier in this chapter, the potential for sexual harassment and sexual assault incidents to occur in program housing is a genuine concern that warrants careful consideration in determining how to organize student rooming assignments or make homestay decisions.

Students may have specific disabilities or medical conditions requiring housing accommodations, so a post-acceptance health disclosure process is recommended. (See Chapter 25 of this volume, "Pre-Departure Mental Health Clearance: One Approach to Managing Risk Abroad" (Sterling, 2024) for more information.) Working with partners with experience sourcing accessible accommodations or the flexibility to install special appliances or fixtures when necessary is important as institutions seek to make education abroad available to all students.

A review of student program evaluations will typically yield many comments about accommodations. Although each student will have their ideas about what kind of lodging they should have during their program, budget constraints and the availability of options that meet their expectations in the local context may create disappointment. Providing students with as much information before arrival as possible can help manage expectations and encourage students to be forthcoming about their needs.

In the case of homestays, diligent care should be taken when matching students with host families. Students' psychological well-being requires an environment where they can be their full, authentic selves. This does not mean that students should not be placed in environments where they will be challenged. Still, the homestay should be where they feel comfortable regrouping and reflecting after participating in busy academic schedules and navigating a foreign culture. If a student is subject to microaggressions, overt racism, homophobia, or other harassment, or otherwise feels as though they must hide or apologize for aspects of their identity, it can be damaging to their mental health.

### Accompanying Faculty or Staff

With faculty-directed programs being an accessible and popular education model abroad for US colleges and universities, faculty members are another key stakeholder. It can be tempting for faculty to organize their housing, especially if they are familiar with or from the host country. However, as institutional employees carrying out official business, institutional liability could also be at play for faculty housing considerations.

In instances when an institution or organization is coordinating housing for faculty members, attention must be given to situations in which faculty members are permitted to bring spouses, dependents, or other guests. Clear guidelines outlining who is eligible to stay in the program-affiliated housing, expectations, and liability matters should be provided in writing to all occupants.

Proximity to students is another critical consideration for faculty housing. In every case, it is ill-advised to have faculty members share a room with students. Faculty members and other program staff should not enter a student's room alone or host students in their room. Instead, faculty and student meetings should occur in public spaces such as a hotel lobby or cafe. In instances where faculty are not housed in the same building as students, they should be a reasonable distance from students to provide quick support in the case of an emergency.

### Partners Onsite

Given the complexities of organizing housing for education abroad programs, many colleges and universities depend on relationships with trusted partners and providers. These organizations may bring the benefit of local staff who are familiar with the neighborhoods and cultural practices that inform the selection of safe accommodations. However, their task is challenging as they must balance institutions' stringent health and safety requirements, students' amenities expectations, an often-scarce market, and local realities in the host country. Transparency and expectation setting at the onset of collaboration are essential, as is a willingness to be flexible and understanding on the part of the institutional partner. Providers should have documented procedures for vetting accommodation options available to share with institutional partners, who should inquire about providers' housing policies. Agreements should specify which party is responsible for ensuring the selection of safe accommodations, reference critical points of contact for any housing issues, and clarify who is financially liable in cases where damage occurs. Partners and providers should also maintain procedures for requesting accommodation disclosures to inform appropriate housing selection. Addresses of where participants are lodged should be shared with the partner institution before students depart for their education abroad location.

Onsite staff are essential in the accommodation sourcing process. Often, these individuals possess the requisite local knowledge of neighborhoods that would be safe and appropriate for students to live in and have a good pulse on the market within a particular city. As the people who live and work in the communities where students will live, these individuals can be well prepared to visit potential housing options for a walk-through and safety check, which should be done regularly.

Additionally, onsite staff play a central role in vetting and preparing host families. Interviews with each household member should be conducted, as should home tours, and background checks where appropriate. Moreover, families should receive regular professional development related to hosting an international student. Workshops can focus on student development in the intercultural context, an overview of the organization's expectations for responding to incidents and emergencies, and how to recognize students in distress or suffering from mental health issues and supporting students with diverse identities and backgrounds. (See Chapter 22 of this volume, "Exploring Mental Well-Being Abroad: Historical Overview and Future Landscapes," Thompson, 2024.) After each program, student feedback should be collected and shared with the family to ensure the host family is a good match for receiving international students.

Lastly, it is important to consider international students' impact on the host community. Especially when housing students in apartments where locals live and work, it is imperative to cultivate relationships with the community to promote respect and positive living dynamics for locals and students. Spending time developing such relationships can also help to provide an additional layer of support as neighboring locals help keep watch over the community and can share known incidents or health and safety concerns.

## Operationalizing Housing Safety in Education Abroad

Given the number of stakeholders and all that is involved in vetting housing for education abroad programs, it can be a daunting task, especially for resource-strapped institutions and organizations. Having clearly defined roles and responsibilities for all parties involved in the education abroad process can make it more feasible while setting expectations (Code of Ethics, 2020, p. 23). Roles may change depending on the model of the program.

For instance, for faculty-directed programs, working with vetted onsite program providers can greatly assist institutions and faculty leading programs since they take on much of the work that can only be done onsite. However, this places a large degree of liability on the part of the provider organization; accordingly, liability insurance coverage is essential. Additionally, working with a program provider does not remove all responsibilities from sending institutions and faculty members. Institutions must ensure they have vetted program partners and agree upon roles and responsibilities. This can be accomplished by asking partners to share details about their health and safety processes, checking references, conducting site visits, and regularly reviewing program evaluations. Faculty members leading programs should still inspect housing when onsite and immediately report any concerns to their home institution. While some faculty members can resist working with a program provider due to perceptions that they may lose control over the program, the health and safety benefits that providers bring are plentiful. Sharing legal cases and examples from other institutions where there have been incidents can be powerfully persuasive.

For exchange programs, students typically have the option to live in student housing or can arrange for independent housing of their choosing. If the home institution permits the latter, an independent housing waiver should be developed in partnership with institutional counsel. Details about on-campus housing options should be reviewed, and a site visit should occur whenever possible.

The frequency of how often program housing should be evaluated is a matter of an institution or organization's risk tolerance threshold. However, at a minimum, program evaluations should include questions about program housing to help ensure that issues raised by students are identified and addressed regularly.

## Balancing Health and Safety with Local Cultural Norms

The Forum on Education Abroad's *Standards of Good Practice* state that "each organization shall promote respect for the cultures and values of all involved, including the communities from which the participants come and the communities in which they operate" (2020, clause 4.3.6).

How can this standard be met in instances where the health and safety requests from the sending partner are at odds with what is customary or legally permissible in the host community? In many cases, such requests are the product of institutional, local, or national regulations, and the sending partner may have limited flexibility in forgoing such requests. In these instances, it is important for both partners to engage in transparent and direct communication and to share rationales in an effort to build mutual understanding in support of a path toward finding a mutually agreeable solution.

Consider a host partner's request to receive medical information about program participants. Depending upon the sending institution's policies, this may not be possible. Yet, the host organization has a duty of care to organize accommodations that can meet the health and wellness needs of its participants. In this case, conversations with legal teams on both sides may be necessary to explain the liability and risk at stake and explore alternative arrangements or amendments to policies that reflect these realities.

Increasingly, countries are adopting stringent data sharing and protection laws that have a significant impact on education abroad operations (e.g., the General Data Protection Regulation (GDPR) in the European Union and the Personal Information Protection Law (PIPL) in China). Given the amount of personal information needed to organize accommodation, care must be taken to ensure compliance with these data protection laws. For more information, please reference Chapter 11 of this volume, "GDPR and PIPL Enforcement in Higher Education," by Liu and Bahner (2024).

Finally, differences in vetting practices and standards may exist across cultures, and some practices that are commonplace in one country may not be practiced or even permitted in another. For instance, it is common practice in the United States to conduct background checks on household occupants. However, in other countries, this may not be possible, or if it is, it may not be a common cultural practice and indicate signs of distrust of the local partner. In these situations, open lines of communication are essential to help foster understanding and to find alternative solutions that can reduce foreseeable risks.

## The Clery Act and Housing Abroad

The *Jeanne Clery Disclosure of Campus Security Policy and Campus Crime Statistics Act*, or Clery Act, is a federal statute that "requires colleges and universities to report campus crime data, support victims of violence, and publicly outline the policies and procedures they have put into place to improve campus safety" (Clery Center, n.d.). From a compliance perspective, this is an essential piece of legislation for institutions that receive federal funding to consider in relation to the education abroad programs they operate. From a health and safety perspective, the data captured for Clery compliance can help inform risk management decisions.

Since the introduction of the Clery Act in 1990, there has been an evolution in its interpretation within the context of education abroad. In other words, what responsibilities do institutions that operate education abroad programs have regarding fulfilling their Clery Act reporting obligations?

In the domestic context, US colleges and universities participating in Title IV federal student financial aid programs must disclose information about crime on or around their campuses or off-campus facilities described by the Act. The notion of geography in relation to an institution's campus or off-campus facilities leaves much room for interpretation for its applicability to education abroad programs. The specific language of the act states:

> Clery geography. (i) For the purposes of collecting statistics on the crimes listed in paragraph (c) of this section for submission to the Department and inclusion in an institution's annual security report, Clery geography includes—
>
> (A) Buildings and property that are part of the institution's campus;
>
> (B) The institution's noncampus buildings and property; and
>
> (C) Public property within or immediately adjacent to and accessible from the campus. (ii) For the purposes of maintaining the crime log required in paragraph (f) of this section, Clery geography includes, in addition to the locations in paragraph (i) of this definition, areas within the patrol jurisdiction of the campus police or the campus security department. (Federal Register, Vol. 79, No.202, 2014)

Wilke posits that point B, *noncampus buildings,* "best applies to education abroad [and] is best defined as property owned, controlled or leased by the institution, used for the institution's mission or in relation to its mission not in the same geographic area, and frequently used by students" (2014, p. 6). For an education abroad program, this suggests that apartments leased by an institution where students stay during a program would be considered Clery reportable. In this case, the institution must ensure its employees know their status as a Campus Security Authority (CSA).

While not defined in statute, regulations provide that CSAs include campus police or security department personnel; individuals or organizations identified in institutional security policies; and individuals with security-related responsibilities. The definition at § 668.46(a)(iv) states that a CSA also includes an official "who has significant responsibility for student and campus activities" (Department of Education, 2020).

If a Clery reportable crime occurs in or near the property, regardless of whether it involves a participant or not, it should be reported so it can be included in the institution's data collection. Other forms of accommodation and meeting space rented or leased, such as hotels and classrooms, would also fall under this category, whereas homestays would be excluded.

While compliance and reporting introduce additional administrative responsibilities to onsite staff and program leaders, there are benefits to an institution's risk management strategy. As data are compiled over time, data-informed decision-making can help guide choices of which neighborhoods and accommodation options to select for a program. The Clery Act provides one example of safety-related data that institutions can collect, but many other incidents can occur on programs that are not considered Clery reportable. For these, it is recommended to consult The Forum on Education Abroad's initiative tracking incidents of significant risk to students (Dietrich, 2024). For more information on the Clery Act, please see Chapter 6 of this volume, "Clery Act and Title IX Extraterritorial Application (And Why the Federal Approach Is the Floor, Not the Ceiling)" (Storch and Stagg, 2024).

## Conclusion

Student accommodations on education abroad programs are sometimes an afterthought as the focus is on ensuring a program is academically enriching and includes meaningful opportunities for cultural engagement. However, the choice of housing is a critical element in education abroad program design that directly impacts students' ability to thrive academically and personally in their new cultural context. Ensuring that students' living environments are safe and promote wellness is critical to student success. The education abroad experience invites challenges and places students in situations that are purposefully, at times, uncomfortable. Accordingly, students should expect an accommodation option that provides them with a space that promotes their well-being and in which reflection and rest can occur to sustain them throughout their intercultural experience. Careful consideration about the type of housing in relation to program goals, learning objectives, and risk management must be factored into program development as should the impact of the various stakeholders involved.

## References

Ashmann-Gerst, J. (2004). *Paneno v. Centres for Academic Programmes Abroad Ltd.* https://www.courtlistener.com/opinion/2299104/paneno-v-capa-uk/

Center, R., & Williams, B. (2012). *Foreign Exchange students were sexually abused in a program overseen by the State Department.* NBC News. https://www.nbcnews.com/news/world/foreign-exchange-students-sexually-abused-program-overseen-state-department-flna424764

*Code of Ethics for Education Abroad.* (n.d.). Retrieved 2024 from https://www.forumea.org/code-of-ethics.html

Dietrich, A. (2024). *Student risk report: Data from education abroad programs, January 1–December 31, 2023.* The Forum on Education Abroad. doi.org/10.36366/R.2024SRR.1

Education, U. S. D. of. (2022, May 19). *Campus security.* https://www2.ed.gov/admins/lead/safety/campus.html

Guernsey, L. (1997). *Suit raises questions about liability in study-abroad programs.* https://www.chronicle.com/article/suit-raises-questions-about-liability-in-study-abroad-programs/?sra=true

John J. McConnell, Jr. (2021, February 2). *DOE v. R.I. Sch. of design. Legal research tools from Casetext.* https://casetext.com/case/doe-v-ri-sch-of-design-1

Liu, X.S. & Bahner, E. S. (2024). GDRP and PIPL enforcement in higher education. In J. Pollard & K. S. Priebe (Eds.), *Convergence of litigation, policy, and standards: Building the informed practitioner in education abroad risk management.* The Forum on Education Abroad. doi.org/10.36.366/SIA.5.978-1-952376-41-2.11

Schecter, A. (2012). *Foreign exchange students sexually abused in program overseen by State Department.* https://www.nbcnews.com/news/world/foreign-exchange-students-sexually-abused-program-overseen-state-department-flna424764

Sterling, V. (2024). Pre-departure mental health clearance: One approach to managing risk abroad. In J. Pollard & K. S. Priebe (Eds.), *Convergence of litigation, policy, and standards: Building the informed practitioner in education abroad risk management.* The Forum on Education Abroad. doi.org/10.36366/SIA.5.978-1-952376-41-2.25

Storch, J. & Stagg, A. (2024). Clery Act and Title IX Extraterritorial Application (and why the federal approach is the floor, not the ceiling). In J. Pollard & K. S. Priebe (Eds.), *Convergence of litigation, policy, and standards: Building the informed practitioner in education abroad risk management.* The Forum on Education Abroad. doi.org/10.36.366/SIA.5.978-1-952376-41-2.8

The Forum on Education Abroad. (2020). *Standards of good practice for education abroad.* The Forum on Education Abroad. doi.org/10.36366/S.978-1-952376-04-7

*The Jeanne Clery Act.* (2023). The Clery Center. https://www.clerycenter.org/the-clery-act

Wilke, D. (2014). *Complying with Clery* (pp. 2–10). NAFSA. https://www.nafsa.org/sites/default/files/ektron/files/underscore/ie_novdec14_supplement.pdf

*Woman Sues College Says She Was Raped Studying Abroad.* (1997). Hartford Courant. https://www.courant.com/1997/03/27/woman-sues-college-says-she-was-raped-while-studying-abroad/

Violence Against Women Act, 79 F.R. 62784 (2014). https://www.govinfo.gov/content/pkg/FR-2014-10-20/pdf/2014-24284.pdf#page=33

# 5

## Analyzing the Legal Challenges and Opportunities for Students with Disabilities

**Seth Gilbertson, J.D.**

## Introduction

Entering college can be an exciting time for students, but it may also be a hard time as they adjust to new settings and expectations and cope with unfamiliar impacts on their health and well-being. In recent years, studies have consistently shown an increase in the number of students with self-disclosed physical and mental health-related disabilities. Anyone who works with students on a college or university campus is likely familiar with this trend. Just like their nondisabled peers, many students with disabilities seek to enhance their educational experience by participating in activities that take them out of their comfort zone and offer something new and different—traveling and studying abroad may offer just such an opportunity. As the prevalence of study abroad programs and students with disabilities follow parallel trend lines upward, colleges and universities are tasked with providing an opportunity for all students to participate under substantially similar and equal terms. Study abroad offices must prioritize and address student disability issues within their policies and training in order to maintain an equal opportunity for participation and ensure that they remain in compliance with laws against discrimination as well as their own institutional commitments.

## U.S. Federal Disability Discrimination Laws

The Americans with Disabilities Act (1990) and Section 504 of the Rehabilitation Act of 1973 (hereinafter collectively "ADA laws") mandate equal access to postsecondary institutions for students with disabilities. Both laws identify an individual with a disability as one who has "a physical or mental impairment that substantially limits one or more major life activities; ... a record of such impairment... or [is] regarded as having such an impairment."

Section 504 of the Rehabilitation Act of 1973 was the first federal civil rights law to protect people with disabilities. It prohibits discrimination against people with disabilities in programs that receive federal financial assistance. Section 504 set the groundwork for future legislation protecting people with disabilities, such as the Americans with Disabilities Act.

Since its inception in 1990, the Americans with Disabilities Act has prohibited discrimination against individuals with disabilities across a wide swath of public life, aiming to ensure these individuals have the same rights and opportunities as their nondisabled peers. Almost two decades later, the 2008 ADA Amendments Act (ADAAA) was enacted to address and rectify various Supreme Court decisions that Congress believed had interpreted the ADA laws too narrowly, especially concerning the definition of "disability." The ADAAA significantly broadened the scope of the Americans with Disabilities Act's application to students, giving them greater protections.

Title I of the ADA prohibits discrimination in employment, including the employees of most institutions of higher education. Titles II and III of the ADA cover a broader array of the activities of higher education institutions and are applicable to certain aspects of study abroad programming. Specifically, Title II protects individuals at public colleges and universities operated by state and local governments, and Title III protects individuals at private colleges and universities, which are generally considered private providers of "public accommodations"( Prohibition of Discrimination by Public Accommodations, 2010).

Section 504 is aimed at protecting individuals with disabilities from discrimination based on disability in programs or activities that receive federal financial assistance. Given that most institutions of higher education in the United States receive federal funding through grants and participation in Federal Student Aid (Title IV), Section 504 has important implications for these institutions.

ADA laws place several requirements on how colleges and universities respond once a student has self-identified as having a disability. These include:

- Nondiscrimination: Institutions of higher education that receive federal funding cannot discriminate against students with disabilities. This means they cannot exclude a qualified student with a disability from participating in, deny them the benefits of, or subject them to discrimination under any postsecondary education program or activity.
- Reasonable accommodations: Schools must provide appropriate academic adjustments or modifications to ensure that students with disabilities are not discriminated against in the academic process. These adjustments often include things like extended time on tests, note-taking services, or alternative testing locations, but they can also include things like alternative lesson structures, barrier reduction efforts, and even individualized programming.
- Accessibility: Facilities and services, including web-based and digital materials, must be accessible to students with disabilities. This includes physical accessibility (such as ramps, elevators and keyboard controls) and programmatic accessibility (such as sign language interpreters or captioning services).
- Confidentiality: Once a student has disclosed a disability, that information must be kept confidential. Only those with a legitimate educational need to know should be informed about a student's disability.
- Grievance procedures: Colleges and universities are required to have established grievance procedures for addressing alleged violations. This ensures that students have a formal mechanism to raise concerns or complaints about discrimination or lack of accommodation.
- Designated coordinator: Every postsecondary institution that receives federal financial assistance must designate at least one person to coordinate its efforts to comply with and carry out its responsibilities under the ADA and Section 504.
- Notice: Institutions must provide notice to students, parents, employees, and others that it does not discriminate on the basis of disability.

In essence, the ADA laws ensure that students with disabilities have equal access to educational opportunities at postsecondary institutions. The U.S. Department of Education's Office for Civil Rights (OCR) and U.S. Department of Justice are responsible for enforcing ADA and Section 504 for higher education programs and activities. Many states also have parallel laws that provide supplemental and overlapping protections to students.

## Extraterritorial Application

The ADA and Section 504 are grounded in the principle of nondiscrimination within U.S. jurisdictions and entities that receive federal funding, respectively.

Both laws provide individuals with rights and protections based on their presence and participation in covered programs or activities within the United States, not based on their nationality or immigration status. Therefore, both laws generally afford international students studying in the United States the same legal protections as American students. The ADA laws are less clear about whether American students are protected while studying in foreign countries.

The question of whether a law has an enforceable operative effect outside the boundary of the country of its jurisdictional origin is known as extraterritoriality. There has been a long-standing presumption against extraterritorial application of U.S. legislation within American jurisprudence (i.e., laws enacted by Congress apply only within the jurisdiction of the United States absent clearly contrary legislative intent). The Supreme Court most notably affirmed the presumption against extraterritoriality in *E.E.O.C. v. Arabian American Oil Co.* ("Aramco") (1991).

In *Aramco*, the Court stated that employment protections under Title VII of the Civil Rights Act of 1964 did not apply to overseas conduct, even when the discriminatory conduct is perpetrated by a U.S.-based employer. The case involved a U.S. citizen working for the Arabian American Oil Company in Saudi Arabia who alleged that he faced employment discrimination based on his race and religion. He filed a complaint with the Equal Employment Opportunity Commission (EEOC) under Title VII. The Supreme Court determined that Title VII did not apply outside of the United States because the text of the statute did not specifically indicate such an extraterritorial intent. As a result, U.S. companies were not bound by Title VII when operating outside the United States.

Subsequently, Congress overturned the *Aramco* decision with the enactment of the 1991 Civil Rights Amendments. The Civil Rights Amendments extended the protections of Title VII of the Civil Rights Act and Title I of the ADA to apply to extraterritorially. The Civil Rights Amendment failed to extend Section 504 or Titles II and III of the ADA. This congressional silence—even when faced squarely with the question of extraterritoriality—seemingly reinforces the presumption that Section 504, and Titles II and III of the ADA, do not encompass international activities.

Nevertheless, some courts and administrative agencies such as OCR choose not to recognize the presumption against extraterritoriality and have opined that Section 504 and the ADA are applicable to study abroad programming. Even more choose to overlook the question altogether and simply rule as if extraterritoriality is not a germane issue.

Specifically, as discussed more thoroughly below, at least two federal court decisions do not provide a clear answer regarding extraterritoriality, but signal that Section 504 and the ADA may extend to Americans studying abroad. Four opinion letters released by OCR provide additional contradictory and oblique guidance. Three of the opinion letters do not squarely address extraterritoriality, but employ an analysis that seems to presume extraterritorial application of Section 504. One outlying opinion letter concludes that federal disability laws do not apply outside the United States.

Despite their contradictions and equivocation, these cases and opinion letters can be instructive for institutions to determine how to make reasonable accommodations in their study abroad programs. Realistically, they are also all that we have, so this chapter will analyze each below.

Academic treatment of the question of extraterritoriality of Section 504 and Titles II and III is even more limited. As it pertains to study abroad, the scholarship essentially begins and ends with a law review article from Syracuse University College of Law professor Arlene S. Kanter (2003) (see also Kaplin, Lee, Hutchens, & Rooksby 2019; Whitlock & Charney 2012). Fortunately, Kanter's article presents a compelling argument that there is sufficient justification to carve out an exception to the presumption against extraterritoriality in the case of federal disability law as applied to study abroad. Unfortunately, in the 20 years since it was published, the article and most of its underlying arguments have been largely ignored by judges, regulators, and international education scholars alike.

Kanter posits four bases for her contention:

- The Extraterritorial Application of Disability Discrimination Laws is Consistent with the Policies Underlying Disability Discrimination Laws
- The Language and Legislative History of Laws Prohibiting Discrimination Against People With Disabilities Support Their Extraterritorial Application
- The Presumption Against Extraterritoriality is Overcome When the Conduct Occurs or has an Effect Within the United States; and
- Applying Federal Disability Discrimination Laws to Study Abroad Programs Will Not Result in International Discord or a Violation of Other Federal Laws.

Missing entirely from most of the judicial and scholarly analyses of extraterritoriality is a focus on the situs of the covered activity itself. While it may seem natural to focus on the *abroad* part of a study abroad program, professionals in the field know that months or years of work may go into designing and implementing a week-long program. The overwhelming majority of that work is done in the United States where questions of extraterritoriality are irrelevant. Should the part of the activity that occurs on-location abroad be the only part that may be governed by U.S. law, or should the covered activity be defined so as to include all of the development, planning, promotion, and funding of the program? The manner in which this question is couched in a given case may have a dramatic impact on the outcome.

If a student with a disability in Oregon requests an accommodation from a college official in Oregon for a program that is being planned in Oregon, launched from Oregon, led by a professor who is employed in Oregon, and paid for with institutional funds from an account in Oregon, does it really matter that the accommodation will be provided in Australia? If the program is designed in such a way as to effectively exclude the participation of certain students based on disability, has the violation of the ADA laws not already occurred?

It is increasingly common for colleges and universities to contract with service providers and foreign institutions to provide many of the nonacademic aspects of a study abroad program. This may seem to exempt those aspects from coverage of the ADA laws since so much of the work takes place abroad. However, courts will generally look behind the contract and recognize the institution's legal duty to ensure that its students are treated in a manner compliant with applicable law regardless of whether it provides the program or service directly or indirectly. See the discussion of the *Bird v. Lewis & Clark College* (2000) case and OCR's decision letter in *Arizona State University* (2001) below. It is even possible that a contract purporting to exempt an institution from responsibility for its actions may be rendered unenforceable under the doctrine of *ex turpi causa non oritur action* (from a dishonorable cause an action does not arise) (*Ewell v. Daggs*, 1883).

## Case Law

In *Bird v. Lewis & Clark College* (2000), a federal district court in Oregon held that Section 504 and the ADA applied to study abroad programming. The plaintiff was an undergraduate student who became wheelchair bound while attending Lewis & Clark College. Before studying abroad in a program in Australia, the College gave her assurances that it would accommodate her needs. However, the student was excluded from many of the activities that her peers experienced because of physical barriers that prevented her safe participation. Also, the student had to be carried by peers numerous times because locations were not wheelchair accessible, resulting in embarrassment. The student sued the college on several claims, including a breach of fiduciary duty and violations of the ADA laws.

Regarding extraterritoriality, the court stressed that the plaintiff was an American student participating in an American university's overseas program, taught by American faculty. The court found that the presumption against extraterritoriality should not apply, and if Section 504 and the ADA did not apply to study abroad programs, "students on overseas programs would become the proverbial 'floating sanctuaries from authority' not unlike stateless vessels on the high seas" (Kanter, 2003).Unfortunately, for largely procedural reasons, this part of the court's opinion ruling did not make it into the published decision.

On appeal, the Ninth Circuit Court of Appeals did not address the district court's ruling on extraterritoriality, but denied the plaintiff's Section 504 and ADA claims (*Bird v. Lewis & Clark Coll.*, 2002). Although the Court denied the plaintiff's federal discrimination claims, the Ninth Circuit concluded that the college had violated its assurances to the student. The court seemed to find it particularly troubling that the college had gained the student's trust by accommodating her on its home campus, then betrayed that trust by providing an experience that was fundamentally different than what it had indicated that it and its partners would provide. The college's foreign partner in particular did not seem to fully grasp what it meant to accommodate the student in a manner commensurate with U.S. law and individual student expectations. The dichotomy revealed by the *Bird* decision suggests that extraterritorial application of ADA laws may not be the determining factor when a college or university accepts a duty to accommodate its own statements and actions.

In *Tecza v. University of San Francisco* (2010), a law student at the University of San Francisco (USF) alleged that the school did not accommodate his attention-deficit/hyperactivity disorder and violated his privacy rights during his participation in USF's study abroad programs in Dublin and Prague. Specifically, the student alleged that his professor told other students that he was receiving testing accommodations. Also, while taking an exam in an isolated room, a maintenance person entered and told the student to leave despite having 45 minutes left to complete the exam. Citing *Bird*, the court rejected the student's claims stating the allegations "are not sufficient to sustain claims based on the Rehabilitation Act [and] the ADA...." The court held that the student's experience substantially complied with ADA laws, and study abroad accommodations must be viewed within the context of the totality of the program. Although the court did not address the extraterritorial application of the ADA laws, the court insinuated that such laws apply to study abroad programs.

## Administrative Enforcement

In 2001, OCR Region VIII published an opinion letter taking the explicit position that Section 504 does not apply to study abroad programs. In the

*Arizona State University* (2001) decision, a deaf student requested a sign language interpreter from Arizona State University (ASU) to assist him while he participated in an exchange program at an Irish university. After ASU denied the request, the student filed a complaint with OCR. While the student was entitled to similar accommodations on ASU's campus, OCR determined ASU was not obligated to provide the same accommodations in a foreign country. OCR stated ,"Section 504 and Title II protections of the ADA do not extend extraterritorially… [n]or does either statute otherwise prohibit discrimination on the basis of disability in overseas programs." Published during the same year as the *Bird* decision, some commentators have raised the distinction that ASU's study abroad programming was led by a foreign university, not a U.S.-based institution (Kanter, 2003). OCR did not raise this distinction in its opinion letter, so the idea that there is or should be a distinction remains unexplored by the agency.

Alternatively, and notably after the 2001 opinion letter to ASU, OCR's Eastern Division tacitly accepted the idea that Section 504 and the ADA may be extended extraterritorially in the *Husson College* (2005) decision. A nursing student seeking to study abroad was counseled by Husson College regarding potential difficulties she may experience due to her chronic headaches. The student subsequently withdrew her request to participate. After withdrawing her request, the student filed a complaint with OCR alleging the college denied her the opportunity to participate in the study abroad program. OCR could have dismissed the complaint based on the presumption against extraterritorial application, but did not. Instead, OCR found that the student was not denied participation and that the college acted reasonably in counseling the student about issues she may face during the program. Here, we see another example of how an administrative agency (or court) can imply some application of the ADA laws without explicitly addressing the thorny question of extraterritoriality.

Likewise, before the 2001 ASU opinion letter, OCR took a more liberal view on extraterritoriality when it issued a 1992 decision letter in *College of St. Scholastica* (1992). In that case, a deaf student alleged disability-based discrimination after the college denied her request for a sign language interpreter during a study abroad program in Ireland. OCR determined the college had violated the student's rights because the college did not properly address the student's request for accommodations. The college did not sufficiently investigate the cost and feasibility of providing the interpreter services and lacked a procedure by which the student could internally challenge the decision. While this decision also did not explicitly address the extraterritorial application of the ADA laws, OCR's analysis of the complaint again suggests that the laws have meaningful application to study abroad programming.

Finally, or perhaps originally since it occurred in 1990, at *St. Louis University*, OCR decided a case involving a student with a learning disability that requested accommodations while studying at a university in Spain. The student claimed to need a specific Macintosh-brand computer (remember those!) to help with spelling and punctuation as an accommodation for his disability. When the university provided him with an IBM computer, rather than a Macintosh, the student alleged that the university violated his rights under Section 504 (Apple snobs are not a new phenomenon). OCR's analysis again suggests that the ADA laws apply to study abroad programming because it affirmed that the university had an obligation to provide a computer as a reasonable accommodation. However, there was insufficient evidence that the Macintosh brand was a required accommodation over another computer brand. OCR concluded that the university fulfilled its obligation under Section 504 by accommodating the student with an IBM computer. (As of the date of publication, OCR has yet to weigh in on the iPhone vs. Android debate. Presumably, a BlackBerry would no longer pass muster as a reasonable accommodation under any circumstances.)

## State Laws

State laws play a complementary, but sometimes pivotal, role in ensuring that individuals with disabilities are granted equal access to educational opportunities at colleges and universities, including in the context of study abroad programming. While federal laws such as Section 504 and the ADA provide a foundation, many states have enacted their own legislation to enhance protections and ensure inclusivity within higher education institutions.

While the general principles of nondiscrimination are often consistent with federal law, some states may have specific regulations or provisions that address unique concerns or offer enhanced protections. For instance, certain states might include more detailed guidelines on service animals, accessible technology, or mental health considerations.

State laws generally reinforce the social and political commitment to inclusivity, ensuring that individuals with disabilities can pursue higher education without facing undue barriers or discrimination. Since each state might have variations in its laws, it is crucial for institutions to familiarize themselves with the state-specific mandates in the jurisdictions in which they operate to ensure full compliance.

## Digital Accessibility

Digital accessibility, often synonymous with web accessibility, addresses the need to make digital content and technologies usable by individuals with various disabilities. Digital and web accessibility is an increasing focus of OCR, which has brought hundreds of complaints against institutions of higher education over the past decade. Due in part to this regulatory focus and related civil litigation, the pivotal role that digital accessibility plays in allowing students with disabilities to fully participate in the complete panoply of their institution's educational programs has gained greater recognition. This is as true for study abroad experiences as in any other aspect of institutional programming.

Digital accessibility is more than a technical consideration; it is a fundamental aspect of creating inclusive and equitable educational environments. The requirement that web-based materials aimed at U.S. audiences are accessible is also not bound by concepts of territoriality. By ensuring that digital resources (e.g., forms, policies, schedules), platforms, and tools are designed with accessibility in mind, institutions can remove barriers and provide students with disabilities equal access to information and opportunities. When study abroad programs integrate digital accessibility, they also send a clear message that all students are valued participants, fostering an environment of respect and diversity.

To ensure that study abroad programs are widely accessible and legally compliant, institutions can adopt a series of best practices based on Web Content Accessibility Guidelines or another standard that requires an equivalent level of accessibility for people with disabilities. These standards generally include providing captioned videos and transcripts, designing accessible informational resources and course materials, using technology that supports screen readers, and offering (or requiring) training to faculty and staff on how to create accessible content and course materials. Collaboration between disability support services professionals, study abroad offices, and instructional technologists is essential for implementing and maintaining accessible practices.

Study abroad programs can be more inclusive and legally compliant when they embrace digital accessibility as a core principle. By doing so, institutions ensure that students with disabilities can fully participate in these programs.

## Self-Imposed Obligations

The effort that often goes into understanding exactly where, when, and how the ADA laws apply to study abroad programs often obscures the simple reality that many colleges and universities have bound themselves to even more inclusive and accommodating practices than the law would require. While the popularity of so-called diversity statements may be waning in the face of restrictive litigation and legislation, most institutions still promise equality, diversity, and acceptance in some type of statement or commitment. Take a moment and review your own institution's mission statement(s) and policy language around diversity and inclusion. It is likely that you will find statements that would be hard to square with any practices that fall short of a true commitment to making programs accessible to all students regardless of disability in all but the most extreme cases of hardship or fundamental modification.

The fact is that colleges and universities, like other formal institutions, operate within a framework of policies and procedures. These policies govern various facets, including admissions, student conduct, faculty responsibilities, and other operational considerations. An institution's published statements and policies consequently govern its legal relationship and responsibilities to students. Failure to abide by these guidelines can lead to significant legal, financial, and reputational ramifications in several ways.

## Contractual Relationships

When a student enrolls in a college or university, they are often deemed to have implicitly or explicitly entered into a contractual relationship with that institution. The institution's official statements, policies, handbooks, and guidelines often will serve as terms of this contract. Thus, any deviation from these policies can constitute a breach of contract.

## Process

Particularly (but not exclusively) in public institutions, students are granted certain statutory and constitutional protections, most notably the right to due process. If a university or college does not follow its own procedures during, for example, a disciplinary proceeding, it could violate a student's right to certain process-driven protections. Similar process-based protections may be embedded in an institution's charter or the conditions by which it maintains its state authorization.

## Reputation

From a broader perspective, adhering to policies and official statements is crucial for maintaining the trust of students, faculty, staff, alumni, and the general public. Breaching its own policies may erode this trust and tarnish an institution's reputation, which could have long-term consequences on priorities such as fundraising and enrollment.

## Accreditation and Federal Funding

Most institutions receive accreditation from regional or national accrediting bodies, which set forth certain standards the institution must meet. Not maintaining or adhering to institutional policies could put an institution's accreditation at risk. Furthermore, noncompliance with certain policies, especially those related to federal regulations, could jeopardize an institution's eligibility to receive federal funding or even give the U.S. Department of Education grounds to recoup funds already disbursed.

## Nondiscrimination

Consistently applying policies ensures that all members of the academic community are treated fairly and equitably. Inconsistent application can lead to perceptions of bias or discrimination, which can have legal repercussions under anti-discrimination laws including, but not limited to, ADA laws.

## Policy Considerations: Key Takeaways

The intersection of Section 504 and Titles II and III of the ADA in the study abroad context generally prohibits discrimination against individuals with disabilities who are otherwise qualified to participate in the programming. Study abroad offices are obligated to ensure reasonable accommodations are afforded to individuals with disabilities. Colleges and universities are expected to be flexible in providing accommodations. For example, a change of location, whether for travel or lodging, would be considered a minor alteration that is often feasible to achieve. Students with disabilities who are otherwise qualified should only be denied where the accommodation would constitute a fundamental alteration to the program or the student's participation would be a direct threat to safety. These exceptions are applicable only in extreme situations.

Financial hardship is rarely an excuse for the inability to provide reasonable accommodations. The fact is that providing accommodations will often increase costs; however, the obligation to commit financial resources to providing accommodations is not limited to the specific program or the budget of the institution's study abroad office. The institution must consider the totality of its financial resources to help provide accommodations.

One way to plan for costs in advance is to apply a small surcharge on all students who participate in study abroad. This provides a pool of funds to help dilute the costs of accommodating students with disabilities when necessary. If the office or division creates a separate account to store those funds, then the cost of providing accommodations is set aside and available when it is needed.

Implementing standard policies and procedures will ensure the study abroad office is successful in aiding students living with a disability who would like to study abroad. Study abroad offices should encourage students to inquire about accommodation arrangements as early as possible. To allow students to take this initiative, include comprehensive guidance for students with disabilities in program materials and on study abroad websites. The information enclosed should equip students to make an informed decision regarding their participation. If a program has physical requirements, state them clearly in the application. Further, dedicating a resource webpage (that is accessible) with general information for students often proves to be beneficial. The webpage should provide program resources, explain the ADA and Section 504 requirements, and inform students how they can request accommodations.

Offices that set clear expectations about their disability accommodation services help students decide whether studying abroad—and what programs—would be ideal. Then, if the student chooses to study abroad, they can anticipate the support they will receive from the study abroad office as well as the challenges they are likely to face. In order to do this successfully, administrators must be intimately familiar with the programs they are managing and promoting.

Similarly, study abroad offices need to work with their on-campus participants (such as faculty leaders) and off-campus partners in order to ensure that the requirements and expectations are understood, and modifications and supports are managed appropriately. There is no substitution for an ongoing process of training and coordination.

After the student's program admission, the administrators may make confidential inquiries about accommodation needs. At this point, it may be best to partner with disability services professionals to process information regarding individual needs. Many institutions delegate the disability services office to handle all inquiries due to the strict limitations on disability-related inquiries set by ADA laws and state law. Because offices of disability services are equipped to assist with accommodation requests, they should communicate with the student about the best way to satisfy their needs. Disability services should solicit input from the study abroad office to ensure the accommodations are safe, do not present an undue burden, or fundamentally alter the program. Effort, communication, and documentation are crucial to successfully accommodating students.

The case law and regulatory decisions should serve as guidance for study abroad offices to evaluate their compliance with federal discrimination laws. Administrators should consider the following policy considerations to ensure they are providing disability accommodations in connection with study abroad opportunities:

- Work together with the student as a team; communicate and explain the steps to try and provide accommodations.
- Create a set of policies and procedures to guide study abroad offices with compliance.
- Train staff in the study abroad office to help deal with issues that may arise.
- Train trip leaders to help with accommodations and spot issues before they arise.
- When partnering with foreign institutions, ensure the partner institution understands the necessary accommodations for the student.
- Maintain confidentiality to the greatest extent possible.
- Consider how technology can boost accommodations.
- If you decide to impose certain obligations onto yourself, be sure you can deliver on your promises.
- Consider alternative options—the study abroad office cannot always provide the perfect experience but try to accommodate the student as best as possible. Be creative, resourceful, and compassionate.

Thorough planning and honest dialogue are the best ways to ensure the success of any study abroad programming.

## Conclusion

Although the law on extraterritoriality is unsettled, study abroad administrators should generally establish successful practices as if there is no question that the ADA and Section 504 apply to their programs. The failure to provide reasonable accommodations based on a technicality like the presumption against extraterritoriality may incur fines and costly litigation. Similarly, raising arguments related to resource limitations is generally unsuccessful and may detract from the institution's avowed values and the stated goals of study abroad programming. Complying with federal disability discrimination laws, state law, and institutional policy is the best way to promote an inclusive study abroad operation that accomplishes the fundamental goals of international education and reduces overall risk.

## References

Americans With Disabilities Act of 1990, 42 U.S.C. § 12101 et seq. (1990).
*Bird v. Lewis & Clark College,* 104 F. Supp. 2d 1271 (2000).

College of St. Scholastica, 3 Nat'l Disability L. Rep. (Lab. Rel. Press) P 196 (Sept. 15, 1992).

Discrimination, 42 U.S.C. §12132 (Title II). (1990).

*Equal Employment Opportunity Commission (EEOC) v. Arabian American Oil Co.*, 499 U.S. 244, 111 S. Ct. 1227, 113 L. Ed. 2d 274. (1991).

Equal Opportunity for Individuals with Disabilities, 42 U.S.C § 12181(7)(J). (2010).

*Ewell v. Daggs*, 108 U.S. 143, 149 (1883).

*Husson College, 31 NDLR 180, Case No. 01-05-2005 (OCR 2005).*

*Kanter, A. S. (2003). The presumption against extraterritoriality as applied to disability discrimination laws: Where does it leave students with disabilities studying abroad? 14 Stan. L. &Pol'y Rev. 291.*

Kaplin, W. A., Lee, B. A., Hutchens, N. H., & Rooksby, J. H. (2019). *The law of higher education, sixth edition.* Jossey-Bass, Inc.

Prohibition of Discrimination by Public Accommodations,42 U.S.C. § 12182. (2010).

Rehabilitation Act of 1973, 29 U.S.C. § 701, et. sec. (Section 504) (1973).

St. Louis Univ., 1 Nat'l Disability L. Rep. (Lab. Rel. Press) P 259 (Dec. 12, 1990).

*Tecza v. Univ. of San Francisco,* No. C 09-03808 RS, 2010 WL 1838778 (2010).

Whitlock, J. D., & Charney, A. D. (2012, April 26). *Federal disability laws: Do they translate to study abroad programs?* NACUANOTES, *10*(7).

# 6

## Have Records, Will Travel: FERPA and Access While Abroad

**Michael Pfahl, J.D., Ph.D.**

## Introduction

When the Family Educational Rights and Privacy Act (FERPA) came into effect in the fall of 1974, the Internet was in its infancy (Tarnoff, 2016), and the *Concorde* had just made its first round trans-Atlantic Ocean flight in a little over 6 hours (Lindsey, 1974). Back then, study abroad was still a relatively new phenomenon, with participation well below the 188,753 participants who traveled overseas during the 2021/22 academic year (IIE, 2023; Marion, 1974). But just as higher education has evolved from delivery in a windowless classroom to a custom-designed tour through the sprawling hills of an international destination, FERPA has evolved from its origins as a law primarily focused on the "right to inspect and review" (McDonald, 2011) to a foundation for student privacy on college campuses across the United States. This chapter will provide a further review of this law within the context of education abroad programming.

A law review article published in 1975 after FERPA's effective date grouped the provisions of the new law into three main pillars: access to records, opportunity to correct records, and disclosure of records (Mattessich, 1975). These three main pillars stand today, albeit with further interpretation through several "Dear Colleague" letters issued by the U.S. Department of Education and multiple amendments to the law itself. Within the context of study abroad programming, the application of FERPA focuses primarily on the disclosure provisions and the guidance for enforcement as published (and sometimes clarified) by the U.S. Department of Education (ED).

## Defining an "Education Record"

With so many reasons for institutional units to collect information about students, it is important to remember that while FERPA applies to all "education records," and while that term covers far more than just "educational" or "academic" records, not all student information held by an institution falls under the statutory definition. As provided for in the law, "education records" are defined broadly as "those records, files, documents, and other materials which (i) contain information directly related to a student; and (ii) are maintained by an educational agency or institution or by a person acting for such agency or institution" (Family Educational and Privacy Rights, §1232g(a)(4)(A), 1974, as amended). That definition is immediately followed by a short list of exceptions for specific types of student-related records that are excluded from the definition of "education records," even if they would otherwise meet the statutory definition, such as certain records held by a campus law enforcement agency or by a physician treating the student on campus (Family Educational and Privacy Rights, §1232g(a)(4)(B), 1974, as amended). Additionally, not all information constitutes a "record" subject to the statute. A common example of this is a faculty or staff member's casual personal observations about a student that are outside of the faculty or staff member's duties (such as observations about recent odd behavior, as opposed to knowledge of a student's grade); while a subsequent written record of that information would become subject to FERPA, the personal knowledge does not (McDonald, 2011).

## FERPA Within the Practice of Education Abroad

FERPA's premise is to provide protection for education records collected and held by the institution to the benefit of the student. There is no statement in the law or its implementing text that the purpose of the law was to interfere with the institution's ability to deliver its educational services to the student. In fact, the law itself offers numerous specific instances in which education records may be disclosed without student consent—perhaps none more cited within the study abroad context than the "health and safety emergency" exception (as described below) (Family Educational and Privacy Rights, §1232g(b)(1) (I), 1974, as amended). Most directly relevant to an education abroad practitioner's work is that certain education records of a student may be shared with "other school officials, including teachers within the educational institution or local educational agency, who have been determined by such agency or institution to have legitimate educational interests" (as described below) (Family Educational and Privacy Rights, §1232g(b)(1)(A), 1974, as amended). Other permissible disclosures without student consent include certain disclosures in connection with a "student's application for, or receipt, of financial aid," as well as in certain legal venues in response to a lawfully issued subpoena (Family Educational and Privacy Rights, §1232g(b)(1), 1974, as amended). Narrowing the scope of review further, education abroad practitioners may find themselves most often considering two terms in particular—"legitimate educational interests" and "health and safety emergency."

## Legitimate Educational Interest

Today, most student information is retained in software systems that can be accessed by various institutional employees as directly related to the services those employees provide to the student (i.e., financial aid, bursar, registrar, faculty). As long as the individual employee holds a legitimate educational interest in accessing the education record, generally defined as "job-related need-to-know" (McDonald, 2011), the law allows for the disclosure without consent. However, the individual's status as an institutional employee does not provide *carte blanche* permission to access the education record of all students. The access must be related to the performance of the employee's duties as it relates to serving the student—a decision that must be made on a case-by-case basis. An institution must use "reasonable methods" to ensure that only those employees with a legitimate educational interest in specific education records access those records and ensure that such policy "is effective" and the "institution" remains in compliance" (Family Educational Rights and Privacy, §99.31(a)(1)(ii), 1988, as amended). The full text of the law states:

> An educational agency or institution must use reasonable methods to ensure that school officials obtain access to only those education records in which they have legitimate educational interests. An educational agency or institution that does not use physical or technological access controls must ensure that its administrative policy for controlling access to education records is effective and that it remains in compliance with the legitimate educational interest requirement in paragraph (a)(1)(i) (A) of this section. (Family Education Rights and Privacy, 1988)

## Outside Parties as School Officials

With the growing engagement of outside vendors and contractors in the provision of international support services, among the 2008 Amendments was an adjustment explicitly permitting the disclosure of education records without consent "to contractors, consultants, volunteers, and other outside parties to whom an educational agency or institution has outsourced institutional services or functions"—in effect, an extension of the "school official" principle to encompass outside agents (Family Educational Rights and Privacy, 2008) In its full text amending 34 CFR 99.31(a)(1)(i)(B), the 2008 amendment states:

> A contractor, consultant, volunteer, or other party to whom an agency or institution has outsourced institutional services or functions may be considered a school official under this paragraph provided that the outside party— (1) Performs an institutional service or function for which the agency or institution would otherwise use employees; (2) Is under the direct control of the agency or institution with respect to the use and maintenance of education records; and (3) Is subject to the requirements of §99.33(a) governing the use and redisclosure of personally identifiable information from education records. (Family Education Rights and Privacy, 2008)

Of note, at the time the laws were published, the federal government stated in its implementing regulations that "our experience suggests that virtually all of the more than 103,000 schools subject to FERPA [including 97,382 K-12 schools] will take advantage of this provision" (Federal Education Rights and Privacy, 2008).

To this point and as a means to further document the connection between institution and vendor, standard contract language with vendors should include a provision officially recognizing the contractor as a "school official" and provide assurance that the vendor will maintain any "education records" in accordance with the FERPA laws. These provisions provide documented continuity of service for safeguarding education records and the personally identifiable information contained within them. Contractual affirmations regarding FERPA are also critical in ensuring that the contractor understands their obligations with regard to the same in the event of a disclosure to a third party (whether voluntary through formal request or involuntary such as in the event of data breach). Moreover, as institutions continue to engage more outside contractors to perform supplemental services and functions for study abroad programs, institutions need to remain mindful of the annual obligation to notify current students about their rights under FERPA, including the institution's criteria for determining who constitutes a school official and what constitutes a legitimate educational interest (Family Educational Rights and Privacy, §99.7, 1988, as amended). Therefore, making explicit in this notice that the institution does engage outside contractors and third-party providers within its FERPA policy is good practice.

## Health and Safety Emergencies

In an October 30, 2007, letter written in the wake of the shootings at Virginia Tech, then U.S. Secretary of Education, Margaret Spellings, stated that "nothing is more important to Americans than the safety of their children. FERPA is not intended to be an obstacle in achieving that goal" (Spellings, 2007). This statement was reiterated again in a December 17, 2008, "Dear Colleague" letter written on the heels of the newly published (and long awaited) 2008 Amendments to FERPA, before outlining the U.S. Department of Education's summary of the revisions:

> Although FERPA does not permit disclosures of personally identifiable information on a routine, non-emergency basis, the final laws afford greater flexibility and deference to administrators so that they can bring appropriate resources to bear when there is a threat to the health or safety of students. Section 99.36 in the final laws makes clear that educational agencies and institutions may disclose information from education records to appropriate parties, including parents, whose knowledge of the information is necessary to protect the health or safety of a student or another individual if there is a significant and articulable threat to the health or safety of a student or other individual, considering the totality of the circumstances. The final laws add a requirement that the educational agency or institution record in the student's education records the basis for its decision that a health or safety emergency existed. If, considering the information available at the time of the determination, there is a rational basis for the determination, the Department will not substitute its judgment for that of the educational agency or institution in evaluating the circumstances and making the determination. We believe these changes appropriately balance the interests of safety and privacy. (Simon, 2008)

Since the 2008 Amendments were published, the U.S. Department of Education has periodically released other documents that provide further insight into its interpretation of FERPA's provisions regarding disclosures related to health and safety emergencies (Cole, 2021). In June 2011, the U.S. Department of Education published "Addressing Emergencies on Campus," in which it further defined "significant and articulable threat," stating that

> the phrase "articulable and significant threat" means that if a school official can explain why, based on all the information then available, the official reasonably believes, for instance, that a student poses a significant threat, such as a threat of substantial bodily harm to any person, including the student, the school official may disclose personally identifiable information from education records without consent to any person whose knowledge of the information will assist in protecting a person from threat. (U.S. Department of Education, 2011)

This document provided further guidance regarding disclosure to parents and law enforcement officials, as well as the flow of information relating to "threat assessment teams" organized under a "properly implemented threat assessment program."

In the early days of the COVID-19 pandemic, the U.S. Department of Education released guidance identifying the relevant parties to whom the institution may disclose information in the event of a perceived health or safety emergency, stating that "typically, law enforcement officials, public health officials, trained medical personnel, and parents . . . are the types of appropriate parties to whom [personally identifiable information] (PII) from education records may be disclosed under this FERPA exception [34 CFR 99.36]" (U.S. Department of Education, 2020). The U.S. Department of Education provided further clarity to the conditions under which this exception applies, stating that

> this exception to FERPA's general consent requirement is limited to the period of the emergency and generally does not allow for a blanket release of PII from a student's education records. Rather, these disclosures must be related to an actual, impending, or imminent emergency, such as a natural disaster, a terrorist attack, a campus shooting, or the outbreak of an epidemic disease. (U.S. Department of Education, 2024)

In a document released in April 2023, the ED reiterated that education records subject to disclosure under the health and safety emergency exception may include "certain health records" held by the institution. However, this document, as well as a document published in 2019, included an important distinction between "treatment records" (such as those held by an on-campus clinical resource) and "health-related records" (U.S. Department of Education, 2023). Within the study abroad context, many institutions collect information such as medical release forms or other health disclosures during pre-departure processing ("health-related records"). Specifically addressing this set of records, the U.S. Department of Education states in the guidance that "students' health-related records maintained by schools that are made, maintained, or used for nontreatment purposes, such as medical forms or questionnaires used to screen for eligibility to participate in school-sponsored athletics, are education records rather than treatment records under FERPA," and thus potentially disclosable under the health and safety emergency exception.

## Practical Summary

The U.S. Supreme Court stated in *Gonzaga University v. Doe* that "there is no question that FERPA's nondisclosure provisions fail to confer enforceable rights" (2002). More directly, an individual student cannot successfully sue a university under FERPA. However, violations are not without the threat of consequences as the law does provide that "no funds shall be made available under any applicable program to any educational agency or institution which has a policy or practice" of permitting disclosure of education records (or the personally identifiable information contained therein) without consent or outside of the specifically enumerated exceptions (Family Educational and Privacy Rights, §1232g(b), 1974, as amended). More simply put, "the carrot is federal funding, while the stick is the termination of such funding …" (*Frazier v. Fairhaven School Committee*, 2022). That being said, there is a notable absence in media reporting of a suspension of funding by the U.S. Department of Education for a single, isolated violation related to an unintentional, incidental release of information covered under the laws.

Nevertheless, even without a right to bring individual action and without the immediate threat of the loss of funding (claims of FERPA violations are subject to scrutiny by a review board appointed by the Secretary per Law), FERPA should continue to be viewed by all practitioners as a foundational principle upon which the institution builds its information collection and sharing practices. For example, while the laws allow for disclosure to parents without consent if certain conditions are met, under 34 CFR 99.5 and 99.6, they do not *require* such disclosure. Each institution, therefore, should ensure that it has a written policy and practice to maintain consistency of application of its process for determining if the relevant conditions warrant release under the institution's particular standards. Similarly, while the laws clarified the release of covered information to third parties performing functions on behalf of the institution, practitioners should still scrutinize the way institutional data is transferred to and maintained by these contractors to ensure that only that which is critical to the performance of such services is provided, with all nonrelated information withheld. Practitioners must also be mindful that while FERPA may "permit" certain disclosures without consent in the sense that it does not forbid them, those same disclosures may be subject to additional requirements and prohibitions depending upon the application of the privacy laws within the country hosting the study abroad program, which FERPA does not supersede. In some countries, additional waivers and releases that must be executed separate from the institution's FERPA processes. See Chapters 7, "FERPA in Action: Guide for Education Abroad Practitioners" (Hayes, 2024), and 11, "GDPR and PIPL Enforcement in Higher Education" (Liu & Bahner, 2024), both in this volume, for more information on privacy laws impacting information sharing in other countries.

Accordingly, within education abroad, FERPA should be viewed as it was written—as a law promoting a student's right to access their own records and to have some control over the way those records are shared with others. Just as the law should not be viewed as a barrier to protect human life in the event of a significant threat to health and safety, it also should not be viewed as a blanket approval to share the student's information without consent to any and all who may meet a regulatory exception. Each practitioner should work with their institutional counsel and senior leadership to ensure the consistent and fair application of the law to ensure both the continuity of service to the student but with a mind to the privacy and access components the law seeks to protect.

## References

Cole, J. (2021, May 24). *The Family Educational Rights and Privacy Act (FERPA): Legal issues.* (CRS Report No. R46799). https://crsreports.congress.gov/product/pdf/R/R46799

Family Educational and Privacy Rights. 20 USC §1232g. (1974, as amended). https://uscode.house.gov/view.xhtml?req=granuleid:USC-prelim-title20-section1232g&num=0&edition=prelim

Family Educational Rights and Privacy. 34 CFR 99. (1988, as amended). https://www.ecfr.gov/current/title-34/subtitle-A/part-99

Family Educational Rights and Privacy. 73 F.R. 74806 (final laws December 9, 2008) (to be codified at 34 CFR 99). https://www.govinfo.gov/content/pkg/FR-2008-12-09/pdf/E8-28864.pdf

*Frazier v. Fairhaven School Committee*, 276 F.3d 52, 68 (1st Cir. 2022).

*Gonzaga University v. Doe*, 536 U.S. 273, 287 (2002).

Hayes, A. (2024). FERPA in action: Guide for education abroad practitioners." In J. Pollard & K. S. Priebe (Eds.), *Convergence of litigation, policy, and standards: Building the informed practitioner in education abroad risk management.* The Forum on Education Abroad. doi.org/10.36366/SIA.5.978-1-952376-41-2.7

Institution of International Education (IIE). (2023). New international students enrollment, 2007/08-2022/23. Open Doors Report on International Educational Exchange. Retrieved from https://opendoorsdata.org/data/us-study-abroad/all-destinations/

Lindsey, R. (1974, June 18). Boston to Paris and back in 6 hours and 18 minutes. *The New York Times.* https://www.nytimes.com/1974/06/18/archives/boston-to-paris-and-back-in-6-hours-and-18-minutes-new-york.html

Liu, X. S., & Bahner, E. S. (2024). GDRP and PIPL enforcement in higher education. In J. Pollard & K. S. Priebe (Eds.), *Convergence of litigation, policy, and standards: Building the informed practitioner in education abroad risk management.* The Forum on Education Abroad. doi.org/10.36366/SIA.5.978-1-952376-41-2.11

Marion, P. (1974). Evaluation of study abroad. Presented at the National Convention of the National Association for Foreign Student Affairs. https://files.eric.ed.gov/fulltext/ED089634.pdf

Mattessich, C. M. (1975). The Buckley amendment: Opening school files for student and parental review. *Catholic University Law Review* 24(3), spring 1975. https://scholarship.law.edu/lawreview/vol24/iss3/7

McDonald, S. J. (2011). The Family Educational Rights and Privacy Act: Seven myths and the truth. *Perspectives.* United Educators Insurance. https://campusclimate.unm.edu/resources/ferpa-handouts-all.pdf

Simon, R. (2008, December 17). Dear colleague letter about Family Educational Rights and Privacy Act (FERPA) final laws. U.S. Department of Education. https://sites.ed.gov/idea/files/idea/policy/speced/guid/idea/letters/2008-4/dear-colleague121708ferpa4q2008.pdf

Spellings, M. (2007, October 30). Key policy letters signed by the education secretary or deputy secretary. United States Department of Education. https://www2.ed.gov/policy/gen/guid/secletter/071030.html

Tarnoff, B. (2016, July 15). How the internet was invented. *The Guardian.* https://www.theguardian.com/technology/2016/jul/15/how-the-internet-was-invented-1976-arpa-kahn-cerf

U.S. Department of Education (ED). (2002). Legislative history of major FERPA provisions. https://studentprivacy.ed.gov/sites/default/files/resource_document/file/ferpaleghistory.pdf

U.S. Department of Education (ED). (2011, June). Addressing emergencies on campus. https://studentprivacy.ed.gov/sites/default/files/resource_document/file/emergency-guidance.pdf

U.S. Department of Education (ED). (2020, March). FERPA & coronavirus disease 2019 (COVID-19) frequently asked questions (FAQs). https://studentprivacy.ed.gov/sites/default/files/resource_document/file/FERPA%20and%20Coronavirus%20Frequently%20Asked%20Questions.pdf.

U.S. Department of Education (2023, April 12). Guidance for school officials on student health Records. https://studentprivacy.ed.gov/sites/default/files/resource_document/file/The%20Family%20Educational%20Rights%20and%20Privacy%20Act%20Guidance%20for%20School%20Officials%20on%20Student%20Health%20Records.pdf.

U.S. Department of Education (2024). When is it permissible to utilize FERPA's health or safety emergency exception for disclosures? Retrieved on February 26, 2024, at https://studentprivacy.ed.gov/faq/when-it-permissible-utilize-ferpas-health-or-safety-emergency-exception-disclosures

# 7

## FERPA in Action: Guide for Education Abroad Practitioners

**Anna Hayes**

As discussed in the previous chapter, the Family Educational Rights and Privacy Act (FERPA) is a foundational pillar safeguarding the privacy of student education records. Introduced when the landscape of higher education was vastly different, this federal law has evolved to address unforeseen challenges. To fully understand how FERPA interacts with education abroad policies and procedures, it is essential to recognize the dynamic nature of both the regulatory framework and the international education landscape. With over 188,000 participants in the 2021/22 academic year (Institute for International Education, 2023), study abroad is more available to more participants than ever. FERPA initially focused on a student's "right to inspect and review" educational records, but it has expanded. From traditional classrooms to international destinations, FERPA safeguards student privacy in a rapidly changing academic landscape.

This chapter serves a dual purpose—to provide a contextual understanding of FERPA within education abroad programming and explore its practical implementation in emergencies. The journey begins by revisiting the core principles of FERPA and its historical context, setting the stage for considering its application in some education abroad scenarios. From here, you can consider the most appropriate training for professionals operating within a FERPA context.

### Defining Education Records in the Global Learning Environment

Higher education has changed since FERPA was adopted, and so has the definition of "education records," which encompasses much more student information. Additionally, the field of education abroad has changed in the intervening years. Practitioners must understand both FERPA's scope and the exceptions relevant to study abroad program participants. "Education records," as per FERPA, include records, files, documents, and materials directly related to a student maintained by an educational agency, institution, or person acting for such an entity (U.S. Department of Education, 2021). However, the scope extends beyond specific academic information. Records related to a student's experience in an education abroad program can include enrollment information, grades, course schedules, and health information. While upon first reading FERPA's definition of "education records" seems expansive, subsequent amendments have carved out essential exceptions.

Certain records, such as those held by campus law enforcement agencies or physicians treating students on campus, fall outside the statutory definition (McDonald, 2011).Understanding these exceptions is critical to education abroad practitioners. Understanding an institution's attitude and posture regarding FERPA legislation requires practitioners to work closely with legal counsel and other offices on campus. Consistency and compliance with the broader university's interpretation of FERPA allow education abroad offices to navigate the international nuances within the framework of institutional guidelines.

## FERPA Compliance in Education Abroad: Challenges and Considerations

### Legitimate Educational Interest in Global Learning

Understanding the concept of "legitimate educational interest" under FERPA is crucial for education abroad practitioners. In the traditional academic setting, this principle restricts access to student records to individuals genuinely needing to know for educational purposes (McDonald, 2011). However, when applied to the global learning environment, the scope of legitimate educational interest extends beyond the borders of the home institution.

In the context of international partners or third-party vendors, education abroad practitioners need to understand the limits of "legitimate educational interests" and thoroughly understand the specific roles and responsibilities of individuals involved in global programs. Sharing student information with an international partner, for example, is justifiable if the student is planning to attend as it directly contributes to the educational support and well-being of the student during their international experience (McDonald, 2011).

Education abroad practitioners should establish clear guidelines and draft contractual agreements that outline the legitimate educational interests of all parties, as stated in the *Standards of Good Practice for Education Abroad* (The

Forum on Education Abroad, 2020, clause 4.2.2; 4.2.3). This practice ensures that information is shared responsibly and aligns with the global program's educational objectives and FERPA requirements. Understanding the parameters of "legitimate educational interest" can help practitioners strike a balance between effective collaboration and safeguarding student privacy in the international arena. For additional information about contractual agreements, see Chapter 29 in this volume, "Expectations, Guardrails, and Compliance: Negotiating Effective International Partnership Agreements" (May, 2024).

## Health and Safety Emergencies

In the landscape of education abroad, the health and safety of students are paramount concerns, and as then-Secretary of Education Margaret Spellings stated in 2007, "FERPA is not intended to be an obstacle in achieving that goal." FERPA recognizes the need for flexibility in disclosing information during health and safety emergencies while safeguarding privacy rights and ensuring the well-being of all students.

The FERPA "health and safety emergency" exception permits educational institutions to disclose relevant student information without consent when there is a significant and articulable threat to the health or safety of a student or others (U.S. Department of Education, 2024). This exception is particularly pertinent in education abroad, where students may face unique challenges in unfamiliar environments. Practitioners must be well-versed in the parameters of this exception, understanding that information can be shared with appropriate parties on a "need-to-know" basis, which might include colleagues, emergency response teams, local authorities, or even family members when their involvement is necessary to address the emergency (McDonald, 2011; U.S. Department of Education, 2024).

## Training Program Leaders and Staff

The *Standards* (2020) note that education abroad offices must prioritize training for program leaders and staff on responding to health and safety emergencies (The Forum on Education Abroad, 2020, clause 5.15). FERPA guidelines and practices should also be included in this training as it is a key aspect of health and safety emergency response. As discussed in Chapter 3 of this volume, "Lessons from Legal Cases: Safeguarding Student Health & Well-Being in Education Abroad Programs (Priebe & Hayes, 2024)," program directors are often faculty who may be familiar with on-campus guidelines and resources. Traveling with students internationally requires the faculty to also be familiar with protocols in other settings. Scenario-based training in various emergencies equips program leaders and staff with the skills to make swift, informed decisions. This proactive approach ensures that they can navigate the complexities of FERPA with a focus on privacy and student protection in critical situations. This training method is more than explaining the basics of FERPA—it allows program leaders to consider the unique scenarios and challenges they may encounter in global learning environments.

## Basics of FERPA

The training should cover the basics of FERPA, including its historical context, the rights it affords to students and their families, and the overarching principles that guide the protection of education records. Understanding the core tenets of FERPA sets the foundation for more nuanced discussions on its application in international settings.

## Global Learning Scenarios

Education abroad program leaders may encounter situations that differ from those in domestic settings. Training programs should incorporate case studies and simulations specifically tailored to the challenges of living and learning outside of the United States. These scenarios may include situations where information needs to be shared with international partners, local authorities, or external vendors, requiring a nuanced understanding of FERPA's application.

## Cross-Cultural Competence

Any training related to leading international programs should include the development of cross-cultural competence. Practitioners should appreciate cultural nuances concerning privacy expectations and information sharing. Is the country where the program takes place attuned to individual rights, privacy laws, or a duty to maintain such privacy? Understanding how different cultures approach student privacy increases the likelihood that FERPA compliance is culturally sensitive and respects the values of all parties involved.

## Emergency Response Simulations

Given the significance of health and safety emergencies in the context of education abroad, training should include simulations of emergency response scenarios. Program leaders and staff must be adept at making quick, well-informed decisions while adhering to FERPA guidelines. Simulations provide a practical understanding of balancing privacy considerations with the imperative to protect students in critical situations.

## Collaboration with Legal Counsel

Education abroad offices should include legal counsel in the planning of training sessions. Legal experts can provide insights into the specific FERPA policies of the institution and educate program leaders and staff on university guidelines. This collaborative approach also fosters a culture of proactive compliance, in which individuals understand the importance of seeking legal guidance when faced with ambiguous situations.

## Continuous Professional Development

FERPA regulations and international privacy laws continue to evolve, as noted in Chapters 6, 10, and 11 of this volume (Pfahl, 2024; Liu & Bahner, 2024a, 2024b). Training programs should emphasize the importance of continuous professional development. Regular updates ensure that program leaders and staff remain well-informed about the latest FERPA requirements and interpretations related to the context of education abroad. By fostering a culture of awareness and competence, education abroad offices can navigate the complexities of information sharing while prioritizing student privacy and security.

## Case Studies

A FERPA-informed approach contributes to effective risk mitigation in handling medical emergencies abroad. To fully comprehend FERPA, practitioners should consider the following case studies to put into practice the information discussed in this and the previous chapter. By carefully delineating legitimate educational interests, communicating within the boundaries of FERPA, and collaborating with relevant authorities, education abroad practitioners can protect student privacy and well-being, maintain family communication, navigate legal compliance, and collaborate with emergency services.

### Case Study: Navigating a Crisis Abroad

A group of students from a U.S. university are participating in a semester-long education abroad program in Paris. The students are directly enrolled in the host university's academic courses and taking courses taught by their home institution faculty.

A major terrorist attack occurs near the Eiffel Tower. U.S. and international media report mass casualties. Local infrastructure has been destroyed, communications systems in the city are down, and numerous students are unreachable. The home university faculty and host university's local coordinators responsible for the U.S. students face the challenge of managing the crisis for their institution and their families and friends while supporting the safety and well-being of the affected U.S. university students. As the situation unfolds, FERPA considerations become paramount in managing information related to the affected students.

### Legitimate Educational Interest

Medical professionals, local coordinators, and host university officials may need access to student records to make informed decisions regarding the affected students' well-being. Program leaders must assess the legitimate educational interests of the students involved. Understanding the concept of legitimate "educational interest" within a crisis is crucial for determining who has the right to share and access sensitive information.

### Communication with Families

As discussed earlier in the chapter, FERPA permits the disclosure of information to parents or guardians in health and safety emergencies. In this case, contacting the families of affected students becomes a critical step as students are unreachable to program leaders. However, program leaders must adhere to FERPA requirements, sharing only necessary information while maintaining transparency and privacy.

### Collaboration with Local Authorities

Coordinating with local authorities and adhering to their guidelines is essential for managing the crisis effectively. FERPA's provisions for disclosures to appropriate parties in health and safety emergencies come into play here. The program leaders must navigate this collaboration while upholding FERPA principles and ensuring that information is shared on a need-to-know basis.

### Case Study: Medical Emergency Abroad

A faculty-led field study program takes place in a remote location in Ghana with limited access to medical facilities. During an outdoor activity, one of the students sustains a severe injury, requiring immediate medical attention. The remote location poses challenges for swift emergency medical response, and the program leaders must quickly assess the situation and initiate appropriate actions. Fellow participants demonstrate concern for the impacted student, posting about the event on their social media platforms and asking regularly for updates on the student. In this critical health emergency, FERPA considerations play a vital role in managing information related to the injured student:

*Health Information Disclosure*: FERPA permits the disclosure of relevant educational records that include health information to appropriate parties in cases of health and safety emergencies. The program leaders must assess who needs to be informed, including medical professionals, family members, and university officials, ensuring that disclosures are made within the bounds of FERPA.

However, information about the impacted student should not be disclosed to fellow program participants despite their concerns. In this instance, the program leader should converse with the remaining students, informing them that the student is receiving appropriate care—without disclosing other information—and ask that they respect the student's privacy by not continuing to post about it.

*Family Notification*: Contacting the family of the injured student becomes a priority. As discussed earlier, FERPA allows for disclosing information to parents or guardians in health emergencies, and program leaders must navigate this process while respecting the student's privacy rights.

*Coordination with Emergency Services*: Program leaders must coordinate with local emergency services if treatment and/or evacuation are needed. FERPA provisions guide the responsible and reasonable sharing of information with these services, emphasizing the need-to-know basis in health emergencies.

These case studies highlight the importance of integrating FERPA considerations into emergency response plans during education abroad programs, especially in scenarios involving physical health emergencies. Education abroad practitioners, equipped with a nuanced understanding of FERPA, can navigate such situations while prioritizing student well-being, legal compliance, and privacy protection and navigate health crises abroad while prioritizing student safety, legal compliance, and privacy protection.

## Conclusion

In the dynamic landscape of education abroad, understanding and adhering to FERPA is important for safeguarding student information and ensuring ethical and legal practices. As the scenarios presented in this chapter illustrate, education abroad practitioners face diverse challenges. FERPA considerations play a pivotal role in decision-making and response strategies.

FERPA, enacted in 1974, has evolved from its initial focus on providing students the right to inspect and review their educational records to becoming a comprehensive framework governing these records' disclosure, correction, and protection. Exploring the "legitimate educational interest" with the nuanced application of FERPA in the context of study abroad underscores the delicate balance between privacy and the legitimate needs of educational institutions and their affiliates.

Communication is vital, especially in the context of emergencies or unexpected events. FERPA, while imposing restrictions on information disclosure, provides the necessary framework for responsible and strategic communication, ensuring that relevant parties are informed without compromising students' privacy.

FERPA's emphasis on protecting student records in situations involving data security incidents or emergency evacuations challenges the education abroad practitioner. It is critical that institutions develop and implement robust policies to secure academic records, ensuring that only authorized individuals have access to sensitive information and thus mitigating risks associated with privacy breaches.

FERPA is a regulatory framework that should shape ethical and responsible practices in education abroad. Navigating the complexities of FERPA in diverse scenarios requires a nuanced understanding, proactive planning, and a commitment to prioritizing student well-being and privacy. Armed with this knowledge education abroad practitioners can confidently navigate the intricate terrain of FERPA to facilitate a secure experience for students participating in global learning opportunities.

## References

Institute of International Education. (2023, November 13). *U.S. study abroad 2021/22*. Open Doors Report on International Educational Exchange. https://opendoorsdata.org/annual-release/u-s-study-abroad/

Liu, X. S., & Bahner, E. (2024a). GDPR and PIPL enforcement in higher education. In J. Pollard & K. S. Priebe (Eds.), *Convergence of litigation, policy, and standards: Building the informed practitioner in education abroad risk management*. The Forum on Education Abroad. doi.org/10.36.366/SIA.5.978-1-952376-41-2.11

Liu, X. S., & Bahner, E. (2024b). Global data privacy overview. In J. Pollard & K. S. Priebe (Eds.), *Convergence of litigation, policy, and standards: Building the informed practitioner in education abroad risk management*. The Forum on Education Abroad. doi.org/10.36.366/SIA.5.978-1-952376-41-2.10

May, P. F. (2024). Expectations, guardrails, and compliance: Negotiating effective international partnership agreements. In J. Pollard & K. S. Priebe (Eds.), *Convergence of litigation, policy, and standards: Building the informed practitioner in education abroad risk management*. The Forum on Education Abroad. doi.org/10.36.366/SIA.5.978-1-952376-41-2.29

McDonald, S. J. (2011). The Family Educational Rights and Privacy Act: Seven myths and the truth. Perspectives. United Educators Insurance. https://campusclimate.unm.edu/resources/ferpa-handouts-all.pdf

Pfahl, M. (2024). Have records, will travel: FERPA and access while abroad. In J. Pollard & K. S. Priebe (Eds.), *Convergence of litigation, policy, and standards: Building the informed practitioner in education abroad risk management.* The Forum on Education Abroad. doi.org/10.36.366/SIA.5.978-1-952376-41-2.6

Priebe, K. S., & Hayes, A. (2024). Lessons from legal cases: Safeguarding student health & well-being in education abroad programs. In J. Pollard & K. S. Priebe (Eds.), *Convergence of litigation, policy, and standards: Building the informed practitioner in education abroad risk management.* The Forum on Education Abroad. doi.org/10.36.366/SIA.5.978-1-952376-41-2.3

Spellings, M. (2007, October 30). Key policy letters signed by the education secretary or deputy secretary. United States Department of Education. https://www2.ed.gov/policy/gen/guid/secletter/071030.html

The Forum of Education Abroad.( 2020).*Standards of good practice for education abroad, Sixth edition.* The Forum on Education Abroad. doi.org/10.36366/S.978-1-952376-04-7

U.S. Department of Education (ED). (2021, August 25). *Family educational rights and privacy act (FERPA).* Home. https://www2.ed.gov/policy/gen/guid/fpco/ferpa/index.html

U.S. Department of Education (2024). When is it permissible to utilize FERPA's health or safety emergency exception for disclosures? Retrieved on March 20, 2024, at https://student-privacy.ed.gov/faq/when-it-permissible-utilize-ferpas-health-or-safety-emergency-Exception-disclosures

# 8

## Clery Act and Title IX Extraterritorial Application (And Why the Federal Approach is the Floor, Not the Ceiling)

**Joseph Storch, J.D. and Andrea Stagg, J.D.**

*The last two decades have seen significant shifts in the approach of the U.S. federal government to the application of two critical education, safety, and equity laws in the study abroad environment. In this chapter, we will recount some of the changes in application (due to litigation and regulatory approach) of the Clery Act and Title IX, describe the current vacuum of U.S. federal requirements, and discuss the adoption of these standards (generally, at a minimum) by myriad institutions in their policy expectations for safety and equity in study abroad programs.*

If on President's Day weekend in 2011 a higher education professional asked what the Clery Act and Title IX obligations were for crimes and violations that occur on study abroad programs, the answer would have been brief, "we are aware of none." Starting in February and April of that year, the United States Department of Education (ED) began a series of sub-regulatory guidance statements that could be interpreted as creating and then gradually increasing the compliance obligations overseas, before completely vacating the field in August and October 2020. Concurrent to the whiplash approach of our federal regulator, institutions have voluntarily and steadfastly taken the issue of harm to students overseas—and especially sexual and interpersonal violence and harassment—with increasing seriousness. They have created, and maintained, policies that generally go above and beyond legal requirements at the height of ED's activeness in this space.

## The Clery Act Packs and Unpacks Its Suitcase

### Background

The Jeanne Clery Disclosure of Campus Security Policy and Campus Crime Statistics Act is a federal consumer reporting law initially passed in 1990 and updated several times, most recently in the 2013 Reauthorization of the Violence Against Women Act (Stagg & Storch, 2017). Among other things, the law requires all colleges and universities that accept federal funds to issue an Annual Security Report, including about five dozen policy statements as well as statistics regarding Clery Act crimes and certain arrests and referrals for discipline occurring in certain geographic locations during the three previous calendar years. The primary Clery Act crimes include aggravated assault, burglary, manslaughter, murder, motor vehicle theft, robbery, and sex offenses (rape, fondling, incest, and statutory rape). The following additional crimes are "Clery crimes" if the victim was intentionally selected based on actual or perceived protected category, such as race, religion, national origin, disability, or sex: larceny/theft, simple assault, intimidation, and damage, destruction, or vandalism of property. Aside from issuing these reports annually, the Act also includes ongoing obligations for institutions to issue prompt warnings for certain crimes and emergencies, to maintain a crime log and, for schools that have residential housing, to take certain actions around missing students and fire safety. The law is enforced by the Federal Student Aid office of the Department of Education, which may conduct compliance reviews and levy fines for certain violations.

Neither the Clery Act statute (Higher Education Act, 1965) nor the regulations (Clery Act Regulations) make any mention of study abroad or international education. Historically, the Clery Act requirements do not center "who," but only "where." Statistics are counted based on the location of the incident, not the identity of the victim or accused.

### Clery Handbooks

The Department of Education occasionally issues sub-regulatory documents aimed at assisting the higher education community in complying with the Clery Act, including three editions of a detailed Handbook, followed by an

Appendix. The 2005 Clery Act Handbook (U.S. Department of Education, 2005) makes no mention of study abroad save a brief reference: "Separate Clery Act compliance is required both for U.S. owned foreign institutions as well as branches of domestic institutions that are located abroad" and states that, "If your institution sends students to study abroad or to exchange programs at institutions that you do not own or control, you are not required to disclose crimes occurring there" (U.S. Department of Education, 2005 at 19). The 2011 Clery Act Handbook (U.S. Department of Education, 2011), issued without a relevant change to the statute or regulations, continued that thought, stating,

> If your institution sends students to study abroad at an institution that you don't own or control, you don't have to disclose statistics for crimes that occur in those facilities. However, if your institution rents or leases space for your students in a hotel or student housing facility, you are in control of that space for the time period covered by your agreement. Host family situations do not normally qualify as noncampus locations unless your written agreement with the family gives your school some significant control over space in the family home. (U.S. Department of Education, 2011 at 30)

The Handbook also sought to apply the recently passed missing on campus student requirements to foreign campuses of a domestic institution with student housing facilities (U.S. Department of Education, 2011 at 161).

The 2011 Handbook also called for Clery Act coverage for foreign-located campuses of U.S. institutions (U.S. Department of Education, 2011 at 3, 17, 82, 161, 171, 189). The Department issued a third version of the Handbook in 2016 (U.S. Department of Education, 2016), again without a relevant change to the statute or regulations (Stagg & Storch, 2016). This Handbook included the same language as the previous Handbook about statistics from programs overseas, but then added new text regarding overnight trips (referred to as "short-stay 'away' trips") (U.S. Department of Education, 2016 at 2-25) that did not appear in previous versions. This new text ostensibly added considerable obligations to institutions for tracking travel and attempting to collect crime statistics for a broad range of locations (U.S. Department of Education, 2016 at 2-25 – 2-26). Specifically, the 2016 Handbook stated that if an institution "sponsors short-stay 'away' trips *of more than one night* for its students, all locations used by students during the trip, controlled by the institution during the trip and used to support educational purposes should be treated as noncampus property" (emphasis added) (U.S. Department of Education, 2016 at 2-25). The language "more than one night" was a departure from previous sub-regulatory guidance (U.S. Department of Education, O. of P. E., 2012) received by institutions and their representatives from the Department; previously the Department distinguished between trips of long duration and shorter trips, indicating an example of a trip of three weeks that would be evaluated as noncampus property.

Examples in the 2016 Handbook included written agreements between the institution and a contractor for housing or learning space "for a school-sponsored trip or study abroad program (either domestic or foreign)" (U.S. Department of Education, 2016 at 2-25). The language focuses on whether the institution is sponsoring the program or event, and then whether the institution owns or controls any space involved in the trip by written agreement. Such a written agreement may be the contract or confirmation of booking a hotel. The Department issued several other sub-regulatory documents that continued to confuse those who sought to comply with the Clery Act and would seem to apply the standards for these trips domestically and abroad, again without statutory or regulatory support (Storch, 2016c; Storch, 2016b). Institutions worked to incorporate these new obligations into their Clery compliance plan, requesting information from faculty and staff about all trips of more than one night, domestic and international. In addition, someone would need to document their outreach to police in locations abroad to attempt to collect crime statistical information in the relevant location(s) during the applicable time period. Anecdotally, institutions that dutifully performed this obligation rarely received responses from this outreach.

For fifteen years, though not binding, the Clery Handbooks served as compliance tools for institutions of higher education. Each Handbook was 200–300 pages and contained specific examples and scenarios. So, it was surprising when, without much fanfare, the Trump Administration's Department of Education withdrew the 2016 Clery Act Handbook and replaced it with a 13-page Appendix (U.S. Department of Education, O. of P. E., 2020b). The cover letter (U.S. Department of Education, O. of P. E., 2020a) to the new appendix reproached the Department for treading beyond the borders of what the statute and regulations allow.

> The 2016 edition, as well as the previous versions, created additional requirements and expanded the scope of the statute and regulations. have the force of law or regulations, some institutions may have felt pressured to satisfy the non-regulatory or non-statutory based aspects of the guidance, calculating that the financial and reputational consequences of non-compliance were too great … Following an extensive review of the 2016 edition, the Department concluded that much of the guidance provided was outside of the scope of the relevant statutory … and regulatory … authority. (U.S. Department of Education, O. of P. E., 2020a)

The Department cited to a U.S. Senate report (American Council on Education, n.d.) that excoriated the Department for the length of the Handbook and the burden of Clery Act requirements that went beyond the statute and regulations, including regarding noncampus property and trips of short and long duration, writing that

> [t]he Appendix has also addressed the issues identified in the above-referenced Senate Report regarding reporting crimes that occur during institution sponsored stay-away trips and similar mandates placed upon trips to international destinations, that require institutions to obtain crimes statistics from foreign law enforcement agencies. (U.S. Department of Education, O. of P. E., 2020b)

While the cover letter speaks grandly to the changes, the challenge is that the Appendix itself is silent on the issue. Perhaps the Department meant to address it further in the Appendix and did not include the text in error, or perhaps it was taking a page from the 1980's song and decided to "say it best when [it] says nothing at all." Either way, the Department appears in its latest sub-regulatory communication to have moved away from the expanding application of the Clery Act to a study abroad environment. As of this writing, the Department of Education has not issued further Clery Act guidance during the Biden administration, despite rumors of a new handbook's imminent arrival.

## VAWA Amendments to the Clery Act

The previous sections covered how consideration of study abroad as "Clery geography" has evolved related to crime disclosures or the three-year look back that institutions must do to publish those statistics annually. We have also described how historically Clery obligations were based on the geographic location of an incident, and not the parties involved. Clery Act crimes are disclosed and warnings are distributed to the community regardless of whether the individuals involved are students, faculty, staff, or nonaffiliates with no current or past relationship to the university. If dueling delivery drivers have a fistfight in the quad, and one breaks the other's jaw, that institution just gained a statistic for an aggravated assault on campus, even though the incident does not seem to logically relate to the safety of that particular campus.

In 2013, President Obama signed the Violence Against Women Reauthorization Act of 2013 (VAWA) (Violence Against Women Act, 2013) and regulations followed (Clery Act Regulations, 2014). VAWA institutionalized certain protections and rights for individuals who are victims of sexual and interpersonal violence, including sexual assault, domestic violence, dating violence, and stalking. These new rules on rights and response obligations for higher education institutions did not have the same strict geographic parameters. For example, if an institution receives a report of sexual or interpersonal violence, the school must provide certain information to victims about available options, remedies, resources, and services, regardless of where the incident occurred (Clery Act Regulations, 2014). One interpretation of these provisions is that the obligations apply when the incident took place on study abroad. The Clery Act generally (the statistics-gathering and disclosure) covers a broad range of crimes, but please note this section about response and prevention obligations only relates to domestic violence, dating violence, sexual assault, and stalking.

## Title IX Packs, Unpacks, and Perhaps Begins Repacking Its Suitcase

### Background

Title IX of the Education Amendments of 1972 is a civil rights law that requires equity in access to education, regardless of sex. Tucked into the end of a series of financial aid changes in 1972, the 37 words of Title IX were passed without fanfare, but in the recent decade has become one of the most important tools to address gender equity in the history of the United States. Title IX is enforced by the Department of Education's Office for Civil Rights (OCR), which maintains regional offices to enforce the law through compliance reviews and complaint investigations. The text of the law states on its face that it does not apply outside the United States. "No person in the United States shall, on the basis of sex, be excluded from participation in, be denied the benefits of, or be subjected to discrimination under any education program or activity receiving Federal financial assistance" (Title IX, 1972). For many years before 2017, different regional offices of OCR have said that Title IX does not apply outside of the United States while others insisted that Title IX is applicable outside of the United States and, in fact, is not based on geographic location at all.

### The Obama Administration (2009–2017)

The Obama Administration was responsible for statutory and regulatory changes discussed earlier, as well as significant sub-regulatory changes that generally required schools to take a more substantial and comprehensive approach to responding to and preventing sexual and interpersonal violence. That administration's approach centered the experience of those who experienced harm in its rhetoric around the changes. In and around 2010, higher education attorneys started to notice a more robust approach in the program review resolution agreements that OCR was signing with institutions (Grasgreen, 2010). These agreements were based on the 2001 notice and comment guidance (U.S. Department of Education, 2001) but seemed much more expansive than existing guidance about what institutions were "required" to do to prevent and respond to sexual and interpersonal violence. OCR continued to engage in active enforcement, investigating complaints and initiating additional Title IX compliance reviews, before a guidance document was issued in spring 2011.

In its April 2011 Dear Colleague Letter (DCL) (withdrawn in 2017), the Department stated that Title IX applies "in connection with all the academic, educational, extracurricular, athletic, and other programs of the school . . .," including those activities occurring off-campus (U.S. Department of Education, 2011). The DCL shook the landscape, and higher education legal and compliance professionals scrambled to get a handle on the obligations in the 19-page letter. While Title IX as a whole prohibits sex discrimination in educational programs and activities, the letter was primarily focused on preventing and responding to peer sexual violence. And although Title IX applies to both K-12 and higher education recipients of federal funds, the letter seemed more tailored to addressing issues in the residential higher education context. The DCL described a school's obligation to respond promptly once a school knows or reasonably should know about possible harassment (U.S. Department of Education, 2011 at 4). Such a response broadly includes eliminating the harassment, preventing its recurrence, and addressing its effects (U.S. Department of Education, 2011).

In 2014, OCR supplemented the letter with a 53-page "significant guidance document" titled Questions and Answers on Title IX and Sexual Violence (withdrawn in 2017) (U.S. Department of Education, 2014). The Q&A included a section on off-campus conduct, stating plainly that "under Title IX, a school must process all complaints of sexual violence, regardless of where the conduct occurred, to determine whether the conduct occurred in the context of an education program or activity or had continuing effects on campus or in an off-campus education program or activity" (U.S. Department of Education, 2014).

The guidance was clear that regardless of where sexual harassment or sexual violence occurred, "a school must consider the effects of the off-campus misconduct when evaluating whether there is a hostile environment on campus or in an off-campus education program or activity," acknowledging that students often experience continuing effects of off-campus violence that interfere with their program or activities (U.S. Department of Education, 2014 at 29).

Higher education professionals understood these guidance documents to cover all sexual harassment and sexual violence experienced by the campus community, regardless of location, including while on study abroad. And this was true whether the abroad program was run by a student's home institution or by a partner or other host institution. Even if students were technically enrolled in a different institution for the semester (or year), their home institutions' designated study abroad offices knew exactly where the home institution's students were, how long they would be there, which credits would (or should) transfer, and more. These students on study abroad were very much still "students" of the home institution and could experience sexual harassment or sexual violence abroad that would have an impact on their education programs or activities, both abroad and back home.

Noting the text and the emphasis of the administration, the Obama-era guidance changed the course of Title IX history as far as how institutions of higher education prevent and respond to sex discrimination, including sexual harassment and sexual violence. Before the 2011 DCL, many institutions did not have a clearly designated Title IX Coordinator. Today, many institutions prominently include a link to their Title IX website on their homepage and have an identified coordinator. Larger institutions may have robust offices with a coordinator, deputy coordinator(s), investigators, case managers, and more. Many schools continue the prevention training developed or ramped up around that time, and in many ways, the practices begun in response to this sub-regulatory guidance became the standard or best practice.

### The Trump Administration: Pendulum Swings Back (2017–2021)

The Trump Administration took a decidedly different approach than the Obama Administration. In September 2017, the Department of Education issued a letter (U.S. Department of Education, 2017a) and Q&A (U.S. Department of Education, 2017b) that rescinded Obama-era guidance, including the 2011 DCL and the 2014 Q&A. The newly issued letter and Q&A totaled 10 pages compared to the more than 70 pages of rescinded guidance on sexual misconduct. Importantly, the new, brief guidance did not address international travel. The Department proposed to promulgate regulations to provide stability and clarity to recipients, rather than "rule by letter" (Hefling & Emma, 2017). This was a reference to the Obama-era guidance, which had received criticism from individuals across the political spectrum for seeming to enforce rules that were not written in any law or regulation.

The following fall, the Department issued proposed rules on Title IX (Proposed Regulations, 2018). These rules narrowed campus obligations considerably. The Obama administration guidance had ushered in an era where campuses felt an obligation to respond, in some way, to any sex discrimination that anyone disclosed (or any employee learned about) that happened anywhere in the world. The new proposed rules, which became final in May

2020 and effective that August, focused solely on sexual harassment, which it defined in a new, narrower way. The rules set out required grievance procedures for how to respond to, investigate, and adjudicate reports of sexual harassment as defined by the regulations, limiting the applicability to conduct that occurred on-campus or in a campus program or activity, and in the United States (Proposed Regulations, 2018).

In the preamble to the final regulations, the Department "acknowledge[d] the concern ... that the ... regulations would not extend Title IX protections to incidents of sexual misconduct occurring against persons outside of the United States, and the impact that this jurisdictional limitation might have on the safety of students participating in study abroad programs" (Final Regulations, 2020). However, the Department interpreted the plain language of Title IX, "No person in the United States ..." to mean exactly—and only— what it says, "by its plain text, the Title IX statute does not have extraterritorial application" (Final Regulations, 2020). The Department would read the "plain meaning" to say that Title IX would not cover sexual misconduct that occurs outside of the United States (Final Regulations, 2020).

The 2020 rules, which remain current as of this writing, do not *require* any particular institutional response to known instances of sexual harassment, sexual assault, domestic violence, dating violence, or stalking that takes place on study abroad (or on the other side of town). In fact, if a report alleges prohibited conduct that falls outside the narrow geographic scope of the Final Rule's applicability, the Title IX Coordinator is required to dismiss the complaint. But that is not necessarily the end of the story. The preamble to the Final Rule states,

> Nothing in the final regulations precludes recipients from addressing sexual misconduct that occurs in a recipient's study abroad programs ... a mandatory dismissal of allegations in a formal complaint of sexual harassment because the allegations concern sexual harassment that occurred outside the United States is a dismissal only for Title IX purposes and does not preclude action under another provision of the recipient's code of conduct. (Final Regulations, 2020)

Even after the withdrawal of the Obama-era's influential guidance documents, and the promulgation of the 2020 rules, institutions did not necessarily change their *practices* or *protocols* regarding study abroad or broader institutional policies on prevention and response, including mandatory reporting for employees. Schools continued to train study abroad professionals about their obligations when they learn about sexual harassment or sexual violence, including reporting that information to the Title IX coordinator and/or providing information about resources and remedies to the person who disclosed the harm. And, if applicable, an institution could conduct investigations and adjudicate complaints about prohibited conduct in the context of activities abroad, if the institution had jurisdiction over the responding party. Even if the government no longer *required* such a response, many institutions continued on this course because it was permitted and aligned with stated values and a commitment to community safety.

The Trump era also saw a proliferation in new or updated state sexual harassment prevention and response laws governing the workplace (National Women's Law Center, 2023). In New York, for example, employers are required to provide annual training about sexual harassment prevention to all employees, with special care toward training managers and supervisors, who have an obligation to report such conduct (Combating Sexual Harassment Toolkit, n.d.). The definition of sexual harassment is broader than it is under the 2020 Title IX rules, and it is clear that prohibited conduct need not occur in the physical workplace to require an employer's action under the law (Combating Sexual Harassment Toolkit, n.d.).

### The Biden Administration (2021–2024): A Middle Ground?

The Biden Administration's Department of Education issued regulations expanding the conduct that may constitute sexual harassment under Title IX, forgoing the geographic limitations and acknowledging, as the Department did in 2011, how off-campus conduct may have an impact on a student's education program or activity, such as creating a hostile environment.

In July 2022, the Department of Education proposed new Title IX regulations to be finalized in 2024, effective August 1 of that year (2024 Final Regulations). The preamble to the proposed rules includes examples of how sex-based harassment occurring outside of the program or activity, or outside the United States, may well cause sex discrimination *within* the program or activity. For example, if a student is subjected to sex discrimination in grading on study abroad and becomes at risk of losing their merit-based financial aid award (Proposed Regulations, 2022). While the conduct occurred outside the United States, the impact is felt in the education program within the United States. "When such conduct causes sex discrimination in its education program or activity within the United States, the recipient must address it" (Proposed Regulations, 2022). A second example is cited regarding peer sexual violence during a study abroad program, and how a hostile environment may exist when both students return to campus (Proposed Regulations, 2022 at 41417). This concept is aligned with the Obama-era guidance.

On April 29, 2024, the Department issued its final regulations in the Federal Register (2024 Final Rule). The preamble to the regulations discusses extra-territoriality and is clear that "a recipient does not have an obligation under Title IX to address sex discrimination occurring outside of the United States. However, nothing in these regulations prohibits a recipient from responding as appropriate under its existing code of conduct or other policies pertaining to study abroad programs" (2024 Final Rule at 33532). The final regulations are nearly identical as the proposed regulations discussed above, with one clarification. The proposed rules said: "A recipient has an obligation to address a sex-based hostile environment under its education program or activity, even if sex-based harassment contributing to the hostile environment occurred outside the recipient's education program or activity or outside the United States," 87 FR 41571, emphasis added. The final rules say:

> A recipient has an obligation to address a sex-based hostile environment under its education program or activity, even when *some conduct* alleged to be contributing to the hostile environment occurred outside the recipient's education program or activity or outside the United States. (2024 Final Rule at 33528, emphasis added)

The distinction here is that the conduct that occurred outside of the United States contributing to a hostile environment back in the education program or activity within the United States need not be sex-based harassment; it can be any type of conduct, and if it is sex-based in some way, there need not be an independent determination that it is "sex-based harassment" under Title IX in order for it to "count" toward contributing to a hostile environment. For a detailed discussion of this change, see page 2024 Final Rule at 33530. At the same time, the broad language in the Clery Act around providing notice of response rights and processes for incidents that occur on and off campus remains, as does the open question of whether this applies to study abroad.

## Caselaw on Extraterritorial Application That May Impact Title IX and the Clery Act

Before 2017, case law was split on whether Title IX applied outside of the United States even as the plain language of the law covered "no person in the United States" (King, 2002; Mattingly, 2006; Phillips, 2007). [For an excellent in-depth discussion of each of these cases, see the Journal of College and University Law (Aalberts, Marzen, & Prum, 2015).] The Clery Act, which includes no private right of action, has no cases on point. Yet outside of the Title IX and Clery Act context, two lines of cases, one bubbling slowly and one strengthening recently, could significantly hamper the Department's ability to apply either law to conduct outside the United States without a statutory change by Congress.

Opinions issued over the last two decades on unrelated federal laws have ruled that if Congress intends for a law to apply internationally, it must specifically say so, and agencies or law enforcement may not simply assume international application where unstated. The Supreme Court wrote:

> [t]he question is not whether we think 'Congress would have wanted' a statute to apply to foreign conduct 'if it had thought of the situation before the court,' but whether Congress has affirmatively and unmistakably instructed that the statute will do so. 'When a statute gives no clear indication of an extraterritorial application, it has none.' (RJR Nabisco, 2016; Morrison, 2010; Microsoft, 2007)

Here, neither the Clery Act nor Title IX include specific statutory language applying their requirements outside of the United States (and Title IX includes language specific to the United States), and it is possible that a court would not find favor with extraterritorial application short of clear Congressional authority.

Concurrently, a 2022 Supreme Court case clearly stated the Court's move toward a "major questions doctrine" for regulatory agency action. The Chief Justice wrote that, "in certain extraordinary cases, both separation of powers principles and a practical understanding of legislative intent make us 'reluctant to read into ambiguous statutory text' the delegation claimed to be lurking there ... To convince us otherwise, something more than a merely plausible textual basis for the agency action is necessary. The agency instead must point to 'clear congressional authorization' for the power it claims" (West Virginia, 2022; Biden, 2023). That is to say, a Department of Education interpretation that the Clery Act or Title IX would apply to actions that occur outside of the United States would need to be supported by clear statutory language, not just a plausible textual basis for the application. It is questionable whether a court would find such a clear congressional authorization for applying either law to conduct that occurs internationally.

## Other Efforts to Regulate Safety in Study Abroad

There has been an uptick in state and federal interest in injuries, crimes, and accidents in overseas programs. The State of Minnesota passed reporting legislation (Minnesota, 2014), and multiple members of Congress have proposed legislation, still unpassed, that would add the requirement to the Higher Education Act. For an analysis of the legislation and implementation, please see the *Study Abroad Health and Safety Regulation: Report to the 2015 Legislature* from the Minnesota Office of Higher Education (2015).

Beyond reporting, a number of states, led by New York in 2015, added plain language applying the response principles to incidents that occur on campus, off campus, or while studying abroad (New York State Education Law, 2015).

## Beyond the Legal to the Moral

The above brief history of changes in the federal approach to extraterritorial application of these laws would be dizzying for the vast majority of readers. These shifting sands eclipse the more important point. Of the hundreds of thousands who study abroad annually, there are students and employees on study abroad programs who are exposed to harassment, violence, and other harms on the basis of sex and gender. [According to the Institute of International Education, before the interruption of COVID, well over 300,000 studied abroad every year (Institute for International Education, 2023).] This is not to say that there is something inherently dangerous about study abroad (there is not) or that the rates of prevalence are higher on these programs. [For a detailed analysis of the relative risks of campus versus study abroad, using de-identified insurance claim data, see reports from The Forum (The Forum on Education Abroad, 2016; The Forum on Education Abroad, 2018).] But it is simply to say that there is a non-zero chance that our students will experience this harm during these programs and trips, just as on their home campuses.

Further, if the prevalence differentials generally follow the pattern of campus prevalence, female identifying students may experience harm at higher rates than male identifying students, and transgender and gender nonbinary students likely experience harm at greater rates still. Sexual minorities, students with disabilities, and students from other traditionally marginalized groups may experience harm at elevated rates compared to peers. At the same time, many study abroad professionals have made concerted efforts to reduce barriers to participation and dedicated outreach to members of these groups to experience study abroad (The Forum on Education Abroad, 2020b; Via & The Forum on Education Abroad, 2022).

Our message is simple. When it comes to appropriate, lawful, and equitable response, and equally when it comes to evidence-based and evidence-informed prevention of harms, international programs professionals should not wait for Congress, the president, and the Department of Education to settle on the standards that we must follow. The education abroad professionals should <u>lead</u>.

So, what does leadership in this space look like? It starts with partnerships with institutional experts from Title IX and other equity offices, student affairs, human resources, and related departments, to best understand the approach of the institution to such harms that occur at or near the institution in ways that (with appropriate modifications) can be applied at a distance (Storch, 2016a). It includes discussions with counsel and policymakers so that the policy and procedural approach to harms occurring overseas matches the institutional values, separate and apart from a consideration of the minimums of federal law. Leaders will include different approaches for varied programs with very different risks and resources that span multiple continents. Develop and improve upon proven and promising prevention programming, ensuring it's customized to the specific trip and audience. Build a partnership with leaders and practitioners across the country who have toiled for years to develop standards (The Forum on Education Abroad, 2020b) and best practices (The Forum on Education Abroad, 2020a) for keeping students safe. There are many dedicated professionals who have spent their career centering safety and equity in study abroad. There is far more work to do, but our guidance is not to wait for the dust to settle on Title IX and the Clery Act's obligations—there is important work to do, and important students to serve, *right now*. Let's continue that work!

## References

2014 Minnesota Session Law, Chapter 312-H.F. No. 3172, Section 5.41 (2014). https://www.ohe.state.mn.us/pdf/chapter312.pdf

2024 Final Regulations: Nondiscrimination on the Basis of Sex in Education Programs or Activities Receiving Federal Financial Assistance, § 34 CFR Part 106 (2024). https://www.govinfo.gov/content/pkg/FR-2024-04-29/pdf/2024-07915.pdf

Aalberts, R. J., Marzen, C., & Prum, D. (2015). Studying is Dangerous? Possible Federal Remedies for Study Abroad Liability. *J. of College and Univ. L., 41*(189).

American Council on Education. (n.d.). *Recalibrating regulation of colleges and universities: Report of the Task Force on Federal Regulation of Higher Education, https://www.acenet.edu/Documents/Higher-Education-Regulations-Task-Force-Report.pdf*

Biden v. Nebraska, 600 U.S. ___ ___ (U.S. Supreme Court 2023).

Clery Act Regulations, § 34 C.F.R. §668.46. Retrieved November 27, 2023, from https://www.ecfr.gov/current/title-34/subtitle-B/chapter-VI/part-668/subpart-D

Combating Sexual Harassment Toolkit. (n.d.). *State of New York.* https://www.ny.gov/combating-sexual-harassment-workplace/employers

Comparing college student mortality rates in the U.S. with mortality rates while abroad. (2018). *The Forum on Education Abroad.* https://forumea.org/wp-content/uploads/2018/03/ForumEA-Mortality-Rates-18.pdf

Expanding education abroad access for nontraditional learners. (2023). *The Forum on Education Abroad.* https://www.forumea.org/uploads/1/4/4/6/144699749/forumea_white_paper_2023-%E2%80%8Bexpanding_education_abroad_access_for_nontraditional_learners.pdf

Final Regulations: Nondiscrimination on the Basis of Sex in Education Programs or Activities Receiving Federal Financial Assistance, § 34 CFR Part 106 (2020). https://www.federalregister.gov/documents/2020/05/19/2020-10512/nondiscrimination-on-the-basis-of-sex-in-education-programs-or-activities-receiving-federal

Grasgreen, A. (2010, December 9). Tougher line on sexual harassment. *Inside Higher Ed.* https://www.insidehighered.com/news/2010/12/10/tougher-line-sexual-harassment

Hefling, K., & Emma, C. (2017, September 22). Obama-era school sexual assault policy rescinded. *POLITICO.* https://www.politico.com/story/2017/09/22/obama-era-school-sexual-assault-policy-rescinded-243016

Higher Education Act: Institutional and Financial Assistance Information for Students, 20 U.S.C. §1092(f).

Institute for International Education. (2023). *U.S. Students Studying Abroad, 2021-22.* Open Doors Report on International Educational Exchange. https://opendoorsdata.org/data/us-study-abroad/all-destinations/

Insurance claims data and mortality rate for college students studying abroad, 2016. (2016). *The Forum on Education Abroad.* https://forumea.org/wp-content/2016/04/ForumEA_InsuranceClaims_MortalityRateStudentsAbroad.pdf

King v. Board of Control of Eastern Michigan University, 221 F.Supp. 2d 783 ___ (E.D. Mich. 2002).

Mattingly v. Univ. of Louisville, 2006 WL 2178032 ___ (W.D. Ky. 2006).

Microsoft Corp. V. AT&T Corp., 550 U. S. 437, 454 ___ (U.S. Supreme Court 2007).

Minnesota Office of Higher Education. (2015, January 29). *Study abroad health and safety regulation: Report to the 2015 legislature.* https://www.ohe.state.mn.us/pdf/studyabroadreport.pdf

Morrison v. National Australia Bank Ltd., 561 U. S. 247, 255 ___ (U.S. Supreme Court 2010).

National Womens's Law Center. (2023, October 19). *State workplace anti-harassment laws enacted since #metoo went viral.* https://nwlc.org/resource/state-workplace-anti-harassment-laws-enacted-since-metoo-went-viral/

New York State Education Law Article 129-b, Educ. L. §6440(6) (2015). https://www.nysenate.gov/legislation/laws/EDN/6440

Phillips v. St. George's University, 2007 WL 3407728 ___ (E.D.N.Y. 2007).

Proposed Regulations: Nondiscrimination on the Basis of Sex in Education Programs or Activities Receiving Federal Financial Assistance, § ED–2018–OCR–0064 (2018). https://www.federalregister.gov/documents/2018/11/29/2018-25314/nondiscrimination-on-the-basis-of-sex-in-education-programs-or-activities-receiving-federal

Proposed Regulations: Nondiscrimination on the Basis of Sex in Education Programs or Activities Receiving Federal Financial Assistance, § ED–2021–OCR–0166 (2022). https://www.federalregister.gov/documents/2022/07/12/2022-13734/nondiscrimination-on-the-basis-of-sex-in-education-programs-or-activities-receiving-federal

RJR Nabisco, Inc. V. European Community, 579 U.S. 325 ___ (U.S. Supreme Court 2016).

Stagg, A., & Storch, J. (2016, July). *The 2016 Clery Handbook: New developments and important changes* [White paper]. University Risk Management and Insurance Association (URMIA). https://higherlogicdownload.s3.amazonaws.com/URMIA/9c74ddba-4acc-4dcd-ba3a-d6cd4c945342/UploadedImages/documents/grac/GRAC_WP_CleryHandbook_20160721.pdf

Stagg, A., & Storch, J. (2017, May). *An overview of the Violence Against Women Act (VAWA) Amendments to the Clery Act [White paper].* University Risk Management and Insurance Association (URMIA) Government and Regulatory Affairs. https://higherlogicdownload.s3.amazonaws.com/URMIA/9c74ddba-4acc-4dcd-ba3a-d6cd4c945342/UploadedImages/documents/grac/GRAC_WP_VAWA-Clery_20170530.pdf

Storch, J. (2016a, January). Risk management considerations regarding the Clery Act, Violence Against Women Act (VAWA) and Title IX when students study abroad. University Risk Management and Insurance Association (URMIA) Government and Regulatorty Affairs Blast. https://higherlogicdownload.s3.amazonaws.com/

URMIA/9c74ddba-4acc-4dcd-ba3a-d6cd4c945342/UploadedImages/documents/grac/
GRABlast_Clery_Act_VAWA_TitleIX_20160124.pdf

Storch, J. (2016b, September 26). Sexual and Interpersonal Violence on Study Abroad: Legal and Considerations for Student Affairs Professionals Who Work with International Programs. *The Student Affairs Collective, 15*(1).

Storch, J. (2016c, September 26). Updated: The Clery Act and overseas/distance study: New developments and compliance guidance, 2016 edition. *NACUANOTES, National Association of College and University Attorneys, 15*(1). https://getcleryedge.com/wp-content/uploads/2020/10/NACUA2016.pdf

The Forum on Education Abroad. (2020a). *Guidelines for best practices in responding to sexual and gender-based misconduct.* https://www.forumea.org/responding-to-sexual-and-gender-based-misconduct.html

The Forum on Education Abroad. (2020b). *Standards of good practice for education abroad,* Sixth edition. doi.org/10.36366/S.978-1-952376-04-7Title IX of the Education Amendments of 1972, 20 U.S.C. §1681. Retrieved November 29, 2023, from https://uscode.house.gov/view.xhtml?path=/prelim@title20/chapter38&edition=prelim

U.S. Department of Education, O. for C. R. (2001, January 19). *Revised sexual harassment guidance: Harassment of students by school employees, other students, or third parties.* https://www2.ed.gov/about/offices/list/ocr/docs/shguide.html

U.S. Department of Education, O. for C. R. (2011, April 4). *Dear Colleague Letter.* https://www2.ed.gov/about/offices/list/ocr/letters/colleague-201104.pdf

U.S. Department of Education, O. for C. R. (2014, April 29). *Questions and answers on Title IX and sexual violence.* https://www2.ed.gov/about/offices/list/ocr/docs/qa-201404-title-ix.pdf

U.S. Department of Education, O. for C. R. (2017a, September 22). *Dear Colleague Letter on campus sexual misconduct.* https://www2.ed.gov/about/offices/list/ocr/letters/colleague-title-ix-201709.pdf

U.S. Department of Education, O. for C. R. (2017b, September 22). *Q&A on campus sexual misconduct.* https://www2.ed.gov/about/offices/list/ocr/docs/qa-title-ix-201709.pdf

U.S. Department of Education, O. of P. E. (2005). *The Handbook for Campus Crime Reporting.*

U.S. Department of Education, O. of P. E. (2011). *The Handbook for Campus Safety and Security Reporting.*

U.S. Department of Education, O. of P. E. (2012). *Untitled (Guidance on the Clery Act).* On File With the Authors

U.S. Department of Education, O. of P. E. (2016). *The Handbook for Campus Safety and Security Reporting.*

U.S. Department of Education, O. of P. E. (2020a, October 9). *Clery Act Appendix for FSA Handbook.* https://fsapartners.ed.gov/sites/default/files/attachments/2020-10/CleryAppendixFinal.pdf

U.S. Department of Education, O. of P. E. (2020b, October 9). *Cover letter: Rescission of and replacement for the 2016 Handbook for Campus Safety and Security Reporting.* https://fsapartners.ed.gov/knowledge-center/library/electronic-announcements/2020-10-09/rescission-and-replacement-2016-handbook-campus-safety-and-security-reporting-updated-jan-19-2021

Via and The Forum on Education Abroad. (2022). *Barriers & opportunities in education abroad.* https://www.forumea.org/uploads/1/4/4/6/144699749/via_forum_report_5-17-23_final__1_.pdf

Violence Against Women Act (2013), Pub. L. No. 79 Fed. Reg. at 62,784, 34 C.F.R. 668.46. Retrieved November 29, 2023, from https://www.ecfr.gov/current/title-34/subtitle-B/chapter-VI/part-668/subpart-D

West Virginia v. EPA, 597 U.S. ___ (U.S. Supreme Court 2022).

# 9

## Rethinking and Reframing the Narrative: Reflections on Sexual Violence Prevention in Education Abroad

**Melissa Chambers and Jamie Snow**

## Introduction

Incremental and seismic shifts in public discourse on sexual violence in the first two decades of the 21st century mirrored changes in the social, political, and cultural landscapes of global higher education—and in turn, education abroad (National Sexual Violence Resource Center, 2023). Title IX and the Clery Act, two U.S. federal laws enacted 20 years apart, galvanized campus communities to build a robust response framework to sex- and gender-based violence, bringing about dramatic and lasting changes in education abroad practices. The resulting infrastructures to support victim-survivors of sex-based discrimination, harassment, and violence unquestionably impacted numerous students and began to frame the scope of work for education abroad professionals. Building on years of guidance provided by the U.S. Department of Education's *Dear Colleague* letters and provisions including Campus SaVE (Violence Against Women Act, 2013), The Forum on Education Abroad published guidelines on responses to sex- and gender-based misconduct abroad in 2017 and in 2020. These powerful tools direct education abroad practitioners to best practices for student support and risk mitigation.

Sexual violence (a blanket term referring to unwanted sexual contact, including but not limited to sexual harassment, rape, sexual assault, dating violence, intimate partner violence, coercion, violence against trans and non-binary people, stalking, and more) remains a critical issue directly impacting international education. The current generation of students is growing up with greater advocacy and transparency around sexual health and account-ability for sexual violence than ever before. As discourse continues to shift, practices need to evolve and adapt.

> Young people want sex ed content that goes beyond body parts, pregnancy and STI prevention. They're pushing to ensure sex ed is inclusive and affirming of people of all backgrounds and identities. They are leading the charge forlessons about consent .... (Bruess, 2018)

The culture of consent and speaking out encouraged by the #MeToo movement sharply contrasts with the persistence and prevalence of sexual violence across the globe (New York Times, 2017). Rape culture (a pervasive social environment that normalizes sexual violence) is fueled by social media and pop culture, perpetuated by a number of global leaders, and remains an undercurrent across many cultures (United Nations Women, 2023). Incident management and systems of support for victim-survivors of sexual violence remain largely heteronormative and do not consider the disproportion-ate impact of sexual violence on marginalized communities. In a rapidly changing social and political landscape, it is crucial to advance meaningful dialogue on sexual health and sexual violence prevention informed by inter-cultural contexts and legal realities. This chapter examines current education abroad practices for sexual violence prevention, response, and support of victim-survivors, provides critical points for reflection grounded in cultural, social, and political contexts, and discusses proactive strategies centered on inclusion and intersectionality in education abroad.

## The Context of Sexual Violence Prevention and Education Abroad

As an industry, in the wake of COVID, education abroad practitioners are rebuilding and managing complex issues in the "new normal," including strained budgets, staffing shortages, and calls for increased risk management practices (The Forum on Education Abroad, 2023, p. 14). Practitioners are fac-ing burnout, exhaustion, and collective trauma, but remain mission-driven in the compassionate care of students. Addressing sexual violence preven-tion and response in day-to-day work for education abroad is ambiguous and complex, exacerbated by the lack of collective guidelines and standards for prevention, reporting, tracking incidents, and supporting victim-survivors of sexual violence.

The World Health Organization estimates that globally approximately one in three women worldwide have been subjected to either physical and/or sexual violence in their lifetime (WHO, 2023). The U.S. Department of Justice's Office for Victims of Crime indicates that one in two transgender individuals are victim-survivors of sexual assault (2023). The U.S. Centers for Disease Control and Prevention highlights that marginalized communities, including people of color and people with disabilities, are disproportionately impacted by incidents of sexual violence (2023). These sobering statistics ground the need for care and compassion when addressing these challenging topics related to student safety and well-being.

Given the overall statistics of the pervasive nature of sexual violence paired with anecdotal accounts of education abroad practitioners and emerging research such as the Student Risk Report from The Forum on Education Abroad, sexual violence on education abroad programs occurs frequently and in a myriad of ways (e.g., sexual harassment, intimate partner violence, acquaintance rape) (Dietrich, 2023). According to one study, one in five U.S. students who study abroad experience sexual violence on their programs (Pedersen, 2021). This aligns with national statistics from the Rape, Abuse & Incest National Network (RAINN) on the incidents of campus-based sexual violence (n.d. a). The lives of victim-survivors of sexual violence change in profound ways; studies suggest many students find their education disrupted as a result (Jordan, 2014; Know Your IX, 2023; Lorenzo, 2020). The political landscape in the United States and beyond (especially recent changes in the legislature for reproductive healthcare and ongoing challenges to LGBTQIA+ rights) may create barriers to accessing care for victim-survivors of sexual violence.

Ideally, proactive strategies for institutions and education abroad providers would involve (a) normalizing discussion around sexual health and sexual violence prevention during education abroad pre-departure with an inclusive lens; (b) moving beyond recommendations for how to avoid becoming a victim-survivor, telling rapists not to rape, and encouraging students to intervene as active bystanders; (c) providing greater advocacy and support for sexual violence victim-survivors upon return from programs abroad; (d) implementing comprehensive guidelines for reporting and tracking incidents of sexual violence on education abroad programs; (e) identifying intercultural expertise in incident management; (f) guaranteeing access to medical and psychological support; and (g) offering academic flexibility to ensure semester or program completion after an incident of sexual violence.

In this chapter, we will discuss foundational and practical shifts needed to achieve these goals.

## Impact of Clery and Title IX

At their core, Title IX and the Clery Act share the guiding principle of student care by providing protocols to ensure consistency and equity of institutional responses to sex-based discrimination and violence in all U.S.-based education programs. A challenge for practitioners is determining where responsibilities begin and end between U.S.-based institutions and institutions abroad. Differences in expectations around responsibility may arise based on the type (e.g., university versus provider) and location of the institution.

In 2020, the U.S. Department of Education stated Title IX "only applies to persons located in the United States, even when that person is participating in a recipient's education program or activity outside the United States" (Inside Higher Ed, 2020). Despite this, many U.S.-based institutions still commit to "fostering an environment free from gender discrimination (including discrimination based on gender identity and expression), sexual harassment, sexual misconduct, and sexual violence [that] extends to all students studying abroad" (University of Massachusetts Amherst, 2023). The tension and interplay between what is necessary versus what is right provides many points for reflection.

Similarly, Clery "applies to education abroad programs [only] if the domestic campus controls or operates facilities—such as classrooms or sleeping accommodations— where a Clery reportable crime happens" (Wilke, 2014, p. 3). Implementation of the Clery Act poses further questions about reporting and sharing statistics about sexual violence on programs abroad. The intersection of varying data privacy laws (e.g., FERPA, GDPR) also plays a role in what information may or may not be reported publicly. These clashes in privacy laws may prevent institutions abroad from sharing information about study abroad student experiences without their permission. Data collection and reporting on incidents of rape and sexual violence abroad is low; however, these numbers can be useful when advising students where to study, developing pre-departure and onsite orientation materials, and for incident protocol and process refinement.

Students today are well informed about sexual violence prevention due to mandatory Title IX trainings on their campuses; however, it is unclear how engaged students are with the content. Training fatigue could be a factor allowing students to downplay and minimize potential issues around sexual violence that could come up while studying abroad. For many students, a mindset shift happens when going abroad; they view it as a liminal experience that feels separate from reality, where no bad things can happen (S. Ferst, personal communication, 2023). But the reality is—sexual violence can and does happen anywhere and at any time (Southern Connecticut State University, 2024).

## Current Informed Practice

The 2017 and 2020 The Forum on Education Abroad *Guidelines for Responding to Gender and Sexual Based Misconduct* offer a useful framework for setting up policies and procedures around Title IX, including guiding questions to identify key institutional experts and stakeholders, showcasing where lines of responsibility can be drawn between key stakeholders. However, they also demonstrate how compliance with U.S. law drives the conversation and response. To gain insights for this chapter into current practice around sexual health and safety abroad, interviews were conducted with a number of senior international educators including senior international officers, education abroad directors, and risk managers across diverse institutional types (e.g., U.S.-based and non-US-based comprehensive public and private universities as well as global education providers). Education abroad practitioners need to move beyond current practice to develop engaging prevention and response strategies for more compassionate and care-centered support, in addition to addressing compliance. There is also the need to equip and support staff in navigating sensitive topics with students, honoring emotions that may arise due to personal experiences with rape culture and sexual violence.

### Reporting Protocol and Incident Management

Best practices for initiating reports on instances of sexual harassment and violence vary by institution, program, and availability of professional expertise in sexual health to guide practice. Some of the methods utilized for reporting include online databases, 24-hour emergency phone lines, or in-person reporting to program staff—only some of whom are trained to handle crises of sexual violence. Each of these options has pros and cons. Using a database allows for crime tracking and documentation reporting, which may prevent revictimization. Asking victim-survivors to report on the phone or in-person may provide a supportive and compassionate response in the handling of the incident, but may also require more courage from the victim-survivor to consider reporting at all. A combination of these or offering multiple reporting mechanisms is likely the best option. Often staff feel they must follow protocol (as it is a requirement) even if these protocols can feel at odds with their own personal reactions and desired care for students.

The systems offered by a Title IX investigation and adjudication are not the same as criminal proceedings. Whether or not a victim-survivor chooses to pursue legal action, and the ease and opportunity to do so, varies widely across cultures and laws of the host country. Each situation is unique. It is important to remember the victim-survivor has individual needs and preferences, and may choose not to report, or not to report right away. The effects of incidents of sexual violence on victim-survivors are very personal, varied, and often longer-term (C. Nicolussi, personal communication, 2023). Research highlights how victim-survivors of sexual violence struggle with and/or withdraw from their communities and responsibilities after attacks (Haskell, 2019). Asking a victim-survivor to reiterate their story over again can be traumatizing and should be avoided. Policies and procedures supporting victim-survivors of sexual violence abroad need to include greater levels of support, such as translation services, as well as future-focused care, such as counseling services and leniencies for academic or program completion requirements.

### Defining and Dividing Responsibilities

Definitions around where responsibilities begin and end between U.S.-based institutions and institutions abroad regarding cases of sexual violence can differ drastically. Some consider incidents at any point while abroad (e.g., whether out at a bar, at a residence hall, on-campus) as the responsibility of the host institution. Others only consider incidents occurring on-campus as the responsibility of the host institution. Providers who have in-country staff abroad also discussed confusion about updates to Title IX and how onsite teams struggle to be current when laws change (L. Burgell, personal communication, 2023). This makes communication about expectations regarding support, processes, and consequences for perpetrators (especially when the perpetrators are also study abroad program participants) important to define and identify when establishing new partnerships or programs and developing review processes with existing partners.

Home universities bear the most responsibility for supporting students if an incident of sexual violence occurs; however, what is less clear is who on a campus continues support of the student after returning home. Many education abroad offices offer some form of re-entry programming, but since incidents of sexual violence are on a need-to-know basis, how do we equip our staff at home to support returning students and alumni who may have experienced some degree of sex- or gender-based discrimination or violence?

Often, returning students and alumni are encouraged to share their stories; what are the protocols when those stories have the complexity or heaviness of difficult moments abroad?

Resource availability is a huge factor. Not all offices have positions dedicated to the development of a wide variety of protocols or to manage them consistently. In the 2022 State of the Field Survey published by The Forum on Education Abroad, only 20 percent of respondents reported adequate staffing levels post-COVID (2023). In the best-case scenario, all education abroad offices would have a position dedicated to health and safety (including risk and crisis management) for education abroad (Pulse, 2022, p. 3). The Forum on Education Abroad sets the standards for global education health and safety topics in the United States; one solution is to offer health and safety materials for free to international education professionals seeking to improve their own processes and protocols.

## Cultural Context is Key

International education resources regarding sexual violence prevention are typically designed via the lens of U.S. education abroad practitioners. Title IX and the Clery Act are U.S.-based regulations. The application of these laws while abroad is murky for many professionals. Monocultural approaches to risk management in international education do not give enough context to comprehensively develop solutions and strategies.

As usual, we have begun the debate by focusing on the U.S. side of the issue.

> We talk about legality and risk management from an American point of view. We discuss what must be done to prepare our students, ensure that our overseas sites are adequate, and create crisis management teams on our campuses. The debate must be broadened to fully include our partners outside the United States (Stubbs, n.d.).

Interviews conducted for this chapter with European university staff who host American students highlighted that awareness of Title IX and the Clery Act is extremely low. Of those non-US-based practitioners interviewed for this chapter, most had not heard of Title IX or the Clery Act prior to being interviewed. However, in response to the #MeToo movement, awareness is increasing in the region about the prevalence of sexual violence on study abroad programs, the need for formalized processes, and increased participant support in these situations.

To place these conversations in context, in 2018, approximately 9 million women in the European Union (EU) aged 15 and above were raped; however, only 8 out of 31 countries recognized rape as sex without consent (Amnesty International, 2018). Amnesty International (2020) states further:

> In a great number of European countries, for a crime to be considered rape, the law still requires coercion, the use of force or threats of force to have been used – or the inability to defend oneself. But most rapes do not fit stereotypes such as a 'stranger jumping out of the bushes.'

Presently, 16 out of 31 EU countries "have laws that define rape as sex without consent" (Amnesty International, 2020). This highlights an increased awareness of and support for rape victim-survivors in this part of the world; however, this example also highlights how cultural mindsets and processes vary on the subject worldwide.

Cultural perspectives on dating violence, sexual assault, stalking, and rape impact management (e.g., the understanding of drinking culture, dating cues, club environments, prevention strategies, trans student support) differ not only by country, but also within societies. Differing expectations around these and other related topics can cause frustration between practitioners during incident response as well as lead to more drastic academic or mental health consequences for the victim-survivor. When programs include highly immersive components, such as host families, the boundaries of situations that can and cannot be controlled blur even more (Weidemann, 2009). It is important for education abroad staff to take the cultural context and components of programs into account when building processes and protocols for sexual violence prevention and student support.

## Reframing the Narrative into Building a Community of Care

Creating an active network of support and engagement for program participants and education abroad staff alike is vital to building a comprehensive and compassionate approach to critical health and safety discussions. Sexual violence prevention cannot be a "one and done" topic reserved for orientation. Where possible, onsite staff need training on how to encourage open and ongoing dialogue for prevention as well as how to support students who have encountered incidents of sexual violence. Staff also need instruction on the development and care of pre- and post-program materials, moving beyond the necessary check boxes of compliance to a greater emphasis on empathy, compassion, and care for diverse communities of students. It is best to be proactive versus reactionary, with clear protocols in place before an incident occurs. Making decisions on the fly has the potential to further victimize the victim-survivor.

### Active Bystander Training as a Tool for Prevention

Across many cultures and institutions, sexual health and sexual violence prevention is not a key component of education abroad practitioner training or preparation for student experiences abroad, but should be (Crace, 2018). There is a need to deepen student and staff knowledge to improve information sharing on the topic of sexual violence prevention, including using dating apps abroad, varying cultural definitions of harassment and rape, steps to take after an incident occurs, relevant local laws or practices, and contextualizing beyond heteronormative, white, cisgender victim-survivors. Many institutions currently address these dangers broadly, if at all, when discussing health and safety, mainly by suggesting tips on how to be smart travelers (and largely, telling women what not to do) during pre-departure planning. How can the approach shift? What campus and community resources provide additional expertise?

With the advent of the Campus SaVE Act, including the renewal of the Violence Against Women Act in 2013, institutions invested in bystander intervention (also called active bystander) training across their campuses, such as Green Dot, Step UP! and Bringing in the Bystander. Tools from bystander intervention training could be utilized for prevention of sexual violence in education abroad, including role-playing exercises during pre-departure and onsite orientations or sharing resources with students and staff such as the "Ask for Angela" campaign from the United Kingdom or the "Who Are You?" video from New Zealand (L. Burgell, personal communication, 2023). Active bystander training provides individuals with the skills to *safely* intervene in potentially harmful situations to prevent them from worsening and to check-in on victim-survivors thereafter. Some key strategies of bystander intervention training for sexual violence prevention include (a) creating a distraction to diffuse or change the situation; (b) directly asking the individual at risk if they need help or support; (c) documenting what is happening; and (d) intervening or bringing others into the conversation if it is safe to do so (RAINN, n.d.b; Right to Be, 2024). Bystander intervention training offers opportunities for students to be vulnerable and develop empathy while engaging in meaningful dialogue with each other and program staff, building a compassionate community of care before, during, and after study abroad (VAWA, 2013).

## Impact of Political Change and Social Movements

This chapter would not be complete without addressing the effects of U.S. politics and other political and social changes across the globe on students and education abroad practitioners. Predatory behavior of an alarming number of public figures and an outpouring of reports of sexual violence in the last 5–10 years with #MeToo has helped shed light on the prevalence of these incidents and provide some victim-survivors with the courage to report their own experiences. The normalization of rape culture in addition to violence against LGBTQIA+, BIPOC, and religious communities shape students' experiences and have a direct impact on the work of international educators to support students during vulnerable moments.

Inclusion is key to connecting with education abroad students for sexual violence prevention. Historically, conversations around sexual violence assumed a (likely white) cisgender male perpetrator and a (likely white) cisgender female victim-survivor. There are unfortunately many iterations of sexual violence and rape, specifically where members of marginalized communities are victim-survivors of these incidents. Sexual violence prevention and sexual health discussions often do not consider how intersecting identities may make students more susceptible to sexual violence. There are disproportionate incidents of harm of BIPOC students whose experiences of sexual violence are deeply linked to systemic racism, misogynoir, fetishization, and discrimination (Kaur, 2021; Yongo, 2024). Additionally, the LGBTQIA+ community, especially transgender and nonbinary people, is also disproportionately at risk (NSVRC, 2024).

Many education abroad policies and procedures were designed to support what have historically been the most prevalent groups of study abroad students: cisgender white women. There is a clear need to build a more inclusive framework to support the various ways students identify and how those identities intersect as the field works toward the goal of diversifying education abroad enrollments.

In addition, the 2022 overturning of *Roe v. Wade* meant immediate changes impacting healthcare across the United States due to so-called trigger laws outlawing or restricting abortion. This is a quickly evolving landscape and may prove to have an impact on victim-survivors of sexual violence abroad, specifically when returning to the United States with unwanted pregnancies or in need of health care related to reproductive health or gender-affirming care. It is important to develop a basic understanding of how home university state laws may impact students with these needs and seek support and guidance from subject area experts on campus and in local communities.

### Strategic Approaches to Sexual Violence Prevention in Education Abroad

To create a balanced infrastructure of sexual violence prevention and compassionate support for education abroad students, practitioners and leaders need to first reflect on what gaps exist in their own institutional policies and practices and identify ongoing learning objectives for their teams. Institutions need to establish a strong framework for professional development and training on intersectionality, inclusion, and best practices for sexual health and sexual violence prevention while also brainstorming ways to reframe strategies around incident response and victim-survivor support. In addition to following established guidelines for responding to sexual misconduct provided by The Forum and bound by institutional policy, there needs to be consideration regarding how sexual violence is informed by (but not superseded by) the political and legal realities of the host culture. It is essential to gain a fundamental awareness of the diverse cultural settings in which sexual violence response occurs outside of the United States. Education abroad practitioners should also seek local guidance to acquire further expertise or collaborate with partners that possess in-depth knowledge of the host culture. Education abroad institutions should focus on impactful opportunities for sexual violence prevention by advancing discussion and reflection both before and during experiences abroad.

Strategic approaches to sexual violence prevention and response centered on inclusion will help to ensure that all students feel well-supported. Pre-departure advising and onsite support need to be guided by the numerous ways in which students may identify and how that might impact their experiences abroad. Intersections of identities may indicate a greater risk of potential harm due to the disproportionate levels of sexual violence impacting marginalized communities. Pre-departure orientations should address sexual health and sexual violence prevention but must transcend the conventional dos and don'ts that imply avoiding certain behaviors may prevent becoming a victim of sexual violence. It is important to acknowledge that sexual violence is violence, and is not the fault of the victim-survivor. This reframing moves beyond victim-blaming and toward accountability for potential perpetrators, who should be told not to rape. Engage with subject matter experts on campus, in the local community, and from resources like RAINN or the National Sexual Violence Resource Center to identify best practices for shifting language around sexual violence prevention and support for victim-survivors (RAINN, n.d.c).

Utilizing tools like bystander intervention training is one strategy to encourage education abroad students to develop a community of care for each other while abroad. Hold space for emotions that may arise. Recognize that staff supporting student victim-survivors of sexual violence may be activated or triggered by these events due to their own experiences with rape culture or sexual violence. Compassion, including self-compassion, must extend not only to students but also to colleagues and staff; it is a powerful tool in developing empathy and providing a supportive environment for coping with sexual violence. It is critical that medical and psychological resources are available to all program staff and students.

Research about the prevalence of sexual violence in programs abroad is emerging through new sources, including The Forum *Student Risk Report* (Dietrich, 2024). Additional research is necessary to increase awareness and transparency about the experiences of victim-survivors, potentially serving as a key tool for reframing sexual violence prevention and response for education abroad victim-survivors. Processes and protocols need to be rebuilt in the context of cultural, social, and political realities, considering intersecting identities of students, to ensure all voices are heard and supported. Education abroad practitioners must show empathy for one another in the compassionate care for students and relentlessly advocate for students by exploring and implementing best practices to support their health and well-being. The strategic direction and future of sexual violence prevention and response in education abroad must be inclusive, intersectional, and proactive.

## References

Amnesty International. (2019, Jan 4). *Sex without consent is rape. So why do only eight European countries recognize this?* https://www.amnesty.org/en/latest/news/2018/04/eu-sex-without-consent-is-rape/

Amnesty International. (2020, December 17). *Let's talk about "yes": Consent laws in Europe.* https://www.amnesty.org/en/latest/campaigns/2020/12/consent-based-rape-laws-in-europe/

Anderson, G. (2020, May 11). *Location-based protection.* Inside Higher Ed. https://www.insidehighered.com/news/2020/05/12/new-title-ix-regulation-sets-location-based-boundaries-sexual-harassment-enforcement

Bruess, C., & Schroeder, E. (2018, October 16). *40 years of sexuality education: What's changed?* https://www.etr.org/blog/40-years-of-sexuality-education-whats-changed/

Burgell, L. (2023, July 10). Personal communication [personal interview].

Centers for Disease Control and Prevention. (2022, February 5). *Sexual violence.* https://www.cdc.gov/violenceprevention/sexualviolence/index.html

Clery Center. (2023). *The Jeanne Clery Act.* https://www.clerycenter.org/the-clery-act

Codrea-Rado, A. (2017, October 16). *#MeToo floods social media with stories of harassment and assault.* New York Times. https://www.nytimes.com/2017/10/16/technology/metoo-twitter-facebook.html

Crace, A. (2018). Work to be done for international students' sexual health. *The PIE News.* https://thepienews.com/news/work-to-be-done-for-international-students-sexual-health/

Dietrich, A., Lombardi, M., & Torres, M. (2024) *Student risk report: Data from education abroad programs, January 1–December 31, 2023.* The Forum on Education Abroad. https://www.forumea.org/uploads/1/4/4/6/144699749/forumea-student_risk_report_2023.pdf

Dills. J., Fowler, D., & Payne G. (2016). *Sexual violence on campus: Strategies for prevention.* National Center for Injury Prevention and Control, Centers for Disease Control and Prevention.

Ferst, S. (2023, June 27). Personal communication [personal interview].

Haskell, L., & Randall, M. (2019). *The impact of trauma on adult sexual assault victims.* Department of Justice Canada. https://www.justice.gc.ca/eng/rp-pr/jr/trauma/trauma_eng.pdf

Jordan, C. E., Combs, J. L., & Smith, G. T. (2014). *An exploration of sexual victimization and academic performance among college women.* Office for Policy Studies on Violence Against Women Publications. 38. http://dx.doi.org/10.1177/1524838014520637

Kaur, H. (2021, March 17). *Fetishized, sexualized and marginalized, Asian women are uniquely vulnerable to violence.* CNN. https://edition.cnn.com/2021/03/17/us/asian-women-misogyny-spa-shootings-trnd/index.html

Know Your IX. (2023). *Clery Act.* https://knowyourix.org/college-resources/clery-act/

Lorenzo, L., & Anderson, S. K. (2020). Exploring the academic experience of college student survivors of sexual violence. *Open Access Library Journal, 7(5),* 1–22. doi: https://doi.org/10.4236/oalib.1106288

National Alliance to End Sexual Violence. (n.d.). *Where we stand: Racism and rape.* https://endsexualviolence.org/where_we_stand/racism-and-rape/

National Sexual Violence Resource Center. (2012). *Sexual violence and individuals who identify as LGBTQ research brief.* https://www.nsvrc.org/publications/nsvrc-publications-information-packets-research-briefs/LGBTQ

National Sexual Violence Resource Center. (2023). *Sexual violence.* https://www.nsvrc.org/

Nicolussi, C. (2023, July 12). Personal communication [personal interview].

Pedersen, E. R., D'Amico, E. J., LaBrie, J. W., Klein, D. J., Farris, C., & Griffin, B. A. (2020). *Alcohol and sexual risk among American college students studying abroad.* Prevention Science. https://doi.org/10.1007/s11121-020-01149-9

Pulse International. (2022). *International safety and security positions in higher ed* [White paper]. https://www.pulseinternational.org/_files/ugd/d2e3a2_6fb8c0b24cec43e-dae8659763891a303.pdf

RAINN (Rape, Abuse & Incest National Network). (n.d.*a*). *About sexual assault.* https://www.rainn.org/about-sexual-assault

RAINN (Rape, Abuse & Incest National Network). (n.d.*b*). *Practicing active bystander intervention.* https://www.rainn.org/articles/practicing-active-bystander-intervention

RAINN (Rape, Abuse & Incest National Network). (n.d. *c*). *Tips for talking with survivors of sexual assault.* https://www.rainn.org/articles/tips-talking-survivors-sexual-assault

Right to Be. (2022). *5 Ds of bystander intervention.*https://righttobe.org/guides/bystander-intervention-training/

Stubbs, N. (n.d.). Safety and security issues and their impact on the study abroad field. *Study Abroad: A 21st Century Perspective - Volume 1.* American Institute for Foreign Study Foundation. https://www.aifsfoundation.org/stubbs.htm

The Forum on Education Abroad. (2020). *Guidelines for best practices in responding to sexual and gender-based misconduct.* doi.org/10.36366/G.978-1-952376-10-8

The Forum on Education Abroad. (2023). *State of the field report: Data from the comprehensive 2022 survey.* doi.org/10.363666.R.2022SOF

The White House. (2023, May 25). *Release of the national plan to end gender-based violence: Strategies for action.* https://www.whitehouse.gov/gpc/briefing-room/2023/05/25/release-of-the-national-plan-to-end-gender-based-violence-strategies-for-action/

United Nations Women. (2024). *16 ways you can stand against rape culture.* https://www.unwomen.org/en/news/stories/2019/11/compilation-ways-you-can-stand-against-rape-culture

University of Massachusetts Amherst. (n.d.). *Resources for survivors studying abroad.* Equal Opportunity & Access Office. https://www.umass.edu/equalopportunity/study-abroad

U.S. Department of Education. (2022, November 30). *Interagency task force on sexual violence in education 90-day report.* https://www2.ed.gov/about/offices/list/ope/vawa.pdf

United States Department of Education. (2022). *Questions and answers on the Title IX regulations on sexual harassment (July 2021).* https://www2.ed.gov/about/offices/list/ocr/docs/202107-qa-titleix.pdf

United States Department of Justice. (2014). *Responding to transgender victims of sexual assault.* Office for Victims of Crime. https://ovc.ojp.gov/sites/g/files/xyckuh226/files/pubs/forge/sexual_numbers.html

U.S. Department of Justice. (2014). *Intersection of Title IX and the Clery Act.* https://www.justice.gov/usdoj-media/ovw/media/975341/dl?inline

Weidemann, A., & Blüml, F. (2009). Experiences and coping strategies of host families in international youth exchange. *Intercultural Education, 20*(sup1), S87–S102, https://doi.org/10.1080/14675980903370912

Wilke, D. (2014). *Complying with Clery.* NAFSA. https://www.nafsa.org/sites/default/files/ektron/files/underscore/ie_novdec14_supplement.pdf

World Health Organization. (2023). *Violence against women.* https://www.who.int/news-room/fact-sheets/detail/violence-against-women

Yongo, S. (2024). *Black women struggle to be liked by the world. Here's why.* https://www.forbes.com/sites/sughnenyongo/article/on-the-dystopian-burden-of-misogynoir-on-black-women/?sh=176e70dd5a6dst

# International Laws, Case Studies, and Standards Affecting Duty of Care for U.S. Education Abroad Students

# 10

# Global Data Privacy Overview: A Risk-Based Approach for Colleges and Universities

**Xinning Shirley Liu, J.D. and Emma Snyder Bahner, J.D.**

## Global Data Privacy Trends

Globally, the trend is clear: More and more countries are moving toward data privacy laws that, like the European Economic Area's (EEA) General Data Protection Regulation (GDPR) (Regulation 2016/679, 2016), have broad, comprehensive privacy requirements. Many jurisdictions have either recently enacted or are in the process of drafting new data privacy laws and regulations, including, for example, India's 2023 Digital Personal Data Protection Act (DPDPA, effective date yet to be determined), Québec's 2021 Act to modernize legislative provisions as regards the protection of personal information (Bill 64, effective September 2023), Thailand's 2019 Personal Data Protection Act (effective June 2022), and Argentina's 2023 bill currently pending before congress (Bill 64., 2021; Digital Personal Data Protection Act, 2023; Mensaje 83/2023, 2023; Personal Data Protection Act, 2019). While some laws and regulations mirror the GDPR, which many U.S. postsecondary institutions are familiar with, others differ in essential ways.

Additional global data privacy law trends noted by data privacy experts include

- An increase in data localization laws—meaning data must be stored and processed in the location where it originated—and strict cross-border data transfer regulations (Parekh et al., 2022)
- An increase in countries seeking data adequacy status from the European Commission—in other words, a determination from the European Commission that the country's data privacy laws provide an "essentially equivalent" level of data protection to that which exists within the EEA (Cooper & Somaini, 2024)
- An increase in cyberattacks, particularly ransomware—making it more critical that organizations have robust cybersecurity response plans and be aware of breach reporting obligations (Morgan & Osborne, 2023)

Along with the increase in data privacy regulations, many experts believe that there will also be an increase in enforcement, prompted by government regulators, data privacy advocates, law firms, and consumers, who are increasingly aware of and better equipped to enforce, promote, and exercise data privacy rights (PricewaterhouseCoopers).

International data privacy laws apply to common postsecondary institution activities, including international student recruitment, applications, and admissions; online programs; study abroad and other international programs; alumni outreach; and certain research activities. Even institutions without extensive international programs are likely affected by overseas data privacy laws. For example, many institutions with international student bodies and alumni are required to provide detailed privacy notices to prospective students, enrolled students, and alumni to comply with transparency obligations under laws like the GDPR, and many institutions frequently must enter into Standard Contractual Clauses or other data privacy compliance terms with international academic and research partners to comply with laws like the GDPR.

In recognition of the many ways international data privacy laws apply to common postsecondary institution activities and the increasing compliance risks resulting from the trends noted above, many U.S. institutions, particularly institutions with extensive international programs, have begun taking a risk-based, comprehensive approach to data privacy compliance. Such an approach involves, at an institution-wide level, assessing the institution's global data privacy compliance risk exposure; implementing compliance measures, such as publishing privacy notices, obtaining consent to process personal data, completing data privacy impact assessments, localizing personal data processing activities, and developing processes for responding to individuals' requests to exercise their data privacy rights; and designating individuals or teams who will keep abreast of this rapidly evolving area to ensure that all their global activities remain compliant.

### Regional Data Privacy Law Statistics

Across the world, 71% of nations have in place one or more laws related to data privacy and/or data security, and an additional 9% are currently considering draft data privacy/security legislation (United Nations Conference on Trade and Development, n.d.). Only 15% of countries worldwide have not enacted data privacy or security legislation and are not considering such draft legislation. Of the 15% of countries with no data privacy/security legislation or draft legislation, 50% of such countries are in the Asia-Pacific region, 33% are in the African region, and 17% are in the North/South America region.

### Comprehensive vs. Sectoral Data Privacy Laws

While over 130 countries have enacted data privacy/security laws, not all such countries have enacted comprehensive data privacy legislation like the GDPR. Many countries, like the United States, have no federal comprehensive data privacy law and instead have several sectoral data privacy laws that apply to specific industries. For example, your institution is likely subject to multiple U.S. sectoral data privacy laws, such as those related to education (e.g., FERPA), finance (e.g., GLBA), health care (e.g., HIPAA), and research (e.g., the Common Rule) (Family Educational Rights and Privacy Act of 1974; Gramm-Leach-Bliley Act, 1999; Health Insurance Portability and

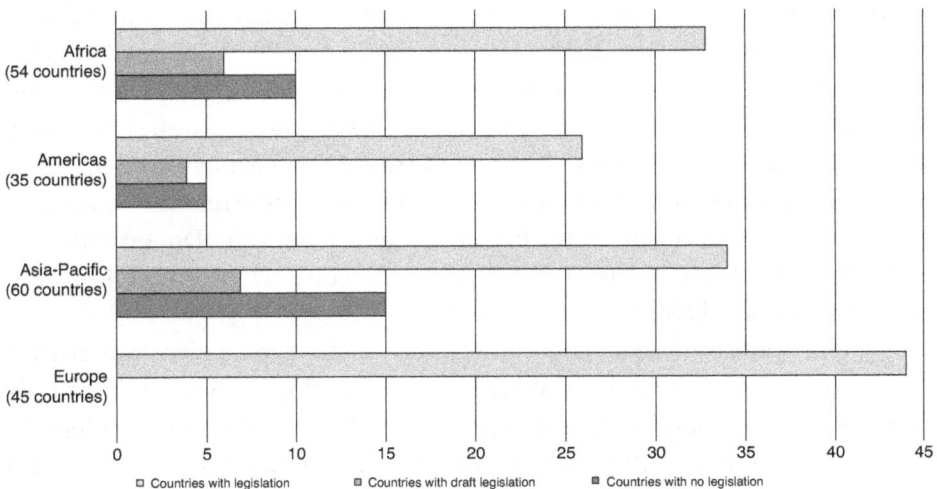

**Figure 10.1.**   Data Privacy/Security Legislation Regional Overview

Accountability Act of 1996; Protection of Human Subjects, 2009). However, even when a country has no federal comprehensive data privacy law, it may have one or more comprehensive data privacy laws enacted at a state, provincial, or another local government level (e.g., 14 U.S. states have comprehensive data privacy laws, 5 of which are potentially applicable to nonprofit postsecondary institutions) (XL Law & Consulting, n.d.). To complicate matters further, a country may have comprehensive data privacy laws at both the federal and local government levels (e.g., Canada's Personal Information Protection and Electronic Documents Act, PIPEDA, and Québec's Bill 64).

Unlike sectoral data privacy laws, comprehensive data privacy laws apply broadly, regardless of industry, to all entities engaged in the processing of "personal data" (which is typically defined very broadly to essentially include any information that relates to an identified or identifiable individual, as explained in further detail below), subject to some limited exceptions that vary from law to law (e.g., Canada's PIPEDA and Australia's Privacy Act apply only to entities that process personal data for commercial purposes). Since 1995, when the EEA adopted its first comprehensive data privacy law, the Data Protection Directive (Directive 95/46/EC, 1995), and even more so after the EEA replaced its Data Protection Directive with the GDPR in 2016, there has been a strong trend globally toward adopting comparable comprehensive data privacy legislation. While the United States is yet to enact such legislation, many other countries where U.S. postsecondary institutions often engage in activities involving personal data processing have enacted comprehensive data privacy legislation like the GDPR, including China, India, South Korea, Taiwan, Vietnam, Japan, Saudi Arabia, Ghana, Kenya, Nigeria, Australia, Brazil, and Canada (Act on the Protection of Personal Information, 2003; Data Protection Act, 2012; Data Protection Act, 2019; Decree 13/2023/ ND-CP, 2023; Digital Personal Data Protection Act, 2023; *Geren Xinxi Baohu Fa (个人信息保护法) [Personal Information Protection Law]*, 2021;*Lei Geral de Proteção de Dados Pessoais [General Personal Data Protection Act]*, 2018; Nigeria Data Protection Regulation, 2019; Personal Information Protection Act, 2011; Personal Information Protection and Electronic Documents Act, 2000; Personal Data Protection Act, 1995; Personal Data Protection Law, 2021; Privacy Act 1988).

When countries or local governments enact comprehensive data privacy legislation, they typically do not repeal their existing sectoral data privacy laws. As a result, many countries have comprehensive data privacy legislation broadly applicable regardless of industry, supplemented by sectoral data privacy laws that additionally apply under certain circumstances. For example, suppose your institution conducts research in the EEA or any country mentioned in the preceding paragraph. In that case, your institution's activities in those countries may be subject to each country's laws governing data privacy in human subject research and each country's comprehensive data privacy law (Office for Human Research Protections, 2022).

## Extraterritorial vs. Domestic Data Privacy Laws

Many countries' data privacy laws apply to U.S. postsecondary institutions only to the extent that they process personal data domestically within a country's borders; this is generally the case with most sectoral data privacy laws. However, with the GDPR's adoption in 2016 and setting the trend for the exterritorial application, more countries are following suit. For example, since 2016, China, India, Vietnam, Saudi Arabia, Kenya, Nigeria, Thailand, and Brazil have each adopted comprehensive data privacy laws with domestic and extraterritorial scopes (Data Protection Act, 2019; Decree 13/2023/ND-CP, 2023; Digital Personal Data Protection Act, 2023; *Geren Xinxi Baohu Fa (个人信息保护法) [Personal Information Protection Law]*, 2021; *Lei Geral de Proteção de Dados Pessoais [General Personal Data Protection Act]*, 2018; Nigeria Data Protection Regulation, 2019; Personal Data Protection Act, 2019; Personal Data Protection Law, 2021).

Under their domestic scopes, comprehensive data privacy laws usually apply broadly to any personal data processing that a postsecondary institution performs within the country's borders. Under their extraterritorial scopes, many comprehensive data privacy laws apply when a postsecondary institution processes personal data in relation to offering goods or services to individuals located within the country (e.g., offering its educational services) or monitoring or analyzing the behaviors of individuals located within the country (e.g., performing behavioral based targeted advertising) (*Geren Xinxi Baohu Fa (个人信息保护法) [Personal Information Protection Law]*, 2021; Digital Personal Data Protection Act, 2023; Regulation 2016/679, 2016). Many other comprehensive data privacy laws apply more broadly any time an institution processes the personal data of individuals located within the country or processes personal data originating from within the country, regardless of the institution's purpose for processing (Act on the Protection of Personal Information, 2003; Data Protection Act, 2012; Data Protection Act, 2019; *Lei Geral de Proteção de Dados Pessoais [General Personal Data Protection Act]*, 2018; Nigeria Data Protection Regulation, 2019; Personal Data Protection Law, 2021).

Should your postsecondary institution operate exclusively within the United States, you should carefully analyze the comprehensive data privacy laws in every country (including laws enacted by states, provinces, or other local governments) from which your institution obtains personal data. You need to determine which of those laws apply to your institution's data processing activities that take place within the United States. Furthermore, if your institution has operations within a foreign country (e.g., study abroad, student exchange, cooperative programs, or other international programs; international entities, campuses or alumni foundations; research activities), then in addition to analyzing each country's comprehensive data privacy laws, you should also evaluate each country's sectoral data privacy laws to determine whether such laws apply to your institution's data processing activities that take place within the foreign country.

Identifying countries from which your institution obtains personal data and countries in which your institution operates typically involves an institution-wide effort as a variety of departments engage in international activities. Such an institution-wide initiative often requires buy-in from senior leadership, which can often be obtained by analyzing enforcement actions (as further discussed in Chapter 11 of this volume, Liu & Bahner, 2024) and explaining the potential impact and likelihood of an enforcement action against your institution. If your institution is subject to many privacy laws in different countries, analyzing enforcement actions and assessing their potential impact and likelihood will also help you to prioritize your compliance efforts and dedicate more resources toward complying with the laws that present the greatest risk.

Some departments that are often key partners in implementing data privacy compliance initiatives include Admissions, International Programs, Advancement, Research, and Marketing as these departments typically engage in high volumes of international activities. These departments should work closely with your legal counsel to identify countries from which your institution obtains personal data and countries in which your institution operates, and then rely on the legal department to determine which data privacy law(s) apply to your institution. As your institution navigates the complex web of intersecting data privacy laws, the legal department should remain a key partner in interpreting the laws and drafting and negotiating legal terms (e.g., contractual terms, consent language) to comply with the laws.

## Similarities Among Comprehensive Data Privacy Laws

U.S. postsecondary institutions engaged in international activities are often subject to many comprehensive data privacy laws. Complying with all applicable data privacy laws is a daunting task, and in the short term, it is often impossible given a lack of resources. As discussed above, you can take a risk-based approach to data privacy compliance by analyzing enforcement actions and assessing their potential impact and likelihood to prioritize your compliance efforts and dedicate more resources toward complying with the laws that present the greatest risk. As part of your risk-based approach, you can also focus on some key commonalities across comprehensive data privacy laws to significantly mitigate your institution's compliance risks under the most comprehensive data privacy laws without fully understanding each law's many intricacies.

In implementing a risk-based approach, it is critical to understand that comprehensive data privacy laws are extremely intricate, not only in the manners in which they are written but also in the manners in which they are interpreted, and as such, there is no one-size-fits-all compliance method. Taking a risk-based approach by implementing measures to comply with key commonalities will reduce but not eliminate compliance risks. Therefore, you must also carefully assess compliance gaps and enforcement risks in cooperation with legal counsel and senior leadership to prioritize your compliance efforts and ensure that any compliance shortfalls are within your institution's risk tolerance or implement compliance measures to address shortfalls that exceed your institution's risk tolerance.

## Material Scopes

The vast majority of comprehensive data privacy laws share essentially the same definition of "personal data" (referred to as "personal information" under some laws) (Data Protection Act, 2012; Data Protection Act, 2019; Decree 13/2023/ND-CP, 2023; Digital Personal Data Protection Act, 2023; *Geren Xinxi Baohu Fa (个人信息保护法) [Personal Information Protection Law]*, 2021; *Lei Geral de Proteção de Dados Pessoais [General Personal Data Protection Act]*, 2018; Nigeria Data Protection Regulation, 2019; Personal Information Protection Act, 2011; Personal Information Protection and Electronic Documents Act, 2000; Personal Data Protection Act, 1995; Personal Data Protection Law, 2021; Privacy Act 1988; Regulation 2016/679, 2016). Under such laws, "personal data" is most often broadly defined to include any information that relates to an identified or identifiable individual, excluding anonymous information. In determining whether the information relates to an "identifiable" individual, the laws would generally require your institution to consider whether the data can possibly be used by the institution or by a third party, alone or in combination with other information that is available to the institution or third parties, to identify an individual.

In determining whether it is possible to use data to identify an individual, and thus whether the data falls within the scope of most comprehensive data privacy laws, some laws, such as the EEA's GDPR (the enforcement of which is detailed in Chapter 11), require your institution to consider only means reasonably likely to be used to identify an individual (i.e., data falls within the scope of the laws only when it is possible to use the data to identify an individual using a method that your institution or a third party is reasonably likely to actually implement) (Regulation 2016/679, 2016, recital 26). Under such laws, anonymized information falls outside the scope of the laws when your institution and third parties cannot identify an individual using any method of re-identification that your institution or a third party is reasonably likely to implement, considering the totality of the circumstances, including, without limitation, cost, time, and available technology. Other laws, such as China's Personal Information Protection Law (PIPL), impose a stricter standard and consider information to be anonymized, and thus outside the scope of the law, only when it is impossible for your institution and third parties to identify an individual using any means whatsoever (*Geren XinxiBaohu Fa (个人信息保护法) [Personal Information Protection Law]*, 2021, arts. 4, 73).

Provided that "personal data" is defined so broadly and that definitions of "anonymous data" vary from law to law, when erring on the side of caution, you may assume that any given comprehensive data privacy law protects any information that can be used, alone or in combination with other existing information, to identify an individual.

## Underlying Principles

Most comprehensive data privacy laws are based on some shared fundamental principles, including lawfulness, transparency, purpose limitation, data minimization and storage limitation, accuracy, and integrity/confidentiality (Data Protection Act, 2012; Data Protection Act, 2019; Decree 13/2023/ND-CP, 2023; *Geren Xinxi Baohu Fa (个人信息保护法) [Personal Information Protection Law]*, 2021; *Lei Geral de Proteção de Dados Pessoais [General Personal Data Protection Act]*, 2018; Nigeria Data Protection Regulation, 2019; Personal Information Protection Act, 2011; Personal Information Protection and Electronic Documents Act, 2000; Personal Data Protection Law, 2021; Privacy Act 1988; Regulation 2016/679, 2016). By implementing policies, procedures, and practices consistent with these fundamental principles, your institution can reduce (but not eliminate) compliance risks from the most comprehensive data privacy laws.

**Lawfulness**. To ensure lawfulness, your institution should document a legitimate business purpose for every activity that involves processing personal data, and you should work with your institution's legal counsel to determine whether applicable data privacy laws allow your institution to process personal data for each purpose and whether such laws require your institution to obtain an individual's consent before processing their data for each purpose. Once all purposes are documented, your institution should periodically review them as processing purposes often evolve as institutions discover new ways to use personal data. The recommended frequency for review varies depending on the size and breadth of an institution's processing activities, but many institutions may benefit from reviewing their processing purposes each year.

**Transparency**. The transparency principle requires your institution to clearly notify individuals of the institution's multiple processing purposes and means. While some laws, such as China's PIPL, expressly require an institution to publish privacy notices (*Geren Xinxi Baohu Fa (*个人信息保护法*) [Personal Information Protection Law]*, 2021, art. 17), other laws, such as the GDPR, require an institution to provide individuals with certain types of information regarding the institution's data processing activities without specifying how the institution must deliver such information (Regulation 2016/679, 2016, arts. 13, 14). Regardless of whether a particular law requires an institution to publish privacy notices, many institutions find that publicly posting privacy notices, such as on your institution's website, is the only practical way to comply with the transparency principle underlying most comprehensive data privacy laws. By publishing privacy notices, your institution may comply with transparency obligations by directing individuals to relevant sections of the privacy notices (e.g., via hyperlinks) before you collect their personal data, thereby avoiding the need to recite lengthy privacy notices each time you collect personal data.

**Purpose Limitation**. Under the purpose limitation principle, your institution should collect personal data only for specified, explicit, and legitimate processing purposes, and it should avoid processing personal data in a manner incompatible with the purposes for which the data was originally collected. If your institution needs to process personal data for a purpose incompatible with the original purpose for which it was collected, your institution should obtain the data subject's fully informed consent.

**Data Minimization and Storage Limitation**. In accordance with the data minimization and storage limitation principles, your institution should collect only the minimum amount of personal data needed, and store personal data in an identifiable form for no longer than necessary to fulfill the processing purpose for which it was originally collected. The data should be anonymized if your institution needs to store personal data beyond the required period to satisfy the original processing purpose. For example, if using study abroad enrollment data to track participation rates and associated statistics, your institution should store only aggregate data that cannot be used to identify individual students rather than storing the original enrollment forms.

**Accuracy**. To ensure accuracy, keep personal data current and promptly correct or erase any inaccurate personal data.

**Integrity and Confidentiality**. The principles of integrity and confidentiality relate to information security and protection against unauthorized access and accidental loss. Ensure your institution implements reasonable and appropriate technical and organizational security measures concerning the risks involved.

## Differences Among Comprehensive Data Privacy Laws

When implementing a risk-based approach to data privacy compliance, recognizing key differences among comprehensive data privacy laws is essential to understanding key commonalities and assessing compliance gaps and enforcement risks. Obligations related to consent and cross-border transfers are two areas where comprehensive data privacy laws tend to differ most.

### Obligation to Obtain Consent

Most comprehensive data privacy laws allow your institution to process an individual's nonsensitive personal data for specific enumerated purposes, also called "legal bases," without obtaining the individual's consent. Still, such legal bases vary from law to law (Act on the Protection of Personal Information, 2003; Data Protection Act, 2012; Data Protection Act, 2019; Decree 13/2023/ND-CP, 2023; Digital Personal Data Protection Act, 2023; *Geren Xinxi Baohu Fa* (个人信息保护法) *[Personal Information Protection Law]*, 2021; *Lei Geral de Proteção de Dados Pessoais [General Personal Data Protection Act]*, 2018; Nigeria Data Protection Regulation, 2019; Personal Information Protection Act, 2011; Personal Information Protection and Electronic Documents Act, 2000; Personal Data Protection Act, 1995; Personal Data Protection Law, 2021; Regulation 2016/679, 2016).

Many laws and regulations, such as the GDPR, allow your institution to process nonsensitive personal data without consent whenever (inter alia) necessary to fulfill your institution's legitimate business interests when such legitimate interests are not outweighed by an individual's personal interests or data privacy rights and freedoms (Data Protection Act, 2012; Data Protection Act, 2019; *Lei Geral de Proteção de Dados Pessoais [General Personal Data Protection Act]*, 2018; Personal Information Protection Act, 2011; Personal Data Protection Law, 2021; Regulation 2016/679, 2016). Other laws, such as the PIPL, do not include a comparable "legitimate interests" legal basis (Act on the Protection of Personal Information, 2003; Decree 13/2023/ND-CP, 2023; Digital Personal Data Protection Act, 2023; *Geren Xinxi Baohu Fa* (个人信息保护法) *[Personal Information Protection Law]*, 2021; Nigeria Data Protection Regulation, 2019; Personal Information Protection and Electronic Documents Act, 2000; Personal Data Protection Act, 1995).

Laws like the PIPL require your institution to obtain an individual's consent far more often than laws like the GDPR. Given these stark differences, coupled with the fact that enforcement actions against education institutions often involve situations where the institution did not have a sufficient legal basis for processing personal data (as discussed further in Chapter 11), consent requirements are a type of obligation that you should work with legal counsel to most carefully assess compliance gaps and enforcement risks when implementing a risk-based approach to data privacy compliance.

### Cross-Border Transfer Obligations

Comprehensive data privacy laws vary significantly in how they allow or prohibit the transfer of personal data outside the country. Some laws, like Canada's PIPEDA, do not contain any provisions addressing cross-border transfers and treat such transfers the same as in-country transfers (Personal Information Protection and Electronic Documents Act, 2000). Other laws, such as India's DPDPA, empower local regulatory authorities to prohibit transfers to certain countries and generally allow transfers to countries that are not prohibited (Digital Personal Data Protection Act, 2023, art. 16).

Many laws, such as the GDPR, take the opposite approach by empowering local regulatory authorities to enable transfers to certain countries and prohibiting transfers to other countries unless certain safeguards (e.g., standard contractual clauses) are in place (Regulation 2016/679, 2016, arts. 44-50). Other laws, like the PIPL, take an even stricter approach by requiring institutions to implement certain safeguards and often obtain individuals' consent before transferring their data anywhere outside the country, while also empowering local regulatory authorities to prohibit transfers to certain countries, organizations, or individuals (*Geren Xinxi Baohu Fa* (个人信息保护法) *[Personal Information Protection Law]*, 2021, arts. 38-40).

Due to this extraordinary degree of variation, your institution should carefully analyze each applicable law's cross-border transfer provisions in each instance where your institution receives or provides personal data outside the country of the applicable law.

## Recommendations

- Work with key stakeholders (e.g., Admissions, International Programs, Advancement, Research, and Marketing) and your institution's legal department to identify countries from which your institution obtains personal data and countries in which your institution operates and determine which data privacy law(s) apply to your institution.
- Analyze enforcement actions and assess their potential impact and likelihood to prioritize your compliance efforts and dedicate more resources toward complying with applicable laws that present the greatest risk.
- Reduce compliance risks under most comprehensive data privacy laws by implementing practices consistent with the common principles of lawfulness, transparency, purpose limitation, data minimization and storage limitation, accuracy, and integrity and confidentiality.
- When implementing a risk-based approach to data privacy compliance, work with your institution's legal department and senior leadership to carefully assess compliance gaps and ensure that any compliance shortfalls are within your institution's risk tolerance or implement compliance measures to address shortfalls that exceed your institution's risk tolerance.
- Designate individuals or teams who will keep abreast of rapidly evolving data privacy laws to ensure that all your global activities remain compliant.

## References

Act on the Protection of Personal Information. (2003). *Act on the Protection of Personal Information (Act No. 57 of 2003)*. https://www.cas.go.jp/jp/seisaku/hourei/data/APPI.pdf

Bill 64. (2021). *An Act to modernize legislative provisions as regards the protection of personal information.* https://www.assnat.qc.ca/en/travaux-parlementaires/projets-loi/projet-loi-64-42-1.html

Cooper, D., & Somaini, L. (2024, January 17). *European Commission retains adequacy decisions for data transfers to eleven countries.* Inside Privacy. https://www.insideprivacy.com/cross-border-transfers/european-commission-retains-adequacy-decisions-for-data-transfers-to-eleven-countries/

Data Protection Act (2012). https://nita.gov.gh/theevooc/2017/12/Data-Protection-Act-2012-Act-843.pdf

Data Protection Act (2019). https://www.odpc.go.ke/dpa-act/

Decree 13/2023/ND-CP. (2023). *Decree 13/2023/ND-CP on Personal Data Protection.* https://thuvienphapluat.vn/van-ban/EN/Cong-nghe-thong-tin/Decree-No-13-2023-ND-CP-dated-April-17-2023-on-protection-of-personal-data/564343/tieng-anh.aspx

Digital Personal Data Protection Act, 2023 (No. 22 of 2023). https://www.meity.gov.in/writere-addata/files/Digital%20Personal%20Data%20Protection%20Act%202023.pdf

Directive 95/46/EC. (1995). *Directive 95/46/EC of the European Parliament and of the Council of 24 October 1995 on the protection of individuals with regard to the processing of personal data and on the free movement of such data.* https://eur-lex.europa.eu/legal-content/EN/TXT/?uri=celex%3A31995L0046

European Commission. (n.d.). *Adequacy decisions.* European Commission. https://commission.europa.eu/law/law-topic/data-protection/international-dimension-data-protection/adequacy-decisions_en

Family Educational Rights and Privacy Act of 1974, 20 U.S.C. § 1232g.

*Geren Xinxi Baohu Fa (个人信息保护法) [Personal Information Protection Law] (promulgated by the Standing Comm. Nat'l People's Cong., August 20, 2021).* http://en.npc.gov.cn.cdurl.cn/2021-12/29/c_694559.htm

Gramm-Leach-Bliley Act, 15 U.S.C. § 6821 (1999).

Health Insurance Portability and Accountability Act of 1996, Pub. L. No. 104-191.

*Lei Geral de Proteção de Dados Pessoais [General Personal Data Protection Act]. (Lei no 13.709, de 14 de Agosto de 2018).* https://www.planalto.gov.br/ccivil_03/_ato2015-2018/2018/lei/L13709compilado.htm

Liu, X. S., & Bahner, E. S. (2024). GDPR and PIPL enforcement in higher education. In J. Pollard & K. S. Priebe (Eds.), *Convergence of litigation, policy, and standards: Building the informed practitioner in education abroad risk management.* The Forum on Education Abroad. doi.org/10.36366/SIA.5.978-1-952376-41-2.11

Mensaje 83/2023. (2023). *Mensaje 83/2023 proyecto de ley de protección de datos personales.* http://www.argentina.gob.ar/sites/default/files/mensaje_proyecto_leypdp2023.pdf

Morgan, S., & Osborne, C. (2023, July 7). *Global ransomware damage costs predicted to exceed $265 billion by 2031.* Cybercrime Magazine. https://cybersecurityventures.com/global-ransomware-damage-costs-predicted-to-reach-250-billion-usd-by-2031/

Nigeria Data Protection Regulation. (2019). *Nigeria Data Protection Regulation 2019.* https://nitda.gov.ng/wp-content/uploads/2020/11/NigeriaDataProtectionRegulation11.pdf

Office for Human Research Protections (OHRP). (2022, February 7). *International compilation of human research standards.* HHS.gov. https://www.hhs.gov/ohrp/international/compilation-human-research-standards/index.html

Parekh, S., Reddin, S., Soller, H., & Strandell-Jansson, M. (2022, June 30). *Localization of data privacy regulations creates competitive opportunities.* McKinsey & Company. https://www.mckinsey.com/capabilities/risk-and-resilience/our-insights/localization-of-data-privacy-regulations-creates-competitive-opportunities

Personal Data Protection Act. (1995). *Presidential Decree Ref. No. ROC-President-(I)-Yi-5960.* https://law.moj.gov.tw/Eng/LawClass/LawHistory.aspx?pcode=I0050021

Personal Data Protection Act. (2019). *Personal Data Protection Act, B.E. 2562.* https://www.mdes.go.th/uploads/tinymce/source/%E0%B8%AA%E0%B8%84%E0%B8%AA/Personal%20Data%20Protection%20Act%202019.pdf

Personal Data Protection Law. (2021). https://sdaia.gov.sa/en/SDAIA/about/Documents/Personal%20Data%20English%20V2-23April2023-%20Reviewed-.pdf

Personal Information Protection Act. (2011). *Act No. 10465, Mar. 29, 2011.* https://elaw.klri.re.kr/eng_mobile/viewer.do?hseq=46731&type=lawname&key=personal+information+Protection+Act

Personal Information Protection and Electronic Documents Act. (2000). https://laws-lois.justice.gc.ca/eng/acts/p-8.6/page-1.html#h-416885

Pricewaterhouse Coopers. (n.d.). *Privacy megatrend: Rise of privacy enforcement.* PwC. https://www.pwc.com/us/en/services/consulting/cybersecurity-risk-regulatory/library/seven-privacy-megatrends/rise-privacy-enforcement.html

Privacy Act (1988) https://www.legislation.gov.au/C2004A03712/latest/text

Protection of Human Subjects, 45 C.F.R. § 46 (2009).

Regulation 2016/679. (2016). *Regulation (EU) 2016/679, of the European Parliament and the Council of 27 April 2016 on the protection of natural persons with regard to the processing of personal data and on the free movement of such data, and repealing directive 95/46/EC (General Data Protection Regulation).* https://eur-lex.europa.eu/legal-content/EN/TXT/PDF/?uri=CELEX:32016R0679

United Nations Conference on Trade and Development. (n.d.). *Data Protection and Privacy Legislation Worldwide.* UNCTAD. Retrieved February 16, 2024, from https://unctad.org/page/data-protection-and-privacy-legislation-worldwide

XL Law & Consulting P.A. (n.d.) *State law map for higher education institutions and non-profits.* Retrieved February 16, 2024, from https://privacy.xllawconsulting.com/#/map

# 11

# GDPR and PIPL Enforcement Trends and Risks for Postsecondary Institutions

**Xinning Shirley Liu, J.D. and Emma Snyder Bahner, J.D.**

## Introduction

Currently, over 150 countries have enacted data privacy laws and regulations (Greenleaf, 2022). The European Economic Area's (EEA) General Data Protection Regulation (GDPR) (Regulation 2016/679, 2016) and the People's Republic of China's (PRC or "China") Personal Information Protection Law (PIPL) (*GerenXinxiBaohu Fa* (个人信息保护法) *[Personal Information Protection Law]*, 2021) are two international data privacy laws and regulations most frequently applicable to activities at U.S. postsecondary institutions.

## GDPR and PIPL Penalties

Maximum penalties under both the GDPR and PIPL are enormous. The GDPR authorizes maximum administrative penalties of up to $22.1 million per violation, or 4% of total annual revenue per violation, whichever is greater (Regulation 2016/679, 2016, art. 83(5)). Similarly, the PIPL authorizes maximum administrative penalties of up to $7.2 million per violation, or 5% of total annual revenue per violation, whichever is greater (*GerenXinxiBaohu Fa* (个人信息保护法) *[Personal Information Protection Law]*, 2021, art. 66).

The GDPR requires administrative fines to be "effective, proportion-ate and dissuasive" (Regulation 2016/679, 2016, art. 83(1)). In determining the penalty amount, the GDPR requires regulatory authorities to consider all applicable aggravating and mitigating factors, including (*inter alia*) the nature, gravity, and duration of a university's violation; any action(s) a university took to mitigate harm to affected individuals; a university's security measures; and whether a university self-reported its violation (Regulation 2016/679, 2016, art. 83(2)).

The PIPL, by contrast, does not require administrative fines to be effec-tive, proportionate, or dissuasive, and regulatory authorities are not required to consider any aggravating or mitigating factors (*GerenXinxiBaohu Fa* (个人信息保护法) *[Personal Information Protection Law]*, 2021, art. 66). However, before imposing a fine, regulatory authorities must issue a corrective order, and regulatory authorities may only impose a fine if a university fails to make adequate corrections within the deadline provided by the corrective order (*GerenXinxiBaohu Fa* (个人信息保护法) *[Personal Information Protection Law]*, 2021, art. 66).

## GDPR Enforcement Trends

As of August 11, 2023, XL Law & Consulting has tracked 56 GDPR enforce-ment actions that resulted in administrative fines against educational insti-tutions, including postsecondary and continuing education, secondary, and pre-secondary institutions (XL Law & Consulting, 2023a). Many tracked GDPR enforcement actions were officially published in a non-English language; the analyses of such actions are based on unofficial English translations. The European Commission does not publicly provide a central repository con-taining all GDPR enforcement actions, so the tracked enforcement actions do not necessarily represent all the GDPR enforcement actions that resulted in fines against educational institutions. Nevertheless, the 56 tracked actions produce valuable takeaways for your institution.

### Average GDPR Fines in the Education Industry

Educational institutions are, to date, a relatively small target of GDPR enforce-ment actions. The 56 actions against educational institutions represent three percent of the total GDPR enforcement actions tracked (XL Law & Consulting, 2023a). Enforcement actions against educational institutions also generally result in lower fines, with average fines of $24.8 thousand and $2.5 million, respectively (XL Law & Consulting, 2023a). This sizable discrepancy may be largely due to the GDPR's requirement for fines to be proportionate relative to the defendant's revenue, as nonprofit educational institutions on average tend to generate less revenue than for-profit businesses in other industries.

Despite the low frequency and relatively small penalties in actions against education institutions, some institutions have incurred substantial fines. The largest was a fine of $300,589 issued to a Norwegian K-12 public school district that self-reported a data breach stemming from an inadequately secured third-party software application (Norwegian Data Protection Authority, 2020). In Italy, a private university incurred the second largest fine, $236,262, where a student filed a complaint regarding the university's requirement to use remote proctoring software to take exams during the COVID-19 pandemic (Italian Data Protection Authority, 2021).

## Educational Institutions Subject to GDPR Enforcement Actions

Postsecondary and continuing education institutions may be at greater risk of enforcement penalties compared to other educational institutions. XL Law & Consulting has tracked 25 enforcement actions against postsecondary and continuing education institutions alone, representing 45% of the total tracked actions against all educational institutions (XL Law & Consulting, 2023a).

## Common GDPR Violations Enforced Against Educational Institutions

Nearly three-quarters of tracked enforcement actions against educational institutions involved violations where the institution processed personal data without a sufficient legal basis or failed to implement adequate information security measures (XL Law & Consulting, 2023a).

In an earlier examination of the tracked enforcement actions, it was observed that insufficient legal basis violations were most commonly incurred by institutions that published students' or employees' personal data for non-journalistic/ expressive purposes without obtaining consent … Such enforcement actions typically ensued after students or employees discovered that their personal data had been published online without their consent and exercised their rights to complain directly to supervisory authorities, or they demanded the institution to unpublish their personal data and did not have their demands fulfilled. While theoretically consent is not required to publish personal data if there is another applicable legal basis, in practice consent is usually required because there are few situations where any other legal basis would allow an educational institution to publish students' or employees' personal data for purposes other than

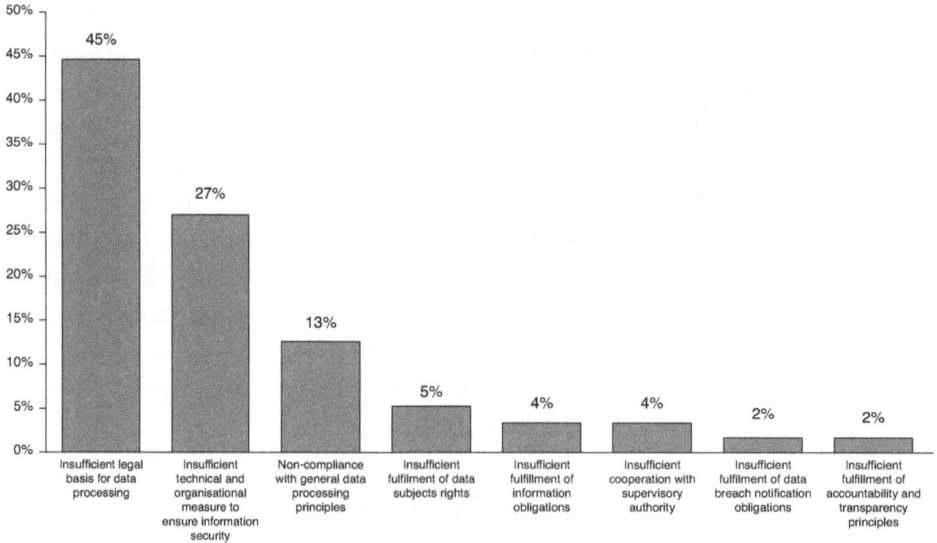

**Figure 11.1.** Types of Violations Enforced Against Educational Institutions

journalism or academic, artistic, or literary expression (Regulation 2016/679, 2016, art. 6) (XL Law & Consulting, 2023a).

Data breaches typically preceded enforcement actions based on failure to implement adequate information security measures; some breaches were reported to authorities by affected individuals or third parties, but many were self-reported by the educational institutions themselves (XL Law & Consulting, 2023a). While reporting data breaches promptly may have avoided additional penalties for failure to report, self-reporting did not shield institutions that self-reported from fines, some of which were so substantial they exceeded fines imposed on other institutions that did not self-report (XL Law & Consulting, 2023a).

The responsible parties and types of systems affected represent a wide range in the data breaches subject to enforcement actions (XL Law & Consulting, 2023a). These include:

- External breaches where third-party bad actors gained unauthorized access to personal data.
- Internal breaches where institutions inadvertently granted employees access to personal data that the employees should have been restricted from accessing (XL Law & Consulting, 2023a).

For example, a Spanish postsecondary institution was fined $3,068 after a newly hired employee reported that they were inadvertently granted access to the email account of their predecessor (Spanish Agency for Data Protection, 2022).

And while some data breach enforcement actions involved only internal systems, others involved applications licensed from third-party vendors. For example, an Italian university was fined \$33,170 after a Microsoft Sharepoint mandatory security update allegedly interfered with the University's whistleblower software application, which ultimately publicly exposed of two whistleblowers' personal data (Italian Data Protection Authority, 2020). Such cases highlight the importance of performing proper vendor due diligence at your institution and understanding how third-party applications interact with your institution's internal systems and other third-party applications.

## EEA Nations Enforcing the GDPR Against Educational Institutions

Of the 30 EEA countries that enforce the GDPR, five are responsible for 84% of the tracked enforcement actions against all types of educational institutions: Italy, Spain, Poland, Greece, and Norway. Focusing on actions against higher education and continuing education institutions only, Italy, Spain, Poland, and Greece are the top four enforcement countries, responsible for 80% of enforcement actions (XL Law & Consulting, 2023a).

## Domestic vs. International GDPR Enforcement Actions

As of August 2023, 100% of tracked GDPR enforcement actions against educational institutions have involved institutions with one or more

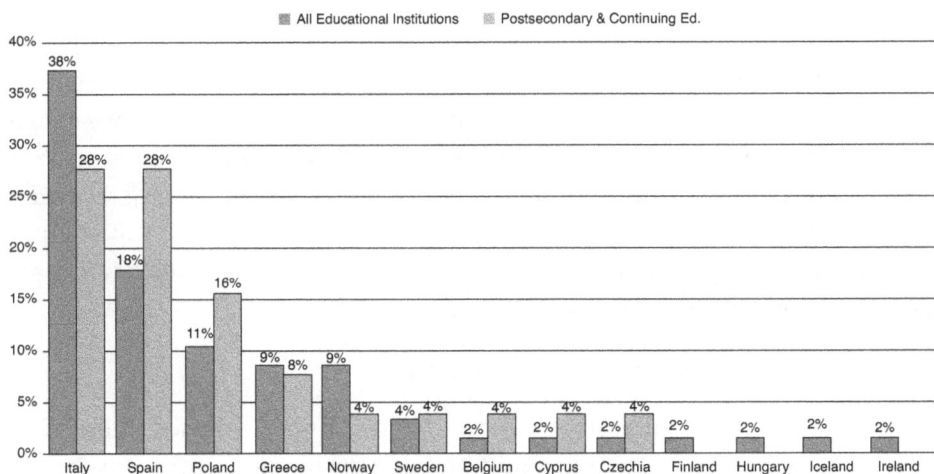

**Figure 11.2.**   Number of GDPR Actions Enforced by Country

physical campuses or offices within the EEA country of enforcement and every enforcement action has resulted from activities that took place within the EEA country of enforcement (XL Law & Consulting, 2023a).

Even though the GDPR also applies to institutions located exclusively outside the EEA insofar as they offer goods or services to people located within the EEA or monitor the behavior of people located in the EEA (Regulation 2016/679, 2016, art. 3(2)), GDPR enforcement actions against educational institutions that have no physical campuses or offices within the EEA are as yet untracked (XL Law & Consulting, 2023a). However, one action was brought against a college located, owned, and operated in Greece, which has a longstanding cooperative education program with a U.S.-based university system (Hellenic Data Protection Authority, 2020). A separate action was also brought against a college in Greece owned and operated by a U.S. nonprofit corporation and accredited by the New England Commission of Higher Education (Hellenic Data Protection Authority, 2021). In light of such actions, you should not assume your institution is beyond the reach of GDPR regulatory authorities, particularly if your institution has any campuses, offices, or other assets within the EEA.

## PIPL Enforcement Trends

As of August 11, 2023, XL Law & Consulting has tracked 1069 PIPL enforcement actions across all industry sectors (XL Law & Consulting, 2023b). Tracked PIPL enforcement actions include all PIPL enforcement actions brought and published by China's central government agencies responsible for PIPL enforcement, the Cyberspace Administration of China (CAC) and Ministry of Industry and Information Technology (MIIT), and by China's provincial government agencies responsible for PIPL enforcement in Shanghai and Beijing (the Shanghai MIIT and Beijing MIIT) up until July 7, 2023 (XL Law & Consulting, 2023b). XL Law & Consulting has not yet tracked any PIPL enforcement actions brought and published by other Chinese provincial government agencies (XL Law & Consulting, 2023b). All PIPL enforcement actions are officially published in Chinese; the following analysis is based on unofficial English translations. While none of the tracked enforcement actions were brought against educational institutions, they nevertheless produce valuable takeaways for your institution.

### Industries of Focus for PIPL Enforcement Actions

Thus far, Chinese regulatory authorities have largely focused their PIPL enforcement activities on organizations that provide app-based goods and services (XL Law & Consulting, 2023b). XL Law & Consulting has not yet tracked any PIPL enforcement actions against traditional educational institutions, but 114 of the tracked enforcement actions (11%) were against organizations that provide app-based services that are related to the education industry (e.g., open online course platform providers and vocational training app providers) (XL Law & Consulting, 2023b).

Although no U.S. postsecondary institutions have been subject to PIPL enforcement actions, countless U.S. institutions were notified in March 2023 that their access to certain publications housed within China National Knowledge Infrastructure (CNKI), China's largest online academic database, was partially suspended (Yang, 2023). The suspended publications include massive databases critical to university research (Yang, 2023). The CNKI told institutions that it must complete a CAC cross-border transfer security assessment before allowing access to parties outside the PRC (Tongfang Knowledge Network Technology Co., Ltd., 2023), in compliance with the PIPL and related measures (Cyberspace Administration of China, 2022).

## PIPL Enforcement Mechanisms

Only one tracked PIPL enforcement action has thus far resulted in administrative fines, while the rest have mostly resulted in corrective orders (XL Law & Consulting, 2023b). Notably, the administrative fine (imposed against DiDi Global, a Chinese company incorporated in the Cayman Islands that provides rideshare services and a variety of other app-based services) was $1.2 billion (XL Law & Consulting, 2023b), making it the second largest data privacy fine to date (Husain, 2023).

Corrective order compliance deadlines have varied on a case-by-case basis, ranging from six to 30 days, with regulatory authorities giving offenders, on average, 13 days to comply with the corrective orders (XL Law & Consulting, 2023b). While 30-day corrective orders are not uncommon, the vast majority (80%) of tracked corrective orders allow less than 20 days to correct violations, and almost half (44%) have allowed one week or less to correct violations (XL Law & Consulting, 2023b). In practice, it often takes U.S. postsecondary institutions many months to implement PIPL compliance measures, so you should not wait until your institution receives a corrective order to begin doing so.

## Domestic vs. International PIPL Enforcement Actions

Like GDPR enforcement trends, XL Law & Consulting has not yet tracked any PIPL enforcement actions against U.S. institutions with no offices, campuses, or other assets located within the PRC(XL Law & Consulting, 2023b). Furthermore, almost all tracked PIPL enforcement actions were brought against organizations incorporated in the PRC, with only two of the 1069 tracked enforcement actions brought against organizations incorporated outside the PRC (both incorporated in the Cayman Islands) (XL Law & Consulting, 2023b). For now, Chinese regulatory authorities appear to be most focused on enforcing the PIPL against organizations incorporated in the PRC. Still, such enforcement actions can potentially disrupt research and academic operations at your U.S. postsecondary institution when such operations are reliant upon receiving data from Chinese organizations, as demonstrated by CNKI's sudden suspension of research database services.

### Chinese Provinces Enforcing the PIPL

The PIPL is most frequently enforced against organizations in China's three most populated areas, Beijing, Shanghai, and Guangdong. Regulatory authorities have brought 853 PIPL enforcement actions against organizations in those three areas, accounting for almost 80% of all tracked PIPL enforcement actions (XL Law & Consulting, 2023b). If your institution has offices, campuses, partners, or vendors in Beijing, Shanghai, and Guangdong, you should pay close attention to PIPL enforcement actions in these areas.

### Common PIPL Violations

Of the tracked PIPL enforcement actions, 38% included violations for the illegal or excessive collection of personal data, and 20% involved handling personal

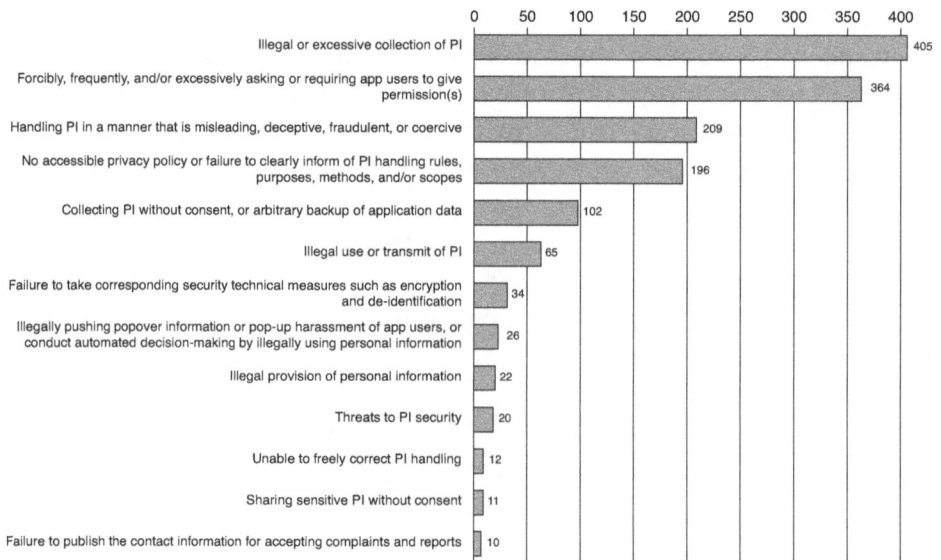

**Figure 11.3.** Common PIPL Violations

data in a misleading, deceptive, fraudulent, or coercive manner (XL Law & Consulting, 2023b). Additionally, 18% included violations related to privacy policies, including failure to have a privacy policy, failure to make a privacy policy easily accessible, and lack of clarity or transparency in a privacy policy, and 10% included violations for collecting personal data without consent or arbitrarily backing up personal data (XL Law & Consulting, 2023b).

## Enforcement Trend Key Takeaways

You can reduce your institution's GDPR and PIPL compliance risks by taking the following actions:

- Document an appropriate legal basis for every processing activity that is subject to the GDPR or PIPL. Pay particular attention to activities that generally require consent as a legal basis.
- Create/refine processes for responding to demands to exercise GDPR or PIPL rights. Fulfill each demand as quickly and completely as possible. When declining to fulfill a demand, as permitted in accordance with applicable exceptions, explain the reason(s) for declining.
- Implement globally recognized information security standards. Regularly review your institution's data privacy and security policies, procedures, and practices.
- Conduct and document thorough vendor due diligence.
- Draft/refine your institution's data breach policies and procedures to ensure that they address GDPR and PIPL requirements.
- Begin GDPR and PIPL compliance initiatives now; do not wait to receive a corrective order.
- Understand that in the short term, it is usually impossible to fully comply with all international data privacy laws applicable to your institution. Take a risk-based approach to prioritize your institution's data privacy compliance efforts.

## Conclusion

Enormous penalties under the GDPR and PIPL have rightfully caused concern among U.S. postsecondary institutions. Such institutions may be comforted by the fact that fines against educational institutions are generally much smaller and less frequent than those against organizations in other industries. Still, they should keep in mind that, in addition to fines, enforcement actions may result in other serious consequences (e.g., corrective orders or suspension of services). While enforcement trends show that institutions with campuses, offices, or other assets within the EEA or PRC are at greater risk of GDPR or PIPL enforcement actions, all institutions subject to the GDPR or PIPL should implement measures to comply with the laws to protect their institutions from legal, financial, and reputational risks.

## References

Cyberspace Administration of China. (2022, July 7). *Outbound data transfer security assessment measures.* http://www.cac.gov.cn/2022-07/07/c_1658811536396503.htm

*GerenXinxiBaohu Fa (个人信息保护法) [Personal Information Protection Law] (promulgated by the Standing Comm. Nat'l People's Cong., August 20, 2021).* http://en.npc.gov.cn.cdurl.cn/2021-12/29/c_694559.htm

Greenleaf, G. (2022). Now 157 countries: Twelve data privacy laws in 2021/22. *Privacy Laws & Business International Report, 176*(1), 3–8. https://papers.ssrn.com/sol3/papers.cfm?abstract_id=4137418

Hellenic Data Protection Authority. (2020b, June30). *HDPA - 18/2020.* GDPRhub. Retrieved December 7, 2023, from https://gdprhub.eu/index.php?title=HDPA_-_18/2020

Hellenic Data Protection Authority. (2020, October 29). *HDPA - 33/2020.* GDPRhub. Retrieved December 7, 2023, from https://gdprhub.eu/index.php?title=HDPA_-_33/2020

Husain, O. (2023, February 27). *The 25 significant data breach fines &violations (2012–2023).* enzuzo. https://www.enzuzo.com/blog/biggest-data-breach-fines

Italian Data Protection Authority. (2020a, January 23). *Garante per la protezionedeidatipersonali - 9269618.* GDPRhub. Retrieved December 7, 2023, from https://gdprhub.eu/index.php?title=Garante_per_la_protezione_dei_dati_personali_-_9269618

Italian Data Protection Authority. (2021, September 16). *Injunction order against "Luigi Bocconi" Commercial University of Milan –16 September 2021 [9703988].* GPDP. https://www.garanteprivacy.it/web/guest/home/docweb/-/docweb-display/docweb/9703988

Norwegian Data Protection Authority. (2020, October 13). *Decision to fine Bergen municipality.* https://www.datatilsynet.no/en/news/2020/decision-to-fine-bergen-municipality/

Regulation 2016/679. (2016). *Regulation (EU) 2016/679, of the European Parliament and the Council of 27 April 2016 on the protection of natural persons with regard to the processing of personal data and on the free movement of such data, and repealing directive 95/46/EC (General Data Protection Regulation).* https://eur-lex.europa.eu/legal-content/EN/TXT/PDF/?uri=CELEX:32016R0679

Spanish Agency for Data Protection. (2022, May 20). *Resolution of termination of the procedure for voluntary payment* (File No. EXP202102806). https://www.aepd.es/es/documento/ps-00581-2021.pdf

Tongfang Knowledge Network Technology Co., Ltd. (Beijing). (2023, March 17). *Notice of suspension of partial services.* https://www.eastview.com/wp-content/uploads/2023/03/Notice-of-Suspension-of-Partial-Services.pdf

XL Law & Consulting P.A. (2023a, January 11). *GDPR enforcement tracker.* Retrieved December 7, 2023, from https://privacy.xllawconsulting.com/#/tracker/gdpr

XL Law & Consulting P.A. (2023b, July 29). *PIPL enforcement tracker.* Retrieved December 7, 2023, from https://privacy.xllawconsulting.com/#/tracker/pipl

Yang, L. (2023, March 30). *China to limit access to largest academic database.* Voice of America. https://www.voanews.com/a/china-to-limit-access-to-largest-academic-database-/7029581.html

# 12

## Specific Issues with International Laws, Case Studies, and Standards: Overview from the Perspective of an Overseas Receiving Institution

**Sunanda Holmes, J.D.**

The U.S. legal framework for managing risk can create incentives to put over-seas receiving institutions ("host institutions") and sending institutions at odds with each other because it encourages *shifting* risk from the sending institutions to the host institution or to the students participating in study abroad programs. But risk may also be managed through strategies to *reduce* the risk to all parties involved in study abroad experiences, including, most importantly, the students themselves. This chapter provides an overview of why keeping this distinction in mind is so important from the perspective of a host institution using as an illustrative example the author's experience at the American University in Cairo (AUC) and other campuses abroad. First, a focus on overall risk reduction encourages sending institutions and host institutions to recognize their common interests, instead of creating potential conflicts of interest, and encourages sending institutions to avoid defaulting to a one-size-fits-all approach in which host institutions are not treated as truly equal partners. Second, it encourages both sending and host institutions to re-examine the rhetoric they use regarding the purpose and benefits of a study abroad experience and the ways in which that rhetoric may unintentionally increase risk as a practical matter unless all parties engage deeply with each other to appropriately prepare and support students during the study abroad experience.

When a sending institution evaluates the legal risks associated with study abroad programs and with partnering with specific host institutions, it is tempting to start and end by considering the duty of care or legal responsibility that each institution has, or does not have, for its students. "Duty of care" implies that individuals and organizations have legal obligations to act toward others and the public in a prudent and cautious manner to avoid reasonably foreseeable injury (or risk) to others. There is a substantial body of case law in the United States addressing the limits of universities' duties of care and providing a blueprint for prudent steps for sending institutions to take to manage risk by having students sign waivers and releases, and through contractual provisions (such as indemnification provisions) shifting responsibility to host institutions (Hoye & Rhodes, 2000). A prime example is the *Thackurdeen vs. Duke Univ.* case (2018), where the court dismissed claims arising from a student's drowning death while on a trip to the beach as part of a study abroad program on the grounds that the student had signed a valid general waiver and release assuming liability for participating in the program's activities. Under this framework, risk reduction measures such as educating students about risk are presented primarily as a necessary predicate to obtain a knowing, voluntary, and enforceable waiver and release— not primarily as a meaningful tool to allow students to make well-informed choices once they are in the host country (Pfahl, 2021).

It may also be tempting for sending institutions to take this blueprint and adopt a one-size-fits-all approach to risk management in which host institutions are asked to both assume liability and the bulk of responsibility for providing practical education and support to help students understand and avoid risk (Bryan, 2022). Sending institutions may see clear advantages to this approach: it can result in internal rules or guidelines that are easier and less costly for the sending institution to implement, and requires less consultation, engagement, and learning with host institutions. Further, to some extent, host institutions are likely better positioned to educate students about cultural norms and practical safety concerns in the local community, for example, by having students from the host institution conduct peer-to-peer orientation sessions. Host institutions may feel that they are not in a position to object to assuming these risks and responsibilities, given that study abroad programs may be more important to their "livelihoods and well-being," resulting in "power differences" between "sending institutions and partners abroad" (Bryan, 2022, p. 49).

These power differences arise in part because of the potential rewards to foreign institutions of hosting U.S. students on their campuses, both as full-time undergraduates and in shorter study abroad programs. In part, host institutions are motivated to host study abroad experiences because educators know that to solve global problems, it is crucial to shape empathetic global citizens, and international education is a cornerstone of their making. These educators and students alike understand the value of global education as a way to enrich the academic and social experience of their national students and achieve learning and problem solving across nations, cultures, and societies. But as a practical matter, host institutions may also see significant financial and reputational benefits from hosting U.S. students—and therefore see greater risks if they lose study abroad partnerships. For example, by hosting students from abroad, universities in the Global South and East may serve an important role in providing enrichment of the intellectual environment in their larger community as well.

A moral case may be made for sending institutions to avoid a one-size-fits-all approach, especially when partnering with host institutions in the Global South and East, where a sending institution's one-size-all approach to risk management may perpetuate "colonial legacies in higher education" (Bryan, 2022, p. 51; see also Rizzotti & Cruz-Feliciano, 2023, pp. 1–2), and may rest at least in part on biases or potentially incorrect assumptions about the availability or reliability of services that help minimize risk to students safety in the Global South (Bryan, 2022). For example, AUC provides for its community (including students from abroad) advisory and support services that will be readily recognizable to U.S. sending institutions, such as offices for international scholars, an Office of Institutional Equity that address complaints of prohibited discrimination and harassment, and an Ethics HelpLine for anonymous reporting of complaints, among others.

Host universities will also have practical objections to a one-size-fits-all approach. Some host institutions may be subject to U.S. law to some extent due to commitments unrelated to study abroad, such as conditions in grants, and some may be subject to U.S. law because, like AUC, they are U.S. nonprofit, tax-exempt entities and therefore base their policies or practices at least in part on those required by U.S. law. These types of host institutions operate within three frameworks: U.S. laws, the law of the jurisdiction in which their campus is located, and their own policies, which are often informed by or based on U.S. laws or benchmarked against U.S. universities. At such host institutions, many of the university's policies and practices that shape the student experience may be modeled after, and adopt, standards articulated in U.S. laws, including the Civil Rights Act of 1964, Title IX, Family Education Rights Privacy Act, the Americans with Disabilities Act (especially with respect to the concept of providing reasonable accommodations), and the Foreign Corrupt Practices Act, among others. But other host institutions may not be subject to U.S. laws at all, except to the extent a sending institution insists on U.S. choice of law and forum provisions in relevant contracts or partnership agreements.

Further, like all institutions abroad, host institutions must primarily be concerned with the legal framework and cultural norms of the country where their campuses are located—and those frameworks and norms may not provide the same blueprint for recognizing duties of care and managing and allocating risk as that provided by U.S. law. Regardless of a host institution's legal obligations, failing to provide a safe experience for international students, whether on or off campus, is not only of concern to the host institution as a moral and ethical matter, but it can cause severe reputational harm both nationally and abroad, and can have a significant negative impact on attracting international students in the future—to the detriment of the university's educational mission.

A one-size-fits-all approach may thus have the effect of imposing on the host institution what is in effect a higher duty of care, and of meeting otherwise-inapplicable U.S. standards for international students. (See the article "Americans abroad: International educational programs and tort liability" by V. Johnson 2006 recommending that sending institutions seek U.S. choice of law clauses, while acknowledging that this may impose greater liabilities on host institutions than would exist under local law.) The sending institution, in its eagerness to shift risk, may even demand more from the host institution with respect to guaranteeing the safety and security of the hosted students than it guarantees for its own students in the United States. Per The Forum on Education Abroad's *Standards of Good Practice for Education Abroad,* when entering into any relationship with a host institution, it is important for sending institutions to consider these concerns and the fairness or equity of the institutional agreements between the parties (2020, clause 4.2). For more on partnerships, see chapter 29, "Expectations, Guardrails and Compliance: Negotiating Effective International Partnership Agreements" by Peter May (2024).

From the host institution's perspective, sending institutions may fail to adequately recognize the power dynamic described above, and may also fail to adequately recognize that regardless of the legal allocation of risk between the sending institution, the host institution, and the students participating in the student abroad program, it is the host institution that will likely experience long-term reputational damage should harm come to any U.S. students. The host institution may forever be listed as a "no go" university by many sending institutions in the future; while U.S. institutions have nearly endless options to send their students to other host institutions around the world, the host institution may forever be marred by a negative traumatic incident involving a U.S. student, which may have had nothing to do with its actions or the lack thereof. This has many costs: the prestige of hosting American students is lost, requiring a re-doubling of efforts to again attract American students. Furthermore, depending on the host country's U.S. Department of State advisory level, the host university might face a withdrawal of funding and a semester or potentially years with no American students. Ultimately, a host institution's ranking and even their accreditation reviews may be affected— university ranking organizations consider the number of international faculty and students on a campus for their calculations, and a major component of accreditation assessments is student life/experience.

Thus, as a practical matter, host institutions are interested in developing agreements, policies, and procedures relating to hosting students from the United States that are designed to truly reduce risk, enabling students to have meaningful substantive experiences while keeping them safe and out of trouble to the greatest extent possible. As the *Standards of Good Practice* reflect, sending institutions have an important role to play in educating and preparing students, and all parties are best served by a collaborative approach to risk reduction (The Forum, 2020, clause 4.2; 6.1). In order for students' academic and personal experience from a study abroad program to be safe and meaningful, both sending institutions and host institutions must be on the same page, with the same goals and objectives and speaking a common language. Keeping the student "front and center" in the minds of both institutions can go a long way to finding common ground without blaming either institution through pre- and post-planning, training/building awareness, and follow-up to fully integrate the expectations of students with the realities of the international setting to ensure a safe academic and social experience for the U.S. students along with their host country counterparts.

It is also important for sending institutions to acknowledge that while the risks that host institutions seek to plan for and prevent are not all unique to study abroad students, they can nonetheless be magnified when international students are involved. For example, consider a student who consumes alcohol at party, underestimates the intoxication level of a fellow student, thinks they have consent, and has sex—only to find themselves facing a complaint, an unfamiliar resolution process, and possible criminal charges.

How is this situation complicated when the legal rules regarding consent and alcohol consumption differ from those in the United States? How is this situation further complicated if there are no laws governing the investigation and resolution of the complaint, unlike in the United States, where students have come to expect certain procedural rights? As another example, imagine that students have come to feel very comfortable on the host campus, venture further into the city, get harassed for their appearance—perhaps because they are expressing their gender identity in a way that is less common in the host community—and look to the host institution for intervention and support with respect to this off-campus incident. Will the host institution assist, even if it has no obligation to do so? Will the sending institution face repercussions if the host institution does nothing, and the students claim the discrimination they experienced negatively affected their ability to learn, leading to repercussions when they return home?

Actively working with host institutions to reduce these risks is important. In our experience, the complicating factors with respect to the above risks when international students are involved are most frequently the following. First, the host country's laws may shape or limit host institution policy in ways the U.S. students do not anticipate. Second, the host university's policies and procedures will also likely assume application/enforcement in the context of cultural norms of the host country. Third, experience suggests that host institution staff may feel pressured to act quickly or be more involved when a U.S. student raises concerns, instead of simply following normal policies and procedures, in part because of the possibility of greater media attention or appearing unwelcoming to international students. Sending institutions must anticipate and prepare for these issues, foster understanding, challenge students to be curious and open to new ways of doing things, establish relationships, and maintain clear channels of communication with host institutions when issues arise.

Equally important, as sending institutions endeavor to implement the recommended best practices regarding the specific issues addressed in the remainder of this chapter, keep in mind that the way study abroad experiences are promoted (by both sending and host institutions) can create expectations that are at odds with each other. On the one hand, they often convey the message that students should seek out new experiences and adventures and focus on nonacademic learning and growth. Renner and Roach (2011) reported findings that the "significant expectations" of students for study abroad programs include "language fluency, building relationship[s] with the host nationals, learning about a new culture, and personal change" (p. 8). Another study found that pre-study abroad, students expect to be "shape[d] and change[d] . . . in a positive way" by their experience (Bell, 2016, p. 200). At the same time, institutional and other messaging about study abroad experiences do not typically convey that students should have new or greater concerns about their safety than they would on their home campuses, even as they may be taking new risks. As just one example, Egypt's Ministry of Higher Education promotes the country as a study abroad destination and has created a website to encourage international students to study in Egypt, boasting a safe and secure environment for students, including women in public places, etc. (Study in Egypt, n.d.).

These goals can work against each other: the more "fun" the students have, the more risks they take, and the more they get to know the national students on the campus and venture for off-campus activities, the more they will learn and encourage future students from their home institutions to study at the host institution—but, at the same time, their safety and security may be more at risk. Students often want to experience everything their host country and region have to offer on a limited budget, so they may try to cut costs and take unnecessary or unmitigated risks to participate in student-led and run activities.

In addition, it is important to keep in mind that at many host institutions, experience will have shown that the risks the host institution faces are often exacerbated by U.S. students' incorrect assumptions and U.S.-centric expectations. American students may wrongly expect that the equivalent of U.S. legal standards apply, that they are safe doing things the same way they do them at home, or in some instances, may even have heard that the host country is "safer" than the United States. (Sometimes, this can be fostered by the host institution because they want to make a good impression on American students.) American students may also come into contact with law enforcement in a context where they would not expect to do so in the United States, such as when another program participant or local student experiences a mental health crisis. In some countries in the MENA region and beyond, a mental health crisis that includes a perceived suicide attempt may be viewed by law enforcement as a crime and may result in the American student being required to participate in an investigation that includes the disclosure of information they might expect to be considered confidential. It is important to have preparation and clear lines of communication so that even in an emergency or traumatic situation, U.S. students have access to resources to understand their rights with respect to law enforcement and the consequences of interacting (or choosing not to interact) with law enforcement. It is also important for U.S. students to understand when the host institution is or is not likely to intervene or participate in their interactions with law enforcement.

Students may also underestimate the challenge of adapting to a new academic system (Bell, 2016) and even wrongly expect that because they are on a study abroad experience, they are not subject to all of the same rules as the host institutions' students and that exceptions will be made because of the understanding that they are there to experience more than just academic life, for example, to travel to many sites, or enjoy the night life, etc. For example, faculty may perceive that study abroad students come to a foreign country with the expectation of receiving an "easy A"—that they come to be tourists, go to the beach, see the sights, and don't focus on their schoolwork. Faculty members may feel the students are not as invested in the academic experience and expect more latitude than professors would give to national students, which may cause resentment on both sides. In response, the host institution's faculty members could create unique academic cultural experiences in their classroom for their foreign and national students that might go a long way in creating memorable, yet challenging academic experiences. The sending institutions can reinforce this expectation, too: study abroad is not just a party. These perceptions really matter within the host institution and affect the ability of the staff and faculty who partner directly with the home institution on study abroad programs to ensure that others at the university who interact with visiting students provide a positive experience in line with your expectations.

Finally, sending institutions should implement the recommendations in the following chapters, and interact with host university staff in the spirit that we all hope our students will approach their study abroad experience: with curiosity, open-mindedness, respect for the professionalism and experience of the host university counterparts, and a willingness to learn from their experience. While it is possible that a host institution will view U.S. law and U.S. university policies as setting standards in certain areas, such as the handling of sexual misconduct complaints, it may also rightfully question or challenge different assumptions and values embedded in those laws and policies. Engaging with host universities in a true partnership—rather than with the expectation that they will blindly meet any requirements and adopt U.S.-inspired policies and practices—may be a surprisingly rewarding part of maintaining a study abroad program.

## References

Bell, R. (2016). Concerns and expectations of students participating in study abroad programmes: Blogging to reveal the dynamic student voice. *Journal of Research in International Education, 15*(3), 197–207. https://doi.org/10.1177/1475240916669028

Bryan, D., Viteri, C., Murphy Hatz, C., Csoman, K. R., Pilaquinga, E. M., & McGrath, E. (July 20, 2022). Reimagining risk management: Decolonizing crisis response through holistic partnership building in education abroad. *Frontiers: The Interdisciplinary Journal of Study Abroad, 34*(3), 44–72. The Forum on Education Abroad. https://doi.org/10.36366/frontiers.v34i3.672

Hoye, W. P., & Rhodes, G. M. (summer 2000). An ounce of prevention is worth...the life of a student: Reducing risk in international programs. *Journal of College and University Law, 27*(1), 151–185.

Johnson, V. R. (2006). Americans abroad: International educational programs and tort liability. *Journal of College and University Law, 32(2),* 309–359.

Pfahl, M. R. (2021). Enhancing enforceability of exculpatory clauses in education abroad programming through examination of three pillars. *Journal of College and University Law, 46*(1), 93–120.

Renner, J., & Roach, E. D. (fall 2011.) A comparative study of international and American study abroad students' expectations and experiences with host countries in selected institutions of higher education. *Journal of Academic Administration in Higher Education, 7*(2), 1–11. https://core.ac.uk/reader/214085130

Rizzotti, A., & Cruz-Feliciano, H. (2023). Introduction. In A. Rizzotti& H. Cruz-Feliciano (Eds.), *Voices from the South: Decolonial perspectives in international education.* The Forum on Education Abroad. doi.org/10.36366/SIA.3.978-1-952376-32-0.1

*Safety & Security.* Study in Egypt. (n.d.). https://study-in-egypt.gov.eg/living-in-egypt/26?name=safety-security

*Thackurdeen v. Duke Univ.,* 1:16CV1108 (M.D.N.C. Mar. 23, 2018).

The Forum on Education Abroad. (2020). *Standards of good practice for education abroad, Sixth edition.* doi.org/10.36366/S.978-1-952376-04-7

# 13

## Sexual Misconduct: A Host University Perspective

Sunanda Holmes, J.D. and Catherine Williams, J.D.

Preventing and responding to sexual misconduct, which includes both sexual harassment and sexual assault, is one of the most challenging responsibilities any university has toward its students. It is also an area where the law has evolved rapidly, including in response to the global #MeToo movement. This chapter discusses the different standards and legal requirements that host universities often grapple with in responding to sexual misconduct claims involving students participating in study abroad programs on their campuses—differences that may even include how sexual harassment, sexual assault, and sexual misconduct are defined. It also discusses some of the special considerations that may shape host universities' policies and practices for preventing and responding to sexual misconduct and suggests best practices to ensure that students' expectations and needs are met when issues of sexual misconduct arise during their study abroad.

### The Legal Context

U.S. institutions sending their students abroad—and students themselves—often expect host institutions to understand and have adopted standards for preventing and responding to sexual misconduct that are informed by U.S. law and, in particular, by Title IX. (For information on Title IX, refer to Chapter 8, "Clery Act and Title IX Extraterritorial Application (And Why the Federal Approach Is the Floor, Not the Ceiling)," by Joe Storch and Andrea

Stagg, 2024.) These expectations are reinforced by standards such as the *Standards of Good Practice for Education Abroad* (The Forum on Education Abroad, 2020b), which requires that host universities "have policies that govern student matters, including … sexual misconduct … [,]" and that include disciplinary process and an appeal process (clause 5.1.6), and the *Guidelines for Best Practices in Responding to Sexual and Gender-Based Misconduct* (The Forum on Education Abroad, 2020a) (the "Guidelines"), which anticipate that host universities will investigate and adjudicate sexual misconduct cases, and have "confidential resources" as defined under Title IX to provide support in such cases (Guideline 4.2).

Host universities may well be able to meet these expectations. Although many countries do not have an equivalent to Title IX that encourages a uniform approach to handling sexual misconduct complaints—or even requires that universities address these matters at all (Rubiano-Matulevich, n.d.)—host universities have an interest in maintaining a safe and welcoming educational environment for their students. They may even be leaders in their countries in raising awareness around sexual harassment and assault and adopting policies and practices to prevent and address sexual misconduct. For example, the American University in Cairo (AUC), which serves as a host institution for many students, has adopted a written policy prohibiting sexual harassment and discrimination, which provides for prompt, thorough, and fair investigation of complaints; it also has support resources in place for students who have concerns about sexual harassment, including an Office of Institutional Equity, and provides training on sexual harassment to students, including to incoming study abroad students.

Title IX itself generally does not apply to institutions abroad, at least with respect to sexual misconduct that occurs outside the United States, such as that occurring on the host university campus. However, sending institutions may have Title IX obligations to their students with respect to conduct occurring abroad. The extent and nature of these obligations have varied with changes in the federal administration, which has added confusion and complexity to how host and sending institutions address training and grievance procedures. For example, the Title IX regulations that took effect in 2020 expressly state that grievance procedures for sex discrimination (including harassment) must be adopted only for discrimination "occurring against a person in the United States" (34 C.F.R. § 106.8(c)). The Biden administration proposed updated regulations that preserve this rule, see 87 Fed. Reg. 41390, at 41571 (proposed July 21, 2022) (proposal to amend 34 C.F.R. § 106.11 to state that Title IX regulations apply to discrimination "occurring in the United States"), but nonetheless impose obligations on the sending institution if the incident(s) occurring abroad may have the continued effect of limiting equal access to education programs and services in the United States—in other words, upon the student's return to the sending university (87 Fed. Reg. 41390, at 41571). Furthermore, the amended regulations explain, if one student from a home institution sexually assaults another while studying abroad, and the latter student is unable to participate fully in their classes upon their return due to the assault, the home institution must take action (87 Fed. Reg. 41390, at 41403). Sending institutions should apprise host institutions of this requirement and request that any incidents of sexual misconduct occurring abroad are reported to them and support services are provided to the student(s) jointly by both institutions, both during and after the incident.

It is also important to keep in mind that host universities' policies and practices are informed, and in some cases limited (at least from the U.S. perspective), by local laws. There may be significant differences between the legal frameworks that govern U.S. and host universities' policies and practices for preventing and addressing sexual misconduct. Accordingly, the starting point for training and supporting students with respect to sexual misconduct and identity-based discrimination is developing and maintaining a meaningful understanding of what local laws technically apply, and how they are applied and enforced in practice (The Forum on Education Abroad, 2020a, Guideline 1.1). Host universities can and should be willing partners to help identify similarities and differences in the relevant legal frameworks.

For example, AUC's policy is informed by Egyptian law, which has both constitutional and statutory prohibitions on discrimination on the basis of sex, among other protected characteristics: Article 53 of Egypt's Constitution states that all citizens "are equal before the law … and may not be discriminated against on the basis of religion, belief, sex, origin, race, color, language, disability, social class, political or geographic affiliation, or for any other reason," and Articles 35, 88, and 92 of Labor Law No. 12 of 2003 prohibit sex and gender discrimination. As at the federal level in the United States, Egypt does not, however, have an express prohibition on discrimination on the basis of sexual orientation or gender identity and expression. While AUC has chosen to adopt a policy prohibiting discrimination on the basis of gender identity and expression (among other things), and while AUC's policy against sexual harassment expressly provides that same-sex harassment is prohibited and covered by the policy, there is no legal requirement that AUC adopt this policy and no substantial legal precedent informing AUC's interpretation or application of this policy.

Furthermore, AUC implements its policies in a context where criminal laws differ materially from those in the United States, and where expectations for enforcement may also be different. In Egypt, for example, sexual harassment (not just sexual assault) is a crime; under section 306(bis)(a) of Egypt's Penal Code, "harass[ing] others in a public or private place by making forward actions, insinuations, or hints that are sexual or pornographic whether by signals, words, or actions and by any means including wired or wireless or electronic or through any other tech communication methods" is punishable by up to 5 years in prison and a significant monetary fine. Furthermore, if the perpetrator has occupational authority—such as a faculty member, teacher, or mentor in an educational setting—or exercises any kind of pressure when committing the crime, the criminal penalties are more severe (Abdelaal, 2021).

As another example, in Egypt, as in 40-plus other countries, same-sex sexual conduct has been criminalized (Human Rights Watch, 2023). Countries may also have morality laws that, for example, prohibit displays of public affection, criminalize certain sex outside of marriage (and do so differently for men and women), and/or regulate the use of drugs and alcohol—which in our experience often play a role in sexual misconduct claims involving students—that are more restrictive than in the United States (Robinson, 2023). These criminal laws will inevitably inform a host university's policies and practices because they affect the remedies that are available to students (or risks students may face) outside the university context, and, crucially, may also have a strong chilling effect on students' willingness to report certain types of misconduct.

## Special Considerations Shaping Host Universities' Policies and Practices

Host institutions are likely to be responsive to sending institutions' questions and concerns about sexual misconduct complaints not only because those concerns are of equal importance to the host institution with respect to its own students but because maintaining a good rapport with U.S. institutions—and recruiting and retaining U.S. students—can be extremely important to the host institution. Regularly hosting students from the United States provides an enriching academic and social environment for the national students adds to the prestige of the host university (Zhao, 2008).

Host institutions are likely cognizant that international students may, with good reason, be particularly concerned about—and therefore require additional support with respect to—reporting sexual misconduct to the police. Students face practical difficulties in reporting crimes abroad, such as language or distance barriers. As a practical matter, enforcement of laws relating to sexual misconduct may be limited in meaningful and unexpected

ways. There are numerous barriers to robust enforcement of Egypt's criminal sexual harassment law, such as the requirement that a reporter of sexual
harassment must bring the perpetrator to the police station/police or at least
keep them in custody, and an unwillingness of police officers to refuse to file
or document such cases (Abdelaal, 2021). Other challenges, which are not
necessarily unique to Egypt, include the reluctance to report sexual harassment due to lack of confidentiality, victims' fear of being blamed for the
harassment or of suffering reputational harm, the embarrassment of information becoming known to family members and colleagues, and the fear of
being subjected to further harassment/misconduct (including by the police)
(El Deeb, 2013; International Labour Organization, n.d.).

At the same time, host institutions may have very different approaches to
responding to sexual misconduct complaints, and it is important for sending
institutions to understand the special considerations that may underlie their
policies and practices.

First, host university policies and practices are designed primarily to
address the needs and concerns of their national students. Because of concerns about underreporting, host institutions may allow more anonymous
reporting or provide more confidentiality than sending institutions subject to Title IX. For the same reasons, and to address national student concerns about reputational harm and retaliation (e.g., concern about parents
learning of pre-marital sexual conduct), host institutions may choose not
to have hearings to resolve sexual misconduct complaints and/or may provide information to the responding party on a more limited basis than might
be required under Title IX regulations. It is important that sending institutions not assume that these differences mean that host universities are
unequipped to resolve sexual harassment complaints in a prompt, thorough,
and fair manner. But just as norms around what constitutes appropriate due
process for resolving such complaints continue to be debated in the United
States, there may be different views on what procedures best strike the balance between encouraging reporting and allowing the host university to take
prompt measures to keep students safe on one hand, and ensuring that any
allegation that sexual misconduct occurred is investigated without bias and
with adequate opportunity for the accused to respond to the allegations.

Second, labor laws and other legal protections may differ from those
in the United States such that the process for investigating complaints and
imposing discipline, terminating an employee, or expelling a student provides different types of protections to the respondent in a sexual misconduct
case than a sending institution and its students may expect. For example,
Egyptian labor laws require, among other things, that the investigator be of

equal or greater seniority to the person being investigated, and investigations may include obtaining signed, written statements from the complainant and witnesses in Arabic. Host universities may also have to contend with the practicalities of operating under different privacy laws or under a greater risk of civil claims, such as defamation claims, which may be threatened or even brought in court against not only the university but also complainants, witnesses, and individual employees who participate in investigating and resolving complaints. These considerations, like those discussed above, may also lead to investigations and complaint resolution proceeding with significantly greater anonymity and/or confidentiality than would be permissible under Title IX.

Third, U.S. students' perspectives or worldviews may not be shared and/or well understood by national and international students, staff, and faculty at host institutions. Like universities in the United States, many universities abroad draw their students and faculty from a wide range of countries and must contend with multiple and differing approaches to social and cultural norms relating to sex and gender identity. In our experience, examples of differences may include:

- Understandings of consent, including whether affirmative consent is required.
- Understandings of when sexual advances are welcome, including the persistence of stereotypes that wearing certain types of clothes and/or wearing make-up, or conduct such as giggling or laughing out loud, invites sexual advances (Mansour, 2021).
- Norms around alcohol use, including an understanding of whether consuming alcohol may in and of itself be perceived as communicating an openness to sexual advances, and also an understanding of how likely students are to have meaningful experience with alcohol consumption (and thus how alcohol consumption is likely to affect their ability to consent).
- Norms around sexual experience prior to or outside of marriage.
- Norms around public displays of affection, including what constitutes a public display of affection. For example, in some cultures, two men may hug or walk arm-in-arm without their conduct being interpreted (in the context of their culture) as a public display of affection, while the same conduct between a man and a woman would be understood as a public display of affection. These differences may lead to misunderstandings about, for example, how accepted same-sex relationships or displays of romantic interest are in the local community.

Fourth, some U.S. students may find that host institutions (or their staff) feel compelled to over-respond to their complaints regarding sexual misconduct, in part due to fear of negative reputational repercussions if the matter is not handled to the student's (or the student's family's) satisfaction. For example, host institutions' staff may be more inclined to report alleged assaults of foreign students to the police to demonstrate that the institution took the matter seriously. Relatedly, in some cases, our experience shows that U.S. students may underestimate the risks they face in certain circumstances because they find that generally, they are treated as "special" and welcomed with great hospitality. For example, a female student from the United States who is invited to a party with other students and who has generally felt safe and welcomed in the host institution's environment may underestimate the degree to which her wearing certain clothing or even simply attending a party at which alcohol is served might be viewed as communicating an openness to sexual advances or conduct.

Fifth, LGBTQIA+ students may face additional challenges with respect to differing norms (and criminal laws), and it is particularly important for the sending and host institution to be aware of and be prepared to address these challenges. Even where same-sex conduct is legally prohibited and LGBTQIA+ students lack legal protections, host universities can create a safe environment for all students within the confines of their campuses, including by prohibiting discrimination on the basis of sexual orientation and gender identity and expression; by explicitly including same-sex conduct in the definition of prohibited sexual harassment; and by providing training to their own staff and students on this issue. However, it is critical for sending institutions to recognize that the host university may not be able to publicly comment or intervene on students' behalf with respect to off-campus incidents, such as police harassment of individuals who are perceived to be non-gender-conforming or same-sex couples who publicly display affection. In contexts where same-sex conduct is criminalized, it can also be useful for gay, lesbian, and bi/pansexual students coming from abroad to understand that they may be viewed as safer to approach than local students—including with conduct, comments, or questions that may or may not be welcome—by gay, lesbian, and bi/pansexual members of the local community.

## Recommendations

The following recommendations draw on the insights and legal frameworks discussed above.

1. Establish, but do not rely exclusively on, detailed contractual commitments: It is easy to require that host institutions have anti-discrimination
   and anti-harassment policies and procedures in place (The Forum on
   Education Abroad, 2020a, Guideline 4.1.1). But a written study abroad
   participation agreement can go further, including by establishing detailed
   procedures for providing notice if and when certain misconduct occurs
   involving the home institution's students, regardless of whether they are
   complainants or respondents, and regardless of whether the conduct
   occurs on or off campus. For example, a sending institution may consider
   requiring that notice be provided to its education abroad and/or Title IX
   office with respect to any sexual misconduct complaint involving their
   student, and may also consider requiring notice to the U.S. Embassy/
   Consular Service in the host country if their student is arrested or is a
   victim of criminal conduct. Both institutions may also require students
   to consent in advance to their parents being contacted if the student is
   arrested or involved in an incident including the unlawful use of alcohol
   or drugs.

2. Develop an informed understanding of policies and practices: The leaders
   of your study abroad programs (both administrators and program leaders) should have access to, and should understand, not only the details of
   the policies and procedures in place at the host institution and the relevant local laws (The Forum on Education Abroad, 2020a, Guidelines 5.1
   and 5.2), but also how local norms inform those policies and procedures,
   how sexual misconduct complaints by (or against) your students will be
   dealt with in practice, and how likely it is that relevant local laws will or
   will not be enforced. These details will likely not be covered by the host
   institution's written policy. Sending institutions and their students will
   want to understand, for example, whether the host university is obliged
   to inform, or has a practice of informing, governmental authorities or
   parents of incidents that occur on campus; whether the local police are
   likely to be helpful in responding to cases involving sexual misconduct;
   whether the local police and local students are likely to respect expectations of privacy (e.g., even if it is not permitted by law, are local police who
   see students in what they perceive as gender-non-conforming dress likely
   to demand to see their personal phones and check for photos indicating a same-sex relationship, and are local students likely to comply); and
   whether the host university has a practice of investigating and responding to incidents that occur off campus. Sending institutions will also want
   to understand what resources are available to students, including what
   office is responsible for handling sexual misconduct complaints and

whether campus clinics or counselors may be available (The Forum on Education Abroad, 2020a, Guideline 5.2.4).

3. Establish clear channels of communication: Identify the specific individuals at your institution and the host institution responsible for communicating to each other regarding sexual misconduct involving your students (The Forum on Education Abroad, 2020a, Guideline 4.2) and establish when notice will be provided of such incidents. Understand precisely what information you are likely to receive—and what information you will not receive—when your student is involved in a sexual misconduct case. While the host institution may have privacy constraints on what they can share, particularly if the complaint also involves students, faculty, or staff who have privacy rights under local laws, they should be able to provide sufficient information for you to take appropriate follow-up steps when student(s) return, including the nature of the incident and any interim measures taken or other support provided to the complainant. Please note that the requirements to share information may also result in underreporting and a study abroad complainant may not receive the support resources they might need for fear of being punished by their home institution, or not being able to engage in other study abroad programs later in their student life.

4. Establish emergency procedures (The Forum on Education Abroad, 2020a, Guideline 5.1.2): Establish an incident response contact tree and decision-making tree in the event of any emergency event. Define what types of incidents qualify as "emergencies" that necessitate activating the emergency response plan. Appoint someone (or a team) from the sending institution who will be available 24 hours/day due to the time difference between the countries.

5. Set student expectations: Provide awareness to students as early as the promotion and recruitment process—and especially through pre-departure activities and orientation—to both set expectations relating to sexual misconduct and inform them of the resources available in the event they experience sexual misconduct, so they are not hearing the information for the first time when they are coping with a traumatic event. Training should be sensitive to cultural differences and not assume that the American approach is superior or more binding than that of the host institution. Without flaming fears of the unknown or perpetuating stereotypes, sending institutions can prepare students to be vigilant and aware that when they study abroad, they are subject to local norms and mores regarding not just consent and understanding of what constitutes sexual harassment (The Forum on Education Abroad, 2020a, Guideline 6.1), but also regarding

dress, alcohol consumption, public displays of affections, and premarital sex, even if they do not agree with them. They can also help prepare students to learn about those norms and mores rather than simply expecting to be able to impose their own. Student-led training at the host institution may be particularly useful in helping students from sending institutions understand local norms. Similarly, training that takes intersectionality into account—for example, the possibility or likelihood that White students from the United States may be subject to different norms or expectations than students of color—will also better prepare students and help them avoid risks.

6. Short-term learning and study abroad: Provide the same support described above in terms of developing an informed understanding and setting student expectations for students participating in short-term programs (e.g., faculty-led programs).

7. Finally, U.S. institutions should not assume that host countries or institutions' laws, policies, or practices, if not identical to their own, are "uncivilized," "wrong," or "backward." Rather, host and sending institutions should remain curious and understand the differences in each other's requirements, and also in their practical experience, to define ways to ensure students' safe and meaningful participation in study abroad programs.

By adopting these best practices, sending institutions can help ensure that study abroad programs provide a safe and welcoming environment for all students, and that students understand any differing expectations as to how their own conduct may contribute to that environment; that any claims of sexual misconduct are promptly and sensitively addressed such that students experiencing sexual misconduct may continue to participate in the study abroad experience as fully as possible, even if the claims are not addressed in precisely the manner they would be in the United States; and that both the sending and the host institution are able to provide additional support (or take additional measures) with respect to returning students as necessary to meet sending institutions' obligations under U.S. laws.

## References

Abdelaal, H. (2021, December 14). *Sexual harassment laws in Egypt: Does stricter mean more effective?*. The Tahrir Institute for Middle East Policy. https://timep.org/2021/12/14/sexual-harassment-laws-in-egypt-does-stricter-mean-more-effective/

Anti-Harassment and Non-Discrimination Policy. American University in Cairo. (n.d.). https://documents.aucegypt.edu/Docs/Policies/Anti-Harassment%20and%20Non-Discriminatison%20Policy%208-5-20.pdf

Constitution Art. 53 (2014) (Egypt). https://www.constituteproject.org/constitution/Egypt_2014#s189

Designation of coordinator, dissemination of policy, and adoption of grievance procedures.34 C.F.R. § 106.8(c) (2020). https://www.law.cornell.edu/cfr/text/34/106.8

El Deeb, B. (2013). *Study on ways and methods to eliminate sexual harassment in Egypt.* UN Women. https://s3-eu-west-1.amazonaws.com/harassmap/media/uploaded-files/287_Summaryreport_eng_low-1.pdf

Human Rights Watch. (n.d.). *#OUTLAWED: "The love that dare not speak its name."* Maps of anti-LGBT Laws Country by Country | Human Rights Watch. https://features.hrw.org/features/features/lgbt_laws/

International Labour Organization. (n.d.). *Sexual Harassment in the World of Work.* https://www.ilo.org/wcmsp5/groups/public/---dgreports/---gender/documents/briefingnote/wcms_738115.pdf

Labor Code (No. 12/ 2003) (Egypt). http://www.egypt.gov.eg/english/laws/labour/default.aspx

Mansour, R.S. (2021, March 12). *A qualitative study to explore understanding and perception of violence against women among undergraduate students in Egypt.* Violence and Gender. https://doi.osrg/10.1089/vio.2020.0058

Nondiscrimination on the Basis of Sex in Education Programs or Activities Receiving Federal Financial Assistance, 87 Fed. Reg. 41390 (proposed July 21, 2022) (to be codified at 34 C.F.R. § 106). https://www.federalregister.gov/documents/2022/07/12/2022-13734/non-discrimination-on-the-basis-of-sex-in-education-programs-or-activities-receiving-federal

Penal Code, Article 306 (2014) (Egypt). https://harassmap.org/laws/law-text

Robinson, K. (2023, January 11). *Iran isn't the only country with Morality Police.* Council on Foreign Relations. https://www.cfr.org/in-brief/iran-isnt-only-country-morality-police

Rubiano-Matulevich, E. (n.d.). A guidance note for preventing, reporting and responding to sexual assault and sexual harassment in tertiary education institutions. https://thedocs.worldbank.org/en/doc/397161582585064307-0090022020/original/guidancenotefinal.pdf

Storch, J., & Stagg, A. (2024). Clery Act and Title IX extraterritorial application (and why the federal approach is the floor, not the ceiling). In J. Pollard & K. S. Priebe (Eds.), *Convergence of litigation, policy, and standards: Building the informed practitioner in education abroad risk management.* The Forum on Education Abroad. doi.org/10.36.366/SIA.5.978-1-952376-41-2.8

The Forum on Education Abroad. (2020a). *Guidelines for best practices in responding to sexual and gender-based misconduct.* doi.org/10.36366/G.978-1-952376-10-8

The Forum on Education Abroad. (2020b). *Standards of good practice for education abroad, Sixth edition.* http://doi.org/10.36366/S.978-1-952376-04-7

Zhao, M., & Wildemeersch, D. (2008). Hosting foreign students in European universities. European Education. https://www.tandfonline.com/doi/pdf/10.2753/EUE1056-4934400104?casa_token=AC1IDe6ctpIAAAAA:fAgWl9b9hWAE5eTZssNr-jxh2R_-vbqs-74dejoJGmn4_04wB1KJwdthFnrrQLlIRsUOELYX6pYXG

# 14

---

# Traveling Abroad with Medication

**Christine Sprovieri and Jennifer Fullick, Ph.D.**

## Introduction

International laws and conventions create complex barriers and benefits to medication access for students in education abroad programs. However, it exceeds the duty of care for the education abroad professional to have full knowledge of all medications' status globally. This chapter provides a two-pronged risk-mitigation approach for the education abroad professional supporting students who may desire or need to travel abroad with medication. The first prong includes a framework for pre-departure advising on barriers to accessing medication while abroad; the second prong provides resources you could leverage to cast a wide net of support. In summary, while an infinite number of variables may create obstacles for students, this practical guidance for education abroad professionals aids in creating opportunities to minimize risk abroad.

## Overview

"Medication access is a complex, multidimensional issue that must consider not only patient-specific challenges, but also health system limitations, among others" (Holland et al., 2021, p. 1627). Similarly, students on education abroad programs face challenges when considering access to medication abroad. For example, some nonprescribed medications, often referred to in the United States as "over-the-counter" medications, such as Benadryl, depending on dosage, may require a prescription in Japan (Weinstein, 2022). Additionally, some medications may be entirely restricted. The rise of Americans diagnosed and prescribed medications for attention-deficit/ hyperactivity disorders can create significant complications when options are limited for treatment medication abroad (CHADD, 2020). Moreover, there can be additional necessary medical equipment and appliances needed, for example, for medications requiring injections or wearables while sleeping. To support students with these needs, your role as an education abroad practitioner must include an approach that allows each traveler to consider their unique journey.

## A Framework for Assessing Access Barriers

The *Standards of Good Practice for Education Abroad* indicate that, at minimum, you should prepare students before departure with "information related to accessing physical, mental, and emotional health and well-being services" (2020), while "recognizing that not all countries have in place the same support and infrastructure." Therefore, it is critical for you to "work with other responsible parties and students to determine how their needs may be met on the program; and advise students on other program options if their needs cannot be met" (The Forum on Education Abroad, 2020). The challenge regarding the capacity to advise within the context of medications abroad is the impossibility of having full knowledge of barriers to accessing all medications in all countries where your students may travel.

Malene Torp from the Danish Institute for Study Abroad notes, "You see what you know; if you don't know anything, you don't see anything" (Fischer, 2009, para.14). This underscores the fact you should be upfront with students about what they should do to prepare before embarking on an education abroad program with medication. Preparing students for their global experiences and helping them learn about their destination from a risk standpoint can also empower them as educated travelers to have safe and productive travel experiences. While no one can ever remove all risk, nor could they guarantee a traveler's safety, the better you prepare *before* you depart, the more likely you will *minimize* incidents and be able to mitigate risk while abroad.

Through pre-departure advising, students are better prepared to ask the most salient questions and consider their personal needs within the context of their education abroad journey. Furthermore, it helps students better interpret and develop a foundation of knowledge of potentially what to expect when they go abroad. For this reason, a framework for advising on access barriers before departure is recommended, which guides a student to consider "their medication access journey and characterizes barriers frequently encountered while seeking medication access" (Holland et al., 2021). Suppose quantities are restricted, thereby limiting what the students can bring to cover them for their entire education abroad duration. In that case, students will need to discuss this with their medical or mental health practitioner to devise an alternative plan. If enough time is allotted in advance, students may choose to change medications or alter dosages, which will require a period of adjustment to get used to the new regimen before they travel abroad. Ultimately, this is a decision that students must make individually with their health provider's guidance well in advance of their planned education abroad experience. Sometimes, there may be incompatibilities between the treatment they need and the country in which they intend to study, and further, differences in diagnostic criteria in the United States and abroad. If medications are illegal or not available, even in the generic forms, students may need to rethink the duration of their time abroad and decide on a shorter-term experience to mitigate potential health and safety risks.

Students today manage many emotional, mental, and/or physical health needs with medications and need to continue this while traveling or studying abroad. However, medications that are largely prescribed, dispensed, and legal in the United States may not be lawful or even available in their country of study. Students on any medication, regardless of whether it is prescribed by a medical or mental health professional or dispensed over the counter at their local pharmacy, must investigate further how they can maintain their continuity of care while they are traveling and studying globally. Plenty of advance lead time may also be needed to prepare for their experience, depending on where they are planning to study or travel abroad. Therefore, sooner is better with regard to planning. Gauging risk variables for traveling with medication abroad, you should consider as part of your advising toolkit the following access barriers that may occur at any point during a student's education abroad journey:

## Legality

Some medications that are legally prescribed or nonprescribed "over-the-counter" medications in the United States are illegal to possess or bring into other countries (and vice versa). For example, narcotics (such as Vicodin®, codeine, or morphine) or psychotropic drugs (including antidepressants or amphetamines like Adderall®) that may be commonly prescribed in the United States to manage certain physical ailments or mental health conditions could be outright illegal in the student's destined country(ies). Utilizing information from the International Narcotics Control Board is very useful for understanding regulations by country. Committing legal infractions, even unwittingly, could subject the student to confiscation, fines, deportation, or worse, land them in prison or even have them face the death penalty if convicted. Rules and regulations, of course, vary by country and nations such as the United Arab Emirates, Japan, and Singapore have incredibly stringent laws surrounding the usage of certain kinds of drugs that may be freely prescribed or obtained without a prescription in the United States but considered a controlled substance elsewhere. These countries, among others, have been known to impose "judicially sanctioned" repercussions that could subject students to caning, whipping, or flogging for certain illegal drug offenses (OSAC, 2019). In Japan, for example, you are required to obtain permission in advance if you intend to bring a medication containing a controlled substance for your personal medical use (see "*Transportability and quantity restrictions*") and some medicines may not be brought in at all (Narcotics Control Department, n.d.). According to the Japanese Stimulants Control Act (1951), violations of these laws could mean hefty fines and up to 10 years imprisonment.

## Transportability and Quantity Restrictions

Students may be prescribed certain medications by a U.S.-based medical or mental health provider and have valid prescriptions; however, they may not be able to bring the required amount with them for the duration of their stay in the host country. Barriers may include U.S.-based insurance restrictions on the amount of medication that can be disbursed, the amount the policy will cover at one time, the temporary limited availability of some high-demand medications, or simply the illegality of a traveler to physically carry a large quantity of medication with them when they arrive at border control. Whatever the amount students may be bringing with them, it is imperative that they carry all medications—including over-the-counter, prescriptions, and even vitamins—in their hand luggage, clearly label it, and bring it in their original containers (Mohn, 2018). All medication will need to go through security protocols; however, any medically required liquids, gels, or aerosols may be exempt from maximum amount limitations but must be presented to security personnel or equivalent for inspection (TSA, n.d.). It is also useful for students to carry a letter from their treating physician describing exactly what the medication is and why it is being prescribed, and a translation of this letter into the local language of their destination and the language of any countries in which they have layovers. Finally, it is important to advise students against arranging for someone to mail their medication to them during their study abroad based on TSA regulations and restrictions on mailing medications.

In some cases, border control officials will want evidence that any large quantities of drugs are being used for personal use and proof that there is no intention for importation of the medication to be resold while in-country. Students may also be required to obtain advance permission by completing official forms from the host government to transport certain medications in their host country. Japan, for example, requires completion of a*yunyukakun-insho,* an import certificate that students will need to present to the customs officer upon arrival in-country (Embassy of Japan, 2023). It is very important to research this in advance, and if this documentation and permission is needed, you must include details about the generic names of the drugs, not specific brand names (Mohn, 2018).

## Availability

Even if certain medications are legal to consume or possess while in the host country, some brands, categories, modalities, or dosages may not be considered commonplace or regularly available in the host country. Similarly, if a prescribed medication is unavailable or difficult to obtain in the host country, this could present another layer of complication for the student. Consider recent post-COVID-19-pandemic shortages impacting global supply chains, which can limit the quantity of accessible medication depending on the country. Medications could be brought in-country only to be lost, stolen, get damaged, or expired. Some prescribed treatments may also require refrigeration, administration by trained medical professionals, or other special handling. Therefore, despite the facility of being able to transport the medication, the student must create a sound plan with the guidance of their treating healthcare provider for the "what ifs" that inevitably could arise. A student or international education professional can also consult with their international health insurance or assistance provider for availability and planning.

## Necessity

Ultimately, you must include in the advising framework the consideration of the necessity of the medication and the risks involved should a student be unable to use that medication. During pre-departure advising students should be advised to find alternative locations that may have fewer barriers to access of their medication, or a program of shorter duration, therefore allowing the student to confidently travel with their needed medications. Finally, as indicated by The Forum's *Standards* (2020), the pre-departure phase encourages advising *against travel* should a student clearly not be able to access their needed medications within their chosen destinations.

## Leveraging Resources

In addition to advising students pre-departure, an international education professional also has an opportunity to encourage students to leverage multiple avenues of support. Some avenues to consider:

*Health Insurance:* Students may not be aware and assume that they are only able to use one insurance plan and related services while abroad, which is not necessarily the case. Explore with the student their personal and institutional insurance options, and relevant support services, which may include advising on medications while abroad and options for securing additional prescriptions, quantities, and appointments with prescribing physicians abroad, in advance of travel. (See Chapter 33 in this volume by Joan Rupar 2024 for more information on international health insurance.)

*Third-Party Education Abroad Provider Organizations:* Some education abroad program provider organizations have specialized staff to support the health and safety of students abroad. Many have long-standing working relationships with local physicians and other experts equipped to navigate specialized requests.

*Emergency Support Services:* Providers of 24-hour or crisis response frequently have experience in obtaining medication and prescription refills globally. Contact them well in advance of travel to inquire about how to access.

*Local/in-country support:* Nongovernment organizations (NGOs) or other partners abroad may have experience in specific medications and restrictions locally.

*Local Healthcare/Nationalized Systems and Resources:* Some countries may have publicly available resources and support worth exploring.

## Implications for Education Abroad Practitioners

Students may not be aware of the significant barriers to using their medications abroad until after arrival in-country; they may not disclose or they may develop conditions while abroad; and/or they may lose medication or face regulatory changes during their program abroad. For these reasons, it is critical to also consider the less ideal scenario of advising students about medication after they are already onsite.

In this scenario, the two-prong approach can still be applied, but will most likely face increased limitations. First, students should be advised to consider access barriers and if there are any that can be overcome. Furthermore, all resources again may be leveraged; however, some may no longer be viable. Conversely, some may be used in an escalated or emergency service mode; for example, a student without life-saving medication may be eligible for expedited or escalated medical support services. Your role as the education abroad professional is to take a holistic approach to advising by considering factors such as the impact of flying home to obtain medication as well as the student's ability to maintain enrollment in their academic program. When advising a student who is already abroad about new or shifting medication needs, you should also be mindful of the student's limited window of time in-country to obtain medication and how to mitigate any negative impact on an unforeseen truncation of their education abroad experience.

## Conclusion

A student's ability to access medication abroad is complex and unique to their individual circumstances. Looking into the future, politics, economics, and increases in natural disasters due to global warming may continue to impact and complicate barriers to accessing medication. Furthermore, as the demographic of students studying abroad evolves, students with more complex medical needs or varying levels of resources may emerge. While it is not possible to comprehend each medication barrier globally, the education abroad practitioner can equip themselves with a framework for guiding students through a planning process to consider pre-departure and leverage a web of resources to provide information with the end goal of providing students with necessary information to make informed choices on risks related to travel and medication abroad.

## Advising Resources

International Narcotics Control Board (https://www.incb.org/)
Overseas Security Advisory Council (https://www.osac.gov/)
U.S. Department of State - Your Health Abroad (https://travel.state.gov/content/travel/en/international-travel/before-you-go/your-health-abroad.html)
U.S. Embassy Abroad (https://www.usembassy.gov/)
U.S. Centers for Disease Control and Prevention - Travelers' Health (https://wwwnc.cdc.gov/travel/page/travel-abroad-with-medicine)

# References

Children and Adults with Attention-Deficit/Hyperactivity Disorder (CHADD). (2020, 16 January). *Know before you go: International travel with ADHD medications.* https://chadd. org/adhd-weekly/know-before-you-go-international-travel-with-adhd-medication/

Embassy of Japan: Information and Culture Center. (2023). *Study in Japan: A Guide for U.S. Students.* Washington, D.C.; Embassy of Japan.

Fischer, K. (2009, February 20). *Short study-abroad trips can have lasting effect, research suggests.* The Chronicle of Higher Education. https://www.chronicle.com/article/short-study-abroad-trips-can-have-lasting-effect-research-suggests-1541/

The Forum on Education Abroad. (2020). *Standards of Good Practice for Education Abroad,* Sixth Edition. doi.org/10.36366/S.978-1-95236-02-3

Holland, L., Nelson, M., Westrich, K., Campbell, P., & Pickering, M. (2021). *The patient's medication access journey: a conceptual framework focused beyond adherence.* Journal of Managed Care Specialty Pharmacy, 27(12), 1627-1635.

Mohn, T. (2018, January 19). *How to make sure you travel with medication legally.* The New York Times. https://www.nytimes.com/2018/01/19/travel/how-to-make-sure-you-travel-with-medication-legally.html

Narcotics Control Department. (n.d.). *Import / export narcotics by carrying: Narcotics Control Department.* https://www.ncd.mhlw.go.jp/en/application2.html

Overseas Security Advisory Council. (2019, February 15). *Traveling with Medication.* OSAC. https://www.osac.gov/Content/Report/93c0b3f6-1d6e-4bef-a78d-15f4ad938dd3

Rupar, J. (2024). Navigating International Insurance for Global Education. In J. Pollard & K. S. Priebe (Eds.), *Convergence of litigation, policy, and standards: Building the informed practitioner in education abroad risk management.* The Forum on Education Abroad. doi.org/10.36.366/SIA.5.978-1-952376-41-2.33

Stimulants Control Act. (1951, June 30). Act No. 252. Chapter VIII Penal Provisions, Article 41-2 (1). https://www.japaneselawtranslation.go.jp/en/laws/view/2814/en

Transportation Security Administration (TSA). (n.d.). *Disabilities and medical conditions.* Disabilities and Medical Conditions | Transportation Security Administration. https://www.tsa.gov/travel/special-procedures?field_disability_type=1011

Weinstein, J. (2022, October 4). *No Pepto in France or Sudafed in Japan: What to know about meds banned in other countries.* The Atlanta Journal Constitution. https://www.ajc.com/travel/no-pepto-in-france-or-sudafed-in-japan-what-to-know-about-meds-banned-in-other-countries/6POCK5GAZNB2FCDG6KABWUGIRQ/

# 15

## Risks of Protest Participation While on Education Abroad

### A.J. Leeds

This chapter explores the risks posed to students by protests and participation in protests. Discussion will include the new youth activism movement, the environment, and how these may impact students in education abroad programs. Several cases will describe students' detentions and arrests not just for their involvement in an active protest but also for being associated with a protest movement at home. The risks posed by protests and the impact on student programs are examined, such as the large-scale protests in Hong Kong in 2020. The risks to students who decide to actively participate in protests are complex and potentially long-lasting. Lastly, this chapter offers best practices you can share with students and how students can be prepared before they go abroad.

Youth activism has changed since the early 2000s. Taking a new form and referred to as alter-activism, emphasis is placed on "lived experience and process; a commitment to horizontal, networked organization; creative direct action, *[such as gluing themselves to roadways or attacking valuable artwork;]* the use of new information and communication technologies (ICTs); and the organization of physical spaces and action camps as laboratories for developing alternative values and practices" (Juris & Pleyers, 2009). This is not a break from previous forms of youth activism but more an expansion of past ideas. Alter-activism is more globalized, more networked, more collaborative, and far more shaped by new technologies than its predecessors (Juris & Pleyers, 2009).

For students studying abroad, this change is important. Young activists have taken the lead in protests and advocacy around issues, including climate change, abortion rights, and gun violence (Rose, 2019). This means students are more likely to be part of protests or activist groups on campus and are often connected to a global network of other likeminded youths. As instantiated by Valenzuela (2013), "technology and the use of digital media has changed the way youth participate in activism globally, and youth are more active in media than older generations." This means that movements and activism are no longer limited to local groups and locations. In past movements, such as the civil rights movement in the United States, it was rare to see global solidarity or protests stemming from those movements or protests. This contrasts sharply with protests led by the Black Lives Matter (BLM) movement after the death of George Floyd. Activism and protests in the United States occurred, but similar protests against social injustice in countries around the world also erupted. Many students are likely to be motivated by these globally connected movements and therefore may try to participate in activism or protests while abroad.

Foreign governments are also adjusting to the new trends in globally connected activism. China currently reviews social media accounts; travelers should not expect Internet privacy. Anyone traveling to China could have their communications may be monitored at any time, and authorities may review the content stored or accessed on your electronic devices (Government of Canada, n.d.). In the worst cases, this might also result in detainment or exit bans (Department of State, 2023). In Israel, the government refuses entry to those that are part of the Boycott, Divestment, and Sanctions (BDS) movement, which has the stated goals of "end[ing] international support for Israel's oppression of Palestinians and pressure Israel to comply with international law" (Liebermann, 2017). Under the Mexican Constitution Chapter three article 33, foreigners cannot participate in political affairs including protests and can be detained or deported as a result (The Political Constitution of the Mexican United States, 2005). Some countries also restrict or limit the types or subjects a protest can address. This can include banning women from protests and banning of LGBTQ protests (Amnesty International, n.d.). This directly relates to student activists and how their activities at home might impact them when they study abroad.

## Case Example: Cairo, Egypt

On November 21, 2011, three U.S. students were arrested in Cairo, Egypt. An Egyptian Interior Ministry official said that the students were arrested "on the roof of an American University in Cairo building, where they were throwing firebombs at security forces fighting protesters in Tahrir Square" (Memmott, 2011).

The three students were studying at the American University in Cairo (AUC) and came from three different universities (CBS, 2011). At the time an AUC spokesperson stated, "There's a lot of very contagious passion right now. Students from the U.S. don't always realize what it's like to live in a country without free speech or other civil liberties, and sometimes are motivated to work to change those conditions" (CBS, 2011). Several students arrested had posted about going to the protests on social media before they were arrested (Goodman, 2011). With support from the U.S. Embassy in Cairo and university officials, the three students were released on November 26, driven to the airport by Egyptian police, and returned to the United States (Matheson & Al-Shalchi, 2011).

The case of the U.S. students at AUC is an example of how students can get caught up in local affairs. Students studying abroad often do not understand that free speech might be significantly different than in the United States and often might become involved to protest that difference. Students are likely to not understand the police response to protests or the consequences of being arrested.

## Case Example: Jerusalem, Israel

On October 2, 2018, a graduate student from Florida was detained by Israel at Ben Gurion Airport (Doubek, 2018). The 22-year-old U.S. citizen with Palestinian grandparents landed with a valid student visa to pursue a master's program in law with a specialization in human rights and transitional justice at Hebrew University. They were initially stopped and questioned about the origin of their surname and father's identity. The student was forbidden to enter the country and received a deportation order based on suspicions that they were a boycott supporter (Atack, 2018). "The Boycott, Divestment, Sanctions (BDS) movement works to end international support for Israel's oppression of Palestinians and pressure Israel to comply with international law" (BDS National Committee, n.d.). After the detention, the Israeli Minister for Public Security and Strategic Affairs, Gilad Erdan, accused the student of leading a chapter of the Students for Justice in Palestine, which he referred to as "extreme," "hate-filled," and "violent" (Debre, 2018). The student had relinquished any BDS views and stopped activities that the Israeli Knesset (parliament) enacted a law against in 2017. This law bans any foreigner who "knowingly issues a public call for boycotting Israel" from entering the country and identified 20 activist groups from around the world whose members could be denied entry upon arrival (Liebermann, 2017).

The student's detention lasted over two weeks, one of the longest in a boycott-related case, in "'not so good' conditions, in a closed area with little access to a telephone, no internet, and a bed that was infested with bed-bugs, according to her lawyers" (AlJazeera, 2023). The Israeli Supreme Court eventually overruled this deportation order, allowing the student to continue studies in Israel (Doubek, 2018).

The case of the Hebrew University student detained and denied entry due to their activities at home reflects the changes in how governments are monitoring activists worldwide and how they might deal with activist in the future. As youth activism continues to grow beyond borders and connect people, it is likely that some governments will move to stop this spread to their own countries by denying entry to activists. Governments will also increase monitoring of social media for critical comments about the government, which could get students in trouble without them even directly participating in protests.

## Case Example: Ho Chi Minh City, Vietnam

On June 10, 2018, a Yale graduate student was arrested in Vietnam. The student was on vacation in Vietnam before returning to his master's program at the University of Singapore. After arriving in Ho Chi Minh City, the student began documenting the demonstrations against a proposed economic law that would give foreign investors 99-year leases on land in three designated special economic zones across the country. Many in Vietnam felt that this would result in large areas being owned by the Chinese companies (BBC, n.d.). On June 10, the student joined protests, stating on Twitter (now named X) "how enormous of an achievement" the demonstrations were for the Vietnamese people (BBC, n.d.). According to family and friends, the student was "beaten over the head and dragged into the back of a police truck" (Fuchs, 2018). State media said the student was "causing trouble; the government denied using force" (Fuchs, 2018). The student was then held without being charged or being able to contact anyone. The U.S. Secretary of State raised this case with Vietnamese officials (Quackenbush, 2018). The U.S. Embassy was eventually able to meet with the student. He was found guilty of "causing public disorder" after a one-day trial on July 20, 2018. The maximum penalty for causing public disorder is seven years in prison, but the student was only required to pay a fine and was immediately deported from Vietnam (BBC, n.d.).

This case exhibits the complications and impacts an arrest can have as the student was detained with no outside contact for several days and then held for trial for roughly 40 days (Quackenbush, 2018). Beyond the impact of arrest and detainment, students should understand the consequences of being deported, especially due to a criminal conviction. Not only will a deportation like this limit or deny entry to return to the country, but it might also impact the ability to receive a visa or gain entry to other countries as well.

## Understanding the Risks

What are the overall risks for education abroad students when there are protests or civil unrest? Risks can be divided into two categories. The first category is the risks and impacts to students when there are protests in the areas that they are studying. Examples of this would be the yellow vest protests in France starting in 2018 (Cigainero, 2018) and the Hong Kong protests in 2019–2020 (Cheung & Hughes, 2019). Each of these protests was different from the other and posed different risks to education abroad students. The second category is the risks and potential impacts of students that actively participate in protests. There are many reasons a student might find themselves going to a protest. Students might be curious about what the protest is about or what the issues are surrounding the protest. Others might simply want to join the excitement and crowd that can be found at protests. Lastly, the student might be an activist on campus or at home and have a direct connection to the issues and feel that they can help make a difference here and at home. Regardless of why a student finds themselves at a protest the risks are largely the same. Even if they do not participate directly in the protests, they can still fall under scrutiny by law enforcement.

Disruption is the most common impact felt by students when it comes to protests. The protests might disrupt roadways, causing delays, or strikes might cause the cancellation of flights or trains, particularly those used for local travel. These disruptions might be a result of direct actions by protesters, such as the blocking of roadways. During shutdown protests and strikes there might be pressure on bus services and car services to stop working. Law enforcement might also take steps to limit the mobility of travel for protesters by canceling public transportation during certain times, or restricting access to areas. Petty crime is also a concern during protests as the large crowds make it easy for pickpockets and other criminals to operate.

The deployment of weapons like mace and tear gas is also a risk factor for people involved in protests and nearby areas. Tear gas can be blown in the wind, impacting areas blocks away. For instance, during the Hong Kong protests hundreds of tear gas canisters were used, making it difficult for people that worked or lived in the nearby communities (Leung, 2019). This is more acute if the student has any illness that might impact breathing. Beyond this, police might deploy rubber bullets, bean bag rounds, water cannons, or other deterrents to disperse crowds, which can result in serious injury and in rare cases death. Depending on the protest and the country, live ammunition might be used by law enforcement or the military.

Arrest is of great concern in this scenario. Countries have a high degree of variability when it comes to free speech and protests. Certain countries curtail or even have total control over what acceptable speech is, as seen in the cases above. Countries also have a variety of ways that they respond to protests and how they determine who to arrest. In certain places, simply being near the protest is reason enough to be arrested by police. Also, filming protests, the military, or the police, might be grounds for an arrest. There is also the risk of assault by officers while they break up or contain protests. Striking protesters with batons or clubs is not uncommon during protests. These risks are also likely to be increased for students as foreigners at protests will likely be targeted by law enforcement because they might see them as outside agitators or working with foreign governments to cause unrest. Regardless of the truth of these accusations, they will likely be used in the media when talking about foreigners arrested at protests.

The most pressing concern for those responsible for the health and safety of students on education abroad programs is the risk of serious injury or death. Large protests are fast moving and often unpredictable. A protest that has been peaceful all day might turn violent in the dark of night. Groups might be at protests with the intent to confront or attack law enforcement. In some areas, law enforcement might respond rapidly and forcefully to break up protests, leading to injury and in the worst case, crush deaths as crowds flee the area. The risks from protesters should also be considered. Attempting to cross a blockade in many countries could be met with violence. The risks are also not just to people participating in protests but to those who find themselves in the wrong place at the wrong time. In 2016, a University of California Davis graduate student was killed during a protest in Ethiopia; the student, a postdoctoral researcher in plant biology, died when the vehicle she was riding in was struck by rocks thrown by protesters (NBC News, 2016).

## Preparing Students to Make Good Choices

What can be done to prepare students going on education abroad programs for the risks involved in protests? U.S. and foreign governments around the world advise their citizens to avoid all protests during international travel and most U.S. institutions recommend their students follow this advice. While this is good advice for students, this new era of globalized youth activism requires expanding upon it because students may find themselves at protests. Professionals responsible for preparing students to go abroad should discuss what to do if a student is accidentally in the middle of or near a protest. You can ask students to think about questions around protests, which might discourage them from participating. You can discuss what protests look like and what happens during a normal protest. For example, the typical time, location, escalation, police response, protester response, and likelihood of violence and/or property destruction. Most countries have a unique way of protesting that is largely predictable (Anonymous Subject Matter Expert, 2024). You can discuss what happens if a student is arrested in a foreign country, what the program can and cannot do to help, what the U.S. government or the student's government can and cannot do to help, and likely treatment the student will receive if arrested.

Most education abroad professionals are not security experts or know about specific countries' laws; so how is this information found? First and foremost is to tap into local knowledge. Education abroad programs do not operate solely from your home campus. Third-party program provider staff, and especially local nationals, will have a great deal of information about protests. They will likely know how common they are, where people gather for protests, how the protests will look, and what the police response will likely be. In addition, you can leverage the U.S. State Department by contacting the local Regional Security Officer (RSO). If your institution is a member of the Overseas Security and Advisory Council (OSAC), you can contact one of their regional intelligence analysts. You can also look at numerous travel advisories from countries outside of the United States. It can also be beneficial for students to receive a briefing from local law enforcement when they arrive, especially on programs of longer duration. This will allow the students to ask questions and for law enforcement to explain rules or laws that might be different from their home campus and country.

What advice should be given to students? First, you shall provide basic information; avoid protests whenever possible and follow the guidance provided by the program administrators. If they find themselves in a protest area, move away from the area, preferably not on the same street as the protest. Do not attempt to cross any blockade. If there is a large area disrupted by the protest, find the nearest safe place to stay until it is safe to move. Avoid being near known protest locations and government buildings.

Practitioners can educate students on protests. This can include areas where protests are likely to happen. In almost every major city, there is a location where people gather to protest. It might be a park, a major intersection, or a government building. Discuss how protests work in the country. This might include information on how law enforcement responds to protests, are they largely peaceful, and what applicable laws might apply in the country.

If the country prohibits the filming or taking of pictures of protests or law enforcement, this is valuable information for students that are so quick to snap pictures or film an event and then post it to social media. What kinds of disruptions can students expect during a protest? Climate activists are routinely blocking streets as part of their direct-action plans (Moulson, 2019). In Central America, protesters often set up blockades to prevent the movement of goods in the city and in border regions can block crossing points (Buschschlüter, 2023). This means that students will need to check routes before leaving, give themselves extra time to get to their destination, and review bus or train schedules for disruptions.

Lastly, there is a need to acknowledge that protests might be appealing to students traveling abroad. Institutions often give the direction to "avoid all protests" and do not address what happens if students are at a protest because they were already advised not to be there.

You can discuss the following questions to encourage critical thinking:

- As a foreigner is it legal or illegal for them to protest?
- What would they do if they were arrested?
- Do they speak the language?
- Is it likely that police speak English?
- Do they know where they will be held?
- How long could they be in custody before charges are brought?
- Do they know how to get a lawyer in the country?
- How will they pay for a legal defense?
- What are the services that can be offered by the U.S. Embassy?
- Could they face jail time?
- Could they be deported?
- If they are charged or deported, might that affect their ability to travel to other countries?
- If they are injured in a protest and require medical attention, are hospitals required to report to police?

Often students think of protests from their own local perspective. For U.S.-based students, they have constitutionally protected rights to protest. Simply having conversations about the consequences will often lead to students avoiding protests. In addition, students should be made aware of possible academic consequences, professional consequences, and possible damage to the reputation of the university they are representing while abroad. However, there are some students that will feel strongly about a cause and will not be persuaded to avoid them. With risk communication and student education, the likelihood is increased that education abroad students can avoid the worst possible outcomes.

## References

Al Jazeera. (2018, October 18). *U.S. student Lara Alqasem claims victory in Israel boycott case.* https://www.aljazeera.com/news/2018/10/18/us-student-lara-alqasem-claims-victory-in-israel-boycott-case#:~:text=Lara%20Alqasem%2C%20who%20was%20barred,her%20alleged%20support%20for%20BDS.&text=Lara%20Alqasem's%20legal%20team%20says,her%20to%20study%20in%20Israel

Amnesty International. (n.d.) *Protect the protest.* https://www.amnesty.org/en/what-we-do/freedom-of-expression/protest/

Anonymous Subject Matter Expert. (2024, March 20). *The Anatomy of a Protest.* [OSAC webinar].

Atack, P. (2018, October 15). *U.S. student barred from entering Israel.* The PIE News. https://thepienews.com/news/us-student-barred-from-entering-israel/

BBC. (n.d.). *Vietnam to deport U.S. student Will Nguyen for 'public disorder.'* https://www.bbc.com/news/world-asia-44896125

BDS National Committee. (n.d.) *What is BDS?* BDS. https://bdsmovement.net/

Buschschlüter, V. (2023, October 10). *Guatemala paralysed as pro-democracy protests run into second week.* BBC News. https://www.bbc.com/news/world-latin-america-67064814

CBS News. (2011, November 22). *3 U.S. students arrested amid Cairo protests.* https://www.cbsnews.com/news/3-us-students-arrested-amid-cairo-protests/

Cigainero, J. (2018, December 3). *Who are France's Yellow Vest protesters, and what do they want?* NPR. https://www.npr.org/2018/12/03/672862353/who-are-frances-yellow-vest-protesters-and-what-do-they-want

Cheung, H., & Hughes, R. (2020, May 21). *Why are there protests in Hong Kong? All the context you need.* BBC. https://www.bbc.com/news/world-asia-china-48607723

Debre, I. (2018, October 9). *U.S. student detained in Israel over alleged boycott support.* AP. https://apnews.com/article/59cb3c23483f436ea91fefd4b8ed54c0

Doubek, J. (2018, October 19). *Detained American graduate student allowed to study in Israel, court rules.* NPR. https://www.npr.org/2018/10/19/658728519/detained-american-graduate-student-allowed-to-study-in-israel-court-rules

Fuchs, C. (2018, June 15). *U.S. citizen reportedly detained in Vietnam after protests.* NBC News. https://www.nbcnews.com/news/asian-america/u-s-citizen-reportedly-detained-vietnam-after-protests-n883481

Goodman, J.D. (2011, November 22). *3 Americans arrested in Cairo.* The New York Times. https://archive.nytimes.com/thelede.blogs.nytimes.com/2011/11/22/3-americans-arrested-in-cairo/

Government of Canada. (n.d.) *China travel advice.* Retrieved February 5, 2024, from https://travel.gc.ca/destinations/china

Juris, J. S., & Pleyers, G. H. (2009). Alter-activism: Emerging cultures of participation among young global justice activists. *Journal of Youth Studies, 12*(1), 57–75. https://doi.org/10.1080/13676260802345765

Leung, H. (2019 December 4). *Tear gas is now a fact of life in Hong Kong. Residents are wondering what it's doing to their health.* Time. https://time.com/5743663/tear-gas-hong-kong/

Liebermann, O. (2017, March 7). *Israel travel ban: Boycott supporters to be turned away.* CNN. https://www.cnn.com/2017/03/07/middleeast/israel-bds-boycott-law/index.html

Matheson, K., & Al-Shalchi, H. (2011, November 25). *U.S. students arrested in Egypt released.* The Ledger. https://www.theledger.com/story/news/nation-world/2011/11/25/us-students-arrested-in-egypt-released/26461331007/

Memmott, M. (2011, November 22). *Reports: Three American students arrested In Cairo.* The Two-Way. https://www.npr.org/sections/thetwo-way/2011/11/22/142645225/reports-three-american-students-arrested-in-cairo

Moulson, G. (2019, October 7). *Climate protests block roads across Europe.* PBS.https://www.pbs.org/newshour/world/climate-protests-block-roads-across-europe

NBC News. (2016, October 6). *UC Davis academic Sharon Gray killed by protesters in Ethiopia.* https://www.nbcnews.com/news/world/uc-davis-academic-sharon-gray-killed-protesters-ethiopia-n660691

Quackenbush, C. (2018, June 20). *American arrested in Vietnam confesses on state television.* Time. https://time.com/5316815/vietnam-william-nguyen-apology/

Rose, S. (2019, June 3). *'Our rage and terror give us power': what drives young activists?* The Guardian. https://www.theguardian.com/books/2019/jun/03/young-people-are-full-of-rage-and-terror-and-that-gives-us-power-meet-the-activists

Senado de la Republica. (2005). *The Political Constitution of the Mexican United States.* Retrieved February 5, 2024, from https://www.senado.gob.mx/comisiones/puntos_constitucionales/docs/CPM_INGLES.pdf

U.S. Department of State. (2023, June 30). *China travel advisory.* Retrieved February 5, 2025, from https://travel.state.gov/content/travel/en/traveladvisories/traveladvisories/china-travel-advisory.html

Valenzuela, S. (2013). Unpacking the use of social media for protest behavior: The roles of information, opinion expression, and activism. *American Behavioral Scientist. 57*(7): 920–942. https://doi.org/10.1177/0002764213479375

# 16

# Marijuana Abroad: Reconsidering Best Practices

**Andrea Campbell Drake**

## Introduction

Best practices within the field of education abroad will point to a host of expectations around supporting students' overall health and well-being. The Forum on Education Abroad *Standards of Good Practice for Education Abroad* (2020) repeatedly calls on organizations to have policies and procedures that attend to participants' physical and mental health. More specifically, The Forum on Education Abroad and NAFSA: Association of International Educators' *Responsible Education Abroad: Best Practices for Health, Safety, and Security* (2021) centers the idea that responsible personnel and responsible organizations more generally should both "provide participants with up-to-date health, safety, and security information so that each participant can make informed decisions about participation in the program" (p. 5) while they also "maintain and communicate to participants current knowledge about location-specific laws, regulations, and protections that may or may not be accorded to participants" (p. 7).

With a clear charge at hand to support study abroad students' health and well-being, one of the biggest challenges in recent years has come with the decriminalization and legalization of marijuana. At this point, marijuana is well documented as a medication that can be used to support a wide variety of health issues, with conclusive evidence that marijuana effectively treats chronic pain, nausea and vomiting, and symptoms related to multiple sclerosis, with potential use for other conditions though studies are limited (The National Academies of

Sciences, Engineering, and Medicine, 2017). College students are increasingly turning to marijuana products for a variety of health concerns, in addition to recreational use of marijuana that one study showed was increasing (North & Loukas, 2023). How can the international education field reconcile the challenge of supporting student health and potential medical marijuana use while also managing up-to-date information around the wide variety of laws both domestically and internationally around marijuana? What are the implications to advising students to stop using marijuana? What are the implications to picking up a different (potentially stronger) but legal drug such as a selective serotonin reuptake inhibitor (SSRI)? In light of these new questions, best practices around students' use of medical marijuana should be revisited and perhaps reworked.

## Legalization Efforts in the United States

To understand the current state of marijuana use at colleges and universities, we first should look at the larger context of legalization of marijuana in the United States. To be clear, the U.S. Drug Enforcement Administration (DEA) has considered marijuana to be in the most severe drug category as a Schedule I Controlled Substance since the 1970s. According to the DEA, "Schedule I drugs, substances, or chemicals are defined as drugs with no currently accepted medical use and a high potential for abuse. Some examples of Schedule I drugs are: heroin, lysergic acid diethylamide (LSD), marijuana (cannabis), 3,4-methylenedioxymethamphetamine (ecstasy), methaqualone, and peyote" (n.d.). It should be noted that fentanyl, referenced by the Center for Disease Control and Prevention (2023), as the most common drug involved in overdose deaths, is listed by the DEA as a Schedule II Controlled Substance, thus considered having a lesser potential for addiction or use disorder.

With the DEA listing marijuana alongside heroin and LSD, and in a category stronger than Fentanyl, certain bodies of the federal government continue to consider marijuana not only illegal but dangerous. Meanwhile, an increasing number of states have moved to legalize marijuana, for medical use, recreationally("adult-use") or both. Legalization efforts started in 1996 with California becoming the first state to legalize medical cannabis. In 2012, legal recreational use was approved in Washington state and Colorado. Since then, a flurry of states followed. As of November 2023, Ohio became the 24th state to legalize recreational marijuana, while marijuana use for medical purposes is now legal in 38 states. In 2022, as part of the decriminalization process, President Biden pardoned individuals who were convicted for simple marijuana possession under federal law, and he ordered a review of marijuana's listing as a Schedule I drug (Matthews & Hickey, 2023).

In May 2024, the U.S. Department of Justice submitted a proposed regulation to reschedule marijuana from a Schedule I to a Schedule III substance under the Controlled Substances Act. This recommendation follows a comprehensive review by the Department of Health and Human Services and signals a significant shift in federal marijuana policy, potentially easing restrictions on cannabis research and aligning federal law more closely with the growing number of states that have legalized marijuana for medical and recreational use. The DEA is now, at the time of publication, reviewing this proposal, which reflects an acknowledgement of marijuana's accepted medical use and potential benefits (United States Department of Justice, 2024).

With today's college students born after this latest trend in legalization began, many are finding marijuana use a common theme on and off college campuses. In states like Massachusetts, legalization allows use of recreational marijuana for those who are over 21 years old, but medical marijuana is legal for those who are over 18 years old. In states that have legalized, the influx of cannabis retailers is dramatic, and dispensaries are generally easy to find. A recent survey (2023) found that nearly 40% of the 14,000 University of Texas Austin students use marijuana, with products like vapes making it easy and common to smoke on and off campus (Abdulahi, 2023).

## Medical Uses of Marijuana

In consideration of marijuana use on college campuses, it can be hard to differentiate between medical marijuana and recreational marijuana use, but the distinction is important. There is increasing literature on the legitimate, impactful use of marijuana to treat a wide variety of ailments—both physical and mental. The Massachusetts Cannabis Control Commission, a state agency charged with implementing and administering the laws associated with the legalization of marijuana including the certification of healthcare providers with the ability to prescribe medical marijuana, has identified the following medical conditions as qualifying for medical marijuana access: cancer, glaucoma, HIV/AIDS, hepatitis C, Lou Gehrig's disease (ALS), Crohn's disease, Parkinson's disease, multiple sclerosis, as well as "other debilitating conditions as determined in writing by a certified physician" (n.d.).

In addition to physical ailments, research is underway to support the idea that marijuana, and its extract cannabidiol (known as CBD), could have benefits for mental health including for treating insomnia, anxiety, and PTSD (Grinspoon, 2020). Anxiety and depression have been listed as mental health conditions that have been accepted as qualifying for a medical marijuana card in Massachusetts (Massachusetts Cannabis Information, n.d.). One of the major challenges in understanding the implications of marijuana as a medical treatment is the lack of clinical trials and studies due to the restrictions placed on marijuana by the federal government and major funding agencies.

College campuses have seen the impact of marijuana use for medical purposes since its legalization especially (National Institutes of Health, 2021). Christine Horn has been a Nurse Practitioner at the University of Massachusetts Amherst University Health Services for over 15 years and confirmed an increase in marijuana use since its legalization. She works with students with medical marijuana cards for various reasons, including chronic pain, vocal cord dysfunction, anxiety, and insomnia. She has also found that more students are obtaining marijuana without getting a Medical Marijuana card since the cards were expensive to get upfront and marijuana is easily accessible at dispensaries across the state, including several within walking distance of campus (C. Horn, personal communication, July 27, 2023).

## Implications for Study Abroad

As legalization efforts continue across the United States, and more students become familiar with the uses of medical marijuana, there is no question that marijuana is a drug that is here to stay. When it comes to implications for education abroad, there are several areas to consider. With marijuana so commonly available in states like Massachusetts that have legalized marijuana, it would not be hard for students to forget that it is illegal to travel with marijuana out of state or by air. Airports are federal jurisdictions regulated by the Transportation Security Administration (TSA). According to the TSA, "marijuana and certain cannabis infused products, including some Cannabidiol (CBD) oil, remain illegal under federal law except for products that contain no more than 0.3 percent THC on a dry weight basis or that are approved by FDA" (n.d.). The TSA might make some allowances for small amounts of medical marijuana for personal use, but this is not guaranteed, and it is at the discretion of the TSA officer. The TSA website (n.d.) states that if any illegal substance is discovered during a security screening, a TSA officer will refer the matter to local law enforcement, where laws and punishment may vary.

Apart from the inability to legally travel *with* medical marijuana, there is the fact that many countries still consider marijuana to be illegal with very harsh penalties. The legalization movement has made progress internationally, but there remains a wide spectrum of positions on marijuana classification and use. As of 2021, seventy countries worldwide have legalized medical marijuana in some form (New Frontier Data, 2021). For the vast majority, this might mean decriminalizing marijuana with allowances for home cultivation and possession for medical purposes but no apparatus for legal sales. In 26 countries, medical patients have legal access to cannabis. Yet only ten countries worldwide have legalized cannabis for recreational use (Kagai, 2021).

Even within the list of countries that have legalized or normalized marijuana use in some form, the devil is in the details. For example, Uruguay was the first country to legalize marijuana for people 18 and older, but there are still restrictions around obtaining a government-issued permit. Jamaica may come to mind as a country that has legalized marijuana as it is readily available for travelers to purchase and has a significant cultural practice around marijuana use, but recreational use of marijuana is illegal there. Britain has issued advice to its travelers to Jamaica about the arrest of British nationals for marijuana possession and the harsh prison conditions there (UK Foreign Travel Advice, 2024).

Several countries are famous for their especially harsh drug laws, including marijuana. All forms of cannabis are illegal in the United Arab Emirates, Indonesia, Japan, Saudi Arabia, Singapore, China, Iran, and Malaysia (with minimal medical allowances). The sentences for cannabis use, possession, or trafficking can range from heavy fines, long prison sentences, or even the death penalty (Sabaghi, 2022b). In Asia, while some countries such as Thailand have moved to legalize marijuana, resulting in a major boom for the marijuana tourism industry, other countries have taken new steps to curb marijuana use and sale, including Hong Kong's recent criminalization of CBD that makes possession and consumption of any amount of CBD punishable by seven years in prison and a fine of approximately US$128,000 (Yeung, 2023).

Most students from the United States study abroad in Europe. According to the 2023 Open Doors Report, eight of the ten leading destinations for study abroad in the 2021–22 academic year were in Europe (Institute of International Education (IIE)). Nearly 30 countries in Europe provide patients with access to some form of legalized medical marijuana. There is an ongoing movement across Europe to legalize marijuana with proponents pushing for a regulated market. Germany, the Czech Republic, Luxembourg, Malta, Switzerland, and the Netherlands all have campaigns underway to legalize further and permit marijuana use (Gilchrist, 2023). The individual laws and customs around marijuana use within Europe vary, with some marijuana use tolerated for recreational purposes in places like the Netherlands (technically illegal, though decriminalized) while other countries like France have one of the strictest cannabis policies in the European Union. Possession of cannabis in France could result in a prison sentence of up to one year and a fine of over $4,000. Although in practice France has an on-the-spot fine of 200 euros, which is reduced to 150 euros if paid within 15 days. France has limited allowances for medical marijuana, but it is still in a pilot phase and not available to non-French citizens (Sabaghi, 2022a). In Spain, routinely listed as one of the top destinations for U.S. students, there is no federally regulated program for legal cannabis. However, various provinces have permitted private clubs to allow members to buy and consume cannabis. This cannabis club scene has exploded in the last ten years especially in Barcelona, a very popular tourist and study abroad destination. Tourists' ability to purchase and consume marijuana in these clubs has been allowed through a legal loophole that Spanish courts might overturn (Sabaghi, 2024). Meanwhile, students smoking marijuana on the street can be arrested, detained, and charged with possession of an illegal substance. In Italy and Portugal, it might be possible to obtain medical marijuana if students are prescribed it by meeting with an Italian or Portuguese doctor, but the process is complicated and not guaranteed.

## Rethinking Best Practices

With the considerable variety in tolerances, laws, and customs around marijuana use abroad, education abroad practitioners encounter a great challenge about the best way to advise students. Until recently, advisors would generally deter students from any marijuana use abroad, including for medical purposes. Given the harsh penalties, the risk did not seem worth the reward in permitting medical marijuana use during a study abroad experience. Yet, the world is shifting slowly in its perception of medical marijuana. College students are increasingly using medical marijuana for a wide variety of concerns and medical practitioners continue to prescribe marijuana products. Is it, therefore, ethical to ask students to cease use of an effective health plan and perhaps replace it with an unknown (to them) medication?

There are still a host of complications around medical marijuana use abroad. In terms of access, since we know students cannot travel with any marijuana product, if they plan to use medical marijuana in-country it will have to be acquired locally. If we look at countries where medical marijuana is legalized, we must then investigate whether someone who is not a resident/citizen of that country is permitted to use medical marijuana. If yes, who prescribes it? Will an Italian doctor prescribe medical marijuana to an American college student only there for a semester? If yes, where does the student go to obtain medical marijuana? Is access readily available at local pharmacies? If yes, what is the cost, and is it affordable for the student? If it is affordable and the student successfully acquires the local medical marijuana, is the type and potency at the right level to treat the student's health conditions? Does it need to be adjusted periodically, and is that an easy concern to address?

Medical marijuana access and use in a limited number of countries is complicated, but perhaps not impossible. Emergency assistance providers should be willing and able to help students navigate this complex process. Education abroad advisors and international education organizations can be on hand to support the student as well.

If the student is determined to go to a country that does not recognize medical marijuana, or where it is not accessible to nonresidents, the student needs to understand what other medical options might be available (in consultation with their prescribing physician) as well as the significant impacts of marijuana detox. In situations where a student is using medical marijuana to treat mental health concerns and a healthcare professional suggests moving the student to a legally available prescription medication, such as a selective serotonin reuptake inhibitor (SSRI) or serotonin and norepinephrine reuptake inhibitors (SNRI), the impact of moving students to those medications should be seriously considered. Properly adjusting these medications can take months and require frequent visits with a prescriber.

In addition to concerns about starting another medication, if the student decides to stop using marijuana, the impacts of cannabis withdrawal syndrome should be seriously considered and planned. Cannabis withdrawal syndrome has come to light recently as a significant medical condition that can include mood and sleep disturbances, appetite decline, weight loss, and restlessness. According to research, cannabis withdrawal syndrome impacts about half of cannabis users after abrupt cessation or significant reductions in use (Weinstein & Gorelick, 2012). Withdrawal symptoms usually develop within 24–72 hours of stopping cannabis use, peak within 2–5 days, and resolve within 2–3 weeks. This timeline runs up against some of the most challenging days of a study abroad program, when a student might also be dealing with time zone changes and cultural adjustment (Connor et al., 2022; Metrik & McCarty, 2023).

If a student can plan for a successful detox from marijuana, they should work with their doctor, psychiatrist, or another member of their medical care team to consider other options that can be considered to manage their medical condition. For mental health concerns, there is strong evidence that talk therapy can be beneficial in managing a variety of symptoms. Luckily, access to mental health counselors is becoming more common in study abroad programs, with many universities adding access to 24/7 remote mental health counselors.

A health self-disclosure process will be key for practitioners to work with students effectively. Many universities have some variety of a health form, which asks students to self-disclose any physical or mental health conditions or concerns. Perhaps adding a question about medical marijuana use would be a good place to prompt students to consider implications to travel abroad. Whether or not a self-disclosure form is used, universities should prompt students to think through the impacts of marijuana use abroad and have a clear understanding of the legality and logistics of marijuana use in their chosen destination. (See Chapter 14 of this volume, "Traveling with Medication," by Christine Sprovieri and Jennifer Fullick 2024 for more information.) The gradual, cultural shift that encompasses the legalization movement and allows for more understanding of compelling medical uses of marijuana will support this. However, cultural stigma around marijuana use persists. It is a barrier to self-disclosure for students, and it is a barrier to practitioners looking to properly support students on a study abroad program.

## Conclusion

Given the evolving landscape of marijuana use among college students, coupled with the complexity and ever-changing nature of domestic and international laws and regulations around marijuana, this topic warrants significant attention in the education abroad field. There is no one-size-fits-all approach to such a dynamic situation, though education abroad practitioners would be remiss to entirely ignore the subject of marijuana use abroad. In some cases, with the appropriate planning and risk mitigation, it may be possible to support a student in legally accessing marijuana used for medicinal purposes. It is also important to consider how replacing medicinal marijuana use with an alternative legal drug could have adverse side effects. In any case, this is an important topic that requires continued research and discussion, and perhaps a special note in The Forum's *Standards of Good Practice*.

## References

Abdulahi, S. (2023, February 22). *Marijuana use on campus grew as legalization spread.* Inside Higher Ed. https://www.insidehighered.com/news/2023/02/23/study-increased-marijuana-use-college-campuses

Connor, J. P., Stjepanović, D., Budney, A. J., Le Foll, B., & Hall, W. D. (2021). Clinical management of cannabis withdrawal. *Addiction, 117*(7), 2075–2095. https://doi.org/10.1111/add.15743

Drug Enforcement Agency (DEA). (n.d.). *Drug scheduling.* https://www.dea.gov/drug-information/drug-scheduling

Gilchrist, K. (2023, May 11). *These European countries are pushing to legalize weed—but the EU is not on board.* CNBC. https://www.cnbc.com/2023/05/11/germany-czechia-luxem-bourg-netherlands-push-to-legalize-cannabis.html

Government of the Netherlands. (n.d.). *Toleration policy regarding soft drugs and cof-feeshops.* https://www.government.nl/topics/drugs/toleration-policy-regarding-soft-drugs-and-coffee-shops

Grinspoon, P. (2020, April 10). *Medical marijuana.* Harvard Health Blog. https://www.health.harvard.edu/blog/medical-marijuana-2018011513085

Institute of International Education. (2023, November 13). *Leading destinations for U.S. study abroad students 2021/22.* Open Doors Report on International Educational Exchange. https://opendoorsdata.org/data/us-study-abroad/leading-destinations/

Massachusetts Cannabis Information. (n.d.). *How to get a medical marijuana card in Massachusetts.* https://massachusettscannabis.org/mmj-card

Matthews, A. L., & Hickey, C. (2023, November 7). *More U.S. states are regulating marijuana.* CNN. https://www.cnn.com/2023/04/20/us/states-where-marijuana-is-legal-dg/index.html

Metrik, J., & McCarty, K. N. (2023). Cannabis withdrawal. In D. C. D'Souza, D. Castle, & S. R. Murray (Eds.), *Marijuana and madness* (pp. 285–298). Cambridge University Press. https://doi.org/10.1017/9781108943246.028

National Academies of Sciences, Engineering, and Medicine (2017). *The health effects of can-nabis and cannabinoids: The current state of evidence and recommendations for research.* National Academies Press. https://doi.org/10.17226/24625

National Institutes of Health. (2021, September 8). *Marijuana use at historic high among college-aged adults in 2020.* https://www.nih.gov/news-events/news-releases/marijuana-use-historic-high-among-college-aged-adults-2020

New Frontier Data. (2021). The global cannabis report: Growth and trends through 2025. https://f.hubspotusercontent10.net/hubfs/3324860/Reports/NFD-GlobalCannabisReport.pdf

North, C., & Loukas, A. (2023). Marijuana use behaviors on Texas college campuses. *Addictive Behavior, 141,*107634. National Library of Medicine. https://doi.org/10.1016/j.addbeh.2023.107634

Sabaghi, D. (2022a, March 7). *France enters the medical cannabis industry.* Forbes. https://www.forbes.com/sites/dariosabaghi/2022/03/07/france-enters-the-medical-cannabis-industry/?sh=5705e13d1a0d

Sabaghi, D. (2022b, March 30). *You can risk death penalty for cannabis in these countries.* Forbes. https://www.forbes.com/sites/dariosabaghi/2022/03/30/you-can-risk-death-penalty-for-cannabis-in-these-countries/?sh=5a7697117c8e

Sabaghi, D. (2024, January 4). *Barcelona City Council threatens to shut down cannabis social clubs.* Forbes. https://www.forbes.com/sites/dariosabaghi/2024/01/04/barcelona-city-council-threatens-to-shut-down-cannabis-social-clubs/?sh=28aec8443331

Sprovieri, C., & Fullick, F. (2024). Traveling Abroad with Medication. In J. Pollard & K. S. Priebe (Eds.), *Convergence of litigation, policy, and standards: Building the informed practi-tioner in education abroad risk management.* The Forum on Education Abroad. doi.org/10.36366/SIA.5.978-1-952376-41-2.14

The Forum on Education Abroad and NAFSA: Association of International Educators. (2021). *Responsible education abroad: Best practices for health, safety, and security.* https://www.forumea.org/responsible-education-abroad-best-practices-for-health-safety-and-secu-rity.html

The Forum on Education Abroad. (2020). *Standards of good practice for education abroad, Sixth edition.* doi.org/10.36366/S.978-1-952376-04-7

Transportation Security Administration (TSA). (n.d.). *Medical marijuana.* https://www.tsa.gov/travel/security-screening/whatcanibring/items/medical-marijuana

UK Foreign Travel Advice. (2024, January 15). *Local laws and customs. Jamaica.* https://www.gov.uk/foreign-travel-advice/jamaica/local-laws-and-customs

U.S. Department of Justice. (2024, May 16). *Justice Department submits proposed regulation to reschedule marijuana*. Office of Public Affairs. https://www.justice.gov/opa/pr/justice-department-submits-proposed-regulation-reschedule-marijuana

Weinstein, A. M., & Gorelick, D. A. (2011). Pharmacological treatment of cannabis dependence. *Current Pharmaceutical Design, 17*(14), 1351–1358. https://doi.org/10.2174/138161211796150846

Yeung, J. (2023, February 1). *Hong Kong is criminalizing CBD as a 'dangerous drug' alongside heroin*. CNN. https://www.cnn.com/2023/01/31/business/hong-kong-cbd-ban-businesses-intl-hnk/index.html

# Shifting Sands: Evolution of Understanding Risk

# 17

## The Identity Kaleidoscope: Formation, Expression, and Experience Informing the Shared Enterprise of Mitigating Risks

**Mark Beirn**

## Introduction

In previous chapters, the authors examined legal cases and policies that shape the way education abroad practitioners support the health and safety of students abroad. They identified certain identity categories that are factored into this important work. Departing from the legal case study and policy analysis in the first two parts of the volume, "The Evolution of Our Understanding of Risk" section begins with a focus on the formation of identities. This introduction will delve into the conditions that lead to the construction of identities, such as race, ethnicity, gender, sex, (dis)ability, religion, nationality, marital status, age, criminal background, citizenship, and immigration status, thus setting the stage for an examination of how these identities are regularly defined and redefined through law and legal decisions; by community and social practices; in protest and political action; through migration and (im)mobility; and inscribed and reinforced by the physical environment. Undergirding the work of education abroad professionals with the specific cultural contexts and historical processes that have defined these identity categories allows the field to modify current approaches to global risk management and build communities of support in areas that have been historically neglected or marginalized.

Students' identities are rooted in social interaction, academic work, and political action on and off campus. As such, the work to understand the value and power of identity creation is assisted by a brief discussion of key academic theories and milestone events that underscore identity categories. A brief overview of intercultural communications, intersectionality, queer theory, disability and crip theories, and critical race theory will provide the intellectual scaffolding for a subsequent discussion of identity formation, reassignment, mimicking, and masking in a complex process of legal and social negotiations in the United States, broadly defined, and beyond. The following chapters will focus on theory and praxis outside the United States, providing additional frameworks, best practices, and advice on working with students engaged in education abroad at critical moments in their identity formation. Taken a whole, this section presents a critical analysis of student positionality and proposes actions to navigate the uneven and shifting power dynamics of higher education to aid education abroad practitioners in identifying and mitigating risk to reduce the potential for harm.

Education abroad professionals will be prompted through this section to consider various ways the identities our students shift in and out of are shaped, defined, challenged, and reassigned. Drawing attention to this allows education abroad professionals to recognize the kinds of identity-based risks not conventionally covered by insurance products, healthcare providers, and risk assessments. These processes must factor into the work you do, from the obvious to the less apparent inequities these students may face. Education abroad professionals must think expansively about the kinds of resources and responses necessary to support all students, and ways to recognize and respond to injury or violence that occurs as a direct or indirect response to one's individual or collective identity.

## Defining Risk in the United States

In *Freaks of Fortune: The Emerging World of Capitalism and Risk in America*, historian Jonathan Levy (2012) locates the historical foundations of contemporary American "risk" within a racial and gendered transatlantic capitalism that sought financial instruments like insurance to protect against bodily harm (harm to able bodies, white bodies) and loss of property (including women, enslaved African and indigenous Americans, and whiteness). Recognizing the historical roots of risk and parameters of risk mitigation in the United States is a critical step in advancing your ability to identify the gaps in current approaches, while also recognizing and then inhibiting the intentional or unintentional impulse to view identities as a risk factor instead of an asset to student travelers. Anything short of this would numb your tongues instead of advocating for students in the face of discrimination and identity-based violence, both physical and psychological, whether at customs and immigration checkpoints, in a doctor's office, on public transportation, or within campus environments.

Students come to education abroad offices with some aspects of their identities more fully formed than others. Indeed, identity factors often drive student interest in pursuing an education abroad experience. Practitioners of education abroad must prepare themselves and these students for the "identity-based risks" discussed by Brittani Smit in the upcoming chapter "Preparing for and Mitigating Identity-based Risk On-Site" (2024), that do not abate when traveling abroad. These risks, the "isms" and "obias" of the world, include racism, sexism, ageism, ableism, homophobia, anti-Semitism, Islamophobia, and anti-Asian discrimination do not go away; they manifest in new ways that exacerbate the already challenging experiences of education abroad, whether as state-sanctioned violence or community trauma. These categories of differences such as race, age, ability, religion, sexual orientation, gender identity, and national origin are dynamic and essential aspects of identity that make discussions of student development and risk management essential. Overlooked or unacknowledged, these factors can lead to dangerous situations and an erosion of trust between education abroad practitioners and the students you seek to support throughout their sojourns abroad. Trust is at the foundation of this work.

## Theoretical Frameworks

Education abroad practitioners will be familiar with intercultural communication theories that examine how individuals from different cultural backgrounds interact, exchange information, and negotiate meaning (Hofstede, 1980; Philipsen, 1982). They offer a framework for understanding how students from different backgrounds navigate their identities within a complex higher education environment. Central concepts such as cultural identity, intercultural competence, and identity negotiation are pertinent to exploring the dynamics of student identity on U.S. college campuses. Students bring a myriad of cultural backgrounds, leading to interactions that shape their

identity negotiation processes. Studying abroad has been central in promoting intercultural competence (Bennett, 1993; Paige, 2003), the ability to
interact effectively with people from different cultures, seen as essential for
students to navigate diverse social practices, spaces, and values. Yet, implicit
within intercultural communication is an assumption of a host culture and
a visiting culture operating in a balanced power dynamic. Power hierarchies
are more or less absent as students are taught how to unlock the essential
qualities of the host culture in order to adapt and assimilate effectively.

As a corrective to this, intersectionality provides intercultural communications with an analytical framework for interrogating the identity, culture, and power imbalances inherent to education abroad. Responding to
second-wave feminist theory, Kimberlee Crenshaw (1989) posits that individuals' identities are shaped by and in relation to the interconnected web
of social categories, such as race, gender, class, sexuality, and ability. When
discussing student identity on college campuses, intersectionality provides
a kaleidoscopic lens to understand how these factors influence experiences,
perspectives, and opportunities. Intersectionality reveals that identities are
relational and subject to imbalanced power structures. Student experiences
cannot be understood in isolation from one another. This opens up space to
consider multiple factors of difference, such as race, ability, gender identity
and expression, (dis)ability, nationality and immigration status, and more,
revealing the shifting power dynamics embedded in these relationships.

A person's race, gender, sexuality, disability, and socioeconomic status
interlock to form a complex identity in relation to extant power structures
(Collins, 1990). Intersectionality highlights the ways in which identity formation is influenced by the interplay of various factors and experiences. The
following theories provide texture to this concept of intersectionality.

Queer theory challenges conventional notions of gender and sexuality
binaries rooted in either the biological or the social (Saraswati & Shaw, 2021).
It emphasizes that identity is not fixed but fluid and constructed within social
and historical contexts. Often providing a view from the periphery of society,
Queer theory highlights the impact of heteronormativity and cisnormativity
on identity formation, illustrating how individuals navigate societal expectations (such as marriage, children, monogamy, and dress) to express their
authentic selves. Queer theory acknowledges the multiplicity of sexual and
gender identities, underscoring the importance of allowing individuals to
define their identities beyond normative boundaries.

Crip theory, also known as disability theory or disability studies, is an
academic and activist framework that critically examines the social, cultural, political, and historical aspects of disability. It challenges traditional

understandings of disability, moving beyond a medical or individualized perspective to explore disability as a complex intersection of identity, culture, and social experience. Crip theory seeks to disrupt ableist norms, advocate for disability justice, and promote the empowerment and inclusion of disabled individuals. In her book, *Feminist, Queer, Crip*, Alison Kafer (2013) challenges society to approach disability not merely as a problem to be solved but integrated and accounted for beyond the prescriptions of law.

Absent in the aforementioned theories is race and its social constructions. Critical race theory (CRT) scrutinizes the ways in which race becomes a category of difference that allows for de jure and de facto discrimination and segregation (Crenshaw, 1989). As a process, racism—be it anti-Blackness, anti-Semitism, Islamophobia, etc.—is embedded within societal structures and institutions. CRT exposes the power dynamics that perpetuate inequities along racial lines and shape how individuals navigate their racial identities in communities and with governments and state actors. By highlighting how legal and social frameworks influence identity formation, marginalized racial groups challenge systemic racism and construct identities rooted in resilience, resistance, protest, and political action.

Taken together, these theories provide a framework that highlights identity formation is not linear, but a dynamic process influenced by personal agency, societal norms, law, and structural inequalities. Acknowledging the complexities of identity formation requires a holistic approach that embraces diversity, challenges normative constructs, and empowers marginalized groups to reshape their identities within a complex and ever-evolving landscape.

## Processes of Identity Formation

The work of translating markers of identity from the U.S.-American context into other cultural, linguistic, historical contexts can be challenging, yet understanding their construction can reveal important ways to support international travelers. For example, discussing the constraints of translating BIPOC—Black, Indigenous, People of Color—from a U.S.-American context into the French context opens up an opportunity to discuss the legacies of French colonialism, racism, and social and linguistic hierarchies (Lechene, 2023). It is prudent to retool our machinery to account for identity formations that so often present themselves as "risk" instead of points of entry for cultural engagement. What follows is a necessarily incomplete discussion of the ways in which identities are shaped and defined through law, social practice, mobility and migration, protest and political action, and in the built environment. In understanding the logic of these processes, education abroad professionals may more effectively equip student travelers.

## Law and the Legal Construction of Identity

The relationship between identity and laws in the United States and elsewhere is intricate and multifaceted. Laws both reflect and shape societal norms, offering opportunities for empowerment and recognition, while also perpetuating exclusion and marginalization. Whether it is gender identity, racial designation, citizenship, (dis)ability, marital status, or more, the legal landscape plays a role in influencing how individuals perceive themselves, how society perceives them, and the rights and privileges they can access.

Michael Omiand Howard Winant (1986) developed the concept of "racial formation theory" to explain how laws and legal practices construct and transform race by social, economic, and political forces. Using the U.S. Census and state definitions of race, Omi's work challenges the notion that race is a fixed biological concept by emphasizing its historical legal construction and change over time (Omi, 2001). According to Omi, racial classifications written into the U.S. Census contribute to the transformation and codification of racial identities in the United States every 10 years. These categories extend far beyond the White/Black binary and include a variety of categories that reflect the imprecise and mercurial nature of race as a category of difference. He highlights how the Census has evolved from categorizing individuals into broad racial groups based on external physical characteristics to more intricate classifications that reflect social and cultural perceptions of race. The staying power of Census racial categories also perpetuates the idea that racial categories are objective and unchanging, despite their fluid and context-dependent nature. The Census shapes the way people identify themselves and how they are recognized by society, including our campuses.

Laws also play a pivotal role in shaping societal norms and values. In a 2014 talk at Washington University in St. Louis, Omi discussed a legal case from 1983 involving Susie Guillory Phipps, a white woman from Louisiana who learned at the age of 43 that the state of Louisiana had classified her as "colored" on her birth certificate following an antiquated legal racial calculus. Phipps sued the State of Louisiana unsuccessfully to have her racial identity changed to reflect her own understanding of her identity. She prevailed only when the law was revoked by the state legislature. Omi cites this case as an example of the ways in which legal decisions and law shape individual identities even if they are at odds with one's own self-perception. Understanding how identity categories such as a race can change under different legal jurisdictions can help you to prepare students for the possibility of racial reassignment while traveling abroad.

Legal frameworks reflect cultural and moral values, often impacting how individuals perceive themselves and others. Others are aspirational. For example, landmark civil rights legislation such as the Civil Rights Act of 1964 reflects a shift in society by providing legal protections for unequal treatment and discrimination. Legal rights and protections granted by laws contribute to identity formation. For marginalized groups, achieving legal recognition and protection can empower individuals to embrace their identities and assert their rights. However, laws can also be wielded as tools of marginalization and exclusion. Historical instances such as the Jim Crow laws in the U.S. South or its antecedents in laws of separation in New England demonstrate how legal frameworks can reinforce systemic racism and shape identities (Luxenberg, 2019). Laws that legitimatize some behaviors and others that criminalize certain behaviors or stigmatize specific identities, often along lines of gender or sexual expression, contribute to a sense of belonging for some while alienating and stigmatizing others.

Immigration laws provide an illuminating example of how legal frameworks can shape identity. The United States' complex immigration policies influence how individuals are categorized, labeled, and treated. Laws such as the Chinese Exclusion Act of 1882, the Immigration Act of 1924, or the more recent Executive Order and Presidential Proclamations collectively and informally known as the Muslim Ban reinforced racial hierarchies and influenced how immigrant groups were racialized and criminalized in law and society (The United States Government, 2021). The language used in legal documents can have significant implications for identity. Terms such as "alien," "illegal immigrant," "terrorist," or "criminal" carry connotations that can shape public perception, restrict access to resources, inhibit mobility, and influence an individual's self-concept. Language choice in laws can reinforce stigmas, hinder integration, and perpetuate negative stereotypes.

### Social Practices: Negotiating Identity Within Community and Culture

Social practices play a vital role in shaping identity, both at the community and individual levels, offering individuals a sense of belonging and shared heritage. Festivals, rituals, and traditions serve as social practices that connect individuals with their cultural roots (Cohen, 1988), while career pathways, fashion choices, and foodways offer opportunities for expression and connection. Cultural identity, shaped by these practices, becomes a dynamic expression of shared values, beliefs, and history, influencing how individuals perceive themselves within a broader cultural context.

Language plays a pivotal role in identity construction, reflecting cultural affiliations, social roles, and individual perspectives (Gee, 2014). The words chosen, linguistic nuances, and communication styles contribute to the development of identity. Encouraging students to engage in the language(s) of their host cultures reduces risk. Language as a social practice is not only a means of conveying information but also a powerful tool for expressing and negotiating one's identity within diverse social settings.

Social practices surrounding gender roles also significantly impact identity formation. The expectations and norms associated with masculinity and femininity influence individuals' self-perception and behaviors (West & Zimmerman, 1987). Family structures, educational systems, and media representation reinforce or challenge these gender norms, contributing to the complex mosaic of gender identities. The advent of social media has introduced novel dimensions to identity formation, representing a contemporary form of social practice. Platforms like Facebook, Instagram, and X (formerly Twitter) provide spaces for individuals to construct online personas, engage in self-presentation strategies, and connect with virtual communities (Boyd, 2014). However, the digital realm also introduces challenges, including the potential for stereotype reinforcement and the impact of online interactions on self-esteem (Valkenburg & Peter, 2011). For education abroad professionals, these practices present challenges for our students as they cross legal jurisdictions where social media surveillance is pervasive.

Identity formation is not confined to singular social practices but rather emerges from the interconnectedness of various elements. Cultural practices, language use, gender roles, and digital interactions collectively shape the complex fabric of individual and collective identities.

### Migration and Mobility: Crossing Borders and Belongings

Migration often involves individuals leaving familiar cultural landscapes and engaging with new ones, leading to shifts in cultural identity. As people adapt to and adopt elements of the host culture, they undergo a process of acculturation and exchange (Curtin, 1984). The negotiation between the heritage culture and the host culture becomes a central aspect of identity formation (Berry, 1997). Cultural identity, shaped by the interplay of migration and acculturation, reflects the fusion of diverse cultural elements. The complexity of this process is evident in studies exploring the experiences of immigrants, such as those by Phinney (1990) and Schwartz et al. (2011), which highlight the dynamic nature of cultural identity as individuals navigate multiple cultural influences. Studies by Massey et al. (1993) and Portes and Rumbaut (2006) illustrate the impact of migration on economic identities, emphasizing the ways in which individuals negotiate their roles within new economic contexts. Economic success or challenges experienced during migration can significantly shape one's self-perception and sense of identity.

Recognizing that when students navigate migration, whether relocating to or within the United States for higher education and then again outside the United States to study abroad, they grapple with shifting social and legal contexts that contribute to their evolving identities. Students may experience a change in the way they are identified legally and socially when traveling abroad. A student from a rural background moving to an urban campus faces the intersection of rural–urban dynamics with other identity markers, such as class, race, and gender. An undocumented student confronts the anxiety of deportation or being denied reentry along with the stigma of being the subject of heated political discourse in the United States. International students coming to the United States for education are often racially reassigned to fit into a U.S.-centric racial category. Students traveling on U.S. passports may suddenly become aware of or identify with their own identity as American nationals in ways they did not have to when they were at home.

An essential component to international mobility is the passport. More than just a mere travel document, passports have a profound impact on the formation of identity when crossing borders. Beyond facilitating international mobility, passports play a role in shaping how individuals perceive themselves and how they are perceived by others, reflecting nationality, sex/gender, cultural ties, legal status, and the broader concept of belonging. Passports encapsulate a person's lived experiences, social positioning, and humanity as seen through the eyes of the state and facilitate access to resources and infrastructure.

Undocumented students often find themselves in a liminal space, navigating the complexities of being in a country without legal authorization. The constant awareness of their undocumented status shapes their educational, social, and personal experiences, influencing the construction of their identity. Studies by Gonzales (2011) and Teranishi (2010) highlight the challenges faced by undocumented students, including the fear of deportation, limited access to educational resources, and the constant negotiation of a dual identity—straddling the cultural ties of their heritage and the legal challenges in their host country. These challenges become integral to the formation of identity as undocumented students grapple with the tension between their personal aspirations and societal constraints.

Passports carry profound symbolic significance in the context of identity formation for migrants. For undocumented individuals, the absence of a valid passport or residency authorization becomes emblematic of their marginalized status, limiting their mobility and reinforcing their sense of invisibility. The concept of "symbolic violence," as introduced by Bourdieu (1991), helps us understand the impact of lacking a valid passport on identity. The denial of official documentation reflects the exclusion and inequality experienced by undocumented individuals, contributing to the construction of an identity marked by societal constraints.

### Protest and Political Action

Protests and demonstrations are often platforms for students to voice concerns, advocate for change, and negotiate their identities on college campuses and in their own communities. Guidance provided to students domestically on how to engage in protests safely is often more robust and nuanced than the restrictions abroad informed by the U.S. Department of State Travel Advisory to avoid local protests. A.J. Leeds's chapter, "Risks of Protest Participation While on Education Abroad" (2024), bridges the gap between campus guidance and study abroad policies with examples of overseas protest movements and how practitioners should respond to support student safety and well-being. Demonstrations not only address immediate issues but also play a crucial role in shaping the identity of individuals and communities. Identities around racial categories, sexuality and gender, veteran status, and (dis)ability, to name a few, have emerged through protest as diverse student groups advocate for rights and representation through activism, conflict, and dialogue with different stakeholders.

Research by Gordon (2018) and Ahmed (2012) explores how activism within area studies fosters critical consciousness and shapes identities. Students involved in protests often develop a sense of belonging within their respective areas of study, challenging traditional narratives, and contributing to the construction of a more inclusive identity. Area and ethnic studies academic programs gained prominence during the civil rights and social justice movements of the 1960s and 1970s as students expressed desires to challenge Eurocentric and monocultural approaches to education and to ensure that the experiences of underrepresented communities are acknowledged and studied. Many students felt that traditional curricula ignored the contributions and experiences of African American, Latinx, Indigenous, Asian American, and other marginalized communities. Protests were often sparked by the lack of representation in existing courses and the need for courses that addressed social inequalities, racial justice, and cultural diversity.

Similarly, campus protests focused on gender and disability issues have provided spaces for individuals to challenge societal norms, advocate for inclusivity, and negotiate their identities. Studies by Fine and Asch (1988) and Erevelles (2011) emphasize the importance of activism in shaping identities within the context of gender and disability. Participation in protests allows individuals to challenge ableism, sexism, and other forms of discrimination, contributing to the development of a more empowered and intersectional sense of self.

Protests advocating for veterans' rights on college campuses served as a platform for military-affiliated students to address issues such as educational access, mental health support, and recognition of their service. Woodward and Schulenberg (2015) and Kim (2011) have shown how engaging in activism allowed veterans to negotiate their identities in a civilian setting and challenge stereotypes associated with military service. Protests become spaces for veterans to assert their unique identities, share their perspectives, and bridge the gap between military and civilian life, contributing to the formation of a more holistic identity beyond their service roles.

There are countless examples and ongoing movements in American history that demonstrate how protests have not only influenced legal frameworks but also shaped social perceptions of identity and rights. They also underscore the interconnectedness of activism, law, and social change in shaping collective identities and advancing equality. Acknowledging these connections can help build and sustain trust between students and practitioners during study abroad programs, while opening opportunities to discuss locally specific actions.

## Built Environment: The Social Production of Space and Identity Expression

Finally, the built environment serves as a powerful canvas upon which identities are painted, contributing to the complex interplay of social constructs. As individuals navigate their surroundings, the design, accessibility, and cultural context of the built environment contribute to shaping their sense of self. Urban theorists, such as Henri Lefebvre, provide valuable insights into the ways in which the built environment shapes social practices and identities. Lefebvre's "The Production of Space" posits that space is not merely a neutral backdrop but a socially produced construct that reflects power relations, cultural norms, and societal structures (1991). Constructed and naturalized spaces, for example, campuses, dorms, parks, airports, street corners, and crossings, reflect and reproduce societal norms. While abroad, students engage in study, research, professional development, and community engagement in diverse settings such as urban and suburban campuses, in rural communities, on remote field stations, and aboard sailing vessels.

The college campus is not merely a collection of structures; it is a canvas upon which the intricate tapestry of student identities is woven. The built environment, encompassing spaces such as toilets, bedrooms, disability access points, and areas marked by racial, transgender, and gender dynamics, plays a pivotal role in shaping intercultural and intersectional identities and reinforcing or liberating societal hierarchies. Spaces marked by racial and gender dynamics, such as lecture halls adorned with Eurocentric art or portraits of statesmen, may perpetuate feelings of exclusion among students of color. These spaces symbolize colonial influences and contribute to the construction of an intersectional identity that navigates both racial heritage and the pursuit of education.

One of the most highly politicized spaces over the past decade is the public toilet. Toilets embody more than just physical functionality; they serve as embodiments of identity and access. The design of accessible toilets reveals societal attitudes toward disability. These spaces can be liberating or stigmatizing, depending on their design and placement. They intersect with the experiences of students with disabilities, shaping their sense of belonging within the campus community. Gender-segregated restrooms reinforce a binary understanding of gender identity, influencing transgender and nonbinary students' sense of belonging. This shaping of identity through spatial design illustrates Lefebvre's assertion that space is a product of social and power relations (1991).

The presence of gender-neutral restrooms communicates inclusivity and recognition of diverse gender expressions. Their absence, conversely, underscores the exclusion of transgender and nonbinary students from the campus narrative. Nevertheless, frank and open conversations about toilets and bathrooms on campus and abroad can be a starting point for rich comparative conversations about gender, privacy, public access, hygiene, and infrastructure.

Bathrooms are also sites of power imbalance and segregation. While plenty of sociological research has suggested that our muted, passive interactions with most strangers in restrooms are governed by strict yet unspoken behavior codes, Mary Anne Case, a professor at the University of Chicago Law School, has found that a significant amount of active networking takes place in men's rooms. Case's exploration of gendered spaces within legal contexts provides a theoretical foundation for understanding how bathrooms become sites of identity negotiation (Case, 1996). The legal and societal regulations surrounding restrooms contribute to the reinforcement or resistance of traditional gender norms, influencing individuals' self-perception and societal expectations.

Residence hall rooms offer a unique vantage point to examine intercultural interactions. Shared living spaces bring together students from diverse backgrounds, fostering cross-cultural encounters. These spaces become sites of negotiation and mutual learning, where students engage with others' traditions, customs, and perspectives. However, residence hall rooms can also be fraught with challenges. Cultural differences in decorating styles and personal preferences can lead to misunderstandings and discomfort. The built environment shapes the ways in which students approach these encounters, either fostering cultural exchange or reinforcing divisions.

Rooms designated for disability access underscore societal attitudes toward difference and inclusion. The placement and design of ramps and elevators communicate the institution's commitment to accommodating diverse needs. Yet, these spaces can also be segregated, reinforcing a sense of otherness. Similarly, spaces marked by racial dynamics, such as multicultural centers, can create a sense of belonging and empowerment, but they can also limit students' intersectional identities and lead to tokenization if they merely serve as symbolic gestures without substantive support.

The built and physical environment is a critical medium through which intercultural and intersectional student identities are constructed and reflected. Recognizing the profound impact of the physical environment enables institutions to reimagine their campuses as spaces of inclusion, empowerment, and transformation.

## Conclusion

Student identities are dynamically shaped by a web of interconnected factors—laws, social practices, migration, protest, and the built environment—each interacting with gender, sex, race, religion, disability, age, and more. Through the lenses of intercultural communication theory, intersectionality, queer theory, crip theory, and critical race theory, this chapter's introduction highlights the intricate ways in which these influences inform students' identity formation and their plans to study abroad. It underscores the importance of recognizing and navigating the complexities of these intersections to create inclusive educational environments that honor a multiplicity of identities and experiences in the shared enterprise of mitigating risk and reducing harm.

# References

Anzaldúa, G. (1987). *Borderlands/La Frontera: The New Mestiza.* Aunt Lute Books.

Bennett, M. J. (1993). Towards Ethnorelativism: A developmental model of intercultural sensitivity. In R. M. Paige (Ed.), *Education for the intercultural experience* (pp. 21–71). Intercultural Press.

Berry, J. W. (1997). Immigration, Acculturation, and Adaptation. *Applied Psychology, 46*(1), 5–34.

Bourdieu, P. (1991). *Language and Symbolic Power.* Harvard University Press.

Boyd, D. (2014). *It's complicated: The social lives of networked teens.* Yale University Press.

Case, M. (2010). Why not abolish laws of urinary segregation?.In H. Molotch & L. Noren (Eds.), *Toilet: Public Restrooms and the Politics of Sharing* (pp. 211-225). New York University Press. https://doi.org/10.18574/nyu/9780814759646.003.0022

Cohen, A. P. (1988). Culture as identity and practice. *Anthropological Theory, 1*(1), 17–28.

Collins, P. H. (1990). *Black feminist thought knowledge, consciousness, and the politics of empowerment.* New york, NY: Routledge.

Crenshaw, K. (1989). *Demarginalizing the intersection of race and sex: A Black feminist critique of antidiscrimination doctrine, feminist theory and antiracist politics.* University of Chicago Legal Forum, 139-167.

Crenshaw, K. (1991). Mapping the margins: Intersectionality, identity politics, and violence against women of color. *Stanford Law Review, 43*(6), 1241–1299.

Curtin, P. (1984). *Cross-cultural trade in world history.* Cambridge University Press. https://doi.org/10.1017/CBO9780511661198

Davis, L. J. (2013). *The disability studies reader.* Routledge.

Delgado, R., & Stefancic, J. (Eds.). (2001). *Critical Race Theory: The cutting edge.* Temple University Press.

Dicker, R. (2018). *Title IX: A brief history with documents.* Routledge.

Gee, J. P. (2014). *An introduction to discourse analysis: Theory and method (4th ed.).* Routledge.

Gitlin, T. (1987). *The Sixties: Years of hope, days of rage.* Bantam Books.

Gonzales, R. G. (2011). Learning to be illegal: Undocumented youth and shifting legal contexts in the transition to adulthood. *American Sociological Review, 76*(4), 602–619.

Gordon, L. R. (2018). *What fanon said: A philosophical introduction to his life and thought.* New York, NY: Fordham University Press.

Hall, S. (1992). *The question of cultural identity.* In S. Hall, D. Held, & T. McGrew (Eds.), *Modernity and its futures* (pp. 274–316). Polity Press.

Harris, C. I. (1993). Whiteness as property. *Harvard Law Review, 106*(8), 1707.https://ssrn.com/abstract=927850

Hofstede, G. (1980). *Culture's consequences: International differences in work-related values.* Sage Publications.

Holsaert, F., Prescod, M., Noonan, N., Richardson, J., Robinson, B. G., Young, J. S., & Zellner, D. M. (2012). *Hands on the freedom plow: Personal accounts by women in SNCC.* University of Illinois Press.

Jacobson, M. F. (1998). *Whiteness of a different color: European immigrants and the alchemy of race.* Harvard University Press.

Kafer, A. (2013). *Feminist. Queer. Crip.* Indiana University Press.

Kennedy, R. (2002). The racialization of legal interpretation. *The Yale Law Journal, 112*(4), 625–751.

Lechene, J. [@joris.lechen, @joris.explains] .(2023, August 19). *How do you translate social constructs in another language?* [video] TikTok. https://www.tiktok.com/@joris_explains/video/7268979275691298081

Leeds., A. J. (2024). Risks of protest participation while on education abroad. In J. Pollard & K. S. Priebe (Eds.),*Convergence of litigation, policy, and standards: Building the informed practitioner in education abroad risk management.* The Forum on Education Abroad. doi.org/10.36.366/SIA.5.978-1-952376-41-2.15

Lefebvre, H. (1991). *The production of space.* Oxford: Blackwell.

Levy, J. (2012). *Freaks of fortune: The emerging world of capitalism and risk in America.* Harvard University Press.

Luxeburg, S. (2019, February 12). The forgotten northern origins of Jim Crow. *Time.* https://time.com/5527029/jim-crow-plessy-history/

Mamdani, M. (2002). *When victims become killers: Colonialism, nativism, and the genocide in Rwanda.* Princeton University Press.

Massey, D. S., Arango, J., Hugo, G., Kouaouci, A., Pellegrino, A., & Taylor, J. E. (1993). Theories of international migration: A review and appraisal. *Population and Development Review, 19*(3), 431–466.

Omi, M. (2001). Racial formation. In R. Delgado & J. Stefancic (Eds.), *Critical Race Theory: The cutting edge* (pp. 65–77). Temple University Press.

Omi, M. (2014, September 26). *Racial categories and the instability of race.* [Presentation]. Washington University seminar, St. Louis, MO, United States.

Omi, M., & Katagiri, Y. (2006). Race and equality in U.S. Census and identity formation in the United States. *Daedalus, 135*(2), 55–66.

Omi, M., & Winant, H. (1986). *Racial formation in the United States: From the 1960s to the 1980s.* Routledge.

Orrenius, P. M., & Zavodny, M. (2018). *Immigrants' changing labor market assimilation in the United States. IZA World of Labor, 403.*

Paige, R. M. (2003). The intercultural development inventory: A critical review of the research literature. *Journal of Intercultural Communication, 6,* 53–61.

Philipsen, G. (1992). *Speaking culturally: Explorations in social communication.* State University of New York Press.

Rosen, R. (2000). *The world split open: How the modern women's movement changed America.* Penguin Books.

Sedgwick, E. K. (1990). *Epistemology of the closet.* University of California Press.

Saraswati, L., & Shaw, B. (2021). Feminist and queer theory: An intersectional and transnational reader. Oxford University Press.

The United States Government. (2021, January 21). *Proclamation on ending discriminatory bans on entry to the United States.* The White House. www.whitehouse.gov/briefing-room/presidential-actions/2021/01/20/proclamation-ending-discriminatory-bans-on-entry-to-the-united-states/

Tsui, B. (2015, December 14). Choose your own identity. *New York Times.* https://www.nytimes.com/2015/12/14/magazine/choose-your-own-identity.html

Tushnet, M. (2010). *Defining civil rights in the 21st century.* Princeton University Press.

U.S. Census Bureau. (2020). *Questions planned for the 2020 Census and American Community Survey.* Retrieved from https://www.census.gov/programs-surveys/decennial-census/2020-census/planned-questions.html

Valkenburg, P. M., & Peter, J. (2011). Online communication among adolescents: An integrated model of its attraction, opportunities, and risks. *Journal of Adolescent Health, 48*(2), 121–127.

West, C., & Zimmerman, D. H. (1987). Doing gender. *Gender & Society, 1*(2), 125–151.

Westwood, S., & Callahan, J. L. (2019). Creating inclusive campus environments: Advancing intersectionality in college student affairs. *Journal of Diversity in Higher Education, 12*(4), 347–360.

# 18

## Preparing for and Mitigating Identity-Based Risk On-Site

**Brittani Smit, Ph.D.**

## Introduction

According to the Open Doors Report on International Educational Exchange, 32% of U.S. students studying abroad identified as students of color in the 2021–2022 academic year compared to 22% ten years earlier (Institute of International Education [IIE], 2022). Although there is still work to be done to achieve equity in access, particularly concerning the percentage of students of color studying abroad, this shift in demographics marks a significant step in the ongoing diversification of the field of students studying abroad in the United States. As practitioners work toward increasing access to education abroad for historically underrepresented students from various groups, it is crucial to pay equal attention to acknowledging and addressing the unique challenges they may face due to discrimination and bias abroad. In today's social and geopolitical climate, identity-based factors such as race, ethnicity, gender, sexual orientation, and religion can significantly influence how individuals are perceived, treated, and integrated into the host community. This leads to challenges and opportunities that necessitate thoughtful advising and support for positive and safe education abroad experiences.

Despite the growing emphasis on diversity, equity, inclusion, and belonging in education abroad, both students and program providers can overlook or underestimate the risks tied to identity-based discrimination. Students may focus on academic and cultural enrichment, disregarding potential identity-related challenges. Similarly, providers may not adequately address these risks through-out the lifecycle of the education abroad program or offer sufficient staff training. This chapter underscores the significance of onsite personnel in risk advising and delves into their role, factors impacting awareness, legal considerations, and best practices, and includes a real-world case study, with the aim of emphasizing the collective responsibility of all stakeholders in fostering inclusivity and recognizing the role of identity in student well-being.

## Understanding Identity-Based Risk in Education Abroad

For the purposes of this chapter, the term "identity-based risk" refers to the potential harm, discrimination, or challenges that students may face due to social identity bias and attitudes toward aspects of their identities. For instance, a student from a marginalized racial or ethnic group might face xenophobia or racism while studying abroad, resulting in feelings of isolation, anxiety, and reduced participation in academic and social activities. Similarly, students may encounter prejudice, discrimination, or even legal consequences in certain countries based on their gender identity and sexual orientation, depending on the country's legal and prevailing cultural stance on LGBTQIA+ rights. Such experiences can lead to emotional distress, compromised mental health, incidents of physical violence, and litigation, and may even cause some students to withdraw from their education abroad program altogether (Center for Collegiate Mental Health, 2024).

Furthermore, discrimination can have broader repercussions beyond individual students. Incidents of discrimination can impact the experience of the entire cohort in the case of cohort-based programming. These incidents can tarnish the reputation of the education abroad program, the home institution, and the host institution, especially if not addressed adequately or if there is negative media attention. Such occurrences might dissuade prospective students from participating in similar programs or hinder institutional partnerships with specific countries. Therefore, recognizing and proactively addressing identity-based risks is paramount for creating a safe and inclusive environment for all education abroad participants. By acknowledging these potential challenges, program providers can implement strategies to mitigate risks and support students who may be more vulnerable to identity-related issues.

## The Role of Onsite Personnel in Risk Advising

Onsite personnel play a crucial role in the success of education abroad programs due to their unique position as local organizations or institutions responsible for facilitating the program. Their proximity to the host community and direct engagement with students provides them with valuable insights into the local context, culture, and potential challenges that students may encounter based on their identities. This firsthand knowledge makes them essential stakeholders in risk advising as they are best equipped to identify and address identity-based risks effectively.

However, on-site staff may hesitate or be unable to identify and support students through identity-related issues for various reasons. Firstly, they may lack comprehensive training to recognize identity-based challenges, leading to the underestimation or overlooking potential risks. Additionally, the fear of cultural insensitivity or miscommunication might hinder their ability to address sensitive identity-related matters effectively. Also, significant variations exist in how diversity, equity, and inclusion concepts are understood, interpreted, and put into practice between the United States and other countries. This disparity may lead to confusion and misunderstandings for both students and onsite staff.

Despite these challenges, through support and collaboration, on-site personnel can significantly impact the safety and well-being of students as they navigate identity-related concerns abroad. Education abroad offices and risk management teams can offer resources, training, and guidance to enhance risk advising capabilities and support onsite staff. This assistance may encompass cultural competency training, tools for responding to identity-based incidents, guidelines for collaborating with local organizations, and resources for cultivating a more inclusive environment. Additionally, comprehensive pre-departure preparations can be developed to educate students about potential challenges related to different identity groups and the available resources. It is crucial for onsite staff to earnestly embrace this responsibility as a core aspect of student safety and well-being, emphasizing the importance of providing clear, honest information about potential identity-based risks. However, in order to offer such resources and support, it is important to first build the capacity of staff to acknowledge and address these issues openly.

## Overcoming the First Hurdle: "The Conspiracy of Silence"

Derald Wing Sue's (2016) groundbreaking book, *Race Talk and the Conspiracy of Silence: Understanding and Facilitating Difficult Dialogues on Race*, sheds light on the pervasive "conspiracy of silence" that hinders open and honest dialogues on racial issues, often driven by discomfort, fear of offending others, and a lack of skills to engage in constructive conversations about race.

Applying Sue's insights to the context of education abroad programs, we can draw parallels between the conspiracy of silence concerning discrimination and bias and the hesitancy of onsite personnel to address identity-based risk.

In the context of international education, identity-based risk can include issues related to race, ethnicity, gender, sexual orientation, and religion, among others. These risks can stem from cultural differences, discriminatory practices, and legal disparities in the host country. These topics are often considered taboo, and in an industry that typically advertises smiling faces encountering jaw-dropping vistas, the realities of discrimination and bias present a challenging counter-narrative. Onsite staff are typically positioned as ambassadors and guides for host countries, a position that seemingly requires reticence, or at the very least, cautious word choice when addressing less-favorable aspects of host countries. Consequently, onsite staff may hesitate to openly address identity-based risks. This reluctance could stem from a desire to portray the country positively, fear of offending students or host communities, or a lack of cultural competency in engaging in such conversations. As a result, crucial discussions about potential risks and challenges related to students' identities may be avoided or downplayed.

To effectively mitigate identity-based risk, onsite personnel must be open, clear, and forthcoming about these issues, acknowledging that while everyone's experience is unique, there may be certain patterns or societal factors. Creating a safe and inclusive environment for all students requires addressing the unique challenges that students from different identity groups may encounter abroad. By breaking the conspiracy of silence and initiating honest discussions about identity-based risk throughout the education abroad experience, on-the-ground providers can better prepare students for potential challenges and offer appropriate support.

## Legal Considerations Across Borders

In the United States, the ethical and legal stance against discrimination of students is unequivocal, with discrimination based on race, nationality, gender, and disability being not only unethical but also illegal. This is upheld by key U.S. legislations: the Civil Rights Act of 1964 safeguards against racial discrimination; the Education Amendments of 1972 protect students from sex-based discrimination; and the Americans with Disabilities Act of 1990, the Americans with Disabilities Amendment Act of 2008, and Section 504 of the Rehabilitation Act of 1973 provide protection for students with disabilities.

These legal safeguards have been extensively tested and applied within the domestic U.S. context. However, as Sara Easler (2019) points out in her thesis *A Litigation Analysis of the Extraterritoriality of U.S. Federal Laws in International Education,* it remains unclear to what extent these protections extend beyond U.S. borders. The existing legal precedent has yielded mixed and inconsistent outcomes, with some cases raising questions about whether U.S. laws apply beyond national borders. This absence of clear guidance on rights and institutional responsibilities in extraterritorial situations creates uncertainty for both students and institutions regarding rights and obligations outside the United States. Therefore, in navigating these intricate legal and ethical considerations, the collaborative efforts of educational institutions, legal experts, and international education professionals are pivotal to ensure comprehensive protection for students abroad.

## Best Practices in Identity-Based Risk Mitigation for On-the-Ground Providers

In the absence of clear guidance regarding the extent to which U.S. laws apply to education abroad programs, providers should proactively adopt best practices in identity-based risk mitigation that encompass the entire education abroad journey. As outlined below, this includes pre-departure preparation, establishing a clear code of conduct and robust monitoring and support systems, conducting programming that connects students to local communities and providing cultural competency training for staff.

### Pre-Departure and Onsite Orientation

Before students embark on their education abroad experience, on-the-ground providers should implement comprehensive risk assessment protocols (Fischer, 2010). As outlined in sub-clause 6.1.11 of The Forum's *Standards of Good Practice for Education Abroad* (2020), this involves identifying potential identity-based risks in the host country and developing strategies to minimize them. Additionally, collecting identity-related information from previous students can help tailor support and resources to individual needs. Furthermore, aspects of identity such as "race and ethnicity should be explicitly addressed in advising, in materials for prospective applicants, and in orientation programming before departure and in-country" (Almassri et al., 2023, p. 44) to help students navigate culture shock and prepare them for the challenges they may face specifically related to their identities. This approach should be taken in regard to other dimensions of identity such as religion, gender identity, and disability as well, and onsite staff should model openness and willingness to address identity-based issues and acknowledge differences in experience based on identity.

## Cultural Competency and Antibias Training

Staff should undergo training in cultural competency and bias mitigation to better support students with diverse identities. Other important aspects of anti-bias training include awareness of the ways various identities intersect (Crenshaw, 1988) and the ability to recognize microaggressions and support students who are the target of microaggressions and bias (Almassri et al., 2023). Additionally, students should have the opportunity to attend programming that addresses identity-based risks and fosters inclusivity. These sessions can help promote intercultural dialogue among students and build empathy and mutual respect. They also provide an avenue through which students can share concerns related to their identity with onsite staff and each other and receive guidance and support.

## Monitoring and Support Systems

Establishing reporting mechanisms for incidents related to identity-based risks is crucial for two reasons. First, they enable the identification of discernible patterns of discrimination over time, guiding proactive interventions. Second, continuous incident monitoring ensures swift and targeted responses to uphold student well-being and rights. These reporting mechanisms should include ways for students to report incidents to both on-site staff and others as well, ensuring that participants are protected and able to report without fear of retribution. These reporting avenues facilitate seamless communication among stakeholders, including students' home and host institutions, legal experts, and both onsite and administrative international education professionals. As outlined in sub-clause 4.4.3 of The Forum's *Standards of Good Practice for Education Abroad* (2020), this collaborative approach not only addresses challenges comprehensively but also bolsters the safety and inclusivity of education abroad programs.

## Establishing a Clear Code of Conduct

Many organizations work across multiple countries, each governed by unique legal frameworks and rights encompassing gender, sexual orientation, relationships, substance use, speech, and disability protections. Given these international and domestic variations, a clear code of conduct helps establish a baseline of expectations for students, serving as a useful reference point for on-site staff, as outlined in sub-clauses 5.1.6, 6.1.8, and 6.2.2 of the *Standards of Good Practice for Education Abroad* (2020). Amid these intricate international and domestic variations, a clear code of conduct helps establish a baseline of expectations for students, which serves as a useful reference point for on-site staff. This code not only safeguards students but also harmonizes expectations across borders, mitigating the risk of misunderstandings, conflicts, and legal entanglements. This code should comprehensively address speech and expression, providing clarity about expectations across diverse cultural and legal contexts. This fosters an environment conducive to learning, respectful dialogue, and minimizing potential risks associated with conflicting viewpoints.

## Community Connection and Support

Identifying and establishing connections with underrepresented and marginalized communities in the host country offers invaluable benefits for students arriving in new contexts where they lack a frame of reference for understanding how they may be treated. As one example, Bingham et al. (2023) highlight that, particularly for LGBTQIA+ students, local community connections can provide valuable insight into the acceptance, visibility, and tolerance of their identity, aiding in risk identification and mitigation. Onsite staff can aid in this regard by maintaining relationships with communities related to various identity groups and sharing this information with students (The Forum on Education Abroad, 2020, clauses 4.4.5 and 4.4.6). By fostering relationships with local communities, students gain insight into potential challenges and learn skills for navigating cultural nuances. These networks enhance students' well-being, enrich their cross-cultural experiences, and allow them to learn from and connect with community members with whom they can relate.

## Case Law: King v. Board of Control (2002)

One of the most notable litigation outcomes related to identity-based discrimination in an education abroad program is the case of *King v. Board of Control* (2002), in which six African American female students from Eastern Michigan University embarked on a faculty-led education abroad program to South Africa (Easler, 2019). During this program, they were subjected to identity-based discrimination and sexual harassment by fellow male students and a male teaching assistant. Incidents of harassment began early in the program as male students invaded female students' rooms without consent, publicly used derogatory language, and engaged in sexually explicit behavior. The students attempted to report the incident onsite but were unable to do so satisfactorily, so they ultimately opted to cut their program short due to the ongoing mistreatment and filed a federal claim based on Title IX. The court ruled in favor of applying Title IX, asserting that failure to act against the sexual discrimination would unjustly hinder access to educational opportunities, including education abroad. In this instance, as women of color, the plaintiffs experienced discrimination based on both their race and gender, which as Kimberle Crenshaw's theory on intersectionality highlights, results in compounded risk. This case highlights the vulnerability of programs that do not implement adequate safeguards, such as training for staff and sufficient reporting mechanisms, ultimately resulting in exposure to litigation (Easler, 2019).

## Conclusion

As the demographics of education abroad participants continue to evolve, the need to address unique challenges tied to discrimination and bias becomes increasingly pressing. By acknowledging and navigating the complexities of identity-based risk, program providers can equip students with the knowledge, support, and resources they need to thrive while abroad. This involves breaking the "conspiracy of silence" and openly addressing the potential challenges tied to social identities, fostering intercultural dialogue, and developing robust reporting mechanisms. Through comprehensive pre-departure orientation, cultural competency, and antibias training, and fostering connections with local communities, on-site personnel can empower students to navigate challenges and seize opportunities, ensuring a transformative education abroad journey. Moreover, the creation of clear codes of conduct that address freedom of speech within diverse cultural and legal contexts can help facilitate productive cross-cultural interactions.

By collaboratively embracing best practices and fostering a culture of inclusivity, stakeholders, including on-the-ground providers, educational institutions, and legal experts, can coalesce to create safer, more transformative education abroad experiences for all students. The commitment to identity-based risk mitigation is a shared responsibility that extends across borders. By weaving this commitment into the fabric of education abroad programs, institutions send a powerful message that all students, regardless of their identities, deserve an enriching and safe education abroad experience.

## References

Almassri, A., Welch, Z., & Brunsting, N. (2023). Integrating study abroad research and practice: African American and Black Students in focus. *Frontiers: The Interdisciplinary Journal of Study Abroad, 35*(2), 40–51. https://doi.org/10.36366/frontiers.v35i1.848

Bingham, W. P., Brunsting, N., & Katsumoto, S. (2023). A systematic literature review on LGBT+ U.S. students studying abroad. *Frontiers: The Interdisciplinary Journal of Study Abroad, 35*(1), 152–187. https://doi.org/10.36366/frontiers.v35i1.736

Crenshaw, K. W. (1988). Toward a race-conscious pedagogy in legal education. *Nat'l Black LJ,* 11, 1.

Center for Collegiate Mental Health. (2024, January). 2023 Annual Report (Publication No. STA 24-147). https://ccmh.psu.edu/annual-reports

Easler, S. M. (2019). *A litigation analysis of the extraterritoriality of U.S. federal laws in international education* [Doctoral dissertation, University of South Carolina]. Scholar Commons.

Fischer, K. (2010, May 26). Study-abroad missteps remind colleges of need to train trip leaders. *The Chronicle of Higher Education.*https://www.chronicle.com/article/study-abroad-missteps-remind-colleges-of-need-to-train-trip-leaders/

Institute of International Education. (2022). Open Doors Data. *United States Study Abroad Student Profile.* https://opendoorsdata.org/data/us-study-abroad/student-profile/

King v. Board of Control of Eastern Michigan. 221 F. Supp. 2d 783 (E.D. Mich. 2002).

Sue, D. W. (2016). *Race talk and the conspiracy of silence: Understanding and facilitating difficult dialogues on race.* John Wiley & Sons.

The Forum on Education Abroad. (2020). *Standards of Good Practice for Education Abroad, Sixth Edition.* The Forum on Education Abroad. doi.org/10.36366/S.978-1-952376-04-7

# 19

# Building Cultures: Preparing International Staff for Understanding Diverse Identities of U.S. Students

**Christina Thompson and Ebony Ellis**

## Introduction

In recent years, post-COVID, an increasing number of U.S. students have been enrolling in study abroad programs. This trend can be attributed to various factors such as globalization, students' curiosity to learn about different cultures, and gaining a competitive edge in the job market. In the 2021/22 academic period, the total number of U.S. students participating in overseas study programs for academic credit was recorded at 188,753 (Institute for International Education (IIE), 2023b). According to the Institute of International Education (IIE) (2023a), during the 2021–22 academic year, 32% of the U.S. students who studied abroad identified as students of color. In the 2011–12 academic year, IIE reported that 24% of students identified as students of color.

For the purpose of this chapter, the term "diverse U.S. student identities" in the context of education abroad includes individuals from a variety of backgrounds, including but not limited to racial and ethnic minorities, students with disabilities, LGBTQ+ students, first-generation college students, and those from various socioeconomic backgrounds. This diversity is not limited to racial, ethnic, or gender identity. Still, it extends to encompass a wide range of experiences, identities, and perspectives that students bring to their study abroad experiences.

Bingham et al. (2023) wrote about the importance of tailored risk management strategies, personalized safety plans, and policies that are cognizant of the varied vulnerabilities and requirements of students from different backgrounds, all of which are necessary for a secure and supportive learning environment. This chapter explores effective strategies and resources for education abroad practitioners to assist U.S. students in their academic experiences abroad while addressing the unique challenges and risks associated with a diverse student body. The authors will explore an adapted model of Bronfenbrenner's (1977) ecology of human development, emphasizing one's spheres of influence during key times to mitigate risk management proactively in education abroad. Additionally, the chapter will explore the Global Education Equity Empowerment Framework, aligning it with The Forum on Education Abroad's *Standards of Good Practice for Education Abroad* (2020) and integrating foundational principles of equity and inclusivity into the broader context of global education. Thompson and Ellis (2023) developed this framework to reimagine and support a more flexible and nonlinear approach to risk management and safety for onsite staff supporting students abroad.

## Understanding the American Student Identity

As a diverse group, U.S. students bring a wide range of experiences, challenges, and perspectives to study abroad programs. The following examples provide a glimpse into the multifaceted nature of American student identities. While not exhaustive, they concentrate on several predominant issues, such as high financial need, equity deserving students' of diverse gender identity and sexuality, and the ways in which colorism may increase the perceived risks associated with participating in education abroad programs (Woodson, 2020; Bingham, Mitchell, & Brunsting, 2023; Wood, 2023). These selections are intended to highlight critical areas of concern within the broader spectrum of student experiences.

Recognizing the complexity of identities among U.S. students is key to fostering a supportive environment when they are abroad. It is essential to acknowledge the multifaceted nature of discrimination, race, gender, and the importance of an intersectional approach in addressing the unique challenges faced by individuals with overlapping identities (Crenshaw, 1989). Bryant and Soria (2015) mention that LGBTQIA+ students may encounter specific challenges in regions with socially conservative views on sexuality and gender, impacting their safety and well-being. Mitic and Wolniak (2022) found that students with higher financial need to face significant barriers in participating in study abroad programs. Their research underscores the importance of financial aid and support in enabling study abroad experiences for students from underserved backgrounds. While Mitic and Wolniak (2022) noted that study abroad participation was not significantly influenced by ethnicity or gender among low-income students, they emphasized that socioeconomic status often plays a more critical role in accessing these programs than other identity-based traits.

Students may face distinct challenges in countries where they are in the minority, such as racial or ethnic discrimination. These challenges are accentuated by the dynamics of colorism, impacting social status and opportunities, as highlighted in the study by Hunter (2007). Woodson (2020) writes that colorism, once conceived solely as a skin color issue, is now acknowledged to encompass a broader spectrum of influences, particularly within the African diaspora. In addition to skin tone, attributes such as hair texture, body image, and perceived attractiveness are recognized as significant contributors to colorism (Woodson, 2020). Woodson mentioned that colorism has been incorporated into these multifaceted dimensions and acknowledges its global prevalence, often associated with preferences for the European aesthetic (Woodson, 2020). While extensively studied in specific cultural contexts, the global impact of colorism on diverse societies has been largely underexplored (Woodson, 2020). Recognizing and addressing these multifaceted challenges is part of a risk management issue in international education programs to ensure equity and accessibility for all students, irrespective of their racial or ethnic backgrounds. This proactive approach is key to fostering an inclusive and equitable environment in international educational settings (Hunter, 2007).

Addressing the distinct challenges that diverse student groups face in international education, such as the racial and socioeconomic barriers highlighted by Hunter (2007) and Thompson and Ellis (2023), advocates for a comprehensive support framework to assist onsite international staff. This need for an understanding of student experiences abroad connects with Bronfenbrenner's (1977) Ecological System Theory and its concept of "Spheres of Influence" in global education. Applying this theory enables practitioners to support better diverse U.S. student groups, such as LGBTQIA+ students navigating cultural challenges in conservative societies or students of color experiencing racial discrimination or colorism in minority settings. Bronfenbrenner (1977) advocates for the development of programs that are responsive to both the immediate personal and cultural needs of students and the broader institutional and societal dynamics influencing their experiences. Bryan et al. (2022) mentioned that when actively working to mitigate risk management challenges onsite for students from diverse backgrounds, the first step is to recognize the opportunities when you can prevent potential risk management issues and establish trust with the student and the onsite partner to avoid harm such as discrimination.

## Understanding the Spheres of Influence in Global Education

Bronfenbrenner's (1977) model, with its layered approach, provides a valuable perspective on the different environmental factors influencing a student's international experience. From the "microsystem" of immediate environments like family or school to the broader societal and cultural contexts in the "macrosystem," this theory equips education abroad practitioners with a framework to create inclusive and adaptive strategies to mitigate risk onsite. It is important to note that when you discuss the spheres of influence in a global education context, you are referring to various levels of impact and power possessed to support students on a global scale. These spheres of influence can range from individual to organizational action, and

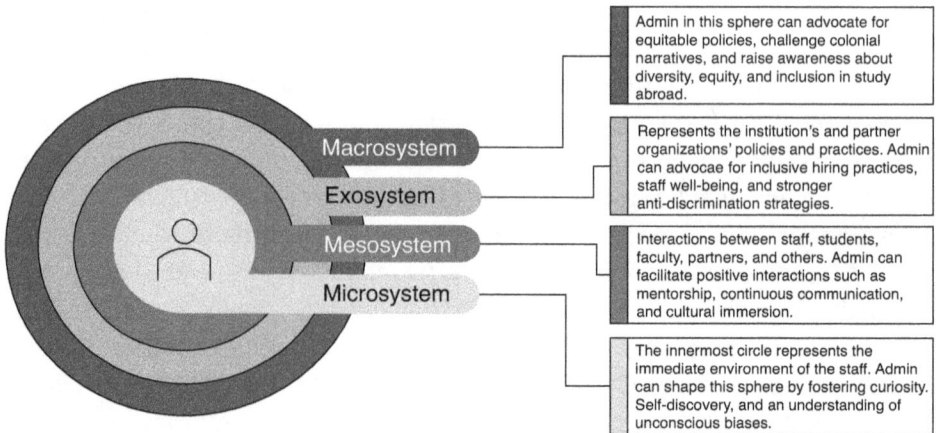

**Figure 19.1.** Understanding the Spheres of Influence in Global Education: A Bronfenbrenner-Inspired Framework

Notes: This figure was adapted from Bronfenbrenner, U. (1977). Towards an experimental ecology of human development. American Psychologist, 32(7), 513—531. This figure conceptualizes the spheres of influence in global education through a Bronfenbrenner-inspired framework, depicting the interrelated systems that impact global education risk management, policy, and practice. It promotes the importance of intervention in risk management between the macrosystem, exosystem, mesosystem, and microsystem, emphasizing the role of administration in fostering equity, inclusion, and diversity across all levels.

they collectively shape the trajectory of a student's international experience. Drawing from Bronfenbrenner's (1977) Ecological System Theory, you can better understand the multifaceted environments and dynamics at play during a student's time abroad, especially matters of risk and safety.

Starting with the "microsystem"—the immediate, direct environments such as family or school—the model expands outward to the "mesosystem," which represents the interconnections between these immediate environments. Further out, the "exosystem" encompasses external environments that indirectly impact the individual, like parental workplaces or community services. At its broadest level, the "macrosystem" embodies overarching societal and cultural norms and policies (Bronfenbrenner, 1977). Figure 19.1 was adapted for application within global education.

- **Microsystem**: This is the student's immediate environment, where education abroad practitioners can influence by developing programs that nurture curiosity, self-awareness, and an understanding of unconscious biases. These efforts create a supportive, inclusive atmosphere crucial for mitigating risks related to personal interactions and cultural misunderstandings. For example, this might involve developing programs focused on identity, where students can explore self-awareness and the supporting staff can work proactively to mitigate issues of racial discrimination or stereotypes during the development of the program. Bush et al. (2022) mentioned a program developed in Senegal as a way to disrupt the typical narrative of African American students studying in South Africa. Bush et al.'s (2022) study highlights the need to be intentional in location selection. For instance, South Africa's colonial past, practice of colorism, apartheid history, and ongoing racial issues it may not offer African American students the healing and transformative environment they seek from racial trauma experienced in the United States, necessitating a deeper examination of these choices (Bush et al., 2022).
- **Mesosystem**: This layer involves interactions between students, staff, faculty, and partners. By enhancing mentorship, communication, and cultural immersion opportunities, we can foster a deeper understanding of students' needs and address risks arising from miscommunications or cultural differences. For example, Bryan et al. (2022) highlight that the updated forum guidelines illuminate the complex aspects of making risk management decisions, stressing the need for involving students as active partners in their study abroad programs. Furthermore, Bryan et al. (2022) advocate for the collaboration between institutions and students in the development of onsite risk management strategies, which empowers students to play a more significant role in their safety plan.

- **Exosystem**: This sphere includes institutional and partner organization policies. Advocating for inclusive policies and robust mechanisms to address discrimination or harassment can mitigate risks related to institutional biases and support a safe environment for all students. For example, this may include a collective review of policies intended to address issues of student discrimination onsite between partners. Bryan et al. (2022) argue that in partnerships between Global North and Global South areas, using a relationship-focused method is a way to challenge colonial attitudes. This happens when partners examine their own biases, truly listen to each other, and break down power structures that favor one group (like Western universities) over another (such as local communities) (Bryan et al, 2022).
- **Macrosystem:** At this broadest level, societal norms and policies are influential. Education abroad practitioners can challenge and reshape this sphere by advocating for equitable global education policies, debunking colonialist narratives, and underscoring the importance of diversity and inclusion. This approach addresses broader societal risks, such as systemic discrimination or social-cultural insensitivity. For example, Bryan et al. (2022) mentioned that sharing power in discussions goes beyond just including diverse participants; it involves actively allowing their inputs to reshape and co-create the conversation, empowering education abroad practitioners to influence and reform.

The *Standards of Good Practice for Education Abroad* note that "each organization shall commit to planning, delivery, evaluation, and assessment for continuous improvement" (The Forum on Education Abroad, 2020, clause 5.2.1). Also, it mentions that "responsible parties shall endeavor to recruit and advise students from all segments of the student population, including those who are historically underserved by their organization's programs (2020, clause 6.1.3) and in clause 6.1.3.1." "Responsible parties should develop strategies to increase participation by historically underserved groups." Within these spheres, there is the opportunity to implement strategies that promote diversity, equity, and inclusion while also addressing the various risks associated with studying abroad. Moving forward, with an understanding of these spheres of influence and their application, the subsequent step involves self-assessment through case studies in the next section.

## Self-Evaluation: Navigating Through Reflection and Growth

The training provided to your onsite staff must be thorough, covering not only the historical and cultural nuances of the host country but also incorporating practical strategies for inclusivity and risk mitigation (Johnson et al., 2022). As cited in the *Standards*, "Each organization shall commit to planning, delivery, evaluation, and assessment for continuous improvement" (clause 5.2.1.). This will enable staff to constantly refine their approaches and respond effectively to the dynamic challenges students may face in different environments (Bennett, 2011).

Thompson and Ellis developed the "Global Education Equity Empowerment Framework" and first published it in an LinkedIn article in 2023. The tool aims to redefine the understanding of equity as risk management among education abroad practitioners using continuous reflection and self-evaluation. This framework encourages you to identify and challenge inherent biases, adapt to diverse international contexts, and prioritize safety and risk mitigation within an organizational setting. It comprises three key components: "Global Education," focusing on cross-cultural understanding and risk awareness; "Equity," which emphasizes fairness, justice, and proactive strategies to address historical imbalances in international education; and "Empowerment," advocating for agency and confidence across all constituencies while highlighting the importance of managing risks. When practitioners apply this framework, the hope is that practitioners are motivated not only to rediscover themselves as individuals but also to comprehend the

## Global Education Equity Empowerment Framework (updated 12/2023)

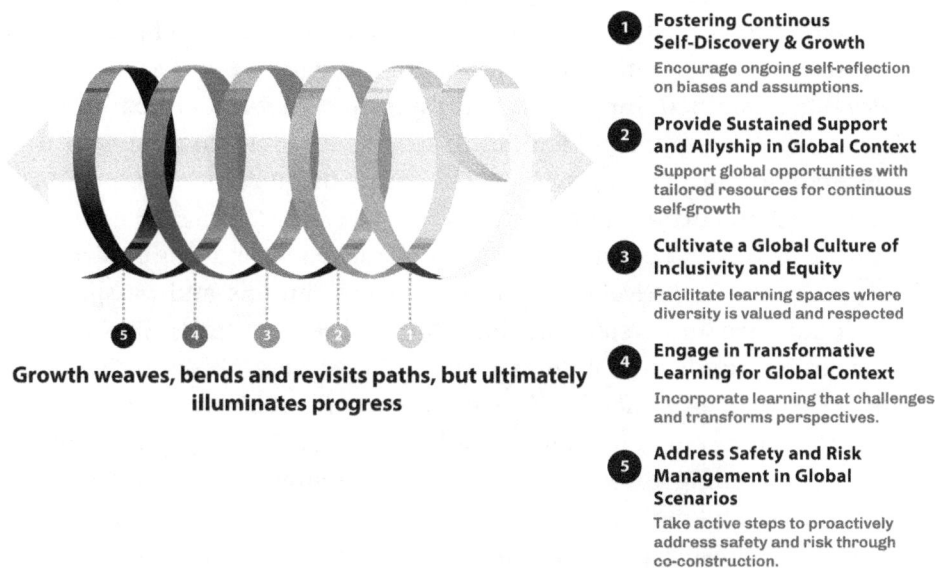

**1 Fostering Continous Self-Discovery & Growth**
Encourage ongoing self-reflection on biases and assumptions.

**2 Provide Sustained Support and Allyship in Global Context**
Support global opportunities with tailored resources for continuous self-growth

**3 Cultivate a Global Culture of Inclusivity and Equity**
Facilitate learning spaces where diversity is valued and respected

**4 Engage in Transformative Learning for Global Context**
Incorporate learning that challenges and transforms perspectives.

**5 Address Safety and Risk Management in Global Scenarios**
Take active steps to proactively address safety and risk through co-construction.

**Growth weaves, bends and revisits paths, but ultimately illuminates progress**

**Figure 19.2.**   Global Education Equity Empowerment Framework

Note: Figure 19.2, Source Thompson, C., & Ellis, E. (2023, August 29). Foundations of Inclusive Global Education: Exploring Global Equity in Action. Linkedin.com.

various cultures, viewpoints, prejudices, and obstacles that influence the global world in alignment with the *Standards of Good Practice for Education Abroad* (The Forum on Education Abroad, 2020).

1. **Fostering Continuous Self-Discovery and Growth**: The Forum on Education Abroad's *Standards* advocate for each organization to create frameworks for scrutinizing, pinpointing, and rectifying systemic biases and shortcomings within their policies, practices, and programs (2020, clause 4.4.3). This promotes a culture of continuous personal exploration and evaluation among education abroad professionals, particularly in understanding and addressing their own biases and preconceptions in diverse and international contexts. Implementing regular meetings, maintaining reflective journals on global learning experiences, and participating in professional development workshops with an international focus are strategies to support this endeavor. This kind of introspection and evaluation helps staff manage risks, acknowledge areas for growth, and recognize progress.

   For example, it is beneficial for staff members to maintain reflective journals throughout and following the education abroad program. These journals should document their experiences, provide space for self-reflection on biases and interactions with students, and detail the handling or resolution of any risk-related issues linked to their students (The Forum on Education Abroad, 2022, section I). They can also participate in debriefing workshops and discussions to unpack these reflections and learn from each other's risk management strategies

2. **Provide Sustained Support and Allyship in a Global Context**: It is the obligation of responsible entities to furnish a secure environment that fosters learning for every student (The Forum on Education Abroad, 2020, clause 5.2.7). Furthermore, Section C of the *Code of Ethics for Education Abroad* highlights equity, diversity, and inclusion and emphasizes the commitment to actively engage with diverse groups and perspectives with patience, understanding, humility, and respect (p. 4). This reflects the desired conduct we wish to instill in our learners. This is in alignment with the *Code of Ethics for Education Abroad*'s (2022) collective goal to broaden access to education abroad, fostering an inclusive atmosphere that is welcoming, respectful, and safe for everyone. We aim for equitable treatment of all individuals, rejecting intolerance and dedicating efforts to eradicate disparities within our organizations and communities (The Forum on Education Abroad, 2022, section C).

   Support education abroad practitioners in navigating the unique challenges of global education by providing tailored resources for professional development and acting as allies in cultural navigation, language barriers, and other opportunities for equity building onsite. This support should include resources for individual well-being, emphasizing the importance of creating conditions for people to cope amid uncertainty, rapid change, and potential risks. For example, a staff member who experiences difficulties in communicating in the host country's language during an education abroad program is offered resources to undertake a starting language course. Moreover, mental health resources are made available to the team to assist in navigating any stress or challenges encountered throughout the program.

3. **Cultivate a Global Culture of Inclusivity and Equity**: Prioritize creating a culture that values diversity and equity and recognizes global nuances and differences in approaches when outside the United States. This involves creating an environment where all members feel valued and respected, diversity is seen as a strength, and systemic inequities are actively challenged. This necessitates a commitment to anti-bias development to support and enhance diversity, which may contrast with the dominant culture in the host country. By addressing the complexities of colorism, for example, and its broader implications, educational programs can support the development of an inclusive and equitable atmosphere, ensuring that all students and staff are recognized and respected, irrespective of their racial or ethnic backgrounds. This proactive approach is crucial for fostering an inclusive and equitable environment in international educational settings, as highlighted by both Hunter (2007) and Woodson (2020).

For example, the education abroad office should advocate for team diversity through inclusive hiring practices, strategic campus or community partnerships, implement a clear antidiscrimination policy, and regularly conduct learning opportunities on equity, inclusivity, and risk management in global education. Regarding The Forum on Education Abroad's *Code of Ethics* (2022) on sustainability, the focus is on integrating sustainable environmental practices with academic and program objectives, recognizing that sustainable outcomes result from informed and judicious choices, benefiting relationships, economic well-being, cultural traditions, and the global ecosystem (section H). The impact of our initiatives on the environment, as well as on the economic and cultural structure of host communities, is a critical consideration. Similarly, each organization is mandated to cultivate respect for the cultures and values of all stakeholders, including both the communities from which participants originate and those within which they engage (The Forum on Education Abroad, 2020, clause 4.3.6).

4.  **Engage in Transformative Learning for Global Context:** In preparing individuals for study abroad programs, training centered on cultural understanding and risk management is key. This type of training not only challenges participants to question their preexisting beliefs but also emphasizes the potential risks involved in altering one's mindset—an essential yet often uncomfortable step toward growth (Jarman et al., 2022). Such risk, while challenging, serves as a motivator for deep self-reflection and learning, necessitating both time and commitment to new ideas or re-evaluated concepts. Staff, therefore, must undertake significant self-reflection to navigate these changes effectively, thereby enhancing their ability to support students in their own journeys of personal development and adaptation to new cultural perspectives.

    The importance of advocating for global perspectives and cultural understanding is underscored by The Forum *Code of Ethics* (2020), Section B, Advocacy, highlighting the critical role of education abroad in fostering curiosity and making a positive impact on the world (p. 51). As such, education abroad professionals are called to embody and promote the Forum's mission, which is to continuously seek innovative ways to enhance the qualip9ty and safety of education abroad experiences. By connecting the concepts of advocacy and risk management, educators can create more impactful and transformative experiences for all participants involved in study abroad programs.

    For example, to foster an environment conducive to student growth, specific support mechanisms such as mentoring, access to counseling services, and participation in cultural immersion activities are helpful. These supports enable students to navigate their paths toward understanding and integrating into new cultural contexts, with ready access to guidance when needed.

5.  **Addressing Safety and Risk Management in Global Scenarios:** According to the *Standards of Good Practice* (2020), sections 6.2.8 (p .36) and 5.1.7 (p .28) emphasize the importance of supporting students in safety management by offering essential resources and ensuring that organizations have specific policies and procedures for security and risk management. These policies are designed to safeguard the health, safety, and well-being of both students and staff. Furthermore, section 6.1.11 stresses the responsibility of providing students with the necessary resources to navigate safety concerns effectively (The Forum on Education Abroad, 2020).

    For example: To take this a step further, you can consider disrupting traditional top-down risk management methods by engaging both educators and students in the co-construction of safety plans (Bryan et al.,

2022). This collaborative approach ensures that safety measures are not just comprehensive but also deeply relevant to the varying contexts of the students and their needs. Another approach is to create a diverse risk management task force that includes not only staff and local partners but also student representatives. Host regular interactive workshops where all constituents can share insights, discuss potential scenarios, and collaboratively develop emergency response strategies. This should be complemented with a robust feedback system, allowing for continuous evolution and adaptation of safety protocols to meet the ever-changing demands of global educational environments (Thompson & Ellis, 2023).

## Case Studies

The following case studies explore the various scenarios encountered by students and their support networks during their time abroad. These examples aim to shed light on the practical application of the theories discussed, highlighting the significance of recognizing and catering to the diverse needs of students. It is important to note, however, that these case studies do not encompass all possible situations nor cover the full spectrum of diversity. They serve as a starting point for exploring how theoretical concepts can be implemented in real-world contexts to foster equitable and inclusive global educational experiences.

## Case Study 1: LGBTQIA+ Students in a Country with Anti-LGBTQIA+ Laws

### Background

A faculty-led program is guiding a group of U.S. students to a nation known for its socially conservative stance on LGBTQIA+ rights, including laws that restrict or ban diverse expressions of sexuality, gender, and gender fluidity. Within this student group, there are LGBTQIA+ individuals who have expressed concerns regarding their safety and acceptance while participating in the program. There is a student who identifies as gender nonconforming and has expressed a preference to reside with either female-identifying students or other individuals who also identify as non-gender-conforming.

### Application of Theories

- Recognizing that LGBTQIA+ students may face unique challenges in socially conservative countries, the program administrators should be prepared to advise and recommend resources to manage their expectations.

- Spheres of Influence in Global Education
  - Microsystem: This is the immediate surroundings of the student, such as their classrooms and living spaces. Actions here involve creating inclusive and engaging programs that help students understand themselves and others better, aiming to prevent misunderstandings and foster a supportive environment.
    - Personalized Support: Offer tailored pre-departure sessions for LGBTQIA+ students, addressing specific concerns related to safety, cultural norms, and legal aspects concerning LGBTQ+ rights in the host country (Bingham et al., 2023).
    - Safe Housing: Ensure housing arrangements accommodate the needs of gender nonconforming students, allowing them to reside with peers who respect their identity and creating a supportive living environment (Bingham et al., 2023).
    - Visible LGBTQIA+ Symbols with Considerations: Displaying Safe Zone stickers or similar symbols can signal support for LGBTQIA+ students if legally feasible. Catalano (2021) points out, however, that the effectiveness of these symbols depends on the genuine commitment and training of staff. Such measures need to be more than symbolic, underlining the importance of an informed and sustained effort to create a truly supportive environment for LGBTQIA+ students.
  - Mesosystem: This layer connects different parts of a student's life abroad, like the relationships between students, faculty, and local communities. Enhancing mentorship and communication here helps understand and meet students' needs, addressing any communication gaps or cultural differences effectively.
    - Sensitivity Training: Include sensitivity and inclusivity training for education abroad staff, faculty, and participants within the program model. This training should cover topics like understanding LGBTQIA+ identities, using inclusive language, recognizing unconscious biases, and responding appropriately to LGBTQIA+ concerns. Catalano (2021) shares that research indicates that facilitators of LGBTQ+ diversity education interventions often volunteer for these roles and may not have the appropriate training or lived experiences to support them.
    - Cultural Immersion Activities: Engage students in activities that require active sense-making and interaction with the local community. This not only helps bridge cultural gaps but also enriches

students' understanding of their own identities in relation to others (Bingham et al., 2023).

- – Critical Reflection Sessions: Incorporate regular sessions where students critically examine their preconceptions and the dynamics of power and privilege in their host and home cultures. This will encourage a deeper understanding of interpersonal and systemic power dynamics, which is essential for transformative learning (Bingham et al., 2023).

- Exosystem: This refers to external influences and systems that indirectly impact students' experiences and outcomes while studying abroad outside of the United States.
  - – Educational Partnerships: Collaborate with local LGBTQIA+ organizations to provide students with access to community resources, support groups, and safe spaces within the host country. This type of partnership can offer a direct line of support for students and educate program staff about local LGBTQIA+ issues and resources (Bingham et al., 2023).
  - – Feedback Mechanisms: Establish clear channels for students to provide feedback on their experiences, especially regarding feelings of safety, acceptance, and inclusion. Use this feedback to make ongoing adjustments to the program and address any incidents of discrimination or harassment swiftly and effectively (Bingham et al., 2023).

- Macrosystem: This is the widest layer, encompassing societal norms and policies. Actions here involve advocating for fair education policies and challenging existing narratives to address larger issues like systemic discrimination and promote diversity and inclusion.
  - – Promotion of Inclusive Narratives: Use the program as a platform to advocate for broader societal acceptance and understanding of LGBTQ+ identities. Encourage students to engage in respectful dialogue and learn about diversity and inclusion (Bingham et al., 2023).
  - – International Networking: This approach addresses the complex challenges faced by LGBTQIA+ communities, as emphasized by Angelo and Bocci (2021) in their analysis of the Council on Foreign Relations. Angelo and Bocci (2021) share that despite progress, substantial advocacy and protection against discrimination and violence based on sexual orientation and gender identity are still needed globally. In alignment with Angelo and Bocci's

(2021) recommendations, to promote global LGBTQIA+ rights and understanding, it is recommended to actively participate in international forums, forge alliances with LGBTQIA+ groups worldwide, and engage in cross-border collaborations. This approach fosters international cooperation and mutual learning, enhancing the effectiveness of efforts in advancing LGBTQIA+ causes globally.

- Global Education Equity Empowerment Framework Approach: Proactively equip staff with the reflective skills and self-awareness to specifically support LGBTQIA+ students, addressing the risk of inadequate support and empowering them with language to advocate for their students in the country (Thompson & Ellis, 2023).

### Faculty/Staff Reflective Questions

1. How did your perception of cultural differences regarding sexuality, gender, and gender fluidity impact your understanding of the risks faced by LGBTQIA+ students? How did this influence your approach to risk mitigation in the program?
2. Can you recall instances where you felt challenged in supporting LGBTQIA+ students due to cultural barriers or safety concerns? How did you manage these risks and provide support in these moments?
3. Based on your experiences, what suggestions do you have for improving staff training and resources to better identify and mitigate risks for LGBTQIA+ students in future programs?
4. What specific strategies or approaches did you adopt to navigate and bridge the cultural differences and challenges faced by LGBTQIA+ students, thereby reducing their risk of harm or discrimination?
5. How has managing this program shaped your perspective on the risks associated with global LGBTQ+ rights? What role do you see for educational staff in advocating for and mitigating these risks?

### Facilitator Notes

1. Begin the debrief by creating a safe space with a community pact for open dialogue. A community pact should include suggestions from the participants on what they need to feel comfortable and respected, encouraging open, honest dialogue. Establish ground rules for respectful communication and active listening, ensuring every voice is heard and valued in a nonjudgmental environment.
2. Emphasize the importance of respecting different perspectives.

3. Encourage staff/faculty to share their experiences, both positive and challenging.
4. Emphasize the importance of continuous learning and growth.

## Case Study 2: Low-Income Students in a High-Cost City

### Background

A faculty-led program is organized in one of the world's most expensive cities. Among the participants are students from lower socioeconomic backgrounds who are concerned about managing their finances during the program. Unfortunately, due to an underlying diabetes condition, one student suffered an injury earlier in the program that is not healing correctly. Due to limited financial resources, the student is unable to afford a visit to the doctor.

### Application of Theories

- Recognize that students from lower socioeconomic backgrounds may face financial challenges and may feel alienated amongst peers who do not have such constraints.
- Spheres of Influence in Global Education
  - Microsystem: This is the immediate surroundings of the student, such as their classrooms and living spaces. Actions here involve creating inclusive and engaging programs that help students understand themselves and others better, aiming to prevent misunderstandings and foster a supportive environment.
    - Resource Mapping and Support Networks: Lusardi and Messy (2023) emphasize the significance of financial literacy for young people, underscoring the need for pre-departure financial management training to mitigate students' financial distress. Their research indicates that financial education is critical for navigating complex financial environments, particularly for students facing the challenges of managing finances in new, high-cost settings abroad. A practical approach to enhance students' financial skills includes presenting scenarios that mirror various aspects of student life overseas, like accommodation and transportation. This could involve students creating a monthly budget, factoring in currency exchange rates and potential expense fluctuations, effectively preparing them for the financial realities of studying abroad.

- Mesosystem: This layer connects different parts of a student's life abroad, like the relationships between students, faculty, and local communities. Enhancing mentorship and communication here helps understand and meet students' needs, addressing any communication gaps or cultural differences effectively.
  - Peer Support Circles: Combining the approaches of forming small student groups and incorporating structured peer discussions, as suggested by Martinot et al. (2022), can enhance faculty-led programs. By organizing students from diverse economic backgrounds into small groups and holding regular, inclusive meetings, these programs can foster open conversations about financial management and economic challenges. Additionally, structured peer discussion sessions after academic activities, guided by insights from Martinot et al. (2022), emphasize the role of peer and teacher support in enhancing student engagement. This dual approach not only deepens understanding but also builds a supportive community among students from varied socioeconomic backgrounds.
- Exosystem: This refers to external influences and systems that indirectly impact students' experiences and outcomes while studying abroad outside of the United States.
  - Financial Literacy Workshops: Offering student-specific workshops to educate administrators and students on the context of study abroad may help address institutional and individual budget management in cities where the cost of living is higher for the student. This is also important when understanding international healthcare systems. This directly supports students in navigating their immediate challenges, including managing finances and accessing medical care (Leap et al., 2022).
- Macrosystem: This is the widest layer, encompassing societal norms and policies. Actions here involve advocating for fair education policies and challenging existing narratives to address larger issues like systemic discrimination and promote diversity and inclusion.
  - Policy Change: Whatley (2017) explores how financial aspects such as student loans, grants, family contributions, and financial need affect decisions to study abroad. The study shows that loans often discourage students from studying abroad, while grants have the opposite effect. Students from wealthier families or those with greater financial need are less likely to study abroad. This points

to the necessity of making global education more accessible and argues for better financial aid solutions to increase study abroad participation. At this level, administrators can impact by advocating with their campus leadership and local politicians.

- Global Education Equity Empowerment Framework Approach: Focus on staff understanding socioeconomic challenges, ensuring risks of inequity are addressed by personalized coaching for students on financial best practices before, during, and after the program (Thompson & Ellis, 2023).

## Faculty/Staff Reflective Questions

1. How did you assist students in identifying and managing the risks associated with financial challenges during the program (e.g., health care coverage, food insecurities, etc.)? What specific actions were taken to mitigate these risks?
2. Were there moments when you felt unequipped or overwhelmed in addressing the financial risks faced by students? How did you respond to these situations, and what could have better prepared you?
3. What measures can be implemented to better equip staff in identifying and mitigating financial risks for students from diverse socioeconomic backgrounds in future programs?
4. Which strategies or resources did you find most effective in aiding students with their financial management, particularly in reducing their risk of financial hardship?
5. How has overseeing this program shaped your understanding of global socioeconomic disparities and their specific risks to students? What broader risk implications have you observed?

## Facilitator Notes

1. To begin the debrief, create a safe space. A community pact should include suggestions from the participants on what they need to feel comfortable and respected, encouraging open, honest dialogue. Establish ground rules for respectful communication and active listening, ensuring every voice is heard and valued in a nonjudgmental environment.
2. Encourage students to share their strategies and challenges.
3. Emphasize the importance of empathy and understanding.
4. Discuss potential improvements for future programs to better support students from all socioeconomic backgrounds.

## Conclusion

In this chapter, the authors integrate conceptual frameworks to explore preparing international staff to understand the diverse identities of U.S. students. These standards provide a comprehensive set of guidelines and benchmarks that can enhance the effectiveness and efficiency of education abroad programs. The Forum *Standards of Good Practice for Education Abroad* emphasizes the critical importance of continuous improvement and inclusivity within education abroad programs (2020, clause 5.2.1). Organizations are urged to engage in careful planning, delivery, evaluation, and assessment to enhance program effectiveness and adapt to the evolving challenges students face. Additionally, the standards call for an active effort to recruit and advise students from all segments of the student population, particularly those historically underserved and other equity-deserving students, by the organization's programs, as stated in clauses 6.1.3 and 6.1.3.1 (2020).

This approach aims to foster an environment that supports learning for every student, underscored by an emphasis on equity, diversity, and inclusion as outlined in clause 5.2.7 of the *Standards*. To address and rectify systemic biases, organizations are encouraged to create frameworks for continuous self-reflection and improvement, aligning with clause 4.4.3 of the *Standards* (The Forum on Education Abroad, 2020). The framework proposed by Thompson & Ellis (2023) and the use of the adapted model based on Bronfenbrenner's (1977) Ecological System Theory provides a useful foundation for shaping your risk management approach, emphasizing the interconnectedness of your students and supporting staff experiences within sociocultural environments and the importance of equity and empowerment. This effort is supported by implementing practices that respect the cultures and values of all stakeholders (4.3.6) and advocate for global perspectives and cultural understanding, highlighting the critical role of education abroad in fostering curiosity and making a positive impact, as stated in Section B, Advocacy, of the *Code of Ethics* (The Forum on Education Abroad, 2022). In addition, ensuring student safety and effective risk management is emphasized in the *Standards,* clauses 6.2.8 and 5.1.7, alongside the responsibility of providing essential resources for students to navigate safety concerns effectively (clause 6.1.11).

An integral aspect of your approach is the collaborative development of safety and risk management plans with students, as emphasized in this chapter. This participatory approach ensures that the solutions you create are contextually relevant, taking into account the unique needs and perspectives of each student. By involving students in the planning process, you empower them to actively participate in their own safety and well-being. These principles and directives serve to promote more inclusive, safe, and enriching experiences for all participants in education abroad programs, advocating for a global education system characterized by continuous growth, equity, and empowerment.

To translate these principles into action, the authors suggest implementing specific actions and policies drawn from the case studies. This may involve establishing viable signs of inclusion (Catalano, 2021), offering comprehensive financial literacy training to address the financial challenges students face (Leap, Tignor, & Udowitch, 2022; Lusardi & Messy, 2023), and crafting contingency plans tailored to diverse cultural contexts (Hoffman, 2016). These strategies are designed to proactively address the diverse needs of students and foster a supportive environment. As noted in The Forum *Standards of Good Practice for Education Abroad* (2020), it is essential to recognize the ongoing need for reflection and adaptation of your practices to meet the evolving needs of students in global education settings. Just as global circumstances change, your approaches to education abroad must evolve and ensure that you remain responsive and adaptable in an ever-changing world, as noted in the *Code of Ethics* (section I).

In closing, we extend a call to action to you; as Education Abroad practitioners, let us collectively commit to a future characterized by continuous growth and adaptation in our practices for risk management (The Forum on Education Abroad, 2020; Hunter, 2007; Thompson & Ellis, 2023; Willinsky, 1998). By embracing the principles of equity, empowerment, co-construction, and continuous improvement, you can contribute to the creation of a more inclusive and enriching global education system. Together, we can shape the future of global education to be even more impactful and transformative, preparing students for success in an interconnected world while proactively addressing the risk.

# References

Angelo, P. J., & Bocci, D. (2021, January 29). The changing landscape of global LGBTQ+ rights. *Council on Foreign Relations*. https://www.cfr.org/article/changing-landscape-global-lgbtq-rights

Bennett, J. M. (2011). Developing intercultural competence for international education faculty and staff. *In The SAGE Handbook of Intercultural Competence* (pp. 333-349). SAGE Publications, Inc.

Bingham, W. P., Mitchell, M., & Brunsting, N. (2023). Considering LGBTQ+ Students' Study Abroad Experiences Across Research and Practice. *Frontiers: The Interdisciplinary Journal of Study Abroad, 35*(2), 29-39. https://doi.org/10.36366/frontiers.v35i1.847

Bryan, D. W., Viteri, C., Murphy, C. C., Csoman, K., Llulluna, E. P., & McGrath, E. (2022). Reimagining Risk Management: Decolonizing crisis response through holistic partnership building in education abroad. *Frontiers: The Interdisciplinary Journal of Study Abroad, 34*(3), 44–72. https://doi.org/10.36366/frontiers.v34i3.672

Bryant, K. M., & Soria, K. M. (2015). *College students' sexual orientation, gender identity, and participation in study abroad.* Frontiers: The Interdisciplinary Journal of Study Abroad, 25(1), 91–106. https://doi.org/10.36366/frontiers.v25i1.347

Bronfenbrenner, U. (1977). Towards an experimental ecology of human development. American Psychologist, 32(7), 513–531.

Bush, L., Jeffers-Coly, P., Bush, E. C., & Lewis, L. (2022). "They are coming to get something": A qualitative study of African American male community college students' education abroad experience in Senegal, West Africa. *Frontiers: The Interdisciplinary Journal of Study Abroad, 34*(2), 257–279. https://doi.org/10.36366/frontiers.v34i2.610

Catalano, C. (2021, September 7). *Reflections on a decade of "Safe zone" education in higher education.* College of Liberal Arts and Human Sciences | Virginia Tech. https://liberalarts.vt.edu/departments-and-schools/school-of-education/insights-from-the-school-of-education/decade-of-safe-zone-education.html

Crenshaw, K. (1989). Demarginalizing the intersection of race and sex: A black feminist critique of antidiscrimination doctrine, feminist theory, and antiracist politics. University of Chicago Legal Forum, (1), 139. https://scholarship.law.columbia.edu/faculty_scholarship/3007/

Hoffman, D. M. (2016). How can we best prepare students for study abroad? Teaching intercultural competence. Journal of Studies in International Education, 20(3), 215-230.

Hunter, M. (2007). *The persistent problem of colorism: skin tone, status, and inequality.* Sociology Compass, 1(1), 237–254. https://doi.org/10.1111/j.1751-9020.2007.00006.x

Institute for International Education. (2023a, November 13). *Race/Ethnicity of U.S. Students Studying Abroad, 2021/22.* Open Doors Report on International Educational Exchange. https://opendoorsdata.org/infographic/race-ethnicity-of-u-s-students-studying-abroad-2021-22/

Institute for International Education. (2023b, November 13). *U.S. Students Studying Abroad, 1989/90-2021-22.* Open Doors Report on International Educational Exchange. https://opendoorsdata.org/infographic/u-s-students-studying-abroad-1989-90-2021-22/

Jarman, M., Burman, M., Purtzer, M. A., & Miller, K. (2022). "Those lessons learned went right out the window once I was atop the soil where it all happened": Transformative Learning in a Study Abroad Course. *Frontiers: The Interdisciplinary Journal of Study Abroad, 34*(4), 26–52. https://doi.org/10.36366/frontiers.v34i4.546

Johnson, M., Titus, B., & Mettifogo, M. (2022). *Training "American" Identity: Engaging On-site Staff in Equity, Diversity, and Inclusion Work.* In N. J., Gozik & H. B. Hamir (Eds.), A House Where All Belong: Redesigning Education Abroad for Inclusive Excellence (pp. 335-360). The Forum on Education Abroad. DOI: 10.36366/SIA.1.978-1-952376-21-4.1

Leap, A., Tignor, S., & Udowitch, E. (2022). *Strengthening the Bridge Between Financial Aid and Study Abroad.* Journal of Student Financial Aid, 51(3), A7. https://doi.org/10.55504/0884-9153.1798

Lusardi, A., & Messy, F. (2023). The importance of financial literacy and its impact on financial wellbeing. Journal of Financial Literacy and Wellbeing, 1(1), 1–11. https://doi.org/10.1017/flw.2023.8

Martinot, D., Sicard, A., Gul, B., Yakimova, S., Taillandier-Schmitt, A., & Maintenant, C. (2022). Peers and teachers as the best source of social support for school engagement for both advantaged and priority education area students. *Frontiers in Psychology, 13.* https://doi.org/10.3389/fpsyg.2022.958286

Mitic, R. R., & Wolniak, G. C. (2022). *Examining the associations between financial conditions and study abroad in diverse, low-income college students.* Journal of Student Financial Aid, 51(3). https://doi.org/10.55504/0884-9153.1800

The Forum on Education Abroad. (2020). *Code of Ethics for Education Abroad* (Third Edition). Carlisle, PA. doi.org/10.36366/G.978-1-952376-08-5

The Forum on Education Abroad. (2022). *Standards of Good Practice for Education Abroad* (Sixth Edition). https://doi.org/10.36366/G.978-1-952376-08-5

Thompson, C., & Ellis, E. (2023). Foundations of Inclusive Global Education: Exploring Global Equity in Action. Linkedin.com. https://www.linkedin.com/pulse/foundations-inclusive-global-education-exploring-equity-ebony-ellis%3FtrackingId=WU7BkLD4RdurydJ0en5nIg%253D%253D/?trackingId=WU7BkLD4RdurydJ0en5nIg%3D%3D

Willinsky, J. (1998). Learning to divide the world: Education at empire's end. University of Minnesota Press.

Wood, D. (2023). Lessons Learned from Low-Income, First-Generation, Technical, and Rural Students (LIFTRs) Who Participate in Education Abroad. *Frontiers: The Interdisciplinary Journal of Study Abroad, 35*(3), 238–273. https://doi.org/10.36366/frontiers.v35i3.833

Woodson, K. (Ed.). (2020). *Colorism: Investigating a Global Phenomenon* (Fielding Monograph Series Book 14). Fielding University Press.

# 20

# Considering Immigration and Visa Challenges with International Student Mobility

**Kelia Hubbard**

For full degree-seeking international students, global mobility is a fundamental part of their experience. Pursuing their educational goals requires relocating from their home country to the United States. Adding an education abroad experience can be exciting but also presents some challenges. International students must consider not only the cost of their travel but also the ramifications of traveling internationally and what documentation is necessary for a successful trip. Specifically, immigration laws and procedures in the United States can make international travel more challenging for international students. According to the Department of State's monthly nonimmigrant visa issuance statistics (U.S. Department of State Bureau of Consular Affairs, n.d.), the F-1 visa status is the most common degree-seeking student visa status used in the United States. The F-1 visa (Academic Student) allows an individual to enter the United States in order to study full time at an accredited academic institution, authorized by the U.S. government to accept international students, and the program must culminate in a degree, diploma, or certificate (U.S. Department of Homeland Security, n.d.). As stated in clause 6.1.16 of the *Standards of Good Practice*, "responsible parties shall communicate the need to comply with host country immigration and/or visa process for students of all citizenship statues" (The Forum on

Education Abroad, 2020). In this chapter, we will explore some of the policies, procedures, and authorities that govern travel for international students in the F-1 visa status and offer best practices in support of clause 6.1.16.1, "responsible parties should support the immigration and/or visa processes with information and required documentation" (The Forum on Education Abroad, 2020).

## Travel Documents

When traveling outside the United States, whether back to their home country or to another location, international students must ensure that they have proper travel documentation. This includes a passport that is valid for at least six months at the time of entering the United States, a valid F-1 visa, and a valid and properly endorsed form I-20 (U.S. Department of Homeland Security, n.d.). Students from Canada and Bermuda do not require an F-1 visa stamp to obtain F-1 status (U.S. Department of Homeland Security Study in the States, 2013b). The form I-20 is the "Certificate of Eligibility for Nonimmigrant Student Status" (U.S. Department of Homeland Security, n.d.) and is issued by the Designated School Official (DSO) at the home institution. The travel signature on page two of the I-20 is valid for one year from the date signed by the DSO. The student can travel internationally multiple times on that same signature, within the one year as long as they meet all other travel requirements. The DSO will explain these requirements to the student prior to traveling. In addition, the student must have an active F-1 record in the Student and Exchange Visitor Information System (SEVIS) (U.S. Immigration and Customs Enforcement, 2024). There are some occasions when a student may not know that their SEVIS record is not active, but for the most part, DSOs take careful action to notify students of any disruption in the SEVIS record and inform students of the actions needed to regain valid F-1 status. These documents will be explored in more depth below.

## Passport

It may seem obvious that a passport should be valid and available to international students for travel and other purposes, but things happen that are sometimes out of the student's control. For example, a student may damage their passport by accidentally including it in their laundry, or have their passport stolen. If a student has a long-term stay in the United States and is from a country experiencing political strife or a change in diplomatic relation with the United States, their passport may expire and they have no avenue to renew it (see, e.g., "Venezuelans can't renew their passports in the U.S. because the two countries don't have a diplomatic relationship," Rose & Peñaloza, 2022). If a student loses their passport or their passport is stolen, most countries will require that a police report be filed before issuing a replacement passport. Some countries may require the student to appear in person at their Embassy in the United States and submit proper proof of citizenship and identity. Once the student can obtain a new passport, their U.S. visa is no longer available because it was stamped in the old passport. A valid U.S. visa is needed to enter the United States. All of these factors add stress to an already stressful situation, especially if international travel is expected to occur soon.

## Valid F-1 Visa

According to the Immigration and Customs Enforcement (ICE), a valid visa is necessary to enter the United States unless a student is from a country that is not required to have a visa such as Canada (U.S. Immigration and Customs Enforcement, 2020). International students can only obtain a visa from outside the United States. The validity period of the visa stamp will vary from country to country. The United States Department of State may allow some students from certain countries to have a visa valid for 4–5 years and multiple entries, while other countries are limited to 1 year of visa validity that can only be used for one entry. According to the United States Code (Issuance of Visas, n.d.), the consular officer has discretion when granting the visa.

Consider the ramifications of the visa on international student mobility for a student who attended high school in the United States for two years and then attends a four-year university. If this student was given a four-year visa to attend high school, by their second year of university the visa is expired and the student's passport is expiring in five months. This student wants to participate in a study abroad in Spain and is from a country that is required to have a visa to travel to Spain. First, the student must follow the procedures to renew their passport through their country's embassy inside the United States. Depending on the timing of the study abroad program's start date, the student may need to pay extra fees to request expedited processing of their passport. The student may also need to appear in person at the embassy to renew the passport—even if it is located far away from campus—and pay extra fees for expedited mail services.

## I-20 Signature

The Certificate of Eligibility for Nonimmigrant Student Status or Form I-20 is issued by the DSO at the university the student is attending. The school officials in the international office with the official title of Primary Designated School Official (PDSO) or Designated School Official, also known as the DSO, are the only officials able to access SEVIS and issue the form I-20. The I-20 is three pages. Page 1 has the student's biographical information, school information, academic program information, and financial support information. Page 2 lists information related to employment authorization and travel signatures. Page 3 provides a summary of the visa status rules and requirements. See the Department of Homeland Security's Study in the States website for a sample of this form (n.d.).

The I-20 is a required part of the travel documentation needed for an F-1 student to be able to enter or re-enter the United States (Immigration and Customs Enforcement, 2020). The DSO supports the travel authorization process by signing on page 2 of the I-20, indicating that there have been no significant changes on the I-20 and the student is eligible to return to the university to continue their studies upon completion of their international travel. The travel signature is valid for 12 months and can be used for multiple trips.

Referencing back to the case status above regarding the visa for Spain since the travel signature is valid only for one year, it could expire prior to the student's return to the United States from a yearlong study abroad program. Since the I-20 travel signature is a key document in the re-entry process, DSOs generally work with students to ensure that students obtain a travel signature during their study abroad program. This is much easier now that I-20s can be signed electronically compared to the pre-COVID days of having to mail I-20s abroad with just the right amount of planning and timing to ensure the student receives the I-20 (U.S. Department of Homeland Security, 2021).

## Study Abroad Authorization

Earlier it was mentioned that the DSO authorizes study abroad participation for F-1 visa holders. There are procedures that the DSO should follow in order to support the international student in participating in a study abroad program but the Code of Federal Regulations (CFR) does not provide specific instructions to authorize study abroad participation. According to the Department of Homeland Security, DSOs should draw from the text from three sections of the regulations "8 CFR 214.2(f)(4), 8 CFR 214.2(f)(5)(iii), 8 CFR 214.2(f)(10)" (U.S. Department of Homeland Security, 2013a) that relate to the topic of study abroad participation and authorization. These three regulatory sections reference status maintenance requirements and guide the DSOs decision-making process. International students with the F-1 visa status are (1) required to maintain full-time enrollment, (2) not travel outside the United States for more than five months (see the Five Month Rule section below), and (3) make progress toward their degree program, among other status maintenance requirements. The DSO must consider status maintenance requirements among the overall procedures needed for an international student to participate in a study abroad program. In addition, an F-1 student is allowed to study abroad after completing at least one term in their F-1 status. If an F-1 student is participating in a study abroad program during the first term of their enrollment, for example, as a participant in a first-year education abroad program, the student will have to report to the school first or not have their visa status start until the term that they are entering the United States for their degree program.

It is important that DSOs and the Study Abroad Office work closely together to ensure that international student has proper guidance and authorization prior to their study abroad travel, as stated the clause 6.1.16.1 of the *Standards of Good Practice* (The Forum on Education Abroad, 2020). International students are responsible for intentionally monitoring their immigration status and following the instructions of their DSO and Study Abroad Advisor. Ultimately the visa holder will be held accountable for maintaining their visa status. A common procedure for authorizing study abroad involves the international student being admitted to the study abroad program including having a formal letter of acceptance from the Study Abroad Office that provides detailed information about the study abroad program and confirms their full-time enrollment during the study abroad program. The student will present this letter to the DSO along with their immigration documents. The DSO will review their travel documentation, and then enter information regarding the study abroad program into SEVIS.

## Five-Month Rule

Another challenging aspect of travel for international students is the five-month rule. The five-month rule instructs DSOs to terminate the status of an F-1 visa holder who is outside the United States for more than five months. According to the Immigration and Customs Enforcement (ICE), one of the basic requirements needed for re-entering the United States from abroad is "You have been out of the United States for less than five months (U.S. Immigration and Customs Enforcement, 2020)," which is documented through departure records. There is an exception to the 5-month rule for students who are on an approved study abroad program, which makes it even more important that the DSO and study abroad advisor are working closely together to document and approve an international student for a study abroad program (U.S. Department of Homeland Security, 2017).

## Other Considerations

It is important to note that Study Abroad Offices are faced with supporting international students that are beyond the oversight of the international office on campus. This is not to say that international offices do not support these students, but international offices may not always have knowledge of all international students who are on campus. The students that universities identify as international may include students who hold a visa status that is not sponsored by the university (e.g., students who have visas via their families or a refugee status) or students who are undocumented or hold the Deferred Action for Childhood Arrivals (DACA) status.

Other visa types that the Study Abroad Office may come across include F-2, J-2, H-4, and a host of other dependent visa classifications. Most dependent visas are issued to individuals who are under the age of 21, and unmarried, to accompany their parents to the United States. The dependent visa status is valid only as long as the primary visa holder maintains their status. Study abroad offices can collaborate with their DSO colleagues for assistance with determining the visa classification and eligibility for travel, although there may be times when the visa holder needs to consult with an immigration attorney depending on the many variables that can exist within visa classifications. A common issue is what DSOs label as "aging out," which occurs when a dependent visa holder approaches the age of 21 where they are no longer eligible to hold a dependent visa status. Most visa holders will be aware of this and seek guidance from the DSO on the best plan to change their visa status from dependent status to an F-1 degree-seeking student status as the primary visa holder. There are complexities and nuances to changing a visa status that study abroad offices may not be aware of and this is another situation that requires partnership and open lines of communication between the study abroad and the international office.

DACA brings different challenges for status holders. DACA does not grant a person legal status in the United States. The DACA status essentially places a temporary respite on deportation proceedings for persons who were brought to the United States as children and do not have a valid immigration status. According to the Immigrant Legal Resource Center, a person granted

DACA status can apply for a travel authorization known as "advance parole" if they are traveling for humanitarian reasons, for educational purposes, or for employment purposes (Immigrant Legal Resource Center, 2015). This sounds great in theory, but the U.S. Department of Homeland Security gives authority to U.S. Customs and Border Protection (CBP) to ultimately decide who is allowed to enter the United States. Some DACA recipients may not feel comfortable applying for advance parole, or using advance parole, for this reason. Immigrants Rising recommends DACA recipients weigh the risks before using advance parole (Immigrants Rising, n.d.). Moreover, over the last 10 years, DACA has been rescinded and restored, causing increased stress and uncertainty for recipients (American Immigration Council, 2021). The risk of being outside the United States when yet another judge halts DACA is understandably too high for some DACA recipients.

The term "undocumented" refers to persons who do not hold DACA status and are not in a valid visa status inside the United States. Persons who are undocumented should not depart the United States as there is no travel authorization that they can hold, and they are at risk of being deported from the United States and denied entry into the United States. Study Abroad Offices may not be able to provide programming outside the United States for all students considered international, and they should be aware of the variables that exist within the international population.

Other considerations that can affect international student mobility are political ideology and staffing at federal agencies. Depending on the governing forces at any moment in time in the United States the options available for international student travel can become more or less challenging. As an example, if there is a more restrictive stance taken toward a specific country as we saw during the travel bans in 2020 (NAFSA, 2021), then the mobility of international students from that country could become very limited. In addition, the nationwide challenges with hiring and retaining employees also affect federal agencies. Therefore, during times of larger employment shortages federal agencies will take longer to process applications such as visas and new employees may take longer to build their knowledge and capacity on regulations and procedures related to student visa types.

## Resources

Keep in mind that international students are responsible for maintaining their immigration status. Whether you are a well-staffed office or a single-person office, use your resources to ensure that you stay educated about the various procedures related to studying abroad for international students.

A key resource is going to be the study abroad colleagues with their vast knowledge and experience working with various countries to obtain visas for study abroad participants and your international office colleagues with their extensive U.S. visa knowledge. If you work in an international office, ensure that you are researching and studying the Code of Federal Regulations and are familiar with what is required for an international student to maintain their status. Use professional organizations such as the Forum on Education Abroad, NAFSA: Association of International Educators, the American Immigration Lawyers Association (AILA), and the President's Alliance for Higher Education. These organizations put out resources related to immigration and global travel matters and changes likely to affect institutions of higher learning and education abroad programming. Go to the source, federal agency websites, to obtain information on their procedures and requirements. Finally, contact other DSOs and study abroad colleagues at other schools to compare policies and generate new ideas to help support the international student population.

Professional organizations:
The Forum on Education Abroad: https://www.forumea.org/
NAFSA Association of International Educators: https://www.nafsa.org/
American Immigration Lawyers Association (AILA): https://www.aila.org/
President's Alliance for Higher Education: https://www.presidentsalliance.org/

Federal agencies that most commonly deal with travel:
Department of State: https://www.state.gov/
Department of Homeland Security: https://www.dhs.gov/
Immigration and Customs Enforcement: https://www.ice.gov/
Customs and Border Protection: https://www.cbp.gov/

## References

American Immigration Council. (2021, September 30). *Deferred Action for Childhood Arrivals (DACA): An overview*. Retrieved April 16, 2024, from https://www.americanimmigrationcouncil.org/research/deferred-action-childhood-arrivals-daca-overview

Immigrant Legal Resource Center. (2015). *Travel for DACA applicants: Advance Parole*. https://www.ilrc.org/sites/default/files/documents/advance_parole_guide.pdf

Immigrants Rising. (n.d.). *Advance Parole: Weighing the benefits and risks*. https://immigrantsrising.org/resource/advance-parole-weighing-the-benefits-and-risks/

Issuance of visas, 8 U.S.C. § 1201. (n.d.). https://uscode.house.gov/view.xhtml?req=granuleid:USC-prelim-title8-section1201&num=0&edition=prelim

NAFSA. (2021, March 11). *Travel Ban: NAFSA Resources*. https://www.nafsa.org/professional-resources/browse-by-interest/executive-order-travel-ban-nafsa-resources

Rose, J., & Peñaloza, M. (2022, October 19). *Thousands of Venezuelan migrants legally in the U.S. are in limbo unable to work.* NPR. https://www.npr.org/2022/10/19/1130026634/venezuelan-migrants-stuck-legal-limbo

The Forum on Education Abroad. (2020). *Standards of good practice for education abroad* (Sixth Ed.). doi.org/10.36366/S.978-1-952376-04-7

U.S. Citizenship and Immigration Services. (n.d.). *Students and employment.* Retrieved March 30, 2024, from https://www.uscis.gov/working-in-the-united-states/students-and-exchange-visitors/students-and-employment

U.S. Department of Homeland Security. (n.d.). *Students and the form I-20.* Study in the States. https://studyinthestates.dhs.gov/students/prepare/students-and-the-form-i-20

U.S. Department of Homeland Security. (2013a, July 15). *May I participate in a study abroad program?.* Study in the States. https://studyinthestates.dhs.gov/2013/07/may-i-participate-study-abroad-program

U.S. Department of Homeland Security. (2013b, October 6). *Questions from Designated School Officials: Which countries citizens do not need to apply for an F or M visa to study at an SEVP-Certified school?* Study in the States, https://studyinthestates.dhs.gov/2013/10/questions-designated-school-officials-which-countries-citizens-do-not-need-apply-f-or-m

U.S. Department of Homeland Security. (2017, January 26). *Questions from DSOs: Do students returning from temporary absences need new visas?* Study in the States. https://studyinthestates.dhs.gov/2017/01/questions-dsos-do-students-returning-temporary-absences-need-new-visas

U.S. Department of Homeland Security. (2021, October 12). *SEVP Policy Guidance: Use of electronic signatures and transmission for the form I-20.* https://www.ice.gov/doclib/sevis/pdf/I20-guidance.pdf

U.S. Department of State. (n.d). *Monthly Nonimmigrant Visa issuance statistics.* https://travel.state.gov/content/travel/en/legal/visa-law0/visa-statistics/nonimmigrant-visa-statistics/monthly-nonimmigrant-visa-issuances.html

U.S. Immigration and Customs Enforcement. (2020, December 28). *Travel.* https://www.ice.gov/sevis/travel

U.S. Immigration and Customs Enforcement. (2024, February 27). *Student and Exchange Visitor Program.* https://www.ice.gov/sevis

# 21

## Approaching Disability Inclusion via Universal Design for Learning, Regulations, and the Standards

**Laurie Laird and Lindsey Pamlanye**

*"Travel abroad is a great opportunity for students and a wonderful way to learn. I hope that everyone–regardless of disability–gains the right to fall and get back up again while taking in an amazing country."—disabled participant in study abroad program (MIUSA, n.d.-a)*

### Accessibility and Inclusion Statement

Disability will be referenced in a variety of contexts throughout this chapter. To adequately portray the diverse experiences in the disability community, identity-first and person-first language will be used interchangeably. The phrases people with disabilities, disabled participants, disabled applicants, and so on will be incorporated without prejudice or preference. Terminology is intended to reflect the spectrum of language utilized not only by disabled individuals domestically within the United States, but with respect to the international context and does not center or privilege the U.S. experience. Within the international disability community, there is a mixed capitalization of d/Disability as not all people with a diagnosed disability identify as members of the Disabled community, especially noted in d/Deaf culture. This chapter will predominantly use disability.

The importance of language in the disability space cannot be understated. Consistent with the principles of the social model of disability, which will be discussed in more depth, disabled people and their experiences are considered the primary authority. As such, the authors' primary recommendation is to privilege the choice of disabled people and to defer to their requested terminology on an individual basis. The authors also acknowledge that language in the field is regularly updated, which is especially true of terms used to describe disability-related identities.

This chapter offers guidance intended to serve as a starting point, not finite instruction. The authors recommend that readers regularly pursue professional development to remain current on disability-related laws and language in both the United States and destination countries. The experience of disability varies from country to country—whether it is the legal terminology, disability culture, or how accessibility is implemented. The chapter content itself is an exercise of disability inclusion and strives to adhere to the *standards of Universal Design for Learning* (UDL) (AHEAD, n.d.). It is written in plain language and incorporates bulleted lists where appropriate. Finally, this chapter aligns with the social model of disability and the Disability Rights Movement's fundamental ethos of centering the authority of disabled people. Staying true to the guiding principle of "Nothing About Us Without Us," among accessibility advocates, this chapter draws directly from the experiences of people with disabilities, including the authors.

## Background

In Chapter 5 of this volume, "Analyzing the Legal Opportunities and Challenges for Students with Disabilities," of this publication, author Seth F. Gilbertson (2024) provides an overview of how the discrimination against disabled people manifests in the United States as well as the legal mechanisms that are in place in relation to risk mitigation for disabled students pursuing education abroad. The Americans with Disabilities Act (ADA) (Americans with Disabilities Act, 1990), Section 504 of the Rehabilitation Act (Rehabilitation Act, 1973), the United Nations Convention on the Rights of People with Disabilities (UNCRPD) (Convention on the Rights of Persons with Disabilities, 2006), and the Web Content Accessibility Guidelines (WCAG) (W3C, 2023) are some key regulations that focus on disability inclusion. The importance of such standards that promote inclusion by protecting against discrimination is largely uncontested. However, the systematic exclusion of people with disabilities that necessitated the establishment of these regulations continues to influence how disability is both experienced and perceived across all facets of society. Institutionalized ableism, internalized ableism, myths, misconceptions, and stigma related to disability continue to impact the lived experience of disabled people internationally. Higher education institutions and collaborating partners are not immune to these influences.

The path to inclusion requires ongoing, intentional attention to dismantle and avoid discriminatory practices at all stages of participant engagement. This especially includes international programming as education abroad professionals strive to incorporate best practices in accessibility and ultimately work toward inclusion. The scope of this chapter does not permit for an extended discussion of all legal aspects related to disability and education abroad. Instead, its primary focus is to build on the discussion in the previous chapter of this volume (Gilbertson, 2024) and offer foundational information that further informs the practical application of best practices for disability inclusion in education abroad to mitigate risk. The content draws liberally from the resources compiled by the National Clearinghouse on Disability and Exchange (NCDE), a project sponsored since 1995 by the U.S. Department of State's Bureau of Educational and Cultural Affairs and administered by Mobility International USA to increase the participation of people with disabilities in international exchange between the United States and other countries. The resources of the NCDE are available for free to support all those involved in international exchange—students, international exchange professionals, disability services professionals, and exchange providers—and include best practices, tip sheets, personal stories, advising forms, and more.

In an increasingly interconnected, interdependent global society, international experiences are promoted as a necessary element of student experience to compete in the current climate that requires high levels of intercultural competence and global citizenship (British Council, 2022, U.S. Department of State, 2021). Yet, disabled students continue to be underrepresented in these opportunities compared with their nondisabled peers. According to the Open Doors Report (Institute of International Education [IIE], 2023), the percentage of students with disabilities who studied abroad in 2019–2020 was 12.4%. Although this number has increased over previous academic years, it continues to fall far below representing the actual percentage of students in higher education who reported a disability at 21% that same year (National Center for Education Statistics, n.d.). Taking these numbers into account and applying principles of UDL, education abroad professionals must develop opportunities that facilitate disabled student participation at all stages of programming—from recruitment to program matriculation, and they must do so while mitigating the associated risk factors. Ensuring that all students—including disabled students—have the opportunity to develop these global competencies requires intentionality on behalf of exchange professionals. This chapter provides guidance for such intentionality.

## Frameworks for Guiding Disability Inclusion

To discuss initiatives of disability inclusion, it is necessary to first establish a foundation for defining disability and how the many facets of disability manifest within the international education sector. Having a working understanding of the core concepts of disability will empower professionals to enter conversations with education-abroad participants, disability resource professionals, education-abroad providers, and other relevant stakeholders, with a sense of confidence and an openness to learn, as well as advocate for change.

As established in Gilbertson (2024), the Americans with Disabilities Act (1990) is a civil rights law that prohibits discrimination against individuals with disabilities in all areas of public life. The ADA defines disability as "a person who has a physical or mental impairment that substantially limits one or more major life activities, a person who has a history or record of such an impairment, or a person who is perceived by others as having such an impairment" (ADA.gov, 2023). The ADA does not specifically name all of the impairments that are covered (ADA.gov, 2023). Relatively structured definitions of disability as described above can give credence to the "one-size fits all" approach to understanding, and by extension, accommodating, disability. This chapter expands on the ADA's description of disability and asserts that education abroad professionals will benefit from developing a well-rounded understanding of disability language and culture to serve participants.

Mike Oliver (2004) offers an alternative framework for defining disability and describes two primary models for understanding disability: the individual (medical) model and the social model of disability. Oliver explains, "the idea underpinning the individual model was that of personal tragedy, while the idea underpinning the social model was that of externally imposed restriction" (2004, p. 20). These two models describe the lived disability experience.

The *standards* of the medical model frame disability as an inherent, individual characteristic to be eliminated or fixed. In this way, being nondisabled is the societal norm and people with disabilities ultimately need "to be cured, fixed, and cared for through medical intervention and therapy" (MIUSA, n.d.-e). The experts on disability under the medical model are professionals, such as doctors, nurses, and scientists. Examples of how the medical model practices manifest in international programming include requiring rigorous means testing, diagnostic proof for reasonable accommodations, and the use of identity-first language.

Conversely, the social model of disability centers on the disabled person as the primary authority. The social model of disability is largely connected to the Disability Rights Movement and aligns with the principle of Nothing About Us Without Us. Rather than defining disability as inherent to the individual, disability is instead considered a product of societal barriers. Environmental and attitudinal barriers are what actually prevent people with disabilities from having equal opportunities in their societies (MIUSA, n.d.-e). Where the medical model classifies disability itself as an impairment, the social model contends that disabled people are impaired by inaccessible environments. The solution therefore is not always in curing individuals but instead reconstructing environments in a way that accommodates all needs. This is a vital distinction for education abroad professionals as it empowers them to be agents of change.

A proven method for creating educational environments that take a proactive approach to inclusion is incorporating principles of Universal Design for Learning (UDL). UDL is an educational framework for adapting to diverse learner needs. Developed by CAST (originally the Center for Applied Special Technology), it emphasizes flexibility in curriculum design, providing multiple means of representation, engagement, and expression (CAST, 2022; Mace, R, et al., 1991). UDL emphasizes adaptable curriculum design, offering multiple avenues for representation, engagement, and expression, and ultimately promotes inclusivity and equitable access. In a practical sense, UDL borrows and builds on the Universal Design concepts utilized in product design and architecture that promote accessibility from the outset. If all users are considered at the concept stage, end products will be more useful and require less reactive adjustments after the final design is complete (AHEAD, n.d.).

UDL takes Universal Design into the educational sphere and promotes inclusive teaching, accommodating various learning styles, abilities, and preferences, fostering an equitable and accessible learning environment. It is directly transferable to the study abroad field because applying its principles to all aspects of international experience—recruitment, advising, studying abroad, program development—means an emphasis on proactive rather than reactive accessibility, and ultimately steps toward inclusion.

Noting that a goal of UDL is to create and enhance environments to meet the access needs for a broad range of diverse participants, Soneson and Cordano (2009) offer a framework for understanding access by considering the functional abilities required to engage in particular environments. They identify four categories of functional abilities: (1) Physical—which includes mobility functional abilities that can manifest as muscle weakness, loss of balance, limited flexibility, dexterity, or ability to walk or climb stairs, and systemic-related functional abilities that can be symptoms of diseases such as lupus, epilepsy, multiple sclerosis, chronic fatigue syndrome, among others; (2) Sensory—which includes sensory differences of individuals who are blind or low vision or deaf/hard of hearing; (3) Cognitive—which includes neurological conditions that affect the ability to listen, read, write, reason, speak, or compute; and (4) Emotional and Behavioral—which include neurological conditions that manifest in behavioral and emotional symptoms.

By analyzing programs through the lens of the types of access that each provides and how that overlays with functional abilities, program providers will be better able to support participants in identifying the best programmatic match and any accommodations that may be required to address their specific functional abilities. Soneson and Cordano's framework further equips education abroad professionals with language that will be beneficial, especially as it relates to the provision of reasonable accommodations (to be discussed later in this chapter). It is important to note that while this framework works on a continuum of functional abilities, there is no hierarchy associated with these abilities. No student should ever be considered "more" or "less" functional based on their type of disability. Instead, consistent with the social model, providers can look to environments and determine what adjustments can reasonably be made to become more inclusive.

## Collaborating for Success

Education abroad programming requires dynamic collaboration to be successful. A wide range of partners—from the participants themselves, host institutions, disability resource advisors, and so on—must come together to ensure that needs are met at all stages of the journey. Soneson and Minder (2020) provide a comprehensive breakdown of these individual roles and their corresponding responsibilities to help prepare colleges and universities for not only meeting the requirements of the law but also working toward creating educational opportunities that achieve universal access and full inclusion. As described in Gilbertson (2024), the application of the ADA in international contexts can be a gray area. However, many forward-looking institutions operate, as much as possible, under the assumption that the law does apply in most education-abroad contexts and work with partners to meet its standards.

The *Standards of Good Practice in Education Abroad* guiding principle 5.1.8 under "Administrative Framework" recommends institutions establish guidelines to support effective partnerships (The Forum on Education Abroad, 2020). Such guidelines offer a natural platform to bring the lens of disability inclusion. Some specific examples include the following:

- Establishing partnerships and formalizing collaboration: This could include specifically stating an institution's commitment to disability inclusion and expectations they have for the collaborating organization with regard to supporting the reasonable accommodation process. Explicitly defining the roles and responsibilities of each organization or party—the student, the disability services office, the study abroad office, as well as the host site or third-party provider—at each stage of the experience is considered a best practice. Providing clear examples and expectations helps to reduce risk and establishes a foundation for open communication and collaboration.
- Responsibility for security and risk management: This would address specifically how the safety of participants with diverse disabilities will be addressed throughout a program and who assumes risk in different contexts.
- Managing privacy, confidentiality, and disclosure practices: With regard to disability disclosure, clear protocols should be established around what information is shared with whom and at what step in the process as well as how these protocols are communicated with the participants. Maintaining privacy while maximizing access to needed resources should be the goal.
- Marketing practices: Digital accessibility should be at the forefront of all marketing efforts. Including images and personal stories of past participants with disabilities in a way that is not exploitative and shares a compelling message that a program is committed to supporting such participants and has a track record for doing so.
- Partnership review: Regularly revisiting expectations and protocols to ensure that they are serving all parties is an important practice. Such reviews should incorporate the input of participants with disabilities.

Institutions such as the University of Arizona, the University of Illinois at Urbana-Champaign, and the University of Minnesota, as well as consortiums like CIEE, have been shifting to a model of disability access that takes UDL principles into consideration, reducing the need for requests of specialized accommodation and the accompanying documentation it requires (Oswald & Webb, 2022).

Digital accessibility is a critical area that affects all aspects of the education abroad journey. Ensuring that websites, platforms used for the application process, communication systems, and survey tools are accessible is an important step in making programs inclusive and mitigating risk. Following the WCAG for institutional websites is a first step. Additionally, program providers need to work with their collaborating partners to verify that they are adhering to the same accessibility standards. Providing alt-text descriptions for images and describing visual content during presentations or webinars further demonstrate a program's commitment to inclusion.

To provide equal opportunities, education abroad programs must consider the accessibility of locations and formats for program activities even before someone with a disability expresses interest in participating in a program. The University of North Carolina at Chapel Hill reached out to disability organizations at destination sites for advice on how to better review access standards (MIUSA, n.d.-b). They collected accessibility information and posted their findings and photos to their website as part of each program page's "Accessibility" tab. Sharing information in this way supports students to make informed decisions when choosing a program.

Stating clearly that opportunities offered to one program participant should be available to all participants will establish expectations about accessibility for all elements of a program, including field excursions. Contractually, programs should not be partnering with third parties that are exclusionary of people with disabilities. Identifying disability-inclusive programming in advance can be a better option for all students and is easily incorporated into all programs, regardless of whether participants with disabilities are taking part. It is important to note that while UDL is best practice, it is not possible to be 100% accessible. For example, what is accessible for someone with a hearing impairment may be inaccessible for someone with a vision impairment. Ultimately, even if an exchange environment is not considered 100% accessible for a participant, that individual still has the autonomy to choose that experience. Institutions, providers, advisors, and so on should continue to create environments and experiences that adhere to the principles of UDL and be prepared to offer reasonable accommodations, and participants will continue to weigh the risk and reward on an individual basis.

It is equally important to ensure that policies do not impose accommodations on a participant with a disability that are unrequested and/or unnecessary and make them a condition for taking part in a program.Restricting the only blind participant in the program from traveling independently, when participants without disabilities do not have this requirement would be an example of this.

Other best practices in working with host site providers and partners include the following:

- Engage partners in access assessments of all program elements considering multiple disabilities and corresponding needs. This would include excursion sites, housing, transportation, websites, learning management systems, and communication platforms, among other elements.

- Invite them to collaborate in researching local disability-related laws and how they are enforced and communicate that to students.
- Ask partners to make connections with local disability organizations that can serve as consultants and offer guidance.
- Include partners in working with a student to identify creative solutions and adaptations that will meet their needs.
- Involve partners in developing detailed descriptions of a program, considering functional abilities required, and any expectations for participants that are integral to the learning and living experience.
- Regularly revisit safety protocols and emergency plans to ensure that they include and meet the needs of diverse participants, including people with disabilities.
- Involve people with disabilities as paid consultants to review itineraries, physical environments, digital resources, and program plans for accessibility.

Sometimes conflicts happen when trying to work with partners with different cultural perspectives to negotiate access solutions or arrange disability-related services at a program location. Take the following proactive steps to encourage a successful collaboration:

- If you encounter attitudes that pose barriers to inclusino, ask your partner about what concerns they have and, one by one, problem-solve around specific issues or dispel misconceptions.
- Identify allies or champions in the local community so that you can engage them for support wthen they have the right connections to help you achieve your goal.
- Change happens different in different cultures and communities. Try to identify how change happens in your partners' context and what motivates reconsideration in this setting. This could include leveraging personal connections, presenting legal or financial arguments, or providing examples of how inclusion happens on your other programs. Employ the appropriate strategy given the culture and context.

## Recruitment

There are proven strategies to encourage people with disabilities to apply for education abroad programs. It is helpful to keep in mind that some disabled candidates may have been excluded from similar programming in the past or been told outright that education abroad is not for them. Make it clear they are welcome and will be supported to find programming that meets their needs.

Some successful practices include (MIUSA, n.d.-c) the following:

- Use welcoming language in promotional materials and consider including a specific statement such as "we encourage people with disabilities and from other diverse backgrounds to apply. We do not discriminate based on disability."
- Ensure that websites, digital resources, and all materials and platforms used throughout the education abroad experience—from marketing collateral to application portals to orientation and program content and evaluation surveys—are accessible and made available in alternative formats, and let potential participants know they are available upon request.
- Include images of people with apparent disabilities in brochures and websites and, if possible, quotes about the impactful experiences of disabled participants.
- Do not rely solely on pictures and videos to convey information about a country and its culture (e.g., food, art, and architecture). Provide rich written descriptions with specific details.
- Share materials and do outreach and in-person training in collaboration with disability services offices, disability student clubs, independent living centers, and other organizations and individuals that regularly engage with diverse groups of people with disabilities.

## Advising

Professionals in the education abroad field often express apprehension about how to approach advising people with disabilities. An unfortunate reality for disabled students is that some advisors, likely acting with the best of intentions, steer them away from sites or programs where the environment may be (from the advisor's perspective) less accessible or less predictable. Each person with a disability is unique. What they are seeking in their experience abroad (personally, academically, and/or culturally) as well as their needs are as varied as they are for nondisabled peers. The approach to supporting people with disabilities should be nearly the same as advising their nondisabled peers. Start with an attitude of "yes." Communicate with the interested student that you are committed to supporting them in achieving their dream of education abroad and together you will work through the process. The core concerns should be identifying the participant's learning goals and what supports are needed for their full engagement in a program. This is true for all participants—regardless of disability status.

Much like gender identity, sexual orientation, economic status, or care-giving responsibilities, disability is only one component of an individual's life experience that must be considered when advising on exchange. People with disabilities have diverse talents, skills, goals, and abilities. Stay conscious of this and let the individual participant guide the discussion regarding their international interests.

An unfamiliarity with different disabilities and terms may contribute to some awkwardness around language use. While it is important to remain informed of best practice, such efforts can quickly become a preoccupation and detract from inclusion efforts. Language should defer to what is being employed by the person with the disability whenever possible. People prefer to refer to their disability in different ways and some avoid labels entirely. The ultimate goal is to make environmental adjustments that support the full inclusion of disabled participants, driven by their instruction.

Disabled participants know their needs better than anybody, and once acquainted with the requirements of a program, they ultimately will make their own choice. In some cases, students may benefit from guiding questions to determine how their needs may call for accommodations or support in another country. Clear program descriptions that adhere to principles of UDL and detail the physical, sensory, cognitive, and other elements of an environment coupled with forms or questionnaires can assist professionals in working with participants. Students with disabilities often require more detailed descriptions of all aspects of a program to determine whether or not participation in that program is viable.

Program providers should not assume that discomfort or risk automatically impacts student eligibility. Advisors should avoid making broad assumptions that a certain country is inaccessible, for example. A hyper-fixation on a student's disability may lead to other factors influencing their eligibility or choices. People with disabilities want opportunities to grow and learn and they have the right to try,regardless of whether or not they succeed in the challenge. These students need encouragement rather than overprotection.

It is not typically expected that education abroad advisors are experts in disability services. Instead, it is more likely that accommodations are under the purview of the institution's disability services and accommodations office. In addition, open communication and close collaboration between these offices are considered a best practice. Participants with disabilities should work closely with all of their relevant advisors, both in and outside of the institution, during their education abroad discernment process.

## Ongoing Support

Advising continues beyond program discernment. Keeping an open mind and an open line of communication with participants supports potential changes to their engagement. No matter how much planningfor accessibility and inclusion abroad is done in advance, discovering new barriers in or having equipment failures is common, so there will almost always be a need for adjustments and contingencies,. Create a plan to revisit accommodations that are in place and identify any new issues and solutions regularly. Asking questions that center on the participant's experience and how the program is meeting their needs and learning goals can help surface potential areas for attention or adjustments.

Program alumni with disabilities can offer valuable insights on how accessibility canbe improved. Invite them to share their story with you and with future participants. While each individual is different, there are universal lessons that can be useful to pay attention to the following:

- How did you access health insurance? Did you encounter any issues?
- What resources were they able to access to support disability-related expenses?
- Were partners or staff abroad ready or was significant negotiation required?
- Could more have been done to identify community resources in advance or plan for more housing choices?

Approach the support process as an ongoing opportunity for learning and program improvement that can inform systemic change related to inclusion. When a barrier is identified, consider it from multiple angles and functional abilities. This can help surface other potential barriers that can be addressed proactively. And look for ways that lessons learned or successful modifications can be applied or adapted to work in other locations or across programs leading to greater impact and not a one-off solution.

## Reasonable Accommodations

The term "reasonable accommodation" designates the various modifications that may be needed so that people with disabilities have the same opportunities as people without disabilities to live full lives in their communities. The *Standards of Good Practice for Education Abroad* defines it as "a modification or adjustment to a course, program, service, job, activity, assessment, test, or facility that enables a qualified individual with a disability to have equal opportunity to attain the same level of performance or to enjoy the same benefits and privileges that are available to an individual without a disability" (The Forum on Education Abroad, 2020, clause 3.41).

Modes of reasonable accommodation vary according to location and culture. Medications that are standard procedure in one locale might require additional documentation, as is often the case for students with ADHD traveling to Japan that require a *Yakkan Shoumi* from the Japanese Department of Health (Mobility International USA, 2022; see also Chapter 14 of this volume, Sprovieri & Fullick, 2024). Students may require extended time for testing and their destination country may offer a lesser amount of extended time. In terms of responding to risk in this context, participants need to be prepared for the adjustment and can potentially practice the new parameters in advance. Alternatively, a participant may make the advance decision about what risk is worth taking and choose a different destination that offers comparable accommodation.

Each participant will have a their own approach to their disability;some will not require accommodations. People with disabilities often own the equipment they need for everyday life and can provide clear, direct instruction about any additional requirements they may have. The right to an accommodation under both Section 504 of the Rehabilitation Act and the ADA is not unbounded. Each institution must assess whether a requested accommodation constitutes a fundamental alteration in the program that is offered or be an undue financial or administrative burden. Retroactive accommodations need not be provided. For example, a participant with a learning disability, upon realizing they arefailing a class, can request additional time to take future tests, but it would be unreasonable for previous test scores be disregarded..

Establishing reasonable accommodations is a process of negotiation between program coordinators, the host institution, and the participant; the goal of which is to ensure that the participant has an accessible—and hopefully successful—education abroad experience. Start by focusing on the barriers the participant with the disability is experiencing. Collaborate with with disability providers to determine whether the participant's requested accommodations are reasonable. Although education abroad providers are not traditionally expected to be disability experts, having foundational knowledge of UDL is a step toward inclusion. One method of intervention is providing education abroad professionals with checklists and other informational tools that can greatly increase their awareness and knowledge in the field. Ultimately, it is important for professionals to be prepared to act as a liaison between participants and relevant access services at both home and destination institutions.

Finally, prepare students for the cultural adjustments involved in studies abroad while disabled. Accessibility looks different in different places. Physical environments and cultural expectations can impact participant perceptions of independence. Advising and pre-departure preparation for participants with disabilities should include advice on what cultural differences may come up and who they can talk to if they need to process it. Connect them with peers with disabilities and local disability organizations so that they can findresources to learn more about what strategies may work as they adjust to the new culture.

A common myth among providers is that reasonable accommodations are complicated and difficult to facilitate. While some that require addressing physical barriers or hiring certified assistants necessitate more planning and may be more problematic in some locations, others accommodations are simple to arrange and do not require much advance preparation, even after the program has begun. The following is an overview of commonly requested accommodations. It is certainly not an exhaustive list, but it provides some context and language for continued discussion.

- Academic accommodations—extended time or flexible deadlines, testing in alternative venues, calculator or laptop access, reduced course load, and regular breaks.
- Alternative formats—captioning, audiobooks, transcription services, instructions read aloud, presentations/materials provided in advance, handouts, and other materials provided digitally.
- Physical environments—accessible housing, classrooms, excursions, and transportation with regard to physical barriers for individuals using mobility aids.
- Independent assistance—sign language interpreters, note-takers, readers, scribes, sighted guides, personal assistants, and additional travel time or early arrival.

The reasonable accommodation process must always begin at that point of disclosure, even if disclosure happens while the program is already in progress. The primary method to mitigate risk in this space is a proactive and collaborative approach to providing reasonable accommodations. It is vital for professionals to understand their roles and responsibilities for providing accommodations. It is also beneficial to identify allies, both at home and destination institutions, and make strides to confront any internal and institutional biases about what makes for a reasonable accommodation. Ultimately providers must create conditions that encourage participants to disclose.

## Encouraging Disclosure

Disclosure is the act of a disabled person sharing personal information about their disability with others. Students are entitled to disclose disability at any point during their education abroad program; however, they are not required to do so. If a student is disabled but does not need any specific accommodations, they may choose not to disclose. It is vital to remember that the choice of whether to pursue accommodations does not make a student more or less disabled. Students who do require accommodations or other types of support to facilitate participation will likely benefit from disclosure, but it is possible that they will avoid doing so if they fear exclusion based on their disability status. Building trust with participants is fundamental to not only encouraging disclosure, but ensuring that disclosure is coming from a place of empowerment and not vulnerability. It is best practice for professionals to engage with participants as a partner in the process of determining accommodations to support full and meaningful participation.

If a participant typically requires accommodations or other forms of support while studying at their home institution, it stands to reason that they will require similar accommodations while abroad. This means that they will likely need to disclose their disability. Many education abroad program policies will then require documentation of a disability to provide specific accommodations. Common risks associated with these practices are that students and program coordinators or providers must then be prepared to possibly translate relevant medical documents or other required materials into the language of the receiving country. This may take additional resources such as time, cost, and potentially further diagnostic testing to satisfy both program and immigration requirements. Ultimately participants must adapt to the processes and cultural practices around disability access in a particular country.

It is also important to remember that any participant can become acutely disabled at any time. It is not uncommon for participants to become ill or injured while abroad. Such participants may have no previous experience with disability, and, by extension, disclosure. These participants may not communicate their needs to their key points of contact. Consider a participant who suffers a broken leg while abroad and becomes a temporary wheelchair user. This participant might not be aware of the reasonable accommodations that are available to them and instead may choose to prematurely end their program and return to their home country. When programs incorporate the principles of Universal Design, inclusion is built in, and unanticipated needs are often already met. For example, program choices to fully include a wheelchair rider will also serve the needs of someone with a broken leg.

There are many factors disabled participants have to consider before they can safely and confidently commit to an education abroad program. While program advisors, administrators, and so on are expertly positioned to provide information that guides participants in choosing a program that best fits their needs, ultimately, the decision belongs to the participant. Advisors may remind students that while, yes, the choice is theirs, they are not alone in this decision process. Participants should consider consulting with their peers, their families, as well as trusted medical professionals. Professionals should address each individual question and use responses to aid participants in discerning the best program for them. Providing as much detailed information as possible empowers participants to make informed decisions.

## Financial Considerations

For some education abroad professionals, the concern of covering the cost of program accommodations for people with disabilities weighs heavy. Cost is seldom recognized as the reason why an accommodation is unreasonable, so anticipating costs and identifying resources for how to cover them is key. Some best practices with regard to planning and collaborating to support participants with disabilities that apply to all types of education abroad programs can help institutions be prepared.

- Consider including a line item of 1–5% of a program's budget so that some funds are available from the start. This can be especially helpful when creating new programs.
- When designing new experiences, draw on the principles of Universal Design to make them inclusive for diverse participants from the start, reducing the need for individual accommodations and associated costs.
- Recommend grants and other resources that may be available to participants, particularly those established for individuals who are historically underrepresented in education abroad, including government scholarships; be mindful of application deadlines and how they align with program timelines.
- Identify possibilities for cost-sharing across institutional departments and consider creating a fund or scholarship specifically for supporting additional costs related to disability accommodations. The University of Illinois—Champaign Urbana established the Enable Abroad Scholarship for this purpose (MIUSA, n.d.-d).

- Work with the disability resources office to provide funds at least equivalent to the cost of on-campus accommodations as many participants are already using accommodations or facilities on campus.
- Funds from vocational rehabilitation or the Supplemental Security Income (SSI) program for students who are using these programs can sometimes be used toward program fees or accommodations overseas.

## Risk of Exclusion

When looking at risk management in study abroad, the natural focus is on risks as they relate to participants and/or the institution. Planning for and mitigating those risks is what is assumed when engaging the topic. Perhaps an aspect of risk that has not been considered is the risk of loss associated with excluding or unintentionally preventing the participation of students with disabilities. Through often untended practices and in worst cases intentional lack of planning, recruitment, or clear processes for requesting reasonable accommodations, institutions run the risk of missing out on the unique perspectives and lived experience that participants with diverse disabilities can bring to the education abroad experience for all those involved. Participation in education abroad is transformative for the individual participant and the many individuals with whom they engage, from peers, to people at the host site, to members of their campus and home communities.

## Conclusion

Education abroad is rapidly becoming a fundamental aspect of higher education, and supporting the inclusion and equal access of disabled students who are historically underrepresented is important work in the field. Supporting people with disabilities is not significantly different from supporting nondisabled students. With preparation and sound protocols in place for communicating available supports and the processes for accessing/providing them, professionals will set themselves up for success in mitigating risk and more importantly making programs inclusive for all.

## Some Key Recommendations From this Chapter

- A student-centered approach that recognizes the student as the expert in their disability and needs is essential. Offer low-barrier ways to request reasonable accommodations confidentially and throughout the process.

- Find allies and collaborate. Developing clear expectations and protocols of the various organizations and parties involved can help professionals be prepared for the unexpected and support successful collaboration.
- Draw on the principles of Universal Design in program development and improvement so that the broadest range of people and functional capacities are included from the ground up.
- Remain open and flexible. Anticipating that needs will change and building the flexibility to respond is an important strategy.
- Share your success stories. Invite students with disabilities and exchange partners to share their experiences to attract other students with disabilities to engage in programs and contribute to ongoing learning for program improvement.
- Pursue ongoing professional development. The fields of international education and disability support are constantly evolving. Invest in training for all those involved and regularly seek the input of students with disabilities who participate in your program as collaborators.
- Reach out for support. The NCDE, AHEAD, NAFSA, Diversity Abroad, and The Forum on Education Abroad have robust resources, websites, trainings, and publications to support educators.

## References

ADA.gov. (2023, December 1). Introduction to the Americans with Disabilities Act. https://www.ada.gov/topics/intro-to-ada/

Americans With Disabilities Act of 1990, 42 U.S.C. § 12101 et seq. (1990).

AHEAD. (n.d.). Universal Design for Learning. https://www.ahead.ie/udl

British Council. (2022, June 14). Developing intercultural communication skills for the hybrid workplace. *Corporate English Solutions.* https://corporate.britishcouncil.org/insights/developing-intercultural-communication-skills-hybrid-workplace

CAST. (2022, February 8). About Universal Design for Learning. https://www.cast.org/impact/universal-design-for-learning-udl

Gilbertson, S. (2024). "Risks of protest participation while on education abroad. In J. Pollard & K. S. Priebe (Eds.), *Convergence of litigation, policy, and standards: Building the informed practitioner in education abroad risk management.* The Forum on Education Abroad. doi.org/10.36.366/SIA.5.978-1-952376-41-2.5

Institute of International Education. (2023). "Profile of U.S. Study Abroad Students, 2006/07 - 2021/22" *Open Doors Report on International Educational Exchange.* https://opendoors-data.org/.

Mace, R., Hardie, G., & Plaice, J. (1991). Accessible environments: Toward universal design. In W. E. Preiser, J.C. Vischer, & E.T. White (Eds.), *Design interventions: Toward a more humane architecture* (pp. 155-176).

Mobility International USA. (2022, March 5). Japan focus: ADHD and traveling with medication. https://www.miusa.org/resource/tip-sheets/yakkanshoumi/

MIUSA (Mobility International USA). (n.d-a).The right to fall. www.miusa.org/resource/personal-stories/kaiti/

MIUSA (Mobility International USA). (n.d-b). Scouting out accessibility overseas. www.miusa.org/resource/bestpractice/scoutforaccess.

MIUSA (Mobility International USA). (n.d-c). 10 Recruitment tips to attract people with disabilities. Retrieved from https://www.miusa.org/resource/tip-sheets/recruiting/

MIUSA (Mobility International USA). (n.d-d). Advocating for access. www.miusa.org/resource/best-practices/advocacy-2/

MIUSA (Mobility International USA). (n.d.-e). Models of Disability: An Overview. https://www.miusa.org/resource/tipsheet/disabilitymodels/

National Center for Education Statistics. (n.d.). Students with Disabilities. *Fast Facts*. https://nces.ed.gov/fastfacts/display.asp?id=60

Oliver, M. (2004). The social model in action: If I had a hammer. In C. Barnes & G. Mercer (Eds.) *Implementing the social model of disability: Theory and research* (pp. 18–31). The Disability Press.

Oswald, G., & Webb, T. (2022). *Universal Design in Study Abroad*. Association on Higher Education and Disability (AHEAD).

Rehabilitation Act of 1973. 29 U.S.C. § 701 et seq. (1973).

Soneson, H., & Cordano, R. J. (2009). Universal Design and Study Abroad: (Re-)Designing Programs for Access. *Frontiers: The Interdisciplinary Journal of Study Abroad, 18*(1), 269–288. https://doi.org/10.36366/frontiers.v18i1.266

Soneson, H., & Minder, S. J. H. (2020). *Education Abroad Advising to Students with Disabilities* (2nd ed.). NAFSA.

Sprovieri C., & Fullick, J. (2024). Traveling Abroad with Medication. In J. Pollard & K. S. Priebe (Eds.), *Convergence of litigation, policy, and standards: Building the informed practitioner in education abroad risk management*. The Forum on Education Abroad. doi.org/10.36.366/SIA.5.978-1-952376-41-2.14

The Forum of Education Abroad. (2020). *Standards of good practice for education abroad, Sixth edition*. The Forum on Education Abroad. doi.org/10.36366/S.978-1-952376-04-7

United Nations Convention on the Rights of Persons with Disabilities, December 13, 2006. https://www.un.org/development/desa/disabilities/convention-on-the-rights-of-persons-with-disabilities/convention-on-the-rights-of-persons-with-disabilities-2.html

U.S. Department of State. (2021, March 25). *Why study abroad?* https://studyabroad.state.gov/value-study-abroad/why-study-abroad

W3C. (2023). *Web Content Accessibility Guidelines (WCAG) 2.1*. https://www.w3.org/TR/WCAG21/

# 22

## Exploring Mental Well-Being Abroad: Historical Overview and Future Landscapes

**Laura Thompson, Ph.D., LPC**

Education abroad programs can provide students with a wide range of benefits, including opportunities for personal growth, the development of greater cultural awareness, new language skills, social network development, increased self-confidence, and creativity (Tamilla & Ledgerwood, 2018). Despite these benefits, there are many potential stressors that students may face while abroad that can negatively impact their mental health and well-being. This is why it is vital that professionals in the field have a basic understanding of mental health and are attuned to some of the factors that may negatively influence students while they are away from home. Research (Ozbay, Johnson, Dimoulas, Morgan, Charney, & Southwick, 2007) has documented the positive impact that social support has on mental health and overall wellness. For students who are studying abroad, even the perception of available support may help reduce feelings of loneliness or mental distress that can be associated with adjusting to life in a new culture (Thompson, 2015). This chapter will provide a brief overview of mental health in the college student population. It will review some of the challenges inherent in education abroad. Finally, it will discuss potential avenues for assistance and offer recommendations so that you are better prepared to support the mental health and well-being of students while they are abroad.

First, it is important to review some important information about mental health. Approximately three-quarters of lifetime mental health disorders have an initial onset by the age of 24 years (Eisenberg, Downs, Golberstein, & Zivin, 2009; Eisenberg et al., 2007; Kessler, Berglund, Demler, 2005; Zivin, Eisenberg, Gollust, & Golberstein, 2009). The ages of college students vary, of course, but the American College Health Association (2013) estimated that most (78.5%) college and university students in the United States are between the ages of 18–24 years, coinciding with the first onset of most mental health disorders (Eisenberg et al., 2007; Mowbray et al., 2006). Furthermore, the increasing number of college students experiencing and reporting mental health issues is widely reported in the literature (Castillo & Schwartz, 2013; Eisenberg et al., 2007; Hefner & Eisenberg, 2009; Mowbray et al., 2006).

Common mental health problems in traditional college-aged students include anxiety (Blanco et al., 2008; Norberg, Norton, Olivier, & Zvolensky, 2010; Steinhardt & Dolbier, 2008; Zivin et al., 2009), depression (Castillo & Schwartz, 2013; Hunt & Eisenberg, 2010; Steinhardt & Dolbier, 2008; Zivin et al., 2009), eating disorders ( Zivin et al., 2009), suicidal ideation (Hunt & Eisenberg, 2010; Zivin et al., 2009), self-harm and other forms of self-destructive and reckless behaviors (Zivin et al., 2009), and substance abuse (Blanco et al., 2008; Castillo & Schwartz, 2013; Cranford et al., 2009). According to the Center for Collegiate Mental Health's 2023 Annual Report, anxiety continues to be the number one reason for which students report to university counseling centers in the United States.

It is also necessary to consider the impact that the COVID-19 pandemic has had on the mental health of students (Salimi et al., 2023). After the U.S. Centers for Disease Control and Prevention (CDC) recommended that schools shut down in the United States in March 2020, students faced the difficult transition of moving from face-to-face classes to online learning platforms, creating academic difficulties for some. Many students had to adjust to living at home with parents again, while others could not return to their homes for a variety of reasons. Those who remained on campuses had to cope with strict rules and regulations related to social distancing, reduced hours for campus support services and facilities, recreation center closures, and a halt to campus clubs and activities and impromptu social gatherings. Lost employment opportunities also impacted students financially.

Disappointingly, for most students studying abroad, experiences were cut short. International students in the United States also faced the uncertainty of not knowing if or when they might return to their home countries due to travel restrictions (Salimi et al., 2023).

During this period, students largely received less social and emotional support from friends, peers, and professors (Babb et al., 2022). It is important to acknowledge that throughout the world, countries varied in terms of their response to the pandemic. As a result, the way host country students, staff, and faculty experienced the pandemic, and post-COVID challenges sometimes differed significantly from the experience of U.S. students.

Globally, increased isolation, a lack of social connection, and increased time spent on social media fueled feelings of loneliness, sleep disturbances, and mental health challenges including anxiety and depression. While the demands for mental health services increased, there were challenges to access for many who sought support.

Even though life has returned to pre-COVID norms, many young adults are still experiencing residual impacts from the pandemic. According to a study conducted by Active Minds (2021), 20% of college students reported that their mental health had significantly worsened under COVID-19. Since the onset of COVID-19, a growing number of students who attend counseling in university counseling centers have reported social anxiety and fears of not being liked by others as concerns (Center for Collegiate Mental Health, 2024). Increasing levels of isolation, social comparison commonly experienced with social media use, and the return to in-person classes after remote instruction are some of the factors that may be contributing to social anxiety (Center for Collegiate Mental Health, 2024).

With the increased number of university students reporting mental health challenges (Lipson et al., 2022), it is imperative that the topic of student mental health remains at the forefront. Furthermore, it is critical that you consider some of the unique stressors that students may face while abroad so that you can help students prepare for their experience and support them while they are abroad.

McCabe (2005) identified a range of stressors students face while studying abroad that may exacerbate preexisting or dormant mental health issues. Feelings of loss and separation can become more pronounced when students find themselves geographically distanced from loved ones. Education abroad students may also feel increased social pressure as they attempt to integrate with new friends in an unfamiliar place. Navigating travel and transportation in unknown territory can pose challenges that provoke stress even in experienced travelers. Adjusting to a new culture, language, food, and living arrangements can also be difficult.

Often overlooked, jetlag and changes in sleep patterns can negatively impact students when they travel abroad. Jetlag impacts circadian processes, particularly when three or more time zones are crossed (Inder, Crowe, & Porter, 2016). It can take one day per time zone for the circadian clock to adjust to a new time zone (Waterhouse et al., 2007), and symptoms of jetlag can include poor sleep, reduced performance in mental and physical tasks, increased fatigue, decreased concentration, and gastrointestinal symptoms (Waterhouse et al., 2007). It is important to note that individuals with mood disorders may be more sensitive to disruption in circadian rhythms. Inder, Crowe, and Porter (2016) reported that transmeridian travel appears to precipitate mood episodes for people with mood disorders, particularly when their adherence to medication is compromised. For these individuals, there is some evidence to suggest that there can be an increased rate of depression with westward travel, and an increased rate of manic/hypomanic episodes with eastward travel (Inder, Crowe, & Porter, 2016).

For students who study abroad, culture shock is a natural part of the adjustment process and is something that will impact most of them to some extent (Furnham, 2005). The term "culture shock" was first used by anthropologists Cora Dubois and Kalervo Oberg (1960) and has been described as the emotional, psychological, behavioral, cognitive, and physiological impact of the cultural adjustment process on an individual (Pedersen, 1995). The challenges and discomfort students may face as they adapt to a new environment may lead them to feel an unexpected sense of shock that can feel disorienting (Furnham, 2005). Culture shock may be experienced more intensely the more the host culture differs from a student's home culture.

Oberg (1960) first described aspects of culture shock including a felt sense of strain resulting from the effort it can take to psychologically adjust; a sense of loss and deprivation as a result of missing friends, possessions, and the comforts of home; feelings of being an outsider and being rejected by the new culture or rejecting aspects of the new culture; confusion in terms of role and identity within the new culture; surprise, anxiety, and sometimes indignation by cultural differences; and feelings of inadequacy in not being able to cope with the new environment. Culture shock is often described as a transitional process that occurs in linear stages (Oberg, 1960; Gullahorn and Gullahorn, 1963), including the "honeymoon stage" when individuals first arrive in a new place and feel enthusiastic about the new environment; the "crisis stage" when cultural differences feel particularly highlighted and individuals struggle with the discomfort of being in a new culture; the "recovery stage" when individuals begin to adapt to the differences; and the "adjustment stage" when life in the new environment begins to feel more comfortable and enjoyable.

In reality, however, the experience of culture "shock" is different for each person and rarely do individuals experience stages in a linear fashion. Furnham (2005) highlighted common reactions to culture shock, including feelings of anxiety, confusion, and apathy. Some individuals may feel alienated and lonely and experience a sense of powerlessness in the new culture.

A lack of self-confidence, distrust in others, irritability, or the experience of psychosomatic symptoms such as a headache or an upset stomach are other ways that culture shock may manifest. Finally, extreme homesickness, over-eating or the lack of an appetite, excessive cleanliness, uncontrollable crying, difficulty concentrating or completing assignments, or sleep problems are other potential symptoms of culture shock. When symptoms of culture shock have a significant impact on a participant's daily mood and functioning or do not seem to improve with time, this may signal that the student is struggling with mental health issues.

Ryan and Twibell (2000) conducted a study and identified key themes that concerned study abroad student participants. The primary concern expressed was related to interpersonal relationships and fitting into a new society. Students also discussed the challenges of meeting friends in a new culture.

Academic achievement is another domain that can be a source of dis-tress for students abroad. They may encounter methods of instruction, testing, grading, and university systems that differ considerably from their home institutions (Ryan & Twibell, 2000). Language barriers can also contribute to academic stress for students abroad (Ali, Yoenanto, & Nurdibyanandaru, 2000) and may make communication with instructors difficult and lead to challenges in completing assignments. Furthermore, they can lead to a sense of pressure due to the extra time that it may take to complete assignments (Ali, Yoenanto, & Nurdibyanandauru, 2000). Limitations in communication and language skills can also contribute to social barriers, leading to increased stress and a sense of isolation for stu-dents (Ryan & Twibell, 2000).

Another factor to consider is that students who are studying in countries with significantly different standards of living may face challenges that are unique to these locations. Health and safety concerns may be sources of stress that impact well-being (Ryan & Twibell, 2000). Sanitation conditions may require students to take extra precautions to avoid getting sick. Other locations may have higher crime rates and necessitate students be more cau-tious in their everyday lives while abroad. Transportation concerns, includ-ing access to transportation, a fear of accidents, and pedestrian safety, may also contribute to student stress, potentially leading to a decline in overall health and mental well-being.

Other challenges may include difficulties with navigating confusing bureaucratic processes and the frustrations of getting simple things accom-plished due to being an outsider in a country. Financial stressors; pollution and climate; having too much or too little personal space; and concerns about returning home, including missing friendships created, and the perceived difficulties of re-entry may also impact students while abroad (Ryan & Twibell, 2000).

For study abroad students from traditionally underrepresented populations, challenges sometimes emerge because of their racial or ethnic identities (Goldoni, 2017), sexual orientation, or gender identity (Bingham, Brunsting, and Katsumoto, 2023). Some students hold several marginalized identities, and the intersection of these identities can exacerbate challenges students may face while abroad. Experiencing racist, homophobic, transphobic, or xenophobic attitudes or incidents can have a detrimental impact on student mental health and well-being while abroad. To learn more about the intersection of mental health and diversity equity and inclusion, identify formation and expression, training international staff for understanding U.S. students' diverse identities, and mitigating identity-based risk onsite, see also chapters 11.2 (McGrath & Lombardi, 2024, 9 (Beirn, 2024), 9.2 (Thompson & Ellis, 2024), and 9.1 (Smit, 2024), respectively.

In addition to the themes mentioned previously, substance use and resulting consequences can also negatively impact the well-being of study abroad participants (Thompson, 2015). In some studies, American college students participating in study abroad programs have been found to as much as double their weekly alcohol use while abroad (Pedersen et al., 2010; Pedersen et al., 2014) and potentially face a range of alcohol-related consequences that are unique to the study abroad context (Hummer et al., 2010; Pedersen et al., 2010). These consequences can include legal problems within local government and legal systems; academic sanctions from both the home institution, the host institution, and/or the study abroad program; finding oneself in dangerous situations with locals in the host country; missing flights or program activities; being disrespectful or offensive to a host family or program staff; and contributing to the negative stereotypes of Americans (Pedersen et al., 2010; Pedersen et al., 2014). Additionally, female students and students in the LGBTQIA+ community may be at greater risk for harassment and sexual assault abroad (Michl et al., 2019), particularly those studying in non-English-speaking countries (Kimble, Flack, & Burbridge, 2013). Alcohol alone, however, may not explain the substantial variance in experience of alcohol-related problems experienced by students abroad. Factors such as lack of familiarity with surroundings and resources, impaired judgment regarding the safety of the immediate surroundings, and language barriers and deficiencies in comprehending the nuances of local culture and laws may increase the potential for negative outcomes (Hummer et al., 2010).

Although mental health and substance use disorders are the leading cause of disability worldwide, the majority of those who need care lack access to high-quality mental health services (Wainberg et al., 2017). Stigma, shortages in human resources, fragmented service delivery models, and lack of research capacity for implementation and policy change are some of the factors that contribute to the mental health treatment gap globally (Wainberg et al., 2017). There are also many cultural constructs about mental health (Watters, 2010). As a result, attitudes about mental health, the way mental health issues are conceptualized and diagnosed, the availability of resources for support, and treatment approaches will vary widely depending on the location of the program. While some countries have well-developed resources for supporting mental health, the majority of countries, particularly less economically developed regions, are lacking resources (Saraceno & Saxena, 2002). In many locations, it may not be possible to find support that aligns with what students are used to in their home countries. Helping students understand the limitations that may exist in support while abroad may help them manage their expectations.

Given the current landscape of mental health and the many challenges students may face while studying abroad, thoughtful attention should be given to preparing students for their study abroad experiences and supporting them once abroad. The following is a list of best practices to guide you in your role:

1.  Orientation programs for education abroad should thoroughly address topics related to mental health, alcohol use, and harm reduction strategies, and help students to development coping and safety skills necessary for navigating life in a foreign culture (Thompson, 2015). The stages and symptoms of cultural transition should be reviewed, and strategies for dealing with homesickness should also be discussed. Furthermore, programs are encouraged to make pre-departure and in-country orientation programs mandatory for all participants (The Forum for Education Abroad 2020, clause 6.1.9).

    According to Goldstein and Keller (2015), understanding students' beliefs about the intercultural adjustment process is imperative because research supports the notion that there is greater satisfaction when expectations of an experience are met or exceeded. Preparing students prior to going abroad can help address some of the realities of an experience so that expectations are more realistically aligned. Goldstein and Keller (2015) also emphasized the importance of students being exposed to high-quality intercultural interventions and informal cultural mentoring in order to help them understand some of the realities they may face while abroad. Per *Standards* clause 6.1.12, "... not all countries have in place the same support and infrastructure as the home institution" (The Forum on Education Abroad, 2020). This can help challenge inaccurate beliefs they may have about the intercultural adjustment process. Having realistic expectations can help students have greater satisfaction with the overall study experience abroad. It is critical that students recognize that not all countries will have the same support infrastructures in place that are available at their home institution, which is why the *Standards* recommend that responsible parties "shall clearly communicate to students the importance of disclosing mental and physical status, accommodation, and other specific needs; and work with other responsible parties and students to determine how their needs may be met on program" (The Forum on Eduation Abroad, clause 6.1.12).

2. Orientation programs should also incorporate preparatory activities to help participants increase self-awareness and cultural awareness. Goldoni (2015) encourages the use of preparatory modules focused on four key areas: students' personal preparation for study abroad; preparation for intercultural communication; preparation for integration; and linguistic preparation. It is recommended that programs utilize a variety of activities that address these areas. For example, encouraging participants to reflect on their identity, life, and upbringing from a cultural perspective, explore questions aimed at developing greater self-awareness, examine stereotypes and prejudices, and learn about cultural communication patterns can assist them in being more culturally prepared.

3. Participants should be encouraged to develop a self-care plan for their time abroad. Self-care plans can include a list of favorite activities and actions that help in challenging moments. Healthy coping strategies such as journaling, connecting with a loved one, getting outside, exercising, meditating, listening to music, dancing, engaging in an art project, breathing techniques, and making a list of things the participant is most grateful for can help. Education abroad professionals can help students identify whether their favorite activities may need to be adapted to the different cultural environment. For example, going for a walk alone or for a run may be unsafe or draw more unwanted attention in the new environment. Given that students are ultimately responsible for their well-being, the topic of self-care must remain at the forefront of their minds. Reminding them about the importance of these strategies is important. Also, it is vital to recognize that student needs for alone

time and downtime may vary. Encourage students to find time alone if they need this for their well-being.

4. Participants who are regularly meeting with a mental health professional prior to departure should create a plan with their mental health provider for managing mental health while abroad. Some practitioners are willing to have virtual appointments while the participant is abroad. Other providers are not willing to do so given licensure considerations. The topic of continuity of care is vital, particularly for students with more significant mental health issues.

5. Medication management must be addressed. It is critical that participants who are prescribed medications have a plan in place for medication management for their time abroad. They should connect with their physicians and mental health providers prior to going abroad. Investigating the legality and availability of medications is critical as some that are prescribed in the United States are not available or permitted in other countries. Other countries only allow a limited supply. Furthermore, some locations may require supporting documentation from a medical provider. Participants should bring copies of all prescriptions and keep medications in the original labeled containers. Travel health specialists can also assist in getting information that is specific to each destination. It is important to emphasize to participants that study abroad is not the time to experiment with discontinuing the use of regular medications. (See chapter 8.2, "Traveling Abroad with Medication," by Christine Sprovieri and Jennifer Fullick (2024) for more information on this topic.)

6. Participants should have insurance that provides coverage for international medical and emergency assistance. Many institutions provide international medical and emergency insurance for their participants, but in cases where it is not included, encourage participants to purchase their own coverage. Per *Standards* clauses 5.1.6 and 5.1.7, "each organization shall have policies and procedures in place regarding security and risk management that prioritize the health, well-being, and safety of students and personnel, including, but not limited to: Risk assessment and monitoring for program locations and activities; Tracking, responding to, and reporting critical incidents; Written emergency plans and protocols; and insurance coverage" (The Forum on Education Abroad 2020).

There are a variety of insurance companies that provide policies for study abroad and international travel. Some of these policies provide mental health support for students abroad including regular counseling sessions, either virtually or in-person. On a rare occasion a student may need to be evacuated due to a crisis or mental health emergency. Some international insurance providers can assist with this process. (Chapter 33 of this volume (Rupar, 2024) discusses international insurance in more detail.)

7.  Identify available resources for mental health support in the locations of your programs.

    Learn about how mental health is viewed and supported in these countries. If possible, establish contacts with providers in those areas and have a list of contact numbers available. It is important to know which hospitals provide care for individuals who are having a psychiatric emergency and which hospitals conduct examinations after a sexual assault. Keep in mind that attitudes about mental health and the way it is viewed and supported vary widely in different cultures. In some locations, it will not be possible to find local mental health practitioners who conceptualize mental health issues and treat mental health from a Western lens. The quality of care may differ significantly from what students may be accustomed to in their respective home countries. Furthermore, health professionals may not speak English. It may be necessary to have a translator available. Per *Standards* clause 6.2.7, "responsible parties shall support students in accessing physical, mental, and emotional health and well-being services" (The Forum on Education Abroad, 2020). As noted earlier, *Standards* clause 6.1.12 states that education abroad professionals and program providers should "work with other responsible parties and students to determine how their needs may be met on the program" (The Forum, 2020).

    It is also critical to familiarize yourself with any public policies or laws that may impact the provision of mental health or sexual assault services in specific locations. In some countries, a student who presents to an emergency department due to suicidal ideation or a suicide attempt may be subjected to an involuntary hold. There are also countries that require police intervention in sexual assault cases and may ask a student to remain in the country if there is a criminal investigation or court proceedings connected to the assault.

8.  If you are connected to a university, create and maintain open lines of communication with the Counseling Center at your institution. You can also encourage students to contact their home institution to see what resources, if any, are available to them. Some universities provide mental health support for their students while abroad. Some also have designated case managers who are available to assist in supporting students and their families when psychological, medical, or other crises arise.

9.  Educate yourself about the topic of mental health by investing in training and professional development. Because study abroad programs often have limited resources, it is critical that there is a community approach to

supporting participants. Study abroad professionals, program faculty, and staff should understand how to identify mental health red flags and appropriately respond to red-flag behaviors. They should also understand when it is best to refer to other resources. Emotional First Aid (mentalhealthteam. com) or Mental Health First Aid are two potential options for training.

This chapter has provided an overview of mental health and a range of considerations and strategies for support that will help guide you in your role as you prepare students for international education experiences. Anticipating that students will inevitably face a variety of challenges abroad that may impact their mental health and well-being is crucial. Proactively preparing students for these realities and encouraging them to utilize self-care strategies and support resources can have a powerful impact on shaping their experiences abroad.

# References

Active Minds. (2021). *The Impact of Covid-19 on student mental health*. Retrieved from https:// www.activeminds.org/studentsurvey/

Ali, S., Yoenanto, N. H., & Nurdibyanandaru, D. (2020). Language Barrier is the cause of Stress among International Students of Universitas Airlangga. *PRASASTI: Journal of Linguistics, 5*(2), 242-256.

American College Health Association. (2013). *National College Health Assessment Spring 2013 Reference Group Executive Summary.* Retrieved from http://www.acha-ncha.org/docs/ ACHA-NCHA-II_ReferenceGroup_ExecutiveSummary_Spring2013.pdf

Babb, S. J., Rufino, K. A., & Johnson, R. M. (2022). Assessing the effects of the COVID-19 pandemic on nontraditional students' mental health and well-being. *Adult education quarterly, 72*(2), 140-157.

Beirn, M. (2024). The Identity Kaleidoscope: Formation, Expression, and Experience Informing the Shared Enterprise of Mitigating Risks. In J. Pollard & K. S. Priebe (Eds.), *Convergence of litigation, policy, and standards: Building the informed practitioner in education abroad risk management.* The Forum on Education Abroad. doi.org/10.36.366/ SIA.5.978-1-952376-41-2.17

Bingham, W. P., Brunsting, N., & Katsumoto, S. (2023). A Systematic Literature Review on LGBT+ U.S. Students Studying Abroad. *Frontiers: The Interdisciplinary Journal of Study Abroad, 35*(1), 152-187.

Blanco, C., Okuda, M., Wright, C., Hasin, D.S., Grant, B.F., Liu, S.M., & Olfson, M. (2008). Mental health of college students and their non-college attending peers: Results from the National Epidemiologic Study on Alcohol and Related Conditions. *Arch Gen Psychiatry, 65*, 1429-1437.

Castillo, L.G. & Schwartz, S.J. (2013). Introduction to the special issue on college mental health. *Journal of Clinical Psychology, 69*, 291-297.

Center for Collegiate Mental Health (2024). *2023 Annual Report.* https://ccmh.psu.edu/ annual-reports

Cook, L.J. (2007). Striving to help college students with mental health issues. *Journal of Psychosocial Nursing, 45*, 40-44.

Cranford, J.A., Eisenberg, D., Serras, A.M. (2009). Substance use disorders, mental health problems, and use of mental services in a probability sample of college students. *Addictive Behaviors, 34*, 134-145.

Eisenberg, D., Golberstein, E., and Hunt, J.B. (2009). Mental health and academic success in college. *The B.E. Journal of Economic Analysis & Policy, 9*, 40-35.

Eisenberg, D., Gollust, S.E., Golberstein, E., & Hefner, J.L. (2007). Prevalence and correlate of depression, anxiety, and suicidality among university students. *American Journal of Orthopsychiatry, 77,* 534-542.

Furnham, A. (2005). Culture shock, homesickness, and adaptation to a foreign culture. In M. A.L. van Tilburg & A. J. J. M. Vingerhoets (Eds.), *Psychological aspects of geographical moves: Homesickness and acculturation stress* (pp. 17–34). Amsterdam University Press. http://www.jstor.org/stable/j.ctt46mv9k.6

Goldoni, F. (2015). Preparing students for studying abroad. *Journal of the Scholarship of Teaching and Learning, 15*(4), 1–20. https://doi.org/10.14434/josotl.v15i4.13640

Goldoni, F. (2017). Race, ethnicity, class and identity: Implications for study abroad. *Journal of Language, Identity & Education, 16*(5), 328–341. https://doi-org.proxy.library.nyu.edu/10.1080/15348458.2017.1350922

Goldstein, S. B., & Keller, S.R. (2015). U.S. college students' lay theories of culture shock. *International Journal of Intercultural Relations : IJIR, 47.*

Gullahorn, J.T. and Gullahorn, J.E. (1963), An extension of the U-Curve hypothesis. Journal of Social Issues, 19: 33-47. https://doi-org.proxy.library.nyu.edu/10.1111/j.1540-4560.1963.tb00447.x

Hefner, J. & Eisenberg, D. (2009). Social support and mental health among college students. *American Journal of Orthopsychiatry, 79,* 491-499.

Hummer, J.F., Pedersen, E.R., Mirza, T., & LaBrie, J.W. (2010). Factors associated with general and sexual alcohol-related consequences: An examination of college students studying abroad. *Journal of Student Affairs Research and Practice, 47,* 427-444.

Hunt, J. & Eisenberg, D. (2010). Mental health problems and help-seeking behavior among college students. *Journal of Adolescent Health, 46,* 3-10.

Inder, M. L., Crowe, M. T., & Porter, R. (2016). Effect of transmeridian travel and jetlag on mood disorders: evidence and implications. *Australian & New Zealand Journal of Psychiatry, 50*(3), 220-227.

Kessler, R.C., Berglund, P., Demler, O. Jin, R., Merikangas, K.R., & Walters, E.E. (2005). Lifetime prevalence and age-of-onset distributions of DSM-IV disorders in the national comorbidity survey replication. *Archives of General Psychiatry, 62,* 593-602.

Kimble, M., Flack, W.F., & Burbridge, E. (2013). Study abroad increases risk for sexual assault in female undergraduates: A preliminary report. *Psychological Trauma: Theory, Research, Practice, and Policy, 5,* 426-430.

Lipson, S. K., Zhou, S., Abelson, S., Heinze, J., Jirsa, M., Morigney, J., Patterson, A., Singh, M., & Eisenberg, D. (2022). Trends in college student mental health and help-seeking by race/ethnicity: Findings from the national healthy minds study, 2013–2021. *Journal of Affective Disorders, 306,* 138–147. https://doiorg.proxy.library.nyu.edu/10.1016/j.jad.2022.03.038

McCabe, L. (2005). Mental health and study abroad: Responding to the concern. *International Educator, 14,* 52-57.

McGrath, B., & Lombardi, M. (2024). Mental health through the lens of equity and inclusion. In J. Pollard & K. S. Priebe (Eds.), *Convergence of litigation, policy, and standards: Building the informed practitioner in education abroad risk management.* The Forum on Education Abroad. doi.org/10.36.366/SIA.5.978-1-952376-41-2.24

Michl, T., Pegg, K., & Kracen, A. (2019). Gender X culture: A pilot project exploring the study abroad experiences of trans and gender expansive students. *Frontiers: The Interdisciplinary Journal of Study Abroad, 31*(2), 32-50.

Mowbray, C.T., Mandiberg, J.M., Stein, C.H., Kopels, S., Curlin, C., Megivern, D., Strauss, S., Collins, K., & Lett, R. (2006). Campus mental health services: Recommendations for change. *American Journal of Orthopsychiatry, 76,* 226-237.

Norberg, M.M., Norton, A.R., Olivier, J. & Zvolensky, M.J. (2010). Social anxiety, reasons for drinking, and college students. *Behavior Therapy, 41,* 555-566.

Oberg, K. (1960). Cultural shock: adjustment to new cultural environments. *Practical Anthropology., 7*(4).

Ozbay, F., Johnson, D.J., Dimoulas, E., Morgan, C.A., Charney, D., & Southwick, S. (2007). Social support and resilience to stress: From neurobiology to clinical practice. *Psychiatry,* 35-40.

Pedersen, E.R., Larimer, M.R., & Lee, C.M. (2010). When in Rome: Factors associated with changes in drinking behavior among American college students studying abroad. *Psychology of Addictive Behaviors, 24,* 535-540.

Pedersen, E.R., Skidmore, J.R., & Aresi, G. (2014). Demographic and pre-departure factors associated with drinking and alcohol-related consequences for college students completing study abroad experiences. *Journal of American College Health, 62,* 244-254.

Pederson, P. (1995). *The five stages of culture shock: Critical incidents around the world.* Greenwood Press.

Rupar, J. (2024). Navigating International Insurance for Global Education. In J. Pollard & K. S. Priebe (Eds.), *Convergence of litigation, policy, and standards: Building the informed practitioner in education abroad risk management.* The Forum on Education Abroad. doi. org/10.36.366/SIA.5.978-1-952376-41-2.33

Ryan, M. E., & Twibell, R. S. (2000). Concerns, values, stress, coping, health and educational outcomes of college students who studied abroad. *International Journal of Intercultural Relations, 24*(4), 409–436.

Salimi, N., Gere, B., Talley, W., & Irioogbe, B. (2023). College students mental health challenges: Concerns and considerations in the COVID-19 pandemic. *Journal of College Student Psychotherapy, 37*(1), 39-51. https://doi.org/10.1080/87568225.2021.1890298

Saraceno, B., & Saxena, S. (2002). Mental health resources in the world: results from Project Atlas of the WHO. *World psychiatry, 1*(1), 40.

Smit, B. (2024). Preparing for and mitigating identity-based risk on-site. In J. Pollard & K. S. Priebe (Eds.), *Convergence of litigation, policy, and standards: Building the informed practitioner in education abroad risk management.* The Forum on Education Abroad. doi. org/10.36.366/SIA.5.978-1-952376-41-2.18

Sprovieri, C., & Fullick, J. (2024). Traveling abroad with medication. In J. Pollard & K. S. Priebe (Eds.), *Convergence of litigation, policy, and standards: Building the informed practitioner in education abroad risk management.* The Forum on Education Abroad. doi. org/10.36.366/SIA.5.978-1-952376-41-2.14

Steinhardt, M. & Dolbier, C. (2008). Evaluation of a resilience intervention to enhance coping strategies and protective factors and decrease symptomatology. *Journal of American College Health, 56,* 445-453. https://doi.org/10.3200/JACH.56.44.445-454

Tamilla, C., & Ledgerwood, J. R. (2018). Students' motivations, perceived benefits and constraints towards study abroad and other international education opportunities. *Journal of International Education in Business, 11*(1), 63-78. https://doi.org/10.1108/JIEB-01-2017-0002

The Forum on Education Abroad. (2020). *Standards of Good Practice for Education Abroad,* Sixth Edition. doi.org/10.36366/S.978-1-95236-02-3

Thompson, C., & Ellis, E. (2024). Building cultures: Preparing international staff for understanding diverse identities of U.S. students. In J. Pollard & K. S. Priebe (Eds.), *Convergence of litigation, policy, and standards: Building the informed practitioner in education abroad risk management.* The Forum on Education Abroad. doi.org/10.36.366/SIA.5.978-1-952376-41-2.19

Thompson, L. K. (2015). *How mental health, sojourner adjustment, and drinking motives impact alcohol-related consequences for college students studying abroad* (Doctoral dissertation, Syracuse University).

Wainberg, M. L., Scorza, P., Shultz, J. M., Helpman, L., Mootz, J. J., Johnson, K. A., Neria, Y., Bradford, J.E., Oquendo, M.A., & Arbuckle, M. R. (2017). Challenges and opportunities in global mental health: a research-to-practice perspective. *Current Psychiatry Reports, 19,* 1-10. https://doi.org/10.1007/s11920-017-0780-z

Waterhouse, J., Reilly, T., Atkinson, G., & Edwards, B. (2007) Jet lag: Trends and coping strategies. *The Lancet.* 369: 1117–1129. https://doi.org/10.1016/S0140-6736(07)60529-7

Watters, E. (2010). *Crazy like us: The globalization of the American psyche.* Free Press.

Zivin, K., Eisenberg, D., Gollust, S., & Golberstein, E. (2009). Persistence of mental health problems and needs in a college student population. *Journal of Affective Disorders, 117,* 180-185. https://doi.org/10.1016/j.jad.2009.01.001

# 23

## Managing the Risks Associated with Mental Health Abroad

Laura Dupont-Jarrett, Ph.D., L.P.

## Introduction

Students' need for paraprofessional support from education abroad staff, as well as professional mental health care, while not documented in large-scale studies, is perceived to be dramatically increasing. It can be understood by its impact on completion rates: The Forum on Education Abroad's recent Student Risk Report (Dietrich, 2024) shows that mental health distress was the most likely reason for early program withdrawal, with 64% of students who experienced mental health crises withdrawing from their program early. Support for students' anxiousness, attention difficulties, and/or mood disorders, compounded by their lack of adequate social support, has become a growing and demanding area of service for study abroad professionals (The Forum on Education Abroad, 2023). This growing service need also requires greater crisis management and creates increased legal risk.

While most litigation involving student mental health abroad has occurred within the K-12 primary and secondary educational context (C. Ryan Gallia, personal communication, November 28, 2023), as mental health crises amongst the college population increase abroad (The Forum on Education Abroad, 2023), the chance of litigation will likely increase as well. The good news is that measures designed to safeguard student health and safety should also help protect organizations against legal accusations of negligence or harm.

The following discussion includes the professional observations and opinions of the author, a mental health expert working at the intersection of the fields of higher education, student mental health, and study abroad, as well as information learned and perspectives heard in discussions and conference sessions with education abroad professionals from both sending institutions and onsite provider organizations.

### How Student Mental Health Needs Present

Students are requiring increasing mental health-related support from staff at U.S. sending institutions. Staff providing pre-departure student support are experiencing increasing numbers of students disclosing mental health conditions, treatment needs (i.e., therapy), and medications, thus increasing the need for pre-departure health coaching and advising (Forum, 2023b). In addition to pre-departure demands, staff from sending institutions are also more frequently involved in helping manage mental health crises that occur while students are abroad. For example, these staff are more often becoming a first point-of-contact when students abroad request an early program return, rather than communicating with onsite staff about this. Post-program completion, staff at U.S. institutions sometimes feel the increased need to communicate with certain students to encourage them to seek professional care to address the cause for the premature program withdrawal, consistent with Standard 6.3.4 (The Forum on Education Abroad, 2020).

Onsite staff for education abroad organizations are experiencing increasing demands on their time and energy to support students' mental health (Barneche et al., 2023; The Forum on Education Abroad, 2023). Anecdotal reports at The Forum and EUASA 2023 European Institute attested to increasing time supporting mental health accommodations requests, encouraging disengaged (and therefore poor academically performing) students, and referring and encouraging students to seek professional mental health care (Zamudio-Suarez, 2023). Academic accommodations due to mental health disabilities has become increasingly common (Field, 2023).

The disconnect between programs abroad and home institutions creates unique challenges for providing a continuity of care. Managing these needs effectively requires substantial time and training, sometimes outside of the skills of an education abroad professional. As a result of the increased demands on staff time and emotional energy (Lucas, 2009), there have been higher rates of employment turnover, resulting in a secondary health and safety risk—less trained and skilled staff (The Forum on Education Abroad,

2023). More training and ongoing mentoring are needed to build the competence of staff teams, especially those with new staff.

## High-Risk Situations

High-risk student situations caused by mental health conditions are infrequent, but require great attention (Hidalgo Bellows, 2021). High-risk situations include student suicides and attempts, overdoses, risky physical health situations due to compromised decision-making (i.e., a student who chooses to go to an unsafe area due to impaired cognition as a symptom of a mental health condition), psychotic episodes leading to the inability to care for oneself, harm to others, etc. These situations also increase the possibility of lawsuits and litigation.

Anecdotally, some education abroad site providers report a number of cases of student hospitalization for consumption of pills as suicide attempts. Anecdotal evidence from U.S. campuses indicates more chronic suicidality (students regularly experiencing and managing thoughts of suicide, but without attempting it), as well as suicide attempts. Their daily functioning and ability to meet their academic responsibilities are being compromised by the need to manage their suicidality, which is true on campus, but exacerbated during cultural immersion.

Some students use alcohol or drugs to "self-medicate" instead of using prescribed medications. This increases the risk of substance abuse incidents and accidental overdoses. While many alcohol- and drug-related incidents and situations are treated as stand-alone problems, they may be rooted in dysfunctional attempts to manage mental health conditions.

In order to understand how things go wrong in student mental health and safety risk management and improve our practices, it can be beneficial to examine relevant past and current legal cases.

## Legal Precedents

Examining past legal cases involving student mental or behavioral health abroad can point to strategies to protect student health and safety and reduce legal liability. There have been very few legal cases involving student mental health during education abroad. Two cases, however, center on erratic, aggressive, or violent student behavior.

### Court Case Summary (Furrh v. Arizona Board of Regents, 1983)

A student brought an action against the University of Arizona because of the way staff handled his mental health episode during a study abroad program in Baja Mexico. The student suffered a delusion that the mafia was going to kill him and fled the group on multiple occasions. This prompted a professor and staff member to tussle with the student at one point and forcibly restrain him. In the lawsuit, the student alleged assault and imprisonment allegations against the university.

## Litigation Outcome

The judge responded to the student's assertion that the restraint was negligent by stating: "if [the professor and staff member] had done nothing, that would have been negligence."

## Implications for Best Practice

The court finding implies that taking action to prevent a student from harming themselves or another person is expected. The finding of no negligence on the part of the university can reassure organizations that their efforts to prevent harm from coming to students is appreciated by the courts, even if not always by the students themselves. However, the statement that doing nothing would have been negligent is concerning, if it implies the opposite— that physically restraining the student was the appropriate response. Asking faculty and staff to physically restrain students who are acting delusional, paranoid, erratic, or violent creates other types of risk. While *Standards* clause 6.2.7 notes that responsible parties should help students access health services, and clause 5.1.7 states that organizations should have emergency plans, a modified approach that could be explicitly articulated would be that responsible parties will seek emergency services on behalf of a student who is in a mental health crisis (The Forum on Education Abroad, 2020). Ideally, an alternative action of calling local authorities would have been viewed by the courts as an equal or better response. In general, it is always best practice to have procedures in place for emergencies, and program leaders trained in what to do for various emergencies. (See strategy #8 below for additional discussion.)

## Court Case Summary (Hindenach v. Olivet College, 2019)

After a scuffle with two classmates was broken up by the professor leading a program to Italy, one student fled into the streets of Florence where he encountered and killed an Italian citizen. He was incarcerated and tried by the Italian courts. The student was found to suffer from major depression with psychotic features and ordered to spend five years in an Italian psychiatric hospital. The student brought legal action against the college, alleging the college negligently failed to monitor the student's mental health while on the study abroad program in Italy, which resulted in his incarceration.

## Litigation Outcome

The court found the college did not have a duty to prevent the injuries suffered by the student because the college could not have reasonably foreseen that the student had psychotic tendencies, would fatally harm someone, be incarcerated, and be forcibly hospitalized as a result of going on a program to Italy, even though the college was aware the student was suffering from depression and anxiety and used antidepressants and antipsychotic medication.

## Implications for Best Practice

Increasing numbers of students are reporting serious, persistent mental illness in their pre-departure health disclosures. However, study abroad organizations cannot be expected to predict nor prevent all harmful behavior that could result from mental illness, nor can they prevent students with health conditions from studying abroad. The court concurred that study abroad organizations cannot be held liable for student behavior and its consequences. The responsibilities of education abroad organizations are to provide safe learning environments (The Forum on Education Abroad, 2020, clause 5.2.7) and provide information about accessing mental health services while on the program (The Forum on Education Abroad, 2020, clause 6.1.10). Best practices include encouraging students to consider their health needs when planning study abroad (strategy #1 below), training staff to help students plan for their health needs abroad (strategy #2), providing students with information on health care abroad (strategy #3), ensuring students have good health insurance (strategy #4), and ensuring there are procedures in place for mental health emergencies (strategy #8).

There are very few cases involving student mental health abroad; however, one notable case centers on a student death by suicide. Instances of suicide—obviously some of the most serious health and safety situations abroad—also cause families a lot of grief and anger, which may make them more likely to seek legal action.

## Court Case Summary (Abrahart v University of Bristol, 2022)

The parents of a student studying abroad in the UK, who died by suicide, sued the university under UK civil law for not providing reasonable care for the student's well-being, health, and safety. They alleged that the university did not do enough despite knowing she had a disability and was in distress, as she had emailed university staff saying she was having suicidal thoughts the day before needing to give an oral presentation.

### Litigation Outcome

The court agreed with the plaintiff, saying the university failed to make reasonable accommodations for her mental health, and thus treated her unfairly.

### Implications for Best Practice

The clear mandate from the court is that institutions are expected to make reasonable accommodations for mental health disabilities (The Forum on Education Abroad, 2020, clause 5.2.5). While disability accommodations are a broad health topic, beyond just *mental* health, organizations should be aware that this court finding clearly assigns liability for failing to meet requests for mental health accommodations (The Forum on Education Abroad, 2020, clause 5.2.5: Each organization shall facilitate reasonable accommodations to enable students of varying needs and disability status to participate in education abroad). This finding of negligence in preventing a suicide due to not making adequate academic accommodations is likely chilling to most instructors and professionals in education abroad (strategy #9 below). This topic is covered in Chapter 4, "Analyzing the Legal Challenges and Opportunities for Students with Disabilities," by Seth Gilbertson (2024).

### Other Potentially Illustrative Cases

Although the following related cases are not perfectly tied to student mental health abroad, it can be helpful to examine them in order to extrapolate best practices for safeguarding student mental health and safety.

### Court Case Summary (Doe V. Rhode Island School of Design, 2019)

A student was sexually assaulted in her study abroad housing. The student alleged negligence to provide safe housing on the part of the institution.

### Litigation Outcome

It was found that the education abroad organization had a duty of care to find reasonable, secure housing for students on the program, and that it was reasonably foreseeable that a student could be the victim of a crime if reasonably safe housing was *not* provided.

*Implications for Best Practice*

One might imagine that a court could, at some time in the future, decide that an education abroad organization has a duty of care to find reasonable mental health care for students, paralleling Standard 6.1.10 (Forum, 2020) or that it is reasonably foreseeable that a student could suffer from mental illness if reasonable health care is *not* provided. Thus, a best practice would be ensuring that each program has student health care insurance, mental health care resources identified, and proactively provides this information to students for easy usage. (See strategy #7 below.)

In general, the courts appear hesitant to impose a duty of care, domestically as well as internationally; see, for example, *Freeman v. Busch* (2003) (C. Ryan Gallia, personal communication, 2023). However, they appear more likely to do so when situations are *foreseeable*—that is a main area of liability. Education abroad organizations often ask and thus know if students have mental health conditions. Even when it is not known which specific students have a mental health condition, the general prevalence rate of mental health conditions amongst the college student population is known (Eisenberg et al., 2023). Thus, the need for all students to be provided with resources for professional mental health care seems foreseeable.

### Court Case Summary (Doe v. Calvin University, Silliman University, and Dwight TenHuisen, 2021)

A student was assaulted by a fellow student; the plaintiff alleged that the organization failed to follow its policies and procedures for protecting students, that a duty of care was owed to students, that there were training failures and deficiencies in the orientation program, and a lack of available personnel.

*Litigation Outcome*

The case has not yet been decided at the time of writing.

*Implications for Best Practice*

Best practices would be to establish policies and procedures and monitor compliance (#8 below), provide staff with training in incident response protocols (#5 & 8 below), ensure students are provided with information about mental health care during orientation (#4 & 7 below), and provide sufficient staffing to respond to student mental health needs (#6 below).

## Court Case Summary (Does v. Spahn and The U.S. Department of State Peace Corps, 2023)

A class-action lawsuit has been brought against the administration of the U.S. State Department Peace Corps, alleging applicants have been denied acceptance based on mental health, thus discriminating against them based on disability.

### Litigation Outcome

The case has not yet been decided at the time of writing.

### Implications for Best Practice

As has generally been understood and practiced in the field of education abroad, students should not be denied the opportunity to study abroad based on mental health conditions, regardless of the severity of the conditions or symptoms, or the availability of treatment during the program (#1 below). This further reinforces the importance of urging students to assess their health support needs themselves (#1, 2, & 3 below), and to train staff to provide support and respond to crises (#4–9 below).

## Best Practices for Student Mental Health Abroad Risk Management

Many practices can be implemented, pre-departure and onsite, to increase student satisfaction and successful program completion rates, protect student health and safety, and decrease risk and liability. The following suggestions are derived from and limited to the above discussion of legal precedents; they are not an exhaustive list of best practices in mental health abroad risk management.

### Pre-Departure Strategies

U.S. institutions can engage in several pre-departure strategies that will likely increase the quality of the student's experience and the likelihood of program completion and success, as well as decreased risk.

1.  First, study abroad organizations should not bar students access to study abroad based on mental health conditions as this would constitute discrimination. Instead, students should be encouraged to consider their health needs when selecting a program destination, length, and type.

Typically, students are encouraged to consider factors such as academics, language, culture, and cost in their program selection decisions. By asking students to also assess their health support needs (mental and physical) and compare that to the resources available at the programs in which they are interested, they can make a well-informed program decision to meet their needs. Some students seem to underestimate the mental health support they will need abroad or expect resources commensurate with the professional support they receive on the home campus. Sending institutions should make efforts to encourage them to be realistic in assessing their needs and selecting programs that will meet these needs. Because encouraging the importance of health planning is not yet a standard in student learning and development, we should endeavor to articulate and recommend it in the future.

2. Study abroad organizations should provide education abroad staff with training to support students in planning for their mental health abroad. Some organizations collect health information from students before departure in order to be aware of and assess the types and level of support they may need. If an organization collects this information, staff should be trained in how to review the health disclosures for key information, and what action they should take in response. Some organizations require students to get a doctor's verification of their "readiness" for study abroad. While this medical "clearance" process is becoming less common (the reasons for such are a topic for a separate discussion), if an organization requires it, mental health should be addressed within it, as well as physical health. This topic is covered in Chapter 11.2, Pre-Departure Mental Health Clearance: One approach to managing risk abroad, by Vanessa Sterling (2024). Staff also need training on where and how to refer students to available mental health resources as they plan. Staff need coaching to increase their competence and confidence in engaging in challenging conversations and pushing students to aggressively plan for their mental health and wellness; for example, how to coach a student who says they plan to "take a break" from their prescribed medication while abroad. These conversations may at times feel counter to the goal of facilitating an easy planning process without barriers, so training and coaching is needed to know how to balance these tensions, consistent with clause 4.3.2 of the *Standards of Good Practice*, preparing personnel for ethical decision-making and practices (The Forum on Education Abroad, 2020).

3. Study abroad organizations should provide students with accurate, realistic information about the mental health support available at each program location (The Forum on Education Abroad, 2020, clause 6.1.10). For

example, programs should communicate the availability of virtual or local, English-speaking mental health therapists, physicians for mental health medications, and critical care units (i.e., inpatient mental health doctors or psychiatrists). Providing this information will assist students in identifying the best fit for their needs and decrease the risk of students being at a location where they are unable to secure the health support they need.

### Onsite Strategies

4. Ensure all students have robust international health insurance that identifies both local and virtual providers, and covers a wide variety of mental health services, locally and virtually.
5. Train onsite staff to have general emotional-support skills (i.e., paraprofessional skills, sometimes referred to as "mental health first aid" skills), how to detect signs of distress, and how to refer students to critical care services (The Forum on Education Abroad, 2020, clause 5.1.7). These skills can increase the likelihood that staff are able to effectively support students in low- to medium-level situations. For example, if staff are shocked and confused by the volume of students with anxiety or using medication for mental health, which is common for the U.S. population (Ketchen et al., 2022), they will be less prepared and experienced in how to support these students. Onsite staff need to be trained to identify students in need of mental health support, to recognize alcohol and substance abuse, and how to respond to suicidality, effectively referring students to professional care, and refraining from playing the role of therapist and overstepping boundaries (Field, 2023).
6. Support onsite staff capacity to attend to student mental health, both ongoing and during crises. Staff working beyond capacity and competence increases the risk they will not detect or appropriately attend to students needing support and referrals (Field, 2023; The Forum on Education Abroad, 2020, clause 5.2.3; The Forum on Education Abroad, 2023a). It also increases the risk that they will be too emotionally exhausted to provide appropriate compassion (Field, 2023; The Forum, 2023a).
7. Each organization that provides support to students abroad should identify available mental health care and provide information to students on seeking that care.
   a. The responsibility of doing so may be through the organization's international health insurer. Health insurance companies can typically be expected to select and vet providers with the necessary legal and professional qualifications and certifications.

    b. While historic practice may have been to provide this information only upon student request, it is now recommended that all students upon arrival be provided with information about how to seek professional mental health care.

    c. The provision of mental health care varies greatly across the globe. Organizations need to understand and explain to students how to access care during different types of programs, the level of capacity (i.e., if there is a lengthy waitlist or not), the availability of English-language providers or translation services, how to access prescriptions for medication, how to seek critical care (i.e., hospitalization), and whether symptoms/conditions such as suicidality, psychosis, etc., are treated at local hospitals.

8. Onsite organizations should have procedures for handling mental health emergencies, and practice seeking emergency services for critical situations. Education abroad staff as well as faculty program leaders and third-party service providers should be trained in these procedures.

9. Finally, sites should carefully review each request for accommodations for mental health disabilities and make all that are reasonable.

While many people in the field of education abroad wonder why U.S. student mental health seems so poor currently, and wish it would simply get better, organizations must be realistic and accept that student mental health will continue being a vulnerability in health and safety risk management. Just like with physical health, mental health conditions are ever-present and not controllable. But many things can be done to reduce the risk of crises or catastrophic harm. By undertaking best practices extrapolated from legal cases, education abroad organizations can best provide care for students and limit risks to health and safety.

## References

Abrahart v. University of Bristol. 5 WLUK 260 (2022).

Abrams, Z. (2022, October 12). Student mental health is in crisis. Campuses are rethinking their approach. *Monitor on Psychology, 53*(7). https://www.apa.org/monitor/2022/10/mental-health-campus-care

American Psychiatric Association. (2022). *Diagnostic and statistical manual of mental disorders (5th ed., Text Revision).* https://dsm.psychiatryonline.org/doi/book/10.1176/appi.books.9780890425787

Barneche, M., Dupont-Jarrett, L., & Nichol-Peters, V. (2023, November 16). *Advancing best practices for supporting student and staff mental wellbeing* [conference session]. The Forum on Education Abroad, 2023 European Institute, Strasbourg, France. https://www.forumea.org/european-institute.html#schedule

Barry, E. (2023). Peace Corps sued over mental health policy. *The New York Times*. https://www.nytimes.com/2023/09/27/health/peace-corps-mental-health.html

Dietrich, A. (2024). *Student risk report: Data from education abroad programs, January 1 - December 31, 2023*. The Forum on Education Abroad. Doi.org/10.36366/R.2024SRR.1

Doe v. Calvin University, et al., 1:21-cv-01071 (2021).

Doe v. Rhode Island School of Design, 929 F.3d 756 (1st Cir. 2019)

Doe v. Spahn, 21-cv-04007-LB (N.D. Cal. Dec. 21, 2021)

Eisenberg, D., Ketchen Lipson, S., Heinze, J., & Zhou, S. (2023). *The healthy minds study: 2022-2023 Data Report*. The health minds network. https://healthymindsnetwork.org/wp-content/uploads/2023/08/HMS_National-Report-2022-2023_full.pdf

Field, K. (2023) Professors struggle with demands to tend to students' mental health. *The Chronicle of Higher Education*. https://www.chronicle.com/article/professors-struggle-with-demands-to-tend-to-students-mental-health#:~:text=One%20in%20five%20respondents%20said,her%20book%20Unraveling%20Faculty%20Burnout.

The Forum on Education Abroad. (2020). *Standards of good practice for education abroad, Sixth Edition*. doi.org/10.36366/S.978-1-952376-04-7

The Forum on Education Abroad. (2023). *State of the field report: Data from the comprehensive 2022 survey*. Carlisle, PA: The Forum on Education Abroad. https://www.forumea.org/state-of-the-field.html

Freeman v. Busch, 349 F.3d 582 (2003).

Furrh v. Arizona Board of Regents, 139 Ariz. 83, 676 P.2d 1141 (1984).

Gilbertson, S. (2024). Analyzing the legal challenges and opportunities for students with disabilities. In J. Pollard, & K. S. Priebe (Eds.). *Convergence of litigation, policy, and standards: Building the informed practitioner in education abroad risk management*. The Forum on Education Abroad.

Hidalgo Bellows, K. (2021). A 'Breaking point" in campus mental health. *The Chronicle of Higher Education*. https://www.chronicle.com/article/we-need-to-address-the-entire-system

Hindenach v. Olivet Coll., 340540, WL 1265074 Mich. Ct. App. (2019).

Hoye, W., Liu, X.S., Pfahl, M. (2022, June 26-29) *Claims abroad: A global survey of study abroad cases* [Conference presentation]. National Association of College and University Attorneys Annual Conference 2022, Pittsburgh, PA, United States. https://www.pathlms.com/nacua/events/2954

Ketchen Lipson, S., Saha Zhou, S., Abelson, S., Heinze, J., Jirsa, M., Morigney, J., Patterson, A., Singh, M., & Eisenberg, D. (2022) Trends in college student mental health and help-seeking by race/ethnicity: Findings from the national healthy minds study, 2013–2021, *Journal of Affective Disorders, Volume 306*, Pages 138-147, ISSN 0165-0327. https://doi.org/10.1016/j.jad.2022.03.038

Lucas, J. (2009). Over-stressed, Overwhelmed, and Over Here: Resident Directors and the Challenges of Student Mental Health Abroad. *Frontiers: The Interdisciplinary Journal of Study Abroad, 18*(1), 187–216. https://doi.org/10.36366/frontiers.v18i1.261

Marijolovic, K. (2023). Trauma and social anxiety are growing mental-health concerns for college students. *The Chronicle of Higher Education*. https://www.chronicle.com/article/trauma-and-social-anxiety-are-growing-mental-health-concerns-for-college-students#:~:text=Trauma%20and%20social%20anxiety%20are%20both%20increasing%20among%20college%20students,Health%20at%20Pennsylvania%20State%20Univers

Masterson-Algar, A., Jennings, B., & Odenwelder, M. (2020) How to run together: On study abroad and the ASD experience. *Frontiers: The Interdisciplinary Journal of Study Abroad, V. 32, Issue 1*. https://frontiersjournal.org/index.php/Frontiers/article/view/436/396

Sterling, V. (2024). Pre-departure mental health clearance: One approach to managing risk abroad. In J. Pollard & K. S. Priebe (Eds.), *Convergence of litigation, policy, and standards: Building the informed practitioner in education abroad risk management*. The Forum on Education Abroad.

Zamudio-Suarez, F. (2023) When student demands are out of control. *The Chronicle of Higher Education*. https://www.chronicle.com/newsletter/weekly-briefing/2023-11-18

# 24

## Mental Health Through the Lens of Equity and Inclusion

Breeda McGrath, Ph.D., NCSP and Marissa Lombardi, Ed.D.

While the COVID-19 pandemic undoubtedly exacerbated the growing mental health crisis in higher education and the field of education abroad, it had been on the rise for some time (Lumpkin, 2021) with universities across the world reporting increasing levels of need for mental health services (Auerbach, 2018). According to a report by Penn State University's Center for Collegiate Mental Health (2016), the number of students seeking help at campus counseling centers increased almost 40% between 2009 and 2015 and continues to rise. We have seen a significant spike in the percentage of university students dealing with mental health issues since the pandemic. In 2020–2021, 60% of students met the criteria for one or more mental health diagnoses, a near 50% increase from 2013 (Lipson et al., 2022). To say that higher education institutions (HEIs) and the field of education abroad have entered uncharted territory on this topic would be a gross understatement (Abrams, 2022; Gallup, 2023).

While there has been an overall increase of anxiety, depression, and stress reported among all college students, students of color and students from other underserved groups regularly experience additional sources of psychological stress compared to their majority peers. There is also a greater level of unmet mental health needs among students of color (Lipson et al, 2018), calling for organizations to ramp up the development of effective and culturally sensitive mental health support systems that reach students of color early on. Discrimination, impostorism, microaggressions, feelings of isolation, and hostile political and campus climates are just some of the issues that can impact the mental health of students of color (Cokely et al., 2017; Museus & Pérez, 2023). As the field of education abroad has worked to build back participation numbers to pre-pandemic levels (The Forum on Education Abroad, 2023), staff are faced with meeting these increased levels of student needs with diminished resources. According to The Forum on Education Abroad's 2022 State of the Field Report, 48% of U.S. institutions reported budget cuts during the pandemic and just "29% of those institutions reported restored budgets in 2022" (The Forum on Education Abroad, 2023). Proactive approaches to addressing student support needs are the best solution and they can be situated in an integrated, equity-centered framework that sees mental health and the well-being of all students as an important foundation upon which education abroad programming succeeds.

## The Changing Landscape

According to Lipson et al (2022), the mental health of college students consistently declined from 2013 to 2021, with the number of students who met the criteria for one or more mental health problems doubling during that time. Prospective participants in education abroad programs today bring a different set of needs and experiences to their programs than in the past, which calls for education abroad professionals to evaluate the support systems that have been in place and consider how they may further develop them to meet the changing needs of students. The general mental wellness of educators and students alike across the field of education abroad and beyond, has been affected by significant health challenges, family losses, isolation, lost opportunities, and community upheaval. The COVID-19 pandemic magnified existing equity gaps in healthcare services, and individuals and groups who have experienced marginalization are facing additional obstacles as state governments across the United States make decisions about access to services and navigate sociopolitical issues around gender and diversity. Decisions about state and cultural values continue to change the landscape of mainstream education and these shifts have an impact on how we are supporting students and staff across institutions and within education abroad.

While better preparation, support, and mental health-related crisis response on-the-ground has been a hot topic in the field of education abroad for some time, not surprisingly, it emerged as one of the top five challenges in The Forum on Education Abroad's 2022 State of the Field Survey findings. Some respondents reported that since the COVID-19 pandemic, a growing number of students are less able to cope with the basic challenges of studying abroad, and more mental health issues are surfacing than ever before. Another notable theme was that students are more overwhelmed and experiencing burnout, which presents significant impediments to participation in education abroad—even at the earliest phases of the process (The Forum on Education Abroad, 2023).

Amid unprecedented increases in demand for care, many universities and education abroad organizations have expanded their efforts to provide mental health support for students, and in some cases, for staff as well. In addition to simply hiring more clinicians, some are trying different approaches and models such as group therapy, peer counseling, a stepped-care model where the students who are most in need receive the most intensive care and additional mental health first aid training for faculty and staff (Abrams, 2022). Some have also begun to ramp up training and professional development for education abroad professionals.

## Mental Health Disparities Among Underrepresented and Marginalized Identities

### Political and Campus Climate

Varying perspectives on the place of equity, diversity, and inclusion in education are driving higher education discussions in a way that has not been seen in over 30 years. Shifts in sociopolitical circumstances, such as the election of Donald J. Trump in 2016, that propagate bigotry may be harmful and affect the mental health and well-being of those who possess marginalized identities (Albright & Hurd, 2020; Museus & Pérez Huber, 2023). For example, a 2020 study found that having marginalized identities was associated with greater experiences of distress related to Trump's presidency and was also associated with increases in anxious symptoms (Albright & Hurd, 2020). Trump's prejudice against women, LGBTQIA+, immigrants, Muslims, Black and Latinx individuals, and other groups increased the psychological toll of coping with discrimination and prejudice. Increased exposure to negative statements on social media in a sociopolitical climate that sanctions negative bias toward several identity groups may lead to feeling less safe. The increase in racist political rhetoric has created stressful and, in some cases, harmful conditions for students of color in HEIs throughout the United States (Pérez Huber & Muñoz, 2021). Other research shows that mental health among college-age students was negatively impacted by the murder of George Floyd, with reports of higher distress about police brutality, increased stress, and worry (Howard et al., 2022).

Students of color and other minoritized groups are being adversely impacted by challenging and even hostile campus climates. Museus & Pérez Huber (2023) note that while hostile climates existed throughout higher education prior to 2016, the racist rhetoric embraced by the prior presidential administration and propagated across the country exacerbated the hostility in campus climates, promoting increased violence toward groups with minoritized racial, religious, socioeconomic, and immigrant backgrounds. (p.17)

It is not surprising that Black students are more than twice as likely as white students to say that the racial climate on their campus is poor (Gallup, 2016). College students have also reported an increase in racist incidents on their campuses that have been associated with negative mental health outcomes such as increased stress, anxiety, depression, and fear (Pérez Huber & Muñoz, 2021).

In addition to the threats of physical violence, culturally exclusionary curriculum, and overtly racist rhetoric in the media, marginalized students are also exposed to more subtle forms of racism such as microaggressions (Williams et al., 2019). Racial microaggressions have been found to cause emotional and psychological distress (Choi et al., 2022) as well as depression (Torres-Harding et al., 2020). Smith et al. (2016) found that the college environment was more hostile toward Black men than other groups and that the Black males participating in their study experienced "various forms of racial microaggressions in academic, campus-social, and public spaces" (p. 8). In many cases, the perpetrators of these racial microaggressions include faculty, staff, and students. It is clear that campus climates can have a significant impact on the mental health and well-being of college students, particularly those from marginalized and minoritized communities.

## Greater Unmet Mental Health Needs

According to multiple research studies (Lipson et al., 2018; Gallup, 2023), college students of color have greater levels of unmet mental health needs relative to their white peers. Racial inequities and biases, which often prevent people of color from seeking mental health services, can lead to poor outcomes if and when they do receive treatment (Williams et al., 2019). Black and Asian students who experience mental health issues are far less likely than white students to discuss or seek treatment for such issues (Russell, 2021), and only 21% of Black students with mental health issues receive a diagnosis compared to 48% of White students (Lipson et al., 2018). According to Gallup (2023),

perceived stigma, and differences in the way racial and ethnic groups define and recognize mental health challenges, may disproportionately influence the willingness of students from some racial/ethnic groups to be open about mental health struggles.

Prior studies have shown that Black and Asian students who experience mental health issues are less likely than White students to seek treatment for such issues. (p.6)

A key challenge in the educational abroad field is how to advocate for, develop, and implement mental health support programs that effectively reach underrepresented students. In order to better chances of doing so, you must recognize the unique needs across different racial and ethnic groups and the significant barriers they face. Considering and developing culturally specific messaging for Black and Latinx/Latine students and other marginalized groups, may be a useful strategy to effectively promote help-seeking (Lipson, et al, 2018). Collaborating effectively across partners and organizations to provide culturally relevant mental health programming, developing curricula that prioritizes the mental health and well-being of diverse students, and promoting connections and belonging throughout the program cycle are some of the key strategies that we can implement to collectively encourage positive student mental health and well-being both at home and abroad.

## Strategies for Building Stronger Mental Health Support Systems

### Reduce Barriers Early On

With students reporting overload and stress (Gallup, 2023; Lumpkin, 2021), reducing barriers early on is important for increasing access to education abroad, particularly for underrepresented students. Where possible, simplifying and streamlining study abroad application and preparation procedures is one way to reduce the initial hurdles facing students. The 2023 Gallup report, *Stressed Out and Stopping Out: The Mental Health Crisis in Higher Education*, notes that "emotional stress" and "personal mental health reasons" were the top reasons that students considered stopping their coursework, across all student populations (p. 4). These are also top reasons that adults aged 18–24 cite for not enrolling in postsecondary education (Gallup, 2023). It is, therefore, important to consider how this might be impacting persistence in education abroad participation.

For many years, data indicates a much smaller percentage of study abroad participants come from underrepresented groups due to a combination of barriers including lack of access and limited support. Research indicates that underrepresented students also access mental health support at lower rates than the majority of students (Lipson et al., 2018). As a result, it is critical that mental health support is accessible before students even enroll in education abroad experiences. Furthermore, supporting underrepresented students' mental health is critical to increasing their access and participation. Chapter 10 identifies some best practices with regard to planning and collaborating to support participants with disabilities that align with best practices in building inclusive programs. Essential steps forward include placing diversity, equity, inclusion, and social justice at the center of programming and support systems from the start and helping students explore the sociocultural contexts to which they are traveling, so that they can plan their systems of support, find communities in which they can feel safe, and prepare for challenging situations emotionally and strategically.

## Utilize the *Standards of Good Practice for Education Abroad*

The *Standards of Good Practice for Education Abroad* are an essential framework for education abroad professionals to consider when developing infrastructure around supporting student mental health and well-being. They provide numerous points at which good practices that support all students can be incorporated. Considering how mental health and well-being can impact student learning and development before, during, and after the international experience, clauses 6.1, 6.2, and 6.3 of the *Standards of Good Practice for Education Abroad* provide an important foundation for prioritizing equity, diversity, and inclusion through the program cycle (The Forum on Education Abroad, 2020). Clause 5.1.5 details that organizations must have policies in place to govern student matters, including those around mental health (The Forum on Education Abroad, 2020). Ensuring that these policies, procedures, and guidelines are regularly reviewed for transparency, equity, and accessibility is essential. These policies also need to be updated regularly in light of changing student demographics and other variables. Some important student characteristics that need to be considered include age, gender identity, socioeconomic status, sexual orientation, political, religious, ethnic, and cultural identity. Preparing participants adequately requires orientation sessions tailored to the needs of these specific groups. Risk assessments, disciplinary protocols, and student conduct sanctions should also be reviewed on a regular basis to ensure that they do not increase the stigmatization of mental health needs and challenges. Prior to traveling abroad, students will benefit from orientation sessions that include opportunities to recognize and discuss their own coping skills and problem-solving approaches. Helping students to anticipate cultural differences and stressful situations as potential moments of growth where they should use both internal and external supports are essential. A strength-based approach to understanding oneself can provide a positive, empowering lens through which challenging situations can be tackled. In addition, scheduling feedback sessions after re-entry where participants can provide input on their experiences can be valuable opportunities for direct action, correction of issues, and stakeholder engagement to improve a site. Providing students with an opportunity to process the challenges they tackled abroad can strengthen their awareness of their resilience and provide valuable details about the site that can help others prepare.

## Collaborate and Communicate Within and Across Organizations

In order to create strong mental health support networks with our HEIs, we must collaborate across units, such as Student Health Services, the Counseling Center, Office of Disability Services, Office of Diversity and Inclusion, as well as onsite partners. Now, more than ever, a comprehensive approach is needed to support student mental health and well-being, one that takes into consideration diverse cultural conceptualizations of mental health and well-being, and the lived experience of our students, including racism, social isolation, and financial stress. By collaborating across units that have a range of student support expertise, both within our own HEIs and with onsite partners, we are better equipped to develop practical approaches.

In 2015, The Steve Fund and The Jed Foundation released an Equity in Mental Health Framework that offers useful recommendations and key implementation strategies to help colleges and universities to promote, support, and institutionalize the prioritization of emotional well-being and mental health support for students of color and all students. While the report was intended to address institution-wide collaboration and commitment, its recommendations, outlined below, are also highly relevant for the education abroad context:

1. Identify and promote the mental health and well-being of students of color as a campus-wide priority.
2. Engage students to provide guidance and feedback on matters of student mental health and emotional well-being.
3. Actively recruit, train, and retain a diverse and culturally competent faculty and professional staff.
4. Create opportunities to engage all sectors of the organization around national and international issues and events.
5. Create dedicated staff roles to support well-being and success of students of color and minoritized students.
6. Support and promote accessible, safe communication lines with campus administration and an effective response system.

7. Offer a range of supportive programs and services in varied formats and cultural approaches.
8. Help students learn about programs and services by advertising and promoting through multiple channels.
9. Identify and utilize culturally relevant and promising programs and practices and collect data on their effectiveness from a variety of stakeholders.
10. Participate in resource and information sharing within and between schools (The Steve Fund and The Jed Foundation, 2017).

When working with partners overseas and at home, education abroad professionals may consider adapting these recommendations to advocate for, support, and promote the emotional well-being and mental health of education abroad participants.

## Offer Ongoing Training for Faculty, Staff, and Onsite Partners

Increasing staff and student mental health literacy is an important foundation of any mental health strategy. While many HEIs have ramped up efforts to support student mental health in recent years, funding and efforts are also needed to ensure that staff and faculty responsible for supporting education abroad participants have the necessary training and resources. As a baseline, staff should have access to ongoing training on topics such as:

- Psychological first aid
- Understanding appropriate boundaries
- Common signs of mental distress
- Intersection of mental health and diversity, equity, and inclusion, and social justice
- Self-care strategies for preventing staff burnout

Staff can benefit from strength-based approaches to self-appraisal and performance appraisals in their roles. Incorporating self-care strategies into staff work may help prevent burnout, especially if the strategies are tailored to an individual's personal style and self-concept. While some might find socializing with friends to be rejuvenating, others may feel restored with mindfulness or meditation or spiritual practices. Additional sources of self-care include spending time on hobbies such as art, reading, sport, music, comedy, gardening, yoga, DIY, craftwork, cooking, and spending time in nature. Travel and language learning not related to work can also be helpful. Maintaining self-care is an essential prerequisite for healthy functioning in order to support student mental health.

The field of education abroad must respond to the changing mental health needs of its participants, and not allow a lack of support or resources to become a barrier to global learning and access to international experiences. Since college students of color and other marginalized identities often face additional stressors and are less likely to access needed mental health support, it is especially important to assess their needs and strengthen their support systems. This may include accessing other sources of support within their cultural, social, familial, and spiritual communities. For some students, making a plan for scheduled conversations with mentors, family members, or spiritual leaders with whom they typically connect while at home can provide a stable support system in moments of uncertainty, vulnerability, or isolation abroad. Our field has a responsibility to consider how units can more effectively collaborate within and across institutions to support the mental health and well-being of those we serve. With mindful planning, collaboration, communication, and ongoing training, we can better support the changing mental health needs of today's education abroad participants.

Resources for Mental Health Support:

- Mental Health First Aid: https://www.mentalhealthfirstaid.org/mental-health-resources/
- Positive Psychology – Strength Based Approach: https://positivepsychology.com/strengths-based-interventions/
- VIA Character Strengths: https://www.viacharacter.org/
- Diversity Abroad: https://www.diversityabroad.org/GlobalImpactExchange
- Anandavalli, S., Borders, L. D., & Kniffin, L. E. (2021). "I Am Strong. Mentally Strong!": Psychosocial Strengths of International Graduate Students of Color. The Professional Counselor, 11(2), 173–187. https://doi.org/10.15241/sa.11.2.173

# References

Abrams, Z. (2022). Student mental health is in crisis. Campuses are rethinking their approach. APA Monitor on Psychology, 53(7). https://www.apa.org/monitor/2022/10/mental-health-campus-care

Albright, J. N., & Hurd, N. M. (2020). Marginalized identities, Trump-related distress, and the mental health of underrepresented college students. American Journal of Community Psychology, 65(3–4), 381–396. https://doi.org/10.1002/ajcp.12407

Auerbach, R. P., Mortier, P., Bruffaerts, R., Alonso, J., Benjet, C., Cuijpers, P., Demyttenaere, K., Ebert, D. D., Green, J. G., Hasking, P., Murray, E., Nock, M. K., Pinder-Amaker, S., Sampson, N. A., Stein, D. J., Vilagut, G., Zaslavsky, A. M., Kessler, R. C., & WHO WMH-ICS Collaborators. (2018). WHO World Mental Health Surveys International College Student Project: Prevalence and distribution of mental disorders. Journal of Abnormal Psychology, 127(7), 623–638. https://doi.org/10.1037/abn0000362

Center for Collegiate Mental Health. (2016, January). 2015 Annual Report (Publication No. STA 15-108). https://ccmh.psu.edu/assets/docs/2015_CCMH_Report_1-18-2015-yq3vik.pdf

Choi, S., Clark, P. G., Gutierrez, V., Runion, C., & Mendenhall, R. (2022). Racial microaggressions and Latinxs' well-being: A systematic review. Journal of Ethnic & Cultural Diversity in Social Work, 31(1), 16–27. https://doi.org/10.1080/15313204.2020.1827336

Cokley, K., Smith, L., Bernard, D., Hurst, A., Jackson, S., Stone, S., Awosogba, O., Saucer, C., Bailey, M., & Roberts, D. (2017). Impostor feelings as a moderator and mediator of the relationship between perceived discrimination and mental health among racial/ethnic minority college students. Journal of Counseling Psychology, 64(2), 141–154. https://doi.org/10.1037/cou0000198

Gallup, Knight Foundation, The Newseum Institute. (2016). Free expression on campus: A survey of U.S. college students and U.S. adults. https://knightfoundation.org/wp-content/uploads/2016/04/FreeSpeech_campus-1.pdf

Gallup. (2023). Stressed out and stopping out: The mental health crisis in higher education. https://www.newamerica.org/higher-education/highered-public-opinion-hub/stressed-out-and-stopping-out-the-mental-health-crisis-in-higher-education/

Howard, L. C., Krueger, E. A., Barker, J. O., Boley Cruz, T., Cwalina, S. N., Unger, J. B., Barrington-Trimis, J. L., & Leventhal, A. M. (2022). Young adults' distress about police brutality following the death of George Floyd. Youth & Society. 2023; 55(6): 1173-1190. https://doi.org/10.1177/0044118X221087282

Lipson, S.K., Kern, A., Eisenberg, D. & Breland-Noble, A.M. (2018). Mental health disparities among college students of color. Journal of Adolescent Health, 63(3), 348-356. https://healthymindsnetwork.org/wp-content/uploads/2019/04/1-s2.0-S1054139X18301915-main.pdf

Lipson, S.K., Zhou, S., Abelson, S., Heinze, J., Jirsa, M., Morigney, J., Patterson, A., Singh, M., & Eisenberg, D. (2022). Trends in college student mental health and help-seeking by race/ethnicity: Findings from the national healthy minds study 2013-2021. Journal of Affective Disorders, 306, 138-147. https://doi.org/10.1016/j.jad.2022.03.038

Lumpkin, L. (2021). A mental health crisis was spreading on college campuses: The pandemic has made it worse. The Washington Post. https://www.washingtonpost.com/education/2021/03/30/college-students-mental-health-pandemic/

Museus, S., & Pérez Huber, L. (2023). Degrees of distress: How higher education institutions help and hurt student mental health. https://collegefutures.org/insights/degrees-of-distress/

Pérez Huber, L. & Muñoz, S. (Eds.). (2021). Why they hate us: How racist political rhetoric impacts education in the U.S. Teachers College Press.

Russell, T. (2021). What to know about depression in Black college students. PsychCentral. https://psychcentral.com/depression/what-to-knowabout-depression-in-black-college-students

Smith, W. A., Mustaffa, J. B., Jones, C. M., Curry, T. J., & Allen, W. R. (2016). 'You make me wanna holler and throw up both my hands!': Campus culture, Black misandric microaggressions, and racial battle fatigue. International Journal of Qualitative Studies in Education, 29(9), 1189–1209. https://doi.org/10.1080/09518398.2016.1214296

The Forum on Education Abroad. (2020). *Standards of good practice for education abroad* (Sixth Ed.). https://www.forumea.org/standards-of-good-practice.html

The Forum on Education Abroad. (2023). State of the Field Report: Data from the Comprehensive 2022 Survey. DOI:10.363666.R.2022SOF

The Steve Fund and The Jed Foundation. (2017). Equity in Mental Health Framework. https://equityinmentalhealth.org/

Torres-Harding, S., Torres, L., & Yeo, E. (2020). Depression and perceived stress as mediators between racial microaggressions and somatic symptoms in college students of color. American Journal of Orthopsychiatry, 90(1), 125–135. https://doi.org/10.1037/ort0000408

Williams, M. T., Rosen, D. C., & Kanter, J. W. (Eds). (2019). Eliminating race-based mental health disparities: Promoting equity and culturally responsive care across settings. New Harbinger.

# 25

## Pre-Departure Mental Health Clearance: One Approach to Managing Risk Abroad

**Vanessa Sterling**

Each education abroad organization or institution sending students abroad should consider how they can best support their students with health conditions when abroad. Currently, there is a debate education abroad practitioners as to whether institutions and organizations should collect and review students' protected health information (PHI), or if that review should be retained by students' healthcare providers. Each organization or institution should determine whether they need to collect and review student health information, and, if so, who should have access to this information and for what purpose.

This chapter approaches the current debate with the perspective that collecting and reviewing students' health information can both assist health diagnoses and is an explicit demonstration of due diligence. From this perspective, it is advisable that institutions design and utilize a standard process for reviewing health information and advising students on how to manage their health—physical, mental, and behavioral—while abroad as an important component of the post-acceptance, pre-departure phase. Further, this chapter focuses on a clearance process for mental health conditions. Why this focus? Many students who study abroad do so while managing health conditions. Discussing mental health can be intimidating, and many education abroad practitioners have little to no training to discuss it confidently. Many fear that if we "say something wrong," we might cause upset or harm to a student. And traditionally college-aged young people are sometimes loathed to discuss any pre-existing mental health conditions as they are assuming (or perhaps hoping) that going abroad will alleviate their symptoms. Add to that the potential legal concerns relating to privacy and discrimination, and it is no wonder that many education abroad professionals feel limited in their ability to conduct pre-departure mental health clearances.

However, there are real benefits to collecting, methodically assessing, and providing mental health resources before students head out on their experiences. If your institution has already determined that it would like to collect information about student mental health, this chapter will guide you in how to properly align goals for a mental health clearance process and work with the information you gather within your practice as an international educator. If your institution has not yet taken a position in this regard, this chapter can be a resource to share with stakeholders when embarking upon a discussion about how to develop an institutional protocol.

## To Ask or Not to Ask?

### The Spector of FERPA

If you ask colleagues in your organization or the broader field of international education if you should ask students about their medical needs, undoubtedly you will hear from many that you "cannot do that because of FERPA (the Family Educational Rights and Privacy Act)." Is that true?

The short answer is "it depends." The longer answer involves considering the type of organization in which you work, the types of questions you ask the student, and how the collected information will be used during the student's time abroad (U.S. Department of Education, 2019). FERPA applies to any institution or organization that receives direct funds from the Department of Education. So, if you work for a higher education institution that receives U.S. federal funding, FERPA rights must be considered and included in any assessment process you build. If you work for an education abroad program provider, FERPA does not directly apply but honoring it may be included in an MOU (memorandum of understanding) or contract. If you work for an organization or institution solely based outside of the U.S., FERPA is irrelevant unless the contract or MOU that you have with a sending institution requires following FERPA stipulations. (See Chapter 5 of this volume, "Have Records, Will Travel: FERPA and Access While Abroad," by Michael Pfahl (2024) for more information.) Furthermore, asking students to self-disclose their personal health information allows you more autonomy in reviewing and responding, as the student's consent is inherent in self-disclosure forms (i.e., the student decides what to share and what not to share).

### Working With Your Legal Counsel

However, if you work for an institution that does receive federal funding, you can still build a clearance process that is FERPA compliant. This requires engaging directly with your legal counsel to discuss the needs you have of a process and how to manage it effectively without incurring unnecessary legal risks.

If your legal counsel takes a more conservative approach, they may initially state that only licensed medical practitioners should evaluate medical information. In a well-designed mental health clearance process, you are not evaluating the "medical aspects," rather whether care for reported conditions is available at the program location. Your reasonable concerns, such as the availability of mental health resources (or lack thereof) in a particular location; legal issues affecting treatment, such as the local availability of certain prescription medications; differing standards of patient care and consent; and the host culture framework all provide an effective counterargument for why you should review the health information alongside a medical practitioner. *Your role is to enhance the advice of medical professionals by adding the international context,* not to replace it. But how can you frame this well for an attorney who may know little to nothing about education abroad?

One salient example is that Adderall, a medication commonly prescribed for ADHD and ADD (attention deficit/hyperactivity disorder), is completely illegal to possess in Japan, but many prescribing physicians outside of Japan do not know this. Given the legal penalties for possession of Adderall in Japan are up to ten years imprisonment, it is a tremendous risk to your institution to rely on physicians alone to discuss a student's ADHD medications if they are going to Japan. (Many other countries, such as South Korea, have a permit system by which students can import Adderall legally, but without the permit, legal penalties are equally severe). Sharing this fact about a medication that is quite commonly prescribed and a study abroad destination that is popular can help your legal counsel see the need for an assessment process! (See Chapter 14, "Traveling Abroad with Medication," by Christine Sprovieri and Jennifer Fullick (2024) for more details.)

### Goals for a Pre-Departure Mental Health Clearance

Consider the goals you want to achieve through your mental health clearance process. The clearance process can provide support for students who manage mental health conditions, contributing to the student's overall success in their program. The clearance process can be a starting point for students to research local regulations about medications and mental health care and outline what services their chosen program can provide. This in turn can help you set expectations with the student about what support services are available. Furthermore, providing the student with guidance and support according to their needs will help the student better adjust once in their host country, thereby contributing to a healthier classroom environment for the staff and other students on the program. Addressing student mental health needs prior to departure works towards organizational goals of inclusivity in that it acknowledges mental health as an important aspect of student life that can be supported abroad.

## Gaining Skills

### What Do You Know?

Many people have little understanding of the various mental health concerns students manage today unless they have previous personal or professional experience assisting someone living with a particular diagnosis. Excellent resources are readily available. Do keep in mind that if you are not a licensed medical professional, you should never use information you read as a basis for providing advice. Review web-based resources such as the National Alliance on Mental Illness (National Alliance on Mental Illness, 2023) and meet with practitioners such as clinicians at your institution's counseling and health centers. The following are basic areas to familiarize yourself with.

### Conditions and Their Potential Impacts

Although college-aged students can have any mental health challenge, recent reporting from U.S. college and university health centers identified the following ongoing or chronic mental health conditions as the most commonly diagnosed among their students: anxiety, depression, ADHD and ADD, and trauma- or stressor-related conditions including post-traumatic stress disorder (PTSD) and acute stress disorder (American College Health Association, 2024). National Alliance on Mental Illness (NAMI) has resources to understand these categories. Encourage students with diagnoses to speak to their treating clinician about potential new challenges that living abroad can pose, even for short-term programs. This is an area where your international expertise can be especially useful, as many U.S.-based clinicians neither understand nor have any experience with the rigors of life abroad, and how being away from one's normal support structures can exacerbate symptoms. Emphasizing that the student is not simply getting a change of scenery or going on an extended vacation is crucial, as that encourages clinicians to engage with how a different environment may affect symptoms and treatment options.

Many students hope that going abroad will remove them from the stressors that contribute to their symptoms, or may cure them of their condition entirely, so you must address this fallacy clearly in the pre-departure phase with all participants.

## Medications and Their Uses

Knowing what medications your students are using will help you research whether they are available and legal in the students' host countries and therefore can be useful in informing your advising and pre-departure preparations. But it is an ongoing conversation based on resources, staff time, and institutional approach to risk management that should determine if you even ask students questions about their prescriptions. An alternative best practice is not to ask, so that you don't create an expectation that there is some sort of intervention or support just because the question has been asked and the answer given.

If you are asking students about medications, the following is a general overview of the five main categories of psychotropic medications with examples: antidepressants, antianxiety medications, stimulants, antipsychotics, and mood stabilizers. Antidepressants include SSRIs (i.e., fluoxetine [Prozac], sertraline [Zoloft], and escitalopram [Lexapro], as well as older-generation drugs [i.e., bupropion, amitriptyline]). Antianxiety medications include both benzodiazepines (i.e., Xanax, diazepam, clonazepam) as well as antihistamines (i.e., hydroxyzine), and beta-blockers (i.e., propranolol). Stimulants are often used by people with ADHD and ADD, such as Ritalin, Adderall, and Vyvanse. Antipsychotics (i.e., risperidone and aripiprazole) are used with those who have experienced psychosis (a temporary loss of contact with reality) or related symptoms either as part of schizophrenia, schizoaffective disorder, or in more advanced cases of mood disorders, such as bipolar disorder or major depression. They can also be used for other concerns, such as mania, OCD, bipolar depression, and general anxiety. Mood stabilizers are used in cases of bipolar disorder (i.e., lamotrigine [Lamictal], Lithium).

Regardless of the diagnosis and medication prescribed, students should remain on their medications unless instructed otherwise by their treating clinician. Medication compliance is critical to maintaining good mental health, but often poses challenges for young people, as it can be inconvenient, may have unpleasant side effects, and involves engaging with medical insurance. Obtaining a supply sufficient for the entirety of their time abroad can require planning and coordination, so be prepared to discuss with the student how they can get what they need before they leave and whether equivalents are available if their medication is not available or legal in their host country.

### International/Host Country Realities

Providing information on what a student can expect abroad is where your work is most valuable, as U.S.-based clinicians and counselors likely have little to no understanding of the resources available to provide continuity of care or crisis support. Work with your program provider or host institution and insurance provider to become familiar with what is available. Assume nothing, ask many questions, and collect the information you learn for future reference. Routinely update this information.

### Differing Medical and Legal Systems

Each country governs its own medical system. Laws and regulations can vary from country to country. Even among countries within the European Union, there can be differences in clinical approaches, inpatient requirements, and information sharing. Areas to consider are definitions of consent for treatment, patient's rights, and whether emergency care takes place in a hospital setting or an auxiliary facility. For example, the Czech Republic uses the asylum model (in-patient, long-term care in a solely mental health facility) for treating psychosis or substance abuse, and the treating physician (not the patient) determines when a patient can be discharged. Some countries like Japan still routinely use passive or chemical restraints in clinical settings. And many countries expect family members to provide daily, non-medical support to people in hospital. Frameworks like GDPR can make the transfer of medical records challenging or impossible. (See Chapters 10 and 11 by Shirley Liu and Emma Bahner (2024a, 2024b) for more information.)

### Permitting for Medications

Medication continuity is important. However, not all medications are available abroad, and some that are legal in the U.S. are expressly illegal in other countries. Japan, South Korea, and Singapore severely restrict many commonly prescribed drugs. Check official government online resources as well as the International Narcotics Control Board (International Narcotics Control Board, 2023) for which medications are allowed to be imported into the country and which are not. Some countries have permitting processes for foreigners carrying prescriptions for personal use, such as the *Yunyu Kakunin-sho* (previously known as the *Yakkun Shomei*) for Japan (Japanese Ministry of Health, Labour, and Welfare, 2021). Students must be aware that the importation of some medications, such as medical marijuana, can have severe consequences, and that a U.S. prescription has no legitimacy in a foreign country. See Chapter 14, "Traveling Abroad with Medication," by Christine Sprovieri and Jennifer Fullick (2024) for more information.

## Boundaries of Responsibility

If you are not a trained mental health practitioner, your role is to provide information that the student can share with their treating clinician about the realities abroad, such as academic expectations, local availability of mental health care, etc. It is not your role to make unilateral decisions about whether an experience is appropriate (or not) for a particular student at a particular time. Focusing on facts, such as the availability of support and the legality of medications, may lead you to conclude that a student cannot receive the care they may need abroad. You can certainly share that information with a student and other interested parties, such as their family (if you are permitted), their program provider or host institution, or their U.S.-based treating clinician (once you have obtained consent from the student, if your institution requires this). However, no one should expect you alone to assess a student's ability to succeed in a program based on their health profile.

## Establishing a Process

Your legal counsel may be hesitant to allow you to review a student's mental health profile due to the concern that this will expose your institution to a discrimination claim. Establishing a routinized process through which all students are evaluated may alleviate this exposure. Let's now discuss how to construct a process in tandem with your legal counsel that will honor both your institution's legal philosophy and risk tolerance while generating the information you need to advise a student appropriately.

## Modalities

There are many options that can work for your assessment. Successful systems account for the technology you have, your office's workflow, and your campus's or organization's external resources. Start with your existing application/assessment process to see if/where you can add separate questionnaires, letters from treating physicians, or other documentation. Some offices prefer to request a full health profile for each student, of which mental health may take a small role. Others use questionnaires powered by yes/no questions that allow students to complete only what is relevant to their personal situation. The questions can be drafted in concert with your legal counsel. Note that you should not request any health information until after a student has been admitted to a program, because doing so can expose you to claims of discrimination.

### Initial Review

All student information submitted should receive a first review. If the student reports no specific concerns, your assessment is complete. If a student reports a history of a mental health diagnosis but not a current one, you may opt to follow up electronically or make a note for your records. If a student shares a current concern that seems to be lower acuity, such as test anxiety or well-managed ADHD, electronic follow-up is appropriate. If a student shares multiple concerns, a meeting (either virtual or in-person) may be advisable.

### Follow-Up

Once your initial review is complete, decide which students require electronic or in-person follow-up. Factors to consider include location and duration of program, the type of program, the level of student support, whether the student expresses a need for regular counseling, and whether there are legal concerns in the host country that the student should understand.

### Timelines

Your review should allow students adequate time to respond to the information you present to them. Contacting students needing follow-up should ideally start eight weeks before departure. This will allow students enough time to obtain an appropriate supply of medication, switch to a new medication, complete permits (if applicable), and/or create a treatment plan with their U.S.-based care provider before departure.

### Emails and Meetings

#### Emails

Standardizing the format of your response makes your process both more efficient and less susceptible to claims of discrimination. If you are sending an electronic response, create a template that includes the following: (a) a thank you to the student for their willingness to share; (b) an acknowledgment that you are not a medical professional, but rather sharing your expertise as an international educator; and (c) that your goal is to encourage the student to create a plan to support their mental health while abroad. Then, you can add other relevant information such as insurance coverage, the program support structures, and if the student will need permission to bring their medications to their host country. To respect FERPA-related concerns, limit the number of parties copied all related emails.

### Meetings

If a meeting is warranted, consider having another member of your organization's professional staff participate, as that person can act as a witness to your discussion with the student, thus reducing the potential for later conflicting reports. Develop a standard script or pattern for your meetings and provide respectful responses to student questions or statements. Take notes and let the student know what the next steps are. Send a follow-up email outlining what you covered in the meeting, highlighting any specific guidance you shared.

### Clarifying Goals

Share that your goal for the meeting is to help the student be successful abroad. Students may be candid in these conversations, and what you hear may include upsetting content. These meetings are not meant to be therapy sessions but rather opportunities for you to transmit information and help the student proactively plan for their health. Sometimes students get emotional while discussing their challenges, and that may impact you as well.

## Sharing Information Appropriately

### Recording Documentation

Once you have completed your assessment of each student, make a quick note in their file. Use consistent terms and avoid making judgments about the suspected diagnoses. You may find it useful to create a list of students with more complex profiles and/or specific support needs in order to efficiently guide any necessary follow-up.

### Transmitting Information Internationally (FERPA, GDPR, etc.)

Sometimes it is necessary to share some of the information gleaned from this process with those supporting your students abroad. As this is sensitive data, be mindful of how you share this. Consult your organization's IT department to determine the safest transmission method, remembering FERPA requirements, GDPR (General Data Protection Regulation) if a student is going to a country in the European Union, and other state data maintenance requirements, such as the California Consumer Privacy Act (CCPA). Keep the information to a minimum and avoid speculation or opinion.

### Make a Call

If you feel a more candid conversation with your on-site staff or host institution is necessary, send an email to the person who needs to receive the information requesting a phone call or a virtual meeting. If you need to follow up afterward, discuss what should be in writing. This serves dual purposes. It allows you to limit the "paper trail" as each email becomes an official record regarding a student that can be requested legally while ensuring that your partners abroad are aware of your student's needs.

## Is the Mental Health Clearance Process Worth It?

Working with students one-on-one through a mental health clearance is time intensive but is also invaluable. It allows those receiving your students abroad time to adequately prepare to support your students in the way you would expect. It also creates space for those abroad to let you know when that support is not possible and to consider other options before a student departs for their experience. The process can also help students learn to be proactive about their health needs, which is an important life skill.

## Final Thoughts

This is hard work in an area that many international educators often find uncomfortable and sometimes intimidating. You may learn powerful and upsetting information about your students. Emotions can run high. You may at times feel out of your depth. This is completely understandable. Leveraging the support your institution/ organization provides, such as through an employee assistance program (EAP) or other short-term counseling resources, can be important to making this work emotionally sustainable for you and your colleagues.

## References

American College Health Association. (2024). American College Health Association National College Health Assessment Spring 2023 Reference Group Summary. https://www.acha.

org/documents/ncha/NCHA-III_SPRING_2023_REFERENCE_GROUP_EXECUTIVE_SUMMARY.pdf

International Narcotics Control Board. (2023, December 1). *Travelling Internationally with Medicines Containing Controlled Substances.* Retrieved from International Narcotics Control Board: https://www.incb.org/incb/en/travellers/index.html

Japanese Ministry of Health, Labour, and Welfare. (2021). *Information for Those Who Are Bringing Medicines for Personal Use into Japan.* Retrieved from Ministry of Health, Labour and Welfare of Japan: https://www.mhlw.go.jp/english/policy/health-medical/pharmaceuticals/01.html

Liu, X.S., & Bahner, E.S. (2024a). GDPR and PIPL Enforcement in Higher Education. In J. Pollard & K. S. Priebe (Eds.), *Convergence of litigation, policy, and standards: Building the informed practitioner in education abroad risk management.* The Forum on Education Abroad. doi.org/10.36.366/SIA.5.978-1-952376-41-2.11

Liu, X.S., & Bahner, E.S. (2024b). Global Data Privacy Overview. In J. Pollard & K. S. Priebe (Eds.), *Convergence of litigation, policy, and standards: Building the informed practitioner in education abroad risk management.* The Forum on Education Abroad. doi.org/10.36.366/SIA.5.978-1-952376-41-2.10

National Alliance on Mental Illness. (2023). *Mental Health Conditions.* Retrieved from nami.org: https://www.nami.org/About-Mental-Illness/Mental-Health-Conditions

Pfahl, M. (2024.) Have Records, Will Travel: FERPA and Access While Abroad. In J. Pollard & K. S. Priebe (Eds.), *Convergence of litigation, policy, and standards: Building the informed practitioner in education abroad risk management.* The Forum on Education Abroad.

Sprovieri, C., & Fullick, J. (2024). Traveling abroad with medication. In J. Pollard & K. S. Priebe (Eds.), *Convergence of litigation, policy, and standards: Building the informed practitioner in education abroad risk management.* The Forum on Education Abroad. doi.org/10.36.366/SIA.5.978-1-952376-41-2.14

U.S. Department of Education. (2019, December). *Joint Guidance on the Application of FERPA and HIPAA to Student Health Records.* Retrieved from studentprivacy.ed.gov: https://studentprivacy.ed.gov/resources/joint-guidance-application-ferpa-and-hipaa-student-health-records

# 26

# Building the Partnership: Best Practices for Engaging Counsel

Ashley Krutz-Ordner and Miko McFarland

## Introduction

Advances in technology and globalization make international activity more accessible than ever before, and it is exciting to see the growing number of college students developing their cross-cultural skills by going abroad. As organizations increasingly recognize the value of education abroad as a high-impact practice, the resources and infrastructure needed to effectively mitigate and manage risks associated with the activity must also rise to meet the new demand. This effort is hardly one-dimensional, as an organization's international footprint involves a myriad of stakeholders. One of the most critical partnerships needed to support international activity, and its inherent risks, is with your general counsel. General counsel is a cornerstone of the infrastructure required to effectively administer and manage international activity, especially when it comes to participant duty of care. They are essential to contract management, navigating the organization's liability, and advising on policies that impact participant health, safety, and security.

This chapter explores the fundamental aspects of working with your general counsel, including the role counsel plays, considerations for education abroad practitioners, and each party's scope of responsibility. The chapter also includes expert advice from legal practitioners who explore more complex topics such as contract negotiation, global human resources, and seeking external counsel. Finally, a tabletop discussion is also provided to help you and your general counsel consider a hypothetical scenario that illustrates the complexity of an organization's international activity.

While this chapter aims to be as comprehensive as possible, it is important to point out that the guidance offered in this chapter may not apply to every organization or institution type. For example, public or state-funded institutions may have different reporting obligations than private ones. U.S. states might have varying laws and compliance requirements. Institutions with a highly centralized structure may approach the work differently than their decentralized counterparts. It is important to know how your organization's profile impacts its risk management calculus.

## Maximizing Your Partnership

### Understanding Why

Before delving into the details of working with general counsel, let us take a moment to recognize the "why" that drives your work and your organization. Because comprehensive internationalization yields a variety of academic, economic, and cultural benefits to the campus community, the reasons why your organization engages in international activity like education abroad will depend on the organization's mission, strategic priorities, and vision of your leadership. U.S. higher education has traditionally enjoyed a high demand for international collaboration, which has allowed for the development of innovative educational pathways, exciting education abroad programs, and a diverse student population that serves the U.S. economy well.

With the exception of the recent COVID-19 pandemic, the Institute for International Education (IIE) Open Doors Report indicates that the number of U.S. students who participate in education abroad has steadily increased year on year (IIE, 2021). "For institutions of higher education, education abroad programming continues to represent an essential component for ensuring competitiveness in their institutions as well as an opportunity for students and faculty alike to remove the traditional boundaries of the classroom in exchange for an entire world of learning possibilities" (Pfahl, 2021, p. 94). Moreover, education abroad is a research-proven high-impact practice that provides students with a significant advantage by positively contributing to students' retention and persistence to degree completion (Bhatt et al, 2020).

The number and variety of education abroad programs have also soared over the past two decades. For-profit and nonprofit provider organizations have entered the market to meet the growing student demand for international activity and to facilitate programs where universities may be limited in resources and capacity. The Forum's 2022 State of the Field Report shared that, on average, 44% of education abroad program portfolios are made up of provider programs (The Forum on Education Abroad, 2023). Today's college students have the luxury of considering a vast menu of programs and experience types, from structured faculty-led short courses to more individualized, independent exchange semesters to professional internship placements. Programs can specialize in a variety of academic disciplines and experiential learning, with varying levels of on-site support and inclusions. There is almost certainly something for everybody and every interest, but it also means that institutions must be prepared to support a diverse student body, with complex needs, within a myriad of educational and cultural contexts.

The boom of internationalization and global mobility has also led to the expansion of infrastructure needed to effectively coordinate education abroad programs, ensure compliance with international regulations, and manage risks. Within the past decade, higher education has seen an emergence of highly specialized practitioners whose focus is to understand, track, and establish best practices in international health, safety, and security measures. Today, many organizations that maintain a robust global footprint now have a dedicated international risk manager who works closely alongside leadership, general counsel, and the education abroad unit to coordinate international risk management efforts. This specialized position allows institutions and organizations to prioritize their international risk and crisis response in a consistent and coordinated manner across all program and participant types. A member-led organization, Pulse International, brought international risk managers together to advance best practices and information sharing across the field: "Since Pulse's initial inception in 2010, the number of professionals in international safety and security in higher education has increased ten-fold. As of June 2023, Pulse International has over one-hundred and sixty members, representing over one hundred organizations/institutions from five countries (Australia, Canada, South Africa, Spain, and the United States)" ("About Us," n.d.).

In sum, understanding the context and rationale that drive your organization's international activity should be foundational to approaching your partnership with your general counsel. The field of education abroad has grown, evolved, and professionalized significantly over the past two decades, so relying on past personal experience to understand it may no longer be the most relevant perspective. We must take time to understand today's education abroad landscape to appreciate how far we have come as a professionalized field and to anticipate what the future may hold.

## Establish a Strong Foundation

Participant duty of care is a constantly evolving obligation and should be viewed as a continuum. Unfortunately, there is not an easily defined duty of care checklist and you cannot have one simple conversation with your general counsel to have duty of care "completed"—it is a cycle that requires continual work and evaluation. Nonetheless, there are steps you and your organization can take to establish a strong foundation for your duty of care discussions.

To get started, it is important to have a firm grasp on your organization's identity, strategic priorities, and international portfolio. First, review your organization's mission statement and values to determine how education abroad fits within the larger vision. As a standard of best practice, you should understand how your work aligns with the mission, values, and goals of the organization (The Forum on Education Abroad, 2020, p. 22-23). Not only can this framework be beneficial to evaluate your current expertise and strengths, but it can also help you identify new and emerging risks for your organization. What are your organization's strategic goals, and how do they impact your work? For example, if you have strong programs in Europe but your organization is looking to start offerings in Asia, then you are likely to encounter new risks related to the growth of your operating landscape. Similarly, if your organization is historically strong in faculty-led programs but is looking to expand independent experiential learning abroad, then you might be faced with a learning curve related to new risks.

Next, identify who is involved in international activity at your organization. As mentioned earlier, some institutions have a centralized unit that oversees all internationalization efforts, others may be more decentralized in nature. If your organization falls into this second category, you should take time to explore the opportunities available, identify leadership, and understand their training and experience. Do you have an institution-wide standard for international activity? Is there consistency among policies and procedures for different units? If not, start conversations with your general counsel here, as there is a lot of risk to manage when an organization lacks central standards and consistency.

To further facilitate organization-wide discussions, especially with faculty and staff representing different areas, it is essential that your organization adopt an established lexicon for international activity. For example, are stakeholders at your organization using the term "exchange" to capture a broad range of experience types? How can you define and differentiate these opportunities from each other? Be sure to take the time to work across your organization to create and adopt clear definitions for these terms, with your duty of care in mind. For example, a "sponsored program" might be an experience that is completely vetted by your organization through a comprehensive due diligence process, whereas an "independent experience" is student-identified and not vetted by you. By using a well-defined lexicon, you avoid miscommunications and set clear expectations for different international activity types.

Once you have a common lexicon, you can define your organization's risk appetite and tolerance by establishing clear and transparent guidelines. For example, a U.S.-based organization might choose to define its risk appetite and tolerance using the U.S. Department of State Travel Advisory levels—a public-facing resource (U.S. Department of State, n.d.). The organization might have a statement to the effect of "any international travel to a U.S. Department of State Level 1: Exercise Normal Precautions is acceptable" but clarify that "any travel to a Level 4: Do Not Travel is strictly prohibited." While it is best to use more than one intelligence resource when determining a location's full risk, the U.S. Department of State example demonstrates how an organization might define risk tolerance in a way that stakeholders can easily identify and understand. Also, consider activities that you may find to be higher risk or outside of your risk appetite. For example, your organization may be completely comfortable with internships that are designed to teach a student about business practices abroad, but more cautious in regard to clinical practices in a healthcare setting (i.e., the ethical nuances of a student's placement, especially when it comes to practices students would not typically have access to in a U.S. setting). A clear definition of unacceptable risk provides your organization with an essential foundation, one that can then be used to inform your best practices, policies, and procedures.

Once you have identified your stakeholders, established clear definitions, and refined your organization's risk appetite and tolerance, you can begin to explore your approach to education abroad and duty of care. While we have already defined the legal concept of duty of care in this book, also consider how this definition aligns with your organization's ethical approach and identity. Per the *Standards of Good Practice*, each organization must adopt ethical principles and guidelines that inform their decisions and behavior (The Forum on Education Abroad, 2020, clause 4.3.1). Furthermore, every organization must prepare staff or faculty to perform ethical decision-making and practices (The Forum on Education Abroad, 2020, clause 4.3.2). If you have not done so already, this is also a good time to review The Forum on Education Abroad's *Code of Ethics*, which has excellent information on shared values and professional principles in the field (The Forum on Education Abroad, 2020). In addition to these resources, here are some additional questions to consider:

- Does your organization have an internal code of ethics? Look to your organization's core values to understand which values are important to uphold.
- How do you prepare and train employees to make ethical decisions?
- Are there overlapping ethical codes and guidelines (i.e., best practices for students in healthcare) that are applicable, but maybe not specific to education abroad?
- How would you define your organization's identity and approach to risk?
- How would you define your personal risk tolerance and how does it align with your organization's risk tolerance?
- Do you and your organization have a clear definition of what is not acceptable, and a hard line "no"?
- Or are you open to a review process—asking the participant to explain the risk to reward of the experience and having a designated committee review it?

### Clarification on Role and Scope of Work

U.S. institutions typically have a robust infrastructure to effectively manage their domestic operations and risks, but the same level of multi-departmental or institutional-wide oversight may not be in place for international activities. Therefore, much of the responsibility for the development, implementation, and subsequent liability falls directly to the unit(s) which are already solely responsible for international activities and decision-making. Does the level of infrastructure, or lack thereof, reflect the actual risks associated with international activities? Not necessarily. It does mean, however, that general counsel will likely be working more closely with international offices because there is less infrastructure to support these activities.

The education abroad practitioner and general counsel have distinct roles when it comes to international risk. What areas of expertise and knowledge do each of you bring to the conversation? For example, education abroad professionals are familiar with best practices in programming and the professional organizations that drive innovation. As education abroad professionals work directly with students and programs, they have valuable firsthand knowledge which makes them well suited to identify areas of concern and risk. Education abroad offices also have knowledge of historical precedent with regard to risk decisions and critical incidents. For example, is there a history of concerning behavior among participants in a particular program that may require a unique approach? Or is there a history of an on-site host failing to meet expectations in response to student incidents?

On the contrary, general counsel's legal expertise means that they can effectively advise on risk mitigation for international activities and applicable

U.S. federal and state laws, or case law, that should be considered. General counsel also has knowledge of organizational precedent and can help maintain institutional-wide consistency. General counsel "often have the luxury of being able to fully focus on the whole, while central departments or program administrators will be relatively more focused on their own perspective. Lawyers can help bridge this gap" (Anderson et al., 2011, p. 5).

It is also important to point out that the general counsel is not in the position of making decisions on behalf of the organization. In other words, the general counsel should not be expected to have the final say on international activities. Rather, the appropriate leadership must be responsible for decision-making, with general counsel's guidance: "Directions or guidance, particularly in the academic realm, should almost always come from executive or academic administrators with designated authority. At the same time, lawyers represent the institution and will need help to ensure that the institution's interests are protected" (Anderson et al., 2011, p. 4). Therefore, an organization's leadership must also be willing and able to accept the risk and uphold a decision.

Keep in mind that general counsel is not a universal expert in law and there will be situations where you will need to seek outside counsel—especially for context on international laws or operating laws in a particular country. For more information and advice on working with outside counsel, please review the "Working Effectively with Outside Counsel" chapter in this volume (Ferreira, 2024). There will also be situations where U.S. law or a particular risk concern will require the expertise of other internal stakeholders. In these situations, it is best practice to create a team of experts to inform the discussion. Examples of other experts who could be consulted:

- Export control
- International data and privacy protection
- Information technology services
- Risk management and insurance
- Compliance and ethics
- Research integrity
- Records retention
- Audit, investigation, and advisory services
- Campus police
- Senior leadership or cabinet
- Academic leaders (i.e., Deans and Department Chairs)
- Human Resources
- Diversity, Equity, Inclusion
- Dean of Students or student conduct

- Mental health or counseling services
- Disabilities resources
- Title IX compliance
- Environmental health and safety

For example, if you are working on a particular situation that involves international research activities with employees and students you may need to consult: general counsel, export control, Global HR, and academic affairs. By creating a robust team, you will have all of the experts at the table to inform a decision—which creates legitimacy and buy-in. If your organization has a lot of international employment and HR-related concerns, please be sure to reference the chapter in this volume on "Employment and Compliance in Education Abroad: Guidance for Working with Global Human Resources" (Rae, 2024).

## Working with General Counsel

### Contract Principles

Stakeholders across your institution will always pursue international collaborations, from a faculty member who wants to co-publish research with an overseas colleague, to an advisor who received an email about an interesting new internship abroad, to an administrator who just returned from a conference excited about a connection they made with a potential international partner. In all cases, such stakeholders are carrying out activities as a representative of the institution, so there needs to be a standard process for documenting, negotiating, and formalizing the details of partnerships that develop.

An institution's international collaborations almost always require formal recognition. A good starting place would be The Forum on Education Abroad's *Standards of Good Practice*, in particular Administrative Framework 5.1.8 which outlines best practices in partnership agreements (The Forum on Education Abroad, 2020c). The types of agreements used to guide international activity vary from non-binding agreements, like a Memorandum of Understanding (MOU), to binding contracts that define a scope of work with specific terms and conditions. MOUs are most commonly used to formalize a partnership because they recognize an intent to collaborate more generally between two entities. MOUs are usually non-binding but may use language that references potentially binding actions. For example, you develop a formal partnership with a partner to exchange graduate teaching assistants, but the MOU also includes language about a scholarship that will be awarded to participating students (which is binding).

As mentioned earlier, a critical part of your due diligence is making sure that you are consulting the appropriate subject-matter experts at your organization. General counsel can help you consider the risks associated with an international activity captured in an agreement. Even with non-binding or more "friendly" agreements, general counsel should still be consulted to consider if binding terms and conditions are necessary to protect the organization: "Lawyers can help clients understand the principles underlying the inclusion of such clauses and often, the benefits that accrue to both parties by setting forth clear duties and obligations at the beginning of the relationship" (Anderson et al., 2011, p. 6). As your organization reviews any potential MOU, ask the following questions:

- Is this partner wanting to deviate from your organization's standard contract language?
- Is this partner proposing to outsource core academic services or other functions that fall under the institution's accrediting body?
- Does the contract involve the use of institutional and/or Title IV funds?
- Does the activity outlined in the contract involve the sharing of data or information that is traditionally protected by U.S. federal or state laws?
- Is the contract requiring something that the partner is unable to provide due to their own laws and regulations? (e.g., GDPR)
- Does the contract address an area of expertise (e.g., IT, Financial Aid, and Insurance) that falls outside the scope or expertise of your office?

Education abroad also utilizes binding contracts that clearly define the scope, terms, and conditions of a specific activity or program. For example, you may be working with an education abroad provider to develop a Master Services Agreement (MSA) that outlines the inclusions, deadlines, and costs associated with administering a faculty-led program. Because these types of agreements require both parties to fulfill specific responsibilities associated with the scope of work, your general counsel must review all terms and conditions to ensure that the institution can fulfill the obligations as they are written. One way to streamline this process is to proactively work with general counsel to establish template language to use in contract negotiation. For example, your institution may have very specific data security requirements that are non-negotiable. With template language, you can articulate this early on to your partner before reaching the stage of a final draft. Another example is adjudication, as most public institutions are unable to adjudicate outside their state. You could work with your general counsel to establish template language for adjudication terms. You can learn more about international partnership agreements, and their nuances, in Peter May's chapter in this volume, "Expectations, Guardrails and Compliance: Negotiating Effective International Partnership Agreements" (2024).

Regardless of where the conversation begins—with the faculty member co-publishing research, the advisor championing a new program, or the administrator who wants to establish a partnership—the signing should always conclude with a consistent and formally recognized signature authorization. The education abroad office, general counsel, and senior leadership should establish documented signature authority (and delegated signature authority if necessary) to standardize who at the organization is authorized to represent the organization's interests in international agreements and contracts.

Establishing signature authority:

- Minimizes risk to the organization and to the individual.
- Ensures greater transparency of international activity.
- Coordinates all organizational international activity into a central repository.
- Maintains consistency across all agreed-upon contract terms.
- Ensures that any fiscal responsibility can be upheld.

It is ideal to have a separation of duties with three distinct roles covered by your organization: main party of interest for the content review, general counsel for the legal review, and the signature authority. If you condense these roles into one (i.e., the main party of interest is also the signature authority), you may fail to get a full multi-faceted and unbiased review of the contract. Typically, senior leadership will appoint an official(s) who are authorized to represent the organization.

Keep in mind that signing a water-tight, mutually agreed-upon contract is not the end, it is just the beginning. Ensuring that all stakeholders involved in the international activity understand the terms of the agreement and are operating within its terms is where the real work begins: "Accountability, for both the university and vendor, also means making sure that employees outside of general counsel are aware of the contract and its provisions, especially if it coincides with their day-to-day work" (The Chronicle of Higher Education, 2023, p. 29-30). Ongoing collaboration with your general counsel and other subject matter experts is the name of the game, and the contract is your playbook.

### Waivers and Release Forms

As student learning expands from traditional on-campus and U.S.-based models, organizations will naturally see an increase in their potential exposure to risk as activity increases. Furthermore, this increase in potential risk is often coupled with conversations about organizational exposure to liability (Pfahl, 2021). In general: "The courts that have ruled in cases involving attempts by students, their parents, or their estates to hold an institution liable for an injury or death of a student have generally held that a university's duty of care to its students is similar to that of a business invitee, but conversely courts have generally upheld the principle that the university itself is not generally the 'insurer of the safety of its students' absent further action and affirmation" (Pfahl, 2021, p.95). In other words, while organizations have a duty of care to advise participants of "reasonably foreseeable risks," recent rulings have also implied that participants are expected to act in the interest of their own safety as well (Pfahl, 2021, p.95–98). Additionally, organizations must also "prepare students to manage their safety by providing resources related to concerns including, but not limited to: physical risks, behavior, property crime, liability and legal issues, sexual misconduct, identity-based discrimination, and country specific recommendations" (The Forum on Education Abroad, 2020c, clause 6.1.11).

As each case is judged based on unique specifics and the discussion of duty of care and liability is so robust, many organizations have turned to waivers as a solution (Pfahl, 2021). While most education abroad professionals collaborate with general counsel to discuss the specific language in a waiver, it is becoming more and more important to also consider how the waiver is delivered and signed by a participant. What are the important steps in the execution of a waiver? Per Pfahl (2021), "this process at a minimum, should be developed to satisfy three pillars of enforceability in that the student's consent to the conditions provided therein must be made knowingly, voluntarily, and with valuable consideration" (p. 96). Here are some recommendations for applying the "knowingly, voluntarily, and with valuable consideration" pillars (Pfahl, 2021, pp. 96–119):

- Provide a pre-departure process that seeks to educate the student on reasonably foreseeable risks, especially ones they may face as a part of the experience.
- Educate students on how they might mitigate these risks, if possible, and which risks will always remain.
- Provide students with this information early on (i.e., not right before they get on the plane).
- Make sure that it is clear that participation in the activity is voluntary, and that students know they have options (i.e., they do not have to go abroad on this experience, or accept these risks if they fall outside their personal tolerance/appetite).

- Give students time to reflect and consider if they want to assume these risks, and ultimately sign the waiver.

A best practice for waivers and general release forms is to approach the process as an educative and informative one—not just something to check off as a legal requirement for duty of care. As a part of this, be mindful of the language, tone, and content you use to make sure that it is helpful and informative for your students. Rather than using a lot of legal jargon that might be difficult for students to digest, consider using language that is readable and understandable. Provide students with the opportunity to ask questions if there is something that they do not understand and make sure that they know how to and who to contact with their questions. Incorporate the risk information into your pre-departure orientation (it never hurts to reiterate and repeat) and, again, give students clear options for communicating their questions and concerns. If your organization works with higher-risk locations and/or activities, then also consider what specific language and guidance you can incorporate for those participants. For example, highlighting information provided by the U.S. Department of State Travel Advisory, the Centers for Disease Control and Prevention health notice, or a larger institutional/ethical recommendation (i.e., "Please keep in mind that you should not participate in medical procedures while abroad, but can observe") are all excellent ways to provide students with additional information and credible resources for their "valuable consideration."

### Seeking Legal Advice

In addition to contracts and waivers, there will also be complex instances where you will need to consult general counsel. For example, you have a participant in a country where the on-site situation has become dangerous but is not yet assigned an elevated U.S. Department of State Level 3 or 4 advisory (which is a marker in your policy for high risk). In this instance, you could approach your general counsel with plans to evacuate the student due to safety and review how certain actions may/may not be appropriate. Additionally, proactive discussions on hypothetical scenarios will help calibrate your response for future situations. We recommend using tabletop discussions with your entire team to review, discuss, and debrief potential actions and your duty of care.

### Tabletop Discussion

Before completing the tabletop discussion below, take a moment to review the *Standards of Good Practice* and complete the prompts for self-assessment

(The Forum on Education Abroad, 2020c; The Forum on Education Abroad, 2020b). The prompts are a great resource for identifying concerns and topics to discuss further with the general counsel.

Tabletop example:

A faculty member plans to bring their child (16 years old) with them while they accompany a faculty-led program in Guatemala. The faculty will be paying the child's travel expenses out of pocket, but uses the institution's travel booking system/agent to arrange flights. The on-site provider in Guatemala has a policy that guests are allowed to stay in faculty housing but are not permitted to join program activities. However, the faculty member is a single parent and must bring their child in order to lead the program.

Recommended questions:
- What are the potential risks and implications for the institution, program, and participants? How does this scenario impact the institution's overall risk management strategy for the program?
- What is the institution's policy for accompanying guests on international travel? Does that conflict with general HR policies regarding accommodations for single parents on campus (if applicable)?
- How does the host's policy align or conflict with the institution's policy? What did the contract stipulate? Is there room for exceptions?
- What is the institution's duty of care toward the faculty member and child? How does that change if the guest is younger (i.e., 5 years old) or older (i.e., 18+ years)?
- What liability or insurance considerations should be considered?

## Summary

Internationalization efforts and education abroad yield many dividends for an organization, its stakeholders, and its participants. With added value, it is no surprise that organizations are eager to expand on opportunities that enhance their global reach and reputation. Organizations have a duty to balance providing new and meaningful opportunities abroad with their responsibility to provide duty of care and mitigate risks. The partnership you establish with general counsel early on is foundational to facilitating your current international activity and growth. From establishing a lexicon to understanding roles, your organization can now approach this partnership in a way that will optimize strengths and expertise from both the education abroad practitioner and general counsel.

In addition to The Forum on Education Abroad, there are other resources that can foster professional development for education abroad and general counsel. For example, the National Association of College and University Attorneys (NACUA) offers resources and training for its members. More specifically, the training module "Navigating University International Programs" is offered for new attorneys in higher education. Additionally, the Overseas Security Advisory Council (OSAC), a partnership between the U.S. Department of State's Diplomatic Security Service and the U.S. private sector, offers free resources and events that support U.S. organizations international risk management. As mentioned previously, Pulse International can also be an excellent resource that bridges the work of education abroad and international health, safety, and security. Risk management professionals in higher education may also look to the University Risk Management and Insurance Association (URMIA) for best practices.

Ultimately, managing your organization's duty of care for international activity is not a solo endeavor. Our field is rapidly evolving and professionalizing and requires, now more than ever, a network of professionals who can support the myriad of international activities. Therefore, look to those who have subject matter expertise and bring them into the conversation, especially your general counsel. Collaboration and transparency will not only enhance the quality of your international activity but also result in positive experiences for your participants. In the end, facilitating safe and enriching learning experiences is our common purpose.

## References

Anderson, A., Nicholson, W., O'Neil, C., & Wang, W. (2011). Emerging Institutional Models for Managing International Activity: Legal Counsel's Role. The National Association of College and University Attorneys, 1–12. https://www.higheredcompliance.org/wp-content/uploads/2018/10/xv-11-04-2.doc

Ferreira, W. (2024). Working effectively with outside counsel. In J. Pollard & K. S. Priebe (Eds.), *Convergence of litigation, policy and standards: Building the informed practitioner in education abroad risk management*. The Forum on Education Abroad. doi.org/10.36.366/SIA.5.978-1-952376-41-2.27

Institute for International Education. (2021). Open Doors Report on International Educational Exchange. https://opendoorsdata.org/data/us-study-abroad/

May, P.F. (2024). Expectations, Guardrails, and Compliance: Negotiating Effective International Partnership Agreements. In J. Pollard & K. S. Priebe (Eds.), *Convergence of litigation, policy and standards: Building the informed practitioner in education abroad risk management*. The Forum on Education Abroad. doi.org/10.36.366/SIA.5.978-1-952376-41-2.29

Pfahl, M.R. (2021). Enhancing Enforceability of Exculpatory Clauses in Education Abroad Programming Through Examination of Three Pillars. *Journal of College and University Law*, 46(1), 93–120. https://heinonline.org/HOL/LandingPage?handle=hein.journals/jcolunly46&div=7&id=&page=

Pulse International. (n.d). About Us. Pulse International. Retrieved August 1, 2023, from https://www.pulseinternational.org/about-us

Rae, L. (2024). Employment and Compliance in Education Abroad Programming: Guidance for Working with Global Human Resources. In J. Pollard & K. S. Priebe (Eds.), *Convergence of litigation, policy and standards: Building the informed practitioner in education abroad risk management.* The Forum on Education Abroad. doi.org/10.36.366/SIA.5.978-1-952376-41-2.28

The Chronicle of Higher Education. (2023). The New Learning Partnerships. The Chronicle of Higher Education Inc., 29-20.

The Forum on Education Abroad. (2020a). *Code of Ethics for Education Abroad, Third Edition.* doi.org/10.36366/G.978-1-952376-08-5

The Forum on Education Abroad. (2020b). *Meeting the Standards of Good Practice for Education Abroad: Prompts for Self-Assessment.* doi.org/10.36366/S.978-1-952376-05-4

The Forum on Education Abroad. (2020c). *Standards of Good Practice for Education Abroad Standards of Good Practice, Sixth Edition.* doi.org/10.36366/S.978-1-952376-24-5

The Forum on Education Abroad. (2023). *State of the Field Report: Data from the Comprehensive 2022 Survey.* doi.org/10.363666.R.2022SOF

U.S. Department of State. (n.d.). Travel Advisories. U.S. Department of State, Bureau of Consular Affairs. Retrieved August 1, 2023, from https://travel.state.gov/content/travel/en/traveladvisories/traveladvisories.html

# 27

## Working Effectively with Outside Counsel

**William F. Ferreira, J.D.**

Outside counsel operates as a trusted extension of the in-house legal team. Typically, outside counsel attorneys are law firm practitioners in private practice who work closely with the internal Office of General Counsel to support the education abroad function. Although technically sitting "outside" the institution, external attorneys are anything but "outsiders." Academic institutions draw on deep relationships with external counsel to deliver specialized experience, industry know-how, and second opinions on legal and business challenges.

### Role of Outside Counsel

Outside counsel serves to supplement the vast store of institutional legal experience to facilitate programs and solve operational challenges before they become problems.

First, outside attorneys offer a depth of experience that may not exist within the institution. The question—How are institutions generally handling Issue X and Y in education abroad?—is ripe for consultation with experienced outside counsel. Law firms advise dozens of universities and academic institutions on international programs. Outside counsel has learned their best practices, their recurrent problems, and a broad range of solutions in varied markets across the United States and the world. So rather than providing advice limited to what one institution has experienced, outside counsel offers insights into the best solutions developed across the whole education abroad industry. In effect, outside counsel often provides the broad industry "mapping" and strategic advice that institutions cannot draw from internal experience only. And because of their broad experience, outside counsel does not need to "reinvent the wheel"—they bring templates and solutions already tested in a range of situations and geographies.

Second, outside attorneys can mobilize a global team and offer country-specific legal expertise. A cardinal rule of legal ethics—a rule that often prompts consultation with outside counsel—is that a lawyer may not practice law in a jurisdiction in violation of licensure requirements or represent that they are admitted to practice law in a jurisdiction where they are not licensed (American Bar Association (ABA) Model Rules of Professional Conduct, 2023, Rule 5.5). In-house legal teams rarely have staff attorneys who are licensed outside the United States. But outside law firms do. Firms often have offices and lawyers licensed in the many jurisdictions in which study abroad occurs. Specialized local country capability—whether on employment, tax, litigation, data privacy, or education regulation—is a key feature of the outside counsel relationship. And the benefit goes beyond just legal matters. Opining on local norms and customs, or checking document translations for consistency, is just as important as local law acumen.

Third, outside counsel provides objectivity, credibility, or even a second opinion on education abroad matters. Schools often engage outside counsel to help preserve relationships between the internal attorneys and the ultimate internal client, whether a particular department, faculty member, or unit. Because in-house attorneys often have day-to-day interaction and rapport with their internal clients, it can be preferable to bring a relatively neutral outside point of view to a particularly complex or sensitive international education matter. And where internal investigations or audits are necessary, the legitimacy of an outcome often depends on the fairness and credibility of the review process—a feature that sophisticated independent counsel can supply on a confidential and privileged basis.

Finally, outside counsel serves as a trusted advisor across both the business and legal terms of an arrangement. Oftentimes, outside firms have worked for an institution for years—even decades—and appreciate the institution's unique culture and values. They possess institutional history and legacy information that outlasts the turnover within the client institution. For example, a longtime outside firm can say things like, "The former Provost tried that 10 years ago and here's how it played out." Combining this institutional knowledge with day-to-day work on the toughest international education initiatives and pressures, counsel can "look around the corner" and help predict how a particular issue or project may land within the institution and within the marketplace.

## Issues to Bring to Outside Counsel

Consider three real-life scenarios, modified slightly:

1.  An institution learned that it had several foreign nationals working on an education project in Country Z. Documentation confirmed that the institution contracted the workers as "independent contractors." However, in substance, the workers were employees of the institution because Country Z (like most countries) elevates the substance of the relationship over contractual form. In fact, foreign labor authorities disregarded the independent contractor designation and deemed the workers employees, subject to host country employment law, payroll, and income tax withholding. Under Country Z law, to employ workers without a registered corporate affiliate in-country was a civil offense that carried assessment of back taxes and penalties.
2.  An institution encountered a dispute with an education abroad provider. The dispute focused on whether the institution complied with host country law and the terms of its contract with the provider. The parties disagreed on the appropriate interpretation of host country law and whether the contract terms were breached. A formal claim was filed in a foreign country's judicial system.
3.  A group of students left their study abroad location for a weekend trip to a neighboring country. Upon return, they were denied re-entry to the country in which they were studying. The allegation? The students did not hold an appropriate visa to leave the study abroad country and then re-enter 3 days later. Students were detained in a holding cell in the airport.

All three scenarios can cause unease among education abroad professionals. And all three scenarios are obvious candidates for outside counsel involvement. But all three scenarios are defensive in nature—reacting to and resolving a calamity or some unexpected turn of events. Institutions with long experience in education abroad know that *proactive* engagement with legal counsel may help avoid these situations.

Various institutional activities abroad merit proactive discussion with outside counsel. Host country registrations, licenses, permissions, and other forms of official legal status abroad almost always require review with local counsel. The following activities, among others, are illustrative triggers for a call to local counsel:

- Awarding a degree in the host country—including dual and joint degrees.
- Employing local nationals or third-country nationals in the host country, or posting U.S. employees to long-term positions in the country.
- Executing a lease for host country office space, or acquiring land and other real property there.
- Opening an institutional bank account in the host country.
- Conducting scientific or medical research programs in the host country.
- Transferring sensitive personal data to points outside the host country.
- Bringing experimental drugs, devices, controlled substances, or medical supplies into the host country.
- Purchasing equipment or motor vehicles in the host country, titling these assets in the name of the institution, or buying insurance for these assets in the host country.

Though far afield from what may be claimed as "education law" within the host country, local counsel can help to ask the right questions, assess the situation, and gauge the institution's compliance obligations and risk profile relative to these activities.

Outside counsel also brings perspective to internal exercises such as policy development, templates, contracts, travel abroad waivers, and data privacy consent documentation. For example, policies related to health, safety, and security in education abroad, and policies related to sanctions and export control compliance, benefit tremendously from the critical eye of counsel familiar with the kinds of claims that constituents may lodge, the interests that regulators must protect, and how specific language (e.g., in a travel abroad waiver) will play out in a judicial setting. Institutions increasingly maintain forms for documents like privacy notices and study abroad contracts, particularly contracts with education abroad providers, exchange programs, and collaborative degree programs. Outside counsel's repository of templates—including agreements with the same foreign counterparties and countries—bring efficiency and valuable intelligence to the institution.

## Protecting Attorney-Client Privilege

A fundamental aspect of any relationship between an institution and its counsel is the principle that the lawyer must not reveal information that the institution discloses in the context of seeking legal advice (ABA Model Rules of Professional Conduct, 2023, Rule 1.6). The lawyer also cannot be compelled by any third party to disclose such information. The reason is simple–clients must be able to speak openly and candidly with their attorneys in order to receive the best possible legal advice. This kind of trust is a "hallmark" of the attorney–client relationship and the basis for the attorney–client privilege.

While there are variations from jurisdiction to jurisdiction (and country to country), the general rule is that the attorney–client privilege attaches where there is a communication made between a client and their attorney that is made in confidence and for the purpose of seeking legal advice (American Law Institution, 2023). Conversely, the attorney–client privilege does not protect facts or communications not made for the purpose of legal advice (although legal advice need not be the only purpose of the communication). As should be evident, copying a lawyer on an e-mail, or having a lawyer in the room for a meeting, or marking a document as "confidential" and subject to "attorney–client privilege" does not mechanically bestow attorney privilege on the information, absent a legal advice purpose.

Protecting attorney client privilege is paramount to an effective working relationship with outside counsel. A few basic steps can go a long way. First, education abroad practitioners must understand and appreciate the circumstances in which attorney–client privilege applies (as described above).

Second, practitioners should avoid revealing privileged materials and take reasonable steps to prevent privileged information from being disclosed. For example, the following actions may damage the privilege or even have the effect of waiving the privilege:

- Forwarding counsel's advice to third parties outside the institution.
- Sending the following to third parties: contracts and agreements that contain counsel's confidential comments or changes (e.g., margin comments intended for internal consumption only).
- Drafting meeting notes or minutes that record legal advice and sharing those notes externally.
- Inviting third parties to join legal advice communications with counsel.
- Posting on social media or listservs about sensitive matters on which the institution seeks legal advice.
- Revealing to third parties the summaries or results of counsel-led investigations.

A final note about internal investigations. Institutions often engage outside counsel to conduct reviews, audits, or investigations of sensitive regulatory and other legal matters, such as labor and employment controversies.

For the attorney–client privilege to apply to such an investigation, generally the investigation must be done at the direction of counsel and managed by counsel. Any action taken by nonlawyers as part of the investigation should be at the direction of counsel in order to preserve the privileged nature of the investigation.

## How to Identify Non-U.S. Counsel

Competent English-speaking lawyers are essential to success of education abroad. In general, outside counsel should be engaged only through the institution's Office of General Counsel (OGC). The OGC typically coordinates and directs outside legal services provided to the institution. And for good reason—OGC must keep a record of exactly who is advising the institution in order to avoid legal conflicts or duplication of advice down the road.

Finding responsive and competent counsel in far-flung non-U.S. jurisdictions can be a challenge. The first port of call always should be to in-house counsel, who can guide the process to identify appropriate outside counsel. The OGC may have contracts and relationships with global law firms specialized in international academic and research initiatives. Such firms can make a referral or recommendation within their network of offices or locations. Peer institutions and bar associations also could make recommendations.

Beware of lawyer lists supplied by embassies and governments, or international "ranking" directories—many such lists are not kept up-to-date and often do not include individuals experienced in the nonprofit sector.

For several reasons, making a public posting online or on a listserv seeking lawyer referrals often is a discouraged approach as it can inadvertently generate discussion or reveal information that the institutions preferred to keep confidential.

## Engagement Terms for Non-U.S. Counsel

When establishing a relationship with outside counsel, the arrangement should be documented in writing. Normally such arrangements are recorded in an engagement letter, as required by the rules of professional legal ethics. The outside firm should be able to provide a standard engagement letter. (If they cannot supply a standard engagement letter, then this may be a red flag.) The letter should specify the scope of representation, an indication of the legal team involved, and the law firm's partner in charge of the matter. Typically, the supervising partner is responsible for the quality of advice and the management of legal services to the client.

In many cases, an institution's home country outside counsel firm may engage foreign counsel on behalf of the institution, in which case the relationship with foreign counsel is run through the home counsel and consistent with the home firm's normal terms.

Engagements should address logistics issues such as billing terms, including the basis and frequency of billing, out-of-pocket expenses incurred on behalf of the client (such as filing fees or travel costs), and the due date and currency of payments.

Importantly, engagements of non-U.S. counsel should address confidentiality and attorney–client privilege. Varying attorney–client privilege regimes exist, and respect for the privilege is not uniform around the globe. Auditors and government regulators in other locations have sometimes ignored the attorney–client privilege. One step to protecting privilege— but by no means the only step—is to indicate clearly that the non-U.S. firm will keep confidential all information obtained from the client and will only disclose it with the client's written consent. Such confidentiality obligations should survive expiration or termination of the engagement. Furthermore, the non-U.S. counsel should not be permitted to use the client's name or logos in any advertising, promotional material, press release, public announcement, website, or other media, written or verbal, without approval from the client.

Legal conflicts of interest can be a significant issue abroad. These issues arise when non-U.S. counsel undertakes a matter that is related to a matter in which it advises the institution and in which the counsel's other client is adverse to the institution. The concept of a "conflict" is much more narrow in several parts of the world compared to the United States. But conflicts are to be avoided. The engagement should require counsel to confirm that it does not have any conflicts of interest in accepting the engagement and that counsel will undertake to ensure that no conflict of interest arises during the period of the engagement.

Finally, it goes without saying that all parties must act ethically and in compliance with law, including applicable antibribery law. Non-U.S. counsel should (a) commit to comply with all applicable U.S. and non-U.S. law antibribery measures, such as the U.S. Foreign Corrupt Practices Act ("FCPA"), and (b) commit not to directly or indirectly offer, give, promise to give or authorize the giving of any money, loan, gift, donation, or other thing of value to induce a government official to do or to omit from doing any act in violation of their lawful duty in order to obtain any improper advantage or to induce a government official to use his or her influence improperly to affect or influence any act or decision.

# References

American Bar Association. (2023). Text of the model rules of professional conduct. ABA. https://www.americanbar.org/groups/professional_responsibility/publications/model_rules_of_professional_conduct/model_rules_of_professional_conduct_table_of_contents/

American Law Institution. (2023). Restatement of law, third, of law governing lawyers. American Law Institute Publishers. ALI

# 28

# Employment and Compliance in Education Abroad Programming: Guidance for Working with Global Human Resources

L. Raven Rae, J.D.

Delivering education abroad programs often utilize a mix of U.S.-based staff, ex-patriates, host country nationals, and third-country nationals, each of whom present different issues in compliantly engaging them under the appropriate legal framework. As a higher education organization based in the United States, one of the preliminary challenges to overcome in developing competencies in international human resources management (IHRM) is unpinning the underlying mindset and assumptions from U.S. employment law. Human resources (HR) in the home country and local counterparts or partners must work together to ensure that your organization is operating legally and mitigating risks. The Forum on Education Abroad's *Standards of Good Practice for Education Abroad* offer guidelines for governing personnel matters, conduct, and training (2020, clause 5.1.5).

To do so, your institution needs to develop competencies in international employment concepts, collaborate with local counterparts in host country HR or management offices, and communicate regularly and effectively with local staff, local counsel, and accountants/payroll agents so that HR issues understood locally are also visible to the larger institution. Successful International Human Resources Management (IHRM) involves structuring these relationships so that risks are anticipated and mitigated. Since your international staff is in a position to learn about incidents and to be among the first to respond to them, being able to rely on them to discharge your statutory obligations becomes extremely important in risk management. Having IHRM as a partner in communicating these expectations and including them in onboarding checklists and annual performance reviews will help ensure that key international personnel are not missed.

Across cultures, your Global HR staff will need to understand that some of these policies and requirements will be understood differently depending on cultural norms. Some U.S.-based policies might seem contrary to ordinary aspects of life or to laws in each country. For example, you may have an anti-nepotism policy that prohibits hiring family members or close relatives, but in some places if a person holds a good job, they might be culturally expected to try to find similar posts for their family members. Or, you may have an antidiscrimination policy that prohibits discrimination against LGBTQIA+ individuals, in a country where homosexuality is criminalized and even discussing it might be seen as illegal "promotion" of homosexuality. A nuanced and sensitive presentation of how these policies protect your students and your organization is warranted. Your HR staff should be able to explain the legal necessities of providing training and meeting those obligations while still respecting cultures and differences because the fact that another jurisdiction is not compelled to follow U.S.-based laws does not absolve your institution of complying with them in its overseas offerings.

A dilemma may arise where local law contradicts U.S -based laws. In those instances, HR must confer with local counsel, weigh the risks, and determine the best course of action that respects local employees and laws, and discharges duties related to management. See Chapter 27, "Working Effectively with Outside Counsel," by William Ferriera (2024) for more information.

There are some additional key differentiators in IHRM; for example, at-will employment is largely not an operative concept outside the United States, rather employees have very specific benefits and rights to continued employment. In addition, U.S.-based statutory requirements that have extraterritorial relevance, the liability insurance landscape, and developing case law around duty of care makes managing and training international staff of paramount importance in meeting institutional obligations and mitigating risk.

Identifying which jurisdiction's laws apply to the employment relationship and establishing the necessary knowledge, skills, and abilities within your IHRM function to perform HR tasks compliantly are key to meeting IHRM objectives. This chapter addresses the knowledge base required to develop your IHRM capacity and provides a roadmap to identify and navigate some perennial issues in managing your global workforce. It presumes that you directly engage at least some internationally based personnel that require oversight and management. The information contained herein is not legal advice; however, it is informed by the author's experience directly engaging employees in the field of international education, development, and exchange in more than 60 countries.

## Structural Considerations Impacting IHRM Needs

Successful IHRM requires the establishment of open and collaborative relationships between home office HR and host country counterparts and staff. If your organizational structure includes a controlled entity, branch, representative office, subsidiary, or other affiliated entity whereby you are hiring employees directly, you will need localized procedures and employment contract templates, and the ability to determine which home office policies are applicable and which ones need to be tailored to the particular employment law of the host country. Your home office IHRM staff should be able to liaise with local counsel, other relevant partners, and counterparts to integrate the entirety of your global workforce.

Engaging an employee abroad often creates a need to register a local entity to comply with tax withholding and social insurance contribution requirements. Your institution will likely need an employer identification number in order to set up accounts with social benefit administrators in the country and purchase insurance and other personnel-related products and services. Registration may not be necessary if you are working entirely through a partner who is providing and hiring the staff or using a special purpose entity such as a Professional Employment Organization (PEO)or Employer of Record (EOR). These special purpose entities serve as an employer of record and provide various HR administrative services. Seek legal advice to determine whether the scope of your activities and your need for paid labor suggests an obligation to establish legal presence.

PEOs and EORs (Professional Employer Organization and Employer of Record, respectively) have proliferated in recent years, and many of them claim to be capable of meeting all your IHRM compliance needs. Their value to the organization is dependent upon the nature of the work you need to be performed in the foreign jurisdiction, how much supervision or oversight is needed or preferred, and whether the functions performed by staff create onsite presence or are limited to electronic deliverables. The use of PEOs and EORs are not necessary if you are able, through your own local entity, to hire directly, or if a local partner is providing and managing personnel. However, if you need work done by a local employee before your registration is finalized, or from a jurisdiction where you have no need to invest in a registered entity or are not ready to commit to the creation of an entity, a PEO may be able to meet some short-term needs.

Some of the services that PEOs provide include local payroll and benefits compliance, tax withholding, social benefits contribution, tracking of paid time off and overtime, nexus with their networked lawyers and accountants, ensuring local procedural rules are followed, and providing you documentation of their administrative and personnel actions. They do not provide direct legal or tax advice, they do not provide liability insurance, nor do they perform substantive performance management, quality control, or training. In other words, your organization remains responsible for the performance of employees engaged through the PEO, and your actions as an employer may still give rise to labor claims or other litigated matters. PEOs are not necessarily suitable for expats who are seeking to work remotely from another country for extended periods of time. U.S. citizens (ex-pats) or third-country nationals who seek to work from a host country may still need a work permit and their presence has the potential to create a permanent establishment or tax residency if it continues, so it is best to consult with local counsel in those scenarios.

Telework requests or requests to be based in a country other than the country of hire can come from U.S.-based employees or candidates who want to work abroad or from third-country nationals who want to move to accept a new role in your organization, or for personal reasons. Your IHRM department will need a cohesive policy and approach to telework and remote work requests. Despite the practical reality of mobility in your workforce, the regulatory environment does not flex to the same degree. Those arrangements still potentially require IHRM oversight, administration, and set-up to make sure the presence of an employee in an international location is not inadvertently creating compliance costs, obligations and liabilities for your institution.

## Key Internal and External Partners

Once your institution determines that it needs or already has employees abroad, you will need internal stakeholders who have the capacity and knowledge to manage and support those employees, as well as external partners who can supplement implementation efforts in-country. Internally, educating your senior leadership on some of the responsibilities associated with employing staff abroad will help them budget sufficiently for localized legal and tax advice, salaries, fringe benefits, mandatory salary increases and bonuses, insurance, and severance, and to understand the complexities involved in IHRM. It will also be important to ensure HR staff have experience or are trained in key issues involving an international workforce, and/or have a dedicated IHRM specialist whose job it is to onboard and separate international staff compliantly and coordinate the support and services those employees need. For example, all the services noted as being available through PEOs are incumbent upon your HR department to perform as if you are not using a PEO: tracking of attendance and paid time off, income tax withholding and deductions, social benefits contributions, health insurance, etc. They will need to be able to explain a pay stub, answer questions about localized benefits, and explain HR policies to employees in other countries.

The two most important external partners for assessing your obligations as an international employer are local counsel and local accountants/payroll agents who can ensure that you are meeting your obligations as an international employer. These advisors are essential to understanding the framework (labor law, collective bargaining units, taxation, entity formation, etc.). Another potentially useful partner is a translator who can ensure that applicable IHRM policies and communications made to local staff are fully understood in local language(s).

Drafting a localized HR Manual with the advice of local counsel may be useful and, in some locations, may be required. Your home office IHRM team will need to coordinate with their counterpart in the country and/or with local counsel to determine how best to tailor home office policies with local requirements. These localized manuals are important documents that set expectations and convey your key definitions, benefits, policies, and procedures consistently with local law and home office values. Translating your manual into the local or official language(s) of the country is essential to ensure you have transmitted the information in an understandable and culturally respectful way.

## Essential IHRM Knowledge and Skillsets

In addition to a solid understanding of the employment regulations and *standards* of the host country, effective IHRM management requires sound reporting and record keeping. IHRM's ability to produce a reliable list, or headcount, by location, of paid personnel around the world is essential for managing and mitigating compliance risks. Maintenance of accurate records of how (and where) they are paid, their wages, compensation or salary amounts, enrolled benefits, years of service, time worked and paid time off, social benefit contributions, and a copy of their current contract are also vital to meeting your IHRM compliance needs. If your institution has decentralized hiring practices, it can be challenging to know for certain how many people you employ and whether local compliance thresholds have been crossed. For example, if a regional dean hires a gardener or security guard for your foreign office and the local director pays them in cash once a week, does your IHRM office know that? How are you ensuring that the employee is being treated in accordance with local law?

The importance of basic recordkeeping and transparency in overseas hiring is of utmost importance in understanding your institution's liability and employer obligations for several reasons. First, having an accurate list of paid personnel [whether Independent Contractor (IC) or employee] provides a window into potential compliance exposure and provides a jumping-off point for self-review or audit for a variety of purposes, including IRS Form 990 reporting (the IRS' "primary tool for gathering information about tax-exempt organizations, educating organizations about tax law requirements and promoting compliance" (Internal Revenue Service (IRS), n.d. a), securing insurance coverage for those employees/locations, budget planning for fringe benefits, mandatory salary increases, or other costs. Second, having this information and keeping it current allows you to track when your employee count may trigger certain obligations or entitlements in a jurisdiction. For example, some countries require employers of more than 10 employees to set up and contribute to a provident fund or other retirement or pension fund. If you cannot accurately determine whether you have 9 or 10 employees, you may miss, or be unable to avoid, thresholds that have significant liabilities attached to them.

A useful way to develop a solid understanding of your global HR footprint is to request a periodic report from local program leadership that contains the information described above, which can be reviewed with local counsel to determine if all obligations are being met. Ideally, institutions can form a cross-functional team including HR (home and local), finance, operations, and program leaders. This task force can review the reports and conduct regular compliance check-ins with all major stakeholders present. Meeting regularly to review host country status will help maintain an updated and informed source of information about your global HR platform.

The reported categorical information about each paid worker is important because it is what feeds into your obligations upon termination. Take note that the list should include all workers who are paid by your institution and should clearly identify those who are classified as consultants or independent contractors for two reasons: first, listing all paid workers allows your

HR office to review the IC relationships and make sure they are properly classified, and secondly because if any of those contractors have been misclassified they will count toward your employed personnel totals and that could implicate some of the thresholds mentioned above.

## Initial Classification as an Employee Versus Contractor

A successful IHRM function requires a clear internal process for properly classifying an employee versus an independent contractor. U.S.-based institutions may consult IRS's criteria for determining classification online (IRS, n.d.b). Each country has its own similar framework for making these types of determinations. Local counsel will be able to provide you with country-specific criteria. As you evaluate employment classification cases, a useful lens to consider them with is to construe the word "independent" as operative. If a local hire does not perform similar independent work for other organizations, relies on income from your assignments, does not represent themself as a consultant in the subject area, does not have a registered entity through which they perform their services, does not carry liability insurance, does not advertise, and other indicators of not being engaged in this work apart from your institution, there is a high risk that a local labor court would find them to be an employee, even in cases where you've signed an Independent Consultant Agreement and perhaps even disclaimed the employment relationship within that agreement. Classification of a worker as a contractor simply because there is no alternative compliant means of engaging and paying a local hire, or because the budget has not been allocated enough to cover fringe benefits, for example, increases the risk and likelihood that the relationship is improper.

In addition, some countries outside the United States determine employee rights differently and will often view that an employment relationship exists, especially if there are indications that the contractor is treated like an employee. For example, if your contractor goes to staff meetings, reports to a supervisor, has their performance evaluated, has student-facing responsibilities and interactions, gets paid without submitting invoices, requires training, does not have concrete deliverables and a defined time period in which to complete them, or if the scope of work is ongoing and covers duties that would ordinarily be done by employees in the ordinary course of business, these activities tend to show an employment relationship.

The consequences of an erroneous classification can be significant, involving back taxes, interest, penalties, and social benefit contributions in arrears. Contractor agreements that place responsibility on the contractor to remit their own taxes are ineffective because the duty to deduct withholdings rests with the employer so you may be found to be jointly and severally liable for the unremitted tax and benefit contribution amounts.

A leading IHRM practice that mitigates misclassification, beyond making the initial determination correctly as described above, is to limit the engagement of independent contractors to entities, rather than individuals. Even if it is an individual that is sought to perform services, it is not difficult for individuals with marketable skillsets to form a limited liability company (LLC) or to associate with a preexisting entity. Contracting legitimately with an entity for the provision of services rather than directly with an individual tends to preclude direct labor claims. In addition, requiring contracting entities to carry their own insurance and collecting the insurance certificates further solidifies the status of the service provider as a fully established independent enterprise rather than an employee.

Once the employment classification is determined, a secondary area of classification involves whether an employment relationship is of indefinite term, sometimes referred to as "permanent" or whether it is a fixed-term contract with a defined expiration. Indefinite employment protects the worker from termination unless there is "just cause," which is typically narrowly defined within the labor laws. Many countries have very specific termination procedures that must be followed and in most of these cases, employees are entitled to severance payments. Therefore, your IHRM function needs to track contract renewals and plan for conversion to permanent employment if for quality control you want to keep staffing turnover low, as opposed to hiring new personnel every other year before one becomes "permanent." Many jurisdictions allow and recognize fixed-term contracts as long as other compliance obligations are met. It is important to work with local counsel to draft employment contract template to ensure that it contains all permissible and mandatory provisions.

There are a couple of important caveats to fixed-term contracts. The first is that if a labor court determines you have improperly terminated early or unfairly, pay for the remainder of the contract period is a common remedy. Secondly, fixed-term contracts, in many countries, cannot be renewed repeatedly. Some countries limit renewals to no more than once, for a total of two consecutive terms, while others have different thresholds for permanency. If a fixed-term contract is renewed consecutively beyond the threshold, and without a significant break in the engagement or if it is not expressly renewed but the employee continues with the same course of performance, those relationships can automatically convert to indefinite employment as a matter of local law. Once the employment relationship is indefinite, all the rights of employment and protection from termination are attached regardless of the contract terms.

## Payroll and Benefits Capabilities

In most cases, your staff members will either be (a) U.S.-based employees who are traveling, being paid wholly within the United States, and whose work in/from an international location is extremely temporary and brief, such as a site visit; or (b) they are local citizens or residents in certain countries subject to all applicable employment laws and tax treatment of the host country. If you notice any employee located abroad in one location for any significant length of time in the same country, then they may particularly long enough to be able to establish tax residency (often around 6 months or 183 days). If employees in that category are who is not having taxes deducted and remitted by you as an employer in that or some other jurisdiction, it should raise a red flag in your HR office so that you do not accrue back tax liability. Your payroll function (whether in HR or Finance) needs to be able to liaise with local accountants who can calculate proper salaries, tax withholdings, and benefit contributions.

Some common benefits associated with international employees that you will need to review with local counsel/accountants and that your IHRM staff will need to know are: state-sponsored health insurance, 13th month (and sometimes 14th month) bonuses or holiday pay, paid national holidays, minimum paid vacation leave, minimum paid sick leave, minimum parental leaves, government-mandated benefit amounts (such as those paid out during COVID), and mandatory salary increases; all dependent on the jurisdiction. Certain categories of employees, for example, administrative staff, teachers, or director-level employees, may also be part of designated collective bargaining units within a country, each of which have related rules and benefits associated with those categories.

## Training Your International Staff

International education carries with it the need to make sure your international staff is trained, not just on their local job responsibilities, but on the policies, laws, and regulations impacting higher education and your standards of conduct and duties of care (The Forum on Education Abroad, 2020, clause 5.2.2.2). Some of these organizationally relevant requirements might include:

- Code of Conduct
- Family Education Rights Protection Act (FERPA)
- Data Privacy
- Title IX
- Sexual Harassment

- Anti-Discrimination
- Jeanne Clery Disclosure of Campus Security Policy and Campus Crime Statistics Act (Clery Act)
- Safeguarding
- Whistleblowing
- Americans with Disabilities Act (ADA)
- Diversity, Equity, Inclusion, and Accessibility
- Foreign Corrupt Practices Act
- Grievance Policies

Not all of these will be the responsibility of HR to substantively convey; however, it can be helpful if IHRM can, in a centralized way, track who received training in what topics, with attendance dates and signed acknowledgments. Documenting that your staff abroad have received this training is important to ensure they are handling your student issues adeptly and that your institution is in compliance with applicable requirements. Training may need to be done in multiple languages and accessible formats, and your IHRM staff may also need to explain the overarching relevance of these laws and policies to the programs in that country.

## Identifying and Resolving Labor Matters in International HR

Being responsible for employees in international locations can have associated costs and processes that are a function of laws more protective of employee rights than U.S. law. Your IHRM staff needs to build a skillset associated with performance management that is consistent with employee expectations and rights abroad. For example, you should not make final decisions around termination, nor should you inform, verbally or otherwise, of an intention to terminate an employment relationship before consulting with local counsel. Employees are entitled to very specific process if an employer wishes to make a unilateral termination decision, whether it is based on unsatisfactory performance, other financial or business rationales, or even "for cause." In most cases, such a unilateral decision will require notice and payment of a severance amount that is determined by a formula, typically a multiple of a week or month of salary times years of service. Some countries cap this amount and others do not. Some jurisdictions, like South Africa, require a consultative process for some terminations whereby the employer must explain its rationale and give employees input that must be fairly considered before determining whether to move forward with the termination and perhaps even an opinion on how the employee to be terminated is chosen.

Furthermore, the law in some countries prohibits terminating an employee who is out on sick leave and requires a significant percentage of their salary to be paid for the duration of the leave. If you need to hire a replacement worker, your budget needs to be enough to cover the sick pay and the interim employee. Make sure your IHRM staff has also investigated whether insurance is available in such countries to cover the cost of paying the salary during the sick leave.

Dismissal "for cause" is not guaranteed abroad. Not performing the job duties well does not amount to grounds of "for cause" dismissal. Those are more widely reserved for serious misconduct such as fraud, theft, violence, patterns of clear insubordination, job abandonment or failure to meet attendance requirements, or some other clear violation of the law. Poor-performing employees are usually owed progressive discipline and chances to cure their performance, and even if you can demonstrate unsatisfactory work, labor courts will often require you to negotiate a termination by mutual agreement, and coming to that agreement usually means paying an amount pegged to severance obligations. Having to pay a poor-performing employee a large severance upon termination is not a welcome outcome for most U.S.-based employers but given the protectiveness of labor courts and the burdens of proof, plus legal costs in defending unfair dismissal claims, it is often the more cost-effective option to separate without the risk of a judge disagreeing and perhaps even reinstating the employee. Active performance management with knowledge of the expected processes and costs is therefore an essential tool for controlling and planning for that expense.

You may see a tension between taking decisive action and following the letter of the labor law in each jurisdiction. For example, if a student lodges a complaint against a staff member abroad for causing some kind of harm, U.S.-based laws and guidance, and other important sensitivities, might call for immediate separation from the employee in order to prevent further harm; however, the labor law of the country might expect a more deliberative process, which could add to the harm alleged by the student and still not result in grounds for termination.

## References

Berkowitz, P. M., Müller-Bonanni, T., & American Bar Association. (2006). *International labor and employment law*. Chicago, Ill: Section of International Law, American Bar Association.

Ferreira, W. (2024). Working effectively with outside counsel. In J. Pollard & K. S. Priebe (Eds.), *Convergence of litigation, policy and standards: Building the informed practitioner in education abroad risk management*. The Forum on Education Abroad. doi.org/10.36.366/ SIA.5.978-1-952376-41-2.27

Ferreira, W., Rae, L., & Ball, S. (2023, June 28). *International Employment- How to Manage a Global Workforce (Without Losing Too Much Sleep)* [Conference presentation]. National Association of College and University Attorneys Annual Conference, Chicago, IL.

Internal Revenue Service. (n.d. a) *Form 990 resources and tools.* https://www.irs.gov/charities-non-profits/form-990-resources-and-tools

Internal Revenue Service. (n.d. b) *Independent contractor (self-employed) or employee?* https://www.irs.gov/businesses/small-businesses-self-employed/independent-contractor-self-employed-or-employee

Keller, W. & Darby, T. (2014). *International labor and employment laws series.* ABA Section of Labor and Employment Law, Fourth Edition.

The Forum on Education Abroad. (2020). *Standards of good practice for education abroad, Sixth edition.* doi.org/10.36366/S.978-1-952376-04-7

# 29

# Expectations, Guardrails, and Compliance: Negotiating Effective International Partnership Agreements

Peter F. May, J.D.

## Introduction

Academic collaborations between U.S. and foreign higher education institutions represent a key pillar of every comprehensive internationalization strategy. Negotiating contractual agreements in support of such collaborations requires detailed attention to a range of important topics. Effective international agreements (a) clearly identify the parties and their authorized representatives; (b) set forth the parties' mutual vision for the collaboration and their desired outcomes; (c) define mutual programmatic expectations (in as much detail as possible); (d) set forth applicable guardrails relating to the parties' conduct, including provisions on agreement governance, communications, milestones, deliverables, compensation and payment, and intellectual property; (e) address compliance and other legal and regulatory responsibilities, including accreditation (where applicable); and (f) address risk allocation between the parties (for matters known, foreseeable, and unknown), including applicable law, dispute resolution procedures, and liability for third-party claims. Clause 4.2, Collaboration and Transparency, of the *Standards of Good Practice for Education Abroad* addresses many of the foregoing issues (The Forum on Education Abroad, 2020). This chapter will provide an overview of the elements of an effective cross-border agreement, including agreements for study abroad.

One common threshold question in this arena relates to the use of the term "partnership." *Black's Law Dictionary* defines legal partnership as "[a] voluntary contract between two or more competent persons to place their money, effects, labor, and skill, or some or all of them, in lawful commerce or business, with the understanding that there shall be a proportional sharing of the profits and losses between them (n.d.)." There does not need to be a written agreement for two or more individuals or entities to create a legal partnership, and perhaps most importantly, in most jurisdictions, partners are jointly and severally liable for losses, including losses due to claims made against the partners by third parties. In most cases, academic collaborations are not intended to be "partnerships" in the legal sense, but rather contractual agreements between independent legal entities. In the study abroad context, *Standards* clause 3.33 (Partnership) defines partnership as "a formal or informal agreement between two or more responsible organizations to manage and operate education abroad programs" (The Forum on Education Abroad, 2020). University counsel will often style an academic collaboration agreement as a "Cooperation Agreement," "Memorandum of Agreement," or "Collaboration Agreement" to avoid the implication that the parties are jointly carrying on a business for profit as general partners. This chapter will use the term "Partnership Agreement" as a catch-all, with the understanding that no reference to legal partnership should be implied.

A second common question concerns the use of the ubiquitous "Memorandum of Understanding (MOU)." MOUs typically memorialize the intentions of the parties to engage in one or more collaborative activities, usually after an initial set of meetings between key institutional representatives. MOUs signal executive sponsorship of a particular project by senior administrators (e.g., President, Provost, Dean) and should set up clear communications paths for negotiating and finalizing a comprehensive legal agreement. While frequently more than aspirational, MOUs often declare their nonbinding nature. The parties must take care, however, to examine each MOU provision to clarify those (if any) that are intended to be legally binding. An MOU issue familiar to many in the international education field is the premature "announcement" of the new partnership by a prospective partner, including the reproduction of university trademarks and logos (e.g., on a website) without prior written approval. Binding provisions around the use of the parties' trademarks and the confidentiality of sensitive party information that will be shared during further negotiations, for example, should also be strongly considered, even in the case of the more aspirational MOU.

## The Parties

A fundamental provision of any international partnership agreement sets forth the legal name, legal form (e.g., an "individual," a "corporation," a "non-profit corporation"), legal domicile (state and/or country of organization), and legal address of each of the parties. This provision ensures that each party (a) discloses its full legal identity to the other party, (b) identifies the location at which the party may be addressed for legal and administrative issues, including disputes, and (c) if a corporate entity, discloses the name and office of the institutional official authorized to form a legally binding commitment.

In the international context, correct identification of the parties is essential. The scale of the agreement and/or level of investment may require additional due diligence on a party. Deficiencies in a party's corporate good standing (e.g., possible involuntary dissolution), litigation history, or other matters, such as presence on one or more lists of prohibited parties (e.g., the U.S. Treasury Department's list of Specially Designated Nationals and Blocked Persons (SDNs) (U.S. Department of Treasury, 2024) may impair the agreement's enforceability or expose a party to unreasonable risk of harm or loss. For parties domiciled in higher risk locations, the context may require additional due diligence on members of a party's governing board and/or senior management group.

Finally, in the academic context, parties often desire to identify a particular school or research unit of another party. While generally acceptable, the legal entity should be identified first and completely (e.g., "Acme University, a non-profit corporation organized under the laws of the State of Vermont, USA, with its principal office at 100 Main Street, Montpelier, Vermont, USA, 05343, represented by its Acme School of Architecture (hereinafter referred to as ASA)." As noted above, a determination must be still made as to the legal authority of the individual executing the agreement (a President or Provost generally has the power to bind an institution; a Dean or Department Chair may not).

## The Vision

Early in the agreement text, whether in a Preamble or a Background section, the parties should recite their vision and/or motivation for entering into the agreement (The Forum on Education Abroad, 2020, clauses 4.2.2; 4.2.3), including the highest level outcomes of the agreement activities. This sets the tone for the agreement and for the ongoing engagement of the parties. Particularly where language barriers or cultural differences exist, a draft vision statement can help identify potential mismatches in expectations. For example, if an agreement addresses undergraduate academic exchange, but one party views the arrangement as primarily a recruitment channel for additional students, negotiating this high-level vision can help ensure alignment between the parties. A clear vision statement also helps to orient and guide institutional stakeholders implementing the agreement years down the road, potentially after initiating individuals have moved on to other projects or other institutions.

## Defining Expectations: The Scope of Work

A clearly defined Scope of Work that describes the relevant activities to be pursued, as well as the specific allocation and assignment of "functional roles or tasks to responsible parties" (The Forum on Education Abroad, 2020, clause 4.2.2), serves to further ensure that both parties understand the scope and scale of their agreement. Activities should be outlined in as much detail as possible, with particular focus on those that may require significant investment of human or financial resources. If third parties or subcontractors are essential to the conduct of any activity, the party responsible for engaging and managing these resources should be clearly identified, with an efficient approval process by the other party in the event of needed substitutions or changes. Especially in the case of longer-term collaborations, there should be mechanisms in place to revisit aspects of the Scope of Work that may change with the passage of time or due to changed circumstances (The Forum on Education Abroad, 2020, clause 4.2.4).

Involving counsel in the early stages of development of the Scope of Work can yield many benefits, including surfacing legal and/or compliance issues that may need to be addressed by the parties before execution of the agreement. A common example is the deployment of human resources by a party (e.g., faculty, staff, research assistants) in a foreign jurisdiction where the party does not have a legal presence or the ability to compensate staff in compliance with the foreign jurisdiction's employment and tax rules. To support the smooth conduct of activities, the administration of funds (especially those involving foreign bank accounts) should be carefully planned with consideration of the local jurisdiction's banking regulations. Counsel can assist with structuring the agreement activities to achieve successful and efficient outcomes, while avoiding the unintentional exposure of a party to unacceptable risks.

Finally, a thorough Scope of Work will assist counsel in assessing whether various legal and compliance provisions will be essential terms to be negotiated in the final agreement. Examples include provisions governing data privacy and the use of personal information by the parties, intellectual property provisions governing the ownership of publications, data, and other work product generated during the term of the agreement, and attention to anti-money-laundering and anti-terrorist financing regulations with which the programmatic stakeholders may be less familiar. For research collaborations potentially involving the generation of patentable or licensable intellectual property (software, medical devices, etc.), the parties may need to enter into separate agreements concerning ownership, pre-filing disclosure restrictions, and the assignment to one or the other party of the obligation to pursue intellectual property protections in the name of the parties.

## Guardrails

Effective partnership agreements set forth provisions designed to clarify expectations around roles and responsibilities, define the parties' financial contributions and payment structures, and attempt, as best as possible, to anticipate unforeseen circumstances and how the parties will navigate them. Certain "Guardrails" can help set the conditions for clear ownership of agreement tasks, proactive communication, and efficient escalation of issues or disagreements before they have a chance to grow into more substantive conflicts.

### Agreement Governance

Agreement governance, including clearly defined communications channels, is often overlooked and/or underappreciated at the time of drafting. Ideally, every agreement (and especially long-term agreements with multiple work streams), should have at least two roles enumerated. The first, an "Agreement Coordinator," takes primary responsibility for the entirety of the agreement and the general stewardship of the relationship. Agreement Coordinators should have sufficient status and authority within their institution's organizational structure to ensure prompt attention by more senior officials when issues arise. Periodic meetings of the Agreement Coordinators (monthly, quarterly, annually) should be scheduled and maintained to ensure regular communication of issues and concerns, and the prompt review of reports, milestones, and deliverables. For more complex agreements, such as hosted overseas branch campuses, dual-degree programs, or multiyear research collaborations, the parties may wish to consider creating governance bodies, such as an academic affairs committee or a finance and operations committee, which draw upon individuals within each party that have the range of expertise needed to ensure sound decision making. Such governance committees may be particularly important in demonstrating to institutional accreditors that a party is maintaining sufficient academic oversight and control over agreement activities.

The second recommended role, especially for more complex agreements, is the "Activity Coordinator." Activity Coordinators take primary responsibility for day-to-day monitoring of programmatic and administrative commitments made by the parties. Activity Coordinators should have sufficient academic knowledge and administrative skills to ensure that more granular issues can be identified and resolved promptly. In the study abroad context, Activity Coordinators may have additional responsibilities as the first point of contact for student-related health or safety issues. Activity Coordinators convene periodic meetings of relevant stakeholders and document issues and recommendations for consideration by the Agreement Coordinator and other senior officials.

### Milestones and Deliverables

Every international partnership has a life cycle and rhythm of activities. Written milestones and deliverables should be included in the partnership agreement, where possible, with fixed due dates and mechanisms for review and acceptance of deliverables. Milestones and deliverables will vary considerably depending on the scope and scale of the agreement activities, the needs of external funding sources (if applicable), and other factors. A simple academic exchange agreement will contain milestones around enrollments and deliverables tied to the provision of agreed academic programs, the issuance of transcripts, etc. Major agreements for research, especially research that may produce intellectual property intended for licensing or other exploitation by the parties or a third-party sponsor, should have much more detailed milestones and deliverables, including written reports, research publications, etc.

### Compensation and Payment

With a well-developed vision, detailed expectations set forth in the Scope of Work, and input from counsel on anticipated legal and compliance issues (and related costs), the parties can develop a financial model to ensure that each party receives fair compensation or other recognition for the inputs they will contribute directly to the collaboration, as well as for reasonable institutional overhead relating to faculty and staff salaries, administration of the agreement, use of a party's preexisting intellectual property (including trademarks), and other items. Each party should take the time to understand and inventory all anticipated direct costs (personnel, facilities, travel and accommodations, equipment, licenses, taxes, etc.), plus a contingency.

Dialog around costs peculiar to a party's home country's legal or regulatory environment is essential (e.g., VAT, social security obligations, worldwide income tax). Taxes based on net income derived from the agreement should normally be assumed by the party incurring the tax (e.g., if the party is taxed as a for-profit entity). For larger scale agreements, the parties should make provision for inflation and, especially, for currency fluctuations (where budgets or payments are denominated in a specific currency). Payment schedules should be thought through carefully and should take into account the rhythm of expenditures of each party (e.g., in some cases start-up costs will be heavy in the beginning and a front-loaded payment schedule will be desirable/necessary). For larger projects, financial due diligence is also essential, with the parties exchanging financial statements (audited, where possible) and other documentation to ensure that each party has the resources to meet their obligations. If financial concerns arise, creative use of letters of credit, escrow accounts, and other mechanisms can assist the parties in getting comfortable that no one will be left "holding the bag." Additionally, for larger scale agreements, provisions related to audit rights, including a commitment to good-faith cooperation with selected auditor(s), should be included (whether or not such rights are ever exercised).

## Intellectual Property

Finally, with respect to agreements involving the development of intellectual property, such as copyrighted material (e.g., curricula, publications) or patentable technology, the parties should ensure that sufficiently detailed provisions are included with respect to such matters as joint ownership, ownership of preexisting materials, pursuit of patent protection, nondisclosure, attribution, cross-licensing, etc.

## Compliance: Legal and Regulatory (Including Accreditation)

In consultation with counsel, each party should assess the legal and regulatory landscape applicable to the agreement and the activities to be conducted. Foreign counsel should advise on the legal and regulatory implications for a party engaging directly in activities in a foreign jurisdiction. Where a party seeks to require another party to comply (as a contractual matter) with the provisions of foreign laws or regulations, significant discussion (and even training) should occur. For exchange and study abroad agreements, this often comes up in the context of Title IX, obligations under FERPA, and policies and procedures relating to critical incidents, crisis management, and the administration of financial aid. Where applicable, accreditation requirements relating to matters such as program advertising, teach-outs, or prohibitions on implying accredited status based on another party's institutional accreditation, should be set forth in the agreement.

Beyond the typical general agreement of the parties to take reasonable steps to comply with all applicable laws and regulations, additional provisions relating to compliance may be desirable. Suggested relevant topics include:

- Data Privacy and Protection
- Security and Reporting (e.g., Clery Act obligations)
- Anti-Trafficking
- Anti-Money Laundering
- Anti-Terrorism (including screening of individuals and transactions)
- Prohibited Boycotts
- Anti-Bribery
- Export Controls
- Preservation of Tax-Exempt Status

Given the increasing scrutiny of college and university cross-border activities by U.S. regulators and accreditors, comprehensive legal and compliance provisions can assist in demonstrating the parties' commitment to understanding and mitigating risks. The Biden administration's recent re-constitution of the Homeland Security Academic Partnership Council with a view to addressing "malign" influence by foreign governments and other overseas actors, which U.S. Secretary of Homeland Security Mayorkas called a "persistent and increasing" problem for higher education further illustrates this point (Fischer, 2023).

## Allocating Risk

Once vision, expectations/Scope of Work, guardrails, and compliance matters have been addressed, the final task in negotiating a partnership agreement will be developing provisions that relate to allocating risk between the parties. Common provisions in this arena address representations and warranties, governing law, termination, dispute resolution, indemnification, and insurance.

## Representations and Warranties

Representation and warranties require each party to confirm certain facts about themselves (which may be related to other agreement provisions), and without which a party may be hesitant to proceed with the agreement. These provisions will vary significantly from agreement to agreement, but, at a minimum, the parties should provide assurance to each other that the party is duly incorporated, validly existing, in good standing in their legal jurisdiction, and has the power and authority to enter into the agreement. In addition, the parties should assure that the agreement, if executed, will not conflict with the terms and conditions of any other agreement to which the party is subject, or cause a party to breach the terms of another agreement (e.g., if there is an exclusive agreement with another party relating to the recruitment of students or the delivery of study abroad programming). For larger scale agreements and especially those relating to or requiring the use of specific technology, assurances regarding the ownership of key assets and/or technology should be sought, along with a statement that there is no litigation or other claim, pending or threatened, that relates to such assets or technology, that might prevent their use. Similarly, with respect to institutional accreditation(s) and/or relevant licenses, the parties should assure one another that such accreditation(s) and licenses are valid as of the date of the agreement (and will be maintained during the agreement's term), and that any change in status will be communicated promptly.

Well-drafted representations and warranties prompt the parties to review their own "state of the union" and can surface issues that, if not addressed before signing, might derail the agreement. For example, in the study abroad context, if a hosting institution hesitates to agree to a representation that it has developed and maintains a comprehensive emergency response policy and procedures, this may give pause to the sending institution as to whether the risks of entering into the agreement outweigh the benefits. Finally, in the event of a contract dispute between the parties, the party alleging a breach will have the opportunity to assert additional breach of warranty claims in their legal complaint, should it turn out that a representation or warranty in the agreement was inaccurate when made.

## Governing Law

The law that will govern a partnership agreement and any legal dispute arising out of it is sometimes a contentious issue. Each party would understandably prefer to see the law of their home country and/or state apply as that is the law with which they (and their attorneys) are most familiar. Similarly, if there is litigation, the parties would each prefer to litigate in courts that are close to home (and perhaps favorable to them), and which are most knowledgeable of the applicable law. This area of contract law can be quite complex, so counsel should be sought, especially if a party agrees to subject itself to the law (and the courts) of a foreign jurisdiction. As a general matter, courts will usually enforce choice of law provisions contractually agreed to by the parties, provided that the selected jurisdiction has at least some minimum connection to the parties themselves or to the agreement activities (Born, G., & Kalelioglu, C., 2021). Finally, in situations where for political, cultural, or legal reasons a party cannot agree contractually to the application of foreign law, the parties may consider omitting reference to governing law altogether, leaving the matter for future determination by a court, which will apply the applicable choice of law principles during its consideration of the dispute.

### Termination

Generally, at the time of agreement negotiation, parties are in sync with the proposed vision and expectations/Scope of Work, excited to get to work, and have a healthy amount of goodwill toward one another. Thinking through the conditions under which the agreement may be terminated before the end of its term, however, is a very important discipline. While termination provisions vary significantly from agreement to agreement, two typical scenarios prevail. The first, "Termination for Convenience," allows a party to terminate the agreement without justification of any kind. Usually there is a notice period to allow for the orderly conclusion of activities, and, frequently, with respect to agreements for study abroad or other academic programs there is a commitment by the parties to continue to conclude any currently running academic programs. Termination for Convenience can be especially useful where the vision or expectations/Scope of Work are not being fulfilled to a party's satisfaction, but the time and effort to prove a breach or to engage in mediation or other dispute resolution processes are not worth the expense.

The second common provision, "Termination for Cause," generally provides a mechanism for terminating the agreement in the event of a breach. Some provisions allow for a window of time following written notice in which the other party may be provided the opportunity to rectify or "cure" the breach to the other party's reasonable satisfaction. Before exercising the right to terminate, a party should consult legal counsel (including foreign counsel in the event the agreement is governed by foreign law), to ensure that the facts and circumstances, and potential consequences of termination, are well understood.

Finally, many partnership agreements include *force majeure* provisions, which excuse performance of agreement obligations during periods where performance is not possible due to conditions beyond a party's reasonable control (such as floods, strikes, natural disasters, pandemics, and other emergencies). If the *force majeure* condition continues beyond an agreed period (e.g., 60 days), generally either party may provide notice to the other of their desire to terminate.

## Dispute Resolution

Ideally, conflicts between parties will be resolved through the communication channels set forth in the agreement, most commonly via the Agreement Coordinators. Should resolution at this level fail, it is helpful to include both formal and informal dispute resolution mechanisms in the agreement. These provisions are often progressive, mandating good faith discussion between officials at increasingly higher levels of authority. Agreements frequently include the use of nonbinding mediation, with the goal of resolving a dispute without resort to more costly formal legal proceedings such as binding arbitration or litigation. At every stage, given the very high costs of pursuing formal legal action (especially in a foreign jurisdiction), the parties will need to evaluate, in consultation with counsel, the risks and benefits of pursuing any particular dispute resolution path.

## Indemnification and Insurance

Indemnification and insurance are key aspects of risk allocation in international agreements. In essence, indemnification provisions provide a contractual mechanism to seek redress where a party suffers financial or other harm as a result of a breach of the agreement by the other party, or the negligent or intentionally harmful acts of the other party or its employees or agents. For example, in the study abroad context, if a student brings legal action against one party due to the negligent acts of the employee(s) of the other party, a claim for indemnification may be made against the other party, which will be required to compensate the aggrieved party for its litigation expenses and any damages that may be awarded. Some indemnification provisions provide that the indemnifying party may assume control over (and directly cover the costs of) the defense of a legal action brought against the other party. In this case, the party entitled to indemnification will want to include language allowing its full participation (through counsel) in the proceedings and reserving the right to approve any final settlement(s).

International activities present unique risks that should be discussed with institutional risk managers before any agreement is signed. This will ensure that losses (including the cost of defense) arising from incidents or disputes relating to the agreement or any agreement activities will be covered (where possible) by the institution's insurance policies (regardless of any right to indemnification). In some cases, domestic insurance policies will exclude coverage for activities outside the institution's home jurisdiction, in which case special coverage may need to be obtained to address the risks associated with agreement activities (e.g., many domestic general liability policies do not cover losses incurred in countries where the U.S. State Department has designated a country as particularly high risk). Beyond investigating the available insurance coverage for a party's own institution, each party should commit in the agreement to obtain and maintain types and levels of insurance adequate to cover foreseeable risks related to its contractual obligations and the agreement activities.

## Growing Challenges

In the past decade, the implementation of international academic partnerships has been impacted heavily by several national and international trends. The introduction and escalating enforcement of sweeping privacy and data security regimes, such as the updated (2021) E.U. General Data Protection Regulation (GDPR) (Directorate-General for Justice and Consumers, 2021), China's new Personal Information Protection Law (PIPL) (XL Law & Consulting P.A., 2022), and China's new Law on Data Security (Junck et al., 2021), have required universities to review and update data security policies and procedures, create additional disclosure documentation, develop new forms of consent for participants and other data subjects (including research subjects), and ensure the appropriate safeguarding of personal information collected and held by university stakeholders and their international partners. See Chapter 7.1, "GDPR and PIPL Enforcement," by Xinning Shirley Liu and Emma Snyder Bahner (2024) for more information on these laws.

The U.S. Treasury Department's Office of Foreign Assets Control (OFAC) continues to add to its list of Specially Designated Nationals and Blocked Persons (SDNs), most prominently with the recent additions of Russian, Syrian, Iranian, and Israeli individuals and entities with whom U.S. institutions may not enter into transactions due to terrorism and/or money laundering concerns. Similar lists maintained by the United Nations, the U.K. and other countries require ever deeper commitment by universities to screening relevant transactions and potential international partners. Universities are also paying more attention to compliance with the U.S. Foreign Corrupt Practices Act (FCPA) and similar legislation in jurisdictions where their partners are domiciled or active.

Finally, in the area of research, the Biden administration has recently reinforced its policy view that Foreign Malign Influence is pervasive in higher education, leading to the theft of research and intellectual property by foreign state and corporate actors, with a particular focus on China. International partnerships with Chinese and Russian partners should be scrutinized carefully by counsel and senior institutional administrators (Fischer, 2023).

## Conclusion

International partnerships are a key pillar in any college's or university's comprehensive internationalization strategy. Given the many legal and regulatory risks applicable to international activities, effective partnership agreements ensure alignment of the participating parties in the areas of vision, expectations/Scope of Work, guardrails, and the allocation of risk. Given increasing U.S. and international scrutiny with respect to sensitive research collaborations and higher risk countries, institutions and their counsel must be proactive in ensuring appropriate due diligence and the development of comprehensive agreements with international partners.

## References

Born, G., & Kalelioglu, C. (2021). Choice-of-law agreements in international contracts. *Georgia Journal of International and Comparative Law. (50)*1, 44-118. https://digitalcommons.law.uga.edu/gjicl/vol50/iss1/3/

Directorate-General for Justice and Consumers. (2021, June 4). *Standard contractual clauses for international transfers*. European Commission. https://commission.europa.eu/publications/standard-contractual-clauses-international-transfers_en

Fischer, K. (2023, September 13). Latitudes: Among Chinese students at U.S. colleges, political pressures and discrimination grow more acute. *The Chronicle of Higher Education*. https://www.chronicle.com/newsletter/latitudes/2023-09-13

Junck, R.D., Klein, B.A., Kumaki, A., Kumayama, K.D., Kwok, S., Levi, S.D., Talbot, J.S., Vermynck, E., & Zhang, S. (2021, November 3). China's New Data Security and Personal Information Protection Laws: What They Mean for Multinational Companies. Skadden. https://www.skadden.com/insights/publications/2021/11/chinas-new-data-security-and-personal-information-protection-laws

Liu, X.S., & Bahner, E.S. (2024). GDPR and PIPL Enforcement. In J. Pollard & K. S. Priebe (Eds.), *Convergence of litigation, policy, and standards: Building the informed practitioner in education abroad risk management*. The Forum on Education Abroad.

The Forum on Education Abroad. (2020). *Standards of good practice for education abroad, Sixth edition*. doi.org/10.36366/S.978-1-952376-04-7

The Law Dictionary. (n.d.). Partnership. In *Black's Law Dictionary, 2nd Ed*. Retrieved September 15, 2023, from https://thelawdictionary.org/partnership/

U.S. Department of Treasury. (2024, March 12). *Specially designated nationals and blocked persons list (SDN) human readable lists*. Office of Foreign Assets Control. https://ofac.treasury.gov/specially-designated-nationals-and-blocked-persons-list-sdn-human-readable-lists

XL Law & Consulting P.A. (2022). *Personal information protection law of the People's Republic of China (PIPL)*. https://pipl.xllawconsulting.com/

# 30

---

# Who Can Go Where for What Purposes and Under What Conditions: Building an Institutional International Travel Policy

**Shaun Jamieson and Patrick Morgan**

## Overview

### What is an International Travel Policy and Why is it Important?

This chapter aims to understand the purpose of an international travel policy and best practices for how to develop and implement a travel policy at your institution. In its most essential form, an international travel policy is a written document that addresses who can go where for what purposes and under what conditions as "official travelers" while considering the essential, or non-essential, nature of international travel. Accordingly, some institutions may view international activities as mission-critical and deem it necessary to support high volumes of international travel, even to high-risk locations as appropriate, while other institutes may view international activities as supplemental and not essential to their mission. While it may seem straightforward, the complexity of modern colleges and universities, existing policy structures, and numerous external factors pose challenges for developing an international travel policy. Nevertheless, establishing guidelines around international travel is a foundational step toward meeting your duty of care by avoiding unacceptable risk, outlining travel eligibility, mitigating and managing acceptable risk, and being able to identify, communicate with, and support travelers in crisis.

## Purpose of International Travel Policies

### Why International Travel May Require a Specific Policy

Unlike policies for on-campus or domestic operations, policies specific to international travel are distinct and crucial for two reasons. First, international travel involves complexities that do not exist in domestic travel. International travelers may be in unfamiliar surroundings, in a new culture, and with varying levels of support that differ from what travelers are accustomed to on their home campuses. Health, safety, and security risks may vary depending on location; international and country-specific laws may necessitate different compliance requirements; and security, law enforcement, and access to medical and mental health care and medications may differ broadly from your traveler's home setting.

Second, U.S. higher education institutions must have resources to support travelers, develop protocols and guidelines to effectively manage risk, and provide emergency response support that may differ from supporting travelers in the U.S. Federal regulations may affect your travelers and operations abroad differently than they impact domestic travelers and operations.

An effective international travel policy will follow The Forum on Education Abroad's *Standards of Good Practice for Education Abroad*, clause 5.2.4, which states, "Each organization shall provide risk management, preparedness, and emergency response measures for all programs and ensure insurance coverage is in place" (The Forum on Education Abroad, 2020). A well-constructed travel policy should connect travelers to resources such as travel accident insurance (including medical), political, military, and natural disaster evacuation insurance (abbreviated as PEND), your institution's emergency support and assistance provider, consular support when appropriate, and destination-specific information about risks and mitigation strategies. A policy can address compliance risks associated with export control and research security, which may impact both the individual and the institution. Institutions also have a vested interest in effectively managing international travel to better prepare and protect their travelers, create efficiencies, control costs, and control risks to their reputation.

## Policy Documents are an Articulation of Your Institution's Mission and Values

Policy documents in an institution do not exist as objective dispassionate artifacts that stand apart from the reality and culture of the organization. An organization's culture involves "the creation of shared systems of meaning that are accepted, internalized, and acted on at every level of the organization" (Morgan, 2006, p.138). When drafting a policy, consider the language and tone used within the document and how it will contribute to your institution's culture and values through this shared process. A well-crafted policy should convey its purpose and need within the context of your institution's mission, values, expectations, and priorities. These could include risk aversion or tolerance, promoting or restricting international activities, supporting or constraining travelers, protecting the individual or the institution, or simply whether your policy is advisory or compulsory. You may want to address explicitly or implicitly the degree of academic freedom considered in your policy as well, especially with regard to what constitutes essential travel. In addition to the administrative goals of the policy, the document should also reinforce and support the mission and strategic goals of the institution as a whole. Aligning the two supports buy-in from leadership and compliance from those the policy is intended to guide.

### Limitations of International Travel Policies

Creating an effective international travel policy can help control your institutional risks and manage your institution's travel footprint. However, travel policies should not be considered procedural documents. As described in the University of Wisconsin-Madison Policy Library, "A procedure is a description of the operational processes necessary to implement policy" (*Is It a Policy, Procedure, or Guideline?*, 2022). It is "a way of doing something driven by the completion of the task with a focus on satisfying the rules" (*Standards*, clause 3.38). For example, procedures may include the processes to register travel, obtain travel accident and political and natural disaster insurance, determine high-risk travel, petition to travel to high-risk destinations, and so forth.

Despite its benefits, the existence of a travel policy alone does not eliminate the need for a comprehensive travel risk management (TRM) program. A policy is a critical tool in your TRM toolkit but ultimately is merely a tool that complements or governs your institution's TRM procedures.

### Consider the Existing Policy Landscape

When developing a new policy or revising an existing one, consider your international travel policy in the context of your institution's existing policies and structures. You may not need to address certain areas covered by other policies, or you may need to reconcile possible conflicts or inconsistencies.

Several common institutional policies or practices may exist already and have significant interplay with a proposed international travel policy. Common examples of institutional policies may include:

- Existing (domestic or international) travel policies requiring travelers to register trips and enroll in travel tracking systems. These can exist as part of domestic travel policies, procurement agreements with travel vendors, or central travel office management procedures.
- International insurance that may already be offered to employees and/or students as part of their overall insurance portfolio. Existing policies associated with these insurance programs could require enrollment prior to travel or articulate how claims are handled.
- Financial procedures associated with travel that may be already established, whether or not they have guidelines specific to international travel. These may require updates or modifications in order for your international travel policy to complement them.
- Policies, and sometimes entire offices, that may be dedicated to managing export control regulations. These offices regularly collaborate with international travelers to manage the risks associated with the transfer of certain information, technologies, and materials to individuals or entities outside the country.

## Developing Your Own Policy

### Determine Policy Scope and Stewardship

Scope can be broken into two categories: the operational and strategic goals of the policy and the type of travel the policy governs. You should determine the overall scope of your policy by setting some of the operational and strategic goals that will be accomplished through your policy and identifying which types of travelers it will govern.

Policies may align with strategic goals that are more compliance-focused or mission-focused, though they likely contain elements of both. Your institution may be risk-averse and compliance-focused and therefore restrict all higher-risk travel. Alternatively, your institution's strategic goals and mission may necessitate international endeavors and require accepting some risk. In this latter instance, it may be necessary to make mission-focused decisions to allow essential higher-risk travel, such as research travel by graduate students or faculty that is deemed mission-critical.

In terms of traveler type, is this policy intended for enterprise-wide travel or for a specific area of the institution such as study abroad offices or a particular college? Will this policy govern all travelers or certain types of travel or travelers (e.g., undergraduate students, faculty, staff, and for-credit activities)?

The scope will dictate who best to choose as a policy steward responsible for the ultimate implementation and/or enforcement of the policy. While the policy steward will carry primary responsibility, it may be shared with other offices or individuals and may or may not be the same individual or office that is primarily responsible for implementing a new policy. A policy steward must be able to enforce compliance mandates outlined in the policy, whether that is implementing compliance audits or facilitating compliance with those responsible for compliance. Note that not all policies have compliance mandates. The scope, goals, and stewardship of a policy may evolve as the stakeholder engagement process progresses.

## Identify Key Stakeholders

Early in the ideation phase of drafting an international travel policy, the potential policy steward, acting as the project lead on this policy development endeavor, should identify key stakeholders who will be instrumental in shaping, implementing, and managing the policy. Depending on the policy goals, scope, and institution, key stakeholders may vary, though they often include representatives from the offices or departments of risk management, student affairs, general counsel, education abroad, faculty champions, the senior international officer, a full-time international travel risk manager, and the policy steward. Key stakeholders may be chosen because of their expertise in the subject matter covered within the policy, critical role in implementing or managing aspects of the policy, or even their influence over other stakeholders that will be affected by the policy.

## Articulate the Rationale and Build Support for an International Travel Policy

All too often, structural changes around international travel, including policies, are created following a catalytic event. Catalytic events can range from high-profile incidents, such as the death of a student or detainment of a researcher, or they can be linked to world or regulatory events that affect operations such as the uprisings and anti-government protests during the Arab Spring (2010s), the 2015 Paris terrorist attacks, the COVID-19 pandemic (2019–), or the creation of international research security guidelines with National Security Presidential Memorandum 33 (NSPM-33) (Inabinet et al., 2023). Capitalizing on a catalytic event may provide the rationale for an international travel policy and solidify the necessary support among leadership, but it is not advisable to wait until a crisis occurs to start this work. In the absence of such a catalyzing event, how do you build support for a policy?

A policy may not be approved and will not be as successful without support from high-level leadership and key stakeholders (International Organization for Standardization, 2021). What aspects of international education and travel are important for your leadership? To frame the value of an international travel policy for leadership, emphasize how the policy can advance the mission and strategic goals of the institution; align with organizational culture; mitigate enterprise-wide financial, regulatory, legal, and reputational risks; and demonstrate its clear benefits over its costs.

Tactics for building support may include identifying champions who maintain influence with decision-makers and key stakeholders, leveraging compliance-focused entities such as audits or research compliance, holding focus groups with key stakeholders and potential policy champions, facilitating table-top exercises (gap analysis, crisis scenarios for emergencies abroad, worst-case scenarios for failing to meet regulatory compliance, etc.), benchmarking with peer institutions, and writing formal recommendations or policy objectives based on benchmarking.

### Define Key Terms and Concepts

Once you have defined the scope and identified the stakeholders with whom you will be working, you should collectively begin deciding the key terms and concepts that will be important in your policy's implementation. Recalling that an international travel policy answers the question of who can go where for what purposes and under what conditions, your policy should define the "who" and "where" and define the key terms important to its implementation, or "under what conditions." In practice, the technical meanings of these terms can play a critical role in the way travelers and departments interact with your policy. The exact terms and definitions used will depend on your institutional context and norms, but these questions must be answered:

#### Who: Which Travelers does Your Policy Govern?

Because institutions are engaged in such a wide range of activities with a variety of participants, one of the most challenging aspects of designing an international travel policy will be to define which types of travelers are governed by your policy. Faculty, staff, and students will likely constitute the bulk of your travelers, but many other traveler types may also be participating in your institution's international activity. These could include spouses and family members, volunteers, alumni, affiliates and third-party contractors, visiting scholars, faculty or students from other institutions, recently graduated students, and donors. Your institution's definition of an official traveler should establish which of these travelers are governed by your policy and supported by the institution.

## For What Reasons: What Types of Travel are Official?

Of the faculty, staff, students, or other traveler types that are governed by your policy, only a subset of their activities should be considered official travel for which your institution should assume responsibility. Your policy needs to determine which travel is considered official travel. Policies usually will include travel funded by the institution and travel for which the institution is granting academic credit. However, your institution's travelers may be engaging in many forms of travel that do not conform to either of these qualifiers. Students may travel without receiving credit as a student organization, on a service trip, for an internship experience, for an athletic competition, or to conduct their own research, such as honors, masters, or dissertation research. Faculty may travel using external grant funds, as an invited speaker at a conference, or in connection with official partnerships where third parties are assuming the costs. Depending on what risks and responsibilities your institution chooses to assume, some or all of these types of travel may be governed by your policy.

## Where: What Geographical Areas does the Policy Cover?

Your international travel policy will need to define the geographic area it covers. Does your policy only cover travel to international locations, or does it include travel to or within the United States? Some travel accident insurance and political and natural disaster evacuation insurance cover travel to U.S. territories. If this is the case, does it make sense for your policy to cover travel to U.S. territories, even if your policy does not cover the travel within the United States? Faculty, staff, or students holding non-immigrant visas, permanent residency, or dual nationalities may have a home country that is different from that of your institution. You will need to determine whether their travel to and from their home country is considered international, whether travel to and from campus from that location is considered "official" travel, and whether it is covered by your insurance policies.

## Under What Conditions

The policy should include the minimum requirements for all official travel covered under the policy. Requirements may include registering travel in your institution's official travel tracking system or systems, obtaining travel accident insurance and political and natural disaster evacuation insurance, meeting requirements for eligible travel to high-risk destinations, and/or meeting export control or other federal regulations. The policy may also cover additional requirements for faculty, staff, or departments managing international education experiences, such as faculty-led programming, study abroad, international internships, or official student organization travel, for example, requiring travelers for these purposes to attend a pre-departure orientation or training.

The policy should define what a traveler needs to do in order to travel on official travel, but it may not be necessary to outline the specific procedures to meet these requirements. Procedures can be outlined elsewhere, such as on the website of the unit managing the procedure.

### Consider Your Institution's Needs and Limitations When Operationalizing Your Policy

For your policy to be effective once implemented, it should be tailored to the unique operational and cultural context of your institution. How your institution and its leadership approach internationalization is informed by mission, strategic goals, risk management approaches, and availability of resources. A policy, or part of a policy, which has been successfully implemented at another institution may not be a right fit for your own institutional context. Some of the concepts below may be explicitly articulated in your policy document, but others may be managed by administrative mechanisms such as review committees, application processes, or existing complementary policies.

### Consider Your Administrative Capacity

A successful policy should be operationally feasible. Once written, a policy must be implemented, and that implementation requires resource capacity. Any control that is articulated in a policy should utilize capacity and resources that are either already available or that can reasonably be made available prior to implementation. In some cases, a new policy may be a rationale for securing additional resources, but you should carefully consider what aspects of your policy can be realistically implemented given the realities of resource constraints.

### Understand Your Institution's Risk Appetites

Each institution's stakeholders and leadership will have their own willingness to accept or tolerate certain risks associated with international travel (Tsantir & DeRomaña, 2017). This willingness is referred to as the institution's risk appetite.

Risk appetites of the institution and departments or units within it will change over time, may be dependent on stakeholders' and leadership's willingness to accept risk for essential and non-essential travel, and may be influenced by benchmarking with peers. Some institutions may decide to take responsibility only for a small subset of funded or managed travel to a narrowly defined subset of destinations, while others may take responsibility for all individuals at the institution wherever they travel for whatever purpose, including personal travel, and many others will fall somewhere in between these extremes. Involve your institution's chief risk officer in discussions surrounding international travel and write your policy in a way that reflects the institution's overall risk appetite and that allows for adjustments as the institution evolves.

## Determine Your Essential Travel

Your policy should account for how your institution determines what constitutes essential travel. In higher education, travelers are often self-directed and determine their travel plans based on priorities from their research, studies, or other sources. Essentiality needs to be determined in conversation with these priorities rather than be derived directly from them. Because of this, whether or not travel is essential is often a difficult determination to make, and the criteria will be dependent on your institution's mission, values, risk appetites, and strategic goals. Your policy may distinguish essential and non-essential travel, and you should understand how that determination will be made as part of the policy development process, but the actual assessment of whether travel is essential may be determined by another procedure, such as a high-risk review process. One strategy is to tie essentiality to discrete outcomes of the institution's activities; is the travel necessary for a student's graduation, a faculty member's tenure, a staff member's promotion, meeting compliance, reaching recruitment or development goals, and so on? Other rationales will look at the external impact of travel activities. Your institution's travelers may also be engaged in life-saving humanitarian work or groundbreaking research that impacts large populations. The policy itself may define types of travelers that may not be eligible to travel to high-risk locations. Individual risk owners such as the academic college or department responsible for determining degree requirements may also have their own criteria for essential travel.

## Manage Your High-Risk Travel

To meet the *Standard of Good Practice* clause 5.1.7, your policy should outline how to assess risk in program locations (The Forum on Education Abroad, 2020). This should include determining what constitutes high-risk travel and if and how high-risk travel will be permitted. Review and assessment of the risk of travel is a substantive process that should occur as a separate procedure, but your travel policy should outline broadly who is eligible for high-risk travel and what travelers must do, if anything, to petition to travel to eligible high-risk locations.

Risk ratings are a common way to broadly delineate travel that should be considered high risk based on the travel destination (Brockington, 2017). The most resource-efficient way to do this is to rely on destination risk ratings from a third party, such as the U.S. Department of State or an insurance/security provider, to determine a destination's risk. Some institutions may prefer a more resource-intensive approach and develop a bespoke risk rating system. Benefits of a bespoke system include having the flexibility to accommodate special circumstances and/or ongoing developments in a destination and to develop risk ratings that align with an institution's risk tolerance, experience, and global footprint. For example, if an institution has a campus or major partner abroad in a destination, it can dramatically impact their ability to support travelers, and they may want to classify travel to that country at a lower risk than third-party ratings. Similarly, a country may be listed as a U.S. Department of State Level 2 Travel Advisory, but institutions that have bespoke rating systems may consider it high risk based on their criteria.

Once your policy has broadly designated what travel is considered high risk, it should establish who is eligible for high-risk travel and how that eligibility will be determined. The procedure for determining approval will likely fall outside of your policy, but your policy should determine who is eligible to seek approval. Some travel policies have the same travel eligibility requirements for faculty/staff, undergraduate students, and graduate students, while other policies have different travel eligibility requirements for varying groups. For example, graduate students and faculty/staff may be eligible to travel to the highest-risk locations, but undergraduate students may not be eligible to petition to travel to such destinations. Once eligibility for high-risk travel is articulated, your policy should describe what must be done to seek approval or review for high-risk travel. These reviews are commonly handled by one of your key stakeholders such as a global safety or risk management office, a high-risk travel committee, or through departmental or college leadership. Whoever is tasked with reviewing high-risk travel should have an appropriate level of authority or influence over the travelers they are reviewing.

If you are relying on third-party destination risk ratings, you should structure your policy in a way that leaves you some flexibility should those ratings change and become unaligned with your institution's risk appetites or structured in a way that is incompatible with your procedures. For example, when the U.S.

Department of State changed its destination risk ratings from a travel warning system to a travel advisory system in 2018, an institution whose procedures were structured around the former system may have encountered difficulties applying the new system to its existing procedures. When the travel advisories became tied to CDC health notices during the COVID-19 pandemic, most destinations were rated "Level 4 - Do Not Travel" by the U.S. State Department (*Lifting of Global Level 4 Global Health Advisory—United States Department of State*, 2020). Policies that did not allow travelers to be eligible for travel to these destinations through a procedure were unable to consider petitions until the ratings changed, even if the institution would have been comfortable with approving the travel. (See Chapter 15 entitled "History and Usage of Two Critical U.S. Department of State Travel Resources by the Education Abroad Community" by Julie Friend for more information about these changes.)

## Implementing Your Policy

### Identifying Impacted Stakeholders

Once the policy steward, in collaboration with key stakeholders, has developed a framework for an international travel policy, the next step involves gathering input and acculturating the proposed policy with other impacted stakeholders. Gathering input will help your institution meet the *Standard of Good Practice for Education Abroad,* clause 5.1.1, which states that policies "shall be inclusive, equitable, transparent, and consistently implemented" (The Forum on Education Abroad, 2020). Stakeholders that could be impacted by the policy may include administrative staff who support, fund, or organize international travel and education abroad endeavors such as internships, field work, practicums, clinicals, consulting projects, conferences, research, competitions (sports, music, theater, art, engineering, etc.), co-curricular or student organization travel, and others that fall under your definition of official travel. Staff can be education abroad or career services staff that organize or manage education abroad experiences, or they may be staff or business administrators that provide funding, reimbursement, or transfer credit for international travel.

Stakeholders may also include faculty that organically organize their faculty-led programs independent of an education abroad office, manage their own field sites or projects as a principal investigator or director abroad, advise undergraduate or graduate student research, or conduct international research themselves. These faculty stakeholders may reside in academic departments; in Dean's Offices; in the Office of the Provost, President, or Chancellor; or be members of the faculty senate.

Finally, stakeholders may include staff responsible for the health, safety, security, and risk management on campus such as student life, dean of students, student organization and alternative spring break groups, recreation sports, athletics, international center, admissions, health services, public safety and emergency management, risk management, audits, export controls, finance, procurement, and general counsel. Your institution may also have pre-existing stakeholder groups, formal governance units, or unions that may include many of the impacted stakeholders.

### Engaging Impacted Stakeholders

The optimal success of a policy relies on support from impacted stakeholders. The rationale for building support may target ways in which the policy can enable them to conduct their role as faculty, educators, and staff, provide clear pathways and structures to meet policy requirements, and identify their responsibility in meeting policy goals. Involving stakeholders in the process will create ownership and increase the likelihood that official travelers will follow the policy and be compliant when necessary.

You can engage stakeholders in a variety of ways to help gather feedback and build consensus. Many institutional policy processes will require a public comment period, but this can be supplemented by publicized listening sessions where you collect feedback from the community directly. Presenting your proposed policy with stakeholder groups such as faculty senate, student government, or others can also help build support. Holding facilitated tabletop exercises is a great way to both build consensus and test your proposed policy.

Once your policy has the necessary components and has been reviewed by the relevant stakeholder groups, the final step is to adopt the policy according to your institution's internal processes. This may require completing a formal review process for policy approval with a policy review committee or with leadership.

### Compliance and Enforcement Strategies

Once your policy is adopted, travelers will need to follow it. Effective compliance can be accomplished with a combination of awareness, incentives, and consequences. Depending on your institution, some of these avenues may be more accessible to you than others.

You should not underestimate the effectiveness of voluntary compliance. Sometimes your best strategy is to publicize your new policy widely so that travelers are aware of it and understand what is now being asked of them. You can raise awareness through direct communication like institutional websites, newsletters, campus-wide publications, and marketing campaigns, but your stakeholders can also be powerful allies in helping raise awareness. These could include a travel or procurement office, administrators who help arrange and process travel expenses, education abroad staff, academic advisors, and others.

Incentives can also play a key role in driving compliance. When you publicize your new policy, make sure to highlight the potential benefits to the traveler such as resources it provides and support they are afforded during their travels. If travel registration is linked to an incentive, such as having access to or receiving free travel accident insurance and political and natural disaster evacuation insurance, and allows the institution to locate you and provide support in the event of an emergency, be sure to inform travelers of this benefit. Even the high-risk review procedure is one that helps prepare travelers to face risks abroad and should be promoted as a travel preparation and risk mitigation tool rather than an approval or denial process.

While consequences can be an effective way to drive compliance, they are often the most difficult to implement and enforce. When determining consequences, it is important to consider compliance mechanisms where policy stewards become aware of non-compliance and to determine the institutional comfort level of compliance impacts.

In terms of compliance mechanisms, you should consider at what points your office or relevant administrators become aware of official travel and can independently enforce compliance. For example, if travelers are required to book travel through a centralized travel office, connecting purchasing or reimbursement approval to the policy can be extremely effective, but few institutions are willing to deny reimbursements for legitimate travel expenses. Similarly, if administrators are providing funding or credits for an international travel experience, embedding policy requirements in the application process can be effective. Some compliance aspects of travel such as export control restrictions can carry more severe penalties, but they will not impact all travelers. Disciplinary action against employees and students might be an option, particularly for repeatedly failing to follow policy.

In terms of institutional comfort level with compliance, there are important factors to consider. Is your institution willing to revoke funding or credits for official travel that occurred but did not follow policy requirements? If so, who enforces this consequence—the policy steward, the college or department that sponsored travel, the traveler's home department, and so on? If there are compliance mechanisms, it is important to outline expectations for who is responsible for enforcing compliance within the policy. It is also important to be realistic with compliance enforcement when stating compliance expectations within the policy.

## Post-Implementation

### Determining a Maintenance Process and Review Cadence

Creating, adopting, and implementing a policy is not the end of the policy life cycle (Policy, 2023). Rather, a policy is a living document that must be maintained and periodically reviewed, as stated in the *Standard of Good Practice*, clause 5.1.2, to evaluate its application and effectiveness (The Forum on Education Abroad, 2020). Many institutions have internal standards for policy maintenance, which may include a prescribed cadence to evaluate the policy for updates or for decommission. Other institutions may not have a prescribed cadence for maintenance. Either way, as the policy steward or champion, you should determine the cadence of policy maintenance at the time of policy approval. Determining a timeline for policy maintenance will increase transparency and trust with stakeholders and allow you to prepare for the next iteration of policy review and repeat many of the aforementioned steps to gather stakeholder feedback in an effort to iteratively improve the policy.

### Ongoing and Iterative Process Development

The guidance in this chapter will hopefully lead you to successfully build an institutional international travel policy. Even after implementation, your policy may be redefined in future iterations as it is tested by compliance and enforcement strategies and shifting institutional needs. As you did during the initial development, you should continue to revisit and answer the questions of "who can go where for what purposes and under what conditions" as official travelers with the goal of enabling your institution to meet its international objectives and institutional mission. Continue to reassess your institution's unique cultural context, risk tolerance, strategic visions, and mission. As new policies, structures, and administrative capacities develop at your institution, your policy may need to change to adapt or take advantage of new opportunities. Whether you are the policy champion tasked with building your inaugural international travel policy at your institution, or you are a stakeholder working to improve your policy, you will be better prepared to build or retool your International Travel Policy.

## References

Brockington, J. L. (2017). Assessing and Mitigating Education Abroad Risks. In P. C. Martin (Ed.), *Crisis management for education abroad*. NAFSA: Association of International Educators.

The Forum on Education Abroad. (2020). *Standards of Good Practice for Education Abroad, Sixth Edition.* The Forum on Education Abroad. doi.org/10.36366/S.978-1-952376-04-7

Guidance for implementing National Security Presidential Memorandum 33 (NSPM-33) on national security strategy for united states government-supported research and development, January 1, 2022. White House. Retrieved February 17, 2024, from https://www.whitehouse.gov/wp-content/uploads/2022/01/010422-NSPM-33-Implementation-Guidance.pdf

Inabinet, M., Jamieson, S.M., & Molyneux, J. (2023, June 29). *Pulse: Pulling back the curtain and looking to the future* [conference session]. 14th Annual Institute for Health, Safety, Security and Risk Management, Temple University, Philadelphia, PA, United States. https://www.forumea.org/uploads/1/4/4/6/144699749/hsi-program_final_1.pdf

International Organization for Standardization (ISO). (2021). *ISO 31030:2021, Travel risk management — Guidance for organizations.* Geneva, Switzerland: ISO.

*Is it a Policy, Procedure, or Guideline?* (2022, June 2). UW–Madison Policy Library. Retrieved August 25, 2023, from https://development.policy.wisc.edu/2022/06/01/is-it-a-policy-procedure-or-guideline

*Lifting of Global Level 4 Global Health Advisory – United States Department of State.* (2020, December 1). United States Department of State. Retrieved from https://2017-2021.state.gov/lifting-of-global-level-4-global-health-advisory/

Morgan, G. (2006). *Images of organization* (2nd ed.). Sage Publications.

Policy. (2023, June 10). Institutional Integrity and Risk Management. Ethics and Policy. Retrieved from https://ethicspolicy.unc.edu/policy/#policy-lifecycle

*Travel advisories.* (n.d.). U.S. Department of State – Bureau of Consular Affairs. Retrieved August 23, 2023, from https://travel.state.gov/content/travel/en/traveladvisories/traveladvisories.html

Tsantir, S. B., & DeRomaña, I. (2017). Crisis Planning. In P. C. Martin (Ed.), *Crisis management for education abroad.* NAFSA: Association of International Educators.

# 31

## Applying Standards to Travel Risk Management

Henning Snyman, Hilary Douglas, and Gary Collins

## Introduction

Travel has evolved into an integral aspect of academic pursuits, research initiatives, experiential learning endeavors, and professional obligations. Consequently, institutions of higher education must be equipped to offer robust support to their travelers. This assistance should be centered around Travel Risk Management (TRM) propelled by an organization's legal obligation to exercise duty of care toward its travelers (International Organization for Standardization, 2021; The Forum on Education Abroad, 2020, 5.1; 5.1.7).

Around the world, and across diverse sectors such as corporations, NGOs, and academia, a widely embraced best practice in TRM is outlined in the International Organization for Standardization (ISO) 31030, Travel risk management: Guidance for organizations (2021). Rooted in the principles, framework, and processes of ISO 31000, and incorporating key occupational health and safety principles from ISO 45001, ISO 31030 serves as a valuable resource for integrating into an organization's existing risk management processes. It can function either as a component of the overall system or as an independent TRM program.

Effective implementation of TRM, as delineated by ISO 31030, mandates collaborative efforts between organizations and both internal and external stakeholders. It involves anticipating and assessing potential medical and security events, safeguarding data, formulating risk mitigation strategies, and transparently communicating potential risk exposure to travelers. Adequate preparation and guidance significantly diminish the impact of disruptive events, encompassing medical and emergency response advice, information security precautions, and resolution of logistical challenges.

Despite the absence of mandated standards governing how academic institutions approach international travel support, establishing a TRM program based on the International Organization for Standardization (ISO) 31030 (2021) and The Forum on Education Abroad's *Standards of Good Practice for Education Abroad* (2020) offers a structured methodology. This approach facilitates the development, implementation, evaluation, and review of a TRM program, along with a thorough assessment and treatment of travel risks (International Organization for Standardization, 2021; The Forum on Education Abroad, 2020, 5.1; 5.1.5, 5.1.7). Consequently, organizations can move closer to fulfilling their duty of care responsibilities, cultivating resilient "special relationships," mitigating risks associated with international activities, and limiting potential liabilities.

Aligning with the *Standards of Good Practice for Education Abroad* and ISO 31030 yields several advantages, including prioritizing student well-being (International Organization for Standardization, 2021; The Forum on Education Abroad, 2020, 5.1; 5.1.7 and 5.2; 5.2.7), fostering continuous monitoring, evaluation (International Organization for Standardization, 2021; The Forum on Education Abroad, 2020, 5.1; 5.1.4), and adaptation, enhancing safety, legal liability, and risk management, as well as promoting health and safety protocols and emergency response procedures. The widespread acceptance of this guidance can be attributed to its effectiveness and relevance across diverse organizational contexts.

The primary objective of this chapter is to delve into best practices, with a specific focus on operationalizing ISO 31030 within the higher education sector. The discussion will center on effectively integrating ISO 31030 into TRM, elucidating how it aids organizations in meeting various standards and ensuring compliance. While not providing a comprehensive examination of ISO 31030, the chapter will concentrate on core elements that organizations can leverage to construct and implement their own TRM strategies.

ISO 31030:2021 Travel Risk Management Guidance for Organizations is available for purchase online.

## Duty of Care versus duty of care

According to International SOS, the definition of Duty of Care is "a legal obligation imposed on an organization, requiring adherence to a standard of reasonable care while preventing any acts that could foreseeably harm others" (Renaut, 2023).

Corporations and NGOs are required to meet a Duty of Care for their workforce. Use of the term Duty of Care varies in the field of international education given the legal implications (Claus & Yost, 2010). Study abroad is an at-will, fee-paying endeavor and while a "special relationship" exists between the organization and the student in higher education TRM, as established by the courts and elucidated in Chapters 1 (Pollard & Priebe, 2024), 2 (Miller & Pollard, 2024), and 3 (Priebe & Hayes, 2024), respectively, an ethical and moral obligation to support the health, safety, and security of our travelers remains. For the purpose of this chapter, the lowercase "duty of care" will be utilized not as a legal term, but to convey standard best practices for supporting travelers.

## TRM: Enhancing Safety in Educational Journeys

As your institution or organization begins to create or enhance its TRM program, it is imperative to understand your institution, its approach to risk, all the offices and entities that may have roles and responsibilities within TRM, and your travelers.

### Operating Context: Navigating Internal and External Influences

TRM involves a systematic approach to identifying, assessing, and mitigating risks to ensure the safety of individuals traveling on behalf of educational organizations. The effectiveness of TRM is influenced by both internal and external factors.

### Internal Considerations

- Vision, Mission, and Culture: Clearly defined organizational principles (International Organization for Standardization, 2021; The Forum on Education Abroad, 2020, 4.1; 4.1.1).
- Governance and Structure: Roles, responsibilities, and accountabilities within the institution.
- Strategic Objectives: Goals and policies guiding educational initiatives (International Organization for Standardization, 2021; The Forum on Education Abroad, 2020, 4.1; 4.1.2).
- Travel Plans and Standards: Guidelines and regulations for travel activities.
- Risk Management Strategy: Approaches and criteria for managing travel risks.
- Capabilities: Skills and profiles of travelers, resources, and tools for risk management (International Organization for Standardization, 2021; The Forum on Education Abroad, 2020, 6.1; 6.1.11).

*External Considerations*

- Destination/Regions: Political, socioeconomic, cultural, and legal factors.
- Security Factors: Political violence, social unrest, crime, and emergency services.
- Infrastructure Quality: Transportation, telecommunications, and accommodation (International Organization for Standardization, 2021; The Forum on Education Abroad, 2020, 5.2; 5.2.6).
- Health Concerns: Epidemics, pandemics, and local healthcare quality.
- Cybersecurity: Information security during travel.
- Legal Compliance: Adherence to legislation and regulations, such as NSPM-33.

*Sector-Specific Compliance: Aligning with Legislation and Standards*

Organizations should be well-versed in relevant legislation, including, but not limited to, NSPM-33, and understand sector-specific requirements (International Organization for Standardization, 2021; The Forum on Education Abroad, 2020, 5.1; 5.1.5, 5.1.7). This applies equally to the traveler's country of origin, as well as to their destination country.

For research-intensive higher education institutions receiving federal funds above $50 million per year, the National Security Presidential Memorandum-33 (NSPM-33) directs federal agencies and departments to focus on improving research security in the following areas:

1. Disclosure requirements and standardization
2. Digital persistent identifiers
3. Consequences for violation of disclosure requirements
4. Information sharing
5. Research security programs within research organizations, that include:

   - Cybersecurity
   - Foreign travel security
   - Research security training
   - Export control training

Your organization-wide duty of care, travel policies, and continuity plans should be considered when applying risk treatment measures that address these concerns. Consulting the offices responsible for research compliance (IRB), export controls, legal counsel, and risk management are excellent starting points.

## Risk Profile: Adapting to Evolving Contexts

Understanding the risk profile of your organization is essential. Factors influencing the risk profile include industry sector, public image, project specifics, and individual traveler profiles. Regular reviews and communication of changes to stakeholders are necessary. The risk profile of your organization will inform how travel risk is managed and delivered. Third-party TRM providers can assist organizations to deliver certain functions when your internal resources are unable to effectively and efficiently manage travel risk based on your risk profile. Engagement of a medical and security third-party assistance provider should be based on a cost–benefit analysis and be included during the development and implementation of the TRM policy. See Chapter 30, "Building an Institutional International Travel Policy," by Shaun Jamieson and Patrick Morgan (2024) for more information on international travel policies.

## Stakeholders: Collaborative Approach to TRM

Engaging stakeholders is crucial. Whether TRM is a standalone function or integrated into related activities (e.g., is there an organization-wide governing body like a TRM office or does the study abroad office operate independently? Do faculty-led programs operate in conjunction with the study abroad office or separately?), collaboration with offices beyond the study abroad office—campus safety, student affairs, legal teams, third-party study abroad providers (International Organization for Standardization, 2021; The Forum on Education Abroad, 2020, 5.1; 5.1.8) is recommended.

**Table 31.1.** Examples of internal and external stakeholders adapted from ISO 31030 (2021).

| Internal stakeholders | External stakeholders |
| --- | --- |
| Education abroad office | Third-party study abroad programs |
| Health and safety | On-the-ground vendors |
| Security/campus police | Insurance providers |
| IT security | Travel management company |
| Crisis and incident management teams | TRM providers |
| Global travel | Government agencies |
| Human resources | Regulatory and emergency services |
| Risk management | Parents/guardians |
| Legal counsel | Traveler partners/dependents |
| Deans/faculty | Local communities/partners |
| Financial office | Host organizations |

### Traveling Population: Tailoring TRM to Diverse Profiles

Consideration of the destination in the context of an individual traveler's profile (International Organization for Standardization, 2021; The Forum on Education Abroad, 2020, 6.1; 6.1.9, 6.1.9.2) and in-country activities are vital. Factors such as medical history, race, experience of travel, nationality, cultural identity, gender, sexual orientation, religion, age, level of seniority, physical ability, and research topic can all have a significant bearing on travel risk. Different types of travelers, including faculty, staff, students, and accompanying individuals, require tailored TRM approaches (International Organization for Standardization, 2021; The Forum on Education Abroad, 2020, 6.1; 6.1.11, 6.1.12). The regularity and duration of travel also influences travel risk. For instance, a recurring quarter-/ semester-/year-long course requires different considerations than a one-off short-term small group seminar or an independent, remote fieldwork experience. Also, a faculty member that returns to the same research site year after year (even multiple times per year) will require different considerations than a first-time/one-time visit to a higher risk destination.

### Risk Appetite: Balancing Objectives and Risk Management

There should be a balance between your organization's objectives—for instance. academic research or successful study abroad experiences—and the management of risk that could be encountered. Any foreseen risk should be proportionally addressed, and your organization should consider the level of risk that is acceptable in relation to the objectives. In some cases, specific risks cannot be treated effectively and efficiently and therefore travel should be reconsidered. The TRM program should describe the organization's travel risk criteria or travel risk appetite.

## Planning and Establishing the Travel Risk Management Program

### Performing an Organizational Self-Assessment

The following should be done by your organization when developing the TRM program:

Use these questions to focus your organization's TRM efforts and decide next steps.

- Who is responsible for overseeing travel at your organization? Is it one department or multiple?
- Do you have a travel solution or a program in place currently?
- Is travel risk a component of that program or is it primarily focused on expense management?

- Is travel data available to your organization? If so, how do you receive or manage that data?
- Can you confirm support from senior leadership and guarantee the program will be well resourced?
- Who are the internal, and where appropriate, external stakeholders who should be consulted on travel risk to ensure engagement and buy in?
    - Other business units (HR, IT, legal, etc.) must be engaged in the development and promotion of the TRM program.
    - Ensure all staff fully understand the TRM function and how to engage with the program.
- Who will be responsible for implementing the program?
    - Clearly define roles and responsibilities in relation to the duties of implementing the program. The implementation plan should be approved by senior leadership and should integrate the TRM function within your organization's operations.
- What are the risks posed to the organization and the travelers?
    - Understand the risk profile of the organization in relation to the travel destination. Domestic travel should not be excluded, especially if the risk environments within the country differ.
    - Identify the risk(s) posed to the organization and the travelers (International Organization for Standardization, 2021; The Forum on Education Abroad, 2020, 5.1; 5.1.7). Risk posed to the organization and to travelers can affect both parties and increase risk The following are examples:
        - Personal risk to the travelers: medical, assault, detention (legal and illegal), kidnap, theft, robbery, and death.
        - Legal risk can be both criminal and civil.
        - Business continuity risk, the inability to operate due to an incident or failure of the local infrastructure.
        - Reputational risk due to poor incident response.
        - Financial risk, the cost of failed assignments, travel disruptions, taxation, visa or work permit status, insurance, evacuation, and medical repatriation.
        - Risk to data and intellectual property.
        - Risk to productivity/success of a study abroad program.

## Leadership and Commitment: Ensuring Institutional Buy-In

Oversight of your organization's TRM should be the responsibility of senior leadership. The establishment and effectiveness of the TRM policy and objectives are most successful when aligned with your organization's strategic direction and when those at the highest levels are held accountable for risk even if the responsibility of managing such risk has been delegated. Senior leadership, often bound by legal requirements, must ensure that the necessary resources (including funds and staff) are allocated to TRM and that the intended outcomes—program compliance, the safety and security of your travelers—are achieved. The success of TRM relies on effective communication up, down, and across your organization, with senior leadership supporting all internal stakeholders in their individual roles to ensure promotion and "buy in" from all travelers.

The adequate funding of the TRM program and support from the top will ensure that your organization improves and expands the program in line with internal and external changes. The TRM program should be reviewed consistently (yearly) and tested on a regular basis to ensure understanding and continual improvement.

### Policy Development: Institutionalizing TRM

As part of your organization's wider risk management strategy, a TRM policy (International Organization for Standardization, 2021; The Forum on Education Abroad, 2020, 5.1; 5.1.7) is a high-level document sponsored by senior leadership and reflects the organizational TRM program's goals and objectives. The primary objective of a TRM policy is to enhance the safety and security of travelers while minimizing potential risks and disruptions associated with organizational travel. It should be communicated to the organization continuously through information sessions, education, and training. The policy should clearly address all applicable risks and should outline the process and criteria when there may be disagreement regarding the risk level and whether travel should proceed or not.

Finally, the policy should state what is expected from travelers and should align with HR standards, financial reimbursement policies, and organizational code of ethics/conduct.

For more information about travel policy, refer to Chapter 13, "Building an Institutional International Travel Policy," by Shaun Jamieson and Patrick Morgan (2024).

### Travel Risk Assessment

An integral part of your risk management framework is the streamlined risk assessment process (International Organization for Standardization, 2021; The Forum on Education Abroad, 2020, 5.1; 5.1.7), which entails identifying, analyzing, and mitigating risks for travelers. The core objective of this assessment is to pinpoint risks, assess their likelihood, and evaluate their potential impact on both the traveler and the organization. By understanding these factors, you can prioritize risks that necessitate treatment or mitigation. Based on assessment outcomes, the organization can approve, decline, or modify travel arrangements to align them with your institution's overall risk appetite.

### Key Risk Sources

- Travel destination or circumstances
- Accommodation (International Organization for Standardization, 2021; The Forum on Education Abroad, 2020, 5.2; 5.2.7)
- Travel route/type of transport available
- Travel itinerary
- Travel duration
- Traveler and organizational profile
- Geopolitics in travel region
- Legal restrictions
- Cyber threats
- Cultural and religious differences (International Organization for Standardization, 2021; The Forum on Education Abroad, 2020, 5.2; 5.2.7)
- Access to critical infrastructure and resources
- Contextual risk factors such as extreme weather, natural disaster, conflict, epidemic/pandemic, reliability of communications, etc.

Security threats, safety and health hazards should be included in the travel risk assessment. Even in low-risk environments, the presence of threats and hazards can alter the viability of travel.

For short-term education abroad programs, additional considerations involve risks associated with personal activities during nonprogram hours, participation in high-risk activities (e.g., extreme sports), and potential hazards arising from the selection of unsafe or improperly vetted housing, transportation, or local partner organizations (International Organization for Standardization, 2021; The Forum on Education Abroad, 2020, 5.1; 5.1.6 and 5.2; 5.2.6).

For institutions engaged in high-volume travel, leveraging automated risk assessment tools proves effective for lower-risk environments, while higher-risk destinations or group travel may warrant individual, in-depth assessments. For example, pre-trip security and medical briefings generated, and triggered by travel bookings to lower risk environments. Organizations can use technology to obtain traveler profile-specific information through a questionnaire and based on the responses, further risk mitigation measures can be introduced.

**Table 31.2.**   Examples of security threats and hazards from ISO 31030 (2021).

| Security threats | Hazards |
|---|---|
| Crime—petty and serious | Infectious diseases, hygiene, foodborne illnesses, inadequate medical infrastructure (International Organization for Standardization, 2021; The Forum on Education Abroad, 2020, 6.1; 6.1.10) |
| Terrorism | Transportation incidents |
| Cybercrime | Environmental hazards |
| Political unrest or activism | Industrial disasters |
| Hostile governments | Negligent activities |
| Profile specific threats based on the profile of traveler or organization | |

The outcomes of these risk assessments should be meticulously documented and shared with pertinent stakeholders (International Organization for Standardization, 2021; The Forum on Education Abroad, 2020, 6.1; 6.1.10, 6.1.11) to guide decisions on risk treatment options. In instances where technology is employed to authorize low-risk trips, such as utilizing your institution's preferred Travel Management Company, the traveler's acknowledgment of receiving and reading the pre-trip advisory may suffice. Conversely, high-risk trips necessitate a comprehensive security briefing based on a thorough risk assessment to apprise travelers of potential risks and recommended mitigation measures.

Your institution must systematically identify and describe risks that may impact both travelers and organizational objectives, particularly those related to safety, security, and health (International Organization for Standardization, 2021; The Forum on Education Abroad, 2020, 5.1; 5.1.7). In cases where conflicts arise between organizational and individual traveler objectives, the priority must be the individual traveler's health, safety, and security.

Continuous evaluation is imperative for emerging and evolving risks due to the inherent uncertainty they introduce, such as extreme weather, cyber risks, and escalating civil unrest.

The findings of the risk analysis play a pivotal role in assessing and comparing organizational risk criteria against identified risks. Depending on these findings, your institution may choose to cancel travel, proceed with travel as planned, or implement additional safety measures. These measures might include adjusting the itinerary, limiting exposure by reducing the number or profile of travelers, altering the mode of transport, or shortening the duration of travel. The cost and benefit of these measures should be carefully considered and weighed against the residual risk, the traveler profile, and the nature of the identified risk.

## Travel Risk Treatment

Based on the risk assessment, your organization should ensure that controls address risks prior to travel, during travel, during, and after incidents, and once travel is completed (International Organization for Standardization (ISO), 2021, section 7.1). Risks may range from health and safety concerns in the destination country to logistical challenges during travel. Considering the diverse risks involved, tailor control measures to fit the specific destination, the individuals traveling, and their activities. For instance, in a high-risk location, additional security personnel might be assigned, and emergency evacuation plans could be established.

One or several treatment options can be required to modify risk to bring it to a satisfactory level.

### Example

Pre-travel measures:
- Pre-screening for health concerns specific to the destination.
- Providing cultural awareness training for the team (International Organization for Standardization, 2021; The Forum on Education Abroad, 2020, 6.1; 6.1.9).
- Confirming travel insurance coverage for medical emergencies (International Organization for Standardization, 2021; The Forum on Education Abroad, 2020, 5.2; 5.2.4).

During-travel measures:
- Implementing a 24/7 emergency contact system for travelers (International Organization for Standardization, 2021; The Forum on Education Abroad, 2020, 5.2; 5.2.4).
- Providing secure communication tools to mitigate cybersecurity risks.
- Collaborating with local partners for on-ground support.

Post-incident measures:
- Establishing a post-travel debrief to capture lessons learned (Clause 4.1.5).
- Offering counseling services for students and program staff who may have experienced stressful incidents.

The organization should carefully weigh the advantages and disadvantages of each mitigation measure. For example:

Cost–Benefit Analysis: The cost of hiring a local security team is weighed against the potential impact on employee safety.

Impact on Objectives: The disruption caused by increased security measures is assessed against the overall success of the trip.

Holistic Selection: Instead of addressing each risk in isolation, the organization can select mitigation measures that collectively address a range of risks. For instance, a comprehensive travel support package may simultaneously address health, security, and logistical challenges.

### Risk Reduction

Mitigating risks in higher education travel necessitates a comprehensive approach that considers various sources of risk concurrently. For example, choosing secure accommodations close to the activity or work site not only enhances safety but also addresses concerns related to challenging roads or potential traffic accidents (International Organization for Standardization, 2021; The Forum on Education Abroad, 2020, 5.2; 5.2.6). In locations where certain mitigation measures are impractical or prohibitively expensive, a reassessment is vital to align travel objectives with criticality.

Periodic evaluations of the competence of travelers and those involved in the TRM function are essential. This assessment should encompass a thorough review of documents, assessments, and policies, considering the educational background, training, and level of experience of travelers and the TRM team (International Organization for Standardization, 2021; The Forum on Education Abroad, 2020, 5.2; 5.2.2.3). When selecting service providers, verifying accreditation, appropriate licenses, certifications, and regional coverage should be integral to the process.

Ensuring travelers are well-informed before departure and during travel, particularly in escalated situations, relies on sourcing reliable and accurate information. Acknowledgment of pre-trip briefings by travelers should be recorded for compliance purposes. Utilizing mass communication platforms, such as dedicated medical and security assistance service providers, intranets, or social media, ensures effective communication during escalations and should be understood and practiced by all travel stakeholders.

The organization's accommodation policy, spanning hotels, serviced apartments, short-term rentals, or shared economy options, should be risk-based. While low-risk environments may rely on evidence-based questionnaires for selection, higher-risk destinations should involve onsite security assessments by competent and qualified assessors. Data protection, information security, and privacy requirements must align with organizational objectives, the assignment, and traveler needs. Obtaining consent from travelers and implementing measures consistent with data privacy laws are crucial. See Chapter 7, "Privacy & Consent: Global Data Privacy Overview," by Xinning Shirley Liu and Emma Bahner (2024) for more information.

The selection of transportation should align with the travel policy and suit the risk environment. In some cases, implementing a journey management plan, including a detailed travel route assessment, meet-and-greet services, additional security assistance, and appropriate accommodation selection, is necessary based on the traveler's profile and the ground risk level.

Ensuring the fitness of travelers for their journey and guaranteeing access to adequate medical care at the destination are paramount (International Organization for Standardization, 2021; The Forum on Education Abroad, 2020, 6.1; 6.1.10, 6.1.12). For certain travelers, preparing a specific medical response plan may be appropriate in case of health issues abroad.

### Risk Avoidance

To optimize the TRM function and facilitate a rapid response in case of incidents involving faculty, staff, or students traveling abroad, a robust pre-travel authorization and booking procedure is imperative. This process not only enhances visibility for the TRM team but also ensures adherence to any required compliance standards. Moreover, it serves as a mechanism where approval is granted based on an overarching assessment of organizational risk rather than solely focusing on individual travelers' objectives.

Adhering to best practices, the approval hierarchy correlates with the level of risk anticipated for the traveler. The higher the potential risk exposure, the more senior the approver or the larger the approving team within the organization should be. An example of this is where travel to a particular destination is deemed to be high risk, as defined by the TRM Policy, or due to a concern raised by a member of university administration. The traveler in this instance must petition a Travel Risk Committee for an exception to the travel policy. Approval may be contingent on additional mitigation strategies, such as one-on-one pre-departure advising, a robust communications plan, and strict adherence to a detailed itinerary.

Many corporations, NGOs, and academic institutions have a mandatory booking system that clearly outlines the booking channels to be used for all components of travel (including transport and accommodation). Your organization's travel policy and TRM policy should align regarding transport options, accommodation standards, and not restrict the selection of the most secure options based on financial considerations.

The organization's ability to impose restrictions on various aspects of travel, such as travel activities, permissible types of transport, movement times, the number of travelers per trip, trip durations, avoidance of specific events, and considerations for environmental factors, provides an additional layer of risk management and ensures a more secure travel environment for faculty, staff, and students abroad.

### Risk Sharing

Organizations can distribute liabilities and allocate risk in the clauses of a contract with a third-party insurer or third-party provider (educational provider, tour provider, host university, etc.) who might manage one aspect of the program. It is critical to view risk-sharing measures not as a replacement for TRM but as a complementary and essential component. When establishing agreements with third-party insurers or providers, clarity is paramount regarding how risk allocations are managed, whether through contractual transfer, indemnification, or commercial insurance (International Organization for Standardization, 2021; The Forum on Education Abroad, 2020, 5.1; 5.1.8).

For faculty, staff, and students engaged in international travel, it is crucial to ensure the presence of comprehensive general insurance, including liability coverage (International Organization for Standardization, 2021; The Forum on Education Abroad, 2020, 5.2; 5.2.4). This insurance should cover a range of potential incidents, such as medical emergencies (including fatalities), security incidents, evacuation procedures, and repatriation efforts. Some institutions may also consider coverage for canceled or delayed flights, understanding any exclusions and confirming that all third-party service providers possess the minimum required insurance coverage for travelers is of utmost importance.

In cases where travel involves higher-risk destinations or areas prone to incidents like kidnap and ransom, loss of key staff, or conflict risks, specialized insurance coverage should be in place. The utilization of such insurance often involves highly sensitive and confidential considerations, limited to a select few within the organization. The TRM team must be aware of the specifics of these insurance policies, including the escalation process, ensuring their inclusion in comprehensive incident response plans tailored to the unique challenges of faculty, staff, and students traveling abroad. See Chapter 33 in this volume, "Navigating International Insurance for Global Education," by Joan Rupar (2024) for more information on insurance.

### Summary

This chapter outlines the core elements essential for establishing a comprehensive TRM program. A fundamental step involves articulating your institution's mission, goals, policies, procedures, and available resources in the context of TRM (International Organization for Standardization, 2021; The Forum on Education Abroad, 2020, 5.1; 5.1.7). This includes a deep understanding of your travelers—primarily faculty and students— and their specific needs. This foundational knowledge contributes to a holistic comprehension of your institution's risk profile and its appetite for risk.

Identifying both internal and external stakeholders is crucial for delineating clear roles and responsibilities within the TRM framework. Securing buy-in and support from senior leadership becomes instrumental in shaping policy, implementing TRM protocols, and ensuring effective communication throughout the entire process. Once these foundational components are in place, your institution will be well-equipped to assess travel risks systematically and determine the most effective means of risk mitigation. Regular evaluation and refinement will further enhance and optimize your TRM over time.

Institutions of higher education must be intentional about planning TRM. Leveraging the guidelines outlined in *ISO 31030* offers a robust methodology to tailor TRM to align with your institution's values, risk management capabilities, and the necessity to report on global activities. Incorporating these guideline elements into your TRM program ensures a strong foundation that safeguards the health, safety, and security of your institution's travelers, assets, and reputation. Continuous refinement and application of these principles contribute to the ongoing growth and improvement of your institution's TRM initiatives.

## A Comprehensive TRM Program Typically Includes the Following Essential Core Elements

*ISO 31030 (2021)* has a comprehensive implementation plan (Section 5.6). Here are a few essential elements and how to think about them from a higher education perspective.

Destination and time frame:

| Classification and review of destination | How current is the risk assessment? When do risk assessment reviews occur? |
|---|---|
| Dates and times of travel | How will current events, season impact travelers? Will there be an election that may lead to unrest? Will any major cultural events, religious holidays take place during the trip? What is the likelihood of an extreme weather event? |

Traveler-related issues:

| Risk profile of traveler | How may the travelers' identities, experience, medical conditions impact their experience? Encourage travelers to research their destination to understand how their identities, attitudes, values, and outward appearance might be perceived in the host country and impact their experience. |
|---|---|
| Outside of program time | How will you approach outside of program time? Will students have a curfew? When does sponsored travel begin/end? When are travelers covered by organization support, assistance providers, insurance? |
| Traveler training | Is there coursework or a pre-departure orientation prior to travel? What resources will travelers need in advance? Will there be an arrival orientation? |

Process:

| Documentation | What needs to be collected from travelers: Assumption of Risk Waiver, Program Agreement, Emergency Contacts, Communication Plan. How will it be collected? Who will have access? How long will it be stored? |
|---|---|
| Stakeholder training | Who will lead the trip leader orientation? What internal and external resources need to be shared or created- communication plan, incident response guides, emergency numbers? Who will be invited to tabletop training exercises? |
| Travel booking procedures | Does your organization use a central booking system (best practice)? How does the organization stay informed about who is traveling? Which stakeholders can provide support? |

Incident management

| Crisis and incident management team and plan | Have a clearly defined response team with authority to respond to an incident or crisis. Protocols should be clearly laid out in a crisis and incident response guide. |
|---|---|
| Roles and responsibilities | Who is accountable and who is responsible at your organization when an incident occurs? Who needs to be consulted or informed? Who manages the budget?<br>Internally and externally: Who is the first point of contact for minor incidents? Major incidents? Who escalates an emergency? Who reaches out to emergency contacts? |
| Travel assistance | Work with an assistance provider which can provide security assistance during travel, notification of relevant events, emergency safety, security and medical assistance, evacuation, and assistance and support after travel. |
| Travel tracking | Monitoring travelers itineraries/travel registration is a critical part of the TRM program and enables organizations to understand their exposure and enable communication and assistance during an escalation. Travelers can be tracked by either their itinerary, expenditure tracking or active tracking through technology. The selection of a travel tracking system depends on the volume and destination of travel. Higher risk destinations or the profile of the travel might necessitate active tracking and monitoring. |

# References

Claus, L. & Yost, R. (2010). A global view of the university's duty of care obligations. *URMIA Journal*. 29-36.

International Organization for Standardization (ISO). (2021). *Travel risk management — Guidance for organizations (No.31030:2021)*. https://www.iso.org/standard/54204.html

Jamieson, S. & Morgan, P. (2024). Who can go where for what purposes and under what conditions: Building an institutional international travel policy. In J. Pollard and K. S. Priebe (Eds.), Convergence of litigation, policy, and standards: Building the informed practitioner in education abroad risk management. The Forum on Education Abroad. doi. org/10.36.366/SIA.5.978-1-952376-41-2.30

Liu, X.S., & Bahner, E. (2024). Global data privacy overview: A Risk-Based Approach for Colleges and Universities. In J. Pollard and K. S. Priebe (Eds.), Convergence of litigation, policy, and standards: Building the informed practitioner in education abroad risk management. The Forum on Education Abroad. doi.org/10.36.366/SIA.5.978-1-952376-41-2.10

Miller, T., & Pollard, J. (2024). Understanding Legal Terms and Process in the Context of Litigation, Liability, and Risks in Education Abroad. In J. Pollard & K. S. Priebe (Eds.), *Convergence of litigation, policy, and standards: Building the informed practitioner in education abroad risk management*. The Forum on Education Abroad. doi.org/10.36.366/ SIA.5.978-1-952376-41-2.2

National Science and Technology Council. (2022). *Guidance for implementing national security presidential memorandum 33 (NSPM-33) on national security strategy for the United States Government-supported research and development. A Report by the Subcommittee on Research Security Joint Committee on the Research Environment*. https://www.whitehouse.gov/wp-content/uploads/2022/01/010422-NSPM-33-Implementation-Guidance. pdf

Priebe, K. S., & Hayes, A. (2024). Lessons from legal cases: Safeguarding student health & well-being in education abroad programs. In J. Pollard & K. S. Priebe (Eds.), *Convergence of litigation, policy, and standards: Building the informed practitioner in education abroad risk management*. The Forum on Education Abroad. doi.org/10.36.366/ SIA.5.978-1-952376-41-2.3

Renaut, B. (2023, March 28) *Duty of Care by definition*. International SOS. https://www.internationalsos.com/insights/what-is-duty-of-care

Rupar, J. (2024). Navigating International Insurance for Global Education In J. Pollard and K. S. Priebe (Eds.), Convergence of litigation, policy, and standards: Building the informed practitioner in education abroad risk management. The Forum on Education Abroad. doi.org/10.36.366/SIA.5.978-1-952376-41-2.33

The Forum on Education Abroad. (2020). *Standards of good practice for education abroad, Sixth edition*. doi.org/10.36366/S.978-1-952376-04-7

# 32

## Operationalizing Duty of Care in Education Abroad Using The Forum Standards

**Kyle Rausch, Ed.D.**

The Forum on Education Abroad is the Standards Development Organization (SDO) for the field of education abroad, as designated by the U.S. Department of Justice and the Federal Trade Commission. This is an important signification in that it promotes legitimacy of the field of education abroad from the perspective of the federal government while recognizing the need for oversight given the impact, scope, and risks commonly found in education abroad programs. Additionally, the Standards can be an asset to international educators seeking to educate and advocate to the diverse constituents involved in international education within their institution or organization. As such, The Forum's *Standards of Good Practice for Education Abroad* are essential for professionals engaged in the work of education abroad.

International educators recognized the need for a set of standards to promote educational, effective, safe, and ethical education abroad programs before the publication of the first edition of The Forum's *Standards of Good Practice* in 2004. In his International Higher Education Consulting blog, David Comp details the history of standards for education abroad, starting with the meeting of the "General Junior Year Committee" under the leadership of the Institute of International Education (IIE) in 1945. The committee renamed the "Council on the Junior Year Abroad," then held annual meetings for several years to "review the various programs and establish policies on recognition, criteria, and academic standards" (Bowman, 1987). In 1967, Edward Durnall published an article discussing the methods he used for program evaluations, which included six of 15 principles developed at a conference on study abroad held at Mt. Holyoke College in 1960 (Comp, 2007). In the early 1980s, NAFSA: Association of International Educators convened the Task Force on Standards and Responsibilities, resulting in the development of a program of self-regulation and the publication of "Principles for International Education Exchange" in 1981, followed by the first edition of a self-study guide in 1983.

These and other early attempts to establish a set of standards and evaluative frameworks for the field are well documented in David Comp and Martha Merritt's chapter appearing in William Hoffa's *A History of U.S. Study Abroad* (2007). However, much of this early work focused on defining and evaluating learning outcomes as opposed to providing standards related to risk management, health, and safety for education abroad. After The Forum on Education Abroad was incorporated in 2002, the Forum surveyed its members, and the development of *standards of good practice* was ranked as the most critical issue for the field (Comp & Merritt, 2007). The Committee on the *Standards of Good Practice* was convened and worked the following two years to produce the first edition of the *Standards of Good Practice for Education Abroad* in 2004, which included a section on health, safety, and security.

Now in the sixth edition, the *Standards* establish guiding principles, provide an administrative framework, and outline best practices for student learning and development. They are intentionally designed with the entire lifecycle of education abroad in mind. Accordingly, aspects related to duty of care are weaved throughout the *Standards*. Table 32.1 outlines the relevant standards relating to aspects of duty of care.

Noteworthy is the use of the word "shall" in each of these standards. This is intentional and stresses their importance and the duty of care that institutions and organizations have in offering education abroad programs. "Shall" indicates the minimum requirements as established by the International Organization for Standardization, an independent, nongovernmental international organization that brings together experts from diverse fields such as IT, health, transportation, food and agriculture, and others to "agree on the best way of doing things" (International Organization for Standardization, n.d.).

Operationalization of the *Standards* can be challenging as practitioners seek to navigate the complex contextual environments in which they conduct their work. What does the implementation of the *Standards* related to duty of care look like in practice? The Forum's *Prompts for Self-Assessment* (2020) offers a comprehensive set of questions to help professionals consider

**Table 32.1.**

| | |
|---|---|
| 5.2.2.2. Each responsible party shall invest in training specific to program needs. | |
| 5.2.4. Each organization shall provide risk management, preparedness, and emergency response measures for all programs and ensure insurance coverage is in place. | |
| 5.2.7. Responsible parties shall provide a safe environment that supports learning for all students. | |
| 6.1.8. Responsible parties shall communicate expectations for conduct and consequences of behaviors to participants | |
| 6.1.9.2. Responsible parties shall communicate to participants the significance of identities including, but not limited to, racial, ethnic, sexual, gender, religious, ability, citizenship or nationality, and socioeconomic status in relation to the program context. | |
| 6.1.10. Responsible parties shall provide students with information related to accessing physical, mental, and emotional health and well-being services. | |
| 6.1.11. Responsible parties shall prepare students to manage their safety by providing resources related to concerns including, but not limited to | physical risks |
| | behavior |
| | property crime |
| | liability and legal issues |
| | sexual misconduct |
| | identity-based discrimination |
| | country-specific recommendations |
| 6.1.12. Recognizing that not all countries have in place the same support and infrastructure as the home institution, responsible parties shall | clearly convey to students the importance of disclosing mental and physical disability status, accommodation, and other specific needs; |
| | work with other responsible parties and students to determine how their needs may be met on the program; and |
| | advise students on the program options if their needs cannot be met. |
| 6.2.6. Responsible parties shall support students as they navigate identities, including race, ethnicity, sexuality, gender, religion, ability, and socioeconomic status in the local context. | |
| 6.2.7. Responsible parties shall support students in accessing physical, mental, and emotional health and well-being services. | |
| 6.2.8. Responsible parties shall support students in managing their safety by providing resources related to concerns, including | physical risks |
| | behavior |
| | property crime |
| | liability and legal issues |
| | sexual misconduct |
| | identity-based discrimination |
| | communication, social media use, and freedom of expression |
| | country-specific recommendations |
| 6.2.9. Responsible parties shall support students with accommodation needs related to disability status and identity and determine how their needs may be met in the program. | |
| 6.3.4. Responsible parties shall provide resources related to student mental and physical well-being related to program participation. | |

gaps and opportunities. However, concrete examples help clarify what this looks like in practice.

The following vignettes are taken from the author's experience and serve as case studies in operationalizing the *Standards*. The examples highlighted are elemental in nature, and strategically so, to demonstrate how critical it is to consider the *Standards* throughout every aspect of education abroad operations. By considering risk, duty of care, and health and safety before participants are abroad, professionals are better positioned to respond when an incident or emergency arises.

## Case Example 1: Using the Standards to Design Enrollment and Application Processes

Initially, the student enrollment process might not seem to have much to do with duty of care in education abroad. However, risk-oriented enrollment and application processes will include several points during which critical elements related to health and safety can be teased out.

When the author arrived at his present institution, the application process was paper-based. In addition to being less efficient from an administrative perspective, this hinders the ability to quickly access participant information relevant to responding to emergencies or crises from virtually anywhere. Consequently, one of the first tasks was to transition the application process to a fully online application. This presented an excellent opportunity to ensure that the application process aligned with the *Standards*. Standard 6.1.12 states, "Recognizing that not all countries have in place the same support and infrastructure as the home institution, responsible parties shall: clearly convey to students the importance of disclosing mental and physical disability status, accommodation, and other specific needs."

To address this, the author created two post-decision online forms: an *Accommodations Request/Disclosure Form* and a *Health and Wellness Questionnaire*. (Note: Post-decision is after a student has been accepted to a program. It is important not to have health and accommodation disclosures part of the eligibility criteria for acceptance to a program.)

The *Accommodations Request/Disclosure Form* invites students to share if they have any accommodation requests and, if so, if they are registered with the campus Disability Resource Center. An affirmative response then asks the students to give the Study Abroad Office permission to request a copy of their letter of accommodation from the Disability Resource Center. Subsequently, Study Abroad Office staff connect with the Disability Resource Center to obtain a copy of the letter and to discuss relevant accommodations for the abroad experience. This information can then be shared with program leaders, program partners, and onsite staff as needed. Provider organizations and host institutions can ask students to provide a copy of their letter of accommodation to discuss reasonable accommodations and needs in relation to the program location and facilities.

The *Health and Wellness Questionnaire* presents students with a set of 21 health and wellness conditions that may have implications for students participating in an education abroad program and asks students a "yes or no" question if they have one or more of the listed conditions. If they do, students are prompted to complete a *Study Abroad Health Evaluation Form* with their physician and return it to the Study Abroad Office. Additionally, a second question invites students to share other important disclosures such as allergies, dietary restrictions, or other accommodations they may require. The "yes or no" question ensures that sensitive health information is not stored in the application database and refers students to a qualified medical professional for advice on managing their condition(s) abroad.

Students are encouraged to visit the campus travel clinic to discuss their program itinerary in relation to local health issues, recommended immunizations and medications, and personal health concerns within the context of their program's location. The travel clinic has access to Travax® reports that provide detailed information about important health and safety information for travelers.

Both the *Accommodations Request/Disclosure Form* and the *Health and Wellness Questionnaire* are intentionally presented to the student *after* they have been accepted to a program. This is important to assure students that any such disclosures have no bearing on their eligibility to participate in a program. By incorporating these into the enrollment process, the office gathers important information that helps in the aim of meeting clause 6.1.12 of the Standards (The Forum on Education Abroad, 2020c), as the Study Abroad Office can then work with campus and onsite partners to coordinate appropriate support for students to promote their success and well-being while abroad. These processes also address aspects of clauses 5.2.4, 5.2.7, 6.1.9.2, 6.2.7, 6.2.9, and 6.2.4 of the *Standards* (The Forum on Education Abroad, 2020c; see Figure 14.1). For more information on the health clearance process, see Chapter 11.2, "Pre-Departure Mental Health Clearance Process," by Vanessa Sterling (2024).

## Case Example 2: Vetting Program Partners' Ability to Meet the Standards

Increasingly, colleges and universities are turning to third-party program providers to assist them with the development, coordination, and oversight of education abroad programs. The Forum defines a program provider as "an institution or organization that offers education abroad program services to students from a variety of institutions. A program provider may be a college or university, a nonprofit organization, a for-profit business, or a consortium" (The Forum on Education Abroad, n.d.). The benefits of such partnerships are numerous with many institutions citing providers' ability to offer health and safety support as critical to their ability to offer education abroad programming. However, this brings up notions of the transferability of duty of care responsibilities. Institutions engaged in such partnerships must still exercise due diligence in ensuring the partners they are working with meet the essential health and safety needs set forth by the *Standards*.

At the author's institution, the Study Abroad Office implemented an online questionnaire for new partners to complete to help the institution meet its due diligence responsibilities in sourcing vendors and partners. The questionnaire, housed in an online survey platform, contains questions designed to capture information related to all the relevant health and safety-focused standards referenced in Figure 14.1, including:

- emergency preparedness and response
- data collection and stewardship
- orientation focused on health, safety, and security
- insurance
- disciplinary and behavioral policies
- onsite support and staffing details
- student housing
- local transportation
- disability accommodations
- reference checks

Prospective partners are asked to share supporting documentation including a written emergency response plan, documents students are asked to sign, and copies of relevant insurance coverage. A careful review of the questionnaire responses and supporting documentation is carried out and significant gaps in duty of care are addressed with the partner. Institutional/organizational risk tolerance, legal, and other compliance factors inform what is considered significant. It is important that institutions do not expect more from partners than they themselves would be able to provide if they run their own programs.

The vetting of third-party providers should also involve other stakeholders. Whereas professionals in the international education office likely have the requisite knowledge of operational, educational, and logistical needs of a partnership, procurement, purchasing, and risk management offices have additional regulatory parameters that need to be considered (The Forum on Education Abroad, 2020c, clauses 4.2.2; 4.2.3; 4.2.4; 5.1.8).

At times, the responses from potential providers may not meet certain expectations, either from the international education office or other stakeholders. When this occurs, it is important to keep The Forum's *Code of Ethics* in mind, which promote partnerships where "business relationships are mutually beneficial and respectful of each other's goals, principles, and values" and "... establish partnerships that are fair, just, and equitable, and are sensitive to power differentials between organizations" (The Forum on Education Abroad, 2020a). Some prospective partners may lack resources or hold different values or expectations about what is necessary to operate a "safe" education abroad program. When this occurs, international education professionals can help broker a compromise, helping to bridge differences in cultural customs, local regulations and realities, and expectations.

Under the present example, there have been instances where providers completed the questionnaire and stated that they did not have a written emergency response protocol. Rather than immediately disregard the potential for collaboration, this presented an opportunity for a conversation to understand the organization's experience and history in managing programs, introduce legal requirements and expectations from the sending institution, and introduce the provider to The Forum on Education Abroad's *Standards of Good Practice* and other resources. This allows both organizations to improve the experience for participants and further professional development. There certainly may be times when a partnership is not feasible. The inclusion of risk management and legal professionals in the vetting process helps international educators understand their institution or organization's risk tolerance threshold and know when a partnership may not be feasible.

In sum, having a documented process for vetting service providers is essential not only in meeting the *Standards* but also in ensuring that institutions are exercising due diligence in their attempt to transfer duty of care to a third party.

## Case Example 3: Using the Standards as an Advocacy Tool

One of the most practical ways of operationalizing the *Standards* is to use them as a tool in your advocacy for support in gaining the resources, attention, and funding you need to do your job effectively and responsibly. Leveraging the fact that The Forum—and by extension, the *Standards*—is endorsed by the

U.S. Department of Justice and the Federal Trade Commission, the Standards' presence in any proposal can provide a foundation rooted in compliance and best practice that is often highly compelling to senior leaders of colleges and universities.

When the author arrived at his present institution, there were no written emergency response protocols, an ineffective international traveler database, and a decentralized decision-making process for travel to high-risk destinations. Understanding that closing these gaps was essential in his ability to send students abroad responsibly, he worked on a proposal rooted in the *Standards* to advocate for purchasing a new system that would help address many of these concerns. Beyond acquiring a new resource that had a relatively high cost, this ignited a cross-campus discussion about risk management for international travel. In turn, this led to a stronger international travel safety policy and greater clarity in procedures and stakeholders for responding to an international travel emergency.

With clause 5.2.4, the proposal included a brief explanation of The Forum on Education Abroad and the *Standards* to clarify to senior institutional leaders that these needs were identified by reviewing best practices for education abroad as determined by external experts. In the author's case, this brief overview proved sufficient in bolstering the argument. It did not require a deeper explanation of specific standards since leadership trusted that the Study Abroad Office was best positioned to know what resources to consult and how to operationalize these plans. Another key aspect of the proposal was the benchmarking of peer and aspirational institutions. By learning how other institutions were managing risk, making health and safety decisions, and responding to emergencies impacting stakeholders traveling abroad, example rubrics and other templates were included in the proposal, giving senior leaders a more concrete idea of what these processes and resources could look like in practice.

The proposal was well received and resulted in the acquisition of new technology that helped close some of the institutional gaps related to health, safety, and risk management for education abroad. It also led to the creation of the institution's first *Standard Operating Procedures for International Emergencies* and partnerships with the institution's Office of Preparedness and Response, Export Controls Compliance Office, and Campus Police. As can be the case with such far-reaching, high-stakes topics such as risk management for international travel, the process has raised more questions and highlighted other gaps that still need to be addressed. However, the relationships and trust-building process have started and should allow these to be addressed in due course.

## Involving Stakeholders

These examples make it evident that there are several stakeholders to engage when operationalizing the *Standards of Good Practice for Education Abroad*. Given the number of areas that education abroad interfaces with at an institution, there are many *responsible parties*. As defined in The Forum's glossary, a responsible party is an "individual responsible for a specific task or program, including, but not limited to advisor, program leader, education abroad director, and risk manager" (The Forum on Education Abroad, n.d.). Other responsible parties at a college or university could include:

- Chief academic officer (i.e., provost)
- Business manager
- General counsel/legal
- Purchasing/contracts office
- Dean of students
- Campus police/public safety office
- Strategic communications office

Each stakeholder will have their own priorities, expectations, and degree of knowledge of or experience with education abroad and international travel. Accordingly, it is incumbent upon international educators to understand each stakeholder's positionality and needs and tailor communication and requests taking them into account. Assuming positive intent and calling colleagues "in" instead of "calling them out" promotes all stakeholders' shared responsibility in the education abroad risk management enterprise. To be sure, the involvement of stakeholders is a long-term endeavor based on the principles of effective relationship management. However, it is essential to a comprehensive risk management strategy. It allows the study abroad office to be positioned as the trusted office on campus for outbound student mobility.

## Conclusion

The *Standards of Good Practice for Education Abroad*, published by The Forum on Education Abroad, provide the field of education abroad with an industry baseline grounded in research, practice, and critical practitioner reflection and discourse. Their scope encompasses every facet of the education abroad experience and provides the field with a common language and a rubric for practitioners to engage in self and peer evaluation. They are especially important to risk management, health, and safety in education abroad, helping institutions and provider organizations to consider and include health and safety practices at every point in the program development and planning process.

Given how comprehensive the *Standards* are and the broad areas of expertise they call upon, multiple stakeholders need to be involved in education abroad management and coordination, many of which have been mentioned in this chapter. The following inventory builds upon this list. Of course, this inventory is not exhaustive and depends upon institutional and organizational context.

- Senior leadership (president, chancellor, CEO, etc.)
- Chief academic officers (provosts, vice presidents of academic affairs)
- Student affairs leadership (deans of students, vice presidents of student affairs)
- Academic leadership (deans, associate deans)
- Resident/onsite directors
- Risk managers
- Legal officers
- Emergency response planners
- Campus police
- Strategic communication professionals
- Education abroad professionals
- Equity, diversity, and inclusion professionals
- Business managers
- Residential life/student housing professionals
- Disability resource professionals
- Campus health professionals
- Purchasing departments (e.g., for insurance)
- Onsite parties (center/campus faculty and staff, homestay families, etc.)

Due to their scope and the number of stakeholders involved, it can be overwhelming for practitioners to determine how to operationalize the *Standards*. Using them as a lens under which you critically examine policies, processes, practices, and procedures can help you uncover blind spots in your duty of care, health, safety, and risk management operations and assist in advocacy to leadership for the resources you need to offer quality programs that promote participant health, wellness, and safety. The *Standards* can also help you to build stronger relationships across organizational silos and invite engagement from stakeholders who traditionally may have been left out of education abroad matters. By developing strong partnerships with stakeholders, you are better prepared for an emergency, elevate the visibility of the education abroad enterprise, and organically cultivate a wider organizational understanding of the many benefits students can gain from an education abroad experience.

For further examples of operationalizing the *Standards of Good Practice*, consult The Forum on Education Abroad's publication, *Putting the Standards of Good Practice into Practice: A Case Study in Standards-Based Education Abroad Program Design and Implementation* (Wick et al., 2023).

## References

Bowman, J. (1987). *Educating American Undergraduates Abroad: The Development of Study Abroad Programs by American Colleges and Universities. Occasional Papers on International Educational Exchange.* Council on International Educational Exchange. https://eric.ed.gov/?id=ED305007

Comp, D. (2007). *Standards of Good Practice in the Field of Education Abroad.* https://ihec-djc.blogspot.com/search?q=standards

Comp, D. (2009). *NAFSA Task Force on Standards and Responsibilities (1980).* https://ihec-djc.blogspot.com/2009/03/nafsa-task-force-on-standards-and.html

Durnall, E. (1967). Study-Abroad Programs: A Critical Survey. *The Journal of Higher Education 38*(8), 450–453.

Hoffa, W. (2007). *A History of U.S. Study Abroad: 1965-Present* (pp. 451–489). Frontiers Journal.

*International Organization for Standardization.* (n.d.). Retrieved January 8, 2024, from https://www.iso.org/home.html

*Responsible Education Abroad: Best Practices for Health, Safety, and Security* (pp. 2–9). (2021). NAFSA. https://www.nafsa.org/professional-resources/browse-by-interest/responsible-study-abroad-good-practices-health-and-safety

Sterling, V. (2024). 25. Pre-Departure Mental Health Clearance: One Approach to Managing Risk Abroad. In J. Pollard & K. S. Priebe (Eds.), *Convergence of litigation, policy, and standards: Building the informed practitioner in education abroad risk management.* The Forum on Education Abroad. doi.org/10.36.366/SIA.5.978-1-952376-41-2.25

The Forum on Education Abroad. (2020a). *Code of Ethics for Education Abroad.* The Forum on Education Abroad. doi.org/10.36366/G.978-1-952376-08-5

The Forum on Education Abroad. (2020b). *Meeting the Standards of Good Practice for Education Abroad: Prompts for Self-Assessment.* The Forum on Education Abroad. doi.org/10.36366/S.978-1-952376-05-4

The Forum on Education Abroad. (2020c). *Standards of Good Practice for Education Abroad.* The Forum on Education Abroad. doi.org/10.36366/S.978-1-952376-04-7

The Forum on Education Abroad. *Glossary.* (n.d.). Retrieved January 8, 2024, from https://www.forumea.org/glossary.html

Wick, D., Dietrich, A., Lombardi, M., van der Horst, S., & Brostuen, K. (2023). *Putting the Standards of Good Practice into Practice: A Case Study in Standards-Based Education Abroad Program Design and Implementation.* The Forum on Education Abroad. doi.org/10.36.366/R.PTSOGPIP12142023

# 33

## Navigating International Insurance for Global Education

**Joan Rupar**

The *Standards of Good Practice for Education Abroad* stipulate that insurance is one of the critical components of a successful and sustainable international program (The Forum on Education Abroad, 2020, clause 5.2.4).

Institutions have a Duty of Care for all travelers. [See Chapter 1, "Understanding legal terms and process in the context of litigation, liability, and risks in education abroad," by Terence Miller and Julie Pollard (2024) for a detailed discussion of duty of care.] Therefore, travel insurance that provides access to quality healthcare services abroad is critical for university-affiliated international travel. The resources available through a robust insurance package are critical to help travelers in the event of an emergency and they can mitigate liability. Regardless of the type of programming offered, short-term, long-term, or with third-party education abroad program providers, your institution could be at risk for a liability claim. In the event of an incident, everyone involved will be drawn into accountability and liability assessed. This makes the coverage even more important to secure properly.

When education abroad professionals think about insurance, International Travel Accident & Sickness Insurance is often given the most consideration. In addition to this essential coverage, there are other coverages purchased by institutions that help protect the assets of the institution. This chapter will discuss the essentials of worldwide coverage and international travel insurance and provide you with an overview of additional coverage for your institution or organization and important points to consider, including when locally admitted coverage is required, and complex claims requiring engaging multiple policies to fulfill a single claim.

## Oversight of Insurance Regulators

The oversight of insurance bodies in higher education is primarily managed by state regulatory authorities as insurance lines are governed by state agencies. The individual State Insurance departments ensure that insurance providers adhere to specific regulations and standards within their respective states. Since state laws and requirements can vary significantly, insurance providers must comply with different sets of rules depending on the states in which they operate. This state-specific oversight helps maintain the integrity and stability of the insurance market within the higher education sector.

## Key Terms

To understand international insurance, it is important to familiarize yourself with key terms and concepts that differ from domestic coverage. Foreign Packages, coverage designed for U.S.-based organizations operating abroad (Crowe & Paul, 2020), will generally use standard wording for coverage providing excess/Difference in Conditions (DIC) terms that can respond to claims or sit in addition to locally issued coverage. This coverage can also satisfy the requirements of primary coverage for U.S.-issued Excess Liability Policies.

- Nonadmitted—Insurance that is placed from the United States to cover occurrences in another country. Many countries do not permit this cover and in the event of a claim, coverage will indemnify (reimburse) the policy holder versus paying on behalf in country.
- Jurisdiction—The territory where claims/suits will be accepted. This can differ from the coverage territory by only accepting suits within specific countries' borders and not extend to a U.S. suit/claim.
- Public Liability/Civil Liability—Terms often used for what the U.S. market refers to as General Liability. This is commonly requested when proof of coverage is requested in many countries.
- The "coverage territory" can be defined as worldwide for occurrences anywhere in the world, excluding the United States and its territories, and possessions for claims brought anywhere. An exception to this would be countries subject to Trade or Economic Sanctions.

- Controlled Master Policy—Local policy endorsed to a foreign package creating a Controlled Master Program. This structure provides ease of administration, premium payment, taxes, policy issuance, and claim coordination.

For a list of key insurance terms related to education abroad, see the NAFSA resource, International Health Insurance for Study Abroad (Priebe & Smallwood, 2024).

## Worldwide Coverage

There are very important coverages typically purchased by higher education institutions to address international exposures as part of a robust Foreign Package. The lines of coverage generally include General Liability, Automobile, Foreign Voluntary Compensation, and Travel Accident & Sickness Insurance. The coverage applies worldwide, but not for an occurrence within the United States, its territories, or possessions.

Domestic Liability Policies can often have a worldwide coverage territory but stipulate that the claim or suit must be submitted in the United States. This presents a gap of coverage should someone in another country file a claim or suit because the domestic coverage would not respond.

Domestic Workers Compensation benefits vary by state but will offer extraterritorial benefits for temporary travel outside of the United States (Boggs, 2021). Each state will provide this extension of coverage for a defined period of days, usually 180 days. Coverage is rarely provided for endemic disease, medical evacuation, or repatriation of remains. While these issues can be covered by a Travel Accident policy, the faculty/staff would be entitled to receive any lost wages or disability payments.

## International Travel Accident & Sickness Insurance

International Travel Accident & Sickness, sometimes called Travel Accident coverage, is a critical coverage for anyone traveling outside of the United States or away from their home country. This is not to be confused with in-country or major medical coverage, which is intended to provide comprehensive coverage. Travel Accident coverage is temporary and is intended to address emergent health issues or those issues related to an accidental injury during sponsored travel, in accordance with the organization's policy detail. This coverage is essential for education abroad participants because most U.S. health plans have limited or no coverage abroad.

When you think about students traveling and emergent health issues, your duty of care is a delicate balance of providing access to healthcare and mental health providers on a timely basis, appropriate confidential care and treatment, and a program that can pay on behalf of travelers.

Institutions must define what constitutes university-affiliated travel and determine who should be covered by the Travel Accident policy. See Chapter 30, "Who Can Go Where for What Purposes and Under What Conditions: Building an Institutional International Travel Policy," by Shaun Jamieson and Patrick Morgan (2024) for more information on this topic.

Coverage should be structured to meet the specific needs of your institution.

- A "blanket" program ensures all travelers are covered without individual enrollment. Classes of Covered Persons identify eligible persons and can include students, faculty/staff, spouses, dependents, or guests.
- An "enrollment" program only covers travelers who enroll and pay prior to travel.

Plan coverage should include:

- Out-of-Country Inpatient and Outpatient Medical coverage
- Affirmative coverage for Mental Health
- Treatment of Preexisting Conditions
- Prescriptions
- Emergency Medical Evacuation Accidental Death & Dismemberment coverage
- Repatriation of Remains

Institutions can request to include additional coverage and specific services as part of the negotiation process. Common coverages recommended for inclusion (Priebe & Smallwood, 2024) are:

- Routine or Emergency Dental Treatment
- Maternity and Abortion Care (depending on state law)
- Ambulance Services
- Emergency Assistance Services
- Emergency Family Travel Benefit/Bedside Care(to cover travel expenses associated with visiting insured in hospital)
- Evacuation services for political emergencies or natural disasters (commonly referred to as PEND)

Understanding exclusions in international travel accident and sickness insurance policies is crucial for education abroad professionals to provide accurate guidance and support to students studying abroad. Common exclusions in travel accident policies include coverage for routine medical care (including pre-existing conditions) and dental care that might be covered under a different policy, risky behaviors such as extreme sports or dangerous activities, losses under the influence of alcohol or drugs, and losses caused by intentional self-harm (Centers for Disease Control and Prevention, 2023). By being aware of these exclusions, education abroad professionals can advocate for insurance plans that provide sufficient coverage for potential risks students may encounter during their time abroad and manage students' expectations and assist students in making informed decisions about additional coverage (that they may need personally) or safety precautions while abroad. Coverage features included in the plan design can include Trip Cancellation, Trip Interruption, and Trip Delay, referred to as Travel Inconvenience benefits. Other supporting coverage features can be added, such as coverage for lost luggage or assistance with lost documents, and personal liability.

It is advisable that higher education institutions ensure their insurance program offers direct billing as a service so that payments for services rendered will be paid directly to the treating facility or physician on behalf of the student. This eliminates the need for students to pay out-of-pocket for their healthcare needs and may increase the likelihood a student will seek care when needed. When payment must be made at the time of treatment, the responsibility to file a claim for reimbursement lies with the traveler. This is due exclusively to the health "Privacy Rule" (Office for Civil Rights, 2022).

## Security Assistance Providers

Institutions may also align their insurance program with a security assistance provider. Security assistance providers are critical partners in fulfilling your Duty of Care by providing medical and security information and assistance to all travelers. The relationship to your institution can exist in different forms. Some are embedded in the insurance coverage and are recognized as the authorized responder. Others are contracted separately at a separate cost and assistance and arrangements are not necessarily covered by insurance. Furthermore, some will assess case fees that can be 15% of the cost of the services rendered.

Many insurance providers and assistance providers will provide pre-trip medical and security information to travelers. This information can allow a traveler to begin their trip understanding what to expect, if their medication is legal in their destination, and if it can easily be replaced if needed. (For more information on medications abroad, see Chapter 14, "Traveling Abroad with Medication," by Christine Sprovieri and Jennifer Fullick (2024).

It is important to thoroughly assess the services offered by assistance providers and carefully review policy terms. Significant actions like evacuations often require prior approval from the assistance provider for coverage.

If procuring an independent assistance provider, a number of capabilities should be considered.

- Capacity and expertise in your institution's most common travel destinations
- Alignment with Travel Accident & Sickness Insurers
  - Guarantee of Payment Capability
  - Confirmation of Coverage with your insurer
  - Direct Billing Agreements with the insurer
- Case Fee Schedule
- Access to any Local National Employees/Staff

Care should be given to your access to country health, safety, and security information prior to travel. Once traveling, it is important to understand the scope of services available and that may come at an additional cost to the institution. Important considerations include the interaction with the travel assistance provider as well as the course of treatment approval authority. Without this step, there is a possibility that some portions of the response may not be covered by the insurance policy.

### Cancel For Any Reason Coverage

As the world emerged from the pandemic in 2021, travelers were anxious to travel for fear of losing thousands of dollars should travel be canceled or delayed. New coverage was introduced called Cancel For Any Reason (CFAR) (Evans, 2024). The coverage provided some peace of mind that should a condition occur that required a trip to be canceled, there was somewhat of a financial remedy. There was also the reintroduction and improvement of Quarantine coverage as the requirement to isolate caused financial hardship for many.

Medical facilities globally were treating travelers for COVID-19 but were often left with debt (Kaye, et al., 2021). While there could be proof of insurance provided, many smaller medical facilities did not have the operations staff to invoice and chase payments. As a result, many more medical facilities will not treat without an actionable guarantee of payment or cash prior to treatment.

## General Liability

General Liability coverage provides institutions and organizations protection in the event of property damage or bodily injury to another person, entity, or property. The coverage territory of the policy will respond to a foreign occurrence and typically to a suit brought anywhere. Defense costs are in addition to the policy limits.

Some carriers will exclude any suits brought in the United States, which can create a gap in coverage. Exclusions that can often be included and should be challenged for removal include U.S. Suits Exclusion, Injury to Participants Exclusion, Communicable Disease Exclusion, and Terrorism Exclusions. These exclusions would create gaps in important coverage that cannot be otherwise addressed.

Standard limits provided by carriers in the United States are $1 million per occurrence/$2 million aggregate. Institutions typically carry excess limits of liability that apply to their exposures globally. Limits carried by international-based institutions, providers, and vendors will vary by country. This should be taken into consideration when drafting insurance requirements in any contracts issued.

Certificates of Insurance received should also advise the jurisdiction of coverage. This will tell you if the coverage needed crosses borders if a claim or suit is filed in the United States or another country.

It is best practice to review all exclusions and limitations to the coverage. Proof of coverage received from partners or vendors should be carefully reviewed as many locally issued policies will have coverage that will not respond to claims or suits that cross any border. This means, if a provider is negligent and the traveler returns home and files suit, the coverage will not apply.

## Contingent Automobile

Whenever you rent a vehicle, you must purchase the liability coverage from the rental company. This automobile coverage is local statutory (required) coverage that will satisfy the local law in almost every country. There can be terms, conditions, and exclusions in that local coverage not found in U.S. coverage, thus it is advisable to review the terms carefully.

Examples of common exclusions found internationally include drivers under a certain age or driving while legally intoxicated according to the local law limits. When conditions are such that these exclusions apply, coverage can come into play from the Foreign Package, Contingent Automobile liability coverage. The Foreign Package Automobile Coverage is Excess and Difference-in-Conditions insurance, which "provides additional limits of coverage for specific perils when standard markets won't provide adequate limits, adds coverage for perils that are excluded on standard coverage forms, or supplements international policies written by admitted insurers in the applicable foreign countries" (International Risk Management Institute, n.d.).Generally, coverage will respond with a U.S. $1 million limit. Coverage for Physical Damage is also available on a Foreign Package versus a costly addition to the locally issued policy. Some examples of enhanced coverage include access to Emergency Assistance, Legal Assistance, and Bail Bond coverage. These are generally extensions that are required in the event of an accident.

### Workers Compensation

Domestic Workers Compensation (required for all U.S. employees) will provide coverage for "employees" who are outside of the United States for a temporary period of time. The Foreign Package will provide Foreign Voluntary Compensation that will extend the State of Hire Benefits but also include coverage for endemic diseases that is not addressed fully by domestic Workers Compensation. The Foreign Voluntary Workers Comp also brings in coverage for Medical Evacuations as well as Repatriation of remains.

It is important to make certain that the correct coverage is identified when an injury or illness occurs. If an "employee" (faculty member or staff) is injured during sponsored travel, they are entitled to coverage and benefits such as medical payments, disability, and lost wages. Addressing a Travel policy only satisfies part of the financial impact on the traveler. Payment for medical care is one component. If the traveler has continued care and lost wages, that may also be a consideration for coverage.

### "Locally Admitted" Coverage

The consideration to purchase locally admitted coverage in a country can be complicated. It can often be difficult and unnecessary to purchase local coverage if you are not a registered business entity, have a tax identification number, have a local address, or hire local staff. There will be lines of coverage that are best practice to carry, such as local Public Liability or Employers Liability, and others that are required/compulsory to purchase. You should discuss this with your insurance broker or underwriter.

When your institution has a fixed location, is a registered entity, has or hired local staff, consult your insurance broker. Commercial General Liability/Public Liability is almost always available and should always be secured.

Always buy in-country the local automobile coverage for owned or rental vehicles as it is generally compulsory and there is no substitute.

Workers Compensation can sometimes be part of a social scheme that is arranged through payroll tax contributions. This coverage is sometimes insufficient and local law may require you purchase Employers Liability protection. This coverage is to ensure that if the local scheme does not make the injured employee whole, there will be coverage if an employee files suit.

Property coverage should be procured if your institution or organization has property in a country. It can be valuable in the event of a claim as a carrier can then pay that claim to you, in country. If U.S. coverage is used to cover an international location, a claim payment would be made in the United States. Transferring those funds back to the international location may be taxed as income tax. Research this issue carefully.

## A Complex Claim Requiring Multiple Policies

Claims that occur outside of the United States can be much more complex as opposed to on campus in the United States. Factors for consideration include the legal environment, liability to the institution, appropriateness of care, reputation issues, communication with campus and families, tax implications, privacy concerns, and country customary practices.

An event resulting in property damage or bodily injury may require the use of coverage and resources from multiple policies and sources. A car accident is a good way to illustrate the policies that could come into play. It is also one of the most common events that can involve multiple policies. A car accident may involve:

- The local automobile coverage that was purchased with the rental
- The Foreign Package Excess/Difference in Conditions coverage for additional limits
- Travel Accident coverage for medical payments, legal assistance, bail bonds, family travel

Depending upon the severity, the local law will apply and the driver at fault may be detained or expelled from the country immediately. The legal system of that country applies, and variances in legal systems, cultural norms, and privacy regulations can all have a significant impact on how a claim is handled.

When a claim occurs, significant coverage and resources will be needed to manage the claim. Consider the needs of traveler, medical, security, counseling, legal representation, emergency medical response, collaboration with authorities, and even translation assistance.

Ask yourself, what is needed to fulfill your Duty of Care. Carefully review the coverage in your institution's portfolio and access resources accordingly.

## Request for Proposals (RFP) and Renewals

Institutions will typically start to discuss renewal options 120+ days prior to core renewals. As the time approaches to renew your insurance package, education abroad professionals should reach out to Insurance and Risk Management or Finance to discuss the performance of the coverage currently in place. Coverage and resources are put in place to facilitate the student success and growth of those programs. If the coverage is not meeting the needs of your students, it is important to provide feedback and engage as appropriate for your institution.

Many institutions will go through a broker selection process at a timing defined by procurement. This may include an RFP process, where your institution will provide details about the specific insurance requirements, and which will guide potential insurance providers in preparing their proposal. This is another area where you can contribute some ideas on required services and questions to help identify broker candidates who have expertise in international programs and awareness of common education abroad challenges. Refer to the NAFSA resource on International Health Insurance for Study Abroad for a list of key points to include in an RFP (Priebe & Smallwood, 2024).

Responding brokers with this experience will be happy to share their expertise and value in the market. It should be a consideration to ensure the broker is a valued contributor, understands the challenges of the program, and understands how successful programs are built. International insurance can be complicated. You will need a partner who can help navigate the nuances.

In conclusion, insurance plays a crucial role in ensuring the success and sustainability of international education programs. The *Standards of Good Practice for Education Abroad* emphasize the importance of insurance as a critical component of a comprehensive risk management strategy. Travel insurance, particularly International Travel Accident & Sickness Insurance, is essential for providing access to healthcare services abroad and mitigating liability risks for university-affiliated travel.

Institutions have a duty of care for all travelers, which includes providing access to healthcare services, managing liability risks, and ensuring appropriate coverage for emergent health issues or accidental injuries. Robust insurance packages not only provide financial protection but also contribute to fulfilling this duty of care by offering support services such as security assistance and pre-trip medical information.

Key considerations in structuring insurance coverage include defining university-affiliated travel, determining eligible persons for coverage, and negotiating additional services and specific coverage terms. Institutions should also be aware of jurisdictional differences, exclusions, and limitations in international insurance policies to adequately address potential risks and ensure sufficient coverage for students and faculty abroad.

Furthermore, institutions should engage in proactive management of insurance programs through regular review, renewal discussions, and collaboration with insurance providers and brokers. By actively assessing and addressing the evolving needs and challenges of education abroad programs, institutions can enhance the effectiveness of their insurance strategies and support the success and well-being of their students participating in and faculty leading global learning experiences.

# References

Boggs, C. (2021, October 18). *WC extraterritorial/reciprocity statutes by state*. Independent Insurance Agents & Brokers of America. https://www.independentagent.com/vu/SiteAssets/Reference%20Lists/WC-Extra-Recip-Statutes-by-State.pdf

Centers for Disease Control and Prevention. (2023, May 1). Travel Insurance, Travel Health Insurance & Medical Evacuation Insurance. Traveler's Health. https://wwwnc.cdc.gov/travel/yellowbook/2024/health-care-abroad/insurance

Crowe, K., & Paul, N. (2020, February 3). *Covering risks abroad with foreign package insurance*. Risk Management. https://www.rmmagazine.com/articles/article/2020/02/03/-Covering-Risks-Abroad-with-Foreign-Package-Insurance-#:~:text=Often%20sold%20as%20a%20bundle,are%20in%20the%20United%20States

Evans, M. (2024, April 9). *What is Cancel for Any Reason (CFAR) Insurance?* Investopedia. https://www.investopedia.com/what-is-cancel-for-any-reason-cfar-insurance-8599192

International Risk Management Institute (IRMI). (n.d.). Difference-in-conditions. In IRMI Glossary. Retrieved April 20, 2023, from https://www.irmi.com/term/insurance-definitions/difference-in-conditions-insurance

Kaye, A. D., Okeagu, C. N., Pham, A. D., Silva, R. A., Hurley, J. J., Arron, B. L., Sarfraz, N., Lee, H. N., Ghali, G. E., Gamble, J. W., Liu, H., Urman, R. D., & Cornett, E. M. (2021). Economic impact of COVID-19 pandemic on healthcare facilities and systems: International perspectives. *Best practice & research. Clinical anaesthesiology, 35*(3), 293–306. https://doi.org/10.1016/j.bpa.2020.11.009

Miller, T., & Pollard, J. (2024). Understanding legal terms and process in the context of litigation, liability, and risks in education abroad. In J. Pollard & K. S. Priebe (Eds.), *Convergence of litigation, policy, and standards: Building the informed practitioner in education abroad risk management*. The Forum on Education Abroad.

Office for Civil Rights (OCR). (2022, October 19). *Summary of the HIPAA privacy rule.* Health Information Privacy. https://www.hhs.gov/hipaa/for-professionals/privacy/laws-regulations/index.html

Priebe, K. S., & Smallwood, D. (2024). *International health insurance for study abroad.* NAFSA. https://www.nafsa.org/professional-resources/browse-by-interest/international-health-insurance-study-abroad

Sprovieri, C., & Fullick, J. (2024). Traveling Abroad with Medication. In J. Pollard & K. S. Priebe (Eds.), *Convergence of litigation, policy, and standards: Building the informed practitioner in education abroad risk management.* The Forum on Education Abroad.

The Forum on Education Abroad. (2020). *Standards of Good Practice for Education Abroad.* The Forum on Education Abroad. doi.org/10.36366/S.978-1-952376-04-7

# 34

---

# History and Usage of Two Critical U.S. Department of State Travel Resources by the Education Abroad Community

Julie Anne Friend, J.D.

## Introduction

While the U.S. Department of State (DOS) offers many services and resources to both incoming and outgoing travelers, the two most used by education abroad professionals are provided by the Bureau of Consular Affairs (BCA). Pre-departure, the U.S. DOS Travel Advisory system is used primarily as an educational and assessment tool. Country-specific travel advisories provide detailed information about a variety of risks in destinations other than the United States and are written in a manner accessible to students as well as faculty and staff. Once abroad, should a traveler face difficulty or need more timely information or support, each U.S. embassy or consulate houses the office of U.S. Citizen Services. The focus of this office is to support U.S. citizens onsite, whether it be a routine matter or an emergency.

This chapter addresses how the education abroad community uses these services. The first part will discuss the evolution of the U.S. DOS's travel advisory system, the impact of the four-tiered ratings on higher education travel policy development, and what this "new" system means for higher education in the future (The Forum on Education Abroad, 2020, clause 5.1.7). The second part will discuss the most common services useful to the education abroad community and how to access them as well as what the U.S. government cannot do for its citizens abroad (The Forum on Education Abroad, 2020, clause 5.2.4).

## Part One: The U.S. DOS Travel Advisory System

In 2018, the U.S. DOS did something that the education abroad community had been wanting for decades: they overhauled their system for providing health and safety advice to travelers (Morello, 2018). The "new" four-tiered ranking (Figure 34.1) with nine risk indicators (Figure 3, p. 8) and region-specific advice—along with some helpful explanatory graphics—offered a more nuanced approach to risk assessment (Friend et al., 2018; U.S. Department of State, n.d. b). Although the new system forced many, if not most, colleges and universities, as well as corporations and NGOs, to revise their international travel policies, the outcome was clearly positive.

## Background (1978–1992)

Long-time education abroad administrators may remember that in 1978 the U.S. DOS began rolling out advice to travelers with Notices, Cautions, Public

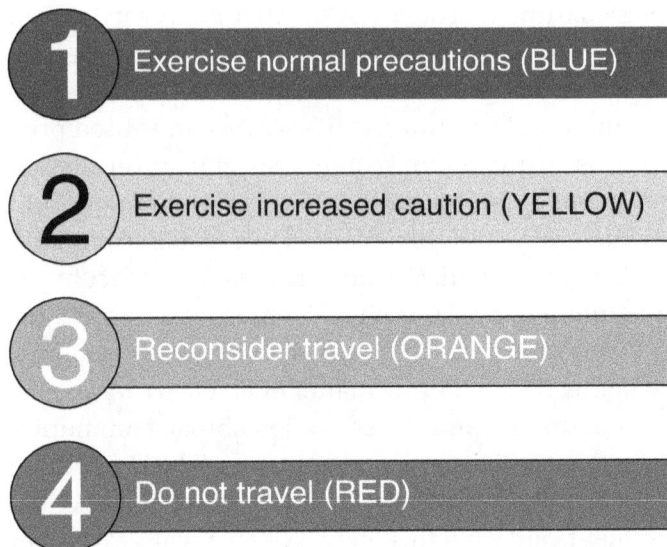

1 Exercise normal precautions (BLUE)

2 Exercise increased caution (YELLOW)

3 Reconsider travel (ORANGE)

4 Do not travel (RED)

**Figure 34.1.** Color-Coded Risk Assessment

Announcements, and Warnings, which were primarily issued to airlines, travel agencies, and passport processing centers to share with clients (Friend, 2010). "For example, in December 1988, the Federal Aviation Authority issued a security bulletin regarding an anonymous but credible, threat to a Pan Am flight out of Frankfurt, Germany" (Friend, 2010, p.3). The information was not distributed to the public. Instead, the Department of State notified several U.S. embassies (Friend, 2010). "On December 21, 1988, Pan Am Flight 103 exploded over Lockerbie, Scotland, killing 259 passengers and crew on board, as well as 11 people on the ground" (Friend, 2010, p. 3; Pan Am 103, 2023).

In 1990, Congress passed the Aviation Security Improvement Act, resulting in the "No Double Standard Policy" (Gilbert, 2023; U.S. Department of State, 2023c). "Under this Policy, any security threat to U.S. citizens that is deemed specific, credible, and non-counterable was to be disseminated to the public via various consular information program documents, including Travel Warnings, Travel Alerts, Country Specific Information [Sheets], and Warden Messages" (Friend, 2010, p. 3; U.S. Department of State, 2023c). "Sources for these consular documents included information from local law enforcement, local media, the intelligence community, and embassy staff as well as a country's own intelligence agency or other similar foreign government agencies ..." (Friend, 2010, p.3; U.S. Department of State, 2023c).

"In 1992, these documents were regrouped into three categories: Warden Messages, Public Announcements, and Travel Warnings" (Friend, 2010, p. 3). One year later, the World Wide Web was introduced to the world, vastly expanding the public's access to information. The Internet Archive Wayback Machine suggests that the DOS began posting Travel Warnings on a website as early as 1994, although most data is circa 1996 and later (Larsen, 2016). It is unclear when colleagues and universities began routinely consulting the DOS's website for travel advice, but the September 11, 2001, attacks influenced higher education's approach to travel risk management. Incident response preparedness, particularly large-scale terror attacks, and the need to know where students were located, even during their free time, became commonplace conference presentation topics (Larsen, 2023).

## Education Abroad's Historical Conflict with the DOS (2007–2018)

By 2007, Public Announcements were renamed "Travel Alerts" and remain in place today. They describe temporary threats or disruptions related to elections, sporting events, civil unrest, outbreaks of disease, or serious impacts of a natural disaster. While informative and useful, given the time-limited impact, Travel Alerts did not have a significant influence on institutional travel decisions. However, many colleges and universities did pay close attention to Travel Warnings, which were often linked to institutional travel policies. By definition, Travel Warnings were assigned to countries with "long-term, systemic, dangerous conditions tied to political, social, economic, or environmental conditions" (Friend, 2010, p. 1). The DOS also asserted that, "in some locations, the U.S. government's ability to assist travelers in distress mat be severely limited due to internal or external travel restrictions" (citation needed, year, p. X). The severity of this description raised concerns for higher education, especially those with limited budgets for private evacuation services. While some Warnings attempted a level of nuance by highlighting region-specific risks (such as the Mindanao region of the Philippines), the overarching message of "do not travel" spoke loudly to university risk managers and campus counsel as well as university presidents and provosts. In other words, many administrators found difficulty in justifying travel to a location where the federal government was telling its citizens not to go.

Most education abroad administrators did not find the DOS's approach very useful at the time. On the one hand, the Travel Warning list was long and, in the eyes of seasoned administrators, too varied for the black and white approach to travel that university leadership preferred. On the other hand, it was useful to have a readily and publicly available source of travel risk information, and inflexible blanket policies (Travel Warning = no travel) made decision-making simple and kept insurance premiums low. When evacuation or general liability insurance policies excluded coverage to Travel Warning countries, it was convenient to defer blame on related travel prohibitions to insurance providers and underwriters. Yet the same travel policies that prohibited university-affiliated travel to any country with a Travel Warning ruled out both Afghanistan (which seemed reasonable to most or all) as well as Israel and Mexico (which seemed unreasonable, at least to some). While not risk-free, significant parts of Mexico and Israel were not only safe, but engagement with these areas was important to many schools' efforts to internationalize curricula. A range of people from national security experts to the layperson international news junkie will assert that the DOS Travel Warnings or other classifications are "political" at least in some cases, insisting that they either reflect our government's displeasure with a country's leadership or aim to influence a country's stance on an area of active diplomacy. Understandably, no U.S. DOS employee will ever confirm or deny this assertion, which therefore made it difficult for study abroad administrators or faculty-led program personnel to advocate travel to certain Travel Warning destinations over others given the lack of evidence that the ranking was based on issues other than health or safety.

As a result, many schools developed complicated review processes that often involved a committee of high-ranking administrators following a rubric or other evaluation criteria to review a written appeal by the traveler or staff/ faculty member leading a group trip. The appeal generally described applicable risk sand mitigation strategies as well as the experience of a trip leader or onsite support staff. While the makeup of review committees varied, some common elements included representation from the President or Provost's office; general counsel; risk management/insurance; health services/counseling center; education abroad; and the faculty senate (Friend, 2010). Ad hoc members, such as area studies faculty members, onsite organizational staff, or security/intelligence experts from public entities, such as the U.S. DOS, or private security assistance providers were sometimes included to provide destination-specific briefings. Some institutions also required the petitioner to give an in-person presentation to the review committee, which resulted in scheduling headaches. Petitioners were sometimes also required to submit letters of endorsement from the sponsoring academic department though they were not always easy to obtain. Requiring wet signatures on hardcopy waivers or releases from students was even more challenging. Resigned resentment of the "bureaucracy" by all involved in the process, especially petitioners with experience traveling to the destination, created open hostility to these procedures and soured working relationships between faculty, education abroad administrators, and senior leadership.

## The "New" Ratings Defined and Described (2018)

On January 10, 2018, the new color-coded, numerical rating system of Travel Advisories was introduced and exists to date (Morello, 2018). Seeking to provide guidance to international educators, The Forum on Education Abroad published an explanation and guidance for the field less than a month later (cite this publication); it contains the best historical example of how Travel Warning countries were initially ranked under the new system (Friend et al., 2018).

Since 2018, world events have increased travel risks—the COVID pandemic, war in Ukraine, war in Israel and Gaza, financial disruption, climate-related natural disasters, and several coup d'états across Africa, to name just a few. But by 2023, college and university travel were essentially "back to normal" (Carrasco, 2022; O'Driscoll, 2022). Today, 211 countries and territories are referenced in this "new" system, and the DOS webpage is updated nearly every day (U.S. Department of State, n.d. b). Most destinations are given an overall rating from 1 to 4, with 4 denoting the highest level of risk. Approximately 79% of countries and territories are assigned a 1 or 2 ranking (U.S. Department of State, n.d b). The following descriptors are taken from the DOS website site and include country examples current at the time of printing (U.S. Department of State, n.d. b).

- *Level 1—Exercise Normal Precautions*: "This is the lowest advisory level for safety and security risk. There is some risk in any international travel. Conditions in other countries may differ from those in the United States and may change at any time."
- *Level 2—Exercise Increased Caution*: "Be aware of heightened risks to safety and security. The State Department provides additional advice for travelers in these areas in the Travel Advisory. Conditions in any country may change at any time."
- *Level 3—Reconsider Travel*: "Avoid travel due to serious risks to safety and security. The Department of State provides additional advice for travelers in these areas in the Travel Advisory. Conditions in any country may change at any time."
- *Level 4—Do Not Travel*: "This is the highest advisory level due to greater likelihood of life-threatening risks. During an emergency, the U.S. government may have very limited ability to provide assistance. The Department of State advises that U.S. citizens not travel to the country or to leave as soon as it is safe to do so. The Department of State provides additional advice for travelers in these areas in the Travel Advisory. Conditions in any country may change at any time."

## Risk Indicators Deemed Useful/Informative

In 2018, the advisories included seven of the now nine risk indicators (see Figure 34.2). The newest risk indicators, *K—Kidnapping or Hostage Taking and D—Wrongful Detention,* were added in 2019 (Overseas Security Advisory Council, 2018). The risk indicators are designed to call the reader's attention to issues of concern immediately and provide specific advice in an organized fashion. The appearance of the risk indicator in the top right corner of an advisory is eye-catching and probably more likely to draw the attention of a student's quick review. Furthermore, such topic-specific details are particularly useful in vetting an itinerary or travel permission request that might expose a traveler to a specific harm. Education abroad professionals tasked with travel risk assessment are pleased with this addition because they offer insight into what might have motivated the overall rating, and allows for a more targeted review of applicable risks (K. Trivedi, personal communication, August 29, 2023; J. Molyneux, personal communication, September 1, 2023).

Travel Advisories at Levels 2-4 contain clear reasons for the level assigned, using established risk indicators and specific advice to U.S. citizens who choose to travel there. These are:

- C – Crime: Widespread violent or organized crime is present in areas of the country. Local law enforcement may have limited ability to respond to serious crimes.
- T – Terrorism: Terrorist attacks have occurred and/or specifi5c threats against civilians, groups, or other targets may exist.
- U – Civil Unrest: Political, economic, religious, and/or ethnic instability exists and may cause violence, major disruptions, and/or safety risks.
- H – Health: Health risks, including current disease outbreaks or a crisis that disrupts a country's medical infrastructure, are present. The issuance of a Centers for Disease Control Travel Notice may also be a factor.
- N – Natural Disaster: A natural disaster, or its aftermath, poses danger.
- E – Time-limited Event: Short-term event, such as elections, sporting events, or other incidents that may pose safety risks.
- K – Kidnapping or Hostage Taking: Criminal or terrorist individuals or groups have threatened to and/or have seized or detained and threatened to kill, injure, or continue to detain individuals in order to compel a third party (including a governmental organization) to do or abstain from doing something as a condition of release.
- D – Wrongful Detention: The risk of wrongful detention of U.S. nationals by a foreign government exists.
- O – Other: There are potential risks not covered by previous risk indicators. Read the country's Travel Advisory for details.

Source: https://travel.state.gov/content/travel/en/international-travel/before-you-go/about-our-new-products.html

**Figure 34.2.** U.S. DOS Travel Advisory Risk Indicators

## University Travel Polices Are Reviewed, Revised, and Renewed

The level of risk that an institution or organization is willing to accept is a business decision unique to that organization (Friend, 2010; Jamieson & Morgan, 2024; Snyman et al., 2024). Most large institutions with complicated and diverse travel profiles have long engaged third-party intelligence assistance providers, such as Control Risks, Crisis24, Global Rescue, or International SOS, to avail themselves of additional resources and services for an annual fee. Such colleges and universities may tie their travel policies to a third-party provider's ratings system or combine various sources to develop a customized restricted travel list.

Smaller schools, or those with more routine travel profiles, may engage with such companies on a more limited basis or rely solely on free, open-source resources, such as the U.S. Department of State's Overseas Security Advisory Council (OSAC). Yet many colleges and universities may not be aware of the free resources and services available to them from OSAC, which is a division of the Bureau of Diplomatic Security in the U.S. Department of State. Its mission is to provide security and risk information to American businesses, institutions of higher education, faith-based organizations, and nongovernmental organizations abroad. Membership is organization-based. Any member organization, such as an institution of higher education, can have an unlimited number of constituent users under a point-of-contact (POC), who manages the organization's relationship with OSAC. OSAC resources and services are free, but some information on their website is password protected for registered users. A commonly used resource in higher education is OSAC's Daily Newsletter that comprises a comprehensive source of world news, alerts, events, and OSAC analytical products on timely issues, such as large-scale sporting events, country-wide elections, the impact of a natural disaster or terror attack. OSAC also produces Country Security Reports that are useful for risk assessments. Constituents are also invited to attend several in-person OSAC-arranged events throughout the year, including their Annual Briefing each November in Washington, DC. If a prospective user does not know their organization's POC or would like more information on membership, they should contact OSACadmin@state.gov (Overseas Security Advisory Council, n.d.).

As a result of the alignment between U.S. DOS Travel Warnings and institutional travel policies that developed over the years, a change to the DOS travel advisory system would require policy revisions at many colleges and universities nationwide. Thankfully, the DOS provided advanced notice of their plans at the OSAC Annual Briefing in November 2017, giving attendees, including representatives from higher education, the opportunity to adapt, align, or change their approach to international travel risk management over the next 2 months. While the DOS did define the new, four-tiered ranking system, it did not provide examples of how countries might be sorted into one of the four categories described.

For institutions that developed their own restricted travel lists as opposed to strict alignment with the Travel Warnings country list, such as the University of Texas at Austin, it was a matter of incorporating the new DOS ratings into an existing rating system (Texas Global, 2023). Likewise, the University of Massachusetts Amherst historically took more than just the

U.S. DOS information into account, so instead of having to change their policy, they integrated the new categories into the institution's established risk matrix used to evaluate high-risk travel (K. Trivedi, personal communication, August 29, 2023). Michigan State University, a leader in public institution international risk management best practices, relies on information from both International SOS and DOS ratings to develop and maintain a customized list of countries that require review (Office for Global Health, Safety and Security, 2023). Similarly, The University of Pennsylvania, an International SOS client, had instead historically linked its undergraduate travel policy to ISOS's ratings, so the impact of the change was minimal (Penn Global, 2018). Today, Penn requires undergraduates interested in only Level 4 destinations to petition for permission to travel (Penn Global, 2018).

For those that relied primarily on the DOS for their travel policies, it made intuitive sense to require petitions (or even deny travel outright, depending on existing risk tolerance for certain travelers) to countries with Level 4 rating, but schools were initially unsure what to do with Level 2 and 3 destinations until the ratings were revealed. As a result, most institutions in this space could draft policy revisions in anticipation of the expected changes announced in November 2017, but they also wanted to wait and see how countries were dispersed across the levels before committing to a particular stance. For example, Northwestern University, which only regulates the travel of undergraduates, following review of the January 10, 2018, reveal, decided to limit its petition requirements to Level 3 and 4 countries with the caveat that undergraduate permission to a Level 4 country may require special circumstances, such as dual citizenship (Office of Global Safety and Security, 2018). In the end, this helped Northwestern resolve the Kenya, Israel, and Mexico question, given that those countries' Travel Warning status was replaced at the time with Level 2 ratings.

Many institutions reserve the right to require review, cancel, suspend or modify a program for any reasons. Florida State University (FSU) cited Ecuador as example of when a Level 2 country might come under review. Given the civil unrest associated with presidential elections during the summer of 2023, FSU required a group of students wanting to attend a conference in Quito near the date of the run-off election to submit a petition for review. Similarly, when the Hong Kong protests and civil unrest led the host institution to shutter its campus in the fall of 2019, FSU evacuated their students, even though the Travel Advisory remained unchanged at a Level 2 (A. Krutz, personal communication, September 7, 2023). Likewise, the University of South Carolina maintains similar administrative flexibility (Global Carolina, 2023). While they do not typically consider a Level 2 destination to be risky, if their third-party security information provider assesses the risk as "high" or "very high" according to the company's internal matrix, the university's review process is triggered. Examples include both Kenya and Johannesburg, South Africa (M. Inabinet, personal communication, September 7, 2023). On the other hand, the University of California at Berkeley "requires travel approval for all DOS levels for study abroad or for student group travel involving coursework/credit. These requests are almost always approved, but this level of screening allows U.S. to better support faculty and departments in planning for risk before sending students" (Office of the Vice Chancellor of Finance, 2023). Such an approach requires that prospective travelers are aware of submission deadlines and turnaround time, so staff have adequate time to evaluate the proposals.

Given the U.S. DOS provided advance notice of these changes, higher education had time to discuss and plan. The transition was smooth, and the timing helped, too. By announcing in November 2017 that the changes would occur in January 2018, institutions had ample time to revise their policies and procedures before summer, a popular time of the year for undergraduate study abroad. In the end, the way colleges and universities manage travel risk continues to vary, but most U.S. colleges and universities tend to apply one of two approaches: they have either developed their own list of destinations requiring special review based on multiple sources of risk information; or they align review procedures to countries with Level 3 and 4 ratings.

## COVID-19 Pandemic and Risk Ratings

In 2020, the COVID-19 pandemic also tested the DOS's ability to adapt to a rapidly changing travel risk environment. As the virus spread into 2020, the DOS decided to align its ratings with the CDC's Travel Health Notice system, which assigned every country a Travel Health Notice Warning Level 3: Do Not Travel, resulting in DOS rating of Level 3 or 4, to (understandably) discourage travel. However, these high ratings remained in place for a few years, forcing colleges and universities who were ready to "open up" travel as early as 2021 or 2022 to revise their travel policies or develop their own list of restricted countries instead of relying solely on DOS rating. It was not until August 2023 when the last countries—mostly small island nations—with Level 3 ratings tied to COVID were downgraded to Level 2.

## Travel Registration: A New Tool for Risk Management

For many years, colleges and universities have used online study abroad application systems that also served as rudimentary travel trackers. This placated leadership when incidents occurred abroad that prompted obvious exposure questions, but may have also exposed gaps in knowledge about non-study abroad student travel (research, performance groups, athletic team travel, conference attendance, etc.). Many institutions also house self-registration travel trackers typically developed by security assistance providers, and these may be used to capture employee as well as non-study abroad travel, but the application of enforcement mechanisms is neither widespread nor uniform if not tied to travel reimbursement or grant/stipend disbursement. For colleges and universities that lagged in tracking non-study abroad travelers, the COVID pandemic highlighted these knowledge and policy and gaps, prompting policy and practice revisions. Post-pandemic, competition fueled innovation as more institutions obtained or refined their use of online application systems and travel tracking platforms. Today, the most sophisticated of these systems allow users to customize approval systems linked to a destination and the traveler's status (individual, group member, graduate or undergraduate, etc.). This is far easier than the previous paper-oriented petition process. Combined with the ability to meet virtually instead of in person, travel policies can be more nuanced, and risk committees can be more agile when managing last-minute review requests.

## New "Other" Ratings Complicated Review

A few years after the DOS introduced the Travel Advisories, they added a new category of "Other" to address even more nuanced and area-specific risks of countries like Mexico and Israel (U.S. Department of State, n.d. b). Within the overall country rating of "Other," there are now region-specific ratings. For example, six Mexican states known for narco-trafficking are ranked Level 4, whereas Quintana Roo (where Cancun is located) and "Distrito Federal" (where Mexico City is located) are rated Level 2. Most recently, Mainland China, which includes the "regions" of Hong Kong and Macau, was rated as "Other," but the internal, region-specific rating assigned China and Macau a Level 3, while Hong Kong retains its original Level 2 rating. (U.S. Department of State, n.d. b). Increased use of the "Other" category may signal the DOS's desire to provide more specific advice for parts of a country that would seem misaligned under a countrywide rating.

Again, the changes were met with mixed reactions. On the one hand, those locations where education abroad programs are common—Mexico City, Merida, and Oaxaca—fell under "internal" Level 2 ratings, where a border state with historically higher risk, such as Tamaulipas, was rated a Level 4. International educators were generally pleased that travel to cities that traditionally host student programs no longer required special review. On the other hand, China, Israel, and Mexico are not the only countries where internal risk varies greatly from one area to another. The U.S. DOS does not explain why these are the only three countries that fall into this category, and there is no formal definition of the "Other" category like that of the Levels 1–4. The category can also confuse travelers because when filtering countries by risk level on the Travel Advisory webpage, these destinations fall to the end of list, after all the Level 4 destinations (U.S. Department of State, n.d. b).

For institutions with travel tracking platforms that incorporated DOS ratings to deploy applicable workflows, such as a request for travel permission due to a Level 3 or 4 rating, this misalignment proved problematic. It took time for both DOS to change the outbound data feed from its numerical rating to an NR (no rating) status, for platform providers to incorporate a non-numerical rating, and campus systems' administrators to create workflows that trigger reviews. In some cases, however, manual workarounds still apply. While these platforms continue to evolve the field is far better positioned to assess and respond to this ever-changing risk environment, and the revised Travel Advisory system is particularly useful to smaller institutions who cannot justify the cost of a third-party intelligence information provider.

## Part Two: U.S. Citizen Services

U.S. Citizen Services ( "CS"), formerly American Citizen Services, supports the Bureau of Consular Affairs ( "BCA") by providing assistance to U.S. citizens living or traveling abroad. It may surprise many educational abroad professionals to learn that the U.S. CS does not serve non-U.S. citizens, which can be a challenge when a college's or university's traveler in distress is not a U.S. citizen. Although exceptions can be made to accommodate special family circumstances, such as a spouse, dependent, or other relative traveling with the U.S. citizen, those exceptions are unlikely to occur in the context of education abroad. (U.S. Department of State, 2023e). This service limitation is one reason why many schools elect to contract with an international insurance and assistance provider as they serve all clients regardless of citizenship. (See Chapter 33, "Navigating International Insurance for Global Learning," by Joan Rupar (2024) for more information on international insurance.) As college communities have grown more and more diverse, it is not uncommon for international students and scholars to participate in university travel programs. As a result, it is important to seek consular services from the non-U.S. citizen traveler's country of citizenship as soon as time permits. Professional relationships often exist between various countries' consular staff in most destinations. U.S. CS may be able to facilitate the involvement of the officials from the traveler's country of citizenship, especially in an emergency. Nonetheless, education abroad professionals should review the most common countries represented by students or scholars on their campuses for planning purposes. They should also advise travelers who are non-U.S. citizens to review their home country's travel guidance to prepare for their time abroad.

U.S. CS offers a wide variety of services to U.S. citizens, some of which are automated (U.S. Department of State, 2024e). Some of the services are targeted to expatriates who may be living abroad for months or even years, and are typically not needed by short-term travelers. For example, expatriates may use U.S. CS to register a marriage, birth or adoption, vote in U.S.-based elections, or renew a passport. Routine services for many travelers include replacement of a lost or stolen passport (U.S. Department of State, 2024e). U.S. embassy-specific websites provide detailed instructions for how to replace a passport while abroad, but a traveler in distress can always contact the nearest embassy or consulate for advice (Passports Abroad, 2022). Replacement passports are not free; the normal fees apply even in this situation (Passports Abroad, 2022). Institutions can have processes in place to provide financial assistance to a traveler who cannot afford the fee on short notice. Travelers may not be prepared to also provide a photo with the necessary paperwork, but consular staff can advise on how to obtain one locally (Passports Abroad, 2022). If the passport was perceived stolen, a police report is useful, but not required (Passports Abroad, 2022). Consular staff may be able to expedite the process if the traveler is near the end of their trip (Passports Abroad, 2022). In most cases, if a traveler follows all the steps outlined on the relevant website, a replacement passport can be issued without significant delay, but it is important to remember that most U.S. embassies and consulates are not open on weekends and holidays (Passports Abroad, 2022). In the case of a "life or death emergency," a replacement passport may be issued within one business day (Passports Abroad, 2022).

U.S. CS also provides emergency assistance to American travelers. Recent updates to the Emergencies section of the U.S. DOS's International Travel webpage provide detailed information about the following emergencies abroad (U.S. Department of State, 2024b):

- Victims of crime
- Missing traveler(s)
- Arrest or detention
- [Emergency] financial assistance
- International financial scams
- Piracy/robbery at sea
- Forced marriage

- Terrorism
- [Government-Assisted] evacuation
- Death abroad

Education abroad professionals should be prepared for the most common (or upsetting!) emergencies involving short-term travelers: (1) the traveler is a victim of crime, (2) the traveler is arrested, (3) the traveler is perceived missing, or (4) the traveler requires a nonmedical evacuation from a dangerous situation, man-made or natural (Erfle & Dietrich, 2020). Education abroad professionals should understand both the services and limits of the U.S. CS in these situations.

## Smart Traveler Enrollment Program

One way to make it easier for consular staff to support a U.S. citizen experiencing an emergency abroad is for the traveler to enroll in the Smart Traveler Enrollment Program (STEP), operated by the DOS (U.S. Department of State, 2024f). There are many benefits of STEP enrollment.

1. Traveler health, safety, and security advice from the U.S. embassy, including changes to the Travel Advisory.
2. Advice and assistance following an emergency in country.
3. Information about routine events in the destination or opportunities like voting while abroad (U.S. Department of State, 2024f).

In an emergency abroad, embassy staff can also use the information in STEP to connect a traveler with their friends or family if the situation has resulted in a loss of contact (U.S. Department of State, 2024f).

Registering is easy, but a complete profile includes more than just dates and destinations. Taking the time to add the names and addresses of accommodations as well as a local contact or purpose for travel can be useful in an emergency. Most travelers do not have this information at hand when starting the registry process, so it is useful to highlight the need for these details in advance. Some travelers are hesitant to provide this data to the government due to privacy concerns, but the United States takes its citizens' privacy seriously given the data provided is subject to the Privacy Act (U.S. Department of State, 2024f). As a result, the Privacy Act does not permit the DOS to disclose any information in the STEP registry to a third party unless noted in the registration (Privacy Act, 1974; U.S. Department of State, 2024f).

While non-U.S. citizens cannot sign up for STEP, they can sign up for the same type of informational alerts available to U.S. citizens (U.S. Department of State, n.d. a). Upon engaging with the STEP website, non-U.S. citizens can select the "Staying at Home? Get Travel Advisories" link (U.S. Department of State, n.d. a). Education abroad staff, parents, spouses, partners, and even friends of travelers can also sign up for alerts in this manner.

## Victims of Crime

A traveler who has been the victim of a crime may not only need to replace a stolen passport, but may also need assistance understanding local police procedures, obtaining support, or contacting family at home. Experiencing crime abroad can be particularly jarring for travelers, especially if the incident resulted in physical, emotional, or financial harm (U.S. Department of State, 2024b). Consular staff are specially trained to support American citizens in these situations and are prepared to fill in knowledge gaps due to language or cultural barriers (U.S. Department of State, 2024b). At the same time, travelers may have expectations of U.S. CS that cannot be realized. For example, consular staff cannot investigate crimes outside of the United States, but they can provide the traveler with list of legal professionals in the community who speak English (U.S. Department of State, 2024b). However, some institutions prefer to refer or recommend attorneys to their travelers based on advice from their own General Counsel. See also Chapter 12.1, "Working Effectively with Outside Counsel," by William Ferriera (2024) that suggests other resources. Likewise, the U.S. CS cannot represent the American traveler in court—even when a U.S. citizen is the victim of the crime—or provide translation services in any official capacity, but the U.S. CS can refer travelers to local organizations who offer these services (Citizen U.S. Department of State, 2024b). Similarly, the U.S. CS cannot pay a traveler's expenses—legal, medical, or otherwise—but they can share information about the financial assistance options available to American travelers abroad (U.S. Department of State, 2024b). Petty crime, especially pickpocketing, is not uncommon particularly in Europe where U.S. study abroad enrollment remains high (Europol, 2019; Erfle & Dietrich, 2020; Institute of International Education, 2023; Dietrich, 2023). As a result, education abroad professionals should be prepared to advise travelers on the support available through U.S. CS if a crime occurs.

## Traveler is Arrested or Detained (by Local Authorities)

Travelers are subject to the law of the country they are visiting, not of their country of citizenship (U.S. Department of State, 2023a). In other words, certain rights that American citizens are accustomed to in the United States might not be available in other countries. Such distinctions are an important part of any pre-departure preparations. However, if a U.S. citizen is arrested abroad, they are afforded certain rights under a United Nations agreement (Vienna Convention on Consular Relations, 1963; U.S. Department of State, 2023b). These rights, in fact, apply to travelers whose country of citizenship is a signatory to the Convention (Vienna Convention on Consular Relations, 1963). The terms "arrest" and "detention" or "detainee" will be used interchangeably, under the assumption that the traveler has been taken into custody by an authority of the law, and that the detainment is lawful.

First, prison authorities are expected to notify the embassy or nearest consulate of a U.S. citizen's arrest. Alternatively, if a friend or family member is aware of the arrest, they can notify the nearest embassy or consulate of the incident (U.S. Department of State, 2023a). Consular officials can visit the detained traveler, explain the local criminal justice process, provide a list of local attorneys who speak English, assure that the detainee is receiving appropriate medical care, and with permission, contact the detainee's family, friends, or employer (U.S. Department of State, 2023a). Consular staff can also visit the detainee regularly and if permitted, provide reading material and vitamins (U.S. Department of State, 2023a). The detainee can also receive regular visits by a member of the clergy that represents their religion (U.S. Department of State, 2023a). There are, however, limits to the services that U.S. CS can provide to travelers. For example, consular staff cannot get a U.S. citizen out of jail, provide legal advice, serve as official translators/interpreters, represent them in court, or pay their bills, such as legal or medical fees (U.S. Department of State, 2023a). As a result, it is important for the traveler to have local representation, which U.S. AC can facilitate. Although it is uncommon for college- or university-affiliated travelers to be arrested abroad, knowing the role of the U.S. CS and having a plan for supporting the detainee is advisable (Erfle & Dietrich, 2020).

## Traveler is Perceived Missing

A U.S. citizen traveler who falls out of contact with friends or family, or fails to show up for class or excursions without an explanation, may be perceived as missing abroad. Most often, the traveler turns up with a reasonable explanation: a lost, stolen, or forgotten phone; a last-minute trip to another location; a new all-consuming romantic relationship; or a not-too-serious illness or injury that has been all or mostly resolved. Other causes may be a misalignment of communication expectations between the friends and family at home and the traveler, who may find it difficult to stay in touch given a robust travel itinerary, the time difference, and lack of cell phone service (U.S. Department of State, 2024d). It may be wise for concerned parties to check other forms of communication, such as TikTok, Instagram, or Facebook, for information on the traveler's location or activities before sounding an alarm. App-based communication platforms, such as WhatsApp, WeChat (China only), Telegraph, or Google Messaging, are often more convenient for travelers abroad.

However, an unreasonable amount of time may pass without any contact with the traveler or an explanation of their whereabouts. There is no clear definition of what an "unreasonable" amount of time might be, but once all communication efforts noted above have been exhausted, the concerned party seek may seek assistance from the nearest embassy or consulate by calling the Overseas Citizens Service Office in Washington, D.C. (U.S. Department of State, 2024d). It is important for the caller to have as much information as possible about the traveler and efforts undertaken to reach them. If the traveler registered with STEP, consular staff will be able to use that information as well (U.S. Department of State, 2024f). If the consular staff reach the traveler, they will pass on messages from the concerned parties (U.S. Department of State, 2024d). Due to Privacy Act constraints, they are unlikely to report back the status of the traveler unless consent is provided (U.S. Department of State, 2024d). Consular staff may also contact local authorities for information such an arrest or hospitalization. If it turns out that the traveler is indeed in distress, the concerned parties' efforts will ensure that support is offered, and in most cases education abroad professionals stateside or abroad will partner with the family as well as U.S. CS to coordinate a response.

While FERPA protects certain privacy rights of students, "the health and safety emergency exception" permits disclosures to "appropriate parties" and defined as "local or state law enforcement officials, public health officials, trained medical personnel, and parents" (U.S. Department of Education, n.d. a). As a result, education abroad professionals are permitted in an emergency to engage in communications with a parent or guardian, without the express need for a waiver, in order to expedite services to a student traveler. The U.S. Department of Education does not expressly define a "health or safety emergency," and instead allows responders to make a case-by-case judgment (U.S. Department of Education, n.d. b). The serious spirit of the exception should be honored; situations requiring such action tend to be extremely grave. For example, the travel is unconscious, and their medical history is needed to optimize treatment. Or, in the case of a missing student, the last known access to financial services on an account shared with parents may give clues to their location abroad.

## Nonmedical Evacuations

Short-term travelers in a location that has experienced a debilitating nat-ural disaster, such as a hurricane or typhoon, may need to evacuate to the nearest safe haven because it is neither safe nor sensible to remain in a loca-tion where damage to local infrastructure is significant and widespread. If resources such as food, water, medicine, or fuel are scarce, it might be deemed irresponsible to deprive locals of these necessities. Another condi-tion that might result in an evacuation is a declaration of war, a coup d'état, or a violent terror attack targeting civilians. In all cases, to remain in country may put travelers at grave risk.

Best practices in education abroad have long stressed the importance of evacuation preparedness (Friend, 2009; The Forum on Education Abroad, 2020, clause 5.1.7). Although the need for evacuation is unlikely, it is still prudent to develop assessment protocols, shelter-in-place plans, and evacu-ation procedures (Friend, 2009). Relying on the U.S. DOS to evacuate univer-sity travelers is unwise given such services are only available to U.S. citizens and qualifying spouses or dependents (Friend, 2009). Government-assisted evacuations are also not free; evacuees must sign a "Evacuee Manifest and Promissory Note (Form DS-5538)" to provide billing information prior to departure (U.S. Department of State, 2024a). For these and other reasons, an institution may elect to engage the services of an evacuation assistance provider (Friend, 2009).

The U.S. DOS also cannot force American entities or nonfederal employee U.S. citizens to evacuate, but institutions should monitor evacuation-related terms used to in consular messaging as part of their assessment process. An authorized departure allows the embassy the flexibility to permit certain employees or groups of employees to leave the country (U.S. Department of Education, 2023d). An ordered departure requires assigned personnel to leave the country (U.S. Department of State, 2023d). That some groups of employees are permitted to depart should trigger an evaluation of risks and exposure by any individual or entity abroad. If an institution's emergency plan relies heavily on consular support, particularly in an emergency, it is worth considering the value of remaining on site if there is a dramatic draw-down of consular staff.

## Conclusion

The DOS's engagement with the public has improved steadily since the 1990s. The increase in multinational corporations and international trade required employers to pay more attention to the health and safety risks of their traveling personnel. Likewise, internationalization efforts U.S. colleagues and universities increased participation in travel by students, faculty, and staff for a variety of reasons. Institutional efforts to reasonably review and manage the foreseeable health and safety needs of travelers, often on a limited budget, led to a reliance on the DOS for pre-departure risk information and onsite support. The 2018 overhaul of the Travel Advisory system—and subsequent improvements— demonstrates efforts by the federal government to adapt to the changing needs of travelers. Higher education's increased participation in organizations like OSAC allows colleges and universities the opportunity to have voice in future upgrades. Similarly, the ongoing updates and improvements to BCA's website (http://travel.state.gov) continue to improve the public's understanding of the resources and services available to American citizens in need abroad. In sum, colleges and universities should feel confident in incorporating applicable DOS resources and services into their risk management plans.

## References

Carrasco, M. (2022, January 19). Study abroad programs resume after pandemic hiatus. *Inside Higher Ed.* https://www.insidehighered.com/news/2022/01/20/students-venture-back-study-abroad-programs

Dietrich, A. (2023). *Student risk report: Pilot data from education abroad programs, January 1 - June 30, 2023.* https://www.forumea.org/critical-incidents--student-risk.html

Erfle, S., & Dietrich, A. (2019). College student mortality on U.S. campuses with rates while abroad. *Journal of American College Health, (68)*8, 900-905. https://doi.org/10.1080/07448481.2019.1634078

Europol. (2019, May 10). *Experts gather for conference on international pickpocketing gangs.* Europol News. https://www.europol.europa.eu/media-press/newsroom/news/experts-gather-for-conference-international-pickpocketing-gangs-0

Friend, J. (2009, November / December). Getting out. *NAFSA's International Educator Health & Insurance Supplement 2010.* https://www.nafsa.org/sites/default/files/ektron/files/underscore/novdec09_gettingout.pdf

Friend, J. (2010, November / December). Travel warnings: Developing effective response procedures. *NAFSA's International Educator Health & Insurance Supplement 2011.* https://www.nafsa.org/sites/default/files/ektron/files/underscore/novdec10_supplement.pdf

Friend, J., Molyneux, J., & Trivedi, K. (2018, February). Your guide to the new U.S. Department of State Travel Advisories. *The Forum Focus.* (Vol. 4, Issue 3). https://issuu.com/forumoneducationabroad/docs/forum_focus_-_february_2018_final

Gilbert, R. (2023, February). *Pan Am 103 and the birth of the "No Double Standard."* American Diplomacy. https://americandiplomacy.web.unc.edu/2023/02/pan-am-103-and-the-birth-of-no-double-standard/

Global Carolina. (2023). High Risk Travel. Education Abroad Office. University of South Carolina. https://www.sc.edu/about/offices_and_divisions/education_abroad/plan_your_experience_abroad/apply/higher_risk_travel/

Jamieson, S., & Morgan, P. (2024). Who can go where for what purposes and under what conditions: Building an institutional international travel policy. In J. Pollard & K. S. Priebe (Eds.), *Convergence of litigation, policy, and standards: Building the informed practitioner in education abroad risk management.* The Forum on Education Abroad.

Larsen, R. D. (2016). A world of warning: exploring U.S. Department of State Travel Warnings and Alerts. [Unpublished doctoral dissertation]. University of Nevada, Las Vegas.

Larsen, D. (2023, May 5). *Knowing who we are.* NAFSA's International Educator. https://www.nafsa.org/ie-magazine/2023/5/5/knowing-who-we-are (Original work published Winter 2002).

Morello, C. (2018, January 10). *State Department updates Travel Advisories to make them more understandable.* The Washington Post. https://www.washingtonpost.com/world/national-security/state-department-updates-travel-advisories-so-theyre-understand-able/2018/01/10/7d54d92e-f614-11e7-b34a-b85626af34ef_story.html

O'Driscoll, B. (2022, November 15). *What studying abroad looks like in a post-pandemic world.* The Economic Times. https://economictimes.indiatimes.com/nri/study/what-studying-abroad-looks-like-in-a-post-pandemic-world/articleshow/95534446.cms?from=mdr

Office for Global Health. (n.d.). *High risk destinations.* Michigan State University. https://globalsafety.isp.msu.edu/students/non-education-abroad/high-risk-destinations/

Office of Global Safety and Security. (2018, September 14). *Undergraduate international travel policy.* Northwestern University. https://www.northwestern.edu/global-safety-security/docs/undergraduate-international-travel-policy.pdf

Office of the Vice Chancellor of Finance, (2023). *Guidelines and requirements for international travel.* Travel. University of California at Berkeley. https://travel.berkeley.edu/policy-and-guidelines/guidelines-and-requirements-international-travel

Institute for International Education. (2023, November 13). *U.S. Students Studying Abroad, 2021/22.* Leading Destinations. Open Doors Report on International Educational Exchange. https://opendoorsdata.org/data/us-study-abroad/leading-destinations/

Overseas Security Advisory Council. (n.d). *About us.* U.S. Department of State. https://www.osac.gov/About/AboutUs

Overseas Security Advisory Council. (2019, February 15). *Understanding the consular travel advisory system.* Research and Information Support Center (RISC). [Member access only]. U.S. Department of State.

*Pan Am 103.* Wikipedia. Retrieved September 8, 2023, from, https://en.wikipedia.org/wiki/Pan_Am_Flight_103

Penn Global. (n.d.). *Heightened risk travel.* The University of Pennsylvania. https://global.upenn.edu/travel-guidance/heightened-risk-travel-0

Privacy Act of 1974, 5 USC § 552a. (1974). https://www.justice.gov/opcl/privacy-act-1974

Pulse: International Safety and Security Professionals in Higher Education. (n.d.) https://www.pulseinternational.org

Rupar, J. (2024). Navigating International Insurance for Global Learning. In J. Pollard & K. S. Priebe (Eds.), *Convergence of litigation, policy, and standards: Building the informed practitioner in education abroad risk management.* The Forum on Education Abroad. doi.org/10.36.366/SIA.5.978-1-952376-41-2.33

Snyman, H., Douglas, H., & Collins, G. (2024). Applying Standards to Travel Risk Management. In J. Pollard & K. S. Priebe (Eds.), *Convergence of litigation, policy, and standards: Building the informed practitioner in education abroad risk management.* The Forum on Education Abroad.

Texas Global. (n.d.). *Restricted regions list.* University of Texas. https://global.utexas.edu/risk/travel/restricted-regions/list

The Forum on Education Abroad. (2020). *Standards of good practice for education abroad, Sixth edition.* doi.org/10.36366/S.978-1-952376-04-7

U.S. Department of Education. (n.d. a). *34 CFR Part 99.36. Family Education Rights and Privacy Act (FERPA). §99.36 What conditions apply to disclosure of information in health and safety emergencies?* Protecting Student Privacy. https://studentprivacy.ed.gov/ferpa#0.1_se34.1.99_136

U.S. Department of Education. (n.d. b). *How does a school know when a health or safety emergency exists so that a disclosure may be made under this exception to consent?* Protecting Student Privacy. https://studentprivacy.ed.gov/faq/how-does-school-know-when-health-or-safety-emergency-exists-so-disclosure-may-be-made-under

U.S. Department of State. (n.d. a). *Get travel advisories.* Smart Traveler Enrollment Program. https://step.state.gov/STEP/Pages/Common/Subscribe.aspx

U.S. Department of State. (n.d. b). *Travel advisories.* https://travel.state.gov/content/travel/en/traveladvisories/traveladvisories.html/

U.S. Department of State. (2023a, February 27). *Arrest or detention of a U.S. citizen abroad.* https://travel.state.gov/content/travel/en/international-travel/emergencies/arrest-detention.html

U.S. Department of State. (2023b, April 6). *7 FAM 400. Arrest of U.S. citizens abroad.* Foreign Affairs Manual (FAM). https://fam.state.gov/fam/07fam/07fam0410.html

U.S. Department of State. (2023c, June 23). *7 FAM 050. No Double Standard Policy.* Foreign Affairs Manual (FAM). https://fam.state.gov/fam/07fam/07fam0050.html

U.S. Department of State. (2023d, September 20). *3 FAM 3770. Travel to post(s) under authorized departure, ordered departure, suspended operations, contingency operations or to unaccompanied / particularly unaccompanied posts.* https://fam.state.gov/fam/03fam/03fam3770.html

U.S. Department of State. (2023e, October 19). *What the Department of State can and can't do in a crisis.* https://travel.state.gov/content/travel/en/international-travel/emergencies/what-state-dept-can-cant-do-crisis.html

U.S. Department of State. (2024a, February 29). *Information for U.S. citizens about a U.S. government-assisted evacuation.* https://travel.state.gov/content/travel/en/international-travel/emergencies/for-evacuated-citizens.html

U.S. Department of State. (2024b, March 4). *Help for U.S. citizen victims of crime.* https://travel.state.gov/content/travel/en/international-travel/emergencies/crime.html

U.S. Department of State. (2024c, March 6). *Safety and security messaging.* https://travel.state.gov/content/travel/en/international-travel/before-you-go/about-our-new-products.html

U.S. Department of State. (2024d, March 6). *U.S. citizens missing abroad.* https://travel.state.gov/content/travel/en/international-travel/emergencies/US-citizens-missing-abroad.html

U.S. Department of State. (2024e, March 8). *Lost or stolen passports abroad.* https://travel.state.gov/content/travel/en/international-travel/emergencies/lost-stolen-passport-abroad.html

U.S. Department of State. (2024f, March 24). *Smart Traveler Enrollment Program (STEP).* https://travel.state.gov/content/travel/en/international-travel/before-you-go/step.html

Vienna Convention on Consular Relations, April 24, 1963, https://legal.un.org/ilc/texts/instruments/english/conventions/9_2_1963.pdf

# 35

---

# Futuring: Envisioning Future Risks in Education Abroad

The editors invited 20 experts from across the field of education abroad to share their outlooks on what they believe will be future issues our field will face, be they legal, regulatory, policy, or risk-related. Here's what they predict.

## The Integrated Vision of the Student Support Continuum in Study Abroad

### Laia Burgell

In envisioning the future of international education, I am interested in a proactive risk management strategy addressing the well-being of students abroad. One notable area that often goes unaddressed is the lack of continuity of mental health support for students throughout their international education experiences. This inconsistency in support increases the risk of crises going unaddressed, potentially leading to more severe consequences for the student's mental health.

Frequently, there is a significant gap in the provision of mental health support when students transition from their home campuses to studying abroad. Despite receiving counseling or mental health services at their home universities, students may fail to disclose their needs when embarking on international programs.

Moreover, when students reach out to on-site staff and receive counseling or mental health support, there is often an interruption upon their return to their home campus. This interruption can again impede the progress made during the study abroad period and leave students without the necessary tools to cope with the challenges they face upon returning home.

I am developing a framework called the Student Support Continuum in Study Abroad that aims to foster a seamless collaboration between students, universities, and study abroad programs. At its core, this framework encourages an open dialogue between all parties to create a cohesive and personalized support system.

This collaborative approach begins before departure and ensures a comprehensive understanding of the student's mental health needs. The final stages aim to facilitate a smooth post-return transition into the university and ensure that any necessary follow-up support is integrated.

The emphasis on open dialogue, pre-departure preparation, and post-return transition within the Student Support Continuum in Study Abroad aligns with a vision for a holistic and personalized approach to student support. As I move forward in my exploration, I intend to focus on the practicalities of implementing this framework and its effectiveness in identifying and addressing individual risk.

*Laia Burgell, Director of Student Life, Barcelona SAE, has 13 years of international education experience in Barcelona, managing the Health & Safety operations, and crafting cultural engagement programs. Burgell is passionate about inclusion, individualized student support, and intercultural competence, as vital components of her work.*

## Gender X: The Future of Traveling in a Binary World

*Ramil Collier*

In October 2021, the U.S. State Department in acknowledgment of the discomforts experienced by transgender non-conforming, non-binary, and intersex people routinely while traveling, issued its first passport with an "X" gender marker. Giving individuals the option to choose X as an alternative to M or F. It is relevant to acknowledge that the "X" designation is not a nonbinary gender marker but rather an abstention to list "sex" on their passport.

A progressive symbol of support but given the trouble that often accompanies being out as non-binary, the education abroad sector must also strive at training staff about gender, the impact of the X marker and, the creation of policies that make study abroad smoother for gender-diverse students.

It's imperative for the Education Abroad Community to understand that willingly outing oneself on their passport could mean inviting danger into the travel experience. Most likely, the X will cause hassle for students while navigating TSA or worse, while abroad in matters that require formal identification. While some may currently pass with the F or M on their passport, an X is a clear indication of one's non-conforming identity.

This is particularly relevant given the waves of anti-trans legislation appearing around the U.S., and even more so when traveling internationally. Students and educators must understand how trans rights are impacted domestically and how they differ throughout much of the world to manage student safety and risk while traveling.

*Ramil Collier, Student Support & Operations Specialist, CEA CAPA Education Abroad, has almost 10 years of experience working in the Education Abroad including serving as the Assistant Director for a Faculty-led program in Ireland during the COVID Outbreak. Collier is a member of The Forum and serves as a leader for the Global Leadership League fostering Diversity, Equity, and Inclusion in Education Abroad.*

## General Data Protection Regulation (GDPR) and GDPR-Like Data Privacy Laws

*David Comp, Ph.D.*

There are a good number of areas in the education abroad risk management space that one needs to be current on and attentive to in our daily work. Currently, more and more of my attention is being diverted towards various regulatory compliance matters that have an international element of some sort.

I know more about the European Union's General Data Protection Regulation (GDPR) than I ever anticipated. The EU's GDPR, arguably the most strict data privacy and personal security law in the world, is not the only international data privacy law we as practitioners need to be aware of. There are ~20 countries across the globe with GDPR-like data privacy laws with a majority being passed since 2018. To be sure, the general premise of these GDPR-like data privacy laws is similar but there are indeed cultural nuisances and legal differences that we need to be mindful of as we work to interpret and negotiate these laws with partners as part of our overall education abroad operations. For example, in Bahrain one may receive a sentence of imprisonment up to one year for transferring data outside of the Kingdom of Bahrain.

I see the number of countries passing GDPR-like data privacy laws growing rapidly and it's a regulatory compliance area I anticipate paying much more attention to in the future. This will require continued collaboration with information technology colleagues as well as with the Office of General Counsel and others to interpret the various data privacy laws and continue to regularly review our policies and procedures within our organizations and be able to pivot our international engagement strategies as needed.

*David Comp, Assistant Provost for Global Education, Columbia College Chicago, has worked in the field of international education for 24 years at Columbia College Chicago and the University of Chicago. Comp has contributed to the field in many ways including presenting and publishing on topics like diversity, standards & ethics, and on data collection & methodology over the course of his career.*

## The Risk of Silence

*Eduardo Contreras, Ph.D.*

In a course I teach on intercultural understanding, I use a beautiful Ted Talk by the Turkish Novelist Elif Shafak called "The revolutionary power of diverse thought." In it, Shafak describes the power of plurality, cosmopolitanism, and global solidarity in the face of authoritarianism, tribalism, and isolationism. She warns listeners not to accept the monolithic and rigid visions offered by demagogues and to consider instead the beauty of diversity and nuance. I invite my students to reflect upon and discuss with one another this quote from the talk, "One should never, ever, remain silent for fear of complexity."

Today, and in the future, I am worried about silence in education abroad on matters that pertain to justice, equity, diversity, and inclusion (JEDI). The field has made significant strides in advancing JEDI efforts in the last few years; however, recent judicial and gubernatorial actions present a threat to JEDI endeavors and could have a silencing effect on the progress we've made in education abroad. For example, in 2023, U.S. Supreme Court decisions banned affirmative action on college campuses around the nation. In the same year, certain state governments passed legislation that terminated JEDI programming in public higher education institutions.

These examples are an outcome of the highly charged polarization in the U.S. today. These forces could not only silence education abroad professionals discussing equity matters, but also force us to rethink or even terminate JEDI policies. We cannot afford to lose focus on pursuing these matters, even in the face of such chilling national and local actions. The situation is deeply nuanced, yet if we aspire to fulfill the highest hopes of education abroad for all students, and if we seek to build on the progress we've made in JEDI matters, we cannot be silent.

*Eduardo Contreras, Vice President for Global Engagement, serves as senior international officer at Baylor University. With over 20 years of experience, Dr. Contreras has a long-term commitment to equity, inclusion, and international* education. He is a board member of The Forum on Education Abroad and is a faculty co-chair for the Harvard Management Development Program.

## Artificial Intelligence Out of Our Hands

*Janette de la Rosa Ducut, Ed.D.*

"You used to use a keyboard?"

People in the future will ask this of their elderly millennials and Gen Z still around.

What we saw in the year 2023 were simply the sprouts of Artificial Intelligence (AI), slowly making its way into education, policy, and risk. Despite the thousands of tools, people still believed that AI meant only "ChatGPT." There are generations that were trained to believe AI would take over our lives, in an insidious way.

But in the future, AI will be less of a novelty. The children of our grand-children will have grown up asking their AI to summarize thousands of reviews on the best travel itineraries. AI will create a checklist of 10 items to uniquely help them prepare for a study abroad program to the Philippines. An AI-generated itinerary will be informed by dependable crime statistics, academic books, personal medical record assessments, and more.

Litigation would have settled the debate on AI more than a decade ago, concluding that it is not just one thing. And that we have trained them with better data or created systems ensuring accuracy of information, so that bias, hallucinations, propaganda, and other ethics/risks are mitigated.

Future issues in risk include whether the law is the appropriate control mechanism for AI. After all, the power to mitigate belongs with the institution that introduces or creates the risk in the first place. Regulations and policies may create parameters. But the governance of AI may require a peer review process, coordinated amongst the purveyors of the most popular tools out there. These are the organizations most aware of the hidden risks which we do not see. And at that point, the biggest AI issue to contend with in the future will be our trust. Of each other, rather than of the tools.

Future generations may use Artificial Intelligence to conduct risk assessments upon itself. And they will do this without a keyboard because technology from the 1900s requiring use of hands is now a thing of the past.

*Janette de la Rosa Ducut, Director, Training & Education, University of California, has over 20 years of experience in education and training in a regulated environment. Over the past decade she has changed the way universities provide training by publishing hundreds of online training courses in risk, health, and safety. She specializes in eLearning, video production, and integrating active learning experiences.*

## Navigating Innovation, Institutional Risk and Student Safety

*Jennifer Engel, Ph.D.*

As we encourage innovative programming in more unusual locations, balancing institutional risk and student safety with learning opportunities abroad will demand even greater attention. As I work with faculty leaders who have unique expertise in "off the beaten track" locations, and consult with colleagues having similar conversations, I'm concerned that the frameworks we collectively have in place to effectively assess and manage the associated risk may struggle to keep up. In recent weeks I've discussed programs that engage students in biological field work via snorkeling expeditions in Malaysia, in shipwreck exploration while scuba diving in the Caribbean, and in collecting elephant behavior data in the fields of Zambia. I'm excited to see these program concepts being proposed and implemented. However, they pose a whole different set of questions, policies, preparation, and evaluation.

What is appropriate for an undergrad to do, and what are their limitations? This question surfaced in reference to their academic preparation and skill set, but it equally applies to students' health, safety, and mental and physical limitations in the field. It also calls into question how to best balance the inherent risks with incredible learning opportunities that wouldn't be possible in any other setting.

We will need to reevaluate the current, and create new, institutional policies in order to effectively guide these activities. New professional standards and current case law will help us discern if the balance of risk appears acceptable in light of the benefits students stand to gain from the experience. I'm grateful to be at an institution that has resources, structures, and people with expertise who I can consult. What concerns me is how we as a field will be able to support institutions with more limited resources and capacity— to help ensure that their students have access to innovative learning abroad opportunities as well.

*Jennifer Engel, Ph.D., Associate Vice President for Education Abroad at Indiana University, provides strategic leadership for education abroad initiatives across the IU system, and has held progressively more complex roles within international education over the past 25 years. She has been involved with*

*The Forum on Education Abroad, NAFSA, and AIEA, holding leadership positions and presenting nationally and internationally.*

## Meeting the Demands of Results-Driven Education

*Nick J. Gozik, Ph.D.*

Over the past several years, we have witnessed growing scrutiny over the value of higher education, fueled by political divisions and an uncertain economic outlook. Such concerns have led to greater emphasis on student learning outcomes, tied to career development, and corresponding shifts in policy and practice both at the institutional level and through accreditation agencies. As President and CEO of the WASC Senior College and University Commission Jamienne S. Studley notes, there are calls to "devote less attention to process and more attention to results". At my institution, Elon University, we have been publishing student achievement and success reports since 2014, as required by our regional accrediting body and federal policy. At the same time, these reports tie to our commitments to high-impact practices (HIPs) and experiential learning—areas that have become ever more popular on U.S. campuses. Education abroad should be ideally situated to meet the demands of a results-driven education, with a promise of offering students cross-cultural skills, a greater sense of independence and adaptability, and real-world experience. However, we often are missing the mark—at least in terms of narrative. The risk of the field being viewed as less central to university and college priorities as they respond to changes in policy presents challenges in the relevancy, funding, and positioning of education abroad— something that is exacerbated by the growing scrutiny of accreditation agencies. But it's not too late, and especially if we are able to innovate and test new models. This could involve more hybrid programming, combining study abroad with internships, research, and community-based learning. It could entail mixing virtual and AI experiences with overseas, on-site programming, thus mimicking the realities of multimodal work experiences. And it could mean seeing study away as not just a one-off experience, yet one component of a four-year, global journey. These and other strategies will re-center student learning and outcomes at the heart of work, helping us answer the call of our stakeholders.

*Nick J. Gozik is Dean of Global Education at Elon University. He has held positions in international education at Boston College, Duke University, New York University, and the University of Richmond, and has taught, presented, and published widely. Gozik holds an M.A. and Ph.D. from New York University.*

## Mental Health as a Foreseeable Risk in Education Abroad

*Marcia W. Henisz*

Given the prevalence of mental health issues in the college-aged population and strong efforts in education abroad offices to expand and diversify participation, it seems increasingly important to me that institutions prepare to address mental health challenges in education abroad. While there is immense value to be gained from international experiences, the poor mental health and limited resilience of many study abroad participants is rapidly approaching a level that could be classified as a foreseeable risk, requiring greater proactive measures to fulfill duty of care of students. Increased societal awareness and acceptance of the need to support mental wellness has made students more open to wellness efforts and has increased student expectation that institutions will provide such support. These needs extend to a term abroad, making lack of preparation a reputational risk. With the popularity of faculty-led programming, education abroad offices must also consider how they are preparing faculty and staff trip leaders to support student wellness and serve as a first responder to a mental health incident.

Liability concerns aside, students that approach the study abroad experience unprepared for its mental challenges have a significant impact on programs. In one recent project I completed for a provider organization, according to program case data, employees spent the equivalent of 156 workdays dedicated to adjustments and mental health challenges of participants. And there was evidence that these figures were underreported! The Forum on Education Abroad's recent Student Risk Report found that 66% of students that experienced mental health distress during their time abroad withdrew from their program (Dietrich, 2023), likely negating the value of the experience abroad. I expect that institutions will need to increasingly look for pro-active measures to support the mental health needs and boost the resiliency of students engaged in education abroad.

*Marcia W. Henisz, Principal & Founder SASSIE Consulting, has over 30 years of experience in international education and is an active member of OSAC and URMIA. Henisz has presented on safety and security at NAFSA, URMIA, The Forum on Education Abroad and OSAC. She is the creator of "Preparing for Wellness Abroad" and formerly served as Senior Director of International Health, Safety and Security at Drexel University.*

## Big Data and International Travel Trends

*Kris Holloway*

I am interested in how we can better harness data on international travel trends to inform our strategic planning and give us tools to make our work easier. Below are business websites and reports that higher education would do well to consider.

The airline industry tracks country-specific vaccination, passport, visa, and other entrance requirements. Airlines are on the front lines of travel, and I've found the International Air Transport Association (IATA) Travel Centre invaluable. Young travelers are more concerned about the travel risks than older travelers (according to Zurich North America); how can staying on top of these regulations help our students feel more prepared?

Skift, Business Travel News and Expedia annually report on travel trends. "Bleisure" (combining business and leisure) trends might mean families and friends of students have more time to spend with them on-site, creating more complex risk scenarios for us. Expedia reported that 25% of travelers booked to destinations after seeing them on shows or movies ("set-jetting"). White Lotus' Season 3 is in Thailand. What happens when locations become "over-touristed"?

The World Economic Forum's Global Risks Report, states the "erosion of societal cohesion" as a top impediment to travel. Civil unrest increases the real risk and perceived risk of being in a different country. How might this impact our students' mental health? The report states "we stand on the edge of a low-growth and low-cooperation era; tougher trade-offs risk eroding climate action, human development, and future resilience." How can knowing about these macro-trends help prepare us to navigate a changing world?

*Kris Holloway, President & CEO, CIS Abroad, entered the field of international education 17 years ago from the non-profit development world. She served in the Peace Corps in Mali and is the author of two narrative nonfiction books, each covering the life of a trailblazing international woman. She is a founding board member of the Global Leadership League.*

## Climate Change and International Education

*Jason Hope*

The future impacts of climate change on international education should not be underestimated. We are already seeing questions being raised about the carbon footprint associated with student mobility, and the pressures and ethical issues attendant to those concerns will only grow in the future. Universities should begin planning now for ways to ensure that their students have access to meaningful intercultural experiences without necessarily needing to travel to do so.

From a security perspective, the effects of climate change will undoubtedly shift the landscape in which we operate in the coming years. Climate contingency planning, including considering ways to support students during intense weather events, may become a regular part of the program development process. Questions that we have never routinely asked, such as whether generators are available in case electricity should fail during heatwaves or periods of severe cold, whether storm shelters are available to use in case of increasingly intense storms, and what the ethical implications are of our physical presence and use of resources in places affected by difficult climate conditions, may become the norm for us.

The population shifts that are predicted to accompany a changing climate will also have security implications for international mobility. The movement of people away from regions becoming increasingly hostile to permanent settlement or where resources are scarce will inevitably cause conflict and social unrest in countries that climate migrants are attempting to reach. These converging challenges may make it more difficult to operate both in the countries most directly affected by a changing climate as well as those likely to experience significant demographic shifts due to climate migration.

*Jason Hope, Director of Global Risk and Strategic Operations, University of Kentucky, has over a decade of international education experience, primarily devoted to health, safety, and security. He is on the board of Pulse and the steering committee of the OSAC academia sector committee. He regularly presents on issues in the field at national and international conferences and events and has published in both academic and practitioner-focused publications.*

## Bias in Health, Safety, and Security: Rethinking Risk Assessment in International Education

*Lily López-McGee, Ph.D.*

In international education and exchange, the presence of potentially biased and prejudicial rubrics to assess health, safety, and security (HSS) may stagnate efforts to diversify the participants and locations of future global programming. Left unexamined, such rubrics to risk assessment have the potential to limit programming to locations and program models that haven't significantly changed over time and replicate problematic views of some world regions.

There must be space for assessing risk through an equity lens. Questions that can make biases more explicit might include the following. Do program leaders have experience navigating the cultural nuances of the region and/or speak the language? Where the location lacks in one dimension (e.g., health-care infrastructure) are there other factors that might mitigate the risk (e.g., program length, less physically intensive activities)? Are there opportunities to examine students' individual preparedness to participate in a program (e.g., level of comfort with ambiguity, resiliency)? Can the program be designed or facilitated to ensure students, faculty, and staff safety (e.g., smaller cohort sizes, shorter localized trips)? How can local staff and community members be involved in the early stages of program development to ensure factors that may not be obvious to U.S. staff are considered or mitigated?

With efforts to broaden participation in programs to less common destinations underway, risk assessment requires change. This is especially important as more students from diverse backgrounds seek opportunities beyond common study locations, curricular programming that is engaged with local communities (e.g., community organizing), and unique program models (e.g., research). Institutions and providers must acknowledge the complex interplay of factors such as the program's design, facilitator/instructor preparedness, and students' unique profiles when evaluating HSS risk. Only then can a more equitable approach to HSS in international education be considered.

*Lily López-McGee, Executive Director, Diversity Abroad, has dedicated more than a decade to capacity building, EDI within global education, and U.S. national security and foreign policy. She has worked for Diversity Abroad and previously supported federal grants at Howard University and UNCFSP. She is a practitioner, researcher, and speaker and has published in industry and academic outlets. She holds degrees from the University of Washington and George Mason University.*

## India's Bold Step in Education Reforms

*Vinita Mehra, J.D.*

The Government of India, in its National Education Policy 2020 (NEP), has proposed encouraging the top 100 international universities to set up campuses in India. As recently as May 2022, the University Grants Commission (UGC)

Regulations has recently promulgated Academic Collaboration between Indian and Foreign Higher Educational Institutions to offer Twinning, Joint Degree and Dual Degree Programmes ("Collaboration Regulations"), replacing earlier regulations which were extremely restrictive. The UGC has also promulgated rules and formed a committee to encourage foreign universities to open a campus in India.

I believe the NEP will provide the following opportunities to universities, as the policies evolve:

- High-performing Indian Universities will be encouraged to set up campuses in other countries, and similarly, selected universities (e.g., the top 1000 in the world) will be facilitated to operate in India.
- India, for its long-term growth, wants to increase its Gross Enrollment Ratio (GER), which is low compared to other BRICS economies. Foreign Universities could assist in this goal by setting up academic collaborations with Indian educational institutions under the Collaboration Regulations, giving an impetus to the recruitment and enrollment of students to such joint programs.
- Shape the transnational, cross-border, offshore, and borderless higher education, which could lead to mobility in higher education, and move from people (students, faculty, scholars) to program (twinning, franchise, virtual) to provider (branch campus) mobility. There could be a concerted development of education hubs.
- Regulation of the unregulated sector like vocational and distance learning education.

With this new policy reform, a quality education could be possible as global universities could consider undertaking academic collaborations and/or establishing their branch campuses in India. But there is also a sentiment that this will increase inequality by increasing the cost of education and create challenges as foreign providers may take unfair advantage of the market. The policy has its fair share of advantages and disadvantages. Time will tell whether the NEP can put India on the map as a leader in Transnational Education.

*Vinita Mehra, Attorney and Leader, Global Business Practice, Kegler, Brown, Hill + Ritter, has over 25 years of experience leading numerous international projects for institutions nationwide, navigating complex regulatory and funding processes for global expansion. As an active member of NACUA, The Forum,* and *AIEA, she regularly presents to educational leaders and university counsel, devising market strategies and recruiting initiatives globally.*

## Potential Impacts to International Travel Accident Insurance Driven by Climate Science

### Jessica Miller

With a focus on international travel accident insurance and associated security evacuation (i.e., PEND) coverage, I am concerned that climate change impacts will drive greater frequency of events requiring evacuation and/or assistance with relocating travelers to safer accommodations following fires, floods, catastrophic storms, and similar events. Beyond immediate damage, local devastation could affect access to water, food, and essential goods and services, resulting in both immediate safety concerns for travelers and ethical questions about strain on limited resources. Additionally, heat-related impacts could drive substantial health concerns in and of themselves, especially in regions that lack access to air-conditioned facilities. Resource scarcity could drive significant civil unrest and increased criminal targeting of those perceived to be wealthy. Collectively, with the increased frequency and severity of claims, I am concerned that natural disaster-related exclusions to coverage will become commonplace and lessen the utility and value of international travel accident policy coverage. This could spur cascading effects on mobility trends since institutions will likely only promote travel to regions less prone to associated risks.

*Jessica Miller, International Program Manager, Office of Risk Management, The University of Texas System, has 16 years of professional risk and program management experience: nine with UT and seven as an Air Force officer. Miller currently holds leadership positions with Pulse and URMIA's International Committee and has presented at numerous events related to international risk, including with The Forum, URMIA, and OSAC.*

## Regulation and Oversight of Education Abroad Providers

### Anthony C. Ogden, Ph.D.

In 2004, the Forum on Education Abroad released its *Standards of Good Practice,* which was arguably a response to an education abroad landscape that was largely unsupervised and unregulated.

Recognizing the looming threat of governmental regulatory oversight, the prescient founders of The Forum anticipated the need for self-regulation. Their foresight was well-placed. By 2007, the New York Attorney General, Andrew M. Cuomo, launched an ill-fated investigation into education abroad practices, issuing subpoenas to a multitude of education abroad provider organizations and academic institutions.

Today, The Forum serves as the Standards Development Organization (SDO) for education abroad, as recognized by the U.S. Department of Justice and the Federal Trade Commission. With its *Code of Ethics* and comprehensive Guidelines, The Forum has become the go-to authority for education abroad standards.

However, a noticeable gap remains: the lack of regulatory oversight of education abroad providers. Providers have undeniably played an influential role in shaping the evolution of education abroad programming. Today, providers offer a wide range of specialized resources, programming, and services that significantly contribute to the advancement of education abroad. Yet, their relative autonomy from regulatory oversight may be nearing an end.

In 2023, the U.S. Department of Education attempted to impose regulatory requirements on institutions that contract with third-party servicers. The directive has been rescinded, for now. To be sure, education abroad providers should anticipate further scrutiny. The following areas warrant immediate attention:

- Financial Transparency. The specter of hidden fees, ambiguous refund policies, private equity investment, high-profile court cases, and potential misuse of student funds looms large.
- Health and Safety Protocols. Ensuring students' well-being requires stringent standards. Issues like subpar accommodations, unsafe environments, inadequate healthcare access, or lapses in emergency response mechanisms can have consequences.
- Legal Compliance. Navigating complex global legal frameworks poses challenges, from credit transfer, data privacy, employment regulations, and operational intricacies.

As education abroad continues its trajectory, a harmonized approach that balances autonomy with accountability is imperative. Collaboration between stakeholders, proactive self-regulation, and a keen focus on student welfare will be pivotal in shaping a robust, trustworthy, and responsible education abroad ecosystem.

*Anthony C. Ogden, Founder and Managing Director, Gateway International Group, is a respected scholar-practitioner with 30 years of experience in international higher education. He has held senior international leadership positions at Pennsylvania State University, the University of Kentucky, Michigan State University and the University of Wyoming. He has published extensively on topics related to international higher education.*

## Sufficient Funding Needed to Manage Growing Risks

*Michael R. Pfahl, J.D., Ph.D.*

Institutions that commit to growing their study abroad portfolios will be faced with increased exposure as courts expand their boundaries of the foreseeable harm to students while further adding to the list of standard programmatic requirements. This exposure gap will widen even further for institutions that consistently underfund their study abroad programs, resulting in less quality programming, unsecure accommodations, and inadequately trained program staff. The inter-institutional competition for resources resulting from the ever-decreasing overall funding pool could result in more programs looking toward untrained volunteers and "chaperones" to lead their students, which, in my opinion, represents the greatest threat to litigation for any study abroad program. These factors, combined with the continued struggle between an institution's legal duty of care and the perceived moral obligations to its students, will open the door for more third-party contractors to assume operational controls while the institution focuses on programmatic branding and enrollment.

Furthermore, institutions that continue to offer study abroad programming under their own flag will find participants who expect the on-campus student experience in the United States to follow them throughout their international journey. For example, students may expect mental health counseling to travel with them, as well as the other services provided to them in their daily campus life. Institutions will continue to juggle with whether to provide these services (perhaps with limitations), or limit expectations with students prior to departure.

In my opinion, institutions need to forego allegiance to return on investment (ROI) and secure sufficient funding levels for each program. This approach reduces exposure through adequate (and trained) staffing, attention to secure housing and transportation, and the adoption of policies that provide for the centralized administration of all study abroad opportunities.

*Michael R. Pfahl, J.D., Ph.D., serves as Senior Associate General Counsel for Kent State University ("Go Flashes"). He received his Ph.D. in Higher Education Administration from Kent State University and focuses his research on international student issues, international comparative higher education law, and study abroad liability.*

## AI and Risk Management

*Julie Pollard*

Applications of Artificial Intelligence (AI) in the risk management space abound. Be it for risk assessment, travel notifications, or training development, professionals are eager to learn ways to ethically capitalize on AI in daily work while recognizing the limitations of these tools. AI presents several challenges as algorithms can possess inherent biases in the data they are trained on. This could result in discriminatory outcomes. If the AI fails to accurately identify or warn of risks that subsequently harm travelers, organizations may face lawsuits alleging negligence in providing adequate warnings. Over reliance on AI and lack of human oversight could yield a similar result. As law tends to lag on regulating technological advancements, it will be interesting to watch for intersections in the AI and duty of care space. Several AI experts on LinkedIn including Dr. Daniel J Hulme from the Department of Computer Science, University College London and Allie K Miller an AI entrepreneur, advisor, and investor are worth following to expand your knowledge on this topic.

*Julie Pollard, Director of International Health, Safety, and Crisis Management, University of California Education Abroad Program (UCEAP) has worked in international education since 2004 including spending ten years in Turkey working in private sector study abroad operations. Pollard is a member of Pulse and has presented at OSAC, NAFSA, The Forum on Education Abroad, EAIE, AIEA, and EURIE on health, safety, and security topics in international education programming. She is co-editor of this book.*

## Fostering Resilience and Professional Growth to Sustain the Field

*Kim S. Priebe*

The rapid evolution of the field of international education presents both opportunities and challenges, with education abroad professionals experiencing expanded roles and responsibilities amidst limited resources and support. The Forum on Education Abroad's 2022 State of the Field Report underscores the pressing issue of high staff turnover, leading to a loss of institutional knowledge and a gap in risk management and crisis response training. The survey highlights that 47% of respondents have been tasked with responsibilities for which they have not yet received training, and risk management and crisis management rank among the top five required skills. Without adequate training, the sustainability of newer professionals' careers is a critical concern. The strain of increased workload and responsibility raises the risk of burnout, which I fear could threaten the long-term viability of individuals and the field as a whole.

The future of education abroad and international health and safety hinges on our ability to foster resilience and professional growth among emerging professionals. To address these challenges, employers must commit to providing professional development opportunities that equip newer professionals (or those with shifting responsibilities) with the skills and knowledge necessary for success. This requires a concerted effort from seasoned professionals and industry stakeholders alike to prioritize mentorship programs that offer meaningful guidance, foster a supportive community, and cultivate essential skills for long-term success. Further, we need to continue to create pathways for new professionals to enter the field.

By fostering a supportive environment and investing in the growth of emerging talent, we can mitigate burnout and retain institutional knowledge—both of which are essential to building a sustainable and resilient future for the field of international education.

*Kim S. Priebe has over 20 years of experience in international education, including serving in international health, safety & security roles with the University of California (UCEAP) and UNC-Chapel Hill, and director of study abroad at NC State University. Priebe is an active member of Pulse, NAFSA, OSAC, and The Forum, regularly presenting on health, safety, and security and contributing to new professional resources for the field. She is co-editor of this book.*

## Neurodiversity in Education Abroad

*Robin Marie Reliford, J.D.*

Within the risk management space, I see a need to increase education and awareness about neurodiversity and supporting neurodiverse students who want to travel abroad. It is estimated that roughly 20% of the global population identifies as neurodiverse. In 2020, the U.S. Centers for Disease Control and Prevention (CDC) estimated that 1 in 36 children are diagnosed specifically with Autism Spectrum Disorder (ASD). Many college students with ASD who participate in international programs do so successfully. Still, others face challenges with academic accommodations, cultural acceptance and adjustment, and group integration, among other things. When this happens, even students who generally excel on their home campus may encounter academic setbacks or withdraw early from their abroad program. More serious cases can involve loss of housing, program dismissal, or even mental health crises.

I anticipate that we will see more students who identify as neurodiverse pursue education abroad opportunities. No one size fits all solution for success exists, but we can start moving towards more inclusive practices to help future students. Increasing awareness and creating space for more information sharing is the first step. Greater pre-departure collaboration between the student, their home institution, family (if welcomed by the student), and their program provider, faculty-leader, or host institution abroad will lead to better understanding of each individual student's needs. It also will help manage expectations of available on-site support. Creating a space where neurodiverse students can seek and receive advice upfront will help students identify the best abroad experience to meet their goals. Additionally, training is needed for program staff and faculty-leaders to better help neurodiverse students overcome challenges that arise on programs and connect them with the appropriate resources. Perhaps most importantly, the power of empathy cannot be overlooked.

*Robin Marie Reliford, J.D., Vice President of Health & Safety, WorldStrides, has worked in international education for 15 years, focusing on health, safety, and risk management. She has extensive experience with program planning and crisis management and is adept at anticipating and responding to student needs. Robin regularly presents at conferences on topics within her field of expertise.*

## Identity-Based Scholarships in the Post-Affirmative Action Climate

### Angela Schaffer

As a scholarship practitioner, I am closely following lawsuits against funders that utilize race and other demographic information in their selection criteria for awards. In the aftermath of the SCOTUS ruling on affirmative action, lawsuits like the American Alliance for Equal Rights vs. Fearless Fund are more common, invoking the first section of the Civil Rights Act of 1866 (also known as Section 1981). This legislation prohibits racial discrimination in the making and enforcing of contracts and was written in the reconstruction era to ensure that contractors would not be selected—or discriminated against—based on their race. I speak regularly with legal counsel familiar with non-profit governance, and look to guidance (and a lot of message board banter) from organizations like the National Scholarship Providers Association and the Council on Foundations as we continue to try to insulate ourselves from the risk of a lawsuit while also staying true to our mission of awarding scholarships to students who come from backgrounds historically excluded from study abroad. Our scoring rubric is designed to recognize and promote students who have financial need based on various ways they identify, including race, community college experience, and being the first in their families to attend college. While students don't receive points for identifying as part of the LGBTQ+ community, we use this information to determine who is eligible for our Rainbow Scholarship; we also closely follow anti-LGBTQ+ legislation in various U.S. states and regularly review updates and resources from organizations like The Point Foundation. At this writing, we are making our scholarship agreements less like contracts, so that we could not be considered in violation of Section 1981. We are also prioritizing ways to protect our scholars' intersectional identities, because we anticipate additional legal action targeting the students we set out to serve.

*Angela Schaffer, Executive Director, Fund for Education Abroad, has worked in international education and exchange for more than 20 years, including roles at institutions (private and public, small and large); international exchange non-profit organizations; and a J-1 Teacher visitor sponsor. Angie is an active member of NAFSA, The Forum, Diversity Abroad, and NSPA (National Scholarship Providers Association).*

## Inclusion in International Education: Navigating Post-SCOTUS Affirmative Action Challenges

*Malaika Marable Serrano, Ph.D.*

In recent years, education abroad organizations such as The Forum on Education Abroad, Diversity Abroad, and NAFSA, have amplified the need to diversify talent pipelines into the field of education abroad. The June 2023 U.S. Supreme Court's (SCOTUS) decision to end affirmative action in the college admissions process undermined years of progress in addressing historic and systemic inequities.

Affirmative action policies in higher education, intended to increase representation of historically marginalized groups. Implications of the SCOTUS ruling for Diversity, Equity, Inclusion, and Belonging (DEIB) in the education abroad space are still being determined, but experts predict there will be an impact on hiring, professional development, and retention of professionals from historically marginalized communities.

SCOTUS decisions that restrict these policies may result in limiting strategic hiring practices and reducing diversity within the field of education abroad and become less representative of the overall student population. As a consequence, if the education abroad field is unable to attract, develop, and retain professionals from marginalized communities, it could result in program designs that lack inclusivity, cultural relevance, and diversity in their content. This, in turn, could have a chilling effect on efforts to attract students from diverse communities and erode progress that has been made in widening access to education abroad for historically marginalized students.

Implications of the SCOTUS decision on identity-based scholarships, grants, paid apprenticeships, internships, training/professional development for specific groups remains to be seen. On the upside, we can—and should—continue to invest in DEIB programs and initiatives that foster inclusion and belonging for all employees.

Clear and consistent, policies, practices, and procedures which are transparent and documented, will drive inclusive hiring, performance evaluation, pay equity, and retention practices. Practitioners, faculty, and organizations alike will need to directly address these challenges to ensure that the demographic representation in our profession reflects the diverse student populations we serve.

*Dr. Malaika Marable Serrano is VP for Diversity, Equity, Inclusion, and Belonging (DEIB) at Guild, where she shapes company-wide processes and systems to create a more equitable workplace. With two decades of experience leading DEIB initiatives in international education, she holds degrees from USC, UMD, and the Università Cattolica del Sacro Cuore. Currently serving on the Boards of NAFSA and Fulbright Canada, she resides in Atlanta with her children.*

## Data + Professional Development = Safer Students

### Melissa Torres

As the field of education abroad continues to professionalize, it will become standard for newcomers to participate in foundational training in order to adequately develop their understanding of the need to have "policies and procedures in place regarding security and risk management that prioritize health, well-being, and safety of students and personnel" (*Standards of Good Practice for Education Abroad*, enhanced sixth edition, pg. 28). EA professionals from institutions of higher education (IHE) and education abroad organizations (EAO) around the world will regularly attend training to keep pace with new and emerging threats to the safety and well-being of EA participants. They will continue to engage in dialogue to share promising solutions or to collaboratively develop new tools and strategies for the benefit of all, a testament to the collective responsibility felt by current and former leaders in the EA field.

With health and safety at the very heart of why The Forum exists and what it does best, our Health, Safety, Security & Risk Management Institute will continue to be the premiere event in this space, bringing together international risk management experts and thought leaders from across the health and safety spectrum, crossing all geographic, functional, and cultural boundaries. The knowledge capital accumulated across 15 annual health & safety institutes will increasingly inform inclusive professional development opportunities and a growing network of EA professionals who have responsibilities for and interest in this area. In the immediate future, all IHEs and EAOs will report critical incidents involving students during education abroad programs, into The Forum's annual Student Risk Report. Responsible parties will use the data to engage in a continuous quality improvement loop to review, respond, and report on emerging risks to health, safety, security & well-being of students, administrators, and faculty.

Finally, as inclusive excellence and the effort to decolonize education abroad transform much of what we do and how we do it, the expertise and knowledge that on-site staff, in-country partners, homestay families, and host institutions hold about the local risk environment, available resources, and strategies for supporting student success will be integral to the development and continuous improvement of policies, processes, and crisis response regarding the safety and well-being of all education abroad participants.

*Melissa Torres, President & CEO, The Forum on Education Abroad, has over two decades of experience in higher education and program development. She led a variety of international initiatives for Brown University, UNC/Chapel Hill, Ohio State and IES Abroad. Melissa regularly presents on current and emerging issues and advocates for international education at state, national, and international levels.*

# Authors

**Emma Snyder Bahner** is a privacy law expert with experience in international and domestic compliance programs, particularly in higher education settings. She frequently speaks publicly on data privacy and other compliance matters affecting higher education institutions, including at national events hosted by the National Association of College and University Attorneys. Emma is licensed to practice law in Colorado and holds a B.A. from the University of Vermont and a J.D. from Penn State Dickinson School of Law.

**Mark Beirn** is Director of International Programs in the College of Liberal Arts & Sciences at University of Illinois, Urbana Champaign. Previously, Mark led global risk management in the Office of Global Engagement at University of California, Irvine, and served as director of study abroad at Tulane University and Washington University in St. Louis, where he is writing his Ph.D. in Urban History. A Fulbright Scholar, Mark's research bridges community activism with urban field work and archival inquiry.

**Melissa Chambers** is grateful for 23+ years transforming students' lives though international education and has expertise developing strategic partnerships for international education, sexual health, sexual violence prevention, and diversity, equity, and inclusion. Author of NAFSA's Sexual Health Abroad (2009 and 2016), Melissa has presented at state, regional, and national conferences and sits on the Rainbow SIG of NAFSA Advisory Board. She holds degrees in Spanish, Creative Writing, and Communication Studies.

**Gary Collins** has over 10 years of experience in global operations and risk management, advising on international mobility and international operations best practices. Gary's work helps institutions and organizations to strengthen international policy and procedures, mitigate risk, plan for emergencies, and help stakeholders overcome global regulatory challenges.

**Hilary Douglas** has held various roles in academia, non-profits, and travel agencies specifically working with undergraduates engaging in public service and/or traveling abroad. She has a Master of Public Administration and currently serves as Program Manager in Global Community Engagement at Stanford University, managing outreach and engagement for global risk.

As the Director of International Health, Safety, and Security, **Andrea Drake** is responsible for developing systems to support students, staff, and faculty traveling abroad as well as the implementation of comprehensive international travel policies. Andrea earned a dual B.A. degree from Northeastern University in International Affairs and Languages, Literature, and Cultures with a minor in Middle East Studies. Andrea earned her Master's in Higher Education Administration from UMass Amherst in 2018.

**Laura Dupont-Jarrett**, PhD, LP, Assistant Director for Education Abroad Mental Health at the University of Minnesota, provides training, guidance, and resources to staff and faculty regarding student mental health and wellness abroad. She's a licensed psychologist who has worked in higher education for 30 years as an advisor, mental health counselor, instructor, trainer, and administrator. She received her MA and PhD in Counseling & Student Personnel Psychology, and her BA in Psychology and French.

**Ebony Ellis,** a leading advocate for cross-cultural communication, has over 17 years of K-16 experience, notably for her innovative work with the U.S. Department of Defense and education abroad. Ebony's work has been featured in many capacities for its innovative intercultural, storytelling, and self-discovery practices. As founder of Aventurine Global, she empowers individuals to embrace exploration and growth. Ebony holds advanced degrees from Albany State University and the University of Northern Iowa.

**William F. (Bill) Ferreira** heads the firm's Global Government Contracts and Education Practice. As a leader on government grants, contracts, and international projects, Bill helps companies, universities, hospitals, academic medical centers, and organizations doing business with the U.S. government and abroad. Drawing on deep experience with global operations, Bill's team has guided campuses in Asia, public health projects in Africa, and academic programs in the Middle East.

**Julie Anne Friend** is the Director of the Office of Global Safety and Security at Northwestern University in Evanston, Illinois. Ms. Friend's scholarship and advocacy related to higher education travel risk management has contributed to the development of standards in the field. Ms. Friend has a Juris Doctor in Law and an MA in English from Michigan State University as well as a BS in Speech Communication from Syracuse University.

**Jennifer Fullick**, PhD is the Associate Vice President for Health, Safety and Wellbeing at The Institute for Study Abroad. With over 20 years in the field of international education, Dr. Fullick is an advisory council member for Mobility International, USA; and contributes to publications on the topics of health and safety in study abroad. Dr. Fullick currently is working on projects to advance the support of mental health and wellbeing in study abroad.

**Seth F. Gilbertson** is a Member at Bond, Schoeneck & King, PLLC, where he specializes in representing and advising institutions of higher education on labor and student affairs issues. Seth was previously Senior Counsel at the State University of New York, where he was the primary counsel responsible for several campuses and practice areas, including international programs. Seth is an active member of the National Association of College and University Attorneys and the New York State Bar Association.

As Duke University's Director of Global Health and Safety, **Anna Hayes** oversees risk assessment, crisis readiness, and faculty training for student travel. With 15 years' combined experience at Duke University, UNC Chapel Hill, and NC State University, she brings extensive expertise in international education. Anna holds a B.A. in Political Science from UNC Greensboro and a Master's degree in International Studies from NC State, and is pursuing a doctorate in Educational Leadership at NC State.

**Sunanda Holmes** is a practicing member of Maryland and DC bars with 32 years of experience in higher education, health care research and policy, international transactions and corporate governance. She is currently the Vice President and General Counsel of the American University in Cairo, a MSCHE accredited 100+ year old liberal arts university with its two campuses in downtown Cairo and New Cairo. Sunanda has worked in and traveled to more than 90 countries and currently lives in Egypt.

**Kelia Hubbard** has worked in international education for over 20 years serving international populations in state and private institutions. Kelia is an expert in non-immigrant visa statuses and has trained international education colleagues at the local and national levels. Kelia is an advocate for international education and approaches her work from an ethical lens ensuring the international office maintains compliance while simultaneously supporting the wellbeing of the international population.

**Shaun M. Jamieson** has over a decade of higher education experience in global risk management and student affairs. Shaun serves as the International Risk Manager for Iowa State University, overseeing the university's international health, safety, security, and risk management initiatives including working with thousands outbound travelers, two foreign campuses, and managing the university's travel risk program. Shaun is Vice President of Pulse International and is chair of the OSAC Academic Sector Committee.

**Ashley Krutz-Ordner** has worked in the field of international education for 13+ years and is currently the Director of International Travel, Safety, and Risk at Florida State University. She serves as the President of Pulse International, and previously served on the NAFSA Region VII Leadership Team. She earned a B.A. at the University of Evansville in Spanish and International Studies, and her M.A. in History from Butler University. She studied abroad in Spain, England, China, and Peru during her education.

**Laurie Laird** is Program Manager of the National Clearinghouse on Disability and Exchange, administered by Mobility International USA (MIUSA). Laurie, who has lived experience with a disability, has worked in higher education, international engagement, philanthropy, and non-profit management for social justice. She has worked with the Global Fund for Women, Santa Clara University, and the University of Portland. Laurie has a B.S. in Psychology and an M.A. in Teaching English to Speakers of Other Languages.

**A.J. Leeds** grew up on the Oregon coast. He was heavily influenced by his grandfather Willard Leeds, who worked in International Education for over 20 years. This relationship led him into the field of international relations and into the study of civil unrest, protests, and coups. After earning his degrees from the University of Portland and University of Denver, he has focused on safety and security working in first Emergency Management and then Travel Security.

**Xinning Shirley Liu,** J.D. is the President of XL Law and Consulting PA, where she advises colleges and universities on operating international programs and activities, domestic and international data privacy, and cross-border research transactions. Shirley is an active member of multiple higher education trade organizations and currently serves on the Board of Directors for the National Association of College and University Attorneys (NACUA). A Fulbright scholar, Shirley is a frequent speaker on international education.

Dr. **Marissa Lombardi** is Executive Director of Training, Programs and Services at the Forum. Prior to that, she served as Vice President of Academic Affairs and Partnerships EF Education First. Previously, she taught in and directed the MS in Global Studies and International Relations program at Northeastern University. Marissa has also served as dean at Lorenzo de'Medici Italian International Institute in Florence, Italy.

**Peter F. May** is an international consultant and attorney with 30 years' experience in the global higher education sector across more than 50 countries.

Peter advises internationally engaged US and international higher education and non-profit institutions on strategy, governance, business structure, strategic program partnerships, contracts, employment, risk and crisis management, compliance, accreditation, and international expansion.

**Miko McFarland** oversees US partnerships and enrollment at Barcelona SAE. McFarland started her career as an adjunct instructor and study abroad advisor at Missouri State University. A leadership position brought her to the University of Kentucky, where she served as the Executive Director of Education Abroad & Exchanges. McFarland is an active member of The Forum and NAFSA, contributing to numerous publications, workshops, sessions in leadership, risk management, operations, and funding models.

Dr. **Breeda McGrath**, a licensed Clinical & School Psychologist, serves as the President of Pacific Oaks College & Children's School in Pasadena, CA. She specializes in child development, psychological assessment, social-emotional learning, cross-cultural psychology, training, and trauma-informed care. Dr. McGrath is also well-versed in ethics, legal issues, and international psychology, focusing on culture, immigration, peace, and conflict.

**Terence Miller**, J.D. has an extensive career spanning over twenty-five years as a senior international officer (SIO). His legal acumen has been instrumental in forging strategic partnerships, managing risks, ensuring regulatory compliance, and driving comprehensive internationalization. He is a Senior Search Consultant at Gateway International Group, LLC, leading the Duty of Care and International Regulatory Solutions.

**Patrick Morgan** is responsible for enterprise-wide health, safety, and security aspects of international operations, including travel policies and risk management procedures, emergency assistance, and the higher risk travel review processes at the University of Michigan. Patrick has worked in travel risk management at U-M since 2011, chairs the U-M International Travel Oversight Committee, serves on U-M's campus health response team, is a member of Pulse, and is a member of the OSAC Council.

**Lindsey Pamlanye** is Program Coordinator of the National Clearinghouse on Disability and Exchange, administered by MIUSA. She holds a BA in Secondary Education and English and an MSc in Equality Studies. Her passion for disability inclusive education abroad stems from her own evolution from a person with hydrocephalus with a desire to travel but believing it impossible, to graduating, working, and living abroad. She is honored to contribute to accessibility and inclusion worldwide.

**Michael R. Pfahl**, J.D., Ph.D, received his Ph.D. in Higher Education Administration from Kent State University and focuses his research on international student issues, international comparative higher education law, and study abroad liability. Dr. Pfahl previously served on the Board of Directors for the National Association of College and University Attorneys (NACUA) and is a past recipient of the association's First Decade Award.

**Julie Pollard** is the Director of International Health, Safety, & Crisis Management for the systemwide education abroad program of the University of California (UCEAP). She has worked in international education since 2005, acquired operational experience in over 80 countries, and spent ten years in Turkey working in study abroad operations for KEI Abroad. Pollard is a member of Pulse and has presented at OSAC, NAFSA, Forum on Education Abroad, EAIE, AIEA, and EURIE on health, safety, and security topics.

**Kim S. Priebe** has over 20 years of experience in international education, including serving in international health, safety & security roles with the University of California (UCEAP) and UNC-Chapel Hill, and director of study abroad at NC State University. Priebe has a master's degree in education leadership and policy studies. She is actively engaged in the field, serving on professional organization boards, regularly presenting at conferences, and contributing to new professional resources, including co-editing this volume of the Standards in Action series.

**L. Raven Rae, J.D.** is an internationally recognized expert on global operations in higher education and international development and exchange. She maintains a curated network of local counsel in over 50 countries and has extensive experience in structuring and managing international portfolios and operations, including statutory, corporate and HR compliance. She often speaks at NACUA on international and higher education regulatory track topics and LGBTQ+ issues, including presenting at their annual conference.

**Kyle Rausch** serves as Executive Director of the Study Abroad Office at the University of Illinois Chicago. He holds an EdD in Leadership and Innovation from Arizona State University, a MS in Higher Education Administration, and a double BA/BS degree in French and International Affairs, both from Florida State University. His research interests include supporting underrepresented students in education abroad, duty of care in international education, and the professionalization of the field.

**Joan Rupar** has worked with insurance and risk management needs of higher education. Specializing in multinational exposures and compliance, she worked as a Senior Executive for a Global Insurance Company with expertise in Foreign Package programs, and engagement with emergency assistance. Joan has helped clients develop effective strategies for coverage solutions and has experience in assisting organizations with global health and safety issues, crisis response plans, and emergency management.

Dr. **Brittani Smit** has extensive experience in delivering high impact education abroad experiences, having served as the Resident Director for South Africa programs for Arcadia University's College of Global Studies, as well as Student Life Manager & Academic Coordinator for the CIEE Global Institute in Cape Town. She currently leads strategy development for inclusive student support and organizational culture as the Associate VP of Diversity, Equity, Inclusion and Anti-racism at IES Abroad.

**Jamie Snow** is Senior International Strategist at the Technical University Munich and heads the internationalization scoring initiative of the Xolas-Arlanto alliance. She has worked on international education and DEI initiatives for 19 years at top 100 universities in the United States, the Netherlands, and Germany. Jamie conducts bystander intervention training for education abroad and tech start-up professionals. She holds an M.A. in International Education from the SIT Graduate Institute.

**Henning Snyman** is Security Director, within the Americas region, for International SOS. Henning worked for over 20 years across Africa and the Middle East, gaining extensive experience within a range of complex environments in a risk management and consulting capacity. He holds a MPICT, which he obtained, cum laude from Macquarie University. In addition, he has a BA in Development Studies and an Honours Degree in Political Studies (Cum laude).

**Christine Sprovieri** oversees global travel risk and emergency response for Brown University. She has experience in global education including volunteering with Peace Corps-Togo and teaching in South America. A Fulbright IEA alumna, member of OSAC's Council and the Pulse Board of Directors, Christine has an MS-International Relations/Global Student Mobility and is completing her EdD, researching ways to bolster pre-travel preparedness to enhance global experiences and promote student resilience abroad.

**Andrea Stagg**'s work includes consulting and training on Title IX, equity, and safety. She has worked with federal and state legislators to develop state laws and follow best practices in campus safety and sexual harassment prevention. She was previously in-house counsel to Barnard College and the State University of New York.

**Vanessa Sterling** is Director of Health and Safety for CET Academic Programs, a third-party provider that operates in nine countries across Asia, Europe, Latin America, and the MENA. She is a certified Mental Health First Aid Responder and Trainer and serves on the Board of Directors of Pulse: International Safety and Security Professionals in Higher Education.

**Joseph Storch** builds systems to simplify compliance and improve response, to invest in prevention. A nationally recognized expert on Title IX, the Clery Act, and climate surveys, he twice testified before the U.S. Senate, drafted legislation and regulations, and provides guidance for associations and institutions across the country. He is the author of over 90 articles and book chapters, presented over 800 conference and training sessions, and led development of innovations serving millions of students.

**Christina 'Chris' Thompson** is an award-winning innovator in global education, celebrated for her dedication to equitable practices. As the founder of COMPEAR Global Education Network and the Global Respectful Disruption Summit, she has pioneered transformative strategies for nearly two decades. Her accolades include the Go Abroad Award for Innovation in Diversity. Chris is currently advancing her expertise through doctoral studies in respectfully disruptive leadership practices at Marymount University.

Dr. **Laura Thompson** is a Licensed Professional Counselor based in Boulder, Colorado. She is the Founder of the Mental Health Team and a Co-Founder of P3 Mental Health Advisors. Laura conducts mental health trainings for organizations including study abroad, secondary and higher education, outdoor/experiential education, gap year, and camps. Laura also teaches graduate courses in counseling for New York University. She holds a Ph.D. in Counseling and Counselor Education from Syracuse University.

**Catherine Williams** has extensive experience advising universities and other non-profits on complying with anti-discrimination and other laws, implementing related best practices, and investigating alleged misconduct and policy violations.

# Index